ATLAS OF THE
NORTH AMERICAN
INDIAN

ATLAS OF THE NORTH AMERICAN INDIAN

Carl Waldman

Maps and Illustrations by Molly Braun

Facts On File Publications
New York, New York • Oxford, England

ATLAS OF THE NORTH AMERICAN INDIAN

Copyright © 1985 by Carl Waldman

Library of Congress Cataloging in Publication Data

Waldman, Carl, 1947–
  Atlas of the North American Indian

  1. Indians of North America. 2. Indians of North America—Maps. I. Waldman, Carl. II. Title.
E77.B6 1984   970.00497   83-9020
ISBN 0-87196-850-9

Printed in the United States of America
10 9

British Library Cataloguing in Publication Data

Waldman, Carl
  Atlas of the North American Indian
1. Indians of North America —— History
1. Title
970.004'97 E77

ISBN 0-87196-850-9

CONSULTANT:

John Trimbur, Ph.D.
Boston University
Permanent Honorary Fellow,
American Studies Program
SUNY at Buffalo

CARTOGRAPHIC CONSULTANT:

Christopher Campbell
Senior Cartographic Analyst
County of Otsego, New York

For Chloe, American,
and Meredith, Native American

Contents

Maps

Thayendanegea or Joseph Brant. New York State Library, Albany.

Preface

Many people find themselves intrigued by the Native American saga. Yet, despite the fact that Indian history is central to that of North America, many people also find themselves poorly informed on the subject. For other than specialists, American and Canadian educational systems pass on little of the rich, exciting, and poignant Indian legacy.

Without a proper educational foundation, the study of the American Indian presents its own special kind of challenge. By focusing on a particular race as a central theme, one takes on the entire span of human history—prehistory to the present. One also takes on as a subject in this case hundreds of different tribes, both extant and extinct, each with a unique history, demography, and culture. Indian studies encompass the various fields of history, archaeology, anthropology, sociology, geography, politics, religion, linguistics, and more. Furthermore, Native American studies can be difficult emotionally in that Indians as a race have been victimized by what has been traditionally represented in public education as progress.

The purpose of this book is to provide an overview, or rather a series of overviews, for understanding the challenging subject of the American Indian, and a framework or frameworks for pursuing further historical and cultural studies. Because of the nature of the material—the great number of tribes and their movement over the centuries—maps are especially helpful in conveying Indian-related information.

There are many ways to organize an American Indian atlas—by general geographic regions, for example, or by states, with summaries of Indian history and culture for each. For purposes of accessibility to the complex material, this book is organized instead by subject, with chapters based on the following seven categories—Ancient Indians, Ancient Civilizations, Indian Life-

ways, Indians and Explorers, Indian Wars, Indian Land Cessions, and Contemporary Indians—necessitating a variety of cartographic approaches.

The subject matter is further broken down into sections with headings. These sections are intended as complete in themselves, but are often interconnected by cross-references when especially helpful. The corresponding maps are for the most part representative in nature and closely tied to the text, rather than exhaustive. With such a wide historical and territorial scope, not every tribe, settlement, battle, or cultural trait can be represented visually. Tribal locations are of course approximate. The maps are generally aligned northward, with modern boundaries frequently used for reference.

As an additional source of information, the book has an Appendix with various lists—a chronology of Indian history, a list of tribes with historical and contemporary locations, lists of United States reservations and Canadian bands, lists of Indian place names, and a list of museums and archaeological sites.

A single-volume reference work on Indians creates a problem of emphasis—how much weight to give the different subjects. Each area of study deserves its own atlas, as does each tribe for that matter. This book, although touching on the Indians of Middle America as part of the North American story, does not even attempt to cover Native South Americans.

It should also be pointed out, especially in light of the particularly holistic Indian world view, that the various categories and classification systems in the book are heuristic devices, applied for the sake of convenience and understanding, and not absolutes. Moreover, nomenclature in Indian studies—applying to both cultural themes and proper names—manifests considerable variation and leaves room for interpretation. Some usage presents a stubborn problem as well in that many terms and concepts have evolved from, if not an outright cultural bias, then at least an implicit cultural vantage point—that of the dominant European/American tradition. Non-Indians should therefore make a special effort to keep in mind the often neglected Indian perspective and empathize with contemporary Indian concerns.

A broad-based work such as this owes much to previous scholars, authors, and cartographers—men like Powell, Hodge, Kroeber, Swanton, Collier, Josephy, Driver, and Highwater—who have

Hunters tracking game. A crayon sketch by Howling Wolf, Cheyenne, while imprisoned at Fort Marion, Florida, 1876. New York State Library, Albany.

dedicated their lives to researching and preserving Native American history and culture. When the information on a given map or in the text is derived from a single source or is of a particularly hypothetical nature, that source will be cited. A bibliography at the back of the book lists general sources and will hopefully aid the reader in continuing studies.

Many people helped with this project. First and most of all, I would like to thank my wife and collaborator, Molly Braun, without whose input and cartographic and illustrating skills this book truly could not have been. I would also like to extend our profound thanks to our author/packager friends Tom Biracree and Frank Coffey who gave us direction for our Indian preoccupation and blazed the trail. The following people were also essential to the project and I would like to express our great appreciation to them: Gerry Helferich, the book's editor at Facts On File, as thoughtful an editor as any author could hope for; Jeannette Jacobs, the book's designer, with her astute eye and wealth of knowledge; John Trimbur, the book's consultant on Indian matters, with his passion for and mastery of the subject; Christopher Campbell, the book's skillful consultant on cartographic techniques and early maps; Susan Brooker, who offered such crucial help down the stretch with design, layout, and mechanicals; and Peter Rosenblatt, for his painstaking help with research, proofing, and paste-ups. A special thanks also to my father, John Waldman, for his encouragement and editing.

I would also like to extend our appreciation to all the other people who helped along the way: Wayne Coffey, for authorial advice; Robin Smith at Facts On File, for support and guidance; Wayne Wright and Cynthia Weigel at the New York State Historical Association, for all their assistance; Marcia Golub, for copy editing; Alan Wexler, for research; Margaret Dunbar, for proofing; Steve Child, Herb Field, Johnny Blair, David Smith, and Joel Weltman, for graphics tips; Mary Davis at the Library of the Museum of the American Indian; Marcel Nolet at the Canadian Department of Indian Affairs; Juanita Spencer at the Bureau of Indian Affairs; my family and Molly's family, as well as all our Indian buff friends in Cherry Valley and elsewhere, for their enthusiasm; Chief Henry, Mary Scott Jacobs, and all the other Native Americans who welcomed us on their homelands; and the Anderson family on the Fort Totten Reservation in North Dakota, for their friendship and inspiration.

Carl Waldman
Cherry Valley, NY
Spring, 1985

Chapter 1
ANCIENT INDIANS

Prehistory is a continuum of survival, countless generations of the human animal passing on a legacy of adaptation. The study of prehistory presents its own special problems, because specific dates, events, and individuals around which to structure the flow of time are not known. Yet, in order to analyze and understand the prehistoric Indian culture, a frame of reference is needed. Definitions, categories, and approximate dates applied by archaeologists and anthropologists, with help from geologists and other scientists, give shape to the long stretch of millennia leading up to the historic Indian.

The system or systems used can be confusing, however. First, the reconstruction of prehistory is of course speculative, and scholars do not always agree. Second, even if they agree on concept, they do not always use the same terms. Third, dating techniques are far from exact; stratigraphy dating, radiocarbon, dendrochronology, archeomagnetism, obsidian dating, and other techniques must allow for a margin of error.

Fourth, cultural stages overlap, with one gradually fading while another slowly becomes dominant. Fifth, there are regional variations in the pace of cultural development, making it difficult to generalize about all of North America; also, different systems of classification are used in different regions and at different archaeological sites. And sixth, exceptions to neat cultural groupings always exist: One particular group might have advanced in a different way and at a faster pace than everyone else around them.

Yet, despite the difficulties involved and the complexity of the subject matter, prehistory, because of the work of archaeologists and other scientists, is accessible to modern man. The story has shape and definition. And it has drama.

BERINGIA

After decades of guesswork and unfounded theories of lost European tribes and lost continents, it is now held as conclusive that mankind first arrived in North America from Asia during the Pleistocene age via the Bering Strait land bridge, also known

as Beringia. There were four glaciations in the million-year Pleistocene, with ice caps spreading down from the north; these were separated by interglacial periods. The Wisconsin glaciation (corresponding to the Wurm glaciation in Europe) lasted from about 90,000 or 75,000 to 8,000 B.C. It is theorized that at various times during the Wisconsin, enough of the planet's water was locked up in ice to significantly lower the oceans and expose now-submerged land. Where there is now 56 miles of water 180 feet deep in the Bering Strait, there would have been a stretch of tundra possibly as much as 1,000 miles wide, bridging the two continents. The islands of today would have been towering mountains. The big game of the Ice Age could have migrated across the land bridge. And the foremost predator among them— spear-wielding man—could have followed them. These Paleo-Siberians were the first Indians, the real discoverers of the New World.

Increasing archaeological evidence, has pushed the estimated date for human arrival in North America further and further back, from about 10,000 B.C. to 50,000 B.C., perhaps even earlier, although there is still no consensus among scholars. Much of

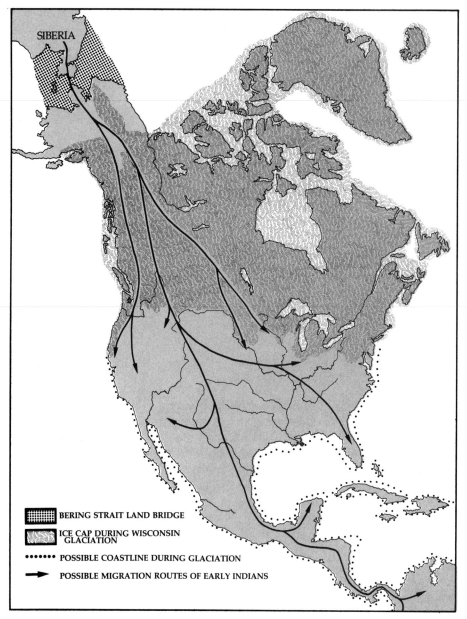

BERING STRAIT LAND BRIDGE

ICE CAP DURING WISCONSIN
GLACIATION

•••••• POSSIBLE COASTLINE DURING GLACIATION

→ POSSIBLE MIGRATION ROUTES OF EARLY INDIANS

1.1 THE BERING STRAIT LAND BRIDGE AND THE MIGRATION OF EARLY INDIANS

along the Alberta–Saskatchewan plains. And finally a third passageway very likely developed in the late Wisconsin along the Yukon, Peace, and Liard rivers.

From these routes early Indians could have dispersed eastward along the river valleys of the Great Plains, westward through the South Pass of the Rockies to the Great Basin, southwestward around the heel of the Rockies to southern California, or southward into Middle America all the way to Tierra del Fuego at the southern tip of the New World. The complete dispersal in all directions probably took centuries or even millennia, as mankind followed the big game.

Later migrations to the New World occurred long after the final submersion of Beringia. About 3,000 to 1,000 B.C., Eskimos, Aleuts, and possibly Athapascans used wooden dugouts and skin boats to cross the Bering Sea.

LITHIC INDIANS (Paleo-Indians)

The Lithic period can be divided, for better understanding, into the Pre-Projectile-Point stage, the Paleo-Indian stage, and the Protoarchaic stage. Sometimes the three categories are referred to as one—Paleo-Indian—or cultures from the Protoarchaic stage are grouped in the later Archaic period. In any case, during the long stretch of centuries after human migration to the New World until the end of the Ice Age, about 8,000 B.C., and for a period afterwards, big-game hunting was the dominant way of life. For the most part, nomadic hunters, wearing hide and fur, and taking shelter in caves, under overhangs, and in brushwood lean-tos, tracked the Pleistocene game—woolly mammoths, mastodons, saber-toothed tigers, American lions, camels, bighorn bison, short-faced bears, dire wolves, giant beavers, giant sloths, giant armadillos, curve-snouted tapirs, musk oxen, native horses, and peccaries, in addition to some smaller mammals.

the disagreement results from the fact that stone artifacts cannot be dated themselves, but can be placed in time by a study of surrounding geology or by radiocarbon analysis of organic matter found along with them. It is the prevailing view, however, that the migration of humanity from Asia did not happen all at once but over many millennia in many waves, the early Indians traveling in small family units or bands. Moreover, the ensuing dispersal throughout North and South America was a gradual process.

The way south was not always clear. In fact, at those times when Beringia existed, the Wisconsin glacier

blocked further southern and eastern migration. Early mankind might have lived in the Alaska region, which was ice-free because of low precipitation, for generations before temporary melts, or interstadials, created natural passageways through the ice. As with the land bridge, it is difficult to establish a time frame for these thaws with any exactitude. Yet geological and archaeological evidence points to an ice-free corridor for several thousand years in the early to middle Wisconsin glaciation along the spine of the Rockies. Then, during another melt 10,000 years later, a second corridor probably formed further east

Archæologists and anthropologists have gleaned what they know of the first Indians from artifacts and bones found at campsites and kill sites.

The Pre-Projectile-Point stage (about 50,000 B.C. to about 25,000 B.C.) bears that name because stone points were not yet used on spears. Artifacts from this period include roughly crafted stone and bone implements, utilized for chopping, scraping, and other applications. The hunters probably used fire to harden the tips of their wooden spears, of which no traces remain. Some famous Pre-Projectile-Point sites include Lewisville, Texas, where early human remains have been found, estimated to be 38,000 years old; and Old Crow Flats, Yukon Territory, where a caribou-bone tool has been found, estimated to be 27,000 years old.

After about 25,000 B.C., new technologies appeared among Lithic Indians. Workable stone—especially flint, chert, and obsidian—was used to craft functional tools, such as knives, scrapers, choppers, and, most important for hunting, spear points. Techniques for shaping the stone included percussion-flaking, or removing chips by striking with a stone, and pressure-flaking, or removing chips by pressing with antler or bone. Paleo-Indian phases are determined by the type of spear point, which usually bears the name of the site where it was first found. The dominant phases are Sandia, Clovis, Folsom, and Plano. The fact that these particular points are not also found on the Asian side of the Bering Strait indicates that the technological evolution surrounding them occurred in the New World.

The Sandia culture (after a site in the Sandia Mountains of New Mexico) lasted from about 25,000 to 10,000 B.C. and was localized in the Southwest. The Sandia lanceolate points, two to four inches long, have rounded bases with a bulge on one side.

The Clovis culture (sometimes referred to as Llano) was much more widespread, as indicated by finds in every mainland state in addition to the original Clovis site in New Mexico. The slender lanceolate points, one and a half to five inches long, were beautifully crafted by pressure-flaking, with fluting (lengthwise channels) on both sides. Clovis points have been found predominantly with mammoth and mastodon bones.

The Folsom culture (after Folsom, New Mexico, and sometimes referred to as Lindenmeier, after the site in Colorado) became dominant about 8,000 B.C. Folsom points are generally shorter than Sandia and Clovis—three-quarters of an inch to three inches long—with a leaflike shape and fluting on both sides that run almost the entire length. It is not certain

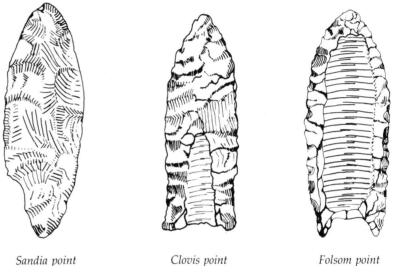

Sandia point   Clovis point   Folsom point

what purpose the long grooves served, since they make the Folsom points more breakable—probably for insertion into the split end of the wooden shaft, possibly to increase the flow of blood from the animal, or possibly to increase spear velocity. Evidence of Folsom hunters has been found over much of North America but especially in the Great Plains, and especially with bighorn bison remains; the larger mammals were already dying out. There is also evidence of new hunting techniques—cooperative group activity in stampeding herds over cliffs or into swamps and bogs for easy kills. Moreover, the atlatl appeared during the dominant Folsom period—a spear-thrower consisting of a wooden stick about two feet long, with animal-hide loops to provide a firm grasp, a

stone weight for balance, and a carved wooden hook at the far end to hold the spear shaft, all serving to increase the leverage of the hunter's arm.

The Plano culture (sometimes referred to as the Plainview, after the site in Texas), like the Folsom, is associated primarily with the Great Plains and the bighorn bison. Plano hunters, active from about 7,500 to 4,500 B.C., made even greater use of organized stampeding techniques. Where there were no cliffs they even constructed corrals to trap animals. They also developed a primitive method of preserving meat, mixing it with animal fat and berries, and packing it in gut or hide containers.

Unlike the Clovis and Folsom Paleo-Indians before them, Plano craftsmen did not flute their points.

There are exceptions to the widespread cultural homogeneity of the Lithic period. The economies of the Old Cordilleran culture of the Pacific Northwest and Columbia Plateau and the Desert culture of the Southwest show traits similar to later Archaic traditions. They can therefore be referred to as Protoarchaic, even though they occurred as early as 9,000 B.C. in what is normally considered the Lithic period. (Some scholars also group the Plano Indians in the Protoarchaic—a bridge to the Archaic—because they demonstrated a more varied economy than Sandia, Clovis, or Folsom people of the Lithic.)

The Old Cordilleran (or Cascade)

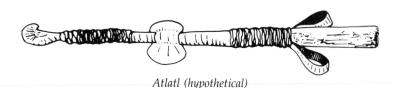

Atlatl (hypothetical)

culture of the Columbia River Valley lasted from about 9,000 to 5,000 B.C., and it probably was the matrix culture for later Indians of the Pacific Northwest and Columbia Plateau. The Cascade spear point is willow-leaf-shaped without any fluting and was used to hunt mainly small mammals. But archaeological finds of fishhooks and tools for the preparation of edible wild plants indicate a wide-based economy.

Likewise, the Indians of the Desert culture, found in the Great Basin area of present-day Utah, Nevada, and Arizona, and existing from about 9,000 to 1,000 B.C., also possessed a primitive foraging society. At Danger Cave in Utah woven containers have been found (the earliest examples of basketry in North America) as well as grinding stones to process seeds. Desert Indians also made twine from hair, fur, and plant fibers, and with it, traps to capture small game.

During and after the final retreat of the northern glaciers, from about 9,000 to 5,000 B.C., many of the large mammals that the Paleo-Indians depended on for sustenance disappeared, first in the lower latitudes, then in the north as well. This pattern of big-game extinction is one of the great mysteries of the Lithic period, and there are various theories to account for it. Climatic change probably played a part. The melting glaciers had created continent-wide a high level of moisture, with lush flora and abundant lakes, rivers, swamps, and bogs. Over the centuries the climate warmed and topography dried up; seasonal and regional variations gradually occurred, probably straining animal life. Yet the large mammals had survived other changes in climate and earlier interglacial periods. Perhaps the difference this time was the presence of the new superpredator— the human animal, with his razor-sharp flint points, his atlatls, his guile, and his organization. The practice of driving entire herds to death unnecessarily is referred to by some scholars as Pleistocene Overkill.

Modern scientists have pieced together a few facts of Paleo-Indian life from archaeological evidence. There are of course gaping holes in our current knowledge, along with a great deal of assumption and hypothesis. For example, in an archaeological sense, the role of the Paleo-Indian woman is invisible because she tended to work in perishable materials rather than stone or bone. Nonetheless, the existence of the beautifully crafted spear points found at campsites and kill sites communicates much about the early Indians, both male and female, and their similarities to modern mankind. They sought food and shelter. They were social. They strived for new technologies. They took pride in their work. They dreamed and they acted. And they survived.

1.2 LITHIC CULTURAL CORE AREAS AND SELECTED ARCHAEOLOGICAL SITES

ARCHAIC INDIANS (Foraging Indians)

The early Indians adapted. Over the eons the climate, terrain, flora and fauna evolved from the Ice Age through the postglacial Watershed Age and into new regional patterns. Generation after generation of Indians, gradually expanding their food base and devising new technologies, adjusted. The Archaic period, which was characterized by a foraging way of life—the hunting and trapping of small game, fishing, and gathering of edible wild plants—lasted from about 6,000 to 1,000 B.C.; i.e., during those centuries the Archaic life-style was dominant. Plano hunters from the earlier Lithic period stayed active until about 4,500 B.C. on the Great Plains.

The Archaic or Foraging period was still essentially a migratory existence. When the food sources ran out in one area, Archaic Indians moved on to another. Yet they were generally more localized than the Lithic hunters. And archaeologists have even found some permanent Archaic sites, as indicated by sizable middens (refuse heaps), especially near lakes and streams.

During the Archaic, a variety of materials—wood, stone, bone, antler, shell, ivory, hide, plant fiber, and copper—were used to make a wide assortment of specialized tools and utensils that fit the requirements of particular regional life-styles. Archaic craftsmen shaped spears, atlatls, bolas, knives, axes, adzes, wedges, chisels, scrapers, mauls, hammers, anvils, awls, drills, mortars and pestles, fishhooks, harpoons, pipes, and containers. Without ceramics, their pipes as well as cooking and storage pots were made of stone. Cloths and baskets of woven plant materials were first crafted during this period. Along with the many tools came new methods of food preparation and preservation. Heated stones were used for boiling water and pit roasting. Baskets and skin containers were used to store food. Archaic Indians were also the

first North Americans to construct boats and domesticate the dog.

Yet survival and practicality were not the only Archaic pursuits. These early Indians also found time to shape some of their rough materials into ornaments. And they developed intricate beliefs and rituals and went to elaborate means to bury their dead.

The Archaic period is often discussed in terms of Eastern Archaic and Western Archaic, with the Mississippi as the divider between them. The East, with its lush, wooded landscape, gave rise to a denser population than the more barren West. The following descriptions of three of the

many Archaic cultures—the Cochise in the Southwest and the Old Copper and Red Paint cultures in the Northeast—will point up geographical variations in adaptation and invention.

The Cochise culture in what is now Arizona and New Mexico was an offshoot of the Desert culture of the Great Basin. It lasted from about 7,000 to 1,000 B.C., leading up to the Golden Age cultures of the region—Mogollon, Hohokam, and Anasazi. A harsh environment defined the Cochise way of life. Lake Cochise once covered a large part of the terrain where the Cochise Indians foraged. As it dried

1.3 ARCHAIC CULTURAL CORE AREAS AND SELECTED ARCHAEOLOGICAL SITES

up over the millennia, succeeding generations had to cope with desert and cliff. Taking shelter in caves and under ledges, Cochise Indians ranged from mesa top to desert floor with the seasons. Food caches provided bases of operations for them. They hunted and trapped small mammals—deer, antelope, rabbits—as well as snakes, lizards, and insects. They gathered up the edible wild plants—yucca, prickly pear, juniper, pinyon—whatever they had learned to use. Cochise millstones—manos and metates for grinding seeds, grains, and nuts—have been found all over the region, evidence of the growing importance of plants in the early Indian diet.

Their extensive use of plants led to a major breakthrough. In Bat Cave, New Mexico, archaeologists have found several cobs of corn from a primitive cultivated species about an inch long, the earliest evidence of agriculture north of Mexico (circa 3,500 B.C.). Contact with Mesoamerican Indians out of the south perhaps spurred this far-reaching development. The Cochise also eventually learned to make pit houses—brush structures over dug holes—and to shape crude pottery figurines, two more elements of later Formative cultures.

Meanwhile, in the Great Lakes region of the East, there existed from about 4,000 to 1,500 B.C. a foraging tradition known as the Old Copper culture. This was a typical Eastern Archaic culture in that the people hunted, fished, and gathered food from a variety of sources. They also devised tools out of the usual Archaic materials—stone, wood, bone, antler, and shell—to exploit the lush, wooded environment. What is remarkable about these people is that, unlike any other Archaic Indians north of Mexico, they made use of still another material—copper. On the south shore of Lake Superior and on Isle Royale they found and quarried deposits of pure metal, both sheets in rock fissures and float nuggets in the soil. At first they worked it as they did stone—by chipping—but then they learned to take advantage of the ma-

terial's flexibility with annealing techniques (alternate heating and hammering), crafting beautiful tools and ornaments. Old Copper artifacts have turned up at Archaic sites throughout the East, indicating the great demand for these unique objects and widespread trading connections.

Another localized Archaic variation occurred in New England and the Canadian maritime provinces, where archaeologists have found numerous graves lined with ground-up red hematite, resulting in the name the Red Paint People. The symbolic use of red—the color of life-sustaining blood—lasted approximately from 3,000 to 500 B.C. The Red Paint People also placed tools, ornaments, and effigies—beautifully crafted of slate, quartzite, bone, and antler—in their graves. At Port au Choix, Newfoundland, the northernmost Red Paint site,

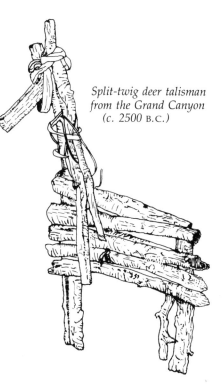

Split-twig deer talisman from the Grand Canyon (c. 2500 B.C.)

100 burials have been located. In some of them, along with the hematite and typical Archaic artifacts, firemaking kits of flintstone and pyrite have been found, one more example of the early Indian's advancing technology.

During the latter part of the Archaic period, from about 3,000 to 1,000 B.C.,

Eskimos, Aleuts, and possibly Athapascans crossed the Bering Sea in small boats and dispersed throughout regions of the Arctic and Subarctic.

TRANSITION AND CULMINATION (Formative and Classic Indians)

As difficult as it is to devise a neat system of classification and a neat chronology for the Lithic and Archaic periods, the task becomes even more problematic with the later cultural stages. With cultural advancement comes diversification: Indians in different parts of the continent progressed in different ways. In archaeological terms, each region has its own cultural sequence and categories (cultures, stages, phases, traditions, etc.). In fact, each archaeological site has its own system of classification, making the study of Indian prehistory that much more confusing.

The term most commonly applied to the Postarchaic period (circa 1,000 B.C. until Contact with the white man) is Formative, the word itself implying transition. Broadly speaking, Formative refers to the spread of agriculture, settled village life, houses, domesticated animals, pottery, weaving, the bow and arrow, and ceremonies and beliefs.

Yet other terms are needed to express degrees of development. In Mesoamerica, for example, where Indians reached the highest degree of organized life—even developing cities—the term Classic is used, implying a cultural culmination, which leads to subdivisions such as Preclassic and Postclassic. Preclasssic for Middle America, then becomes interchangeable with Formative. Moreover, another phrase implying culmination, Golden Age, is sometimes used with advanced cultures north of Mexico, such as the Anasazi, Hohokam, and Mogollon of the Southwest, or the Mound Builders of the East. Indeed, the terminology surrounding

1.4 NUCLEAR AMERICA AND POSSIBLE ROUTES OF CULTURAL DIFFUSION

culture, continued their typically Archaic life-styles into modern times. It might even be said that 19th-century Indians of the Great Plains, with their buffalo hunting, returned to a typically Paleo-Indian nomadic life-style similar to that of the Plano big-game hunters, who also tracked bison.

One other cultural classification should be mentioned. Some scholars use the term Mesoindian, rather than Formative or Preclassic, to distinguish the period in Mesoamerica when agriculture was invented (circa 7,000 to 1,500 B.C.) from the Archaic culture elsewhere on the continent. (See "Subsistence Patterns and Cultural Evolution" in chapter 3.) Pottery was also developed in Mesoamerica during this phase and began to spread northward. Village life followed and eventually city-states. During the Mesoindian, the Formative or Preclassic, and the Classic periods, ideas generally flowed northward out of Middle America, rather than the reverse, as was the case in the earlier Lithic period, and brought about widespread cultural change. Mesoamerica, along with the Andes region of South America, where agriculture also developed, is therefore sometimes referred to as Nuclear America.

Because of the great diversity in Indian culture flowering during and after the Archaic, as well as the resulting complexity of terminology, it becomes necessary at this point in the Indian story to discuss particular cultures and civilizations in detail. The next chapter, "ANCIENT CIVILIZATIONS," will be organized around the cultures themselves rather than around cultural phases, as this one is. In the third chapter, Indian lifeways as they came to exist at the time of Contact with the white man will be analyzed by dividing North and Middle America into geographical regions. In later chapters concerning the Postcontact historic period, the principal frame of reference will be provided by events, tribes, and individuals.

the Mound Builders and Temple Mound Builders is especially confusing. Some scholars refer to all of them as part of a Golden Age. Others speak of the Adena and Hopewell Mound Builders as Formative, and the Mississippian Temple Mound Builders as Classical. Still others use the term Woodland to describe all three, as well as other cultures in the East. Woodland can therefore imply either transition or culmination. To add to the confusion, the term Woodland is also applied to the lifeways of eastern Indians during the years of Contact with the white man.

There are other exceptions to a unified classification system for the Indians of prehistory. The spread of agriculture is the dominant Formative as well as Classical theme, but many Indians in the north, such as those of the Pacific Northwest, came to have many other of the period's typical elements without agriculture—village life, complex social organization, and so on. These Indians also belie the generalization that cultural diffusion of either Formative or Classical elements was slower in the north. And of course other Indians, such as the Eskimos and Aleuts, who arrived on the continent as late as 3,000 B.C., with their unique hunting and fishing

Chapter 2
ANCIENT CIVILIZATIONS

All the necessary ingredients were there: fire, technology, agriculture, religion, houses, and villages. Now civilizations would occur: large centralized populations, and even cities; complex social and religious organizations; and highly refined arts and crafts.

Most full-fledged civilizations would arise where agriculture had first appeared: Middle America (Mesoamerica) and the Andes region of South America. With increasing commerce and conquest among the growing populations, materials and ideas would also pass among them. Mesoamerica would become a densely populated melting pot with extensive interrelations among its peoples. Over the centuries, one particular group of people or tribe would flourish, then fade as others rose to dominance. Great cities would be built, house successive groups of people, then be abandoned, becoming legendary for still others. New art forms would be developed and shared. Religious practices and gods would catch the fancy of peoples far and wide.

And out of religion would spring writing and science.

To the north, in the American Southwest as well as the East and Midwest, other civilizations would flower on a smaller scale but with many of the same cultural elements.

And while all this occurred, other peoples—beyond the villages and planted fields—would wander as always, hunting and gathering.

OLMECS

If any one group of peoples deserves the label "Mother Culture" or "Mother Civilization" of Mesoamerica, it is the Olmecs of the Mexican Gulf Coast's lowland jungles, grasslands, and swamps. In Olmec culture, villages evolved, if not into true cities, then into large ceremonial and economic centers at the least. Tribes evolved into complex social structures. Crafts and handiwork evolved into art and architecture on both refined and colossal scales. Ritual evolved into number and calendar systems and into glyph writing. Agriculture evolved into a network of trading partners. Indeed, this flowering of culture now known as Olmec influenced the other cultures to spring up in Mesoamerica—Maya, Teotihuacan, Totonac, Zapotec, and through them the later Toltec, Mixtec, and Aztec, as well as other peoples far to the north and south.

Olmec celt of dark green jade

Several different Olmec communities flourished, most important among them: San Lorenzo, dominant from 1,200 to 900 B.C.; La Venta (the location of the largest Olmec pyramid), dominant from 800 to 400 B.C.; and Tres Zapotes, which attained its cultural peak about 100 B.C. Olmec culture stretched out beyond the Veracruz region as a result of the establishment of trade routes along rivers, valleys, and mountain passes in the quest for materials—in particular,

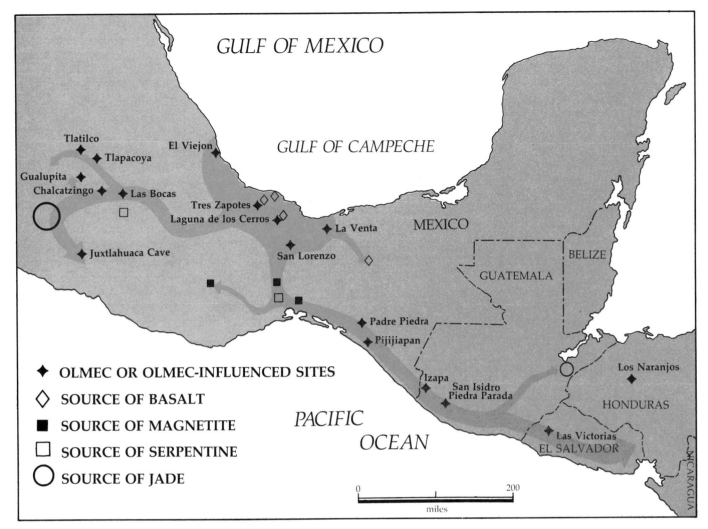

GULF OF MEXICO

GULF OF CAMPECHE

Tlatilco
Tlapacoya
El Viejon
Gualupita
Chalcatzingo
Las Bocas
Tres Zapotes
Laguna de los Cerros
La Venta
MEXICO
Juxtlahuaca Cave
San Lorenzo
BELIZE
GUATEMALA
Padre Piedra
Pijijiapan
Izapa
San Isidro
Piedra Parada
Los Naranjos
HONDURAS
PACIFIC
OCEAN
Las Victorias
EL SALVADOR
NICARAGUA

◆ OLMEC OR OLMEC-INFLUENCED SITES
◇ SOURCE OF BASALT
■ SOURCE OF MAGNETITE
□ SOURCE OF SERPENTINE
○ SOURCE OF JADE

0   200
miles

2.1 OLMEC SITES AND TRADE ROUTES (with modern boundaries). After Coe.

basalt, jade, serpentine, and magnetite—for artistic and ceremonial purposes.

Like most Mesoamerican civilizations to follow, Olmec society was theocratic, with fixed classes of priests, bureaucrats, merchants and craftsmen based in the community centers. A surrounding population of farmers practiced slash-and-burn agriculture (cutting down trees and burning them to make fields) to support the various other stratas of society.

In terms of artifacts, the Olmecs are most famous for mammoth basalt heads (some as heavy as 20 tons), with their thick features and helmet-like headdresses; as well as for statuettes of jade, terra-cotta, and stone, with catlike "baby-faces." The heads, for which the Olmecs dragged overland and floated in by rafts huge quantities of basalt, were possibly representations of chiefs or kings, dressed in headgear for ceremonial ball games. And it is theorized that the snarling or crying baby-faced figurines represented offspring of an Olmec god, the jaguar rain god, and his human female partners, known as were-jaguars. The Great Plumed Serpent, a recurring theme in Mesoamerica (later called Quetzalcoatl), is another common depiction. The Olmecs are also known for large stelae (carved stone slabs); serpentine pavement overlaid in mosaics; concave magnetite mirrors for kindling fires; and white-rimmed pottery.

The progressive Olmecs developed seminal number and calendar systems as well as glyph writing, all of which were to blossom at Mayan sites over the next centuries. In fact, because of linguistic and cultural ties between the two peoples, and because it is not known what became of the Olmecs after their cultural decline, some scholars hypothesize that they migrated southeastward and were the direct ancestors of the Mayas.

MAYAS

The Mayas have been called "the Greeks of the New World." Although misleading with regard to specific cultural traits and perhaps representing a pro-European cultural bias, the comparison expresses the high level of Mayan civilization and intellect. For that matter, the Greeks can be called "the Mayas of the Old World."

The Mayas inherited a rich cultural legacy from earlier Mesoamerican peoples, in particular the Olmecs. Their own greatness resulted not so much from innovation but from refinement of existing lifeways, as revealed in their intricate mathematical, astronomical, and calendrical systems; their hieroglyphic writing, both pictographic and ideographic, and perhaps even with glyphs representing sounds or syllables; their realistic art styles in both painting and relief carving; and their elaborate architecture, including such designs as steep-sided pyramids, corbeled vaults, and roof combs.

The Mayan world, like that of the Olmecs, revolved around ceremonial centers. More than 100 Mayan sites are known in Mexico, Belize, Guatemala, Honduras, and El Salvador. Most of these centers consisted of magnificent stone structures—temple pyramids, astronomical platforms or observatories, palaces, monasteries, baths, ball-courts, plazas, bridges, aqueducts, and reservoirs. Tikal, for example, one of the most important sites of Classic lowland Maya found in Guatemala, had 3,000 structures, including six temple pyramids, spread out over one square mile, and an estimated population of 100,000.

Maya carved shell pendant (minus jade inlays for the drilled holes)

The priests, the keepers of knowledge with their passion for keeping time (there were seven distinct Mayan calendars), performed their functions within the population centers. And the hereditary oligarchs, known as "Sun Children," in charge of commerce, taxation, justice, and public maintenance, also operated out of these centers. Craftsmen also worked

in and around the central complex—stoneworkers, painters, jewelers, potters, and clothiers who fashioned the decorative cotton-and-feather garments. Outside the civic centers were the farmers, living in one-room pole-and-thatch dwellings and practicing their slash-and-burn agriculture, also known as the "milpa" system.

Although Mayan society was rigidly structured into classes, there is no evidence of a larger political system uniting the various population centers or of one dominant capital. The Mayas were not as militaristic as later Mesoamerican civilizations, with-

out huge conquering armies. They did, however, establish far-reaching trade routes. And they were a seafaring people, some traders going forth in large dugout canoes with as many as 25 paddlers.

It is not known why the Mayas of the Classic lowland centers fell into a state of cultural decay about A.D. 900. One theory suggests that an agricultural crisis resulting from a fast-growing population and depletion of the soil led to a peasant uprising against the ruling priests and nobles. In any case, from that time on, Mayan culture thrived primarily to the south in the Guatemalan highlands. A notable

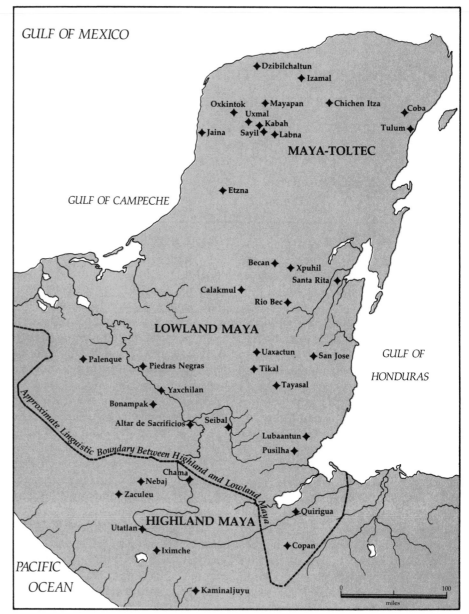

2.2 REGIONS OF MAYAN CULTURE AND SELECTED CLASSIC AND POSTCLASSIC SITES. *After Thompson.*

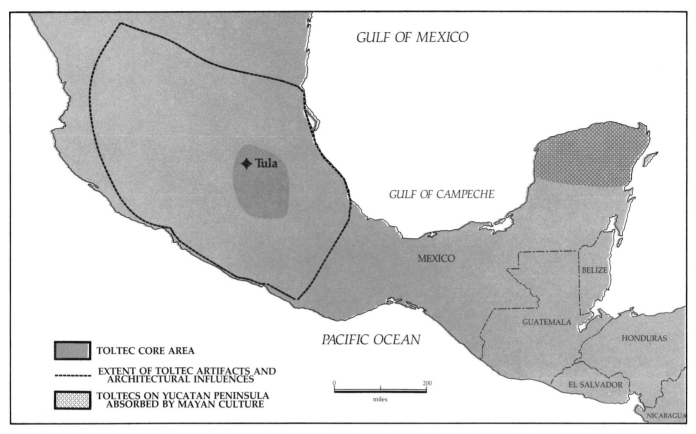

2.3 THE TOLTEC EMPIRE *(with modern boundaries)*

GULF OF MEXICO

◆ Tula

GULF OF CAMPECHE

PACIFIC OCEAN

MEXICO

BELIZE

GUATEMALA

HONDURAS

EL SALVADOR

NICARAGUA

TOLTEC CORE AREA

EXTENT OF TOLTEC ARTIFACTS AND ARCHITECTURAL INFLUENCES

TOLTECS ON YUCATAN PENINSULA ABSORBED BY MAYAN CULTURE

0   200
miles

innovation that reached these southern peoples, probably from Indians in Peru and Ecuador, was metallurgy, including the use of gold, copper, silver, zinc, and tin.

Still another strain of Mayan culture flourished after A.D. 1,000 to the north, on the Yucatan peninsula, after an invasion by Toltec peoples who interbred with the Mayas and adopted their tradition and esthetics. New ceremonial centers, such as Chichen Itza, Mayapan, and Tulum, had their day next.

TOLTECS

They came from the north into the Valley of Mexico—the nomadic Chichimecs, or "Sons of the Dog." Small groups came as early as the 8th century. But it wasn't until the early 10th century that one of these wandering tribes, the Tolteca-Chichimeca, managed to become dominant. Their leader's name was Mixcoatl. Learning from the local cultures, they built a great city of their own—Tula—located

on a defensible hilltop. In 968, Mixcoatl's son Topiltzin came to power. It is difficult to extricate fact from legend, since most of what is known about Toltec history has been passed along through Aztec myths and poems in which both father and son are considered gods—Mixcoatl as a hunting god and Topiltzin as Quetzalcoatl, the ancient Plumed Serpent, whose name he took. Yet it is known that Topiltzin-Quetzalcoatl established a Toltec empire where there had been independent city-states. It is also known that he strived to raise the level of culture among his people. Because of his efforts the Toltec name came to be synonymous with "civilized" in later tradition.

Topiltzin-Quetzalcoatl encouraged architecture, and the Toltecs became master builders: They erected palaces with colonnaded and frescoed halls; they constructed tall pyramids; they built masonry ball-courts. He encouraged agriculture, and the Toltecs developed improved strains of maize, squash, and cotton. He encouraged metallurgy, and the Toltecs crafted fine objects in gold and silver. New forms of pottery also appeared in Toltec culture; and weaving, featherworking, and hieroglyphic writing were further developed.

Tradition has it that the peaceful Topiltzin-Quetzalcoatl fell out of power when he tried to ban human sacrifice, which the Toltecs practiced

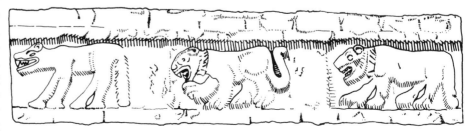

Toltec coyote and felines (detail of bas-relief from a pyramid at Tula)

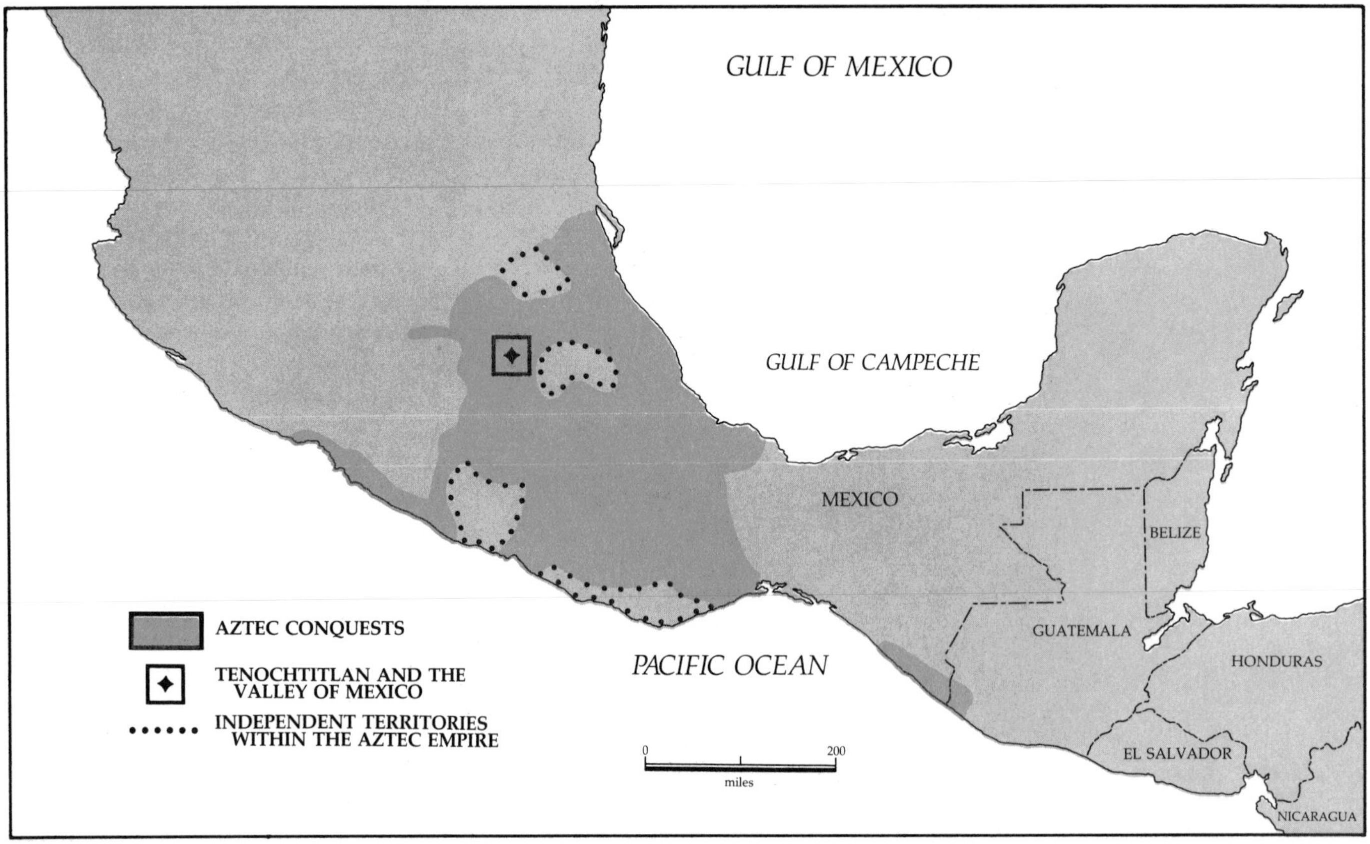
GULF OF MEXICO
GULF OF CAMPECHE
MEXICO
BELIZE
GUATEMALA
HONDURAS
EL SALVADOR
NICARAGUA
PACIFIC OCEAN
0
200
miles
AZTEC CONQUESTS
TENOCHTITLAN AND THE VALLEY OF MEXICO
INDEPENDENT TERRITORIES WITHIN THE AZTEC EMPIRE

2.4 THE AZTEC EMPIRE *(with modern boundaries)*

on a large scale. As a result, his followers—that is, the followers of the benign Plumed Serpent—were overthrown by devotees of the god Tezcatlipoca, deity of the night. The exact nature of the power struggle is not known. Perhaps the two gods stood for theocratic and militaristic elements of Toltec society. Nor is it known what happened to Topiltzin-Quetzalcoatl and his followers after their supposed defeat. Perhaps they were the Toltecs who invaded Yucatan and brought about the Mayan renaissance; the time-scale is right. Whether the great king lived on or not, the legend of Quetzalcoatl became so strong in Mesoamerica that centuries later Moctezuma II, Emperor of the Aztecs, thought that Cortes, the Spanish conquistador, was the returning god.

As for the Toltecs who stayed in power in Tula and the Valley of Mexico, they were plagued by a series of droughts, fires, and invasions of northern nomads. They had come full circle. They had once been the conquering Dog People; now they were being conquered in turn. Tula was destroyed in 1160.

AZTECS

Like the Toltecs before them, whom they came to revere, the Mexicas were a Chichimec people who spoke a Nahuatl language and migrated into the Valley of Mexico from the north. The date given for their arrival in the region is 1168. During the years that followed, they lived as wanderers on the fringes of the local cultures, sometimes serving as army mercenaries with their deadly bows and arrows. Supposedly in the year 1325, with no other choices left to them in the fierce competition for territory, they founded two settlements on swampy islets in Lake Texcoco—Tlatelolco and Tenochtitlan.

Tenochtitlan (the site of present-day Mexico City) proceeded to expand; wickerwork baskets were anchored to the lake's shallow bottom and piled up with silt and plant matter to create *chinampas*, artificial islands for farming. Eventually Tenochtitlan conquered and absorbed Tlatelolco. The residents of Tenochtitlan, who now called themselves Tenochas, then conspired and fought their way to dominance over the valley's competing city-states. Their final coup was an alliance with the Alcohuas of Texcoco against the Tepanecs, other recent arrivals in the valley and the Tenochas' major rival. The Tenochas took a new name—the Aztecs—after the legendary Aztlan from where they

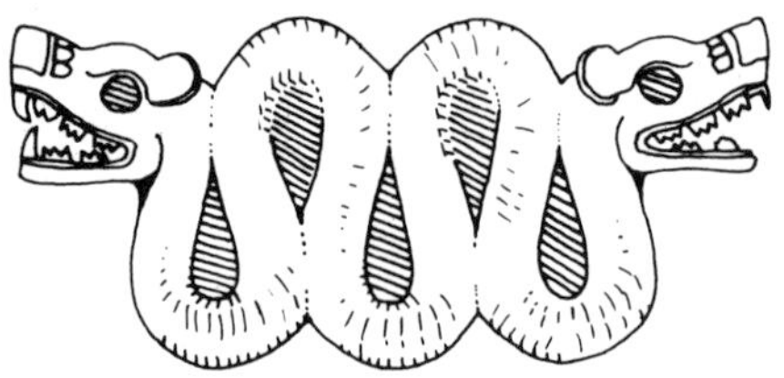

Aztec pendant (mosaic of turquoise with red shell nostrils and white shell teeth)

were supposed to have come, and they eventually subjugated most people of central Mexico. Tenochtitlan became a city of hundreds of buildings, interconnected by an elaborate system of canals, with an estimated 300,000 inhabitants. And the Aztec Empire came to comprise five million people.

Conquest and reconquest served two purposes for the Aztecs. First, it created and maintained their trading empire. Gold, silver, copper, pearls, jade, turquoise, and obsidian were important trade goods; so were the staples of corn, beans, squash, tomatoes, cotton, cacao, mangoes, papayas, and avocadoes, as well as domesticated dogs and turkeys. These same goods were often taken in tribute from defeated peoples who were given nothing in exchange. But the Aztecs wanted more than just goods from the people they conquered; they wanted their very persons. Their second motive for continued military activity was the taking of captives for human sacrifice, which served as a function of the state for keeping order.

Religion permeated Aztec life. Each of their gods—many of the same gods worshipped by earlier Mesoamerican peoples, such as Quetzalcoatl—had its own cult. Huitzilopochtli, the war god, an invention of the Aztecs, demanded the most tribute. Thousands of prisoners were slain at the top of his temple pyramids, their hearts torn out by priests. The Aztecs did not originate human sacrifice in Mesoamerica, but they carried it to new extremes of efficiency and fanaticism.

The priests, although central to Aztec society, were not all-powerful as in other Mesoamerican theocracies. At the apex of the class system was the Chief of Men, selected from a royal lineage by noblemen of the city's clans, each controlling a sector. In addition to the Chief of Men, the priests, and the clan representatives, wealthy merchants and war chiefs shared in the power. Below them all were commoners, including the craftsmen and farmers, as well as a propertyless group of unskilled laborers. Below these were the slaves.

Of all the so-called "lost civilizations," the Aztecs are the best known, being at the height of their power when Europeans arrived. Although the Spanish quickly destroyed much of Aztec culture—temples, sculpture, writings—they also recorded considerable information about it. Yet, despite all that is known about the Aztecs, a puzzling paradox remains. Here was a complex, sophisticated culture with high intellectual pursuits and a refined sense of esthetics; yet here also was a ferocious culture that fed on the ritualistic death of others.

TEOTIHUACAN, MONTE ALBAN, AND OTHER IMPORTANT MESOAMERICAN POPULATION CENTERS

One can approach the history of Mesoamerica either as the saga of different groups of peoples or as that of particular population centers inhabited by successive peoples. The Olmecs, Mayas, Toltecs, and Aztecs were so dominant at their cultural apogees that they are usually given the former treatment, their principal centers discussed along with them. Yet the densely populated Middle America was home to many other Indian peoples with varying degrees of cultural development, from the primitive to the highly sophisticated. Some of these will be touched upon in the following discussion of important historical sites. For additional information concerning the location of other Mesoamerican peoples, see "The Indian Culture Areas" in chapter 3.

TEOTIHUACAN

It is not known who the people were who founded the city-state of Teotihuacan and took it to its prominent

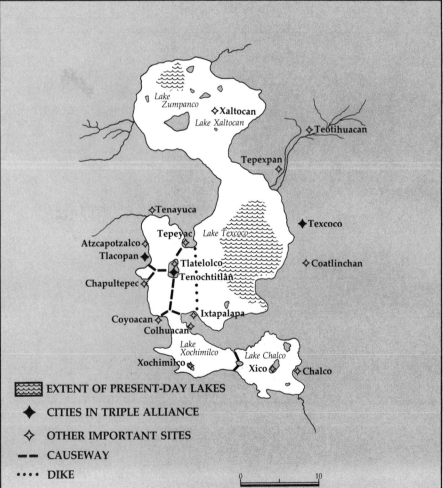

EXTENT OF PRESENT-DAY LAKES

◆ CITIES IN TRIPLE ALLIANCE

◇ OTHER IMPORTANT SITES

— — CAUSEWAY

•••• DIKE

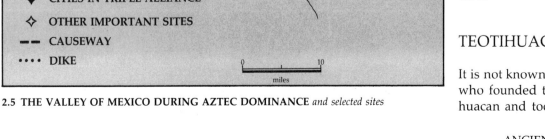

2.5 THE VALLEY OF MEXICO DURING AZTEC DOMINANCE *and selected sites*

role in the Classic period. Whoever they were, while the Mayas flourished to the southeast, the Teotihuacans attained their own cultural heights in the Valley of Mexico. And the cross-cultural influences between the two peoples played a part in the greatness of both.

Teotihuacan, evolving into more than a ceremonial center, became the first true city of Mesoamerica, a well-planned metropolis covering eight square miles with an estimated maximum population of 125,000. The inhabitants built plazas, boulevards, parks, canals, drain conduits, marketplaces, workshops, apartment houses (adobe-and-plaster blocks of one-storied, multiroomed structures), and temple pyramids. Two massive pyramids—the 200-foot-high Pyramid of the Sun and the smaller Pyramid of the Moon—were connected by the city's main thoroughfare, the three-mile-long Avenue of the Dead. The Citadel—a large square enclosure of buildings, including the Temple of Quetzalcoatl—also adjoined the avenue.

Religion and politics were entwined in Teotihuacan's stratified society. Its buildings housed its religious leaders and nobility, as well as merchants and craftsmen, with neighborhoods determined by occupation. Most farmers

Remojades clay figurine

lived in surrounding villages. With agricultural techniques improved beyond the slash-and-burn method— including the use of irrigation and *chinampas*—they produced enough food for a rapidly expanding urban population.

From this dynamic center of religion, commerce, and art, Teotihuacan culture fanned out over much of Mesoamerica. Military themes are minimal in the city's many frescoes, indicating that trade and not warfare played the more significant role in the dispersion of ideas. Many Teotihuacan cultural elements spread to other peoples: hieroglyphic writing, calendar systems, architectural styles, agricultural techniques, and the worship of particular gods, such as Quetzalcoatl (the Plumed Serpent) and Tlaloc (the rain god), as well as the practice of human sacrifice. The city also exported many finely crafted goods— tools; utensils; jewelry; clothing; carvings, especially of obsidian; and tall-lidded, thin-walled, orange-ware pottery.

Teotihuacan's decline came in the 8th century. Drought, agricultural crisis, fire, rebellion, invasion—all or any of these may have played a part. The ruins of the city came to be known to the Aztecs later as the "Abode of the Gods."

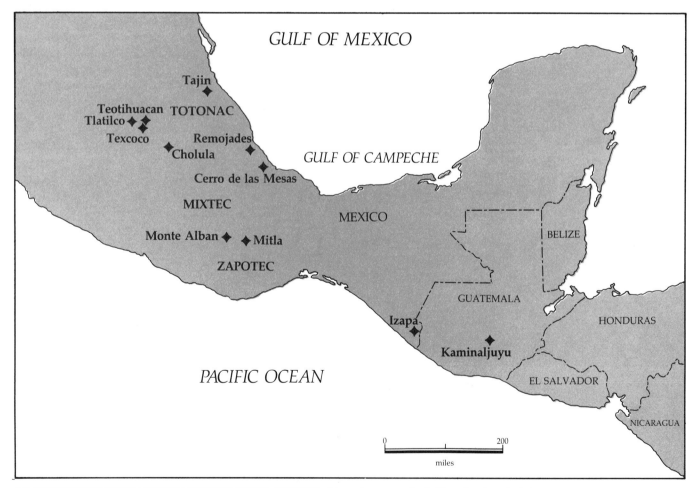

2.6 IMPORTANT MESOAMERICAN POPULATION CENTERS *of lesser known peoples (with modern boundaries)*

KAMINALJUYU

This ancient city-state in the highlands of present-day Guatemala, near the modern site of Guatemala City, was an outpost of Teotihuacan culture, with Teotihuacan-style architecture, although on a smaller scale. Moreover, the tombs of Kaminaljuyu contained luxuries from its parent city. The Teotihuacan interest here probably stemmed from this city's strategic location on the southern trade route and the nearby plentiful source of obsidian.

MONTE ALBAN

Over the course of two millennia the mountaintop site of Monte Alban in Mexico's Oaxaca region evolved from a ceremonial center to a civic center to a royal cemetery. The first shrine was built about 500 B.C., probably by direct ancestors of the widespread Zapotec peoples. Artifacts from this period show Olmec influence, especially in the bas-reliefs of "dancers." During the Classic period the Zapotecs leveled off the site's rocky promontory and built temples, palaces, ball-courts, and residential quarters around a huge central plaza. A priestly hierarchy ruled Monte Alban, and a surrounding rural population of farmers supported it. The great number of richly decorated masonry tombs in the mountainside attest to the wealth of the city's elite.

The Zapotecs abandoned the site about A.D. 900. During the Postclassic period, the Mixtecs, a warlike people from the north, came to dominate the region and used Monte Alban for royal burials. In one of their tombs (Tomb no. 7), over 500 objects of gold, silver, jade, turquoise, pearl, onyx, marble, amber, and other materials have been found.

MITLA

Mitla in Oaxaca became the most important Zapotec ceremonial center after the abandonment of Monte Alban in the Postclassic period. The site is famous for its groups of low horizontal palaces with entire walls of geometric stonework mosaics. As in the case of Monte Alban, the Mixtecs eventually replaced the Zapotecs at Mitla.

TAJIN

It is not certain whether the Totonacs built Tajin, an extensive city in the Veracruz region of Mexico, but it is known that they lived there and used its seven-tiered pyramid with its four sides representing the seasons, its 365 niches for the days of the year, and its unique overhanging eaves. Various connections are postulated: the Totonacs as a branch of the Olmecs, or the builders of Teotihuacan as the builders of Tajin. Tajin's Classic Veracruz style, which may or may not be Totonac, is known for carved objects associated with ceremonial ball games. Tajin was destroyed by fire, possibly set by Chichimec invaders from the north.

TLATILCO

Tlatilco in the Valley of Mexico was an important population center in Formative or Preclassic Mesoamerica. Hundreds of burials containing lavish offerings, especially delicate and cheerfully expressive clay figurines, have been found at the site. Olmec influences are indicated.

IZAPA

Izapa culture, as found at the Izapa site on the border of present-day Mexico and Guatemala near the Pacific Coast, is sometimes viewed as an intermediary culture between Olmec and Classic Maya. Both location and time-scale fit this hypothesis, as do artistic traits.

CERRO DE LAS MESAS

This Gulf Coast site, which attained its cultural zenith during the early Classic period, has revealed elements of various other cultures, in particular Olmec and Teotihuacan. Artifacts include stelae with "were-jaguar" motifs, a large statue of a duck-billed human, and an assortment (782 pieces) of carved jade.

REMOJADES

The Remojades site on the Gulf Coast has given its name to a naturalistic style of pottery abundant in the area. Tens of thousands of hollow clay figurines—of men, women, children, and gods—have been found. Their features were cast from clay molds and accentuated with black asphalt paint.

CHOLULA

At the site of Cholula, southeast of the Valley of Mexico, stands the largest ancient structure of the New World—the Great Pyramid, covering 25 square acres and looming 180 feet. Dedicated to Quetzalcoatl, it was not built all at once but in four successive superpositions by the site's original inhabitants during the Classic period. Later, the Toltecs inhabited the site, and then the Aztecs.

TEXCOCO

Texcoco, on the eastern shore of Lake Texcoco, became the Valley of Mexico's intellectual center under Nezahualcoyotl, an Alcohua king who was also a poet, philosopher, architect, and engineer. His alliance with the Aztecs in the 15th century helped wrest power from the Tepanecs and bring about the eventual Aztec empire. Moreover, Nezahualcoyotl, who became a legendary figure in Middle America, helped design the Aztec city of Tenochtitlan. His own city, Texcoco, is known for its many temples, including the Temple to the Unknown God, its many palaces, and its beautiful gardens.

CIVILIZATIONS OF THE SOUTHWEST

The Southwest, as discussed here, stretches from present-day southern Utah and Colorado through Arizona, New Mexico, and a corner of Texas, into northern Mexico. In this rugged, generally infertile terrain of mountain, mesa, canyon, and desert, Precontact agriculture attained its highest state of development north of the advanced agrarian civilizations of Mesoamerica. Two factors account for this paradox: first, the region's proximity to Mesoamerica, the cradle of Indian agriculture; and second, the harsh environment of the Southwest with its limited game and edible wild plants, making agriculture a practical and appealing alternative.

With the Mesoamerican influence from the south, three dominant cultures or specializations arose out of the earlier Archaic Cochise-Desert tradition: Mogollon, Hohokam, and Anasazi. For each, the adoption of agriculture made sedentary village life possible and brought about the further development of tools, arts, and crafts, especially pottery. And, with extensive interaction, each of the three cultures was influenced by the others. Yet each had distinct characteristics as well.

A fourth culture in the region, the Patayan (or Hakataya), is sometimes treated as a parallel branch of the early Hohokam (their Pioneer stage), but will be discussed separately here. Three other Precontact Southwest peoples—the Sinagua, Salado, and Fremont—are culturally derivative of the major groups, but also warrant brief summaries.

MOGOLLON
("Mountain People")

The Mogollons are named for the small, tortuous mountain range along the southern Arizona–New Mexico border, their culture's core area. These high-valley Indians, descen-

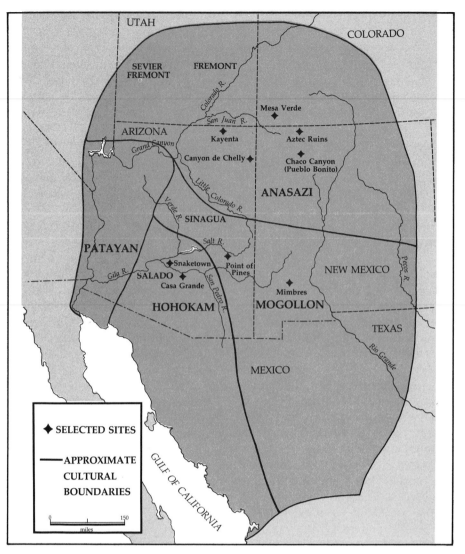

2.7 CIVILIZATIONS OF THE SOUTHWEST (*with modern boundaries*)

dants of the Cochise, are generally considered the first Southwest people to adopt agriculture, house building, and pottery making.

At the culture's peak, Mogollon crops included corn, beans, squash, tobacco, and cotton. Farming methods were primitive, involving the simple digging stick. In fact, the Mogollons continued to depend heavily on small-game hunting, aided after about A.D. 500 by the adoption of the bow and arrow, as well as wild-food gathering, which included roots, berries, seeds, nuts, and insects.

Yet it was the newfound agriculture that led to permanent villages and new types of building among the Mogollons. At sites near mountain streams and along defensible ridges, the Mogollons built their ingenious pit houses—semisubterranean structures

three or four feet in the ground, with log frames and roofs of saplings, reeds, and mud. Because of the sunken walls and the ground's natural insulation, these dwellings were espe-

Mogollon Mimbres black-on-white pottery

cially suited to the region's extreme temperature fluctuations. Some of these structures, larger than the others, served as social and ceremonial centers (kivas). Long into their history, after about A.D. 1100, the Mogollons began building aboveground pueblos as a result of Anasazi influence from the north. Villages grew to as many as 30 structures.

The earliest Mogollon pottery was brown, built up from coils of clay, smoothed over, then covered with a slip of fine clay before firing. Eventually, again because of Anasazi influence, the Mogollons came to paint their pottery, decorating it with intricate geometric designs. The Mimbres group, a Mogollon subculture in what is now southwestern New Mexico, is famous for its stunning black-on-white painted pottery.

The Mogollons are also known for their weaving—clothing and blankets made from cotton, feathers, and animal-fur yarn—as well as basketry and an extensive inventory of stone, wood, bone, and shell artifacts.

Slowly, approximately between the years A.D. 1200 and 1400, the Mogollon culture lost its distinct identity as it was absorbed by the then well-advanced Anasazi. It is thought, however, that Mogollon blood runs in the veins of the present-day Zuni Indians.

HOHOKAM ("Vanished Ones")

Meanwhile, a second Southwest culture had arisen out of the Archaic Cochise-Desert tradition—the Hohokam (the "vanished ones" in the Pima language). These ancient people were concentrated to the west of the Mogollons in the torrid desert lands of the Gila and Salt river valleys, broken only by parched volcanic hills. In their early stages, they demonstrated the three basic traits that define the Mogollon culture—agriculture (in their case on river floodplains), pit houses, and pottery. Yet, because of the inhospitable environment and the scarcity of game and edible plants, a distinct cultural pattern emerged—almost a total commitment to agriculture, made possible by the extensive use of irrigation.

The remarkable Hohokam irrigation systems included diversion dams on rivers with woven-mat valves and an intricate grid of wide, shallow canals, some of them extending as many as 10 miles to the fields of corn, beans, squash, tobacco, and cotton. The advanced agricultural techniques permitted large settlements. At the height of the Hohokam culture, Snaketown, the principal village, which was occupied for 1,500 years

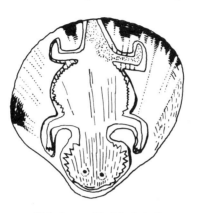

Hohokam acid-etched shell

and is located near present-day Phoenix, came to cover 300 acres with about 100 pit houses, similar to the Mogollon structures but larger and shallower.

There is much evidence for an active Mesoamerican connection in Hohokam lifeways. In fact, some scholars theorize that these people were descended from southern immigrants rather than from the Cochise. In any case, the Hohokam irrigation farming, their dominant red-on-buff pottery, the human figurines of clay, their elaborate textiles, the mosaic iron-pyrite mirrors, the copper bells, the stone palettes, the truncated earthen pyramids, the large ball-courts with rubber balls, and their keeping of macaws as house pets all point to extensive interaction with cultures of Mesoamerica. It should be mentioned, however, that in spite of the probable connection, the peaceful Hohokams rejected the typically Mesoamerican traits of priest-rulers, forced tribute to powerful political centers, and aggression toward one's tribal neighbors.

The Hohokams are also known as possibly the first people in the world to master etching, a process invented sometime after A.D. 1000. Their method was to cover shells with acid-resistant pitch, carve designs on this coating, then bathe the shells in an acid solution made from fermented saguaro cactus fruit. When the coating was removed, an etched design remained.

It is not known why the Hohokams abandoned Snaketown and other settlements, such as Point of Pines, around A.D. 1500, scattering in small groups—possibly it was due to prolonged drought and/or raiding nomadic tribes. It is thought that these small groups became the ancestors of the modern Pima and Papago peoples.

ANASAZI ("Ancient Ones")

Northeast of the Hohokams, in the so-called Four-Corners area of the present-day Utah, Colorado, Arizona, and New Mexico, among the high mesas and deep canyons, was the heartland of the Anasazi people—the "ancient ones" in the Navajo language. Their culture began taking on its distinct characteristics later than the Mogollon and Hohokam, about 100 B.C., but it became by the time of its climax the most extensive and influential by far in the Southwest.

The first stage in Anasazi development is called the Basket Maker period because of the people's mastery in weaving food containers, sandals, and other goods from straw, vines, rushes, and yucca. Over the course of the Basket Maker period, the Anasazis developed and refined their ceramics and agricultural skills, while continuing to hunt and gather. They also began living in semipermanent rounded and domed structures erected over shallow depressions from horizontal mud-chinked logs. These eventually gave way, through southern influences, to the Mogollon/Hohokam-style pit houses.

Yet, after A.D. 750, the pit house, although retained within the culture for social and ceremonial purposes, itself gave way to a radical new form of architecture–the pueblo. In addition to the structures themselves, this originally Spanish word for town or community has come to be applied to the Golden Age of Anasazi culture, the Pueblo period, as well as to modern Pueblo Indians who inherited Anasazi cultural traits. The aboveground structures are constructed of stone and adobe (mud) mortar or entirely of adobe bricks, with beamed roofs of sticks, grass, and mud. Although the Anasazis had originally developed pueblos as single storage rooms, then single-family houses, they soon conceived of the idea of grouping the rooms together with shared walls and on top of one another, ladders connecting the various levels. And, with the levels stepped back in terraces, the roofs of one could serve as the front yards of another below.

Anasazi ceramic male effigy

Elaborately designed multitiered, multiroomed apartment buildings resulted from this Anasazi breakthrough in technology. Pueblo Bonito in Chaco Canyon, started around A.D. 900, is a prime and stunning example. A hugh masonry semicircular structure, its arc connected by a straight wall, this pueblo had five stories and 800 rooms. Other structures sprang up on mesa tops all over the region. And nearby them, on the open plateaus, the inhabitants could grow crops to support these large settlements. Anasazi farming techniques in the Pueblo period included terraced fields and reservoir-canal irrigation systems.

From about A.D. 1000–1300, as Anasazi influence spread outward, the Southwest supported a growing population of builders, farmers, potters, weavers, and other artisans. It was a culturally rich, creative time of intricately painted pottery, brightly colored cotton-and-feather clothing, sparkling turquoise jewelry, meticulous mosaic work, and a whole range of functional tools and utensils. During this Golden Age, many of the mesa-top pueblos were evacuated, probably for defensive purposes, in favor of terraced cliff dwellings in arched recesses of canyon walls; examples can be found at Cliff Palace in Mesa Verde and Mummy Cave in Canyon de Chelly.

Then, starting about 1300, the Anasazis abandoned their great villages entirely and moved elsewhere, many of them southward, some along the Rio Grande, and others along the Little Colorado River. There are various theories for this mass exodus—the prolonged drought of 1276–99 and a change in seasonal rainfall patterns; nomadic invaders, in particular Utes and Apaches; fighting among the various pueblos; a depletion of the wood supply. Whatever the reason or combination of reasons, the evacuees established new, smaller pueblos and passed on many of the Anasazi cultural traits to their descendants, modern-day Pueblo Indians, including Rio Grande peoples and Hopis.

PATAYAN (Hakataya)

The Patayan culture, sometimes called the Hakataya, was centered along the Colorado River south of the Grand Canyon in what is now western Arizona. Like the early Hohokams, with whom they are sometimes grouped, the Patayans hunted and gathered to supplement their nascent farming. Unlike the Hohokams, however, their irrigation methods went only as far as planting their crops in river floodwaters. Moreover, they lived in aboveground brush huts rather than pit houses.

The Patayan people made a brownish pottery, sometimes painted in red, as well as baskets. They also crafted decorations out of seashells from the Gulf of California, which they used for trading purposes.

It is supposed that the Patayans are the ancestors of various Yuman-speaking tribes, including the contemporary Yumas, Mojaves, Cocopas, Maricopas, Havasupais, Yavapais, and Hualapais.

SINAGUA

The Sinagua peoples, thought to have arrived in the region from the north, settled along the Verde River valley in present-day Arizona. A derivative culture, they learned farming techniques from the Hohokams and building from the Anasazis. They were active in the region from about A.D. 500 to 1400; they reached their cultural climax about 1100, which probably was due to the soil enrichment caused by the previous century's eruption of what is now called Sunset Crater.

SALADO

About A.D. 1300, the Saladoans, an Anasazi offshoot, migrated westward from the tablelands into the flat, desert, Hohokam territory of the Gila River. For several generations, they lived peacefully among their hosts and passed along Anasazi adobe building techniques. After about 1400, they moved away.

FREMONT AND SEVIER FREMONT

The Fremont peoples lived to the north of the Anasazis in present-day Utah. The fact that this otherwise unrelated northern culture reveals certain typical Anasazi traits, including pit houses, surface adobe houses, and black-on-grey painted pottery, is evidence of the great extent of Anasazi influence. The Fremont culture is also known for its unique clay figurines.

THE MOUND BUILDERS (Adena and Hopewell Cultures)

In eastern and midwestern North America, because of the bountiful plant and animal life, advanced cultures with sizable populations were able to arise without large-scale agriculture. These were the Mound Builders, or the Adena and Hopewell cultures, centered in the Ohio Valley. The Adena lasted from about 1000 B.C. to A.D. 200; the Hopewell, from about 300 B.C. to A.D. 700.

Although the two shared many cultural traits and coexisted for five centuries, their exact relationship is not known—e.g., to what degree Adena was ancestral to Hopewell, or whether there were conflicts between them. Nor is it known where either of the two peoples originally came from—some scholars have theorized from as far away as Middle America; others, the Great Lakes region—or what happened to them when their cultures faded. Well into the 19th century, theories of lost European tribes were still applied to the hundreds of ancient man-made mounds throughout the East. But of course, as science eventually proved, the earthworks and the artifacts under or near them were aboriginal, another expression of ancient Indian culture.

ADENA

The Adena culture radiated from the Ohio River Valley into territory that is now Kentucky, West Virginia, Indiana, Pennsylvania, and New York. Adena migrants, probably displaced by the Hopewells, later settled near the Chesapeake Bay and in Alabama as well. The Adenas are named after an estate near Chillicothe, Ohio,

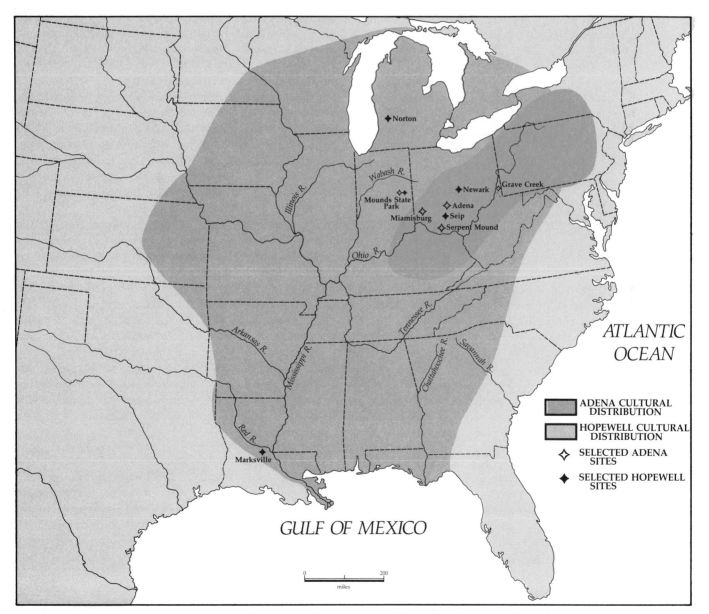

2.8 THE MOUND BUILDERS: *Adena and Hopewell spheres of influence and selected sites (with modern boundaries)*

where a large mound stands in what was the heartland of the culture.

There is some evidence of incipient agriculture among the Adenas—the cultivation of sunflowers, pumpkins, gourds, and goosefoot as food sources. It is known that they eventually grew tobacco for ceremonial use. But they were primarily hunters and gatherers, enjoying, like other Woodland peoples, the rich flora and fauna of their homelands—rich enough, in fact, to support a sedentary rather than nomadic life-style.

The framework of Adena houses had a unique construction. Outward-sloping posts, set in pairs, formed a

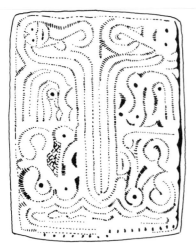

Adena incised stone tablet

circle. Four vertical center posts supported the high ends of the rafter poles that extended downward, beyond the wall posts, to form generous eaves. The walls were wattled and the roof was matted or thatched.

It is the Adena earthworks, however, found in and around their villages, that affirm their high degree of social organization. Conical and dome-shaped burial mounds grew larger and more ambitious over the centuries. In the early stages of the culture, low earthen hillocks were built up, basketful by basketful, over the burial pits of honored individuals. Later, high mounds were constructed over multiple burials, the corpses usually placed in log-lined tombs. With new burials, another layer of dirt would be added to the mound. Often these earthen monuments were sur-

rounded by other earthworks—rounded walls or ridges of earth, usually circular in shape and generally known as "Sacred Circles." Moreover, the Adenas constructed earthen effigy mounds—totemic animals or symbols. The Great Serpent Mound in Peebles, Ohio, is a prime example. A low, rounded embankment, about four feet high and 15 to 20 feet across, extends 1,330 feet in the shape of an uncoiling snake with jaws and tail.

Some Adena grave goods have been found (although not nearly as many as in Hopewell burials), the varying amounts indicating the social inequalities in the culture—engraved stone tablets, often with raptorial bird designs; polished gorgets (armor for the throat) of stone and copper; pearl beads; ornaments of sheet mica; tubular stone pipes; and bone masks. In addition to these ceremonial and ornamental objects, the Adena people also made a wide range of stone, wood, bone, and copper tools, as well as incised or stamped pottery and cloth woven from vegetable fibers.

HOPEWELL

As indicated by disputes over which of the two cultures inhabited certain archaeological sites, Hopewell culture possessed many of the same elements as the Adena. But they were generally on an enhanced scale—more, larger earthworks; richer burials; intensified ceremonialism; greater refinement in art; a stricter class system and increased division of labor; and more agriculture. And the Hopewell culture covered a much greater area, spreading from its core in the Ohio and Illinois river valleys throughout much of the Midwest and East. Moreover, the Hopewell people, whoever they were and wherever they originally came from, established a far-flung trading network. At Hopewell sites have been found obsidian from the Black Hills and the Rockies, copper from the Great Lakes, shells from the Atlantic and Gulf coasts, mica from the Appalachians, silver from Canada, and alligator skulls and teeth from Florida. All evidence implies that the

Hopewell sphere of influence spread via trade and religion (Hopewell is sometimes considered a cult as well as a culture), rather than conquest. Priest-rulers probably had the highest social ranking, with merchants and warlords beneath them.

Supporting even greater concentrations of people than the Adenas, the Hopewells depended more on agriculture and grew a variety of crops. It is conceivable they also traded for food products with other early agriculturalists. Their extensive villages, usually near water, consisted of circular or oval dome-roofed wigwams that were covered with animal skins, sheets of bark, or mats of woven plants.

The Hopewells, like the Adenas, constructed a variety of earthworks. Many of their mounds, covering multiple burials, stood 30 to 40 feet high. Large effigy mounds often stood nearby, as did geometric enclosures. Some of these earthen walls were 50 feet high and 200 feet wide at the base. The enclosure at Newark, Ohio, once covered four square miles with embankments laid out in a variety of shapes—circles, parallel lines, an octagon, and a square.

The Hopewell culture boasted consummate craftsmen, specialists in their structured society. They were masters of the functional as well as the artistic, and worked in both representational and abstract styles. The plentiful and beautiful grave furnishings found by archaeologists include ceramic figurines, copper headdresses and breast ornaments, obsidian spearheads and knives, mica mirrors, conch drinking cups, pearl jewelry, hammered-gold silhouettes, incised

Hopewell stone pipe with frog effigy

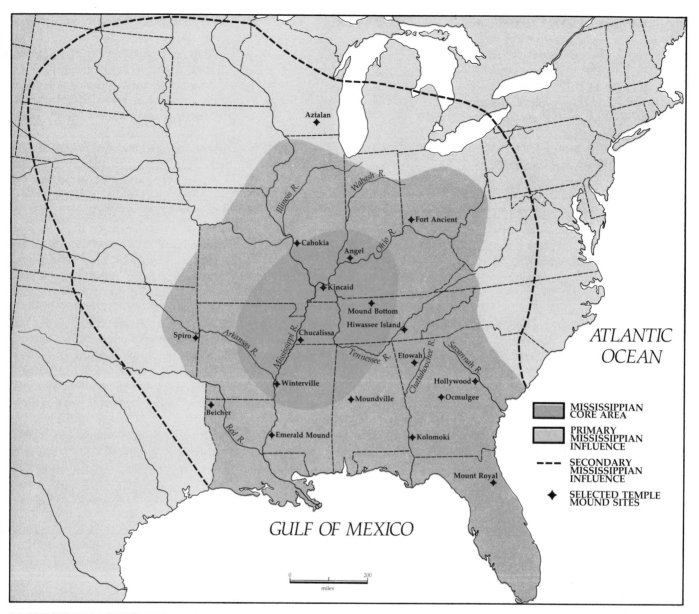

Aztalan

Fort Ancient

Cahokia

Angel

Kincaid

Mound Bottom

Hiwassee Island

Spiro

Chucalissa

Arkansas R.

Mississippi R.

Illinois R.

Wabash R.

Ohio R.

Tennessee R.

Etowah

Chattahoochee R.

Savannah R.

Hollywood

ATLANTIC OCEAN

Winterville

Moundville

Ocmulgee

Beicher

Red R.

Emerald Mound

Kolomoki

Mount Royal

MISSISSIPPIAN CORE AREA

PRIMARY MISSISSIPPIAN INFLUENCE

SECONDARY MISSISSIPPIAN INFLUENCE

SELECTED TEMPLE MOUND SITES

GULF OF MEXICO

0   200
miles

2.9 THE TEMPLE MOUND BUILDERS: *Mississippian sphere of influence and selected sites (with modern boundaries)*

and stamped pottery, and stone platform pipes with naturalistic human and animal sculptures.

But what became of these preeminent artists, these ambitious movers of earth, and these energetic traders? Why did the Hopewell culture perish? As with the decline of Mesoamerican and Southwest cultures, a variety of theories have been put forth—climate changes, crop failure, epidemics, civil war, invasion, or simply cultural fatigue. Whatever the case, another culture would come to dominate much of the same territory. Other mounds would be built, again near the river valleys. And on top of these new mounds would be temples.

THE TEMPLE MOUND BUILDERS (Mississippian Culture)

They were master farmers. They settled near the rich alluvial soil of riverbeds in the Southeast to grow corn, the staff of New World life, as well as beans, squash, pumpkins, and tobacco. They had an elaborate trade network among themselves and with other Indians, and crafted beautifully refined objects. They had a complex social structure and a rigid caste system. They were obsessed with death.

They built mounds, not only burial mounds like the Adenas and Hopewells before them, but also huge temple mounds. These were the people of the so-called Mississippian or Temple Mound Builder culture.

In addition to the obvious Adena-Hopewell influences, Mesoamerican influences, although still not proven, are apparent: Similar farming techniques, similar art styles, and similar use of temple mounds and open village plazas all point to interaction between the two regions. Contact could have come via Indian migrants or traders traveling northward by boat through the Gulf of Mexico or over land routes along it.

As in the case of Mesoamerican cultures, improved agricultural techniques made the Mississippian way of life possible. With enough food, a large population could sustain itself in one place over a long period. Many Mississippian ceremonial and trading centers resulted during the centuries from about A.D. 700 to Postcontact times, spreading out from the culture's heartland along the lower Mississippi Valley, over most of the Southeast from present-day Florida to Oklahoma, but also as far north as Wisconsin.

The largest and most famous Temple Mound site is Cahokia in Illinois, near St. Louis. The village area, extending for six miles along the Illinois River, contained 85 temple and burial mounds, and sustained an estimated maximum population of 75,000. The largest mound, Monk's Mound (because French Trappists once grew vegetables on its terraces), was built in 14 stages, from about A.D. 900 to 1150, basketful of dirt by basketful; by its completion it covered 16 acres at its base and stood 100 feet high. Other important Mississippian centers included Moundville in present-day Alabama; Etowah and Ocmulgee in Georgia; Spiro in Oklahoma; and Hiwassee Island in Tennessee.

Although the Mississippian mounds were rectangular and steep-sided like the temple pyramids of Mesoamerica, they were not stone-faced and their stairways were made of logs; nor were the temples themselves made of stone but, rather, of pole and thatch. Small-

Mississippian marble mortuary figure

er structures on mound terraces housed priests and nobles: the higher the dwelling, the higher the rank. Merchants, craftsmen, hunters, farmers, and laborers lived in surrounding huts, at times meeting in the central plazas to conduct their business.

The Mississippians used a variety of materials from different regions—among them clay, shell, marble, chert, mica, and copper—to make tools, jewelry, and ceremonial objects. Many objects, especially from after 1200, reveal a preoccupation with death, again indicating a Mesoamerican connection: Representations of human sacrifice appear on sculptures, pottery, masks, copper sheets, and gorgets; and certain symbols having to do with death—such as stylized skulls, bones, or weeping eyes—turn up again and again at Temple Mound sites. The diffusion of these symbolic elements throughout the Southeast

has come to be called the Southern Cult, Death Cult, or Buzzard Cult. The religion acted as a unifying force among the different centers, prohibiting warfare among them.

By the early 17th century, the great Mississippian centers had been abandoned. Overpopulation perhaps played a part, or crop loss due to climatic conditions, or political strife. Or perhaps the white man's diseases preceded him inland. In any case, by the time European explorers reached the sites, evidence of the Temple Mound Builders existence was already underground, only to be found centuries later by archaeologists.

One culture with numerous Mississippian traits did survive until the 18th century, however, allowing for extensive contact with whites—that of the Natchez Indians along the lower Mississippi. The French who lived among them and ultimately destroyed them recorded firsthand many of their lifeways. Like the earlier Mississippian peoples, the Natchez had a central temple mound and a nearby open plaza as well as satellite mounds, some of them for houses and some for burials. The Natchez supreme ruler, the Great Sun, lived on one of these. On others lived his mother, White Woman, who was also his adviser; his brothers, called Suns, from whom were chosen the war chief and head priest; and his sisters, Woman Suns. A complicated caste system regulated relationships and behavior. Beneath the royal family were the nobles and the honored men (lesser nobles), plus the commoners, referred to as "stinkards." All grades of nobility, male and female alike, were permitted to wed only commoners. And when a noble died, his or her mates and others in the entourage would give up their lives to accompany the dead to the next world. With the demise of the Natchez culture, Mississippian culture came to an end. (See "The Natchez Revolt" in chapter 5.) Some traits, however, survived among other Indians of the Southeast, such as the Creeks. (See "The Southeast Culture Area" in chapter 3.) But temple mounds would never be built again.

Etowah Mound, Georgia. Photo by Molly Braun.

Chapter 3
INDIAN LIFEWAYS

American Indian culture is an immense subject, covering many aspects of Indian life—subsistence, technology, art, religion, language, and social and political organization. Different tribes, bands, villages, and communities had varying customs, traditions, esthetics, and tools. There are many ways to organize the enormous volume of material—by tribe, by general cultural or geographic areas, or by cultural traits. Indeed, any one of thousands of cultural traits—whether activities, beliefs, or artifacts—can be represented cartographically, showing distribution.

Few books do justice to the extent and variety of Indian culture. This book, since it also treats the sweeping subject of Indian history, must limit itself to an introductory overview. Maps and text on geography, population density, and subsistence patterns, as well as on specific cultural traits—arts and crafts, shelter, clothing, transportation, religion, psychotropics, sociopolitical organization, and language—are presented in con-

junction with maps and discussions of 12 North American culture areas. The culture-area maps show the locations of the major tribes at the time of Contact with whites.

GEOGRAPHY AND CULTURE

When European explorers first arrived in North America, they encountered aboriginal peoples who had worked out stable, long-term adaptations to their local environments and available resources. Native North Americans lived within the balance of nature, and their cultural and religious beliefs expressed a deep reverence for the land and a sense of kinship with wildlife. To the Indian, mankind was just one of many interdependent parts of the universe. Indians for the most part lived on the land as they found it, with minimal ecological disruption. Many of the explorers reported that, except in some regions with particularly harsh environments, there was generally a profusion of natural resources to support Indian population levels. Moreover, they reported how tame and easy to hunt much of the game seemed, which

supports the idea of aboriginal harmony with nature.

Because of the interconnection between Indians and their environment, the study of Indian culture is also the study of geography and natural history—hence, the integrated academic discipline of cultural geography, and also the common use of regional culture or geographic areas as a format for discussions of Indian lifeways. There is generally a direct relationship between geography and culture.

Yet it should also be kept in mind that cultural development in the form of agriculture and trade alter this formula. With plant cultivation and irrigation techniques, harsh and dry environments came to support large populations. And with extensive trade contacts, people needed no longer be so dependent on the raw materials at hand.

The accompanying maps on physiography, climate, rainfall, and vegetation give an overview of the multifarious North American environment. Used in conjunction with the various culture-area maps and tables of cultural traits, one can get a sense of inviolate Indian life minus European intervention and influences.

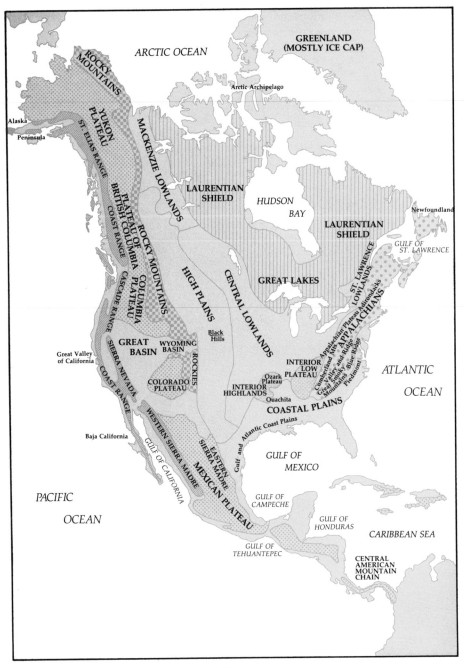

3.1 PHYSIOGRAPHY OF NORTH AMERICA

major traditions—on the one hand, hunting, fishing, and gathering; and on the other hand, agriculture—along with their stages of development. The methods of survival that existed among Indians at the time of Contact had been passed down from earlier generations. And at the time of Contact, different peoples lived the lifestyles of peoples from earlier cultural periods, with varying degrees of technology—some as typically Lithic or Archaic hunters and gatherers, and others as highly organized Classic villagers and farmers. (See also chapters 1 and 2 on "ANCIENT INDIANS" and "ANCIENT CIVILIZATIONS," and the section in this chapter, "The Indian Culture Areas.")

HUNTING, FISHING, AND GATHERING

The Paleo-Indians who crossed the land bridge from Siberia were big-game hunters following the herds of mammoths, bighorn bison, musk oxen, and other large mammals to the grasslands of the interior of the North American continent. During the last glaciation of the Pleistocene, the climate was generally cool and moist on the Great Plains, and a luxuriant cover of grasses stretched for miles, dotted by lakes and marshes. This grassland supported some of the largest herds of mammals ever known, offering an ideal setting for early hunters.

Many of the hunting techniques of later Indian peoples were first applied by Lithic, or Stone Age, Indians. Spears served as the primary weapons, with travel by foot. Yet hunting involved much more than one or several hunters prowling after the large game. The collective hunts of the Paleo-Indians were models of social coordination involving entire bands, women included, and techniques such as driving herds into culs-de-sac or over cliffs. Indeed, the traditional view that hunting was an exclusively male activity, an expression of aggressive male instinct, and the implication that hunting made men dominant in early human societies, has been considerably modified by archaeologists and anthropologists.

SUBSISTENCE PATTERNS AND CULTURAL EVOLUTION

Subsistence was of course central to aboriginal life and culture. The acquisition of food demanded considerable time, energy, and ingenuity. It was the primary focus of Indian technology and a dominant theme in Indian religion, legend, and art. It also affected Indian culture in another broad way: The more time devoted to hunting, fishing, gathering, or growing food, the less time for other cultural pursuits.

The North American Indians ate a wide variety of foods and used a variety of means in acquiring them, depending on geography and availability as well as on knowledge and technology. In order to understand the various means of subsistence at the time of Contact and how they applied regionally, it is necessary to have a general understanding of two

Traditional views of early hunting cultures not only ignore the role of women in hunting, they also underestimate the importance of plants in the diet. Paleo-Indians were gatherers as well as big-game hunters, supplementing their diets with seeds, berries, roots, bulbs, and other food plants. Wild plants were especially important to tribes west of the Rocky Mountains, where game animals were smaller and fewer.

The use of fire was an important part of the technology of early hunting cultures. The technique of inten-

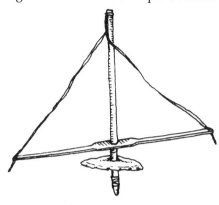

Eskimo pump fire drill

tional burning probably originated in big-game fire drives, but early Indian hunters and gatherers soon learned to use fire for other purposes as well, such as enlarging the area of grassland in order to attract grazing herds and to increase the yield of particular wild food plants. The use of fire, some geographers believe, may have led to the first human modification of the North American landscape, preventing the spread of forests and creating prairies of long grass in some areas. Indians developed various techniques of fire starting: striking a spark with flint and pyrites, or rubbing wood on wood. In the latter method, the fire drill—spinning a shaft against another piece of wood—was often used to create the necessary friction and to heat wood powder. Another implement was the fire plough in which a stick was rubbed over a wooden plane surface.

With the melting of the glaciers, beginning about 10,000 B.C., rising temperatures and lower rainfall led to major changes in the flora and fauna of the interior grasslands. This set the

stage for new cultural adaptations to the postglacial environment. The shift in climate thinned out the plant cover, reducing both the wild harvest for human gatherers as well as grazing lands for animals, and leading to one of the most extensive and controversial extinctions of large mammals, such as woolly mammoths, mastodons, and saber-toothed tigers. This controversy involves the role of human hunters in ending the era of the great herds. Some scholars have argued that the severe climatic changes alone cannot account for the extinc-

tions, because the same mammals had survived previous glacial melts. The difference, these scholars assert, was the presence of hunters in what is sometimes referred to as the Pleistocene Overkill. While the number of Paleo-Indians was relatively small, the great number of remains at excavated hunting sites suggests that the hunters may nonetheless have reduced the mammal population below the critical minimum required to reproduce and survive. The size of the kills also suggests that the early hunters added to the stress of climatic change by dis-

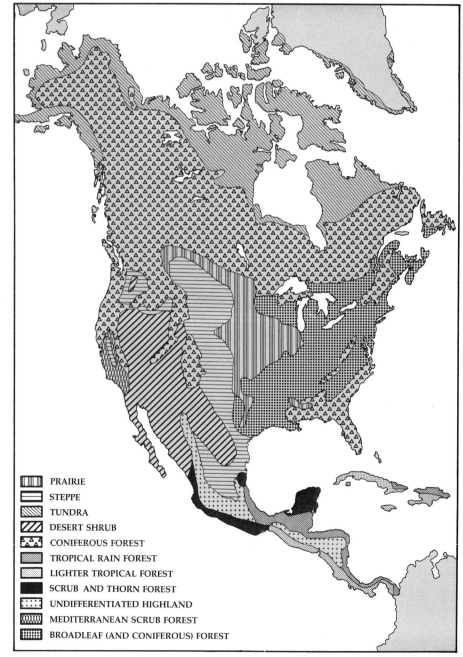

▦	PRAIRIE	
▤	STEPPE	
▨	TUNDRA	
▨	DESERT SHRUB	
▲▲	CONIFEROUS FOREST	
▨	TROPICAL RAIN FOREST	
⣿	LIGHTER TROPICAL FOREST	
■	SCRUB AND THORN FOREST	
⣿	UNDIFFERENTIATED HIGHLAND	
▩	MEDITERRANEAN SCRUB FOREST	
▦	BROADLEAF (AND CONIFEROUS) FOREST	

3.2 VEGETATION OF NORTH AMERICA

rupting the herd psychology and social organization of the large mammals.

As the great herds disappeared in the wake of retreating ice, postglacial flora and fauna established new niches in the altered landscape. The world's water, unlocked from ice, remodeled the coastlines, creating protein-rich tidal pools and marshlands. The expansion of northern breeding and feeding grounds prompted a dramatic increase in migrant water fowl. Alluvial valleys grew in length and breadth along rivers, and the floodplains and marshes were colonized by plants of high usefulness to humans. The northern woodlands, wet prairies, and marshes became ranges for bison, deer, moose, and elk.

With these climatic and physiographical changes, new Indian cultural adaptations and subsistence patterns evolved. The style of hunting shifted from predominantly large-scale drives of mammal herds to individual hunting of smaller animals and birds. Fishing and the harvesting

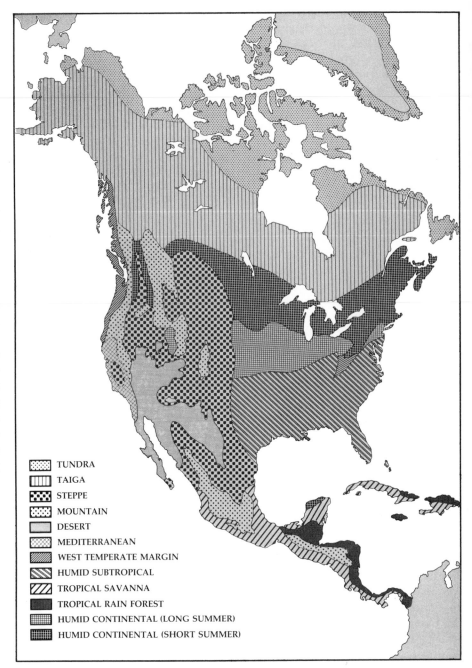

TUNDRA
TAIGA
STEPPE
MOUNTAIN
DESERT
MEDITERRANEAN
WEST TEMPERATE MARGIN
HUMID SUBTROPICAL
TROPICAL SAVANNA
TROPICAL RAIN FOREST
HUMID CONTINENTAL (LONG SUMMER)
HUMID CONTINENTAL (SHORT SUMMER)

3.3 CLIMATES OF NORTH AMERICA

Northwest Coast fishhook and lure

of aquatic resources became more common during the postglacial period. Populations increased in settlements along coastlines and river valleys. In general, the environmental changes now favored a specialized response to local ecozones and a diversification of the sources of sustenance. The shared culture spread by the seasonally nomadic Ice Age hunters dissolved into a number of distinct traditions attuned to the new realities of the postglacial world.

During the Archaic period, between the Paleolithic life of the Ice Age and the later agricultural revolution of the Formative period, the ancestors of the American Indians became increasingly sedentary, working out broad-based economies that insured the sustained vitality of local resources. Archaic Indians learned specialized responses to a remarkable diversity of environments, creating new and appropriate technologies in hunting and fishing equipment—smaller and more finely worked flints for spear points; well-balanced clubs; new missile-

clubs for throwing; snares and traps of many kinds; hooks, lines, lures, nets, harpoons, and the use of poisons and lights for fishing. The atlatl—a wooden spear-thrower with a stone weight (bannerstone) to increase leverage, invented at the end of the Lithic period—also became widespread. The bola—stones joined by cords, used for ensnaring game—was also invented by Archaic peoples. (The bow and arrow and the blowgun would appear among later generations in the Formative period.) For preservation of their catch, Indians

variety of domestic, hunting, and fishing equipment. Some scholars have theorized that plants may have originally been domesticated not for food but for material technology as well as for medicines and poisons.

AGRICULTURE

It is of course impossible to know exactly where the cultivation of plants was first conceived of and applied in the Americas, just as it is impossible to know whether the practice began with an individual, a tribe, or whether it was invented several times over. But it is known that agriculture was developed in both Middle and South America, with knowledge of crops passed among peoples of both locations, and then passed northward. (See "Transition and Culmination" in chapter 1.)

As for archaelogical evidence, the earliest indication of agriculture in Mesoamerica comes from one of the arid caves of Tamaulipas, known as Romero's Cave, near the Gulf of Mexico—cultivated beans, peppers, pumpkins, and gourds, dating back as far as 7,000 B.C., have been found there. The earliest maize found at this same archaeological site dates back to about 2,770 B.C. Older traces of domesticated corn—a variety of hybrid popcorn with a pod dating back to about 4,000 B.C.—have been found in

Mortar and pestle

the southern part of Mexico's state of Puebla. The wild corn from which ancient Indians developed these first hybrid strains no longer grows today, but archaeologists have found traces of the original wild variety in Mexico's Tehuacan Valley.

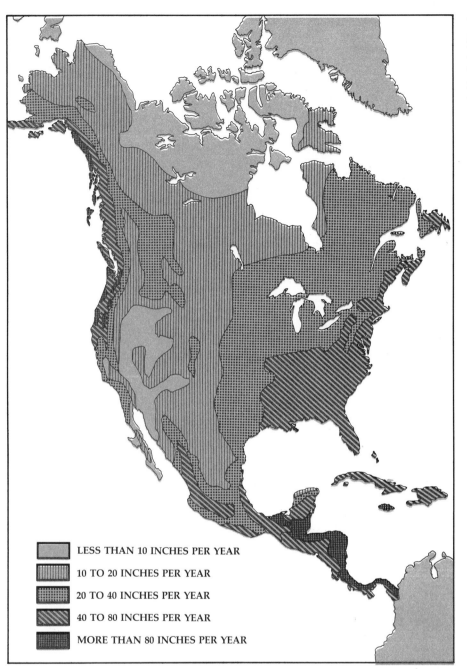

LESS THAN 10 INCHES PER YEAR

10 TO 20 INCHES PER YEAR

20 TO 40 INCHES PER YEAR

40 TO 80 INCHES PER YEAR

MORE THAN 80 INCHES PER YEAR

3.4 AVERAGE ANNUAL PRECIPITATION OF NORTH AMERICA

made jerky, or strips of dried meat, and pemmican, pulverized meat packed with mashed suet and berries. They also hung their food for safekeeping and buried it in caches. Cooking techniques included roasting, broiling, boiling, and baking (but not frying), through direct contact with fire or coals or by heating stones. And it was during the Archaic period that the origins of the revolutionary practice of plant domestication occurred.

Lithic and Archaic hunters and gatherers had already accumulated a considerable knowledge of plant life. Many of the major wild food plants had to be processed to remove toxins as well as prepared for cooking by milling, grinding, and pounding. Indians used baskets for gathering the foods, and stone and wood milling equipment, such as mortars and pestles, and manos and metates, for preparation. Fiber baskets and grinding stones dating back to the Lithic period have been found at Danger Cave in Utah. In fact, ancient basket making and milling cultures may have relied on plant materials for a wide

Meanwhile, in the Andes region along the western coast of South America, Indians were also cultivating plants, especially root crops such as white and sweet potatoes. And, by 3,500 B.C., agriculture had reached at least one location and community in North America—Bat Cave in what is now New Mexico, where cultivated corncobs have been found among other remnants of Cochise culture. (See "Archaic Indians" in chapter 1.) And, in the course of following centuries, agricultural skills, including the use of digging sticks, rakes, and hoes, were spread among peoples

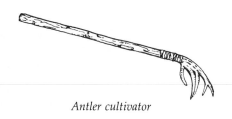

Antler cultivator

throughout much of North America. In many of the regions, such as the Southwest and Southeast, agriculture and the resulting sedentary village life came to be associated with highly organized societies. (See "Civilizations of the Southwest" and "The Temple Mound Builders" in chapter 2.) There

were, however, exceptions to this cultural pattern. Along the Northwest Coast, for example, plentiful food resources without agriculture allowed for extensive social and artistic development.

Of the many plants cultivated in the Americas, maize, or Indian corn, was dominant, perhaps providing more food than all the other crops combined, as it still does in modern Mexico. And it generally holds that wherever there was agriculture among Precontact Indians in North America, there was also maize. Again, the Northwest Coast peoples proved the exception, since some among them grew tobacco but no food crops. The wide dispersion of various domestic strains of corn indicates many early trade contacts among the Indian peoples, both seaborne and overland, as well as tribal migrations. Seeds of course were easy to preserve and transport.

There are 154 other known aboriginal crops in North and Middle America (in addition to the many wild plants gathered for food). All but four of these crops were grown in Mesoamerica; only 18 of the total were grown in the Southwest, and only 12 in the East and Midwest. All except one were diffused from south to north, the exception being the sunflower, which was first cultivated in North America. After maize, the most important staples were beans and squash. But not all these crops were grown for food. Indians also cultivated fiber plants, especially cotton; dye plants; ornamental plants and hedges; hosts for wax and cochineal insects; herbs, medicines, stimulants, and psychotropics. (See "Stimulants, Intoxicants, and Hallucinogens" in this chapter.)

Here is a list of the best-known crops Indian farmers of North and South America developed and gave the rest of the world: corn, beans, squash, pumpkins, tomatoes, potatoes, sweet potatoes, peanuts, cashews, pineapples, papayas, avocadoes, Jerusalem artichokes, sunflowers, chili peppers, cacao (chocolate), vanilla, coca (cocaine), tobacco, indigo, and cotton.

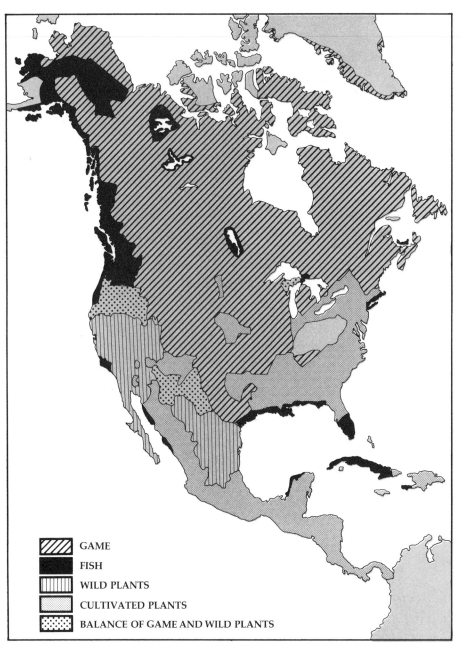

GAME

FISH

WILD PLANTS

CULTIVATED PLANTS

BALANCE OF GAME AND WILD PLANTS

3.5 DOMINANT TYPES OF SUBSISTENCE. *After Driver and Massey.*

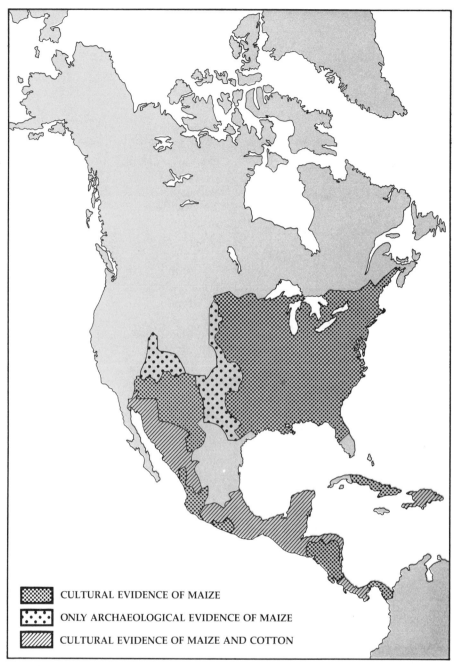

CULTURAL EVIDENCE OF MAIZE

ONLY ARCHAEOLOGICAL EVIDENCE OF MAIZE

CULTURAL EVIDENCE OF MAIZE AND COTTON

3.6 DISTRIBUTION OF MAIZE AND COTTON. *After Driver and Massey.*

INDIAN POPULATION DENSITY AT THE TIME OF CONTACT

The population figure for Native Americans in 1492 is a hypothetical and forever elusive number. Since early estimates were made after European-spawned diseases and warfare had had an impact on native peoples, and since they were regional and unscientific at best, modern scholars have had to devise their own systems of calculation. One variation involves comparative analyses of ecosystems—resources and soil fertility—and their potential in supporting human populations; another involves taking the lowest Indian population figures for different parts of the continent and multiplying them by a fixed number to achieve a total.

Yet such methods have produced enormous discrepancies, from a native population approximation of 15 million for the entire continent to as much as 60 million. In all estimates,

Mesoamerica and the Andes region of South America are attributed the large majority. Figures for Mesoamerica alone vary from seven to 30 million. The number most often heard for the region north of Mexico is one million (750,000 for what is now the United States and 250,000 for Canada) to one-and-one-half million. But some scholars have estimated 10 to 12 million for the same area.

Although the figure is perhaps moot in terms of the number of Indian tribes and life-styles, it has great significance with regard to the degree of white impact. The low point of the Indian population within the United States—less than 250,000—is thought to have occurred at some point between 1890 and 1910. A decline in the native population from about 40 to one, based on an original figure of 10 million for the United States area, is much more staggering to conceive than a ratio of four to one, based on the one million figure.

In any case, regardless of the total figure, comparative population densities for varying regions have bearing on Indian cultural studies as a facet of geography, resources, and means of subsistence, as well as social and political organization. Certain patterns are apparent on the accompanying map. Aboriginal populations were generally densest where agriculture was highly developed or along coastal areas with marine resources. River and lake ecozones also supported denser populations—the St. Lawrence Seaway, the Great Lakes, the lower Mississippi, the upper Missouri, the upper Rio Grande, and the Little Colorado. Conversely, population densities were lowest in extreme environments, such as the Arctic, Subarctic, and Great Basin.

In some areas Indian cultures developed effective forms of birth control to keep their populations in balance with local resources. In many tribes customary practices of avoidance and sexual abstinence gave a religious sanction to population control and produced, in effect, a kind of family planning which spaced the birth of children. Contraception and abortion were also known to some

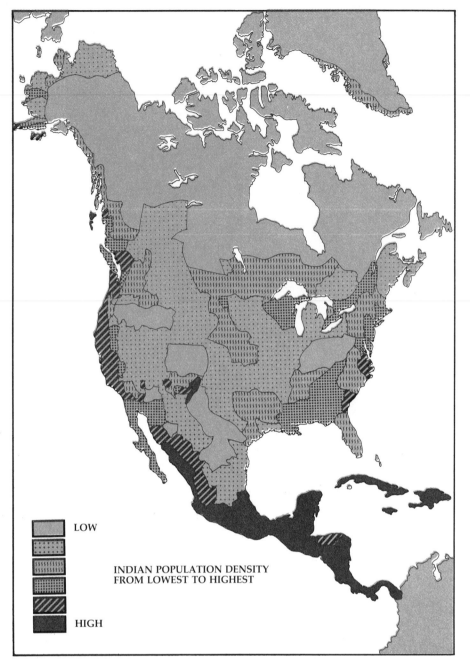

INDIAN POPULATION DENSITY
FROM LOWEST TO HIGHEST

HIGH

3.7 INDIAN POPULATION DENSITY IN 1500. *After Driver and Massey.*

THE INDIAN CULTURE AREAS

In the study of Indians, it is convenient to divide the Americas into geographic regions. Since environment determines many lifeways, tribes within each division share a significant number of cultural traits. The different geographic regions therefore define and delineate culture areas.

There are different schemes for establishing these culture areas. This book will use the common system of 12 divisions for North and Middle America: Northeast, Southeast, Southwest, Great Plains, Great Basin, Plateau, California, Northwest Coast, Arctic, Subarctic, Mesoamerica, and Circum-Caribbean. Some books discuss as many as 18 different areas for the same region. Others combine some of the 12, such as Northeast and Southeast into Eastern Woodlands.

Whichever system is applied, it should be kept in mind that the modern categories meant nothing to the Indians themselves; that tribal territories were vague and changing, with great movement among the tribes and the passing of cultural traits from one area to the next; and that people of the same language family sometimes lived in different culture areas, even in some instances at opposite ends of the continent. In summary, the culture areas are not finite or absolute boundaries, but simply helpful educational devices.

The 12 culture areas, as they will be discussed here, generally represent patterns of Indian life just before Contact with European culture. Nevertheless, some lifeways typical to particular regions, such as horses on the Great Plains, developed because of that Contact.

The tribes whose general locations are visually depicted in the following culture area maps should be considered as representative for each area, rather than exhaustive, and especially important with regard to Postcontact history. For a more thorough ac-

tribes—plants with contraceptive or abortifacient properties were used by certain tribes, and physical means to terminate pregnancies by others. And a few tribes practiced infanticide in order to regulate population growth.

After European Contact, the patterns of Indian population density began to change. Many Indians along the East Coast were displaced early because of extensive British settlement. (See "European Use of Indian Lands and Resources" in chapter 6.) With the introduction of the horse into North America, many tribes migrated onto the Great Plains. (See

"The Indian and the Horse" in this chapter.) Many other tribes were forcibly moved to the Indian Territory which eventually became the state of Oklahoma. (See "The Indian Territory" in chapter 6.) And with outbreaks of disease and warfare, native populations everywhere began to decline. (See chapter 5, "INDIAN WARS," and "The Spread of European Diseases" in chapter 6.) It wasn't until the 20th century that the Indian population began to grow once again. (See chapter 7, "CONTEMPORARY INDIANS.")

3.8 THE INDIAN CULTURE AREAS

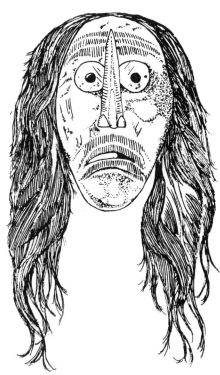

Iroquois false face mask

counting of tribes and subtribes, along with their locations, see the tribal list in the Appendix.

THE NORTHEAST CULTURE AREA

The Northeast culture area, as defined here, covers an expanse of territory east to west, from the Atlantic seaboard across the Appalachians to the Mississippi Valley; and north to south, from the Great Lakes to the Tidewater region of present-day Virginia and North Carolina, and beyond

the Cumberland River in Tennessee. The varying physiography of this area—coast, mountains, valleys, and lakes—has one constant: the forest, both deciduous and coniferous. And for the Indians of this area, the trees of the forest were the primary material for shelter, tools, and fuel, and the animals of the forest were the primary food source. Yet, at the time of Contact with the white man, the Northeast Woodland Indians were not solely hunters and gatherers, but also fishermen and farmers.

The tribes of this region at the time of Contact can be organized into five subgroups, based on variations in

lifeways, and correspondingly the region can be divided into five subareas: 1) the Nova Scotia, New England, Long Island, Hudson Valley, and Delaware Valley Algonquian-speaking tribes (such as Micmac, Abnaki, Massachuset, Narraganset, Wampanoag, Pennacook, Pequot, Mahican, Wappinger, Montauk, and Delaware); 2) the New York and Ontario Iroquoian-speaking tribes (such as Mohawk, Oneida, Onondaga, Cayuga, Seneca, Tobacco, Erie, Neutral, and Huron); 3) the Great Lakes Algonquians (such as Algonkin, Ottawa, Menominee, Potawatomi, and some bands of Ojibway, the rest of whom are considered within the Subarctic culture area); 4) the Prairie Algonquians (such as Sauk, Fox, Kickapoo, Illinois, Miami, and Shawnee), plus the Siouan-speaking Winnebago; and 5) the southern fringe tribes in the vicinity of the Chesapeake Bay and Cape Hatteras, both Algonquians and Iroquoians (such as Powhatan, Nottaway, Meherrin, Secotan, Nanticoke, Weapemeoc, Susquehannock, and Tuscarora).

Exact connections between prehistoric and historic peoples of the Northeast have not yet been determined. It is generally thought that the

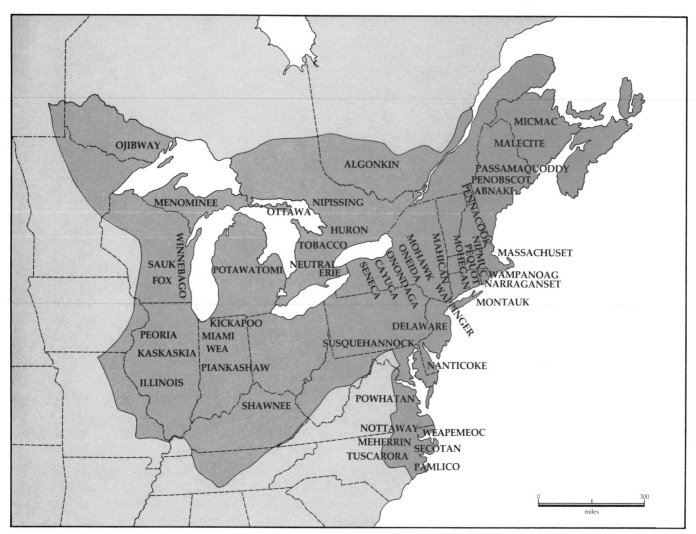

3.9 THE NORTHEAST CULTURE AREA, *showing approximate tribal locations (with modern boundaries)*

Iroquoian tribes were more recent arrivals in the region than the Algonquians and that they probably migrated originally from the south. In any case, regardless of the antiquity

of migrations and lines of descent, it can be said that the Northeast tribes at the time of Contact were the inheritors of earlier Woodland or Formative traditions.

Both the Iroquois and Algonquians had strong tribal (or band) identities above and beyond the basic nuclear families, often living in palisaded villages. The Iroquois came to be known as the People of the Longhouse for their communal houses, whereas the Algonquians generally lived in wigwams. Both Iroquois and Algonquians came to have confederacies of various tribes—i.e., the Iroquois League of Five Nations, the Abnaki Confederacy, and the Powhatan Confederacy.

THE SOUTHEAST CULTURE AREA

The Southeast culture area stretches from the Atlantic Ocean westward to the arid lands beyond the Trinity River in present-day Texas; and from the Gulf of Mexico northward to varying latitudes in the present-day states of Texas, Oklahoma, Arkansas, Missouri, Kentucky, West Virginia, Maryland, Virginia, and North Carolina. This region, like the Northeast culture area with which it is sometimes grouped as the Eastern Woodland culture area, is primarily wooded, much of it with southern yellow pine, but it generally has a milder and wetter climate.

Variations in geography and vegetation within the area include: coastal

Wooden deer head from Key Marco (Marco Island, Florida), probably Calusa

plain, with saltwater marshes, grasses, and stands of cypress; subtropical Everglades; Mississippi River floodplain; Black Belt fertile soil; and the Piedmont Plateau, Blue Ridge, Smoky, and Cumberland mountains of the southern Appalachian chain. The majority of Indians in the Southeast at the time of Contact made their homes along river valleys in villages which served as the dominant form of social organization. Because of commonly sandy soil conditions (except in the Black Belt region), agricultural fields and the corresponding village sites were frequently changed. In general, it can be said that the people of the Southeast were farmers first

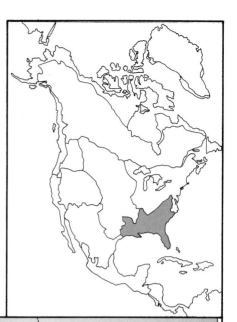

3.10 THE SOUTHEAST CULTURE AREA, *showing approximate tribal locations (with modern boundaries)*

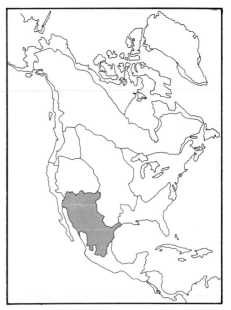

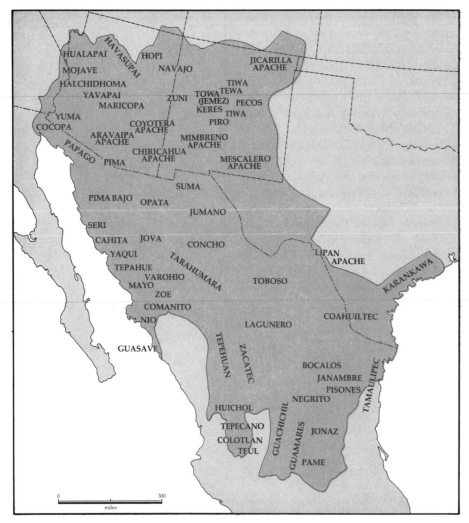

3.11 THE SOUTHWEST CULTURE AREA, *showing approximate tribal locations (with modern boundaries)*

and hunters, gatherers, and fishermen second.

Despite similarities in culture throughout the area, there were many different language families—namely Muskogean, Siouan, Iroquoian, Algonquian, and Caddoan, as well as many language isolates, such as Timucuan, Tunican, Atakapan, Natchez, Yuchi, and Chitimacha, with dialectal variations from village to village. The larger tribes of the area included the Cherokee, Choctaw, Chickasaw, Creek, and Seminole (an offshoot of Creek), referred to by whites as the Five Civilized Tribes, as well as the Catawba, Caddo, Alabama, and Natchez. Some of them, such as the Natchez, are known to have been direct descendants of the ancient Temple Mound Builders, but others must have been later arrivals who came to inhabit many of the same Mississippian culture sites.

THE SOUTHWEST CULTURE AREA

The Southwest culture area, as represented here, extends from the southern fringes of present-day Utah and Colorado southward through Arizona and New Mexico (including parts of Texas, California, and Oklahoma) into Mexico. The constant in this vast region is aridity with the average annual rainfall ranging from less than 20 inches to less than four, most precipitation occurring during a six-week period of summer. Yet topography varies significantly. Contrasts include the southern reaches of the Colorado Plateau with its flat-topped mesas and steep-walled canyons (the Grand Canyon along the Colorado River in Arizona is the prime example

of the latter); the tortuous Mogollon Mountains of New Mexico; the plateaus and sierras of inland Mexico; and the torrid desert country along the Little Colorado River (the Painted Desert), the Gulf of Mexico (the Sonoran Desert), and the Gulf of California. Vegetation, depending on altitude and rainfall, consists primarily of western evergreen, or pinyon and juniper, or desert shrub, cactus, and mesquite.

Within this region of extremes, two essential Indian life-styles developed: agrarian and nomadic. Agriculture north of Mesoamerica reached its highest level of development in the Southwest. And warlike nomads often preyed on the peaceful villagers and farmers. The peoples of this culture area can further be organized as follows: 1) the agrarian Pueblo peo-

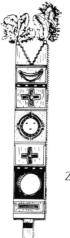

Zuni dance wand

either western or northern evergreens. In terms of plant food, wild roots were the staple.

The Plateau culture area was not as densely populated as the Pacific coastal areas to the west. Nevertheless, more than two dozen distinct tribal groups inhabited the Columbia Plateau, descendants of the Old Cordilleran culture as well as later arrivals. Villages, usually located along riverbanks, became the main political units, with headmen as leaders. Two language stocks were dominant. In the southern regions, stretching from the Columbia River to the Great Basin, language families and isolates of the Penutian phylum were spoken by tribes such as Klamath, Modoc, Nez Perce, Cayuse, Palouse, and Chinook, whose collective ancestors probably settled the area before 6,000 B.C. North of the Columbia, extending into Canada, the most common language family was Salish (of uncertain phylum), with dialects spoken by the Coeur d'Alene, Flathead, Kalispel, Spokane, Lillooet, Ntylakyapamuk, and Shuswap. Their ancestors probably arrived in the region around 1,500 B.C. An exception to this dualistic pattern was the language isolate Kutenai of the Kootenay (perhaps Algonquian-related). Moreover, there were occasional incursions of Athapascan-speaking and Algonquian-speaking bands from the Subarctic and Great Plains culture areas to the north and east.

In later years, people from the Great Plains influenced Plateau inhabitants. The Nez Perces, for example, along with the Cayuses and Palouses, became excellent horse trainers and breeders in Postcontact times.

THE NORTHWEST COAST CULTURE AREA

The Northwest Coast culture area extends more than 2,000 miles from the northern limits of California to the panhandle of Alaska, including western Oregon, Washington, and British Columbia. The widest part in this long coastal strip is only about 150 miles across. A spinelike mountain chain runs the length of the culture area (continuing into the California region)—the Coast Range. The rugged continental landscape drops abruptly to a labyrinth of inlets and islands, the latter formed by the tips of offshore mountains, the largest of which include Vancouver Island, the Queen Charlotte Islands, and the Alexander Archipelago.

The climate here is temperate but moist. The Japanese Current warms the ocean; the ocean in turn tempers and moistens the prevailing westerly winds; and the mountain barrier blocks the vapor-laden breezes, creating abundant rainfall, as much as 100 or more inches a year, and a lush evergreen forest. And meltwaters from mountain glaciers to the east feed numerous rivers running to the sea.

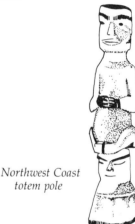

Northwest Coast totem pole

For the native inhabitants of the Northwest Coast at the time of Contact, the oceans, rivers, and forests offered up plentiful fish and game. Even without agriculture other than some cultivation of tobacco, and with only minimal gathering of wild plants,

3.14 THE NORTHWEST COAST CULTURE AREA, *showing approximate tribal locations (with modern boundaries)*

the Northwest Coast Indians had more than enough food to support a dense population. It is said that salmon—the staple at the heart of so many Northwest Coast myths—could have provided for the entire population by itself. And because of the readily available sustenance and building materials for roomy houses and seaworthy boats, the Indians had time enough to achieve an affluent and highly complex society, much of it revolving around the custom of the potlatch, in which an individual's prestige and rank were determined by the quantities of material possessions he could give away. Once again, as in many of the other culture areas, the term "tribe" is used for convenience. Villages, or sometimes kin groups (lineages or extended families), were of greater significance in the social fabric.

Two major linguistic phyla were represented along the Northwest Coast: Na-Dene (spoken by the Tlingit, Haida, and Eyak) and Penutian (spoken by the Tsimshian, Chinook, Coos, Alsea, Siuslaw, and Kalapuya). The other language families present were of undetermined phyla: Salishan (spoken by the Coast Salish, Bella Coola, Chehalis, Clallam, Lumni, Quinault, Tillamook, and Comox); Wakashan (spoken by Bella Bella, Kwakiutl, Nootka, Makah, Haisla, and Heiltsuk); and Chimakum (spoken by the Chimakum and Quileute). These language groups were not neatly segregated geographically. In a broader cultural sense, the tribes can be organized, for purposes of study, into the following: those of the colder northern area, including the Queen Charlotte Islands; those of the central region, in the vicinity of Vancouver Island and the mouth of the Columbia River; and those of the southern region, who shared California-type cultural traits.

THE CALIFORNIA CULTURE AREA

The California culture area corresponds roughly to the present-day state of California, in addition to Baja

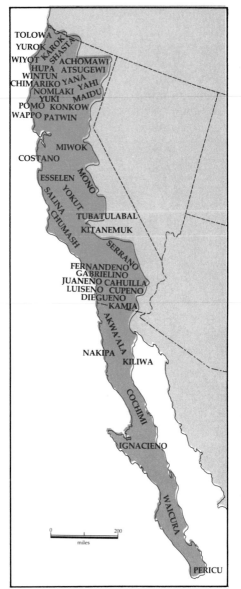

3.15 THE CALIFORNIA CULTURE AREA, *showing approximate tribal locations (with modern boundaries)*

California in Mexico, except along the state's eastern border; there, the Indians at the time of Contact demonstrated life-styles more typical of the Great Basin, Southwest, and the Columbia Plateau. Along the eastern edge of the California culture area, the Sierra Nevada and the Gulf of California provided natural barriers for differing life-styles. To the north, however, no such barrier blocked interaction among peoples, making the dividing line between the California and Northwest Coast areas especially arbitrary, with many shared cultural traits.

Coastal mountains run the length of the culture area, paralleling the Sierra Nevada. In Baja California, the mountains run along the center of the narrow peninsula. The amount of rainfall varies from north to south, with the rugged northern cliff country receiving the most, and lower California and the Mojave Desert the least. Likewise, there are more rivers in central and northern California, many of them converging and flowing to the San Francisco Bay. In the heart of the culture area, the San Joaquin and Sacramento rivers and their tri-

Chumash steatite stingray

butaries form a natural basin, the Great California Valley, between the two parallel mountain ranges.

The shared characteristic of this land of contrasting topography—that which makes it distinct from the other culture areas around it—is the bountiful flora and fauna. For the Indians, acorns were a principal food, along with many other wild plants. Fish, shellfish, deer, and other small game were also staples. Because of the ample means of sustenance, the California region without agriculture supported the densest population north of Mesoamerica. The basic social unit was the family, and groups of related families formed villages, in certain instances with satellite families in the vicinity. To describe the level of social organization beyond the village the term "tribelet" is sometimes applied. There was a high degree of isolation among different tribelets, with little movement of peoples once the group was established.

More than 100 distinct dialects were spoken in the culture area. Foremost among them were languages of the Hokan phylum in the north, as spoken by the Shasta, Pomo, Karok, Chumash, Salina, and Yana (with some dispersion southward and most of the Baja California peoples speaking languages of the Yuman family of Hokan); the Penutian phylum in the central region, as spoken by the Patwin, Miwok, Yokuts, Costano, Wintun, and Maidu; and the Shoshonean family of the Uto-Aztecan phylum in the south, as spoken by the Tubatulabal and Cahuilla. But the Athapascan (Hupa), Algonquian (Yurok), and Yukian (Yuki, Wappo) language families were also found in the northern and north-central regions. In Postcontact times, various California natives came to be jointly known to the Spanish as the Mission Indians. Different peoples also came to carry the names of particular missions; i.e., Gabrielino, Fernandeno, Juaneno, Cupeno, Serrano, and Diegueno. All these peoples, except the Yuman-speaking Diegueno, spoke Shoshonean dialects and probably came late to the region.

THE GREAT PLAINS CULTURE AREA

The Great Plains culture area stretches west, from the Mississippi River Valley to the Rocky Mountains; and south, from varying latitudes in present-day Manitoba, Saskatchewan, and Alberta to southern Texas. This vast region is predominantly treeless grassland—the long grass of the eastern prairies, with 20 to 40 inches of rainfall a year; and the short grass of the western high plains, with 10 to 20 inches of rainfall. There are some

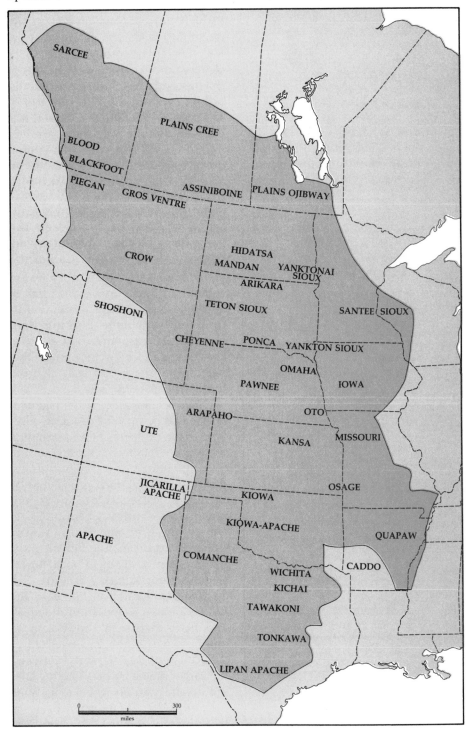

3.16 THE GREAT PLAINS CULTURE AREA, *showing approximate tribal locations (with modern boundaries)*

wooded areas interrupting the fields of grass—stands of mostly willows and cottonwoods along the many river valleys. And in some places geographical features rise up from the prairies and plains, such as the Ozark Mountains in Missouri; the Black Hills of South Dakota and Wyoming; and the Dakota Badlands, plateau and butte country. Otherwise, the region is remarkable for its sameness—miles and miles of perfect grazing land for the large, shaggy-maned North American mammal known as the bison or buffalo.

The Great Plains culture area is unique in the sense that the typical Indian subsistence pattern and related lifeways evolved long after Contact. It was the advent of horses, brought to North America by whites—the first horses since the post-Pleistocene ex-

Sioux ceremonial buffalo skull

tinction of the native species—that made the new life on the Plains possible. With increased mobility and prowess, former village and farming tribes of the river valleys became nomadic hunters, especially of the buffalo. And other tribes migrated onto the Plains from elsewhere to partake of this life-style. With time, varying tribal customs blended into what is sometimes referred to as the Composite Plains Tribe, shaped by the horse and buffalo culture.

It is not known what became of the prehistoric Great Plains hunters of the Plano culture. It is theorized that any remaining Plains inhabitants left the region because of droughts in the 13th century, and that their descendants or the descendants of other peoples did not return until the 14th century. In any case, at the time of Contact, it is believed that the only noncultivators on the Great Plains were the Algonquian-speaking Blackfeet in the north and the Uto-Aztecan Comanches in the south. Most of the region's other early tribes were villagers and farmers, or at least seminomads, with settlements located especially along the Missouri River. As soil became depleted in one area, they probably migrated northward upriver in search of new village sites. Early agriculturalists included the Siouan-speaking Mandans and Hidatsa and the Caddoan-speaking Caddo, Wichita, and Pawnee, and a group that split off from the Pawnee, the Arikara.

Other peoples entered the region at later dates because of droughts elsewhere, the pressures of an expanding white population, or, most of all, to take advantage of the new buffalo-hunting life-style made possible by the horse. These included the Algonquian Gros Ventre, Arapaho, Cheyenne, Plains Cree, and Plains Ojibway from the northeast; the Siouan Assiniboine, Crow, Sioux, Ponca, Iowa, Omaha, Oto, Kansa, Missouri, Osage, and Quapaw from the east; the Kiowa-Tanoan Kiowa from the west; and the Athapascan Kiowa-Apache and Sarcee from the northwest.

Because of the disparity between the earlier prairie farmers and the later high-plains hunters, the Great Plains culture area is sometimes treated as two different areas.

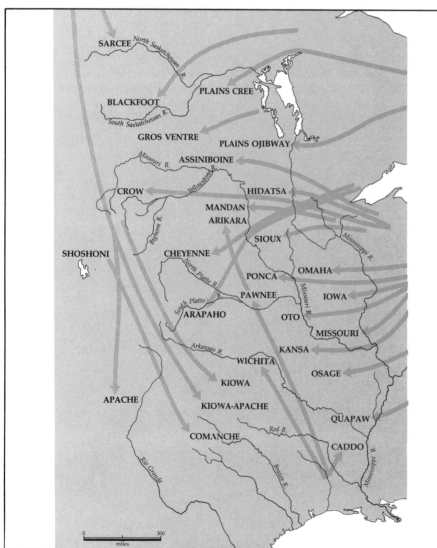

3.17 MIGRATION OF TRIBES ONTO THE PLAINS *(hypothetical routes)*

3.18 THE SUBARCTIC CULTURE AREA, *showing approximate tribal locations (with modern boundaries)*

THE SUBARCTIC CULTURE AREA

The Subarctic culture area spans the entire North American continent, from Cook Inlet on the Pacific Coast to the Gulf of St. Lawrence and New-foundland on the Atlantic. On the north it borders much of Hudson Bay,

Ojibway wooden male effigy doll

and on the south it touches the upper shore of Lake Superior. All in all, the Subarctic covers most of Canada as well as much of Alaska's interior. What is known as the Northern Forest—mostly pine, spruce, and fir, with scattered aspen, willow, and birch—fills up a large part of this im-mense region, opening along its northern limits into the treeless tun-dra of the Arctic. Given the extent of the northern evergreen forest, per-haps a more descriptive and distinc-tive name would be the Boreal culture area (for Northern) or the Taiga cul-ture area (for the kind of forest).

In addition to the coniferous wood-lands, the Subarctic also contains multitudinous lakes, ponds, swamps, bogs, rivers, and streams. The largest of these lakes are, from east to west, the Great Bear Lake, the Great Slave Lake, Lake Athabaska, Lake Winni-pegosis, Lake Winnipeg, Lake Nipi-gon, and Lake Mistassini. Among the largest rivers are the Yukon, the Mackenzie, the Peace, the Saskatch-ewan, the Red River of the North, and La Grande.

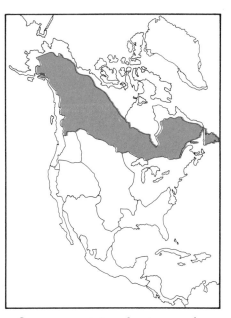

Some mountains do rise up from the generally flat or rolling forest and swamplands. In the west, the Mac-kenzie Lowlands give way to the con-tinuation of the Rocky Mountain chain, which in turn gives way to the Yukon Plateau and the British Co-lumbia Plateau. Much of the Subarc-tic's central region consists of the geological massif and crustal block

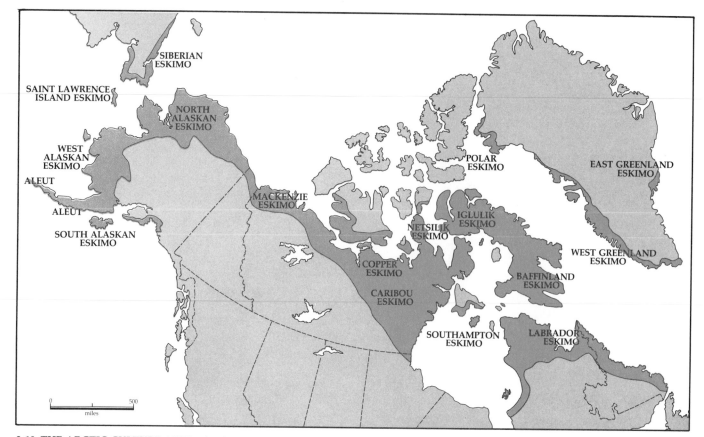

3.19 THE ARCTIC CULTURE AREA, *showing approximate tribal locations (with modern boundaries)*

known as the Laurentian or Canadian Shield.

The scattered and few aboriginal peoples of the Subarctic had to cope with long, harsh, snow-laden winters, as well as summers that were all too short and plagued with clouds of mosquitoes and black flies. Most peoples were nomadic, hunting, fishing, and foraging in small bands united by dialect and kinship. For many bands, life revolved around the seasonal migrations of the caribou between the tundra and the taiga. Other large game included moose, musk oxen, deer, and, in more southern latitudes, buffalo; small game included beaver, mink, hare, otter, and porcupine. To store their catch, the Indians made pemmican by drying, pounding, and mixing the meat with suet. The fur of mammals was as valuable to the peoples for warmth as the meat was for sustenance. Fish and wildfowl also helped provide the necessary nutrition. In the east, birchbark was an especially valued commodity for making boats, cooking vessels, and containers.

Subarctic peoples can be organized linguistically into two groups—the Athapascans to the west and Algonquians to the east, with the Churchill River that extends southwest from Hudson Bay as the approximate dividing line. The Beothuks of Newfoundland, formerly considered as part of the Northeast culture area, are the only exception, speaking a language isolate known as Beothukan. In terms of culture, tribal groups can be analyzed and arranged as follows: the westernmost Athapascans living near and influenced by the Eskimos (the Koyukon, Kutchin, Ingalik, Tanana, Tanaina, Ahtena, Nabesna, and Han); the Athapascans living along the eastern foothills of the northern Rockies (the Kaska, Tahltan, Sekani, Tutchone, Tsetsaut, Mountain, Carrier, Chilcotin, and Tagish); the Athapascans living near the Great Slave and Great Bear lakes (the Slave, Yellowknife, Chipewyan, Dogrib, Beaver, and Hare); plus the western Algonquians (the Western Wood Cree and Swampy Cree); and eastern Algonquians (the Mistassini Cree, Tete de Boule Cree, Montagnais, Naskapi, and northern Ojibway).

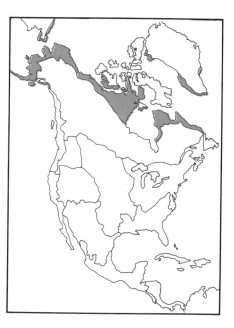

THE ARCTIC CULTURE AREA

The Arctic culture area runs for more than 5,000 miles, from eastern Siberia across the northern stretches of Alaska and Canada all the way to Greenland. Its craggy coastline and rocky

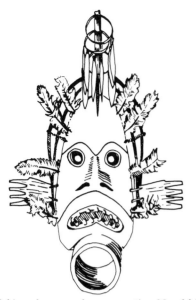
Eskimo dance mask, representing Negakfok, the Cold Weather Spirit

islands touch on three oceans—the Pacific, the Arctic, and the Atlantic. Lying beyond the northern tree limit, and with some parts even within the Arctic Circle, this extreme environment known as tundra has little vegetation other than mosses, lichens, and scrub brush. Few mountain peaks rise above the rolling plains of tundra other than the northern reaches of the Rockies.

Cold and ice are synonymous with the Arctic. Winters are long and severe with few hours of daylight. In latitudes north of the Arctic Circle, the sun stays below the horizon on certain days of the year and, conversely, on certain days of the brief summer, it never dips below the horizon. The Arctic Ocean freezes over in winter, then breaks up into drift ice during the short summer thaw. On land the subsoil stays frozen year-round in a state of permafrost, and the water on the surface does not drain, forming abundant lakes and ponds along with mud and fog. There is less precipitation in the Arctic than in latitudes to the south. Since there are few natural windbreaks, however, gale-force winds stir up surface snow ahead of them, creating intense blizzards and enormous drifts.

The peoples who settled the upper regions of North America out of Siberia came relatively late to the continent, circa 3,000 B.C. And they didn't travel the Bering Strait land bridge as the earlier Paleo-Siberians had done, but came in skin or wooden boats, or perhaps by riding the ice floes. They were of a different stock than other Native Americans, generally of a shorter and broader stature, rounder face, lighter skin, and with the epicanthic eye fold, the small fold of skin covering the inner corner of the eye and typical of Asian peoples. They are known historically as the Eskimos and the Aleuts. The modern descendants of the former, however, prefer the term *Inuit*, meaning "the people," rather than Eskimo, which is an Algonquian appellation meaning "raw-meat eaters."

The Inuits and Aleuts adapted remarkably well to the harsh Arctic environment, with hunting as the primary means of subsistence—especially of sea mammals and caribou—and supplemented by fishing. Those parts of their catch they didn't eat, they used to make clothing, housing, sleds, boats, tools, weapons, ceremonial objects, and even heating and cooking fuel. Wood, extremely rare in the Arctic and usually obtained as driftwood, was a highly valued commodity. The dog, used to pull sleds, sniff out seals beneath the ice, and track land game, was an ally against the elements.

In addition to uniformity of culture, Arctic peoples revealed consistency of language. There is only one defined language family—Eskimo-Aleut (also called Eskimaleut or Eskaleut)—which is considered part of the American Arctic–Paleo-Siberian phylum. To facilitate study, Inuits and Aleuts at the time of Contact are organized into four major cultural groupings: 1) the Aleut, living along the Aleutian chain of islands off Alaska, with the Atka Aleut to the east and the Unalaska Aleut to the west; 2) the Alaskan Eskimo, comprising the North Alaska Eskimo, West Alaska Eskimo, South Alaska Eskimo, and Saint Lawrence Island Eskimo, along with the Yuit of Siberia and the Mackenzie Eskimo of the Yukon; 3) the Central Eskimo, including the Netsilik, Iglulik, Caribou Eskimo, Copper Eskimo, Southampton Eskimo, Baffinland Eskimo, and Labrador Eskimo; and 4) the Greenland Eskimo, including the East Greenland Eskimo, West Greenland Eskimo, and Polar Eskimo.

In cultural terms, the Central Eskimos demonstrated what is considered typical "Eskimo" lifeways—igloos, kayaks, sleds, and dog teams. The Caribou Eskimos of this region, however, were inland people who tracked the animals for which they are named and fished the interior freshwater lakes. Other peoples migrated seasonally to take advantage of both coastal and inland environments. The Copper Eskimos were unique in that they used the plentiful copper surface nuggets found in their territory to craft tools. The Eskimos of southern Alaska had extensive contact with other Indian peoples and adopted certain of their customs. Where there were forests, they lived in above-ground wooden houses. Still other Alaskan Eskimos inhabited semi-underground wood-and-sod houses. The Greenland Eskimos lived in stone-and-turf houses with gut-skin windows. The Aleuts had frequent contacts with the Northwest Coast Indians and, although they, like the Eskimos, also used kayaks and hunted sea mammals, some bands relied on salmon and birds for sustenance. The Aleuts lived in timbered earth-banked pit houses.

THE MESOAMERICAN AND CIRCUM-CARIBBEAN CULTURE AREAS

Two other culture areas—the Mesoamerican and the Circum-Caribbean—are represented visually, along with locations of their major tribes at the time of Contact. They are included here to supply the reader with a frame of reference for the development of culture to the north, in the regions comprising the present-day United States and Canada. Mesoamerica and the Caribbean area are also represented in maps showing the distribution of specific cultural traits later in this chapter. For a detailed discussion of Mesoamerica's Precontact peoples and cultures, see chapter 2, "ANCIENT CIVILZATIONS." For a discussion of Mesoamerica as a sphere of influence, see "Transition and Culmination" in chapter 1, as well as other sections on Indian culture in this chapter.

With regard to the Circum-Caribbean culture area, an in-depth analysis of Precontact lifeways, with an inventory of cultural traits, is more appropriate to a study of South American Indians. The Caribbean and Central American environment—predominantly tropical rain forest—resembles that of South America, and the native population was to a large extent under the sphere of influence of South American peoples (as well as Mesoamerican peoples). In fact, a primary route of migration onto the

Narrow head of stone with crane headdress, Classic Veracruz style

Caribbean islands was northward from South America along the Antilles chain.

However, to summarize them briefly, placing them linguistically and culturally, the Circum-Caribbean peoples spoke languages of the Ma-

3.20 THE MESOAMERICAN CULTURE AREA, *showing approximate tribal locations (with modern boundaries)*

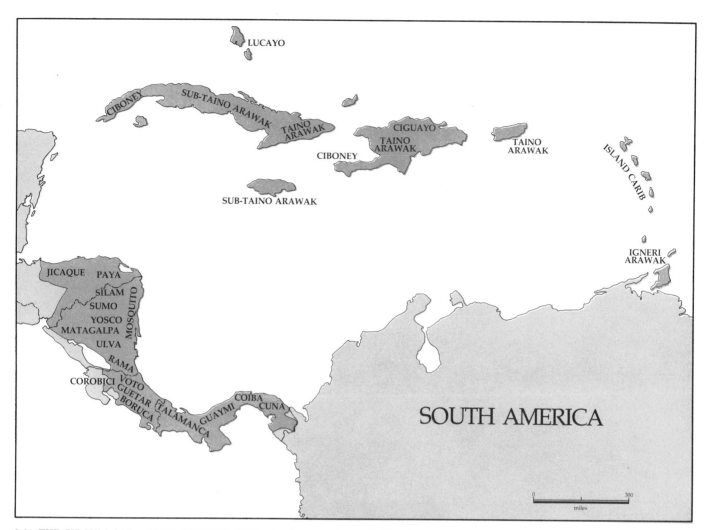

3.21 THE CIRCUM-CARIBBEAN CULTURE AREA, *showing approximate tribal locations (with modern boundaries)*

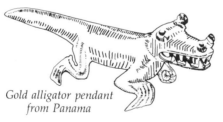

Gold alligator pendant from Panama

cro-Chibchan, Ge-Pano-Carib, and Andean-Equatorial phyla, with some infusion from Mesoamerica of the Aztec-Tanoan and Oto-Manguean phyla in the Central American regions. They were agriculturalists, as well as hunters, fishermen, and gatherers. Maize, cotton, manioc (cassava, tapioca), sweet potato, peanut, and tobacco were the most important crops. The palm tree—both trunk and leaves—served as the primary building material. The dominant form of social organization was the chiefdom—a collection of autonomous bands united politically and religiously under supreme rulers and with social classes. Circum-Caribbean peoples, however, never attained the high levels of social organization or the advanced technologies of the Mesoamerican and Andes cultures.

In Postcontact times, both the Circum-Caribbean and Mesoamerican culture areas relate historically to areas in North America proper; they were explored and settled by Spain as was the American Southwest and Southeast. Yet the later story of Indian peoples, encompassing modern times in Caribbean and Central American countries, necessitates a political and ethnographic context not attempted in this book. Suffice it to say here that the combination of European diseases, the European slave trade, the Spanish exploitation of labor and resources, and the military depredations of the conquistadors exacted a heavy toll in life and culture on the native populations, rendering many tribes extinct. Many of the survivors were absorbed over successive generations through intermarriage, creating (especially in Mexico) a large mestizo, or mixed-blood, population. People of pure Indian stock do remain, many of them living as poor peasant villagers in highland areas.

ART AND TECHNOLOGY

In the discussion of the arts and crafts of Native North Americans—their material culture as well as their dramatic arts, such as dance, music, and storytelling—the formulation of neat categories and groupings is especially problematic. Since there are so many varying artistic and technological traditions at both tribal and regional levels, the phrases "Indian arts" or "Indian crafts" are misleading. There is no one Indian form, as there is no one white form.

Moreover, a true distinction between arts and crafts cannot be drawn. Art for Native North Anericans was not an entity unto itself— art was not just for art's sake—but an integral part of other activities, whether in the creation and decoration of objects with strictly practical purposes, such as hunting and fishing equipment, or in the making of objects for ceremonial ends. Likewise, the dramatic arts were a function of religion and ritual. A hard-and-fast distinction between the utilitarian and the ceremonial cannot even be made, because the Indians considered their rituals essential to their survival.

One can get a sense of the high level of Indian craftsmanship and the integration of form and function by reviewing the various artifacts illustrated throughout this book. This section will organize the subject of art and technology by the various materials used to shape and decorate tools and ceremonial objects, with maps showing the distribution of some of these materials in relation to cooking vessels and other containers, and with an additional discussion of dramatic arts and games. Other aspects of Indian art and technology, as pertaining to subsistence, shelter, clothing, transportation, and religion are treated in other sections of this chapter, as well as in the first two chapters, "ANCIENT INDIANS" and "ANCIENT CIVILIZATIONS."

WOODWORK: Indians were masters of woodwork, especially in the heavily forested parts of the continent, such as the Northwest Coast. They used a variety of tools of stone, shell, copper, bone, horn, and teeth—axes, knives, scrapers, drills, chisels, hammers, wedges, and sanders—to shape a myriad of implements and carvings.

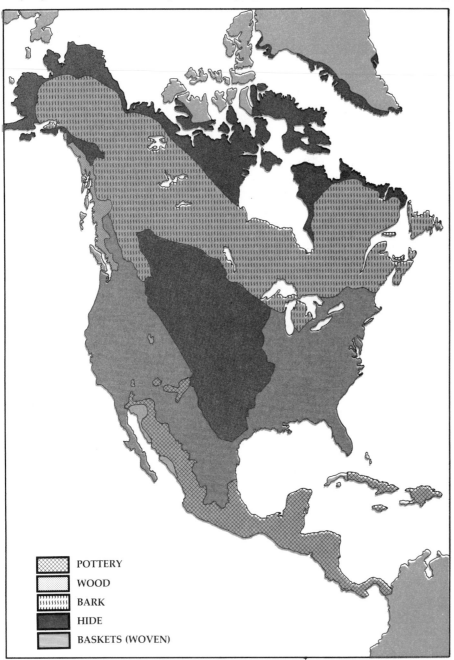

POTTERY
WOOD
BARK
HIDE
BASKETS (WOVEN)

3.22 DISTRIBUTION OF MATERIALS USED IN MAKING CONTAINERS *(non-cooking).*
After Driver and Massey.

Algonkin birchbark container

Among the many wood or bark objects of Native North Americans were houses, boats, sleds, toboggans, snowshoes, bows and arrows, spears, clubs, shields, armor, traps, weirs, digging sticks, hoes, rakes, bed frames, cradles, cradleboards, pipes, boxes, bowls, utensils, flutes, rattles, drums, toys, games, masks, effigy carvings, and totem poles. After the introduction of iron tools by European traders, woodworking enjoyed a new burst of energy and expression.

STONEWORK: Before the advent of iron tools from Europe, stone served as the primary material for jobs involving cutting, piercing, scraping, and hammering. Native North Americans shaped stone into tools by techniques of pressure and percussion flaking (or chipping), as well as drilling, cutting, pecking, grinding, sharpening, and polishing. The flaking properties of flint, chert, and obsidian made them invaluable to Indians for the crafting of points, blades, and other objects. Indians also used soft stones, such as catlinite (pipestone) from the Great Lakes and steatite (soapstone) from the Southeast and Far West to shape pipe bowls, dishes, containers, and ceremonial objects. Gemstones, such as turquoise, were also used to make beads, pendants, gorgets, and other jewelry. Polished slate was another prized medium. Bannerstones were specialized objects, often in the shape of birds (birdstones), thought to be used as weights on atlatls.

SKINWORK: When Indians hunted animals, they sought not only food but also materials for clothing and other objects. Indians used rawhide— animal skins in an uncured form, usually with the fur scraped off—to make sturdy objects, such as shields, bindings, pouches, boxes, drums, and rattles. Indians also developed various techniques to cure leather. The flesh, fat, and sometimes the fur was scraped off the skin, which was then treated with one mixture or another, such as urine or a paste of mashed brains, marrow, and liver, and manipulated by pulling it around a tree, stake, or rope. Eskimo women chewed leather to make it supple. Leather and fur served to make clothing, pouches, sheaths, and blankets. Animal skins in various stages of preparation were also used in the making of dwellings and boats.

TEXTILES: In addition to animal skins, Indians also made clothing, blankets, bags, and mats from woven fabrics. Plant fibers, such as the inner bark of cedar trees, and cultivated cotton, as well as wool from buffalo and other animals, served as the raw materials to make yarn. Only Indians of the Southwest had true looms; elsewhere in North America, Indians used techniques of finger-weaving, including knitting, crocheting, netting, looping, twining, and plaiting. Indians did not use spinning wheels, but spun by hand or on a spindle. In Postcontact times, Indians of the Southwest, especially the Navajos, raised sheep for wool.

BASKETRY: The making of baskets was interrelated with that of textiles in a similar use of advanced weaving techniques. Native North Americans created hundreds of exquisite forms for a variety of purposes—carrying, storage, cooking, and other specialized applications, such as for fish traps or hats. In the process they utilized a variety of plant materials— twigs and splints of wood, inner bark,

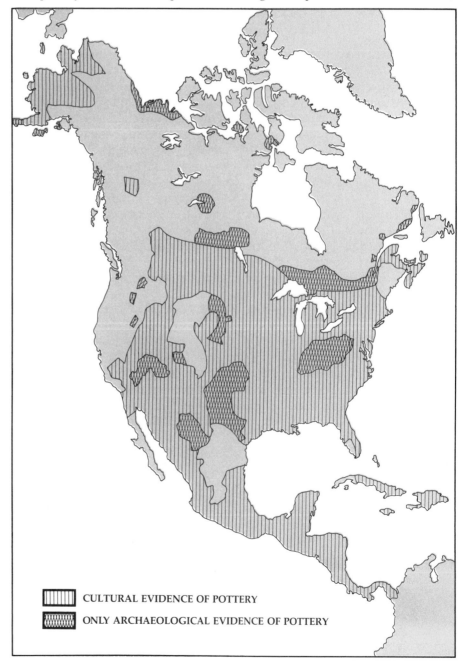

CULTURAL EVIDENCE OF POTTERY

ONLY ARCHAEOLOGICAL EVIDENCE OF POTTERY

3.23 DISTRIBUTION OF POTTERY. *After Driver and Massey.*

roots, canes, reeds, fronds, vines, and grasses. Indians had three basic techniques for their basketwork. Plaited baskets have two elements crossing each other, a warp and a woof.

Iroquois ash-splint basket

Twined baskets have a set of vertical warps and two or more horizontal wefts that twine around each other as they weave in and out of the warps. Coiled baskets have thin strips of wood, fibers, leaves, or grass wrapped into a bundle and coiled into a continuous spiral. Some baskets were covered with resin to hold water.

POTTERY: Pottery making was widespread among the Indians of North America. Only peoples of the Arctic, Subarctic, Northwest Coast, California, and Columbia Plateau had little pottery. Great Plains peoples at one time had skills in ceramics, but they came to abandon it because the vessels proved too fragile for their nomadic life-style. Two basic, virtually independent, pottery areas are recognized—one, the Southwest, and two, the East (with a number of overlapping and cross-cultural subdivisions in the latter, namely the Southeast, Gulf, Central, and Northern,

Acoma Pueblo pottery

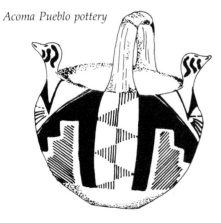

each with distinctive traits). In differing parts of these regions were found two basic pottery-making techniques—coiling, with a coil of clay built up from a base; and modeling and paddling, with clay placed over a jar mold, the potter turning the mold while patting the clay with a stone, then a paddle. Sometimes the two techniques were combined. Firing was accomplished by inverting the pots over stones and building a fire under them; other pieces of pottery were put on top of them, to hold burning cakes of dried dung. For pieces to be decorated, a thin mixture of clay and water, called a slip, was added. Various decorating methods included painting; stenciling; negative designing, which involved painting the background black; corrugation, or smoothing the inside with the ridges of the coil showing on the outside; incising, or scratching the wet clay; engraving, or scratching the hard clay; impressing, or pressing the soft clay with fingers, shells, or other objects; and stamping, or tapping the soft clay with a thong-wrapped paddle. Native North Americans did not use the potter's wheel until Postcontact times. They also used clay to shape effigy figures in addition to pottery vessels.

METALWORK: Although Native North Americans had not entered what is called the Iron Age in other parts of the world, they made extensive use of metals in varying parts of the continent. Early Indians in the Great Lakes region, Indians of the Copper River region of Alaska, and Northwest Coast peoples who acquired metal through trade worked copper that was mined either as sheets in rock fissures or float nuggets in the soil. They developed annealing techniques—alternate heating and hammering—to craft tools and ornaments. Indians also used pieces of meteoritic iron and galena (lead) to make tools—especially chisels—and for inlays. The most extensive metallurgy occurred in Mesoamerica—beautiful craftsmanship in gold, silver, copper, zinc, and tin—introduced from South America during the Classic age. In Postcontact times, the

European influence brought metalwork to other peoples. Metal trade goods were highly valued, not just as efficient tools but also for the raw materials in them. Indians cut up and reworked brass kettles into a variety of tools and trinkets. By 1800, Iroquois peoples of the Northeast had mastered silverwork, and it soon spread to other parts of the continent. Contemporary Indians of the Southwest especially are known for their silver jewelry.

BONE, HORN, ANTLER, AND TUSK WORK: Native North Americans used the bones, horns, antlers, and tusks of land and sea mammals and other creatures in numerous functions, in particular for pointed implements, such as spear, harpoon, arrow, dart, and club points, as well as fishhooks, needles, pins, weaving tools, knives, scrapers, and chisels. They also used these materials to make utensils—bowls and spoons, for example—ceremonial objects, toys, games, ornaments, and jewelry. Deer hooves and turtle and tortoise shells served as raw materials for rattles and other objects.

SHELLWORK: Seashells (and freshwater shells), with a variety of practical and decorative applications, spread all over the continent as trade items. Indians utilized them as blades, scrapers, bowls, and spoons, and in the making of jewelry as beads, pendants, earrings, gorgets, plus decoration on clothing. Other applications included conch shells as trumpets in the Southwest; dentalium shells as a form of money in the Northwest; and quahog clamshells, ground into purple and white beads and strung into wampum, which was used by the Iroquois and Algonquian peoples of the Northeast as a form of money, for ceremonial belts, or for tribal records.

QUILLWORK: Indians of the Northeast, Subarctic, Northwest Coast, and Great Plains used porcupine quills, soaked and softened in water and then dyed, as applied decoration on clothing, bags, boxes, pipes, and other articles. Designs were elaborate, both geometric and representational of animals and flowers.

BEADWORK: In Postcontact times, starting about 1675, eastern Indians began working with European glass trade beads. From the East, the craft spread to other parts of the continent, especially those places where quill-work had been developed. Like quills, beads were applied in a variety of geometric and naturalistic designs on clothing, pouches, quivers, and other articles. Beadwork techniques included weaving and netting, plus spot-stitch and lazy-stitch sewing.

APPLIQUÉ: Techniques of ribbon-and-cloth appliqué, like beadwork, came to Native North Americans in Postcontact times. Pieces of cloth and ribbon were sewn onto leather or textiles in intricate and colorful patterns, some representational. The Seminoles of Florida began using sewing machines at the end of the 19th century, and they became famous for their patchwork skirts and shirts.

FEATHERWORK: Feathers held a special place in Indian culture. Various birds were regarded as sacred, such as eagles, hawks, and owls, and as messengers of the gods. Feathers were used for ceremonial decorations as well as for offerings. Indians placed them on prayer sticks, dance wands, effigy figures, pipe stems, shields, spears, clubs, baskets, and clothing. The Plains warbonnet, with feathers representing exploits, is a dominant Indian image in the public imagination. Indians also used feathers for the practical purpose of stabilizing arrows in flight.

PAINTING, DYEING, AND ENGRAVING: Native North Americans added design to their crafts through painting, dyeing, and engraving. They extracted their paints from a variety of raw materials—earth with iron ore for reds, yellow, and browns; copper ore for green and blue; soot or graphite for black; and clay, limestone, and gypsum for white—and used them to decorate tepees, shields, pottery, ceremonial objects, etc. Paint

was applied with fingers, sticks, brushes, or sprayed from the mouth, and was often held in shells. Body paint was also used for symbolic purposes; i.e., to indicate social position or an intent to make war. Indians extracted dyes from plant sources—berries, roots, barks—to color textiles, basket materials, and quills. Indians also frequently engraved wood, bark, stone, pottery, bone, tusk, etc. Different forms of expression came to be highly developed in different parts of the continent—for example, pottery painting in the Southwest, animal skin painting on the Great Plains, wood engraving along the Northwest Coast, ivory engraving in the Arctic, and bark engraving in the Subarctic.

DRAMATIC ARTS: Music, dance, and the recitation of tales were indispensable to Indian ritual and can be considered a part of religion. Yet they also provided an outlet for individual creativity and expression, and can be thought of as an art form. Both music and dance were valued for their magical power and were used to induce visions, treat the sick, prepare for war, to aid hunting and growing, and to celebrate rites of passage. Indian songs were monophonic—having a single melody—and usually descended from a higher to a lower pitch. Songs and chants, which had some words and some meaningless syllables, could be owned, sold, or inherited in some cultures. Instru-

A game of lacrosse, drawn by Jesse Cornplanter, Iroquois, 1908. New York State Library, Albany.

ments usually accompanied voices and included drums (plank, rod, slit drums, and drums with skin heads), sticks, clappers, rasps, rattles, flutes, flageolets, whistles, and simple reed

Menominee rattle with turtle claw at base

trumpets. Indians danced individually and in groups. Masks and costumes—many of them animal representations—and body paints played a part in dance ritual, which was generally symbolic. Some dances were slow, others frenetic. Indians often played music and danced through the night, often in conjunction with taking hallucinogens. Without written literature, Indians depended on storytelling to communicate tales, myths, legends, and history. Vocal expression and gestures added drama to the spoken word.

GAMES AND TOYS: Indian games were remarkably similar throughout North America, indicating intertribal influence. There were two basic kinds: games of chance and gambling, and games of skill and dexterity. Games of chance included dice, marked sticks, guessing games, and hand games. Athletic games included archery; spear throwing; racing (horse racing in Postcontact times); juggling; lacrosse; poleball, played with a pole and ball; chunkey, played with a ring and pole; snow snake, played by sliding a lance on snow or ice; and shinney, played with a ball and stick; and others. Indians also made a variety of toys for their children out of the materials at hand—wood, cornhusk, bone, ivory, etc. Children also made toys for themselves. Dolls were common, as were animal figures. Other toys were copies of adult objects—boats, sleds, bows and arrows. Still others were for games—balls, blocks, tops, bean shooters, stilts, and string for cat's cradle.

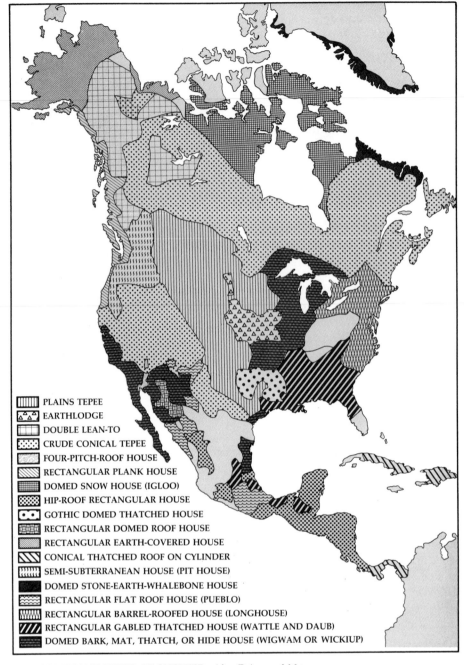

PLAINS TEPEE
EARTHLODGE
DOUBLE LEAN-TO
CRUDE CONICAL TEPEE
FOUR-PITCH-ROOF HOUSE
RECTANGULAR PLANK HOUSE
DOMED SNOW HOUSE (IGLOO)
HIP-ROOF RECTANGULAR HOUSE
GOTHIC DOMED THATCHED HOUSE
RECTANGULAR DOMED ROOF HOUSE
RECTANGULAR EARTH-COVERED HOUSE
CONICAL THATCHED ROOF ON CYLINDER
SEMI-SUBTERRANEAN HOUSE (PIT HOUSE)
DOMED STONE-EARTH-WHALEBONE HOUSE
RECTANGULAR FLAT ROOF HOUSE (PUEBLO)
RECTANGULAR BARREL-ROOFED HOUSE (LONGHOUSE)
RECTANGULAR GABLED THATCHED HOUSE (WATTLE AND DAUB)
DOMED BARK, MAT, THATCH, OR HIDE HOUSE (WIGWAM OR WICKIUP)

3.24 DOMINANT TYPES OF SHELTER. *After Driver and Massey.*

SHELTER

Many of the names are familiar and evoke strong images of the Indian past: tepees, wigwams, igloos, pueblos, and lean-tos. Others perhaps are not so well known: longhouses, hogans, wickiups, earthlodges, pit houses, and chickees. Native North Americans of course constructed a wide variety of house types in addition to that dominant of Indian sym-

bols in white culture, the skin tent known as the tepee (or tipi), using whatever materials at hand: wood, bark, brush, straw, hide, earth, clay, and stone.

Since there was so much diversification from tribe to tribe, with some tribes even living in more than one kind of shelter seasonally, it is difficult to adequately represent such an abundance of information on one map. The accompanying map depicts a regional breakdown of general house types used by the majority of the population for most of a year. The

Chickee

Lean-to

Plank house

Longhouse

Pueblo

Wattle and daub

Wigwam

Tepee

Hogan

Igloo

Earthlodge

Pit house

Wickiup

following is an alphabetical list of particular structures, with definitions and patterns of usage:

CHICKEE: A stilt house, open on all sides, with a platform and a thatch roof (usually four-poled, with split logs for the floor and palmetto leaves for the roof), unique to the Seminoles.

EARTHLODGE: A usually large, dome-shaped dwelling with a log frame and covered with earth or sod, often semisubterranean. Found in many parts of the continent, especially along the upper Missouri.

HOGAN: A conical, hexagonal, or octagonal structure with a log-and-stick frame covered with mud, sod, adobe, and sometimes stone; a Navajo dwelling that traditionally faces east.

IGLOO: A dome-shaped structure made of blocks of ice or hard snow, or of sod and wood, unique to the Eskimos.

LEAN-TO: A temporary, open brush shelter consisting of a sloping single-pitched roof. Western Subarctic peoples constructed double lean-tos with gabled ends.

LONGHOUSE: A long communal dwelling (sometimes over a hundred feet long), either gabled or vaulted, with a door at each end; a log frame with a variety of coverings, often elm bark, it was unique to the Iroquois tribes and the Hurons.

PIT HOUSE: A semisubterranean structure several feet in the ground, with a log frame and a roof of saplings, reeds, and mud.

PLANK HOUSE: A dwelling made of hand-split planks over a log (often cedar) frame, generally rectangular in shape, and found along the Northwest Coast.

PUEBLO: *Pueblo,* the Spanish word for village, refers to a type of Indian architecture of the Southwest as well as to the inhabitants themselves. The

apartment-like multistoried stone or adobe (clay) structures have contiguous flat roofs and receding terraces connected by wooden ladders.

TEPEE (TIPI): A conical tent consisting of an animal-skin (or sometimes bark) covering over a frame of poles, and usually having a smoke hole at the top; found on the Great Plains, as well as in the Northeast, the Subarctic, and the Southwest.

WATTLE AND DAUB: A type of construction using a pole framework intertwined with branches and vines, and covered with mud plaster; found especially in the Southeast.

WICKIUP: A conical or domed hut with a pole frame covered with reed mats, grass, or brush, often with a center fire pit and a smoke hole; found in the Southwest, Great Basin, and California, especially among the Apaches.

WIGWAM: A hut with an arched frame of poles overlaid with bark, animal skin, or woven mats; common to the Algonquian peoples of the Northeast.

Native North Americans also used their building skills to design and erect structures for special purposes. Among these were: 1) the kivas of the Pueblo Indians of the Southwest—underground ceremonial chambers, usually round, with entrances and lighting through the roof, and with fire pits, altars, and *sipapus* (holes in the floor representing the doorway to the supernatural); 2) the temples of the Temple Mound Builders of the Southeast—constructed of pole and thatch on top of mounds; and 3) the sweathouses located in all regions of North America—except among the central and eastern Eskimos and some tribes in the Great Basin and the Southwest—for ritual sweating and purification by exposure to heat, to be followed by a plunge into a stream or lake. Indians designed their sweathouses in two primary styles: small wigwamlike structures with shallow fire pits for pouring water onto hot

rocks, for steam sweating; and large, communal semisubterranean lodges with deep fire pits for direct fire sweating. These latter structures often doubled as clubhouses.

For discussions of the specialized stone, wood, and clay architecture of Mesoamerica—cities, plazas, courtyards, public buildings, palaces, pyramids, temples, ball-courts, monasteries, astronomical observatories, and dance platforms—see chapter 2, "ANCIENT CIVILIZATIONS."

CLOTHING

The prevailing image of the Indian, in terms of clothing, body decoration, and accessories, is that of the Plains Indian dressed in leather, beadwork, warbonnet, and war paint. This style of dress and ornamentation is of course just one of many. As the accompanying map shows, in areas of the continent where agriculture was most developed, animal skins gave way to wild plants and cultivated cotton as primary materials for clothing.

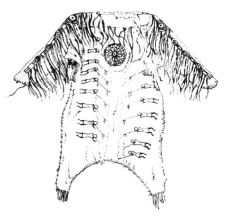

Crow buckskin shirt

Climate and available materials dictated types of clothing that served first and foremost the practical purpose of protection, with modesty and concealment of the body rarely a concern. In warm climates Indians often went naked or wore only loincloths (male) or aprons (female). Dress and ornamentation indicated social position and prestige in some Indian cultures. Indian clothing was often adorned with dyes, shells, quills, and,

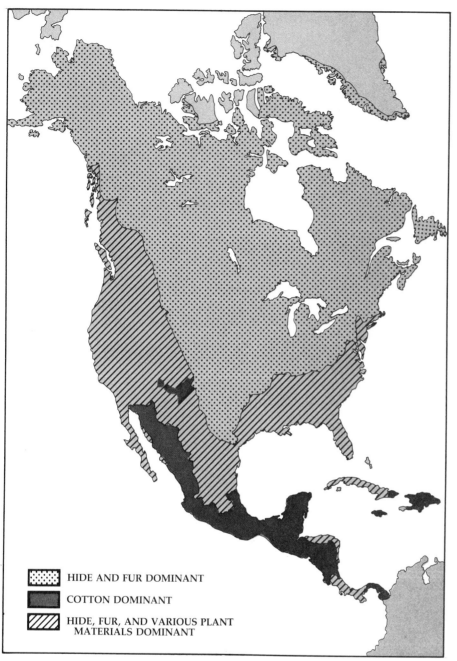

HIDE AND FUR DOMINANT

COTTON DOMINANT

HIDE, FUR, AND VARIOUS PLANT
MATERIALS DOMINANT

3.25 DISTRIBUTION OF CLOTHING MATERIALS. *After Driver and Massey.*

in Postcontact times, beads and ribbons. (See "Art and Technology" in this chapter.)

Among the more common articles of clothing in various styles and materials were breechclouts (or breechcloths), shirts, and leggings for men, and skirts and blouses or dresses for women, plus robes and blankets for both in cold weather. Other common articles were jackets, vests, ponchos, tunics, kilts, aprons, belts, and sashes. Although a great number of Indians went barefoot, for others footwear included leather moccasins—

both single-piece, soft-soled; and two-piece, hard-soled, with a rawhide base. Some moccasins, known as "boot" moccasins, extended high on the calf. Certain early Southwest and Great Basin peoples wore woven or braided plant-fiber sandals. Headgear included feather and plant-fiber headdresses, headbands, and, in the Far West, basket hats and headnets.

The peoples of the Arctic developed specialized clothing for the extreme cold. Using sea mammal, caribou, and polar-bear skins, furs, and intestines, as well as those of small mammals

and birds, the Eskimos crafted insulated and waterproof pants, parkas, boots, and mittens. They tailored their hooded parkas to hang loosely over the body—often in double layers to create the insulating effect of a dead air space—but to fit snugly at the neck, wrists, and ankles. And they insulated their mukluks and mittens with down and moss.

Native North Americans also utilized a wide variety of body decoration in conjunction with their often colorful clothing. People painted faces and bodies with symbolic colors and designs for special rites surrounding warfare, mourning, and clan relationships. Paint served the secondary purpose of protection from sun and wind. Indians in many parts of North America also decorated themselves with tattoos by perforating their skin with sharp implements of stone, bone, or shell, and rubbing in soot or dyes. Indians in the Southeast were known to tattoo their entire bodies.

Jewelry was another form of body ornamentation, with pieces made of shells, animal teeth, claws, stones, and copper. Accessories included earrings—many Indians having pierced ears—necklaces, armbands, headbands, breastplates, and gorgets. In Postcontact times, beadwork and silverwork became widely adopted by Indian jewelers.

The styling and decoration of hair took on special significance in many Indian cultures. As for facial hair, most males plucked whiskers with shell, bone, or wood tweezers, only rarely letting mustaches grow. But there were many individualistic coiffures with little tribal uniformity. Roaches, or hairlocks protruding from shaved heads, were popular in many parts of the continent, as were braids. Indians also used hairdressing, such as bear fat mixed with pigments, as well as interwoven artificial roaches from animal hair. Feathers were often added. To care for hair, combs of wood, bone, and horn were used, and brushes of straw and porcupine tails. The concept of hair as a symbol of strength and individuality contributed to the spread of the scalping custom in Postcontact times.

TRANSPORTATION

LAND, ICE, AND WATER

In the general public's perception of Native North American culture, certain traits receive widespread attention while others are underemphasized. It has been shown, for example, that the tepee is just one of many kinds of Indian shelter. Similarly, in the subject of transportation, it seems that certain modes have come to be represented as particularly Indian. For example, although Indians are often depicted as horse-mounted in popular culture, it is not widely known that, although horses were native to North America during the Ice Age, they were long extinct by the time of Contact and were reintroduced to the native population by Europeans. Another cultural trait receiving great emphasis is the birchbark canoe; in fact, canoes were just one of many types of boat, and birchbark just one of many materials. Likewise, the technology for travel on snow and ice was highly developed among other native peoples besides the Eskimos. And although warfare receives emphasis as a motive for travel among Indians, the majority of journeying beyond tribal territories was for the purpose of trade.

The accompanying drawings give a sense of the diversity of transportation methods and technology. The following section treats the subject of the Indian and the horse. And for a sense of the extent of Indian trails, waterways, and portages throughout North America, for travel both within tribal hunting grounds and beyond tribal territories for trade, see "Indian Trails and White Inroads" in chapter 6.

As for land travel before the advent of the horse, the human foot was the dominant means of locomotion and the human back the dominant means of hauling. The wheel, other than on pottery toys in Mesoamerica, was unknown in aboriginal North America as a mode of transportation (or, incidentally, for pottery making).

Equipment on land included footwear, such as moccasins and sandals (see "Clothing" in this chapter); bundles made from animal skins or wool blankets; carrying baskets; leather or parfleche pouches and sacks; tumplines—leather straps connecting backpacks and bundles to the brow; and cradleboards, made of wood,

Algonkin cradleboard with European floral motif

hide, and/or plant-fiber, for carrying infants (Eskimos carried their babies in their parka hoods or pouches). Dogs were used on the prairies and plains to haul supplies on a travois— a wooden frame in the shape of a V, with the closed end over the animal's shoulders, the open end dragging on the ground, and a plank or webbing in the middle to hold goods. In Postcontact times, the travois was enlarged to fit over a horse and often used to carry the young and elderly— frequently with a top or shade — as

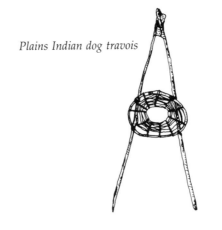

Plains Indian dog travois

well as household equipment, supplies, and trade goods. The travois poles sometimes doubled as tepee poles.

In conditions of ice and snow in the Arctic, dogs were used to pull sleds

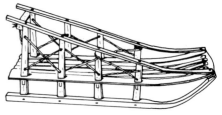

Eskimo sled

of varying shapes, sizes, and materials. Wood or hide platforms were raised off the surface with wood or bone runners. One design utilized whalebone runners, with caribou antlers for crosspieces and *babiche* (rawhide strips) for shock absorbers. Hide was also used for the surface of runners, and a mixture of frozen clay and moss was added to minimize friction and improve wear. Subarctic peoples invented the toboggan, with

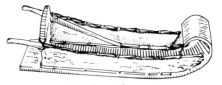

Koyukon toboggan

the wood platforms or beds directly on the ice or snow. Snowshoes were used in northern latitudes by both Arctic and Subarctic peoples: spruce, birch, or willow frames, with rim and crossbars, braced *babiche* webbing with additional thongs for the feet.

Subarctic snowshoe

Eskimos also had crampons to attach to their boots for walking on ice, as well as test staffs, resembling ski poles, to judge the strength and thickness of ice. Native North Americans did not have skis, however.

With regard to water travel, Native North Americans were master boat builders with a variety of techniques and designs. There were five basic types of craft construction:

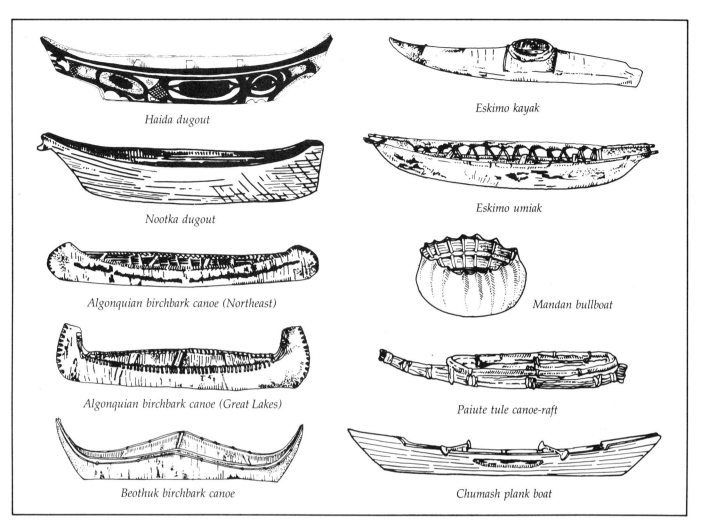

Haida dugout

Nootka dugout

Algonquian birchbark canoe (Northeast)

Algonquian birchbark canoe (Great Lakes)

Beothuk birchbark canoe

Eskimo kayak

Eskimo umiak

Mandan bullboat

Paiute tule canoe-raft

Chumash plank boat

DUGOUTS: These were shaped with woodworking tools, such as adzes, gouges, and wedges, from hollowed-out logs. In the process the logs were sometimes filled with water and heated stones were added, to soften the wood and expand the sides. Separate bow and stern pieces were sometimes added. Dugouts were especially widespread along the Northwest Coast and in the Southeast. Some Northwest crafts, especially those of the Haida Indians, were immense, over 50 feet long, and able to navigate deep ocean waters. Dugouts were too heavy for convenient portage.

CANOES: Coverings of bark, especially birchbark and elm bark, were stretched over a framework of saplings. The making of such canoes was an elaborate process; the sections of bark were sewn together with root fibers and sealed with pitch or tar over the carefully shaped wood frame.

These were light, portable boats, convenient for the interior river and lake systems of the Northeast and eastern Subarctic.

KAYAKS, UMIAKS, BULLBOATS: These were boats made of hide coverings over a wood framework. The Eskimos used this technology to make kayaks—which were one- or two-man boats with all but the paddlers' holes covered—and umiaks—which were large, open boats. Indians of the upper Missouri also made bullboats, circular and cup-shaped craft, similar to the Old World coracles and used primarily for crossing rivers.

RAFTS (or *balsas* as called in South America): These were made from tule reeds tied together into bundles, and were often shaped like pointed boats. The bundles would become waterlogged after a period of use, but would dry out in the sun of Central California.

PLANK BOATS: These were made from small hand-split, holed planks lashed together with leather or plant-fiber bindings and caulked with asphalt. No intact plank craft—a type of boat building unique to the Chumash Indians of Southern California—has been found and reproductions from fragments are hypothetical. It is presumed that these seaworthy craft were designed to ply the water between offshore islands.

In addition to the above kinds of boats, Indians had numerous boating accessories, including wood paddles, stone anchors, shell bailers, and plant-fiber and hide painters for mooring. The aboriginal use of sails is in question, but it is known that shortly after Contact both Arctic and Northwest Coast peoples sailed regularly with sails made from animal skins.

3.26 INTRODUCTION OF THE HORSE INTO NORTH AMERICA. *Lines and arrows indicate approximate diffusion routes of horse-related culture out of Mexico to Indian tribes; dates indicate approximate years horses reached the various areas (with modern boundaries). After Haines and Roe.*

THE INDIAN
AND THE HORSE

The horse and the masterful use of it are generally thought to be typically Indian—buffalo hunting and warfare on horseback. Yet, other than the prehistoric native horse, driven to extinction at the end of the Ice Age, the horse in North America was a Postcontact phenomenon. First introduced to the Indians by the Spanish in the early 16th century, it became the catalyst and an intrinsic element of a new culture, that of the Great Plains.

As Spanish colonies moved northward out of Mexico, so of course did the dominant European mode of land transportation—the horse. Spanish officials outlawed the trafficking of horses to the Indians, but they couldn't prevent the gradual dispersion of the animals to the tribes in the region. The Pueblo Indians originally tended them for the colonists at settlements along the Rio Grande. These newfound skills—caring for and breeding horses—slowly began spreading throughout the native

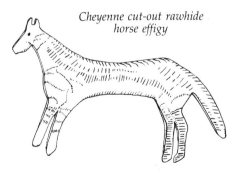

Cheyenne cut-out rawhide horse effigy

population, along with stolen stock. By the mid-17th century, Apaches, Kiowas, and Utes were making the first of what became a typical Plains Indian cultural pattern—raids for horses. Then, during the Pueblo Rebellion of 1680, hundreds of horses fell into Indian hands. Furthermore, some Spanish horses over the years had gone wild and were being tracked down by Indians. (*Mustang*, in fact, is a Spanish-derived word.)

After 1680, equine trade advanced rapidly northward. Southern nomadic peoples, now horse-mounted, bartered horses and products of the hunt with seminomadic or horticultural tribes to the north. Kiowas traded horses to Wichitas, Pawnees, Cheyennes, and Arapahos. Utes traded to Comanches and Shoshonis. Shoshonis traded to Crows and to Columbia Plateau tribes, such as the Nez Perce, Cayuse, and Palouse. (The Cayuse people, who refined the art of horse breeding, passed their name to a kind of pony, and the Palouses gave their name to the the *appaloosa* breed.) Mandan and Arikara villages became northern trading centers. Before long, the Sioux and other tribes east of the Missouri River at that time were also mounted, as were northern tribes such as Blackfoot, Assiniboine, Plains Cree, and Plains Ojibway. Some tribal members took on the specific role of horse merchants. An intertribal sign language evolved to facilitate commerce, and Indians held yearly intertribal horse fairs.

By the latter part of the 18th century, the use of the horse was widespread. Because of the increased mobility, many tribes abandoned village life and farming altogether in favor of the migratory hunting existence. Diversity of cultures blended into similarity, resulting in the so-called Composite Tribe of the Great Plains. The buffalo became the basis of the Plains Indian economy. And the horse, which had made the new life possible, became the dominant symbol of wealth, prestige, and honor, as well as a primary source of intertribal raiding.

INDIAN RELIGION

The subject of religion pervades all Indian cultural studies. Indians were an especially holistic and reverent people, viewing themselves as extensions of animate and inanimate nature. Religion and ritual were a function of all activity—the food quest and other survival-related work, technology, social and political organization, warfare, and art. Religion and magic were fused with practical science—for example, prayer was used in conjunction with practical hunting and fishing techniques, and incantations accompanied effective herbal remedies in the curing of disease. For Indians the natural was inseparable from the supernatural. Myth was a way of understanding reality. Religion played a prominent role in the interpretation of the universe and in the adaptation of human activity to the patterns of nature.

In addition to this holism, other generalizations can be made with regard to Indian religion. Part of the special intimate relationship with nature involved a sense of kinship with the natural world and the attribution of innate souls and human properties to plants, animals, inanimate objects, and natural phenomena. Indian religion generally also involved the belief that the universe is suffused with preternatural forces and powerful spirits. Shamanism was a common form of religious practice, in which individuals sought to control these spirits through the use of magic. Other traits characteristic of most Indian cultures were a richness of myths and legends, ceremonies, and sacred objects; the quest for visions and the use of psychotropic plants to facilitate those visions; music and dance as a part of ritual; and the notion of sacrifice to gain the favor of the gods or spirits.

Apart from these shared traits, however, Indian religion presents a wondrous variety of beliefs, sacraments, and systems. Different tribes or related groups of peoples had dif-

Raising of the Slain Hero *by Jesse Cornplanter, Iroquois, 1908. New York State Library, Albany.*

ferent views of the supernatural world, with varying types of deities and spirits: monotheistic, omnipotent universal spirits, such as the Algonquian Manitou, Iroquoian Orenda, and Siouan Wakenda, who are the sources of all other spirits; pantheistic deities with specific images and attributes, e.g., Quetzalcoatl of Mesoamerica, the Plumed Serpent; ghosts, or the spirits of dead ancestors; animal and plant spirits; spirits of natural phenomena, such as sun or rain gods; benevolent or guardian spirits, such as the Hopi katchinas; and malevolent demons, such as the Algonquian Windigos. Along with these diverse types of supernatural beings, Indian peoples had variegated mythologies and lore concerning the creation and structure of the universe; an array of rites, ceremonies, and sacred objects; and differing systems of religious organization. Some tribes had single shamans or medicine men; others had secret societies or medicine societies; and still others had priesthoods.

In order to help clarify the difficult subject of Indian religion, this section will also discuss the two main cultural currents—the Northern Hunting tradition and the Southern Agrarian tradition—that led up to the great religious diversity at the time of Contact,

as well as religious movements that arose in reaction to whites. For a further sense of the central role of religion in Indian life and the diversity of Indian beliefs and rituals, see also the sections "Art and Technology" and "Stimulants, Intoxicants, and Hallucinogens" in this chapter.

PRECONTACT RELIGIOUS EVOLUTION

The religious beliefs, rituals, and myths of aboriginal America seem to arise from the diffusion and cross-fertilization of two distinct cultural traditions. The older Northern Hunting tradition dates back to the first arrival of Paleo-Siberian peoples in North America during the Ice Age. Their ideology and forms of worship were rooted in the ancient Paleolithic way of life. Hunting and healing rituals and magic, the ecstatic vision trances of shamans, and the worship of a Master of Animals who protects game and regulates the hunt are all characteristic features of the Northern Hunting tradition. Perhaps the purest historic expression of this tradition was in Circumpolar Bear Ceremonialism, in which bears were sacrificed and consumed in a communal meal

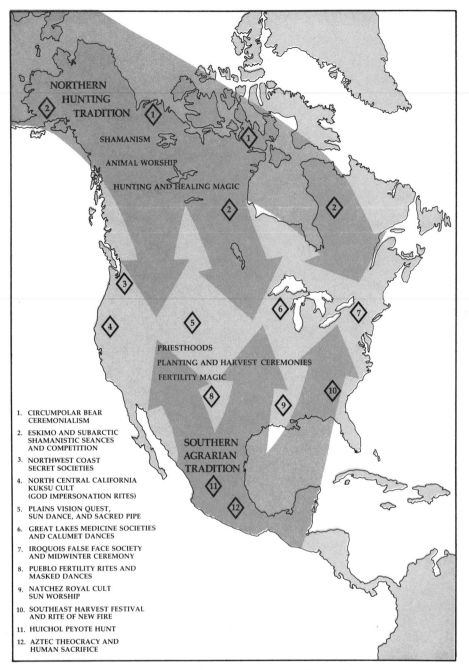

3.27 PRECONTACT RELIGION: *some characteristic practices. After Trimbur.*

1. CIRCUMPOLAR BEAR CEREMONIALISM

2. ESKIMO AND SUBARCTIC SHAMANISTIC SEANCES AND COMPETITION

3. NORTHWEST COAST SECRET SOCIETIES

4. NORTH CENTRAL CALIFORNIA KUKSU CULT (GOD IMPERSONATION RITES)

5. PLAINS VISION QUEST, SUN DANCE, AND SACRED PIPE

6. GREAT LAKES MEDICINE SOCIETIES AND CALUMET DANCES

7. IROQUOIS FALSE FACE SOCIETY AND MIDWINTER CEREMONY

8. PUEBLO FERTILITY RITES AND MASKED DANCES

9. NATCHEZ ROYAL CULT SUN WORSHIP

10. SOUTHEAST HARVEST FESTIVAL AND RITE OF NEW FIRE

11. HUICHOL PEYOTE HUNT

12. AZTEC THEOCRACY AND HUMAN SACRIFICE

commemorating the kinship between humans and Grandfather Bear, the Master of the Mountain. These practices of bear worship existed all along the Arctic Circle, from the reindeer-herding Lapps of Scandinavia across Siberia to the Ainu of northern Japan and on to the Eskimos and Algonquians of the upper latitudes of North America.

As the ancient Paleolithic beliefs and rituals were diffused to the south, they met and intermingled with the younger Southern Agrarian tradition, which was emanating northward,

with the spread of maize, from the Valley of Mexico. In this second tradition, priesthoods and secret cults replaced the individualistic shamans of the Northern Hunting tradition as the religious leaders in society, and hunting magic and rituals were incorporated into agrarian ceremonies devoted to the seasonal cycle of crops. The sacred stories of the Corn Mother, as found in agricultural societies, reinterpreted the ancient myths of the Animal Masters, relocating the generative source of fertility and new life in plants.

In many North American tribes that cultivated maize, vestiges of the older Northern Hunting tradition persisted alongside the planting, fertility, and harvest rituals of the younger Southern Agrarian tradition. The vision quest of the Plains tribes and the sacred pipe, medicine societies, and dog sacrifices of Prairie and Woodland cultures all extended back to ancient shamanistic practices. Even when the ritual calendar was geared to the life cycle of maize, as in the case of the Iroquois and Hopis, winter remained the sacred season, as in the Northern Hunting tradition, the time for animal dances and healing ceremonies. On the other hand, religious practices associated with the Southern Agrarian tradition spread to nonmaize cultures. The Kuksu cult and god-impersonation rites of Northern California, and the secret societies and masked dances of the Northwest Coast, shared elements with the southern priesthood societies and their emphasis on hierarchical ranking and esoteric worship.

POSTCONTACT RELIGIOUS RESISTANCE

In the conquest of aboriginal America, European civilization waged ideological as well as military and economic warfare against the integrity of Native American culture. The European powers that colonized North America sent forth not only armies and traders, but also missionaries to convert the Indians from so-called pagan and primitive ways to Christian religion and Western customs. The resulting effect of Christian missionaries on tribal culture has been every bit as profound as the Indian wars, the fur trade, or European diseases.

In those instances where Spanish, French, or English missionaries succeeded in Christianizing Indians, tribes disappeared as distinct political and cultural entities, their members absorbed into the dominant white culture, usually at the bottom, as in the case of the California Mission Indians, who lived a serflike existence in the Spanish feudal order. In other instances, however, attempts to Christianize the native population met with strenuous resistance. The Pueblo Rebellion of 1680 was one of the earliest revolts against foreign powers. Inspired by the teachings of the prophet Pope, the uprising succeeded, if only briefly, in driving the Spanish from New Mexico and in restoring native religion and culture. (See "The Pueblo Rebellion" in chapter 5.)

Later attempts to drive the Europeans from North America manifested a similar pattern of prophecy and resistance. The pan-tribal movements of Pontiac, Tecumseh, and Black Hawk in the latter part of the 18th and first part of the 19th centuries took much of their impetus from the teachings of the Delaware Prophet, the Shawnee Prophet, and the Winnebago Prophet respectively, native holy men who preached resistance to white culture and a return to Precontact native ways. (See chapter 5, "INDIAN WARS.") The apocalyptic tone of these prophets suggests they borrowed certain themes from Christianity itself, particularly the call of the Old Testament prophets to purify their people of external influences and, through suffering, to prepare for a revitalization of native religion and culture.

Other currents of Indian religious renewal, often combining native and Christian elements, occurred during the same period. In 1799, Handsome Lake founded the Longhouse Religion among the Iroquois, which not only reaffirmed the validity of Iroquois beliefs but also adapted them to the realities of military defeat and cultural subordination, offering Indians a way to make the transition from the older tribal order of clan-held communal property to the new order of the family farm and private property.

Across the Plains and in the Far West during the latter part of the 19th century, more revitalization movements followed in the wake of military defeat and the disappearance of the buffalo. The religious movements of Smohalla and his Dreamers, of John Slocum's Indian Shaker Church, and Wovoka's Ghost Dance Religion developed in an otherwordly apocalyptic direction. The Ghost Dance Religion, which spread from tribe to tribe, culminated at Wounded Knee in 1890, where Wovoka's prophecy that the fallen warriors and the buffalo would return to drive away the whites met the cruel reality of American guns in a massacre that the supposedly magical bulletproof Ghost Dance shirts could not prevent. (See "Wars for the West" in chapter 5.)

At the turn of the 20th century, the last great Indian prophet, Quanah Parker, discovered the Peyote Road and helped found the pan-tribal Native American Church, which spread to the defeated peoples of the Southwest, Plains, Prairies, Great Lakes, as well as to urban areas. By offering a liturgy and the sacrament of peyote, the Native American Church provided a variation on Christian worship that preserved some of the ancient ways and beliefs. (See "Stimulants, Intoxicants, and Hallucinogens" in this chapter.)

3.28 POSTCONTACT RELIGION: *some revitalization movements. After Trimbur.*

STIMULANTS, INTOXICANTS, AND HALLUCINOGENS

American Indians used a variety of plants, some wild and some cultivated, for both religious and practical purposes, as well as simply for pleasure. As for religion and ritual, the mind-altering and hallucinogenic qualities of certain substances facilitated the quest for visions and contact with the spiritual world. Practical applications were medicinal, in which cases psychotropic plants were used as herbal remedies or as painkillers; stimulative, in which cases these same substances were used for energy and bravery; and social, in which cases the sharing of substances created bonds of friendship and loyalty. In many instances, especially in warfare and in peacemaking, the ritualistic merged with the practical. And pleasure was also derived from certain applications.

The South American Indians made use of an especially large number of psychoactive plants, the most well-known being the coca leaf, from which cocaine is derived. In North and Middle America the principal stimulants, intoxicants, and hallucinogens were tobacco, alcoholic beverages, peyote, jimsonweed *(Datura stramonium)*, mushrooms, mescal bean, Black Drink, and ololiuqui.

TOBACCO

Just several generations after Columbus brought knowledge of tobacco to Europe from the Arawak Indians of the West Indies, it came to be widely used and grown in much of the world. The word *tobacco* is a Spanish adaptation of the Arawak term for cigar. Of the more than a dozen known species of the plant, all but a few are native to the Americas, the majority in South America. Knowledge of the plant probably spread from south to north, along with agriculture and maize. Use of tobacco in Precontact times is surmised from archaeological

sites. An extensive pipe culture was invented around the plant. But in addition to being smoked (often with other plants as well), tobacco was also chewed, sniffed, and mixed in drinks. Indians all over North America, except the Arctic, parts of the Subarctic, and parts of the Columbia Plateau, used tobacco in one form or another in Precontact times. And, after Contact, European traders spread use of the plant to these other regions as well.

The smoking, snuffing, and eating of tobacco was part of the ritual surrounding war, peace, harvest, puberty, and death. Indians also burned the plant as incense, sprinkled it in leaf form, or buried it with the dead. Most such uses carried the notion of sacrificial offerings. Secular applications included stimulation in times of stress, such as war or work; curing of disease and wounds; as an anesthetic; and for physical comfort and pleasure. The physiologically active alkaloid in tobacco is nicotine.

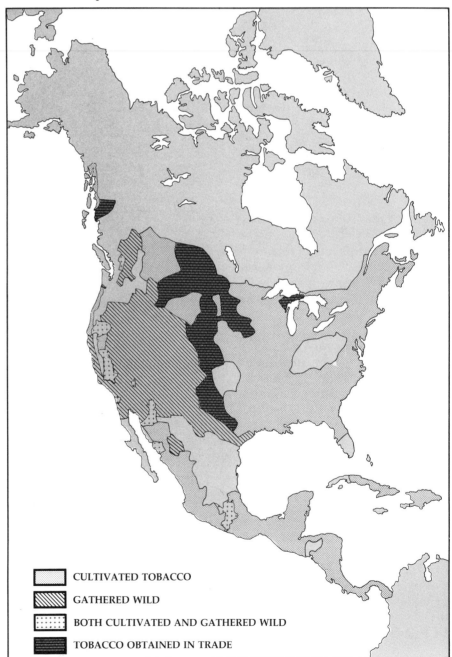

CULTIVATED TOBACCO

GATHERED WILD

BOTH CULTIVATED AND GATHERED WILD

TOBACCO OBTAINED IN TRADE

3.29 USE OF TOBACCO. *After Driver and Massey.*

ALCOHOLIC BEVERAGES

For most North American Indians, drinking alcohol was a Postcontact phenomenon. In fact, alcohol played a prominent role in Indian and white relations in several ways: as a white trade item in exchange for Indian-provided furs; as a negotiating device used by whites to gain the advantage over Indians; and as a catalyst to unrest and violence on the part of both Indians and whites. Yet in certain regions of the continent, especially where agriculture was highly developed—Mesoamerica, the Circum-Caribbean, the Southwest, and Southeast—alcohol was widely used in Precontact times as well.

Indian alcoholic beverages were made from both domesticated and wild plants. There were at least 40 distinct varieties in Mexico alone, such as corn beer, maguey wine, sotol wine, and *balche*, a drink made from fermented honey. Indians of the Southwest made a wine from cacti, and Southeast peoples made a persimmon wine. In much of the Southwest, among the Zunis, Yumans, and Apaches, as well as in the Southeast, the use of alcohol was for the most part secular. Papagos and Pimas of the Southwest, however, believed that the intake of alcoholic beverages would bring rain. Among the Aztecs, intoxication served to induce meditation and prophecy. Public drunkenness, however, was frowned upon and in some instances, among nobles and commoners alike, was punished by death.

PEYOTE

Peyote is the fruit of the nondomesticated *Lophophora williamsii* cactus which grows in northern Mexico and along the Rio Grande Valley of the American Southwest. The rounded top of the plant, protruding aboveground and shaped something like a mushroom, is cut off, dried, and made into the peyote button. Sometimes it is popularly called the mescal

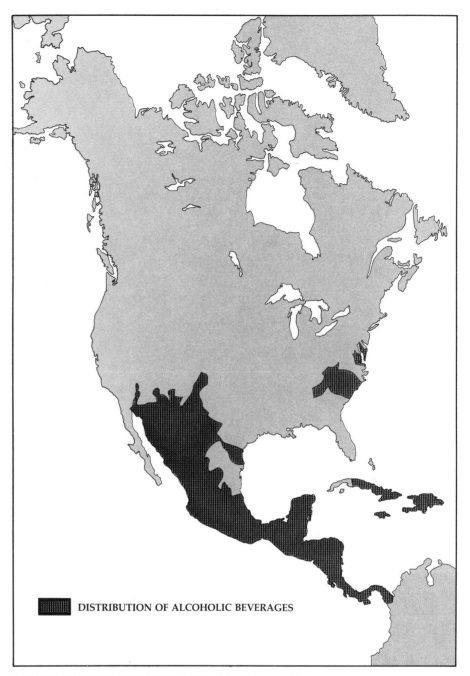

3.30 USE OF ALCOHOLIC BEVERAGES. *After Driver and Massey.*

DISTRIBUTION OF ALCOHOLIC BEVERAGES

button, because of the presence of the hallucinogenic alkaloid mescaline, although peyote is in fact unrelated to the true mescal plant. There are as many as nine alkaloids in peyote, some stimulants and some sedatives, and when the bitter-tasting button is chewed or brewed into a tea, it induces first nausea, then a heightening of the senses, a feeling of well-being, and visions.

Mexican tribes and nomadic Apaches who roamed southward used peyote during Precontact times for both sacred and secular purposes.

Nonritual uses included suppression of appetite and thirst, invigoration in war and work, magical detection of an enemy's approach, prediction of a battle's outcome or the weather, and recovery of lost or stolen articles. Ritual use varied from region to region and from tribe to tribe. In general, it can be said that in Mexico peyote ceremonies surrounded the seasonal quest for food and rainmaking, with participation by both men and women, in conjunction with dancing, racing, and ball games; and that among the Apaches, as well as other nomadic

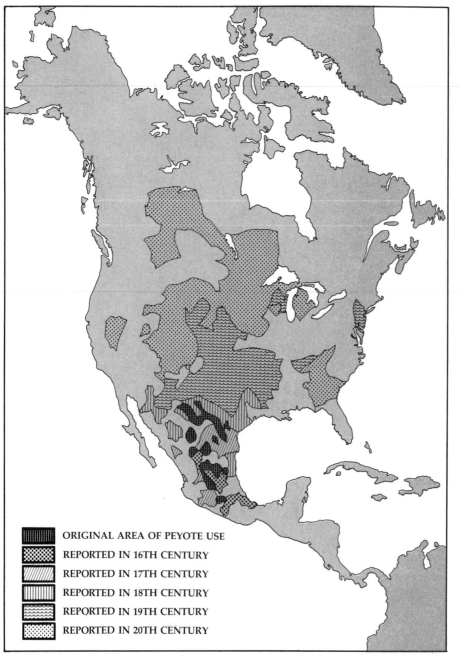

3.31 SPREAD OF PEYOTE. *After Driver and Massey.*

ORIGINAL AREA OF PEYOTE USE
REPORTED IN 16TH CENTURY
REPORTED IN 17TH CENTURY
REPORTED IN 18TH CENTURY
REPORTED IN 19TH CENTURY
REPORTED IN 20TH CENTURY

tribes, like the Comanches who later adopted use of the plant, ceremonies were year-round, with participation only by men, as part of the preparation for war.

In fact, Comanche raids into Mexico were originally most responsible for passing peyote northward to their neighbors on the Great Plains—the Kiowas, Cheyennes, and Arapahos. Peyote culture thus spread through the centuries, with tribal applications and rituals varying. In the late 19th century, however, after the collapse of the Ghost Dance movement in 1890, peyote use evolved into a pan-tribal organized religion, the Native American Church. (See "Indian Religion" in this chapter.) Military defeat, loss of lands, and the confinement of reservation life contributed to the church's rapid growth among western Indians, in spite of attempts to suppress it by Christian missionaries and government officials, and in spite of a ban against the peyote sacrament in Oklahoma Territory in 1898. Nevertheless, not all Indians in the peyote core-area took to the new religion. Most Pueblo Indians, for ex-

ample, maintained their traditional forms of worship.

In 1918, the state of Oklahoma repealed the earlier territorial ban and granted a charter authorizing the Native American Church. By 1930, it was estimated that half the Indian population belonged to the church, which became prominent in the pan-Indian movement of that period. After 1934 and the John Collier administration in the Bureau of Indian Affairs, which advocated Indian self-determination (see "United States Indian Policy and the Indian Condition" in chapter 7), no more official attempts were made to eradicate the religion.

JIMSONWEED

Jimsonweed, or *Datura*, is a tall, coarse annual plant of the nightshade family. Indians in parts of Mesoamerica, the Southwest, and California ingested the plant, usually as a tea made by pounding and soaking leaves, stems, and roots, to induce an effect somewhat similar to that of peyote. In Mexico jimsonweed was sometimes used in conjunction with peyote, but elsewhere the two were culturally exclusive. As with peyote, use was both secular and ceremonial. Medicinal applications included use as an anesthetic for bonesetting and other operations and as an ingredient in panacean ointments.

The popular name jimsonweed, often capitalized, comes from "Jamestown weed," given to the plant by British soldiers stationed in Virginia in 1676, who ate the leaves without knowing the consequences. There is, however, no evidence of Southeast Indians utilizing jimsonweed for its psychoactive qualities.

OTHER PSYCHOTROPIC PLANTS

The term "mescal" is sometimes applied to both mescaline, an alkaloid of peyote, and maguey (*Agave*). The true mescal bean or "red bean," *Sophora secundiflora*, however, belongs to the bean family (*Fabaceae*) and conas for divining purposes. Mazatec medicine men still use the drug today.

Like the teonanacatl mushroom, the seeds of the ololiuqui plant were used in and around the Valley of Mexico for divination. Ololiuqui was also used as a kind of "truth serum."

SOCIOPOLITICAL ORGANIZATION

For most Native North Americans, in fact for most peoples throughout human history, there existed no institutionalized forms of social or political power—no state, no bureaucracy, and no army. Native American societies, as a rule, were egalitarian, without the kinds of centralized authority and social hierarchy typical of modern societies. Custom and tradition rather than law and coercion regulated social life. While there were leaders, their influence was generally based on personal qualities and not on any formal or permanent status. As an early French missionary, Father LeJeune, observed in 1634 of the Montagnais-Naskapis of Labrador, Indians would not "endure in the least those who seem desirous of assuming superiority over others." Authority within a group derived from the ability to make useful suggestions and knowledge of tribal tradition and lore. Among the Eskimos, for example, a person of importance was called *Isumatag*, "he who thinks."

Anthropologists have devised various systems of classification to describe the types of sociopolitical organization among the peoples of North America. Over 20 years ago, Elman Service proposed that American Indian societies at the time of Contact represented a range of evolutionary types—from simple bands through tribes and chiefdoms to the highly organized state of the Aztecs in the Valley of Mexico. While Service's scheme has been challenged and revised by others, it does offer a comparative perspective on the sociopolitical organization of native cultures, where the emergence of institution-

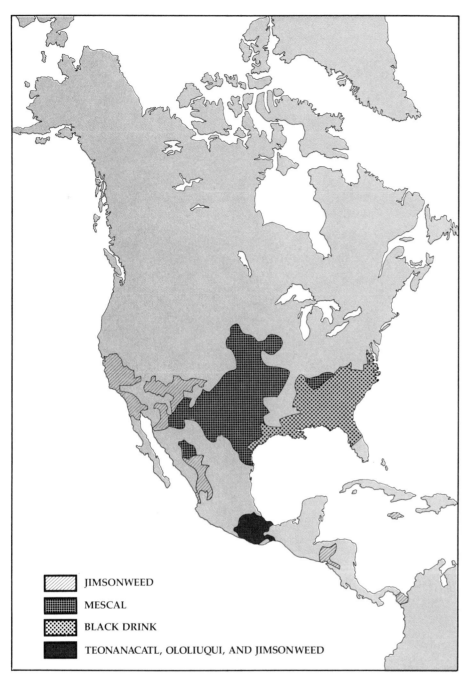

- JIMSONWEED
- MESCAL
- BLACK DRINK
- TEONANACATL, OLOLIUQUI, AND JIMSONWEED

3.32 USE OF JIMSONWEED AND OTHER PSYCHOTROPICS. *After Driver and Massey.*

tains the alkaloid sophorine, the effects of which are similar to nicotine. Various peoples of the Southwest, Great Plains, and a small part of the Southeast ate the mescal bean.

Use of the emetic Black Drink was uniquely a Southeastern phenomenon, other than among the Karankawa Indians of Texas who are generally considered part of the Southwest culture area. The principal ingredient in the drink was the plant *Ilex cassine* (or *Ilex vomitoria*). Tobacco

was also sometimes added. Indians drank the Black Drink ritually as a purgative and stimulant for purification and inspiration before councils, burials, warfare, and seasonal ceremonies, such as the Busk Ritual, also called the Green Corn Festival, an annual renewal rite.

One hears the phrase "magic mushroom." Peoples of Mesoamerica, notably the Aztecs, ingested the mushroom teonanacatl *(Psilocybe)* for its induced sensation of euphoria as well

alized central leadership defines a continuum from the simplest egalitarian societies to the more complex and stratified ones.

Bands were the typical form of social organization of hunting and gathering peoples, such as the Eskimos of the Arctic, the Algonquians and Athapascans of the Subarctic, and the Shoshonis of the Great Basin. These various peoples lived in difficult environments that could support only low population densities. Bands were loose groupings of families, several of which might gather periodically for collective hunts, then disperse again to different hunting grounds. Political leadership remained informal and personal. Cooperation among families was ensured by kinship ties and marriage alliances.

Kinship is one of the most difficult and debated aspects of Indian culture, with a confusion of varying systems. Given the complexity and controversy of the subject, it is touched on only briefly here. Kinship, anthropologists seem to agree, provides a social structure of cooperation and non-violence, a means of maintaining political alliances and economic interaction for societies without law and order. In many respects, kinship systems also govern the social position of the individual. Kinship ties determine lines of descent, which may be through males only (patrilineal), through females only (matrilineal), or through males and females (cognatic). The individual's lineage is often a part of a larger system of intermarrying lineages which determine who one's potential marriage partners may be, and in some cases determine place of marital residence as well; i.e., whether the wife lives with the husband's family (patrilocal) or the husband lives with the wife's family (matrilocal). As a rule among American Indians, the individual's lineage is exogamous, i.e., the individual marries outside his lineage, rather than endogamous, where the individual must marry within his family, clan, or caste.

Among the simplest band societies—the Shoshoni, for example—kinship ties were not emphasized,

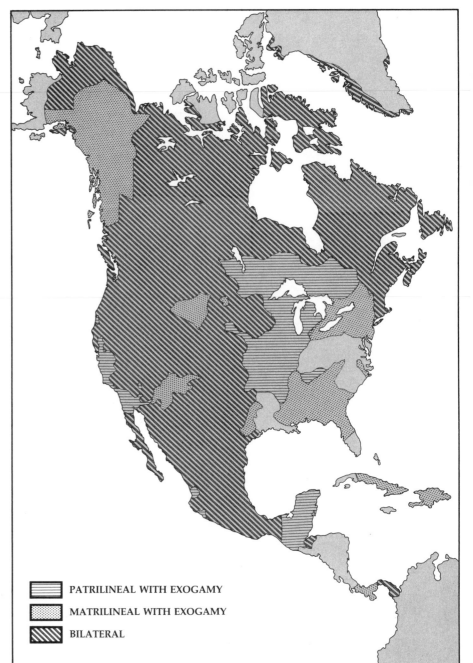

3.33 **CUSTOMS OF DESCENT,** *one aspect of sociopolitical organization. After Driver and Massey.*

and only the taboo against incest served as a marriage rule. Among other bands, such as the Algonquians and Athapascans, there was a tendency to formalize the relationship between cooperating families and to establish a more structured set of rules governing marriage and residence. The Serrano of Southern California were another example of hunters and gatherers with complex kinship systems, including rules of patrilocal residence, lineages reckoning descent in the male line from a common

ancestor, and a moiety structure dividing all lineages into two larger intermarrying groups.

This propensity to formalize kinship relations was taken to another level of organization among societies that can properly be called tribal. With greater population density as a result of agriculture or plentiful wild food sources, native cultures were faced with the problem of establishing stable and cohesive work groups to perform seasonal tasks. The spontaneous division of labor in the natural family came to be replaced in many such societies by invented kin relations and systems of classification that ensured the continuity of social bonds and economic cooperation. The clans of the Northeast and Great Plains tribes, and of the Southwest pueblos, were based on descent from a common mythic ancestor or totemic animal; a system of interdependent and inter-marrying lineages, whose relations of reciprocity established the tribes as larger political entities, was thus created. The principle here is sometimes referred to by anthropologists as "fission and fusion." That is to say, as society segments into autonomous households, clans, and local settlements, the potential political divisions within the tribe are bridged by the cultural similarities of language and custom, the practice of exogamy and marriage alliances, and specialized pan-tribal societies of priests, warriors, and craftsmen. While a society or clan may distinguish itself, none is intrinsically superior to another. Even in cases where wider political and military alliances were established in the form of tribal confederacies—such as the Iroquois League—there was still no sovereign authority beyond the local group, and leadership was confined to headmen and councils of respected elders.

The chiefdoms of the Northwest Coast and Southeast, by contrast, were ranking societies, where descent and community groups were no longer equal in principle but instead arranged hierarchically, with superior authority vested in certain families. Authority was further centralized by the rule of primogeniture, in which status was inherited according to order of birth, the first son ranked highest. Increased political authority allowed chiefs to organize activities of a wider scope—military and trade expeditions, for example, or the building of irrigation works and temples. The chief typically performed the functions of intensifying production, redistributing wealth, and giving his support to craft specialties and the conspicuous consumption of the noble families.

Although chiefdoms were based on a centralized political authority unimaginable in tribal societies, the power of the chief did have its limits. Chiefdoms were theocratic societies in which commoners submitted to the religious authority and the aristocratic ethos of the priest-chief and the nobility; but they were not vehicles of empire in which the ruling class governed by force and maintained standing armies. In the next level of socio-political organization—the true state formation as found in Mesoamerica—kings, like chiefs, were high priests of a ruling theocracy which commanded the religious allegiance of the population. But they were also the heads of a ruling theocracy, controlling political, legal, and military apparatuses, and holding the exclusive right to force.

The Aztec theocracy and warrior-nobles, for example, extended state power throughout much of Mesoamerica, warring against and exacting tribute from other peoples and cultures. Tenochtitlan in the Valley of Mexico, which, with its wealth and splendor, awed the Spanish who visited it under Cortes, and which Cortes himself called the "most beautiful city in the world," was the center of Aztec culture and power. It manifested a metropolitan order far removed from the egalitarian design of band or tribal society, and far more specialized and stratified than even the most organized chiefdoms such as the Natchez. Elaborate social bonds replaced the older kinship ties of traditional Indian culture, and classes of warriors, merchants, and artisans existed alongside the ruling nobility. Whether the *pochteca*, the Aztec merchant class, would have grown in social power to challenge the role of the nobility—as occurred in societies in other parts of the world, and as some scholars have speculated would have happened—is an intriguing question but one cancelled by history in the form of the military conquest of the Spanish conquistadors.

INDIAN LANGUAGES

The number of distinct Indian languages once spoken in the Americas—perhaps as many as 2,200—does much to demolish the frequent misconception of uniformity of Indian culture. The estimate given for Pre-contact tribes is from 200 to 300 for North America and 350 for Mexico and Middle America. The great difficulty in intertribal communication of course shaped intertribal relations. Even for the so-called Composite Tribe of the Great Plains, where a common life-style emerged during the 18th and 19th centuries, it took a manual sign language to break through the many language barriers. Yet, at the same time, while the huge number of languages point up ethnographic diversity, their analysis and classification provides a means of reconstructing tribal genealogies. In fact, lifeways are more subject to change than language. That is to say, a tribe migrating to another geography and life-style takes its language with it. Even though the language might then diverge from its mother tongue, it retains many of its original elements, which can be traced.

There is still much work to be done in the classification of Indian languages. No one, all-embracing system has been established. Yet scholars have come a long way since the pioneering attempts of John Wesley Powell (the 19th-century explorer and director of the Bureau of Ethnology at the Smithsonian). His system of Indian language classification into 56 families, based on word lists of usually no more than a hundred items, has held up remarkably well. But linguists now make use of as many as eight different levels of classification. Even so, there is no standardized terminology. For example, a researcher might come across the terms "family," "phylum," or "stock" to express the same degree of language classification. And the methodology of classification varies; some, like Powell's, are based on word lists, and others are based on glottochronology, a system, devised by Morris Swadesh in 1950, that studies the time it takes for certain cognate words common to all peoples, such as man, woman, sun, or moon, to diverge from a shared mother tongue.

Whatever the method of classification, its purpose is to determine resemblances between languages. Linguists refer to four kinds:

1. Universal: features of speech shared by all languages, such as stops, vowels, and consonants, or shared vocabulary;
2. Convergent: similar features of speech or vocabulary that arise independently or coincidentally in different languages;
3. Diffusional: features of speech, vocabulary, or concepts borrowed from one language by another (for example, the Indian loan word *wampum* in the English language); and
4. Genetic: uninterrupted derivation of linguistic elements from one language to another, with "mother languages" leading to "daughter languages." It is this last category—genetic resemblances—that Powell, Swadesh, and other scholars have tried to establish for the multitudinous Indian languages.

With convergent and diffusional elements confusing the issue, the difficulty of classification is apparent. And unlike biology, in which defined species cannot crossbreed, language is in a constant state of flux. Moreover, with minimal written records, few moments in that flux can be confirmed.

Precontact Indian writing did not advance for the most part beyond pictorial glyphs or pictographs, literal representations of humans, animals, objects, geographical features, or happenings. Some of these glyphs or symbols, however, especially in Mesoamerica, did represent abstract ideas, such as hate or love, and can be called ideographs, or thought-writing. Some Mesoamerican symbols might even have represented syllables or sounds, although the evidence is inconclusive.

In any case, the only true Indian phonetic or sound-writing is the syllabary created singlehandedly by Sequoyah in the 19th century, which reduces the Cherokee language to 85 syllabic characters (unlike an alphabet, which reduces a language even further to phonemes). Various white men also recorded Indian languages in the Roman alphabet, giving linguists Postcontact written sources for their studies.

Other forms of recording information existed among the Indians, such as the Papago calendar sticks with carved notches and Iroquois wampum belts, but these have nothing to do of course with spoken Indian languages and their classification.

The linguistic table that follows for North and Central America and the Caribbean area is based on studies by C.F. Voegelin and F.M. Voegelin, as found in Harold Driver's *Indians of North America,* and by Joseph Greenberg, as found in Alvin Josephy's *The Indian Heritage of America.* (See Bibliography.) Three levels of classification are used: phyla, families, and languages. It should be kept in mind that other historical Indian languages existed of which not enough is known to classify. The accompanying map is after Driver and Massey from *Indians of North America.*

Many of these languages have survived and are spoken by contempo-

Sequoyah, with his syllabary of the Cherokee language. New York State Library, Albany.

rary Indians—over 100 in the United States alone. It is estimated that approximately one-third of all Native Americans still speak their native language, with Navajos, Iroquois, Inuits, Papagos–Pimas, Apaches, and Sioux showing the highest percentages. The languages have persisted despite official efforts to eradicate them, especially in the government-sponsored boarding schools in the early 1920s.

NORTH AND SOUTH AMERICAN INDIAN LANGUAGES: A GENETIC CLASSIFICATION TABLE OF PHYLA, FAMILIES, AND DIALECTS

PHYLUM I: AMERICAN ARCTIC–PALEO-SIBERIAN
A. ESKIMO-ALEUT FAMILY
1. Alaskan Eskimo (Kuskokwim)
2. Central Eskimo, Greenland Eskimo (Trans-Arctic)
3. Eastern Aleut (Unalaska)
4. Western Aleut (Atka, Attua)

PHYLUM II: NA-DENE
A. ATHAPASCAN FAMILY
1. Dogrib, Saschutkenne, Hare
2. Chipewyan, Slave, Yellowknife
3. Kutchin
4. Tanana, Koyukon, Han, Tutchone
5. Sekani, Beaver, Sarsee
6. Carrier, Chilcotin
7. Tahltan, Kaska
8. Tanaina, Ingalik, Nabesna, Ahtena
9. Eyak
10. Chastacosta, Taltushtuntude, Tututni
11. Hupa
12. Kato, Wailaki
13. Mattole
14. Tolowa
15. Navajo
16. San Carlos Apache
17. Chiricahua Apache, Mescalero Apache
18. Jicarilla Apache
19. Lipan Apache
20. Kiowa-Apache
B. TLINGIT LANGUAGE ISOLATE
C. HAIDA LANGUAGE ISOLATE

PHYLUM III: MACRO-ALGONQUIAN
A. ALGONQUIAN FAMILY
1. Cree, Montagnais, Naskapi
2. Menominee
3. Sauk, Fox, Kickapoo

3.34 DOMINANT LANGUAGE FAMILIES. *After Driver and Massey.*

Legend:
- ESKIMO-ALEUT
- ATHAPASCAN
- ALGONQUIAN
- MUSKOGEAN
- SIOUAN
- IROQUOIAN
- CADDOAN
- YUMAN
- COMECRUDAN
- SAHAPTIN-NEZ PERCE
- MAYAN
- UTO-AZTECAN
- SALISHAN
- WAKASHAN
- OTOMIAN
- CHIBCHAN
- ARAWAKAN
- LANGUAGES UNKNOWN OR NO ONE FAMILY DOMINANT

4. Shawnee
5. Potawatomi
6. Ojibway, Saulteaux, Algonkin, Ottawa
7. Delaware
8. Abnaki, Penobscot
9. Malecite, Passamaquoddy
10. Micmac
11. Blackfoot, Piegan, Blood
12. Cheyenne
13. Arapaho, Nawunena, Atsina
B. YUROK LANGUAGE ISOLATE

C. WIYOT LANGUAGE ISOLATE
D. MUSKOGEAN FAMILY
1. Choctaw, Chickasaw
2. Alabama, Koasati
3. Miccosukee, Hitchiti
4. Creek, Seminole
E. NATCHEZ LANGUAGE ISOLATE
F. ATAKAPA LANGUAGE ISOLATE
G. CHITIMACHA LANGUAGE ISOLATE
H. TUNICA LANGUAGE ISOLATE
I. TONKAWA LANGUAGE ISOLATE

PHYLUM IV: MACRO-SIOUAN

A. SIOUAN FAMILY
1. Crow
2. Hidatsa
3. Winnebago
4. Mandan
5. Iowa, Oto
6. Omaha, Osage, Ponca, Quapaw, Kansa
7. Sioux (Dakota)

B. CATAWBA LANGUAGE ISOLATE

C. IROQUOIAN FAMILY
1. Seneca, Cayuga, Onondaga
2. Mohawk
3. Oneida
4. Huron (Wyandot)
5. Tuscarora
6. Cherokee

D. CADDOAN FAMILY
1. Caddo
2. Wichita
3. Pawnee, Arikara

E. YUCHI LANGUAGE ISOLATE

PHYLUM V: HOKAN

A. YUMAN FAMILY
1. Upland Yuman (Hualapai, Havasupai, Yavapai)
2. Upriver Yuman (Mojave, Maricopa, Halchidhoma, Kavelchadoma, Yuma)
3. Delta River Yuman (Cocopa, Kohuana, Halyikwamai)
4. Southern and Baja California Yuman (Diegueno, Kamia, Akwa'ala, Kiliwa, Nyakipa)

B. SERI LANGUAGE ISOLATE

C. POMO FAMILY
1. Coast Pomo
2. Northeast Pomo
3. Western Clear Lake
4. Southeast Clear Lake

D. PALAIHNIHAN FAMILY
1. Achomawi
2. Atsugewi

E. SHASTAN FAMILY
F. YANAN FAMILY
G. CHIMARIKO LANGUAGE ISOLATE
H. WASHO LANGUAGE ISOLATE
I. SALINAN FAMILY
J. KAROK LANGUAGE ISOLATE
K. CHUMASHAN FAMILY
L. COMECRUDAN FAMILY
M. COAHUILTECAN LANGUAGE ISOLATE
N. ESSELEN LANGUAGE ISOLATE
O. JICAQUE LANGUAGE ISOLATE
P. TLAPANECAN FAMILY
1. Tlapanec
2. Subtiaba
3. Maribichicoa

Q. TLEQUISTLATECAN FAMILY
1. Tluamelula
2. Mountain Tlequistlateco

PHYLUM VI: PENUTIAN

A. YOKUTS FAMILY
1. Yokuts, North Foothill
2. Yokuts, South Foothill
3. Yokuts, Valley

B. MAIDU FAMILY
1. Southern Maidu
2. Northwest Maidu
3. Mountain Maidu
4. Valley Maidu

C. WINTUN FAMILY
1. Patwin
2. Wintun

D. MIWOK-COSTANOAN FAMILY
1. Sierra Miwok
2. Coast Miwok, Lake Miwok
3. Costano

E. KLAMATH-MODOC LANGUAGE ISOLATE
F. SAHAPTIN–NEZ PERCE FAMILY
1. Nez Perce
2. Sahaptin

G. CAYUSE LANGUAGE ISOLATE
H. MOLALE LANGUAGE ISOLATE
I. COOS FAMILY
J. YAKONAN FAMILY
1. Alsea
2. Siuslaw, Kuitsh

K. TAKELMA LANGUAGE ISOLATE
L. KALAPUYAN FAMILY
1. Santiam
2. Yoncalla

M. CHINOOKAN FAMILY
1. Upper Chinook
2. Lower Chinook

N. TSIMSHIAN LANGUAGE ISOLATE
O. ZUNI LANGUAGE ISOLATE
P. MIXE-ZOQUEAN FAMILY
1. Mixe
2. Zoque
3. Sierra Popoluca
4. Texixtepec
5. Sayula
6. Oluta

Q. MAYAN FAMILY
1. Huasteco
2. Chontal of Tabasco
3. Chol
4. Chorti
5. Punctunc
6. Moianec
7. Tzeltal
8. Tzotzil
9. Tojolabal
10. Chuh
11. Jacaltec
12. Kanjobal
13. Solomec
14. Motozintleco
15. Mam
16. Aquacatec
17. Ixil
18. Tacaneco
19. Tlatiman
20. Taquial
21. Tupancal
22. Tutuapa
23. Coyotin
24. Quiche
25. Cakchiquel
26. Tzutujil
27. Rabinal
28. Kekchi
29. Pokonchi (Pocomchi)
30. Pokoman
31. Maya

R. CHIPAYA-URU FAMILY
S. TOTONACAN FAMILY
1. Totonac
2. Tepehua

T. HUAVE LANGUAGE ISOLATE

PHYLUM VII: AZTEC-TANOAN

A. KIOWA-TANOAN FAMILY
1. Tiwa (Taos, Picuris, Isleta, Sandia)
2. Tewa (San Juan, Santa Clara, San Ildefonso, Tesuque, Nambe, Hano)
3. Towa (Jemez)
4. Kiowa

B. UTO-AZTECAN FAMILY
1. Mono
2. Northern Paiute, Walpapi, Yahuskin, Bannock
3. Shoshoni, Gosiute, Wind River, Panamint, Comanche
4. Southern Paiute, Ute, Chemehuevi, Kawaiisu
5. Hopi
6. Tubatulabal
7. Luiseno
8. Cahuilla
9. Cupeno
10. Serrano
11. Pima, Papago
12. Pima Bajo
13. Yaqui, Mayo
14. Tarahumara
15. Cora
16. Huichol
17. Tepehuan
18. Nahuatl
19. Nahuat
20. Mecayapan
21. Pipil
22. Pochutla
23. Tamaulipeco

GROUP VIII: UNDETERMINED PHYLA AFFILIATIONS
A. KERES LANGUAGE ISOLATE
B. YUKI FAMILY
1. Yuki
2. Wappo
C. BEOTHUK LANGUAGE ISOLATE
D. KUTENAI LANGUAGE ISOLATE
E. KARANKAWA LANGUAGE ISOLATE
F. CHIMAKUAN FAMILY
1. Quileute
2. Chimakum
G. SALISHAN FAMILY (Salishan and Wakashan placed together by some scholars in MOSAN PHYLUM)
1. Lillooet
2. Shuswap
3. Ntlakyapamuk
4. Okanagon, Sanpoil, Colville, Lake
5. Flathead, Kalispel, Spokane
6. Coeur d'Alene
7. Sinkiuse-Columbia, Wenatchee
8. Tillamook
9. Twana
10. Upper Chehalis, Cowlitz, Lower Chehalis, Quinault
11. Snoqualmie, Duwamish, Nisqually
12. Lumni, Songish, Clallam
13. Halkomelem
14. Squamish
15. Comox, Sishiatl
16. Bella Coola
H. WAKASHAN FAMILY (Wakashan and Salishan placed together by some scholars in MOSAN PHYLUM)
1. Nootka
2. Nitinat
3. Makah
4. Kwakiutl
5. Bella Bella, Heiltsuk
6. Kitamat, Haisla
I. TIMUCUA LANGUAGE ISOLATE
J. TARASCAN LANGUAGE ISOLATE

PHYLUM IX: OTO-MANGUEAN
A. MANGUEAN (Chorotegan) FAMILY
1. Mangue
2. Chiapaneco
B. OTOMIAN (Otomi-Pame) FAMILY
1. Otomi
2. Mazahua
3. Ocuiltec
4. Matlatzinca
5. Chichimeca, Jonaz
6. Pame
C. POPOLOCAN FAMILY
1. Popolac
2. Chocho
3. Ixcateco
4. Mazateco
D. MIXTECAN FAMILY
1. Mixtec
2. Trique
3. Cuicateco
4. Amuzgo
E. CHINANTECAN FAMILY
F. ZAPOTECAN FAMILY
1. Zapotec
2. Chatino

PHYLUM X: MACRO-CHIBCHAN
A. CHIBCHAN FAMILY
1. Cara
2. Chibcha (Muisca)
3. Cuna
4. Guaymi
5. Lenca
6. Mosquito
B. PAEZAN FAMILY
1. Canari
2. Jirajara
3. Puruha
4. Atacameno
5. Mura

PHYLUM XI: GE–PANO-CARIB
A. GE FAMILY
1. Bororo
2. Botocudo
3. Caingang
4. Canella
5. Cayapo
6. Shavante
7. Sherante
8. Manasi
B. PANOAN FAMILY
1. Conibo
2. Shipibo
C. CARIBAN FAMILY
1. Arara
2. Arma
3. Calamari
4. Camaracoto
5. Carib
6. Catio
7. Motilon
8. Quimbaya
9. Yagua
D. GUAYCURUAN FAMILY
1. Abipon
2. Matacoan
3. Mbaya
4. Payagua
5. Charrua

PHYLUM XII: ANDEAN-EQUATORIAL
A. QUECHUAMARAN FAMILY
1. Quechua
2. Aymara
B. ARAUCANIAN-CHON FAMILY
1. Araucanian
2. Chono
3. Ono
4. Puelche
5. Tehuelche
6. Yahgan
C. ZAPAROAN FAMILY
1. Zaparoan
D. ARAWAKAN FAMILY
1. Taino
2. Goajiro
3. Guayape
4. Palicur
5. Campa
6. Chane
7. Guana
8. Baure
9. Mojo
10. Paressi
E. TUPI-GUARANI FAMILY
1. Camayura
2. Mundurucu
3. Parintintin
4. Tupinamba
5. Guarani
6. Chiriguano
7. Siriono
F. JIVAROAN FAMILY
1. Jivaro
2. Palta
G. TIMOTEAN LANGUAGE ISOLATE
H. ZAMUCOAN LANGUAGE ISOLATE

Chapter 4
INDIANS
AND EXPLORERS

The story of the discovery and exploration of North America is as much an Indian story as a European, American, or Canadian one, but it is rarely perceived from the Indian point of view. Indians first discovered the New World (see "Beringia" in chapter 1), and then, when other races and nationalities followed, the Indians received and guided them. The story of North American exploration can therefore be described as one of welcoming and enabling, as well as prevailing and accomplishing. In numerous instances, the Indians enabled the explorers to survive and succeed, providing food and shelter, and showing them the way.

Only a few Indian enablers and guides are well-known—Sacajawea ("Birdwoman"), for example, the Shoshoni woman who guided Lewis and Clark into the wilderness and served as a diplomat to other tribes. However, Chief Guacanagari and the other Arawaks who helped Columbus unload the grounded *Santa Maria* receive little historical mention, as does Donnaconna, Cartier's Huron guide.

In fact, the names of many of the Indian guides who helped make the white explorers successful have not even survived history.

It should be added that some of these Indian guides were forced, in the face of superior arms, to help the whites. At other times, the Indians succeeded in resisting the intruders, killing them or driving them away. In these instances, the story of North American exploration also becomes the story of native resistance.

Sioux catlinite pipe bowl with representation of white man

In any case, whatever the emphasis, the history of exploration is essential to Indian studies. Explorers established first Contact with a large part of the Indian population, and much of what is known about the early tribes and their locations comes from expedition accounts, maps, and records. Moreover, a chronology of explorers, plus their routes and the countries they represented, provides a useful time scale and geography of Indian cultural change.

POSSIBLE EARLY TRANSOCEANIC CONTACTS

North America has been "discovered" at least three times—first by the Paleo-Siberians crossing the Bering Strait land bridge (see "Beringia" in chapter 1), then by the Norsemen at the end of the 11th century, and then by Columbus in 1492. An ongoing dispute in the study of American Indians involves the question of additional pre-Columbian contacts between the Old World and the New.

The presence of Vikings in the New World has been proven archaeologically at L'Anse aux Meadows, New-

New France by Samuel de Champlain, 1632. New York State Library, Albany.

foundland, and backed up by considerable historical evidence from Norse documents. But many other early Atlantic and Pacific crossings and transoceanic connections have been proposed. It has been shown that even before boats were generally seaworthy, small wooden or reed craft could make ocean crossings. Thor Heyerdahl's *Kon-Tiki* and *Ra* crossings demonstrate at least such a possibility. With the extensive sea travel made over the centuries for fishing and trading purposes in more rugged vessels, plus the strong westward ocean current in the South Atlantic and eastward current in the North Pacific, it seems probable that some unintentional drift voyages did occur. It also seems likely that other pre-Renaissance sailors besides the Vikings were curious about what lay over the oceans.

It is a fascinating subject, filled with adventure and mystery, and it would be exciting to know the story of any such early mariners. Yet, with regard to the Indian, even if archaeological evidence should turn up, perhaps too much is made of the transoceanic theme. As it relates to Indian culture, the subject will always remain in the realm of the speculative and the futile since, even if certain contacts are established archaeologically, there is no way to measure accurately the extent of cultural influence. If contacts and influences were more than negligible to begin with, hard evidence probably would already have been found. And there is always the possibility of even earlier or more culturally significant contacts than those found. For that matter, cultural influences might have flowed the other way, with mariners carrying cultural traits learned from the Indians back across the oceans. Or perhaps the Indians were transoceanic mariners themselves. If there were consequential contacts in one direction or the other, it becomes remarkable how many traits were not shared—the practical application of the wheel, for example, used only on toys in the New World, or the cultivation of maize, unknown to the Old World. The two hemispheres developed differently in cultural terms in spite of any such contacts. In terms of human biology, they also developed differently. American Indians show the purest type A, B, and O blood groups, and, in historic times, showed no resistance to European diseases.

Another point should be made concerning transoceanic hypotheses. For years, before the antiquity of the Paleo-Indian presence was established archaeologically, many scholars theorized that the Indians were descended from one lost European tribe or another, as if to explain all peoples and all cultures from one premise. In the 19th century, for instance, many whites, reflecting their cultural bias, refused to believe that Indians, whom they considered as primitives and savages, could have been the Mound Builders. This is not to say that modern scholars who argue in favor of drift voyages or pre-Columbian cultural interactions have the same bias. The point is that without proper attention to Indian culture in and of itself, a focus all too lacking in American education, a preoccupation with speculative transoceanic contacts and influences can detract from the essence of Indian studies.

In any event, the following is a list of some theorized transoceanic contacts and possible cultural relationships. For some entries, geographical regions are cited; for others, the peoples themselves.

PACIFIC OCEAN

1. Japanese to Northwest Coast, perhaps via Hawaii (A.D.): Similarities of decorative motifs. Also, Tlingit armor has a feudal Japanese look. And physical features of Northwest Coast peoples are more Oriental in appearance than those of other Indians, although this is perhaps a result of contact with Eskimos.

2. Northwest Coast to Polynesia or vice versa (B.C. or A.D.): Similarities of decorative motifs.

3. Incas to Polynesia or vice versa (B.C. or A.D.): Similarities of strains of cotton and bottle gourds.

4. Japanese to Ecuador (B.C.): Similarity of Jomon pottery to Valdivia pottery.

5. Indus Valley to Middle Americas (B.C. or A.D.): Similarities of Asiatic game of Parcheesi to Middle American *Patolli*. Similarity of ideographs. Also, the American hybrid of cotton might be a cross between Asiatic cotton and American wild cotton.

6. Chinese to Olmecs (B.C.): Rapid advancement of Olmec civilization.

ATLANTIC OCEAN

1. Africans to Olmecs (B.C.): Negroid characteristics of Olmec sculpture.

2. Egyptians to Middle or South America (B.C.): Similarities in pyramids and reed boats.

3. Egyptians to Mississippi River system (B.C.): Similarities in inscriptions.

4. Libyans to Mississippi River and Southwest (B.C.): Language similarities.

5. Celts to New England, via Iberia (B.C.): Similarities in inscriptions and monuments.

6. Phoenicians to New England (B.C.): Language similarities.

7. Basques to Pennsylvania and to Gulf of St. Lawrence (B.C.): Similarities in language and grave markers.

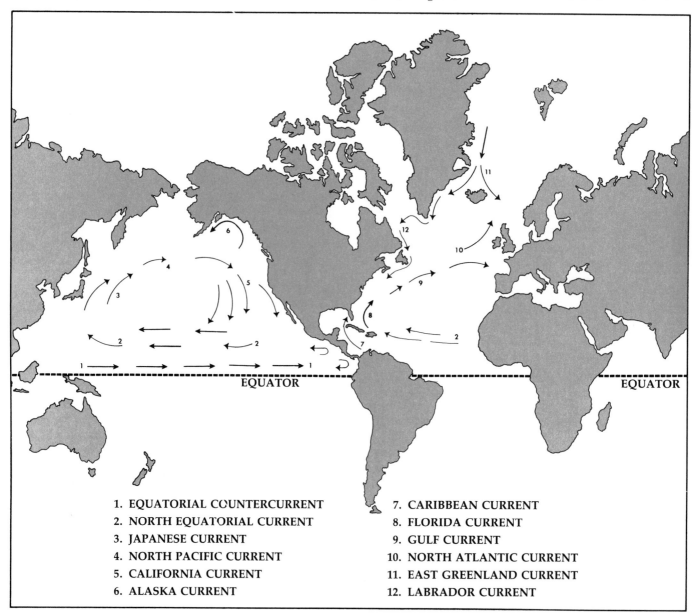

1. EQUATORIAL COUNTERCURRENT
2. NORTH EQUATORIAL CURRENT
3. JAPANESE CURRENT
4. NORTH PACIFIC CURRENT
5. CALIFORNIA CURRENT
6. ALASKA CURRENT
7. CARIBBEAN CURRENT
8. FLORIDA CURRENT
9. GULF CURRENT
10. NORTH ATLANTIC CURRENT
11. EAST GREENLAND CURRENT
12. LABRADOR CURRENT

4.1 OCEAN CURRENTS IN THE ATLANTIC AND PACIFIC, *indicating possible early transoceanic drift voyages*

THE WHITE PENETRATION OF NORTH AMERICA

Excepting the Norsemen, the white exploration of North America lasted more than four centuries—from the end of the 15th into the 20th century. During the colonial stage until the American Revolution, five European nations sent out expeditions under their flags and laid title to territory by right of discovery—Spain, France, England, the Netherlands, and Russia. Portugal was also active in early exploration but established its claims in South America. And Sweden held territory along the Delaware Bay from 1638 to 1654. Individuals of still other European nations made journeys of exploration in the name of the five major claimants. Then, in later years, United States and Canadian explorers crisscrossed the continent and opened the remaining wilderness to further white settlement.

The many reasons that Europeans and their descendants explored the so-called New World are implicit in the concept of the Renaissance, the period which brought Europe out of the Middle Ages; these factors can be broken down and summarized as follows: First, politically, there was a movement away from the feudal system toward the unified and centralized nation-state. Exploration therefore became a national purpose. Economically, there was a growing need for new markets and specific imports for a rapidly expanding population—the Far East, for example, could provide the spices essential to food preservation. Moreover, the economic system of mercantilism or bullionism, in which a nation's wealth and power were determined by its quantities of gold and silver, had become dominant, spurring a search for new sources of precious metals. Furs were another source of wealth and power. In the realm of religion, there was now fierce competition for converts between old-guard Catholicism

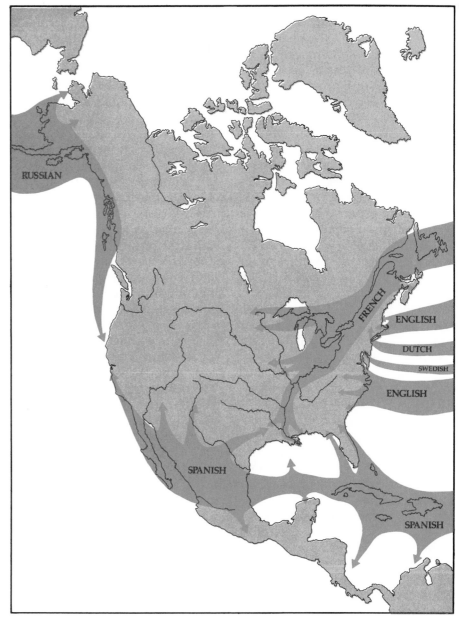

4.2 GENERAL PATHS OF EARLY PENETRATION INTO NORTH AMERICA BY EUROPEAN NATIONS

and the Reformation-spawned Protestantism. With governments having official religions, competition between churches became part of national rivalries and one more incentive to finance expeditions. In the realm of science and technology, there had been major navigational advances, as well as breakthroughs in the related fields of chart making and cartography. European boats, combining the best qualities of the heavy-bodied, square-sail, clinker-built traders of the Atlantic Coast and North Sea, along with the best features of the longer and sleeker triangular-sail, double-mast, carvel-built lateeners of the

Mediterranean, were now ocean worthy. And there were many experienced, skillful, and knowledgeable captains and crews to man them. Finally, in terms of philosophy and inspiration, the Renaissance brought a fresh drive toward knowledge as well as an awakened sense of adventure. Europe therefore was primed for exploration. Nations, churches, and individuals all had multifaceted motivation for exploration—power, prestige, glory, wealth, and curiosity—and the knowledge and means to accomplish it.

Exploration not only evolved out of the Renaissance; it in turn came to influence its development, as reports of North America and its inhabitants revolutionized the European world view. And for succeeding generations who suffered in Europe from overcrowding, poverty, and religious persecution, North America became a symbol of hope and a new life. As time went on, then, land and its settlement became a primary motive for exploration. As it turned out, all these motives, honorable or otherwise, were at the expense of the Native North American population.

It is ironic that none of the first expeditions of exploration for the major colonial powers was carried out by men of those nations. Columbus, who sailed for Spain in 1492, came from Italy, as did Cabot, who sailed for England in 1497. Verrazano, for France in 1524, was also Italian. Hudson, who sailed for the Netherlands in his exploration of 1609, was English. And Bering, for Russia in 1741, was Danish. After these initial voyages of discovery, numerous others followed for the respective nations.

In general, the Spanish penetrated North America from the south, through the Caribbean, Florida, and Mexico; France advanced from the northeast, along the St. Lawrence River, the Great Lakes, the Ohio River, and the Mississippi, with some penetration northwestward from the Gulf Coast; England moved generally from the Atlantic Coast westward, with much additional activity in Arctic waters in search of the Northwest Passage; Holland penetrated northwestward along the Hudson River; and Russia moved from the west out of Siberia into Alaska, then southward as far as California. Then, in later centuries, United States and Canadian explorers generally progressed from east to west, with some penetration eastward from the Pacific Coast.

Also, for purposes of organization and understanding, the history of the penetration of North America can be divided into the following general stages. The 16th century might be called the Spanish stage, with Spain most active in mounting expeditions throughout the West Indies, Middle (and South) America, as well as in-

cursions into the American Southeast and Southwest. The 17th century might be called the colonial period of exploration, with Spain, France, England, and Holland competing for territory along the Atlantic Coast and, to some extent, the Pacific Coast. This period carried over into the 18th century, when Russia joined their ranks and staked claims along the Pacific. During the 18th and into the 19th century, some of these countries, especially England, were active in Arctic waters in the continuing search for the Northwest Passage, a story of exploration unto itself. In a summary of North American exploration, the final stage might be referred to as the United States and Canadian—beginning with the American Revolution—in which both countries explored their western lands. They also both sponsored further Arctic expeditions in the 20th century. During much of the final stage, until 1867 and the sale of Alaska to the United States, Russia continued to play a part in the exploration of North America.

Such a breakdown is of course an oversimplification. One can get a more detailed sense of foreign activity in North America, as well as a sense of early Indian and white contacts in various parts of the continent, from the chronological list of explorers later in this chapter.

THE FUR TRADE

The fur trade, more than any other activity, contributed to the white exploration and opening of the wilderness north of Mexico, and it led to extensive contacts between whites and Indians. All the colonial powers were involved in the mass commercial exploitation of animal pelts and skins—France, England, the Netherlands, Russia, and to a lesser extent Spain—to fulfill the furious demand for furs in Europe, especially beaver pelts for hatmaking. (See "European Use of Indian Lands and Resources" in chapter 6.) Competition among the European nations and among the Indian tribes for the fur trade was a ma-

jor factor in many of the intertribal conflicts and colonial wars. (See especially "The Beaver Wars" and "The French and Indian Wars" in chapter 5.) And reaction to white traders on Indian lands spawned considerable native resistance. (See especially "The Aleut, Tlingit, and Pomo Resistance" in chapter 5.) The world fur market remained vital after colonial times into the 19th century, and it played a significant part in the opening of both the U.S. and Canadian wilderness to white settlement.

Over the course of these centuries, the 17th through the 19th, impact on the Indians as a result of the fur trade came about in various ways. First, as skilled hunters and suppliers of pelts, the Indians were sought after as trading partners and were exposed to white culture. In exchange for their goods, the Indians received European products, both practical, such as iron tools and utensils, and decorative, such as bright-colored cloth and beads. The Indians also received firearms and liquor, both of which had an enormous impact on Indian lifeways. A second and devastating effect from trade with whites was the outbreak of European diseases among the Indian population. (See "The Spread of European Diseases" in chapter 6.) A third effect was the long-term ecological disruption of the food chain by the depletion of fur-bearing mammals. And finally, the fur trade had another long-term impact on the Indians by bringing whites onto their lands. After the white traders, trappers, and hunters came the trading and military posts, and after the posts came the settlers.

In early colonial times, the French most thoroughly exploited the fur trade. Whereas mining and the raising of livestock had a greater economic bearing on the development of the Spanish colonies, and farming dominated the economy and land use of the English colonies, commerce in furs determined French expansion. The French and Indian fur trade began with Jacques Cartier in 1534 along the St. Lawrence River. His original intent had been to find the Northwest Passage to the Orient, but he found

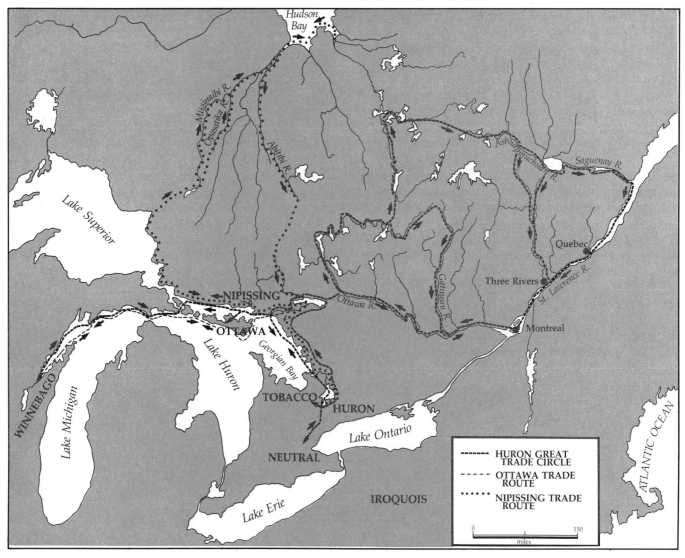

Map labels: Hudson Bay, Missinaibi R., Opasatika R., Abitibi R., Ashuapmuchuan R., Saguenay R., Lake Superior, Gatineau R., Quebec, Three Rivers, St. Lawrence R., Montreal, NIPISSING, Ottawa R., OTTAWA, Georgian Bay, WINNEBAGO, Lake Michigan, Lake Huron, TOBACCO, HURON, Lake Ontario, NEUTRAL, Lake Erie, IROQUOIS, ATLANTIC OCEAN

Legend:
------- HURON GREAT TRADE CIRCLE
- - - - OTTAWA TRADE ROUTE
• • • • NIPISSING TRADE ROUTE

0 ————— 150
miles

4.3 THE HURON TRADING EMPIRE *in the early 17th century. After Hunt.*

instead an untapped source of furs among the Indians who were eager to trade for European goods.

Based on the results of Cartier's expeditions, Samuel de Champlain arrived in New France in 1603, having the express purpose of trading with the Indians for furs. Over the next years, Champlain explored the northern woods and established trade agreements with various tribes to deliver their pelts to French trading posts. Port Royal in Acadia (now Annapolis Royal, Nova Scotia), Quebec City, and Montreal all became thriving centers of commerce.

Eastern tribes, such as the Algonquian-speaking Micmacs, Montagnais, Naskapis, Abnakis, and Crees, were all involved in the French fur trade. Yet the Iroquoian-speaking Hurons, living further to the west,

became the foremost suppliers. From the years 1616 to 1649, the Hurons, in conjunction with the Algonquian Ottawas and Nipissings, developed a trade empire among the Indians from the Great Lakes to the Hudson Bay to the St. Lawrence. Each of the three main trading partners had its own river and portage route for travel by canoe, plus a yearly schedule, linking them up with other tribes as well, such as the Iroquoian Tobaccos and Neutrals. Acting as middlemen, the Hurons traded agricultural products to other tribes for pelts, which they then carried to the French in Quebec City or Montreal, to trade for European wares. In their flotillas of canoes, now laden with such products as textiles, beads, paints, knives, hatchets, and kettles, they then completed the trade circle, returning to the other

tribes to trade a percentage of their take for still more furs.

This complex trade relationship lasted until the mid-17th century, ending with the military and economic expansion from the south by the Iroquois League of Five Nations, who were at the time trading partners of the Dutch. (See "The Beaver Wars" and "Rebellions against the Dutch" in chapter 5.) In the meantime, however, many Frenchmen, some of them sponsored by Champlain and others by the Catholic Church, had already ventured along lakes and rivers, deeper into the wilderness in search of new sources for furs. Many more would follow. The men who earned a livelihood by paddling large canoes into the wilderness Indian-style in quest of furs came to be known as voyageurs. This wilderness profession would lead to another breed of Frenchmen—the coureurs de bois—independent, unlicensed entrepreneurs who defied regulations, many of them living among the Indians, and dealt in furs. Both voyageurs and coureurs de bois would propagate still another wilderness breed—the Metis—mixed-bloods of predominantly French and Cree descent. (See "Canadian Indian Wars" in chapter 5.)

In New France the lure of fur profits and fluctuations in the market proved a more powerful force than official policy and planning. The Company of New France (or Company of One Hundred Associates), chartered in 1627 in order to settle the colony as well as develop commerce, largely ignored the former in favor of the lucrative fur trade. And the Catholic Church, through its Jesuit missionaries, also had its hand in la traite. It was only when trade was choked off by the Beaver Wars that the habi-

tants of New France turned to farming to any significant degree. And even after the company's charter was revoked in 1663 and New France became a Crown colony, royal governors, intendants, and other officials were more concerned with matters of fur commerce and their own investments than other areas of colonial growth, in spite of the efforts of wealthy merchants in France to keep the bulk of profits on their side of the Atlantic. It took a fur market crash in 1696 to again effect another dramatic increase in farming among the settlers of New France.

Nevertheless, despite fluctuations and interruptions, the French fur trade continued to expand into new regions. Under royal management, New France extended its territory from the Great Lakes to the trans-Mississippi area, known to the French as Louisiana. Looking for new Indian markets, the French explored the

Missouri, Platte, and Red river systems of the prairies and plains. They also commonly took the majority of a tribe from the Great Lakes country with them across the Mississippi; the Indian men would protect the explorers and hunt for them, and the women would process the furs and skins.

Meanwhile, French traders expanded their markets in the southern part of the Louisiana Territory, from settlements along the Gulf Coast northwestward along the Mississippi and Red rivers. New Orleans, founded in 1718, became a bustling center of commerce. And during the 18th century, as they had done with the Hurons the century before, the French established a special trade relationship with the Taovayas (the French name for both Wichita and Caddo Indians), who acted as middlemen for them. The Taovayas and coureurs de bois established the Twin

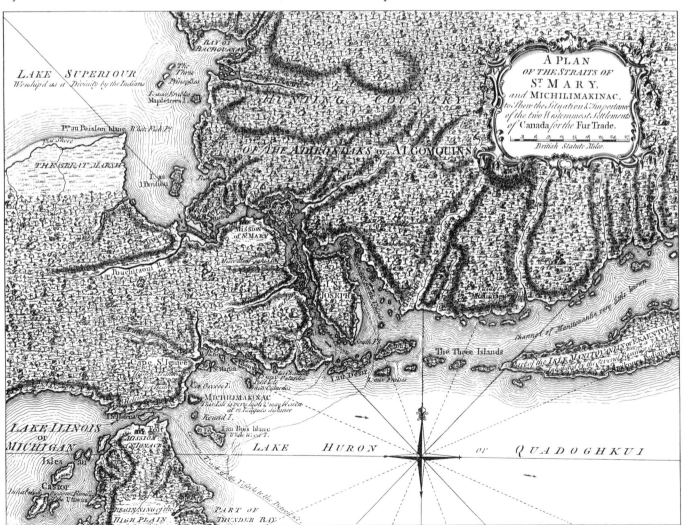

Fur country of the Great Lakes, 1761, with the two westernmost French settlements. Public Archives of Canada.

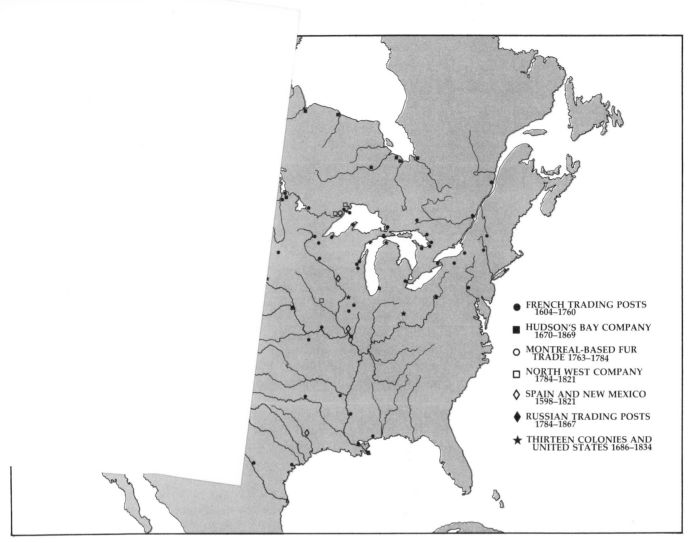

4.4 FUR TRADING POSTS *(For Russian posts in Alaska, see map 5.14.)*

- ● FRENCH TRADING POSTS
  1604–1760
- ■ HUDSON'S BAY COMPANY
  1670–1869
- ○ MONTREAL-BASED FUR
  TRADE 1763–1784
- □ NORTH WEST COMPANY
  1784–1821
- ◇ SPAIN AND NEW MEXICO
  1598–1821
- ◆ RUSSIAN TRADING POSTS
  1784–1867
- ★ THIRTEEN COLONIES AND
  UNITED STATES 1686–1834

Villages of San Bernardo and San Teodoro on the upper Red River just east of the Comanches, with whom they conducted much of their business. The Spanish, resenting the French presence and their sale of firearms to the Comanches, tried to oust the French from the area on several occasions, but without success. Both the coureurs de bois and Taovayas remained active even after 1763 and the takeover of Louisiana by the Spanish. Yet restrictive trade practices by the Spanish finally did dry up the Taovaya source of wealth.

England, which had inherited a trade relationship with the Iroquois from the Dutch in 1664 and whose ships now plied the Hudson River, sought to develop trade especially in the Hudson Bay region. Claim to the area was based on the voyage of Henry Hudson in 1610, but it wasn't until the overland expedition of Pierre Radisson and Sieur des Groseilliers in

1668 and 1669, and the subsequent charter of the Hudson's Bay Company in 1670, that the vast fur-rich area came to be exploited. The English, rather than sending traders inland to collect furs, established trading posts for barter with the Indians at the mouths of the large rivers that drained the Canadian Shield into the bay. Ships could come and go in the summertime when the northern waters were free of ice. And because English goods were generally cheaper and of better quality than French goods, the

English proved themselves competitive with tribes who had previously traded only with the French.

At this time, England did not know the extent of Rupert's Land, as its northern holdings were called, after Prince Rupert, the Hudson's Bay Company's chief backer and first governor. The French also claimed the Hudson Bay and sent out various military expeditions against British posts, with some success, until 1713 and the Treaty of Utrecht, when they abandoned their efforts. Yet France

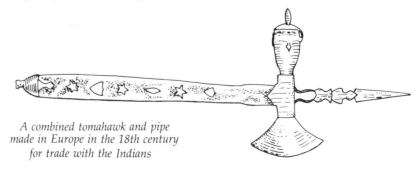

A combined tomahawk and pipe made in Europe in the 18th century for trade with the Indians

continued to play a dominant role in the fur trade until England's ultimate victory in the French and Indian Wars and the Treaty of Paris in 1763.

During the period of conflict between France and England, Russia also began developing its fur trade. Vitus Bering's voyage of discovery in 1741 precipitated a period of intense activity by the *promyshlenniki,* the Russian fur traders who had extended their domain into Alaska out of Siberia. By 1784, the Russians had founded their first permanent North American settlement, on Kodiak Island, as a year-round center of trading. By 1812, they also maintained a settlement in California. (For a more detailed discussion of the Russian fur trade, see ''The Aleut, Tlingit, and Pomo Resistance against the Russians'' in chapter 5.)

The Hudson's Bay Company also encountered fierce competition from the North West Company (chartered in 1784 by Scotsmen), which now dominated the Montreal-based fur trade. Their rivalry spurred a period of extensive exploration in which new Indian contacts were established, especially among the tribes of the Ca-

out of New Orleans, founded the St. Louis Missouri Fur Company. Both enterprises sponsored numerous expeditions into the western wilderness. In 1816, the American Congress enacted a law excluding British traders from the United States. By the time he died in 1848, John Jacob Astor was the richest man in America.

Another American entrepreneur, William Henry Ashley, became a powerful force and amassed a fortune in the fur trade, participating in and backing various expeditions, especially to the Rocky Mountains. Many of the men who worked for and traded with him came to be known as the Mountain Men. Active in the 1820s and 1830s as hunters, trappers, and traders, they traveled the Indian trails and passes of the West. (See ''Indian Trails and White Inroads'' in chapter 6.) Like the voyageurs and coureurs de bois of French Canada, the Mountain Men benefited from their extensive contacts with Indians, learning wilderness survival skills. And in terms of life-style, of all the whites to settle North America, the backwoods seekers of furs had the most in common with the Indians.

Trade was created within the War Department to administer the federal trading houses. The ''factory system'' was abolished in 1822, at which time provisions were made for the licensing of independent traders, who were better able to meet the booming demand for furs.

The international fur market experienced a decline during the 1840s, partly because the beaver hat went out of style. Yet other factors besides changes in fashion account for the end of the centuries-long fur boom—namely the depletion of fur-bearing animals and the advance of farming settlements. In 1867, Russia gave up its North American venture and sold Alaska to the United States, and, in 1869, the Hudson's Bay Company sold off its vast territorial holdings to the Canadian government. As for the Mountain Men and other counterparts, many of them stayed active long after the fur decline, as scouts and guides for the army or as settlers; some became the nemeses of the very people from whom they had learned so much—they were among the only whites skilled enough to track the warring Indians.

Because of the rugged Indian-like life-style of the fur traders—from the French voyageurs and coureurs de bois to the Hudson's Bay Company explorers to the American Mountain Men—they, like the American cowboy, have come to be romanticized. They certainly were stalwart, courageous, and individualistic, and, of all the whites entering the domain of the Indians, perhaps the most appreciative and respectful of Indian ways. But there were also those traders who held the Indians in disdain, using whatever means they could, especially alcohol, to cheat them. Although there is little comparison between the depredations these opportunistic individuals imposed on the Indian and those imposed by the majority of Spanish conquistadors, for example, who sought to conquer, plunder, and enslave the Indian population, certain traders might nevertheless be called the harbingers of an insensitive and exploitative white culture.

North American beaver

nadian West. A ''Nor'Wester,'' Alexander Mackenzie, became the first white man to cross the North American continent north of Mexico. The two companies merged in 1821 under the name of the older company.

The U.S. fur business also began to expand in the early 19th century. In 1808, John Jacob Astor founded the American Fur Company, with various subsidiaries to follow—such as the Pacific Fur Company, with an important trading post at Astoria, Oregon, and the South West Company, operating near the Great Lakes. The next year, the Chouteau family, originally

During these same years, the U.S. government also played a part in the fur trade, through a system of government trading houses, called the ''factory system.'' During the years from 1790 to 1799, the American Congress passed four Trade and Intercourse Acts pertaining to Indian affairs and commerce. Among other regulations, the acts provided for the appointment of Indian agents and licensing of federal traders who could barter with the Indians for furs. In 1802, a follow-up Trade and Intercourse Act codified the four earlier ones. And in 1806, an Office of Indian

A CHRONOLOGY OF NORTH AMERICAN EXPLORERS AND THEIR CONTACTS WITH INDIANS

Thousands of men were involved in exploring the North American wilderness in advance of white settlement. From the following partial list, one can get a view of the overall history of North American exploration by whites and its impact on the native population.

The date or dates cited refer either to specific expeditions or, in the case of certain individuals active in exploration much of their lives, the duration of careers. Names with an asterisk indicate individuals or expeditions having the greatest influence on either later white settlement or awareness of Indians. Those marked are also included in the "Chronology of North American Indian History" in the Appendix.

Although all the individuals listed here were involved in the process of exploration, not all thought of themselves primarily as explorers but perhaps as soldiers, missionaries, traders, trappers, scientists, or painters. The abbreviations after names refer either to nations sponsoring the expedition or to explorers' nationalities; when these differ, both are indicated. Of course, after colonial times many of the expeditions were privately sponsored. It should also be kept in mind that even before the United States and Canada became political entities, certain individuals no longer considered themselves European nationals, although their European nations might be cited here for purposes of identification.

The regions explored are in some instances noted as specific geographic features, such as rivers or valleys; in other instances, as states or provinces; or, if the individual covered a wide expanse of territory, as general geographic areas, such as the Atlantic Coast or the Canadian West.

4.5 INDIAN TRIBES ESSENTIAL TO THE WHITE EXPLORATION OF NORTH AMERICA
(For other tribal locations, see the Indian Culture Areas in chapter 3.)

Nearly all the explorers represented here had contact with the native population. When especially relevant to the expeditions or to tribal histories, specific Indian information is given.

circa A.D. 984
  ***Eric the Red** (Vik.): Greenland.
c. 986
  Bjarne Herjulfsson (Vik.): Sighted northeast coast of North America, probably Newfoundland or Labrador.
c. 1000
  ***Leif Ericsson** (Vik.): Northeast, probably Newfoundland (where L'Anse aux Meadows settlement has been excavated) and Labrador, although

possibly also Nova Scotia, New England, the St. Lawrence Seaway, and other regions.
c. 1004
  Thorvald Ericsson (Vik.): Northeast, Encountered *Skraelings*—either Eskimos or Indians (possibly Beothuks or Micmacs). Attacked a group of nine natives, killing eight. Attacked in turn by a second group of natives in skin boats who fatally wounded Thorvald with an arrow.
c. 1010
  Thorfinn Karlsefni (Vik.): Northeast. Encountered *Skraelings*. Took two native boys to Greenland.

c. 1014

Thorvard and Freydis Ericsson (Vik.): Northeast, probably L'Anse aux Meadows in Newfoundland.

1492–1502

***Christopher Columbus** (Sp.; Ital. descent): West Indies. Watling Island. Contact with Arawaks. Expedition aided by Chief Guacanagari and his men. Columbus gave "Indians" their name.

1497–98

***John Cabot; *Sebastian Cabot** (Eng.; Ital. descent): Northeast Coast. Sightings of Beothuks, Micmacs, Abnakis, Massachusets, and Powhatans. Kidnapped three Micmacs.

1497–1503

***Amerigo Vespucci** (Sp.; Ital. descent): West Indies. South America.

1499–1505

Alonso de Ojedo (Sp.): West Indies. Involved in slave raids on Indians. Killed by poisoned arrow of South American Indian.

1501

Gaspar Corte Real (Port.): Labrador and Newfoundland coasts, Hamilton Inlet, Belle Isle Strait. Kidnapped 57 Beothuks to be sold as slaves.

1506

Vincente Yanez Pinzon; Juan Diaz de Solis (Sp.): Yucatan Peninsula, Honduras. Slave raids on Indians.

1512

***Bartholome de las Casas** (Sp.): Cuba. Missionary to Indians. Made study of and wrote about their customs. Argued for their rights.

1513

***Vasco Nunez de Balboa** (Sp.): Panama. Sighted Pacific Ocean. Used Indian bearers to carry supplies.

1513–21

***Juan Ponce de Leon** (Sp.): Florida. Contacts with Calusas, Timucuas, and Freshwater Indians. Died in Cuba of wound inflicted by Calusas during his second expedition.

1516

Diego Miruelo (Sp.): Florida. Visited Calusas.

1517

Hernandes de Cordoba (Sp.): Florida. Visited Calusas.

1518

Juan de Grijalva (Sp.): Gulf of Mexico, Nicaragua. His reports of Indian riches inspired Cortes Expedition to Tenochtitlan.

1518–22

***Hernando Cortes** (Sp.): Mexico. Conquered Aztecs and other Mesoamerican Indians. Captured Aztec capital of Tenochtitlan. Made alliance with Totonacs, among others.

1519

Alonzo de Pineda (Sp.): Gulf of Mexico, mouth of Mississippi.

1521

Francisco de Orozco (Sp.): Oaxaca. Worked Indians in gold mines.

1522

Cristobal de Olid (Sp.): Michoacan. Battled Tarascans.

1523

Pedro de Alvarado (Sp.): Guatemala. Earlier in career, when under Cortes, ordered an attack on Aztecs in which thousands were killed.

1523–24

***Giovanni da Verrazano** (Fr.; Ital. descent): Atlantic Coast from Carolina to Newfoundland. Encountered numerous eastern tribes.

1525

Estevan Gomez (Sp.; Port. descent): Nova Scotia and Maine coasts. Kidnapped Indians for slaves.

1526

Luis Vasquez de Ayllon (Sp.): Atlantic Coast. Led slave raids on Indians, taking more than 100.

1527

Alvaro de Saavedra (Sp.): Mexico.

1528

Panfilo de Narvaez (Sp.): Gulf of Mexico.

1528–36

***Alvar Nunez Cabeza de Vaca; *Estevanico (Estevan the Moor)** (Sp.): Texas, Mexico, Gulf of California. Survivors from Narvaez expedition. Traveled with and lived among Indians. Contacts with numerous tribes.

1529

Nuno de Guzman (Sp.): Western Mexico. Defeated Tarascans. First contact with Yaquis.

1534–42

***Jacques Cartier** (Fr.): St. Lawrence River. Encountered Beothuks, Micmacs, Montagnais, Algonkins, and visited Huron villages of Stadacona (Quebec City) and Hochelaga (Montreal). Traded European goods to the Indians for furs. Took Chief Donnaconna and other Hurons to Europe after final voyage.

1539

***Marcos de Niza; *Estevanico (Estevan the Moor)** (Sp.): Southwest. Contact with various Pueblo Indians. Estevanico killed by Zunis.

1539

Francisco de Ulloa (Sp.): Gulf of California, Mexico and California coasts.

1539–43

***Hernando de Soto; *Luis de Moscoso de Alvaro** (Sp.): Southeast. First to encounter many of the Southeast tribes. Attempted to assert Spanish dominance over them.

1540–42

***Francisco Vasquez de Coronado** (Sp.): Southwest. Encountered numerous Southwest tribes, including Hopis, Zunis, Apaches, Wichitas, and Pawnees.

1540

Hernando de Alarcon (Sp.): Gulf of California, mouth of Colorado River. Part of Coronado Expedition. Contact with Cocopas, Halchidhomas, Kohuanas, Mojaves, and Hualapais.

1540

Garcia Lopez de Cardenas, Pedro de Tobar (Sp.): Grand Canyon. Part of Coronado Expedition. Contact with Zunis and Hopis.

1540

Juan de Padillo (Sp.): Southwest. Part of Coronado Expedition. Killed by Wichitas.

1540

Melchoir Diaz (Sp.): Arizona, Gulf of California.

1541

Tristan de Luna y Arrelano (Sp.): Alabama River. Part of Coronado Expedition. Contact with Mobiles, Napochis, and Tohomes.

1541

Seigneur de Roberval (Fr.): St. Lawrence River. Part of Cartier Expedition.

1542

Sebastian Moyano de Benalcazar (Sp.): Nicaragua.

1542

***Juan Rodriguez Cabrillo; *Bartolome Ferrelo** (Sp.): California and Oregon coasts.

1551–62

Hernando de Escalante Fontaneda (Sp.): Florida. Held prisoner by Calusas.

1562

***Jean Ribault** (Fr.): South Carolina, Florida. Contact with Cusabos, Saturiwas, Tacatacuras, and Timucuas.

1564–65

***Rene de Laudonniere; *Jacques le Moyne** (Fr.): Florida. Le Moyne painted Timucuas.

1565

***Pedro Menendez de Aviles** (Sp.): St. Augustine in Florida.

1566–67

Juan Pardo (Sp.): Eastern slope of Blue Ridge. Made friendly alliances with various tribes.

1573

Pedro Menendez Marquez (Sp.): Chesapeake Bay.

1576–78

*Martin Frobisher (Eng.): Greenland, Arctic Canada. Sought Northwest Passage. Encountered and kidnapped Eskimos.

1578–79

*Francis Drake (Eng.): California Coast. Encountered Miwoks.

1581

Augustin Rodriguez; Francisco Sanchez Chasmuscado (Sp.): New Mexico. Visited Zuni and Piro pueblos. Rodriguez killed by Zunis.

1582–83

Antonio Espejo (Sp.): Rio Grande, New Mexico. Contact with various pueblos, as well as Jumanos and Yavapais.

1583

Humphrey Gilbert (Eng.): Newfoundland.

1586

*Richard Grenville (backed by *Walter Raleigh) (Eng.): Roanoke Island, North Carolina. Burned an entire Indian village over the issue of a stolen cup.

1585–87

John Davis (Eng.): Arctic Canada. Encountered Eskimos.

1587

*John White (backed by *Walter Raleigh) (Eng.): Roanoke. Painted Indians.

1587

Pedro de Unamuno (Sp.; Port. descent): California Coast.

1590

Sebastian Rodriguez Cirmenho (Sp.; Port. descent): California Coast.

1590–91

Gaspar Castano de Sosa (Sp.; Port. descent): Southwest. Pecos River. Visited Tiwa pueblos.

1592

Juan de Fuca (Sp.; Gr. descent): Northwest. Fuca Straits. Contact with Cowichans, Nootkas, Songish, and Stalos.

1594–96

William Barents (Neth.): Arctic Canada.

1597

Juan de Salas (Sp.): Georgia.

1598

*Juan de Onate (Sp.): New Mexico, Colorado River. Contact personally, or through representatives, with various pueblos. Massacred Keres Indians of the Acoma Pueblo.

1599

Vincente, Cristobal, Francisco, and Juan Zaldivar (Sp.): New Mexico, Texas.

1602–03

Sebastian Vizcaino (Sp.): California Coast.

1602–06

Bartholomew Gosnald (Eng.): Massachusetts Bay, Cape Cod. Contact with Wampanoags. Traded with Indians for sassafras bark.

1603

Martin Pring (Eng.): Maine and Massachusetts coasts.

1603–15

*Samuel de Champlain (Fr.): Northeast. Encountered numerous Algonquian- and Iroquoian-speaking tribes. Battled Iroquois.

1605

George Waymouth (Eng.): Maine Coast. Traded with Indians for furs.

1606

George Popham (Eng.): Massachusetts Coast.

1607

*John Smith (Eng.): Virginia. Battled and captured by Indians of the Powhatan Confederacy. Supposedly saved by Pocahontas, daughter of Chief Powhatan.

1608–15

*Etienne Brule (Fr.): Northeast. Protege of Champlain. Lived among Hurons. Fought Iroquois at Lake Oneida. Visited Neutrals and Susquehannocks.

1609

Francisco Fernandez de Ecija (Sp.): South Carolina. Contact with Santees and Sewees.

1609–10

*Henry Hudson (Neth., then Eng.; Eng. descent): Hudson River, Hudson Bay, Hudson Strait. In claiming Hudson Bay for Netherlands, he encountered Manhattans, Wappingers, and Mahicans.

1612–13

Thomas Button (Eng.): Arctic Canada.

1615–16

William Baffin; Robert Bylot (Eng.): Arctic Canada, Baffin Bay.

1619

Jens Munk (Den.): Ungava Bay, Churchill River.

1620

*Pilgrims (Eng): Plymouth. Contact with Massachusets and Wampanoags.

1626–48

Jean de Brebeuf; Gabriel Lalement (Fr.): Ontario. Jesuit missionaries among Hurons (Lalement joined Brebeuf in 1645).

1630

Alonso Benavides (Sp.): Southwest. Visited Jumanos and Piro pueblos.

1631

*Thomas James; *Luke Fox (Eng.): James Bay.

1631

Pieter Heyes (Neth.): Delaware River. Encountered Delawares.

1633

Jean Nicolet (Fr.): Lake Michigan, Lake George. Protege of Champlain. Encountered Algonkins, Nipissings, and Winnebagos.

1641–46

Isaac Jogues (Fr.): Lake Michigan, Lake George. Jesuit missionary among Hurons. Killed by Mohawks.

1650

Edward Blande (Eng.): Virginia, North Carolina. Contact with Meherrins and Nahyssans.

1650

Hernan Martin; Diego del Castillo (Sp.): New Mexico, Texas. Visited Tewa pueblos and Jumanos.

1654

Diego de Guadalajara; Andrew Lopez (Sp.): New Mexico, Texas. Fought and defeated Cuitoas.

1654

Simon le Moyne (Fr.): Eastern Canada, New York. Jesuit among Iroquois, especially Onondagas. Contact also with Hurons.

1654–69

*Pierre Esprit Radisson; *Sieur de Groseilliers (Fr., then Eng.): Northeast, Midwest. Encountered numerous Algonquian and Iroquoian tribes. Radisson saved by Mohawk family who adopted him. Their trip to Hudson Bay led to charter of the Hudson's Bay Company in 1670.

1660

Jean Pere (Fr.): Hudson Bay to Lake Superior. A Metis (Indian and French mixed-blood).

1669–70

John Lederer (Eng.; Ger. descent): Blue Ridge Mountains, Carolina Piedmont. Contact with numerous tribes.

1669–70

Dollier de Casson; Rene de Brehant de Galinee (Fr.): New York, Great Lakes. Jesuit missionaries among Indians, especially Senecas.

1669–70

Claude Jean Allouez (Fr.): Great Lakes. Jesuit who preached to 22 tribes and baptized 10,000 Indians.

1669–73

*Louis Joliet; *Jacques Marquette (Fr.): Great Lakes, Wisconsin River, Mississippi River, Illinois River. Jesuits who encountered numerous tribes. Accompanied by Miami guides.

1669–87

*Rene Robert Cavelier de la Salle (Fr.): Northeast, Midwest, Mississippi River, Louisiana. Contact with numerous tribes.

1670–89

*Nicholas Perrot (Fr.): Upper Mississippi River. In 1689, formally claims region for France. Contact with Miamis, among other tribes.

1671

Thomas Batts; Robert Fallam (expedition sent out by **Abraham Wood**, a trader) (Eng.): West Virginia. Indian guide by the name of Perceute.

1673

Gabriel Arthur; James Needham (expedition sent out by **Abraham Wood**, a trader) (Eng.): Kentucky, Tennessee. Arthur captured by and escaped from Shawnees.

1765

Henry Woodward (Eng.): Ocmulgee and Chattahoochee rivers. Contact with Creeks.

1675

Fernando del Bosque; Juan Larios (Sp.): Rio Grande. Invaded Coahuiltecan territory.

1678–80

Louis Hennepin; Michel Aco (Fr.): Niagara Falls, St. Anthony's Falls. Captured by Sioux.

1678–79

*Daniel Greysolon Duluth (Fr.): Great Lakes. Negotiated with Sioux for release of Hennepin and Aco, and negotiated treaty between Sioux and Ojibway.

1680

Henri Tonti (Fr.): Great Lakes, Mississippi River. Lieutenant of La Salle. Encountered numerous tribes. Won Illinois Indians to French cause.

1683

Juan Domingo Mendoza; Nicolas Lopez (Sp.): Rio Grande, Pecos River. Contact with Jumanos.

1687

Henri Joutel (Fr.): Louisiana. Part of La Salle Expedition. Visited tribes of Hasinai and Kadohadacho confederacies.

1687–1711

Eusebio Francisco Kino (Sp.): Arizona, California. Converted many Papagos and Pimas. Also encountered Halchidhomas, Maricopas, and Yumas.

1688

Alonso de Leon (Sp.): Texas. Contact with Jean Jery (Jarry), white chief of Indians.

1689–92

*Henry Kelsey (Eng.): Canadian Plains. Explored for the Hudson's Bay Company. Traveled with Indians of various tribes.

1691

Domingo Teran de los Rios (Sp.): Texas. Trinity River to Red River. Contact with various tribes.

1692

Francisco de Vargas (Sp.): Southwest.

1692

Martin Chartier (Fr.): Ohio River, Susquehanna River. Traveled with and settled among Shawnees.

1692–94

Cornelissen Arnout Viele (Neth.): Susquehanna River, Ohio River, Wabash River. Used Shawnee guides.

1692–1700

Jean Couture (Fr.): From Mississippi River to Allegheny Mountains. Coureur de bois (trader) among Indians of the Southeast.

1698

Thomas Welch (Eng.): Charleston, South Carolina, to mouth of Arkansas.

1699

Jonathan Dickenson (Eng.): Quaker shipwrecked on Florida's east coast. Contact with Guales, Ais, Guacatas, and Jeagas.

1699

Father Davion (Fr.): Yazoo River, Missionary to Tunicas.

1699–1725

Pierre Le Moyne d'Iberville (Fr.): Mississippi Delta. Contact with numerous Southeast Indians.

1700

Pierre Charles le Sueur (Fr.): Mississippi River, Minnesota. Contact with Sioux, Otos, and Iowas. Fort attacked by Fox Indians.

1701

John Lawson (Eng.): North Carolina, Allegheny Mountains. Contact with numerous tribes.

1714–16

Louis Juchereau de Saint-Denis (Fr.): Louisiana, Texas. Contact with numerous tribes.

1716

Alexander Spotswood (Eng.): Shenandoah Valley in West Virginia.

1717

Zacharie Robutel de la Noue (Fr.): Ontario, Rainy River, Rainy Lake, Kaministikwia River. Contact with Crees.

1719

Bernard de la Harpe (Fr.): Louisiana, Texas, Red River, Canadian River. Encountered numerous tribes and opened up Indian trade. Brought kidnapped Atakapa Indians to New Orleans.

1719

Claude Charles du Tisne (Fr.): Missouri River, Osage River. Prevented from traveling further westward by prairie Indians.

1720

Don Pedro Villasur (Sp.): Santa Fe, New Mexico, Arkansas River, Nebraska. Killed by Pawnees.

1722–28

Etienne Veniard de Bourgmont (Fr.): Missouri River, Great Plains. Traveled with Missouris and Osages. Contact with Comanches.

1722–31

Pierre Francois Xavier Charlevoix (Fr.): Quebec to New Orleans. Contact with Acolapissas and Tious among others.

1727–43

*Pierre Gaultier de Varennes, Sieur de la Verendrye and sons (Fr.): Canadian and American Great Plains. Encountered numerous tribes. Guided by a Cree named Ochagah. Aided by Assiniboines. Lived among Mandans. One son killed by Sioux.

1729

Chaussegros de Lery (Fr.): Allegheny River, Ohio River. Contact with Fox Indians.

1731

Felipe Segresser; Juan Bautista Grashoffer (Sp.): Arizona. Missionaries to Pimas.

1732

Michael Gvozdev (Russ.): Bering Sea.

1736–37

Ignacio Javier Keller (Sp.): Arizona. Contact with Pimas.

1737

Conrad Weiser (Eng.; Ger. descent): Susquehanna River Valley (Philadelphia to Onondaga). **William Penn's** Indian agent. Lived among Iroquois as boy.

1739–41

*Paul Mallet; *Pierre Mallet (Fr.): Great Plains, Southwest. Pawnees instructed them on their route. Used Indian guides.

1741

*Vitus Bering (Russ., Dan. descent): Aleutian Islands, Kodiak Island, Gulf of Alaska.

1741

Alexei Chirikov (Russ.): Alaska, Alexander Archipelago.

1742

Christopher Middleton (Eng.): West coast of Hudson Bay.

1742

John Peter Salley (Eng.): Virginia Alleghenies. Captured by Cherokees. Lived among them three years.

1747

William Moor (Eng.): West coast of Hudson Bay.

1748

Jose de Escandon (Sp.): Northern Mexico.

1748–50

Thomas Walker (Eng.): Cumberland Gap. Virginia physician.

1749

William Coates (Eng.): East coast of Hudson Bay.

1751–52

Christopher Gist (Eng.): Ohio River, Kentucky.

1754

James McBride (Eng.): Ohio River, Kentucky.

1754–55

*****Anthony Henday** (Eng.): Hudson Bay, Saskatchewan. For the Hudson's Bay Company. Aided by Blackfeet. Contact also with Assiniboines.

1756–65

*****George Croghan** (Eng.; Ir. descent): New York, Pennsylvania, Ohio Valley. Deputy Superintendent of Indian Affairs under *****William Johnson.** Involved in negotiations with numerous tribes.

1758

Christian Frederick Post (Eng.): Wyoming Valley, Pennsylvania. Married Cherokee.

1760–75

*****Daniel Boone** (U.S.): Tennessee, Kentucky. Cumberland Gap. Battled Cherokees and Shawnees.

1766–67

Jonathan Carver (Eng.): Wisconsin River. Contact with Sauks.

1766–68

Marques de Rubl; Nicolas de Lafora (Sp.): Northern Mexico, Texas.

1767–68

William Pink (Eng.): Churchill River, Mackenzie River Basin.

1768

Fernando de Rivera y Moncada (Sp.): Mexico to San Diego. Used Indians as bearers and soldiers.

1768–69

*****Gaspar de Portola; *Junipero Serra** (Sp.): California Coast. Traveled with Indians.

1768–76

Francisco Garces (Sp.): California, Great Basin, Colorado River, Grand Canyon. Mojave guides. Contact with numerous Southwest tribes.

1769–72

*****Samuel Hearne** (Eng.): Churchill River, Coppermine River, Great Slave Lake, Slave River, Arctic Ocean. Explored for the Hudson's Bay Company. Led by Chipewyan guide, Matonabbee. Contact with both Indians and Eskimos.

1772–73

Matthew Cocking (Eng.): Canadian West beyond the Saskatchewan River. For the Hudson's Bay Company. Contact with numerous tribes, among them the Gros Ventres and Sarcees.

1773–77

John Bartram (U.S.): American West. Naturalist.

1774

Juan Perez (Sp.): Pacific Coast. Queen Charlotte Islands. Contact with Haidas and Nootkas.

1775

Bruno Heceta (Sp.): Pacific Coast.

1775

Juan Francisco Bodega y Cuadra (Sp.): Southern Alaska. Contact with Haidas.

1776

Francisco Dominguez; Francisco de Escalante (Sp.): Santa Fe to Wasatch Mountains, Great Salt Lake. Contact with Utes and Paiutes. Used Indian guides.

1776–78

*****James Cook** (Eng.): Pacific Coast, Alaska. Contact with Eskimos and Nootkas. His men bought favors from Indian women.

1778

*****Peter Pond** (Can.): Saskatchewan River to Lake Athabaska. Later, a trader for the North West Company. Contact with Sekanis and Beavers, among others.

1781

Potan Zaikof (Russ.): Prince William Sound, Copper River. Used Aleut guides.

1783

Gregor Ivanovich Shelikov (Russ.): Founded settlement of Three Saints on Kodiak Island. Fur trader among Aleuts and Tlingits.

1786

Jean Francois de la Perouse (Fr.): Lituya Bay. Contact with Tlingits and Haidas.

1789–93

*****Alexander Mackenzie** (Can.; Scot. descent): Canadian West. First to traverse North American continent north of Mexico. For the North West Company. Contact with numerous tribes.

1790–92

Jacques d'Eglise (Fr.): Missouri River. Lived among Missouris.

1791–92

Alejandro Malispina (Sp.): Pacific Coast. Two painters, **Jose Cardeno** and **Tomas Suria,** painted Indians during expedition. Contact with Nootkas, Chumash, and Tlingits.

1791–93

*****George Vancouver** (Eng.): Pacific Coast, Vancouver Island, Alaska.

1792

*****Robert Gray; *William Broughton** (U.S.): Northwest Coast, Gray's Harbor, Columbia River.

1792

*****Alexander Baranov** (Russ.): Alaska, British Columbia, California. Fur trader among Aleuts, Tlingits, Pomos, and other tribes.

1794

Andrew Henry (U.S.): Madison River to Continental Divide. For the North West Company.

1794–95

Jean Baptiste Trudeau (Fr.): Missouri River. Lived among Arikaras.

1797–1811

*****David Thompson** (Can.): Canadian and American West, Columbia River. For the North West Company. Encountered numerous tribes.

1802

Francois Marie Perrin du Lac (Fr.): Missouri River.

1802

James Purcell (U.S.): Osage River to Arkansas River.

1803–06

*****Meriwether Lewis; *William Clark** (U.S.): American West and Northwest. St. Louis to mouth of Columbia River. Encountered 50 tribes. Expedition had Shoshoni woman guide, Sacajawea.

1804

Simon Kenton (U.S.): Allegheny Mountains, Kentucky. Captured by and escaped from Shawnees.

1804

Regis Loisel; Pierre Antoine Tabeau (Fr.): Missouri River.

1804

William Dunbar; George Hunter (U.S.): Louisiana, Washita River.

1805–06

*Zebulon Pike (U.S.): Southwest, Rocky Mountains, headwaters of Mississippi.

1805–20

*Simon Fraser (Can.): Canadian West. For the North West Company. Contact with numerous tribes; among them, Carriers and Sekanis.

1806

Thomas Freeman; William Sparks (U.S.): Louisiana.

1807

Manuel Lisa (U.S.; Sp. descent): Yellowstone River. Fur trader attacked by Arikaras and Mandans.

1807–08

John Colter (U.S.): Grand Teton Mountains, Yellowstone. Contact with Crows. Attacked by Blackfeet.

1811–13

*The Astorians (William Hunt and Robert Stuart, backed by John Jacob Astor) (U.S.): Missouri River, Columbia River, Oregon. Traveled with Crow guides.

1818–24

Alexander Ross (Can.): For the North West Company and later the Hudson's Bay Company. Contact with Nez Perces, among other tribes.

1818–33

John Ross; James Ross (Eng.): Greenland, Arctic Canada. Encountered Eskimos at Thule in northwest Greenland.

1818–41

*Henry Rowe Schoolcraft (U.S.): Ohio River, upper Mississippi River, upper Great Lakes. Indian agent and ethnologist who studied Indians. Contact with numerous tribes, especially Ojibways.

1819–20

Stephen Long (U.S.): Upper Mississippi River, Rocky Mountains.

1819–20

Robert Hood (Eng.): Great Slave Lake, Coppermine River, Kent Peninsula.

1819–27

William Parry (Eng.): Arctic Canada.

1821–22

William Becknell (U.S.): Santa Fe Trail (Missouri to Santa Fe), Cimarron Desert. Trader whose caravan was attacked by different tribes.

1822–33

Hugh Glass (U.S.): American West. Mountain Man. Contact with numerous tribes. Probably killed by Blackfeet.

1823–46

Thomas Fitzpatrick (U.S.): American

West. Mountain Man. Contact with numerous tribes. Later, Indian agent in Colorado.

1824

Jim Bridger (U.S.): Bear River, Great Salt Lake, Yellowstone. Mountain Man. Contact with numerous tribes, among them Bannocks.

1824–25

*William Henry Ashley (U.S.): Missouri River, Rocky Mountains. Fur trader who employed many of the Mountain Men. Attacked by Missouris.

1825–28

Frederick William Beechey (Eng.): Northwest Alaska Coast.

1825–30

*Peter Skene Ogden (Can.): American and Canadian West. For the Hudson's Bay Company. Twice married to Indians.

1825–48

William Sherley Williams (U.S.): American West. Mountain Man among numerous tribes. Killed by Utes.

1826

David Jackson; William Sublette (U.S.): Yellowstone. Mountain Men among numerous tribes.

1826–27

James Ohio Pattie (U.S.): Gila River. Mountain Man among numerous tribes.

1826–28

Jedediah Smith (U.S.): Mojave Desert, California, Klamath River. Mountain Man among numerous tribes.

1828

Jean Louis Berlandier (Fr.): Texas. Swiss-trained botanist who lived among Comanches.

1829

Ewing Young; Kit Carson (U.S.): Salt

Mato-Tope, Mandan Chief. Watercolor by Karl Bodmer. New York State Library, Albany.

River, San Joaquin Valley, Sacramento Basin. Fought Navajos and Apaches.
1829
   Antonio Armijo (Mex.): Old Spanish Trail (Santa Fe to Los Angeles).
1830–31
   William Wolfskill; George Yount (U.S.): Old Spanish Trail (Santa Fe to Los Angeles).
1830–36
   *George Catlin (U.S.): American West. Frontier painter of Indians.
1831–32
   Jacob Fowler (U.S.): Great Plains, Rocky Mountains.
1832
   Paulino Weaver (U.S.): Casa Grande, Arizona.
1832
   Lucien Fontalle (U.S.): Yellowstone, South Pass, Pierre's Hole. Trader for the American Fur Company. Traveled with Delawares.
1832–33
   Nathaniel Joseph Wyeth (U.S.): Missouri River, Rocky Mountains, Northwest.
1832–36
   Benjamin Bonneville (U.S.): Rocky Mountains, South Pass, California.
1833
   Joseph Walker (U.S.): Great Salt Lake, High Sierras, Rocky Mountains. Mountain Man among numerous tribes.
1833
   John Treat Irving (U.S.): Missouri River and Platte River prairies. Nephew of Washington Irving. Lived among Pawnees. Also visited Kickapoos, Otos, and Missouris.
1833–34
   *Prince Alexander Philipp Maximilian (Ger.); *Karl Bodmer (Switz.): Missouri River. Bodmer painted Indians, especially Mandans.
1833–36
   George Back (Eng.): Back River, Arctic Canada. Searched for the missing John Ross Expedition.
1835
   Charles Murray (U.S.): Missouri River and Platte River prairies. Lived among Pawnees.

1836–47
   Marcus Whitman (U.S.): Missouri River, Columbia River. Founded mission among Cayuses. Killed by Cayuses.
1837
   Alfred Miller (U.S.); William Drummond Stuart (Scot.): St. Louis to Wyoming. Miller painted Indians.
1837–39
   Thomas Simpson (Eng.): Great Bear Lake, Coppermine River.
1840
   Robert Campbell (Can.): Pelly River. Contact with Nahanes.
1840–44
   William Hillhouse (U.S.): Ohio, Iowa. Traveled and lived with Sauks and Foxes.
1840–46
   Pierre Jean de Smet (U.S., Bel. descent): Jesuit missionary to Indians. Contact with Coeur d'Alenes, Pend d'Oreilles, Salish, and Blackfeet.
1841
   Charles Wilkes (U.S.): Pacific Northwest. United States Exploring Expedition. Contact with Nez Perces and Tillamooks.
1841–42
   *John Charles Fremont; *Kit Carson (U.S.): Des Moines River, Wind River, Oregon, California. Contact with numerous tribes.
1842–43
   Lawrence Zagoskin (Russ.): Yukon. Studied Indian languages.
1846
   *Paul Kane (Can.): Toronto to Northwest. Frontier painter of Indians.
1847–52
   Rudolph Friederich Kurz (Switz.): Missouri River prairies. Frontier painter of Indians.
1848–50
   John Richardson (Eng.): Mackenzie River, Coppermine River.
1850
   John Franklin (Eng.): Arctic Canada. Died in the Arctic.
1850
   Richard Collinson; Robert McClure (Eng.): Arctic Canada. Searched for missing Franklin Expedition.

1851
   James Savage (U.S.): Yosemite Valley. Contact with Yokuts.
1851–53
   John Rae (Eng.): Arctic Canada. Learned from Eskimos the fate of Franklin Expedition.
1853
   Joseph Ives; Amiel Whipple (U.S.): American West.
1853
   Elisha Kane (U.S.): Arctic Canada
1855
   James Anderson (Eng.): Back River.
1855–58
   Henry Cross (U.S.): American West. Frontier painter of Indians.
1857
   Leopold McClintlock (Eng.): Arctic Canada. Established conclusively fate of Franklin Expedition. Interviewed Eskimos.
1858–66
   Henry Boller (U.S.): Upper Missouri River. Lived among Gros Ventres, Arikaras, and Mandans.
1860–69
   Charles Hall (U.S.): Arctic Canada. Lived among Eskimos.
1865–66
   *Jesse Chisholm (U.S.): Chisholm Trail. Arkansas River to upper Washita River. Half Scottish, half Cherokee.
1869–72
   *John Wesley Powell (U.S.): Colorado River, Grand Canyon. Geologist and ethnologist. Became director of Bureau of American Ethnology and studied Indian languages.
1878
   Andrew Garcia (U.S.): Montana. Lived among Pend d'Oreilles and Nez Perces. Married a Nez Perce.
1878–80
   Frederick Schwatka (U.S.): Arctic Canada.
1889–92
   Wilfred Grenfell (Eng.): Arctic Canada. Took medical services to Labrador Eskimos.
1906–12
   Vilhjalmur Stefansson (Can.): Arctic Canada. Lived among Eskimos.

Chapter 5
INDIAN WARS

The history of the North American Indian since the arrival of the white man is to a large extent one of warfare—a chronicle of hostilities from colonial times through the 19th century. The clash between two cultures—Indian and white, with some tribes aligning themselves with whites against other Indians—is sometimes referred to as the Four-Hundred-Year War (or, in the view of Indian activists struggling for rights, the ongoing Five-Hundred-Year War). This chapter will attempt to organize and summarize this war, or wars, through 1890 and the Wounded Knee Massacre, the incident that has come to symbolize the ultimate defeat of the Indians.

Within the saga of the various conflicts, stated or implicit, is much of the larger Indian story as well—the dispossession of cultures; the movement of tribes; the cession of millions of acres of land; the varying Indian policies of the European colonial powers as well as those of the United States and Canada; and the lives of many great individuals. In order to make the complex subject of Postcontact Indian history more accessible, a following chapter, ''INDIAN LAND CESSIONS,'' will summarize white governmental policies and territorial expansion in relation to Indian displacement and migration. Then, the final chapter, ''CONTEMPORARY INDIANS,'' will bring the North American Indian story up to date.

The subject of the Indian wars is especially charged with emotion. For many of the early white historians, with their pro-European bias, Indians were an obstacle to Manifest Destiny, a menace to peaceful white expansion, and the perpetrators of frontier violence. That long-standing bias in turn fed the popular conception of Indians as villains, with settlers as victims, and frontiersmen, soldiers, and cowboys as heroes. Yet, with a broader historical perspective, the Indians become the greater victims and, in that regard, the greater heroes. Whereas Indian culture creates a sense of wonder, the historical destruction of that culture creates a sense of outrage.

Generalizations or moralizing about one side or another can be misleading. Much is made, for example, of the practice of scalping and which side initiated it. To what extent scalping was an aboriginal custom before Contact is still in dispute; however, whites first institutionalized the practice by placing bounties on Indian heads and scalps. In any case, in the heat of war both Indians and whites readily took to the practice, and both sides commonly committed torture. In the same regard, all whites cannot be blamed for the racism and cruelty of Andrew Jackson or John Chivington toward Indians, and all Indians cannot be held accountable for the cruelty of certain of them against peaceable settlers. There were white soldiers of courage and principle; there were egomaniacs who sought to further their own careers through the murder of Indian women and children. There were peaceful Indians who turned to violence only as a last resort; there were sadistic Indians who, fueled by alcohol, enjoyed violence against any victims, either white or Indian. There were white settlers who, having taken refuge from prejudice and injustice in Europe, sought only to make a new life for themselves; there were elements of frontier riffraff, outcasts from society, and hardened criminals. There were bloodthirsty Indian warriors who showed no mercy; there were playful

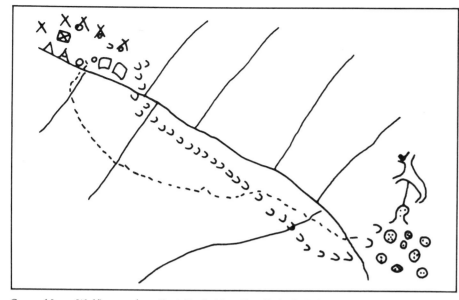

Copy of Lean Wolf's map from Fort Berthold to Fort Buford, Dakota, along the Missouri River, the route he took in a successful raid for Sioux horses. Circles represent lodges of his Hidatsa tribe, with dots showing the number of pillars supporting each roof. Crosses represent Sioux lodges. Combined crosses and circles indicate lodges of intermarried Hidatsas and Sioux. Squares represent dwellings of whites. The square with a cross indicates the house of a white man and Sioux woman. Lean Wolf's original path is shown in footprints and his return in hoofprints. Library of Congress.

warriors who fought only for personal honor with no taste for killing. (As a case in point, the Plains Indians had a custom in which the bravest deed a warrior could perform was to get close enough in battle to touch his opponent with a coup stick without harming him.) There were white settlers, traders, and missionaries who defended Indian rights; there were others who sought only to exploit the Indians for their own personal fortunes. Some white officials viewed reservations as protection for the Indians against an ever-expanding white population; others viewed them as prisons for Indians or even as pens for savage animals. At times, white official policy tried to protect Indians from white individualistic scofflaws on the edge of the frontier; at other times, governmental policy urged the extinction of Indians. And, like their sympathetic counterparts in white centers of government, some Indian proponents of peace, who believed that the long-term hope for their people lay in accommodation with whites, had their efforts undone by a constituency they could not control—in their case often by young, volatile individualistic warriors in quest of personal honor. Some of the Indians

who accommodated whites might be viewed as visionaries, recognizing the inevitable and trying to strike the best deal for their people, and others who did so might be seen as dupes, collaborators, or mercenaries.

The fact that Indians often fought with whites against other Indians during the Contact period was also a natural outgrowth of Precontact lifeways. For the Indians tribal identity was stronger than racial, just as for the whites national or religious identity took precedence over shared race. Some of the intertribal feuding had persisted for numerous generations. And warfare served a variety of functions in tribal culture: as ritual, a rite of passage to manhood or a means of achieving godlike qualities, such as among the Plains warrior societies; as economy, for a source of sustenance through raiding, as practiced by the Apaches of the Southwest; as limited political purpose, a way to establish

tribal confederacies, as in the case of the Iroquois League of the Northeast; and as offical state policy, as demonstrated by the Aztecs of Mesoamerica, who maintained their social structure through military expansion.

Yet, despite the long list of contradictions and exceptions, and despite the fact that the hostilities cannot be viewed simply in terms of Indian versus white, the Indian wars are now generally interpreted as wars of native resistance. And since Indians were generally protecting their people, culture, and lands from invasion and exploitation by outsiders who, more often than not, were white supremacists with the attitude that native peoples were incidental to human destiny, Indian violence is now regarded in hindsight more sympathetically than white violence. Further Indian justification can be argued because the specific causes of uprisings were often the trickery of white traders, the forced sale of Indian lands, forced labor or enslavement of Indians, the suppression of Indian culture, and the violation of treaties by whites through encroachments on Indian lands and failure to pay stipulated annuities—all understandable grievances. One other generalization: The Indians in early encounters with whites for the most part acted with peacefulness, curiosity, and generosity. Given the ultimate threat to them by the white presence, their trusting behavior says a great deal for aboriginal character and reaches modern humanity, through all the ensuing entangled years, with acute poignancy.

In the end, the Indians lost the Four-Hundred-Year War, not for lack of valor or skill. By all accounts they were among history's most effective warriors, and their guerrilla tactics—emphasizing concealment and individual initiative—have been adopted

Plains Indian coup stick

by many modern armies. They were defeated rather by overwhelming numbers—the spillover from an overpopulated Europe. In another sense, it can be said that the Indians were defeated by their own lack of unity. What ifs abound. If the Indians had presented a unified front at various times in history, they might have kept control of the continent until modern times, or at least established an independent Indian country or a state within the U.S. For that matter, if whites had treated Indians in an enlightened and democratic manner, such a political entity also might now exist. These are intriguing scenarios. Given all that Indian culture and philosophy have to offer modern humanity—especially in terms of an ecological world view—many perhaps would like to rewrite history with the Indians having a greater hold on human destiny.

In the descriptions of the various wars, troop and band sizes are often given, as well as casualty figures, to communicate the scope of the fighting. It should be kept in mind, however, that the numbers as presented are more often than not approximations, and that at the time of the conflicts enemy casualties were often inflated in military reports.

THE POWHATAN WARS

It was a tenuous peace from the start, but peace nonetheless. Without it the Jamestown colony established in 1607 would not have survived. Because of disease and starvation, only 150 of the original 900 English colonists remained after the first three years. The Indians of the Powhatan Confederacy of 32 tribes and 200 villages could easily have defeated the struggling settlement in the early years. Why they chose not to do so, despite a good amount of bloody squabbling, is not exactly known.

The decision for peace or war rested primarily with Wahunsonacock—or King Powhatan, as the colonists called him, after the town in which he lived.

His father had founded the powerful confederacy of Tidewater tribes, and Wahunsonacock had further strengthened it. Perhaps his motives for peace were political—a desire to make use of English influence and weaponry to expand his own empire. The relationship between Captain John Smith, who headed the colony until 1609, and Wahunsonacock certainly had much to do with the lasting peace. Both headstrong and both conniving, they held a begrudging respect for each other. Smith even had Wahunsonacock ceremonially crowned as king of the territory in a political maneuver. Legend tells of the role of Pocahontas, the king's daugh-

ter, in preserving the peace—her fondness for the colonists as a child and her saving Smith's life. Her documented marriage to John Rolfe in later years helped maintain stability at a time when the European demand for tobacco had increased, leading to more and more boatloads of settlers, the appropriation of more Indian land, and more bloody incidents.

Whatever the exact reasons for peace, it lasted only four years after Wahunsonacock's death. Although Wahunsonacock's brother Opechancanough, the new ruler of the confederacy, pledged continuing peace, he plotted revenge against the colony for what he considered innumerable

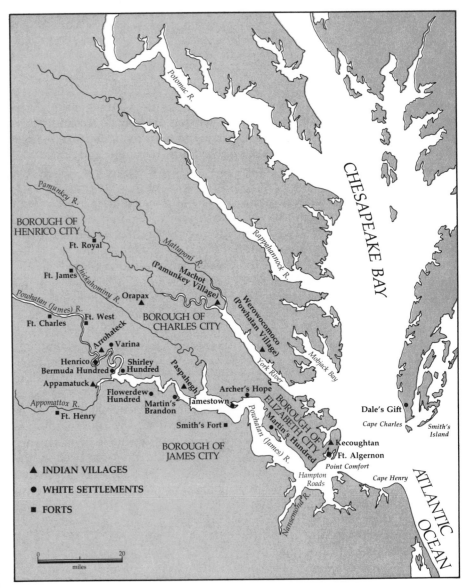

5.1 THE TIDEWATER FRONTIER, 1607–75, *during the time of the Powhatan Wars and Bacon's Rebellion*

offenses against the Indians. Yet, despite Opechancanough's rancor and his apparent grasp of the long-term implications of the mounting colonial population, peace might still have been preserved if the English hadn't executed an Indian named Nemattanou for the suspected murder of a white trader. Soon after this incident, on the morning of March 22, 1622, Opechancanough's warriors swept through the colony's tobacco fields, killing 347 men, women, and children.

From that time on, the colonists' stated goal became one of Indian extermination through any means. Regular patrols attacked and burned Tidewater villages and crops, driving the Indians further inland. Inviting the Indians to a peace council for the purpose of drawing up a treaty, the colonists poisoned the unsuspecting tribal representatives and attacked them; the old and cagey Opechancanough escaped, however. In 1625, about 1,000 Indians were killed in an attack on the village of Pamunkey. Intermittent skirmishes lasted for ten years, until 1632 when, because of mutual exhaustion, a peace treaty was agreed upon.

But Opechancanough had not given up. Again he plotted revenge, and again his warriors attacked, this time on April 18, 1644, when the chief was reported to have been over 100 years old. The Indians killed 400 to 500 English (out of a population now of about 8,000) in swift assaults on outlying settlements mostly on the York and Pamunkey rivers. The colonists, under their governor William Berkeley, soon organized and launched a counteroffensive—small groups of well-armed militiamen roamed through Indian territory, attacking and destroying villages.

In 1646, several months after his return from a trip to England to request additional arms and ammunition from the Crown, Berkeley and a force of militiamen captured Opechancanough. They carried the old, emaciated leader on his litter to Jamestown, where he was shot by an angry guard. While dying, the chief is reported to have said, "If it had been my fortune to take Sir William Berkeley prisoner, I would not have meanly exposed him as a show to my people."

BACON'S REBELLION

In the latter part of the 17th century, frontier attacks on the Indians of Virginia and Maryland grew into a rebellion against royal authority. Since 1646 and the death of Opechancanough, the fragile peace between Indians and whites had often been strained by the growing white demand for land, as well as by mutual acts of violence. In 1675, an incident flared up between settlers and Nanticoke Indians over an unpaid debt. To collect on the money owed, the Indians stole some hogs; when English settlers caught and killed those responsible, the Indians in turn killed a herdsman. Events escalated from there. The English colonists organized a force of local militia, crossed the Potomac River, and killed another 11 Nanticokes. Then they attacked a cabin of innocent Susquehannocks, murdering 14.

After retaliatory attacks on outlying English settlements by the Susquehannocks, a combined force of militia out of Virginia and Maryland surrounded the tribe's main palisaded village. When five chiefs came forward under a flag of truce to parley, some soldiers killed them. The remaining warriors slipped through the siege, killing ten sleeping militiamen on the way, and began another rampage of violence and revenge, killing five settlers for each one of their chiefs. Inquiries into the various atrocities against the Indians led to nothing more than a fine imposed on one Maryland major. Without any further restitution, the Indians continued their raids.

It was at this stage that Nathaniel Bacon became involved. A younger cousin of the 70-year-old governor of Virginia, Sir William Berkeley, Bacon had no tolerance for either royal authority or Indians. He joined a group of vigilantes who had decided to deal with the Indian problem themselves rather than wait for the further mustering of militia, and they took action against the peaceful Ocaneechi and Monacan tribes as well as against the warring Susquehannocks.

Learning of Bacon's activities, Berkeley had his cousin seized, then excused him with a warning. But the angry young Bacon led an army of frontiersmen to Jamestown, and, with the threat of violence, he coerced the Virginia House of Burgesses into commissioning him as commander in chief of the Indian war and into instituting certain economic reforms on behalf of small farmers in their dealings with the aristocracy. Bacon then set off with his followers on a campaign against the Pamunkey Indians, who had been loyal to the whites for years. The Pamunkeys fled to a hiding place in the Great Dragon Swamp between the Potomac and Rappahannock rivers. When discovered, they offered no resistance but were massacred nevertheless.

Meanwhile, in Jamestown, Governor Berkeley rescinded Bacon's commission, claiming it had been extorted from the assembly, and labeled his cousin a rebel and traitor. In response, Bacon led his rebel army from the field to Jamestown. His strategy was to use the wives of the aristocracy to shield his men while they prepared their defenses. After fierce fighting, the rebels captured the city. However, rather than trying to hold it, they put it to the torch. Shortly afterward, on October 26, 1676, Bacon died of what was described as the "bloody flux"— probably tuberculosis. Although Berkeley retook Jamestown, he was soon recalled to England for his mishandling of the entire affair.

With the end of Bacon's Rebellion, the tribes of the region were again peaceful. Ironically, hatred and maltreatment of the Indians had led to much needed civil and agricultural reforms among the settlers. As in the French and Indian Wars and the American Revolution to follow, Indians had been caught in the middle of a colonial dispute.

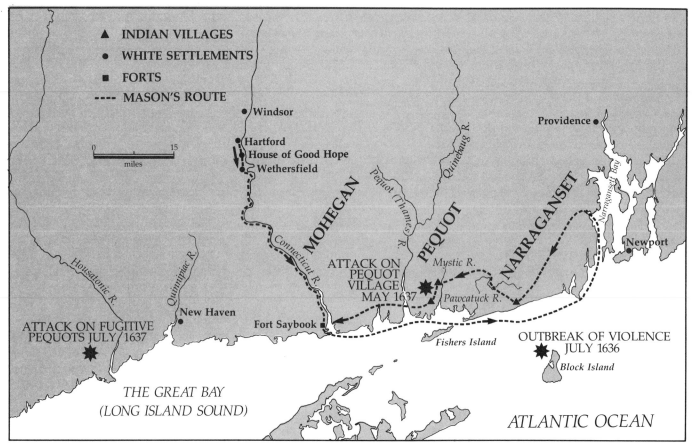

5.2 THE PEQUOT WAR, 1636–37

Map legend:
▲ INDIAN VILLAGES
● WHITE SETTLEMENTS
■ FORTS
---- MASON'S ROUTE

THE PEQUOT WAR

For more than a decade after the founding of Plymouth colony, there was peace between Indians and whites in New England. The Wampanoag sachem Massasoit, most powerful of the region's Indian leaders and loyal in his friendship to the colonists, had more to do with the state of accord than any other individual. Yet, as whites increased in number and spread out over more and more Indian land, the frictions that made war likely also mounted.

The Pequots of the Connecticut River Valley were the first to react to the pressure. Dutch settlers were progressing east and north from the Hudson River; the English west from the Atlantic Ocean; and there was the perpetual threat of the neighboring Narragansets, whom the Pequots mistrusted. As a result, the Pequots developed a defensive and contentious posture. Meanwhile, by trading

with the Dutch they had aroused the enmity of the English. Conditions were ripe for war.

The particular incidents precipitating the Pequot War involved two coastal traders—John Stone and John Oldham—and their deaths in 1633 and 1636, respectively, at the hands of Indians. It is ironic that in both instances it isn't even certain that Pequots actually committed the murders, since Niantics played a part in the first and Narragansets in the second. A shaky peace was maintained for two years after Stone's death, but it could not survive the second similar occurrence. Soon after word came from another coastal trader, John Gallup, who had happened upon Oldham's hijacked boat off Block Island and had skirmished with the Indians aboard, Massachusetts Bay officials rashly ordered a punitive attack. Captain John Endecott and 90 men descended upon Block Island and killed every Indian male they could find, mostly Narragansets as it happened, and burned their villages. Then the force sailed to the Connect-

icut mainland and, against the advice of colonists in Fort Saybrook, who feared a major war, sailed eastward along the coast in search of Pequots, to demand reparations. A minor encounter resulted near the Pequot River, and Endecott's force killed one Indian and burned several villages. Then they returned to Boston.

As the colonists at Fort Saybrook had predicted, the Pequot problem intensified and became theirs. Although the Pequot sachem Sassacus failed to achieve an alliance with the Narragansets (largely due to the intervention of Roger Williams, the founder of Rhode Island), he still went ahead with plans for war. His warriors laid siege on Fort Saybrook during the winter of 1636–37 and attacked outlying settlements wherever they could. The following spring they attacked the settlement of Wethersfield up the Connecticut River and killed nine settlers.

The colonists around New England gathered their forces. Captain John Mason, a professional soldier who had seen action in Europe, was the first in the field, with an army of 80 men out of Hartford, along with a group of Mohegan allies. During the trip south the Mohegans battled a group of Pequots, killing seven of them. At Fort Saybrook Mason's force was joined by a group of men from Massachusetts Bay under Captain John Underhill. Rather than wait for further reinforcements, the small army set out in their boats eastward along the coast. Their original plan had been to attack the Indians from the mouth of the Pequot River, but Mason decided to circle around through Narraganset country and seek additional Indian support for a surprise attack on one of the two main Pequot villages. The troops detoured east by boat to Narragansett Bay, then back west overland. Both Narragansets under Miantinomo and Niantics under Ninigret joined them.

The attack on the stockaded Pequot village took place at dawn on May 25, 1637. Mason divided his men and had them storm the stockade's two opposite gates. Although the colonial forces had the advantage of surprise, the Indians repelled the first attack. But the turning point quickly came when the colonials managed to set the Pequot wigwams on fire and then withdrew. Pequots who fled the raging flames were cut down, many by Narragansets and Mohegans waiting in the surrounding countryside. And those who stayed behind—many of them women and children—burned to death. Pequot casualties in this one battle have been estimated as more than 600, possibly even as many as 1,000. Of the colonists, two died in the attack and about 20 were wounded. Mason's force, on their way to meet the boats in Pequot Harbor, even managed to survive a surprise encounter with a Pequot war party of about 300 warriors that same night.

Mason's men were out in the field again soon afterward, as were other colonists, in search of the remaining scattered Pequots, including Sassacus, the sachem. In July 1637, one colonial force trapped a large group of Pequots hiding out in a swamp near New Haven. Sassacus and several other Indians managed to escape to Mohawk territory, only to be beheaded by members of that tribe anxious to prove to the whites that they had had no part in the Pequot uprising.

The remnants of the Pequot tribe were sold into slavery in Bermuda or divided up among the Mohegans, Narragansets, and Niantics in payment for their help. Use of the Pequot tribal name was forbidden, and Pequot place names were abolished. A once-great tribe and its culture thus perished.

KING PHILIP'S WAR

The origins of King Philip's War between the Indians and the New England colonists were complex. The central issue was land, with the growing white population always needing more of it. The region's Algonquian tribes saw their homelands shrinking as the stream of settlers fanned out from the Atlantic. And to the west lived the Algonquians' traditional enemy, the powerful Iroquois Confederacy.

When obtaining land from the Indians, the whites often managed to defraud them, leading to animosity. Even when transactions were honorable, problems resulted from the Indians failure to grasp the subtleties of English law and the concept of individual ownership of land, an idea alien to them. As far as the Indians were concerned, when they put their marks on deeds, they were granting permission for the use of the land, not ceding their own hunting and fishing rights.

But there were other issues as well, other areas of conflict. The expanding European presence also meant the dilution of Indian culture and the erosion of the Indians' economic base. Colonial missionaries zealously sought to convert the "pagans" to Christianity, creating a large number of "Praying Indians," and along with them a stressful cultural rift within Indian society. Meanwhile, English traders effected the economic subjugation of the Indians, making them dependent on European goods and at the same time saddling them with debts. Many Indians left their homelands, often because of these debts, to work in colonial towns. The resulting proximity of Indian to white led to frequent quarrels—over money, possessions, and insults imagined or real—some of which escalated into acts of violence.

When Indians committed some infraction under English law, they were dragged before colonial courts, a procedure which in itself seemed an injustice to them. They were accountable to their own people, the Indians believed, not to the Crown, and certainly not to Puritan "blue laws." For the New England Indian, humiliation piled upon humiliation, resentment upon resentment.

When a spark in the form of a proud, visionary, and dynamic leader was added to this powder keg, war became inevitable. As a boy, the Wampanoag youth Metacom had seen his father, Chief Massasoit, help the Puritan settlers, offering them land, advice on how to plant corn, and protection from other tribes. As he grew up Metacom had witnessed the mounting colonial injustices against his own and neighboring

Detail of King Philip (hypothetical) from Phelps and Ensign's Travellers' Guide and Map of the United States, *1844. Steve Child Collection.*

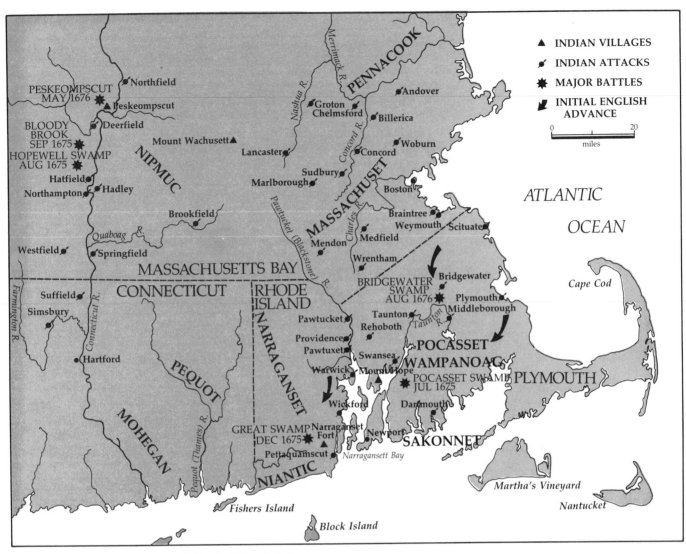

5.3 KING PHILIP'S WAR, 1675–76 *(with colonial boundaries)*

tribes as well as the ravaging effects of the whites' diseases. At the age of 24, Metacom had seen his brother Wamsutta (Alexander), first in succession to Massasoit, die at the hands of the colonists (if not intentionally poisoned, as the Indians believed, at least from disease contracted when Wamsutta was summoned before colonial officials for questioning). Then when Metacom himself had become Wampanoag *sachem*, he was arrested and subjected to harsh questioning. The Plymouth authorities, sensing the new Wampanoag militancy, resorted to harassment in the hope of controlling it.

Metacom (or "King Philip," as the colonists had come to call him) bided his time for four years, yielding when necessary, signing two treaties, even turning over Wampanoag flintlocks as the white officials demanded. His goal

was to achieve an alliance of tribes before making a move to oust the white settlers from New England. His runners journeyed to neighboring tribes in secret council, urging the end of old tribal rivalries and seeking unity of purpose.

War came in June 1675, before the hoped for alliance was in place. The arrest and subsequent hanging of three Wampanoags for the murder of a Praying Indian thought to be a spy precipitated events. Fighting first broke out in Swansea, not far from the Wampanoag village of Mount Hope, after a group of angry warriors killed some cattle. A settler drew the first human blood, wounding an Indian. At the end of the siege, however, nine settlers were dead and two more were fatally wounded.

After this first conflict, the Indians, now unrestrained, swept over other

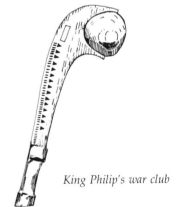

King Philip's war club

outlying settlements. Early Wampanoag successes soon induced the Nipmuc and Narraganset tribes as well as sympathetic warriors from other tribes, even from as far away as Maine, to join the fight. Small bands of Indians attacked settlements all over New England from the Atlantic Ocean to the Connecticut River.

In reaction, the New England Confederation of Massachusetts, Plymouth, Rhode Island, and Connecticut launched several armies. The first major encounter occurred in Pocasset Swamp in July 1675, as colonial forces moved in from the north. Other large-scale fighting took place in August and September along the northern portion of the Connecticut River. The decisive battle was the Great Swamp Fight near Narragansett Bay on a cold and snowy day in December 1675, when the colonists overran the Narraganset stockade.

Several factors contributed to the colonists' ultimate victory. First, they had superiority in both numbers and firepower. Moreover, they were able to make use of their Indian allies (Mohegans, Pequots, Niantics, Sakonnets, and Massachusets) as spies, scouts, and fighting men. The Iroquois also played an important part in the outcome of the war, when they drove Metacom and his warriors from their hiding place north of Albany back into New England, not giving him a chance to recoup his losses. Still another factor was the shortage of Indian food.

The war lasted another eight months after the Great Swamp Fight, with two more Indian routs, one near Deerfield in May 1676, the other near Bridgewater in August. Metacom was shot down soon after the Bridgewater Swamp Fight, betrayed by an Indian informer. His killers dismembered him and took parts of his body as trophies. Colonist forces then proceeded to track down and wipe out any remaining rebel bands until a formal truce was signed. Metacom's wife and son were sold into slavery in the West Indies for the going price of 30 shillings each, as were hundreds of other Indians; some were shipped to Spain as well. The result of the war and its aftermath was the virtual extermination of the Wampanoag, Nipmuc, and Narraganset tribes.

The era of Indian strength had come to an end in New England. The cruel pattern of racial conflict between Indian and white had now been firmly established in the New World. It was a pattern that would repeat itself time and again.

THE BEAVER WARS

The dates are uncertain. Legend blends with fact. Yet it is now thought that sometime about 1560–70, the Huron mystic Deganawida and his Mohawk disciple Hiawatha (not to be confused with Longfellow's fictional Hiawatha) founded the Iroquois Confederacy, or League of Five Nations, including the Mohawks, Oneidas, Onondagas, Cayugas, and Senecas in what is now New York State (the Tuscororas became the Sixth Nation in 1722). The primary motivation was immediate and practical: to end the incessant feuding among close neighbors and achieve an alliance against more distant tribes, thus ensuring survival. But for some—for Deganawida and Hiawatha, certainly—the vision was universal and high-minded: to establish a "Great Peace" that would eventually embrace all the Iroquois' known world. Much later this visionary Iroquois League would provide a model for America's founding fathers in the framing of the Constitution.

But for the early colonists, the League was a powerful force with which they had to contend. The French, penetrating the continent from the northeast, allied themselves with the Algonquian-speaking tribes and the Hurons (an Iroquoian people not part of the League). The Dutch, however, represented by the Dutch West India Company chartered in 1621, made an alliance with the Five Nations. Then, when the British gained control of New Netherland from the Dutch in 1664, they in turn became allies and trading partners of the League.

Trade was the key, in particular the lucrative fur trade. The European presence on the continent upset long-existing balances—the ecological balance, because of the insatiable overseas demand for beaver pelts, and the political balance, effecting new, intense rivalries among the tribes. The 17th century in the northern woods was a time of active commerce, shifting alliances, and eventually, the first large-scale intertribal warfare.

While the Huron-French trade relationship was thriving in New France (see "The Fur Trade" in chapter 4), the Five Nations to the south were depleting their own sources of pelts

The Pacification of Atotarhoh by Jesse Cornplanter, Iroquois, 1906. Deganawida and Hiawatha urge Atotarhoh to join the Iroquois League while other Iroquois flee the snake-ornamented chief. New York State Library, Albany.

and eyeing their neighbors' rich harvests. About mid-century, they decided to make a move on the Huron trade monopoly. There has been considerable debate concerning the Iroquois' motives for their relentless attacks on other Indians, theories about inherent Iroquois personality or cultural traits, the political goals of the Five Nations, the catalyzing effect of the guns supplied to them by the Dutch, and the motive of revenge against the French because of earlier attacks on the Iroquois by the French under Samuel de Champlain. Although relevant, these questions are incidental to the underlying Iroquois motivation—survival. As far as the Five Nations were concerned, if they were to survive either as a confederacy or as separate tribes, they had to replenish their diminishing supplies of furs, which had become their economic lifeblood.

The wars they undertook were long-lasting, with most of the action carried out guerrilla-style by small bands. Yet the following time-scale for major engagements can be determined. Members of the League launched a major offensive against the Hurons in March 1649, routing them easily. The Hurons burned many of their own villages as they scattered in retreat through the northern woods. Jesuit outposts, established by the French, also fell into Iroquois hands—some taken by force, others abandoned by the missionaries. Then, nine months later, the Iroquois attacked and defeated the Tobaccos. War with the Neutrals followed from 1650 to 1651; and then with the Erie, from 1653 to 1656. All these tribes, not far from Seneca territory, were practically wiped out by the aggressive Iroquois. But members of the League also carried out attacks much farther west—against the Ottawas in 1660, and against the Illinois and Miamis from 1680 to 1684. The Iroquois also raided bands of Susquehannocks, Nipissings, Potawatomis, and Delawares. And the Mohawks at the eastern door of the symbolic League longhouse uniting the Five Nations, waged war with the Mahicans of the Hudson Valley, finally making a lasting peace in 1664.

The Iroquois' failure to take the Illinois Indians' Fort St. Louis on the Illinois River in 1684 marked the end of the League's military efforts to es-

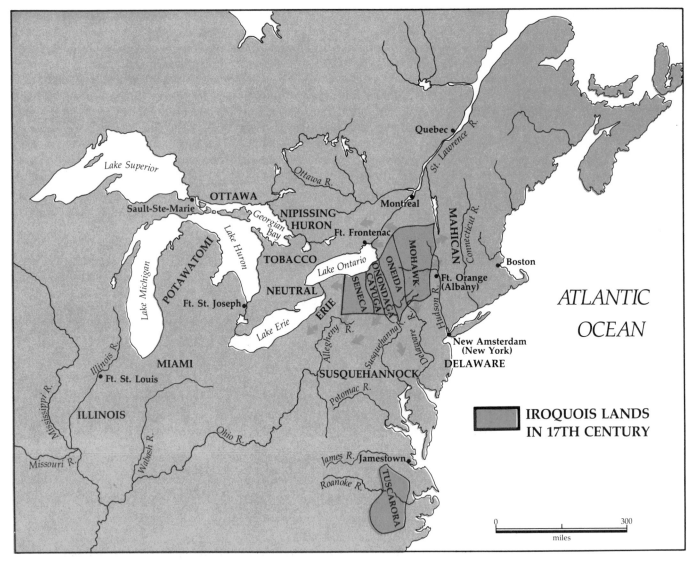

5.4 THE IROQUOIS INVASIONS, 1640–85

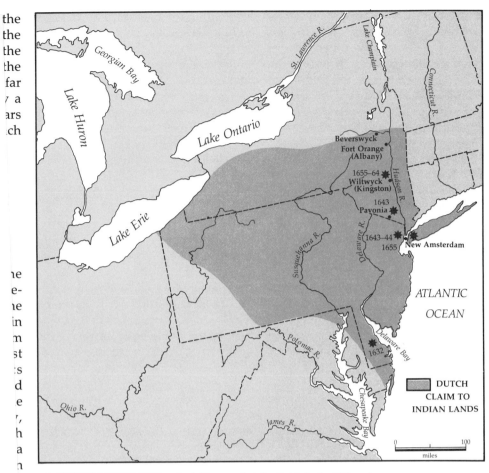

5.5 NEW NETHERLAND *and rebellions against the Dutch in the 17th century (with modern boundaries)*

the
the
the
the
far
a
ars
ch

chartered in 1621, Dutch traders began building more outposts.

The Dutch policy was to treat Indian tribes as sovereign nations and purchase land from them, which served to counter possible claims on the same land by other European countries. The Indians, unfamiliar with the European concept of land ownership and unaware to what extent they were abdicating their own rights, were happy to collect goods for granting use of their territory. Thus, in 1626, local Indians sold the Dutch rights to Manhattan island for 60 guilders worth of trade goods (although the Dutch originally purchased the island from the Canarsees, they had to renegotiate with the Manhattans who actually held the territory). Soon, both New Amsterdam on the island at the mouth of the Hudson River and Fort Orange (Albany) upriver became thriving communities.

In spite of the growing white population and concurrent racial tension,

the Dutch managed for the sake of trade to maintain their policy of neutrality with regard to tribes warring among themselves over fur territory and trade—Mohawks with Mahicans (see ''The Beaver Wars'' in this chapter) and Delawares with Susquehannocks. In 1626, four *swannekens* (the Indian word for Dutch traders) out of Fort Orange broke this policy and joined a Mahican raid on Mohawk territory, in which they lost their lives. Yet, otherwise, Hollanders weathered early unrest among the Indians, even when it was directed at them. In 1632, the Dutch West India Company chose to negotiate with the Delawares after the massacre of 32 settlers at Swaanendael on the west shore of Delaware Bay, appeasing the Indians with gifts and arranging for increased trade with them, rather than calling in the militia.

But, in the following years, this policy of neutrality, peace, and appeasement changed. First, there was a growing Dutch demand for agri-

cultural lands granted under the patroon system. Second, when coastal supplies of furs became depleted, the Dutch no longer needed the help of eastern tribes, and Indian territory was now deemed more important than Indian friendship. Third, the trade monopoly of the Dutch West India Company ended in the 1630s, bringing in a large number of independent traders and making it more difficult to regulate the frontier. Fourth, in 1639, Willem Kieft became governor-general of New Netherland, replacing Wouter Van Twiller. Kieft's solution to the Indian obstacle to Dutch expansion was harassment and extermination, and he set about the task with cruel efficiency.

His first anti-Indian act was to place a new tax, payable in corn, furs, or wampum, on downriver Indians, supposedly to defer the cost of defending them from hostile tribes. Then, in 1641, when violence flared up on Staten Island over the destruction of Raritan cornfields by Dutch livestock, Kieft offered bounties for the heads or scalps of those Indians involved. The next year, in a show of force, Kieft marched at the head of an army through Indian villages in the vicinity of New Amsterdam. And finally, in 1643, the governor-general encouraged what became known as the "Pavonia Massacre" or the "Slaughter of Innocents."

When a party of Mohawks traveled downriver to exact tribute from a band of Wappingers who had survived the Iroquois wars, the Wappingers fled to Pavonia and New Amsterdam for safety. Kieft, however, not only withheld protection and allowed the Mohawks free reign, but also, after the war party had killed 70 Indians and taken others as slaves, sent in Dutch soldiers to finish off the remaining refugees, including women and children. After a night of blood lust and violence, the soldiers returned to New Amsterdam with 80 heads and 30 prisoners. The heads were used as decorations and kickballs; the captives, who were publicly tortured to death, as entertainment.

Enraged by the massacre, bands of Indians began raiding outlying settlements from the Delaware Bay to the Connecticut River Valley. Trading and farming were disrupted all over New Netherland as settlers fled to New Amsterdam, which the Indians held in a virtual state of siege. It was at this time that inhabitants built a defensive wall in southern Manhattan where Wall Street is now located. The uprising lasted for more than a year, until an army of Dutch and English soldiers under Captain John Underhill (who had also fought in the Pequot War) began a persistent and deadly campaign throughout the countryside, tracking down and attacking bands of Indians and destroying villages and crops. At three large Indian encampments—two on Long Island and one in Connecticut—Underhill's men set the lodges on fire and massacred the fleeing inhabitants by the hundreds. By 1644, the Indians, reduced in numbers and starving, were ready to negotiate. Kieft and likeminded officials of the Dutch West India Company stopped short of ex-

termination only because of pressure from traders and farmers who wanted economic stability or who thought the merciless slaughter of Indians immoral and unchristian.

A general state of peace endured until another inflammatory incident, sometimes referred to as the Peach War, occurred in 1655. A Dutch farmer killed a Delaware woman for picking peaches in his orchard, and her family subsequently ambushed and killed the farmer. Word of the dispute spread to other Delaware bands, whose warriors gathered for further revenge. They struck at several Dutch settlements, including New Amsterdam, where they killed several whites and took as many as 150 prisoners. The new governor-general, Peter Stuyvesant, ordered out a militia army which succeeded in freeing most of the prisoners as well as destroying several Indian villages.

The violence shifted north up the Hudson. Esophus Indians rebelled against the Dutch farmers in their midst, attacking the town of Wiltwyck and surrounding settlements, with the goal of driving away the colonists once and for all. Stuyvesant's soldiers sailed upriver. Through his representatives, the governor-general sent word to the Indians, threatening the tribe with destruction unless they agreed to a council. But when a delegation of Esophus chiefs came to Wiltwyck, soldiers murdered them in their sleep. As reprisal, the Indians captured eight soldiers and burned them alive.

Intermittent warfare around Wiltwyck lasted for several years. In 1660, Stuyvesant came up with a master plan for the continuing Indian insurgency. His solution: to hold Indian children as hostages in New Amsterdam to extort good behavior from the various Delaware Indian tribes. The downriver tribes, too weak to resist, consented and permitted the taking of hostages. But Stuyvesant had to send another army to Wiltwyck to round up Esophus women and children. Esophus warriors, remembering the murder of their first delegation, refused to negotiate. Stuyvesant responded by selling Esophus hos-

tages into slavery in the Caribbean. In 1664, the Esophus finally agreed to peace when Stuyvesant called in the Mohawks to terrorize them.

That same year English troops invaded and captured New Netherland, which became New York. Dutch tenure in North America had come to an end.

THE PUEBLO REBELLION AND OTHER REBELLIONS AGAINST THE SPANISH

To the Spanish in New Mexico during the 17th century, the Indians were both serfs to exploit and souls to convert. A governor in Santa Fe, along with his officials and soldiers, ruled the territory; ranchers with land grants developed it; and Franciscan friars based within the Indian pueblos preached their brand of Catholicism. The Indians were exploited by all of them. According to the *repartimiento* system, the Indians owed the Spanish taxes in the form of labor, crops, and woven goods. (See "European Use of Indian Lands and Resources" in chapter 6.) And since they were essential to Spanish economy, the Indians were not driven from their ancestral lands as was so often the case with tribes living near British colonies. Rather, they were welcomed as if they were domestic animals existing only to serve a higher form of life. The question of whether the Indians even possessed human souls was in dispute for a time among the Spanish, until Pope Julius II decreed in 1512 that they were in fact descended from Adam and Eve. In any case, the Spanish considered the Indians heathens and, while striving to "save" them, conveniently lived off their crops and had churches built by them and amassed personal fortunes by selling their handiwork in Mexico and Europe. Moreover, the Christian formula for salvation demanded the suppression of Indian religion and ritual.

The issue of religion was the primary factor in the Pueblo Rebellion. Pueblo medicine men, compelled to practice their old ways in secret, fiercely resented the white presence. Exploitation and cruelty on the part of the Spanish were secondary causes. And the Indians had long memories for past injustices, such as the massacre of almost 1,000 Indians nearly a century before by conquistadors under Juan de Onate following a brief uprising at the Acoma Pueblo.

One medicine man by the name of Pope, a Tewa Indian from the pueblo of San Juan along the Rio Grande, was especially militant. Little is known of his early years other than that he adamantly refused to curtail his katchina worship, centered in the underground ceremonial chambers or passageways to the spirit world known as kivas, and that he refused to convert to Christianity. It is also known

that, as Spanish officials became aware of Pope, they harassed him by arresting him at least three times and even flogging him. He proudly displayed the scars on his back to other Indians as a symbol of resistance. Pope's militancy was such that he even exposed his own son-in-law as a Spanish informer and permitted his death at the hands of his angry followers, whereupon they knew that their leader would stand by his convictions whatever the cost.

Meanwhile, disputes between Spanish civil and religious officials over power and influence in the new territory had undermined the authority of both over the Indians. (In certain instances, the priests argued against lay officials on behalf of Indian rights.) Moreover, the long series of droughts beginning in 1660, as well as raids by the nomadic Apaches, gave converted Indians reason to doubt the effectiveness of the new religion as well as the impetus to revolt. And Pope provided

the leadership necessary for organized resistance and military success.

In the summer of 1680, Pope sent runners throughout the region—to Tewa, Tiwa, and Keres Indian pueblos along the Rio Grande, to Hopi and Zuni pueblos in the west, and even to Apache camps—to spread word of the coming rebellion. Each runner carried a cord of maguey fibers with a specific number of knots to indicate the number of days until the general uprising on August 11. To Christianized chiefs he didn't completely trust, Pope sent knotted cords indicating a later date, August 13. Some did in fact report Pope's plans to the friars in their pueblos, who in turn sent word to Governor Antonio de Otermin in Santa Fe. But Pope's ruse worked. Many Spanish elsewhere—priests and garrisons at pueblos, ranchers at outlying *estancias* and haciendas— were killed in surprise raids. And one pueblo after another joined the rebellion—Taos (Pope's center of op-

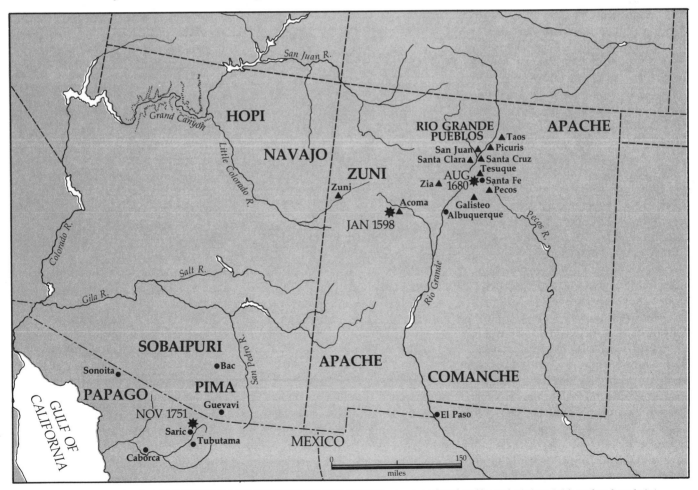

5.6 INDIAN REBELLIONS AGAINST THE SPANISH NORTH OF MEXICO, *showing selected pueblos and missions (with modern boundaries)*

erations), San Juan, Tesuque, Santa Cruz, Santa Clara, Picuris, Pecos, Galisteo, and others.

After successes elsewhere, an army of 500 Indians reached Santa Fe on August 15, where they climbed on top of the abandoned adobe buildings on the town's outskirts. Santa Fe had a garrison of only 50 professional soldiers, but they were armed with brass cannons behind the palace walls, and many citizens were armed as well. On-and-off fighting lasted for days, with the whites usually attacking first in attempts to dislodge the besieging Indians. Indian reinforcements arrived the first day from San Juan and Picuris—the latter under Pope, it is assumed. The fiercest fighting occurred on the third day, when the Indians managed to reach the town's water ditch and divert the supply, and also attack the chapel. After still one more day of indecisive fighting, the Indians finally abandoned their siege and retreated into the surrounding hills.

Several days later, on August 21, the surviving Spanish also left Santa Fe and began the long trek southward to El Paso, passing along the way many dead countrymen, burned-out ranches, and deserted pueblos. By the end of the uprising, 400 Spanish had been killed, including 21 of 33 friars; 2,500 other settlers had been driven back to Mexico. Pope and his followers had repelled a colonial power. Then they proceeded to stamp out any remnants of Spanish culture and religion.

Yet Pope's fanaticism, so critical to the success of the Pueblo Rebellion, now contributed to its undoing. Those Indians who wavered slightly from the Indian way—even, for example, by using practical Spanish goods such as tools—were punished, some even executed. With dissatisfaction growing among his followers, Pope became more and more of a despot. Living in Santa Fe, he even adopted many of the trappings and pretenses of the colonial officials before him, including use of the governor's carriage to ride about town as a symbol of power. When he died several years after the revolt, his al-

liance had all but dissolved. Other factors contributed to the dissolution of Indian unity and the weakening of the pueblos, such as continued droughts and Apache raids.

Spanish troops marching northward out of El Paso several years later met little or no resistance. Zia Pueblo fell to the Spanish in 1689; troops under the new governor of New Mexico, Don Diego de Vargas, occupied Santa Fe in 1692. The Spanish reconquest of New Mexico officially ended in 1692.

Yet, for a decade at least, the conquistadors and other purveyors of an alien culture had been stymied while the Pueblo Indians once again ruled their homeland.

The Pueblo Rebellion was not the only Indian revolt against the Spanish in what was to become the American Southwest. Almost a century before Pope's general uprising, the Indians of the Acoma Pueblo had resisted Spanish domination. During a Rio

Hopi katchina doll of wood and horsehair representing one of the twin war gods

Grande expedition in 1598, Don Juan de Onate sent squads of soldiers to the various pueblos with word that the Indians were now subjects of the Spanish monarch, and must cast off pagan ways and abide by the laws of New Spain, as ordered by official representatives. Rather than submit to

these demands, warriors in the Acoma Pueblo rose up and killed 13 of the Spanish soldiers, including three officers.

A Spanish army returned in January of the following year. Fighting lasted for three days; the royal troops scaled the rugged steep cliffs of the mesa to capture the pueblo on top. Then, after having taken Acoma, the Spanish massacred hundreds of its inhabitants in an orgy of violence. As may as 800 Indians were killed in the fighting and afterwards. Only 80 men were taken prisoner along with 500 women and children. The survivors were sentenced by Onate in a public tribunal. Males over 25 years of age were to have one foot amputated and to undergo 20 years of servitude in New Mexico. Males between 12 and 25 as well as women over 12 were to serve as slaves for 20 years. Children under 12 were to be placed in missions. Two Hopis who were present at Acoma were to have their right hands amputated and set free to spread word of the consequences of Indian revolt. After this example of Spanish colonial justice, it is no wonder that the Pueblos peacefully accepted Spanish intrusion and exploitation for another 80 years, until Pope's revolt.

Other Southwest Indians to rise up against Spanish rule were the Pimas, who practiced irrigation farming along the river valleys of what is now northern Sonora, Mexico, and southern Arizona. During the 1600s, Spanish missionaries, ranchers, miners, and presidio officials intruded upon them in the administrative district of Pimeria Alta, as they did to Indians elsewhere, trying to convert them while exploiting them through agriculture and labor levies. The Pimas of lower Pimeria Alta rebelled in 1695, with some looting and burning of Spanish property and some violence against missionaries, until Spanish soldiers and their Indian auxiliaries rode in after them.

Then, half a century later, in 1751, the Pimas of upper Pimeria Alta, many of them descendants of earlier insurgents who had fled northward, staged a second, more organized rebut not on the scale that Oacpicagigua had planned. For one, the hoped-for alliance with the Sobaipuris and Apaches never developed. And many Papagos and Pimas were too fearful of Spanish reprisals to take part in the violence.

Nonetheless, it took a Spanish army, under Governor Parilla and his presidio captains, months to subdue the rebels, partly by military action and partly by negotiations. A number of rebels were executed, including a relative of Oacpicagigua. Luis supposedly managed to save himself by agreeing to supervise the rebuilding of destroyed churches, although he never carried out his promise. The Pimas remained a recalcitrant presence, helping to slow the Spanish advance northward.

The Apaches, Navajos, and Comanches, traditional raiding peoples of the Southwest and southern Plains, also helped check Spanish expansion. Despite numerous campaigns against them and various administrative schemes, the Spanish could never completely tame these masters of guerrilla warfare. Indians of these tribes possessed a remarkable knowledge of the terrain, plus great endurance and mobility, and rarely risked open combat with a more numerous enemy. Raiding activity continued in the Southwest long after Spanish rule. Both Mexicans and Americans would later have to contend with the region's fierce and proud inhabitants.

THE FRENCH AND INDIAN WARS (The Imperial Wars)

In the late 17th and much of the 18th century, the colonial powers fought a series of wars for control of North America: King William's War (1689–97); Queen Anne's War (1702–13); King George's War (1744–48); and the French and Indian War, or the Great War for Empire (1754–63). They are usually referred to en masse by the name of the last war; i.e., the French and Indian Wars, bestowed from the Anglo-American perspective. Some scholars use a more general name—the Imperial Wars—to designate all four. Others keep the common usage—the French and Indian Wars—but refer to the last of the four as the Great War for Empire.

To add to the confusion in nomenclature, these wars in North America represent just one of many fronts in the European clash for world empire. They correspond roughly and respectively to the following wars abroad: War of the Grand Alliance; War of the Spanish Succession; War of the Austrian Succession; and the Seven Years War.

In any case, from the vantage point of all, these conflicts might just as well be viewed as one long war, broken up by periods of truce. And, in addition to those already mentioned, there were many other conflicts involving Indians during these years: the Tuscarora War (1711–13); the Yamasee War (1715–28); the Cherokee War (1760–61); the Natchez Revolt (1729–30); the Chickasaw Resistance (1720–63); and the Fox Resistance (1720–35). One can even view Pontiac's Rebellion (1763–64) and the related Paxton Riots as a part of the same war or series of wars because, after England's ultimate victory (and to a lesser degree Spain's) against France in North America, it was mostly tribes previously allied with France who rebelled against the now dominant colonial power, England.

As for the Indians and their involvement in the French and Indian Wars, in the broad historical sense they can be regarded as pawns in the long world power struggle. But, during the many conflicts, they were often willing players, choosing sides based on what they considered their best interests in protecting their territories, maintaining trade, or settling old intertribal scores. Moreover, they often fought on one side or another for what the whites offered them—bounties for scalps, regular pay and rations, firearms and blankets. And, as allies in war, the Indians were worth any price. Success in land battles more often than not hinged on their involvement. Yet, whatever the resulting political realignment among the growing white population, the Indians were of course the ultimate losers.

KING WILLIAM'S WAR

War between England and France developed in North America out of economic and territorial competition. The Iroquois League of Five Nations, after their series of wars with other tribes (see "The Beaver Wars" in this chapter), now dominated the western fur trade. With the Dutch out of power, the Iroquois market of choice was the British, who had generally cheaper and higher quality goods to trade. The French in turn resented the growing English-Iroquois fur monopoly, as well as the intrusion by British traders and colonists into lands west of the Appalachians that they had recently claimed. The French knew that the powerful, strategically located Iroquois League was the key to commercial and military dominance in the region. They began a campaign of pressure on the Iroquois member nations to force, if not an Iroquois-French alliance, then at least Iroquois neutrality. The English for their part feared French encroachment from the north, abetted by the powerful Abnaki confederacy of tribes, into New England.

The precipitating incidents of the war involved Abnakis as well as Iroquois. In Maine, Abnakis were enraged when Sir Edmund Andros, the governor of England's northern colonies, led a company of soldiers against the trading post of their friend Baron de St. Castin on Penobscot Bay in 1688, demanding his submission to the English Crown. Next, settlers in Saco, Maine, seized 16 Indians for killing livestock, whereupon Abnakis

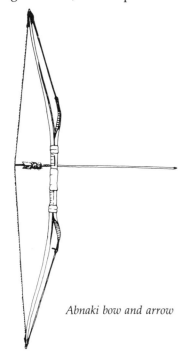

Abnaki bow and arrow

seized a number of settlers, leading to bloodshed on both sides and stepped-up Abnaki raids. (This action and others in the French and Indian Wars are sometimes referred to collectively as the Abnaki Wars.)

Meanwhile, an Iroquois raid in 1689 on the settlement of Lachine along the St. Lawrence River, in which about 200 French colonists were killed and 120 more taken prisoner, gave the French motivation for what the governor of New France, the Comte de Frontenac, called "la petite guerre," or guerrilla-style fighting, against Iroquois and English settlements.

5.7 THE FRENCH AND INDIAN WARS, 1689–1763, *showing tribes plus selected settlements and forts involved in the various conflicts*

Then, in 1690, Frontenac launched a large-scale three-pronged assault into New York, New Hampshire, and Maine, with the purpose of gaining the early military advantage against the English and convincing the Iroquois it was to their advantage to make peace with the French. The Albany party of French Canadian woodsmen and mission Indians, after an arduous winter trek, decided to attack the smaller settlement of Schenectady instead of Albany, killing 60. Frontenac's second force carried out an attack against Salmon Falls, New Hampshire, killing 34 English. In the third action, a combined army of French and Abnakis captured Fort Loyal (Falmouth), Maine, killing more than 100 settlers.

These were small victories, how-

ever, and not enough to bring about Frontenac's hoped-for realignment of power. The Iroquois stayed in the English camp. And England retaliated with a successful naval attack led by Sir William Phipps against Port Royal in French L'Acadie (now Annapolis Royal in Nova Scotia). In a second naval expedition, however, Phipps was unable to take Quebec, his fleet repelled by French cannon.

The following year Benjamin Church, who had also fought in King Philip's War, led a force of 300 into Maine and harassed the Abnakis until they sued for peace. Yet, in 1692, the short-lived truce ended as Indians and French raided York, Maine, killing 48 English and capturing 70 others. The self-perpetuating cycle of raids and counterraids continued.

Finally, in 1697, England and France ended the inconclusive, costly war, signing the Treaty of Ryswick. The French, however, kept up their pressure on the Iroquois and eventually effected their neutrality. First the Oneidas agreed to peace with New France, followed by the Onondagas, Senecas, Cayugas, and, by 1700, the Mohawks.

QUEEN ANNE'S WAR

In 1702, the French had the support of the trans-Appalachian Indians, the promised neutrality of the Iroquois League, the extensive northern territory of New France, settlements on the Gulf of Mexico, and an alliance with the Spanish in Florida. When war again broke out in Europe, it seemed that they held the advantage on the North American battlefield. Nevertheless, in Queen Anne's War as in the earlier King William's War, they could not prevail over the more numerous English colonists.

Because of the recent Iroquois neutrality in New York, most of the fighting occurred in New England, again with frequent Abnaki attacks on frontier settlements. Deerfield, the northernmost settlement on the Connecticut River, was again sacked, as it had been in both King Philip's War and King William's War. Abnakis out of Maine and Mohawks from the Caughnawaga settlement in Quebec killed 49 English settlers and took at least another 100 captive. And once again, the old and now obese Benjamin Church led an army northward in counterraids against French and Indians.

Hard-pressed, the English lobbied for reinvolvement of the Iroquois in forays to Canada. Colonel Peter Schuyler even took three Mohawks and one Mahican to England in 1710, to meet Queen Anne in the hope of winning them over to the English cause, as well as gaining further military backing from the Crown.

Meanwhile, to the south, the French endeavored to gain military support from the Choctaws, Cherokees, Creeks, and Chickasaws by

means of bribery. They had success with the Choctaws and certain bands of Creeks who proceeded to disrupt the Carolina–lower Mississippi trade routes. But the Cherokees remained neutral for the time being, and the Chickasaws, who had been on trading terms with the English for years, stayed in the British camp, creating a balance of power.

In 1702, a British naval expedition plundered the Spanish settlement of Saint Augustine on Florida's eastern coast. The following year, a land expedition of Carolina militia under James Moore moved against Spanish missions among the Apalachees of West Florida. After having butchered many, the British carried away almost all the Indian inhabitants of seven villages, practically destroying the tribe in the process. In 1706, at Charleston, the English repelled a combined French and Spanish fleet.

A state of war continued. In 1710, after Queen Anne had sent the hoped-for reinforcements, the English launched a successful naval attack on Port Royal (Annapolis Royal). But a subsequent naval expedition the next year, under Sir Hovendon Walker, failed when his fleet was shipwrecked in a fog at the mouth of the St. Lawrence. Sixteen hundred sailors and crew died.

Representatives of the European nations negotiated the Treaty of Utrecht in 1713, in which the war-weary and debt-ridden King Louis XIV of France ceded Hudson Bay and Acadia to the English. That same year the Abnakis sued for peace with the New Englanders, pledging their alliance to Queen Anne. But, as before, peace was tenuous and only temporary.

KING GEORGE'S WAR

The so-called War of Jenkins's Ear, between England and Spain in the West Indies from 1739 to 1741, did not involve any Indian tribes, but it led to the later European War of the Austrian Succession and its North American phase, King George's War. The incident which precipitated England's

declaration of war, giving this preliminary small-scale conflict its name, involved a Robert Jenkins, master of the ship *Rebecca*, who claimed that Spanish coast guards had cut off his ear while interrogating him. The underlying cause of the war was the commercial rivalry between the two world sea powers.

Meanwhile, in the North, after Queen Anne's war, Iroquois leaders had expressed their concern to British officials that, despite their neutral stance in the ongoing wars between the imperial powers, the French and their Indian allies would overrun Iroquois territory from the north to reach English settlements on the lower Hudson. As a result, the English built Fort Oswego on Lake Ontario's eastern shore as well as other posts, to block possible invasion routes. The French, claiming that these northern forts were on their territory, in turn built Fort St. Frederick at Crown Point on the western shore of Lake Champlain. In 1744, when war in Europe again led to hostilities in the North American colonies—King George's War—Fort St. Frederick became a major staging post for repeated Indian and French raids on New York and New England frontier settlements.

In 1746 and 1747, the French launched two major inland offensives against settlements in New York and Massachusetts. They captured both Fort Saratoga and Fort Massachusetts, and dragged many of the vanquished to Canada. But Fort Number Four (Charlestown, New Hampshire), defended by only 30 militiamen, managed to repel the invaders.

It was during this period that the Irish-born fur trader and land speculator, William Johnson, who had come to North America in the 1730s to manage his uncle's estates in the Mohawk Valley, actively began seeking Iroquois support, in particular that of the Mohawks, among whom he had settled. Because of his efforts, a group of Mohawks ended their neutrality and accompanied Johnson's colonial force in a foray against Fort St. Frederick. Disputes in Albany over frontier defense appropriations as well as a lack of military coordination with other colonial forces undermined this operation. But Johnson continued to contribute to the war effort by privately financing small, successful raids on French supply lines. And in the French and Indian War to follow, his friendship with the Iroquois would prove critical to ultimate English victory.

Meanwhile, to the south, pro-English Chickasaws and Cherokees warred with the Choctaws and the Creeks, disrupting French trade routes. (See "The Chickasaw Resistance" in this chapter.) But the major military activity in King George's War occurred in Nova Scotia. In 1744, French troops under Joseph Duvivier failed to capture Port Royal (Annapolis Royal). In 1745, a Massachusetts-planned expedition of 4,200 New Englanders under William Pepperrell, with only minimal assistance from royal regular troops, captured the French stronghold of Louisbourg after two months of siege and bombardment. In 1746, a French fleet out of Europe, under the Duc d'Anville, ran into trouble along Nova Scotia's rugged, fogbound coast and also failed to take Port Royal. And, in 1747, a land force out of Beaubassin, under Coulon de Villiers, took the English fort at Grand Pre.

A peace accord was finally reached at Aix-la-Chapelle in 1748. Much to the dismay of the colonists who had fought so hard to take Louisbourg, the fort was given back to the French in exchange for Madras in India.

And once again, as was the case with King William's War and Queen Anne's War, peace was only fleeting.

THE FRENCH AND INDIAN WAR
(The Great War for Empire)

What most historians call the French and Indian War was really the final conflict in a long series of wars among the European colonial powers for world dominance. After a period of peace, undeclared war began again in North America in 1754. Two years of colonial fighting precipitated the Seven Years War in Europe, which lasted from 1756 to 1763. The French and Indian War (a name sometimes applied in plural to all the colonial North American wars since 1689) was the most extensive and most decisive of all the wars, with France losing its hold in the New World. It is therefore sometimes referred to as the Great War for Empire.

Competition over the Ohio Valley triggered this latest colonial military struggle. The English staked their claim to the region on the basis of two treaties: the Treaty of Lancaster (1744) with the Iroquois, who had earlier claimed the area by right of conquest over other tribes; and the Treaty of Logstown (1748) with the Shawnees, Delawares, and Wyandots, negotiated by George Croghan, a Pennsylvania trader. After land grants to the Ohio Company of Virginia in 1749, English adventurers, traders, and settlers began trickling into the Forks of the Ohio region, whereupon France reasserted its territorial claims.

A force of Ottawa and Ojibway warriors under the French trader Charles Langlade moved against the Ohio center of English trade, Pickawillany (near present-day Piqua, Ohio), in 1752; they killed the Miami chief Demoiselle and 13 of his warriors, plus a trader, capturing three other traders. Then the governor of New France, Marquis Duquesne, sent out a force of Frenchmen and Indians to fortify the region. The expedition constructed a chain of posts from Lake Erie to the Forks of the Ohio, including Presqu'Isle (Erie, Pa.), Fort Le Boeuf (Waterford), and Fort Venango (Venango). At this show of power, Indian tribes began returning to the French fold despite the trade advantages the English offered (less expensive and better-quality goods). Among the pro-French Indians in the region for the time being were members of the Ottawa, Algonkin, Wyandot, Nipissing, Ojibway, Potawatomi, Sauk, Shawnee, and Seneca tribes. And the Delawares, who had lost their lands in the east to earlier English expansion and Iroquois aggression, and who now feared the same in the Ohio Valley, likewise offered their backing to the French. With their much smaller colonial population, the French were considered less of a threat to Indian land tenure than the British.

In the fall of 1753, Governor Robert Dinwiddie of Virginia ordered out a force of militiamen, under a 21-year-old major by the name of George Washington, to inform the French garrison at Fort Le Boeuf that their post was situated on English soil. The French, however, refused to leave. The following spring, Governor Dinwiddie sent in a party of woodsmen to build a fort at the junction of the Ohio, Allegheny, and Monongahela rivers (the Forks of the Ohio), as well as a second detachment of reinforcements, again under Washington. Dinwiddie tried to enlist Cherokee, Chickasaw, and Catawba warriors for the expedition but, because of a dispute with fellow colony South Carolina over trade relations with the southern Indians, he failed to do so. Washington, however, managed to secure the help of Chief Half-King and other Mingos at Great Meadows.

On learning that a French patrol was nearby in the Allegheny Mountains, Washington took the offensive with a detachment of 40 provincials plus 12 Mingos; they killed 10 Frenchmen, including a French ambassador, and captured 20 others. The French later charged that their patrol had been on a mission of peace; Washington claimed, however, that the French had indicated hostile intent. In any case, with this minor frontier incident, a world war had begun. In response to Washington's action, the French ousted Dinwiddie's building party from the Forks of the Ohio site; renamed the new post there Fort Duquesne (later Fort Pitt, then Pittsburgh); and, using it as a base of operations, launched an army of 900, including some Delawares, Ottawas, Wyandots, Algonkins, Nipissings, Abnakis, and Mission Iroquois, under Major Coulon de Villiers.

Meanwhile, Washington's men had retreated to Great Meadows, where they constructed Fort Necessity. The

French force attacked during a rainstorm that rendered the English swivel guns useless, and Fort Necessity capitulated. The French allowed Washington and his men, many of them sick and wounded, to march out of the Ohio Valley and back to Virginia. The French, for the time being, had control of the region.

The English recognized the importance of the Iroquois tribes to military success in the north. William Johnson, the New York trader and land speculator who had built Fort Johnson among the Indians of the Mohawk River Valley, kept up his efforts to enlist Iroquois support. Trusted by the Indians because of his sincere admiration for them, his participation in their ceremonies, his ties to them through Indian women, and his more-than-fair trade practices, he made some headway despite their misgivings about being drawn into another colonial conflict. Johnson won over Chief Hendrick (one of the Mohawks who had traveled in 1710 to meet Queen Anne and whose daughter was one of Johnson's mistresses). Then he traveled westward to the village of Onondaga to argue his case before other tribal representatives. In 1754, at Johnson's suggestion, the provincial governors set up a commission under the authority of the Lords of Trade and Plantations to meet with Iroquois leaders at the Albany Congress. But the Iroquois, other than Chief Hendrick's Mohawks, still refrained from any firm commitment.

To the south, the English received valuable help from the Chickasaws who continued to disrupt French trade routes, as well as some support from Creeks and Cherokees. The Choctaws, as always, were pro-French, as were certain Creek bands.

During the first years of war until 1758, the French and their many Indian allies dominated the fighting and thwarted the Duke of Cumberland's master plan for total victory. In 1755, an army of 2,000 regulars and militiamen under General Edward Braddock, along with his aide-de-camp George Washington, set out to capture Fort Duquesne. But a predominantly Indian force less than half that size, under Captain Hyacinth de Beaujeu, massacred Braddock's men in a surprise crossfire before they even reached the post. Less than 500 English escaped to Fort Cumberland; Braddock himself died from wounds.

In a second thrust, a force of New Englanders and Mohawks under William Johnson and Chief Hendrick approached Crown Point on Lake George. They too were ambushed before they reached their destination, by French regulars and some western Iroquois under the German army veteran Baron Ludwig Dieskau. Hendrick was killed in this engagement. But after a retreat southward, Johnson rallied his men at the Battle of Lake George and repelled the French, even capturing Dieskau. Johnson then directed the building of Fort William Henry on the battle site. He later received a knighthood for turning what seemed a certain defeat into an English victory. But for the Mohawks the win was a bitter one: Not only had they lost their leader, but they had fought fellow Iroquois.

The English were also able to claim a victory on the Bay of Fundy, where Colonel Robert Moncton and an outfit

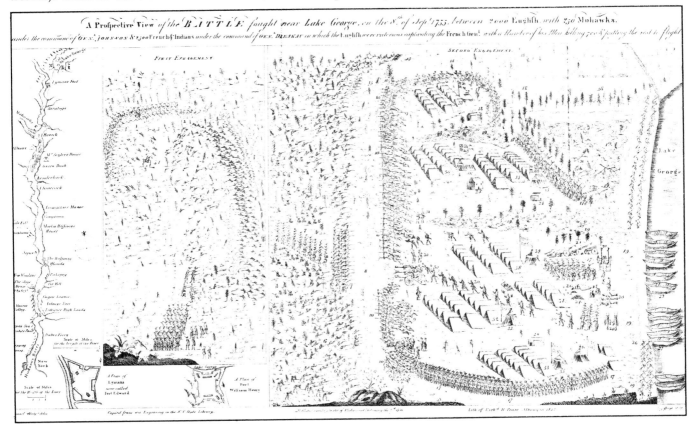

The Battle for Lake George, 1755. New York State Library, Albany.

of New Englanders captured Fort Beausejour. Many of the Acadian settlers in the area, because of their proximity to New England, were consequently rounded up and deported in small groups to various English colonies. Some, however, escaped to Louisiana, where their descendants live today.

A fourth force, under Governor William Shirley of Massachusetts, failed to take Fort Frontenac and Fort Niagara on Lake Ontario. The French had learned of the impending attack from Braddock's captured papers, which referred to Cumberland's master plan, and were prepared to counterattack with superior forces. As a result, Shirley called off his offensive and, after reinforcing Fort Oswego, directed his men back to Albany.

Even with reinforcements, Fort Oswego fell to French and Indian troops led by the Marquis de Montcalm in 1756. And, the following year, his men took Fort William Henry on Lake George, subsequently razing it rather than trying to hold it. The pro-French Indians in this expedition ignored the terms of surrender and massacred many English prisoners.

Yet, in 1758, the fortunes of war began to shift. William Pitt, prime minister and secretary of state of England, also served as commander in chief of the military. In July, sea and land units under Lord Jeffrey Amherst captured Louisbourg in Acadia (Nova Scotia). In August, royal and colonial troops under Colonel John Bradstreet also took Fort Frontenac on Lake Ontario. In November, General John Forbes's troops seized Fort Duquesne which had been abandoned by the French. The one French success that year occurred at Ticonderoga on Lake George, where Montcalm's army managed to repel an attack led by General James Abercrombie along with William Johnson and 300 Mohawks. But, the next year, Ticonderoga also fell to Amherst's army and became a center of operations for repeated raids into Canada by Major Robert Rogers and his Rangers. And an army of 1,400 under General John Prideaux, plus some 900 Mohawks under Johnson, captured

Fort Niagara. All these British victories were aided by England's naval blockade of Atlantic shipping lanes.

Finally, in 1759, a British army under General James Wolfe, and 200 ships under Vice Admiral Charles Saunders, defeated Montcalm at Quebec. Both Wolfe and Montcalm died in the fighting. Montreal fell the following year to Amherst and Johnson's Mohawks. Thus ended all hope for French victory. In the Treaty of Paris, signed three years later at the conclusion of the European Seven Years War, France ceded New France and all of its territories east of the Mississippi to England, ceding West Louisiana (except New Orleans) to its ally Spain, as compensation for Florida, which was passed from Spain to England. There would be further shuffling of these territories in the years to come. Yet France would never again be a major colonial force in North America.

As for the Indians, those who had thrown their support to France would now have to cope with the victorious English. But even those tribes who had backed England were in a weakened position, since the English colonists no longer needed them to fight their war.

REBELLIONS AGAINST THE ENGLISH (During the French and Indian Wars)

THE TUSCARORA WAR

The Tuscaroras of North Carolina, although friendly to the colonists, had suffered at their hands for years. Frontier traders commonly debauched them with liquor, then defrauded them; settlers squatted on their best lands; slavers kidnapped them. When a group of Swiss colonists under Baron Christoph von Graffenried drove them off a tract of land without payment in 1711, the Tuscaroras in retaliation raided set-

tlements between the Neuse River and Pamlico Sound, killing 200 whites, 80 of them children. Graffenried himself was captured and promised not to make war on the Tuscaroras if released. But a settler by the name of William Brice took matters into his own hands. He captured a local chief and roasted him alive. The Corees and other small tribes in the region soon joined the Tuscaroras in further hostilities.

North Carolina sought help from its sister colony, South Carolina. Colonel John Barnwell led a force of 30 militiamen and 500 Indians, many of them Yamasees, against rebel villages. Then, in 1712, with an additional force of North Carolinians, Barnwell attacked the main Tuscarora village, where King Hancock lived. Failing to take it with his first assault, Barnwell returned to New Bern. But the North Carolina Assembly ordered him back for a second attempt. This time, Hancock agreed to sign a treaty, which Barnwell and his men soon violated by taking as slaves a group of Indians they encountered outside the village. The war continued.

In 1713, another colonial army, under Colonel James Moore and including 1,000 Indian allies, marched into Tuscarora territory and attacked the main force of insurgents, killing or capturing hundreds. The 400 prisoners were sold into slavery, at 10 pounds sterling each, to finance the campaign. The survivors of Moore's campaign fled northward and settled among the five tribes of the Iroquois League. In 1722, the league officially recognized them as the Sixth Nation.

THE YAMASEE WAR

Two years after the Tuscarora War, in 1715, the Yamasees of South Carolina also rebelled against the English. Long allies of the whites, even fighting for them against other Indians, they became incensed by degrading maltreatment and exploitation—insults, fraud, forced labor in the wilderness, the encouragement of hopelessly huge debts through rum handouts, and the seizure of wives and children for the slave market to settle those debts. The Yamasees plotted their revenge.

On Good Friday, April 15, 1715, the Yamasees along with Catawbas and other neighboring tribes, launched a well-coordinated attack on traders and settlers, killing more than a hundred and driving many others to the port city of Charleston. Charles Craven, the governor of South Carolina, organized a militia army and, in two campaigns during the summer and fall, he routed and massacred the insurgents almost to the point of tribal extermination. The few survivors fled southward to Spanish Florida.

With the appropriation of Indian lands after the Yamasee War and the Tuscarora War before it, practically all the territory in the Carolinas east of the Appalachians was open to white settlement. And Governor Craven achieved an alliance with the Cherokees to the south, which effectively neutralized the powerful Creek nation. Yet the Cherokees would themselves stage a similar uprising decades later.

THE CHEROKEE WAR

In the early 1760s, the Cherokees of Virginia, the Carolinas, and Georgia had good reason to be apprehensive. They had agreed to supply warriors in the French and Indian War in exchange for a colonial commitment to protecting their families back home from hostile Creeks and Choctaws. But along with this commitment came new colonial frontier posts and garrisons, and interference in Cherokee affairs. And soon after the posts came land-grabbing settlers.

Yet, even with these pressures, the Cherokees probably would not have gone to war against their former allies without a precipitating incident. On returning home through the mountains of West Virginia after helping the English take Fort Duquesne, a group of Cherokees captured some wild horses. Virginia frontiersmen who happened along claimed the horses as theirs and attacked the

Cherokees, killing 12. Then they sold the horses and collected bounties on the scalps, which they said they had taken off enemy Indians. In retaliation, the Cherokees killed more than 20 settlers and declared their independence from English colonial rule.

The conflict lasted two years. It took two armies to defeat the Cherokees. The first—which consisted of 1,500 Scottish Highlanders who had recently fought against French forces and was commanded by Colonel Archibald Montgomery—met heavy guerrilla resistance from Cherokee warriors under Oconostota. After having expelled the regulars, the Cherokees laid siege on Fort Loudon, eventually capturing the starving garrison.

Then, after a period of truce, an army of Carolina Rangers, British light infantry, Royal Scots, and a number of Indian troops set out on a campaign of destruction in Cherokee territory, burning towns and crops. The Cherokees continued to fight from their mountain hideouts, but finally, war-weary and starving, the insurgents agreed to a peace pact with colonial officials, in which they were forced to cede large portions of their eastern lands and to agree to a boundary separating them from the whites.

REBELLIONS AGAINST THE FRENCH (During the French and Indian Wars)

THE NATCHEZ REVOLT

In 1729, the Natchez Indians of the lower Mississippi Valley, the last remnants of the great Temple Mound Building culture of the Southeast, revolted against the French living in their midst. At various times since La Salle's voyage of exploration in 1682 and the subsequent French settlement, acts of violence on the part of both the French and Indians had strained their relationship. To ensure the peace, the French had constructed Fort Rosalie on the bluffs of the Mississippi overlooking the Natchez Great Village. French officials were aided in their diplomatic efforts by the much-loved and peaceful Tattooed Serpent, brother of the supreme ruler known as the Great Sun. But, in the period following the death of Tattooed Serpent, when the Louisiana governor, Sieur Chepart, ordered that

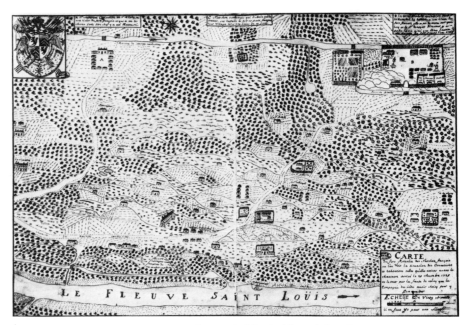

Fort Rosalie before the Natchez War of 1729. Public Archives of Canada.

the Great Village itself be evacuated for his new plantation site, the Natchez rulers met in secret council to choose a course of action. Despite the protestations of the influential pro-French queen mother, Tattooed Arm, the rulers decided on war.

At the time of the first autumn frost, Natchez bands struck at the French in Fort Rosalie and throughout the Mississippi Valley, killing about 250 and taking 300 prisoner. After the capture of Chepart, Natchez warriors would not defile their weapons with his blood and had a member of their lowest caste, a Stinkard, club him to death. Although the Choctaw Indians had promised to join the Natchez, they eventually fought for the French. The Yazoos, however, joined in the uprising, killing a French missionary and the entire French garrison.

In retaliation, the French launched two invasions out of New Orleans into Natchez territory, decimating the tribe. Many captured Natchez were sold into slavery in Santo Domingo. Some survivors settled among neighboring tribes—especially among the Chickasaws, Creeks, and Cherokees—where they gained reputations as mystics because of their ancient Southern Cult religion. Other small bands, hiding out along the Mississippi, continued their resistance against the French.

THE CHICKASAW RESISTANCE

In 1720, when the Chickasaws insisted on maintaining trade with the English and allowing English traders on what the French considered their territory along the Mississippi River, the French sent their Choctaw allies against them. The Chickasaw retaliated with raids on Choctaw villages and on French river traffic, disrupting commerce. In order to break the blockade, the French then offered the Choctaws bounties of firearms and ammunition for Chickasaw scalps. Finally, after four years of persistent Chickasaw raids, French officials arranged a peace treaty with the tribe.

Yet it was only temporary. In 1732,

the Chickasaws refused renewed French demands to expel British traders from their villages along with Natchez survivors from the Natchez Revolt of 1729, whereupon the French again unleashed Choctaw warriors as well as Indians brought in from the Illinois Country. But in 1734, the Chickasaws, striking back, managed to halt commerce on the Mississippi again.

Governor Bienville of Louisiana undertook a military campaign against the Chickasaws in 1736. An army of 400 French regulars and Indian auxiliaries under Major Pierre d'Artaguette approached from the north along the Mississippi; a second army of 600 French and roughly 1,000 Choctaws under Bienville advanced from the south along the Tombigbee. But the two forces failed to meet as planned and were defeated in separate Chickasaw attacks. An army of 3,000 under Bienville three years later failed even to launch an attack because of heavy rains. And still one more invading French army was repelled by the Chickasaws in 1752. At the time of the surrender of New France to England in 1763, the Chickasaws were unvanquished.

THE FOX RESISTANCE

During the early 1700s, the Fox Indians of Wisconsin and Illinois warred against the French and the Ojibways, who were traditional allies of the French and had been armed by them. Because of Fox attacks on Lake Michigan, the upper Mississippi River, and along the portage routes connecting them, trade between New France and Louisiana was disrupted as well as trade between the French and Ojibways.

During the 1720s, the French met in a series of councils to find a solution to the persistent Fox raids. Some officials recommended extermination of the tribe; others, the relocation of the insurgents to a site near Detroit where garrisoned soldiers could keep an eye on them. The latter course was chosen and several French-Ojibway campaigns were launched to round up

hostile bands. Even so, Fox resistance continued well into the 1730s.

Of the many Algonquian-speaking peoples in and around New France, the Fox were the only ones to war with the French.

PONTIAC'S REBELLION

With the fall of Montreal in 1760 and the subsequent French surrender of forts in the Great Lakes region, the tribes of what was then called the Northwest (and later, by historians, the Old Northwest) came under British authority. Most of the Indians assumed at the time that the changing of flags and garrisons at the posts would have little effect on their relationships with whites—that they would continue to receive supplies as they had from the French in exchange for their friendship and use of their land. Colonial representatives who met with them, including Major Robert Rogers, Captain Donald Campbell at Fort Detroit, the trader George Croghan, and Sir William Johnson, also believed such a policy would be maintained by the British and went on record as recommending it in order to keep the peace with the Indians.

Yet Lord Jeffrey Amherst, the British commander-in-chief for America, believed instead that the best way to control Indians was through a system of strict regulations and punishment when necessary, not "bribery," as he called the granting of provisions. So much for diplomacy in the new post-French order. With the discontinuation of supplies came growing Indian resentment. Why should they now be deprived of emergency supplies that had enabled them to survive other winters? How could they hunt without fresh supplies of powder and lead? Why should they share their homelands with whites without a fair exchange? The Indians also sensed a superior and imperious attitude among the British settlers. Intermingling and intermarriage between races—practices common during the

French tenure—was now discouraged.

At the eastern reaches of the Old Northwest, Amherst also granted Seneca lands near Niagara to some of his officers as reward for service in the French and Indian War. Although the grants were overruled in London, the Indians recognized and feared the British pattern of land appropriation and settlement. The Senecas even sent war belts—strings of wampum requesting help—to other tribes in the region, urging a united stand. Nothing came of this early incident, however. No leader had yet emerged to bring the various war-weary tribes together and inspire them to new action. But a leader soon would arise, an individual with a commanding presence, spellbinding oratorical power, strategic shrewdness, and long-term vision: Pontiac, an Ottawa chief.

Little is known of Pontiac's early years, other than that he was born in an Ottawa village, that he had previously fought for the French against the British, and that he had the respect of many Indian tribes for his bravery. As discontentment grew among the Indians, so did Pontiac's following. Like Tecumseh and Black Hawk to follow—other leaders who would try to forge Indian alliances—he had the help of a spiritual messenger, in his case a man known to history only as the Delaware Prophet. The Prophet claimed communication with the Master of Life, and in a revivalist style he preached a return to traditional Indian customs, even excluding the use of firearms. His anti-white stand captured the imagination of many of the Great Lakes and Ohio Valley Indians. Pontiac preached the same message of Indian unity, but allowed for friendship with French *habitants* and the use of guns. The French for their part gave Pontiac

their tacit support in any military endeavor against the English. And French backing of course helped Pontiac's cause with other Indians.

Rumors of war reached Amherst through informers among both the Indians and the French, and through the extensive networks of traders. He sent reinforcements to Detroit—a force of Royal Americans and Queen's Rangers under Major Henry Gladwin, who took over command of the fort from Captain Campbell.

Informers also eliminated any element of surprise in Pontiac's original plan in taking Detroit. He had hoped to attack with his braves—their weapons concealed beneath blankets—during a council in May 1763. But, because of the garrison's readiness, he withheld the signal. Pontiac planned a second attack, attempting to gain entry to the fort with even a larger armed force, under the pretense of smoking the peace pipe. But

5.8 PONTIAC'S REBELLION AND THE PAXTON RIOTS, 1763–64

Gladwin foiled this ruse by allowing only small groups of Indians to enter at any one time. With his warriors restless and beginning to doubt his judgment, Pontiac ordered a siege of the fort and attacks on surrounding settlements. Then he sent war belts to the chiefs of other tribes. This time they were ready. War had once again come to the northwestern wilderness.

It is estimated that 2,000 settlers died that spring and summer. British forts fell throughout the region. Ottawas and Wyandots took Fort Sandusky on the south shore of Lake Erie; Potawatomis took Fort St. Joseph (Niles, Michigan); Miamis captured Fort Miami (Fort Wayne, Indiana); Miamis, Kickapoos, Weas, and Peorias took Fort Ouiatenon (Lafayette, Indiana); Ojibways captured Fort Michilimackinac (Mackinac); Ottawas forced the abandonment of Fort Edward Augustus (Green Bay, Wisconsin); and to the east in Pennsylvania, Senecas, with the help of Ottawas, Wyandots, and Ojibways, took Fort Venango (Franklin), Fort Le Boeuf (Waterford), and Presqu'Isle (Erie).

Other Indian successes included the defeat of Lieutenant Abraham Cuyler's command, which carried supplies in *bateaux* from Niagara to Detroit via Lake Erie. Fifty-six of the 96-man complement died at Point Pelee on May 28. A second, smaller detachment out of Fort Michilimackinac also was defeated early on in the war. Then, at the end of July, Captain James Dalyell, who had managed to get through to Detroit with reinforcements, was defeated at Bloody Run when he tried to foray out against Pontiac's warriors. Twenty of 247 British troops died, incuding Dalyell; 34 more were wounded.

One of the few British victories occurred early in August, south of Lake Erie at Bushy Run. A relief force of 460 men under Colonel Henry Bouquet on the way to Fort Pitt (Pittsburgh) out of Carlisle were attacked by Delawares, Shawnees, Wyandots, and Mingos. By feigning panic, Bouquet's men drew the Indians into a trap and, despite heavy losses, routed them. Two of the Indians killed were Delaware chiefs.

Bouquet's force then helped Fort Pitt hold out against siege. Before his arrival, Captain Simeon Ecuyer had bought time by sending smallpox-infected blankets and handkerchiefs to the Indians surrounding the fort—an early example of biological warfare—which started an epidemic among them. Amherst himself had encouraged this tactic in a letter to Ecuyer. Fort Ligonier and Fort Bedford also managed to last the summer, as did Detroit. The schooner *Huron* broke through Indian lines along the Detroit River in early August, bringing in fresh men and supplies to this important frontier post.

The Indian inability to take Detroit was in fact a primary factor in the dissolution of Pontiac's confederacy, in spite of all the other successes. As winter approached, many of Pontiac's warriors began to lose faith in ultimate Indian victory and to lose interest in the prolonged siege. Moreover, without white trade and provisions, the warriors had to turn their attention to hunting and gathering food for their families before the change of season. On October 20, after an impassioned plea to his followers for a continuation of the siege, Pontiac received a letter from Major de Villiers, the commander of the French Fort de Chartres on the Mississippi River in Louisiana Territory, advising him to bury the hatchet. With the signing of the Treaty of Paris in Europe, the Seven Years War and all hostilities between England and France had officially ended. Pontiac now knew there was no hope of French military involvement. The following day, with his warriors anxious to depart, the dejected Pontiac called an end to the siege. At least he had the satisfaction of knowing that under the Royal Proclamation of 1763, white settlement was prohibited—although belatedly—west of the Appalachians.

Fighting continued elsewhere into the next year. But with time the various tribes of the Old Northwest were pacified. Pontiac, however, hoped for a second general uprising and once again argued his case before various tribes, especially those in the Illinois Country to the west. Although unable to organize the western tribes, he did perhaps sow the seeds for future regional revolt.

Pontiac eventually settled with his people on the Maumee River. As Indian and white tensions once again increased with the influx of settlers who ignored the Proclamation of 1763, Pontiac came to counsel peace. Young warriors drove him and his small coterie of family and supporters from the village because of his new conciliatory stance. Pontiac again traveled westward to Illinois where, in 1769, for unknown reasons—perhaps personal jealousy or revenge on behalf of the English—he was assassinated by a Peoria Indian, who struck him on the head from behind, then stabbed him.

THE PAXTON RIOTS

The frontier attacks on settlers in the Old Northwest fostered among the colonists further hatred and prejudice against Indians. Toward the end of 1763 and Pontiac's Rebellion, this anti-Indian sentiment sparked acts of vigilantism on the Pennsylvania frontier. A group of 75 Presbyterians out of Paxton in Lancaster County, frustrated by the failure of their colony's Quaker-dominated assembly to take a more aggressive stance against Indians, went on a rampage of violence. On December 14, they descended upon a village of Conestoga Mission Indians—a collection of Christianized Susquehannocks and others—and brutally murdered three men, two women, and a boy, scalping them all. The reason the Paxton Boys gave for attacking the Conestogas in particular was that one of the Indians had melted down a stolen pewter spoon.

The remaining Conestogas, who had been away from the village peddling wares, were given refuge by sympathetic whites in the Lancaster jailhouse. Governor John Penn (William Penn's son) issued a proclamation denouncing the incident and prohibiting further violence. Nevertheless, the Paxton Boys gathered again on December 27, broke into the jail, and massacred the remaining 14 Indians, children included.

Benjamin Franklin lambasted the vigilantes in a treatise entitled *Narrative of the Late Massacres in Lancaster County*, referring to them as "Christian white savages." The Paxton Boys for their part denounced Moravian missionaries in Philadelphia who provided for Indians at the public's expense. Then, in February 1764, they marched on Philadelphia to exterminate the city's Indians. The normally peaceful Quakers mobilized themselve to defend the innocent. But a delegation headed by Franklin met the Paxton renegades at their camp outside Philadelphia for negotiations. The Paxton Boys agreed to call off the attack on the condition that henceforth they receive bounties for the scalps of Indians from warring tribes.

LORD DUNMORE'S WAR

Lord Dunmore's War of 1774, like the later American Revolution, represented a rejection of royal authority by the colonists. Moreover, it revealed once again the inevitability of trans-Appalachian white settlement despite the Proclamation of 1763. When Virginia's colonial governor, the Earl of Dunmore, ignored the treaties drawn up since 1763, imposing an Indian boundary line from Lake Ontario to Florida, and granted Shawnee territory west of the Appalachian divide to veterans of the French and Indian War who had served under him, the Shawnees began attacking incoming whites. Dunmore sent a force of volunteers to quell the insurgents, but it was ambushed and routed along the Kentucky River.

Dunmore decided to take more drastic measures and organized an army of 1,500 militia. The Shawnees led by Chief Cornstalk appealed to the Iroquois League for help. Although some Senecas inhabited the land in question, the League refused to go to war with the English, again largely due to the efforts of Sir William Johnson, now the superintendent of the

Northern Indian Department. And, when Sir William died during a conference with the Iroquois at his new home Johnson Hall in New York (north of Fort Johnson), his nephew and son-in-law Guy Johnson inherited his position and continued the peace talks. The Seneca chief Logan was one exception to the Iroquois position and joined the Shawnee cause.

Dunmore's Virginia militia crossed the Appalachians into Shawnee territory. Andrew Lewis headed up one column through the Kanawha Valley. Dunmore himself led a force out of Fort Pitt. The Shawnees crossed the Ohio River to meet Lewis' force in a surprise attack at Point Pleasant on October 6. After a day of bitter fighting, during which the Virginians suffered 50 dead and twice as many wounded, the Indians, who had lost even more men, finally capitulated. Dunmore negotiated a final treaty with Cornstalk in the Scioto Valley.

INDIANS IN THE AMERICAN REVOLUTION

In the War of American Independence, the large majority of Indians took the losing side. As far as they were concerned, the American rebels were simply the pioneers who trespassed and settled on their territory. And for them, despite two centuries of British injustice, representatives of the king and of the established order offered the Indians the best hope of keeping their lands as defined by the Royal Proclamation of 1763, which had established a boundary between Indians and whites. Moreover, British agents had more resources than the Americans with which to bribe tribal leaders for their support. Yet, even so, the British failed in the end to take full advantage of their numerous and powerful Indian allies. If they had properly organized and outfitted the tribes, offering greater backing and responsibility to key Indian leaders such as Joseph Brant of the Mohawks, they probably would have won the war.

American officials also for the most part demonstrated a lack of strategic imagination with regard to the tribes. In fact, the original stated policy on both sides was the encouragement of Indian neutrality. As a result, Indians played only a negligible military role during the first year of fighting. But of course the generals needed men to win. Before long, two bureaucracies—two sets of representatives—were vying for Indian support. The British had an existing system—their Indian Department formed in 1764—through which to deal with the tribes. Three months after Lexington and the "shot heard round the world" of April 1775, the Americans organized their own Indian Department, based on the British structure but with three subdivisions and superintendents—northern, middle, and southern—instead of two. And by the summer of the following year, lines were being drawn among the Indians.

Thayendanegea or Joseph Brant. New York State Library, Albany.

It was in July 1776 that the Mohawk chief Thayendanegea, also known as Joseph Brant, returned from England with Colonel Guy Johnson, the superintendent of Northern Indian Affairs for the British. Brant, born in 1742 in the Ohio Valley while his parents were there on a hunting expedition, had grown up in the Mohawk Valley of New York as friend to Sir William Johnson and Johnson's son and nephew, John and Guy. Joseph's

5.9 THE AMERICAN REVOLUTION, 1775–83, AND LORD DUNMORE'S WAR, 1774,
showing tribes plus selected settlements and forts involved in the various conflicts

In July 1777, one year after Brant's return to America, British and Iroquois representatives met in council at Oswego, New York. Four of the Six Nations—Mohawks, Onondagas, Cayugas, and Senecas—agreed to an alliance with the British with Brant as war chief. But the Oneidas and Tuscaroras decided instead to side with the Americans, due largely to the efforts of the Presbyterian missionary Samuel Kirkland (who had attended Moor's Charity School at the same time as Brant), as well as to Indian agent James Dean.

The opposing tribes spilled one another's blood the next month. During General John Burgoyne's large-scale offensive southward, a British force of 875 men under Colonel Barry St. Leger, including John Johnson's Royal Greens and John Butler's Tory Rangers, plus 800 Iroquois warriors under Joseph Brant and the Seneca chiefs Cornplanter and Old Smoke, marched on Fort Stanwix at the headwaters of the Mohawk River. They failed to take the fort, but, on receiving intelligence from Molly Brant at Johnson Hall, ambushed a relief force of Tryon County militiamen under General Nicholas Herkimer, plus Oneidas and Tuscaroras, at Oriskany. It was an indecisive battle but one with many Indian casualties. Iroquois tribes also fought one another in actions to the east at Bennington and Saratoga. An American and Indian force under General Horatio Gates countered Burgoyne's thrust and won the first major battle for the rebels.

As the pro-British and pro-American factions sought revenge against one another after these campaigns, a state of civil war resulted among the Iroquois. Brant's followers burned the village of Oriska, the home of Oneida Chief Honyery Doxtator. Oneidas and white rebels attacked Mohawks at Fort Hunter and Fort Johnson. Molly Brant fled to the village of Onondaga; about 100 other Mohawks fled to Canada. And, during 1778 and 1779, more violence would follow on the New York and Pennsylvania frontiers, leading to the devastation of Iroquoia.

In the spring and summer of that

sister, Molly Brant, had married Sir William and was the hostess of Johnson Hall. As a boy of 13, Joseph Brant had fought with Sir William Johnson at the Battle of Lake George in the French and Indian War. Sir William, recognizing the boy's abilities, had sent him from the Anglican Mohawk Mission School to Moor's Charity School (later Dartmouth College) to study under D. Eleazar Wheelock. Brant could speak English as well as three of the Six Nations' languages, and during his career he had acted as interpreter for both William and Guy Johnson. He had also served as deputy and secretary to Guy and had accompanied him to Canada because of mounting unrest between loyalists and rebels in the Mohawk Valley.

Then the two had traveled together to England. Brant had become a celebrity abroad, painted by George Romney, befriended by James Boswell, accepted into the Masons, and even received by King George. He had also accomplished his goal of obtaining assurances from the Royal Court concerning Iroquois land rights.

As a result, on returning to America, Brant was steadfastly pro-British. When he arrived in New York by boat, the city was under siege by rebel troops headed by General George Washington. Brant fought briefly at the Battle of Long Island, then slipped northward through enemy lines. On reaching Iroquoia, he traveled from village to village to call his fellow Iroquois to arms against the Americans.

first year, Brant's Iroquois warriors, operating out of Onoquaga and supported by Loyalist soldiers, raided several white settlements, including Sacandaga, Cobleskill, Springfield, and German Flats, burning houses and barns, and driving away livestock. But Brant, merciful toward both Indians and whites, insisted that no attacks be made on the settlers themselves unless they picked up arms to fight.

That same summer, John Butler led a force of Tory Rangers and Indians—mostly Senecas and Cayugas—on a rampage through Pennsylvania's Wyoming Valley along the western branch of the Susquehanna. The Tories and Iroquois captured eight stockades in all, generally allowing the settlers to leave the area unharmed if they surrendered without a fight. The garrison at Forty Fort, however, launched an ill-advised counterattack under Colonel Zebulon Butler (no relation to the Tory John Butler) during which 227 militiamen,

several Continental soldiers among them, lost their lives. This action came to be known as the Wyoming Massacre. And many of those settlers who had fled the Wyoming Valley perished from hunger and exhaustion in the Pocono Great Swamp which came to be called the "Shades of Death."

Other American settlers died that autumn in the so-called Cherry Valley Massacre. Captain Walter Butler, John Butler's son, joined forces with Joseph Brant—about 700 Rangers and Indians combined—for an attack on this small frontier settlement about 50 miles west of Albany near Otsego Lake. On the morning of November 11, the Tory and Indian troops approached the village from the southwest along an old Indian trail. The fort itself had been built under the experienced direction of the Marquis de Lafayette and, defended by the Seventh Massachusetts Regiment under Colonel Ichabod Alden, withstood the attack. But, since Alden had failed to post guards on the trail, many of the

settlers living and working in the surrounding countryside were unable to reach the stockade in time. Brant tried his best to prevent the slaughter of innocents, personally saving several children, but 32 residents were killed, including Alden. Forty others were taken captive to Fort Niagara.

Because of these effective Tory-Indian raids on western settlements and the growing threat to eastern locations as well, Washington ordered a three-pronged invasion of Iroquoia with instructions that it not "merely be overrun but destroyed." General John Sullivan would lead a column out of Easton, Pennsylvania and up the Susquehanna River into New York; General James Clinton would head up a second column out of Albany along the Mohawk Valley across Otsego Lake and down the Susquehanna to meet up with Sullivan's troops, at which point the united force would push northwestward into the Finger Lakes region; in the meantime, Colonel Daniel Brodhead's column would

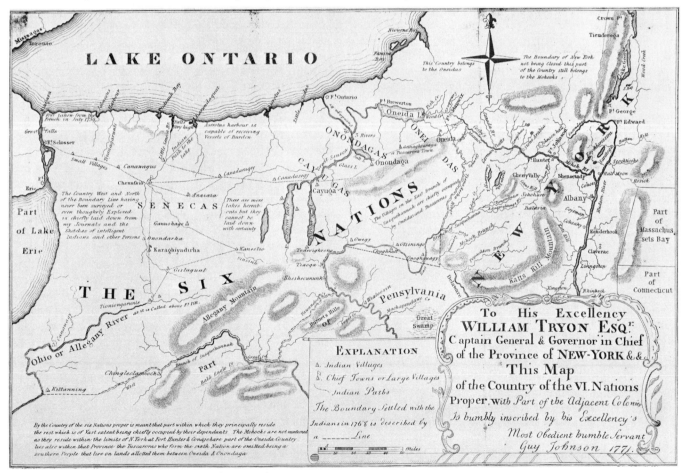

New York by Guy Johnson, 1771. New York State Library, Albany.

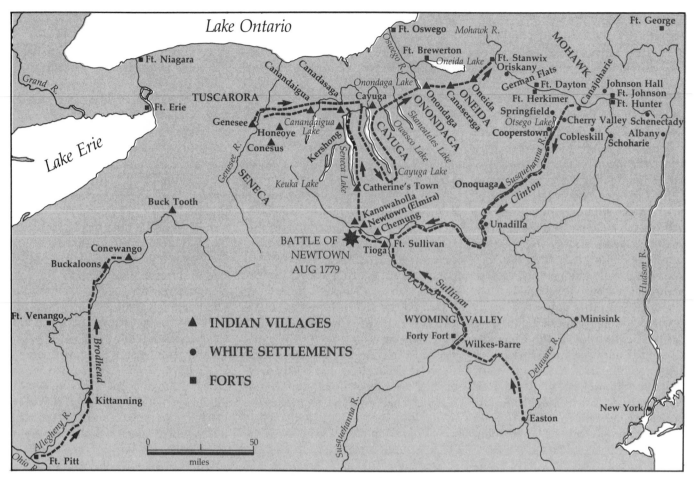

Lake Ontario

Ft. George

Mohawk R.

Ft. Oswego

Ft. Brewerton

Oneida Lake

Ft. Stanwix
Oriskany

MOHAWK

Canajoharie

Ft. Niagara

Grand R.

TUSCARORA

Canandaigua

Canadasaga

Onondaga Lake

Cayuga

Onondaga

German Flats

Ft. Dayton

Ft. Johnson

Johnson Hall

Ft. Erie

ONONDAGA

Canaseraga

ONEIDA

Oneida

Ft. Herkimer

Springfield

Ft. Hunter

Schenectady

Lake Erie

Genesee

Honeoye

Conesus

Genesee R.

SENECA

Canandaigua
Lake

Kershong

Skaneateles Lake

Owasco Lake

Otsego Lake

Cherry Valley

Cooperstown

Cobleskill

Albany

Schoharie

Keuka Lake

Seneca Lake

CAYUGA

Cayuga Lake

Catherine's Town

Onoquaga

Susquehanna R.

Clinton

Buck Tooth

Kanowaholla
Newtown (Elmira)
Chemung

Unadilla

Hudson R.

BATTLE OF
NEWTOWN
AUG 1779

Tioga

Ft. Sullivan

Conewango

Buckaloons

Sullivan

▲ INDIAN VILLAGES

WYOMING VALLEY

Minisink

Ft. Venango

Brodhead

● WHITE SETTLEMENTS

Forty Fort

Wilkes-Barre

■ FORTS

Delaware R.

Kittanning

Allegheny R.

0   50
miles

Susquehanna R.

New York

Easton

Ohio R.

Ft. Pitt

5.10 THE INVASION OF THE IROQUOIS HOMELAND DURING THE AMERICAN REVOLUTION

advance from Pittsburgh up the Allegheny River and assault the Iroquois from the west. Washington also desperately needed these troops in the east, but he considered the immediate resolution of the Iroquois resistance more critical at this stage of the war.

Clinton's army, after having dammed up Otsego Lake at Cooperstown to release the water for transport by boat down the Susquehanna, joined Sullivan's column at Tioga (on the present-day New York–Pennsylvania border), where they built a fort. On August 29, 1779, this combined force of about 4,000 was engaged at Newtown by 600 Tory-Indian troops under John Butler, Joseph Brant, and Old Smoke. The large rebel army killed 22 loyalists and drove the rest away.

Other than occasional Indian and Tory raids on advance patrols, the British mounted no further defense of the region. Brodhead's column, moving up the Allegheny River out of Fort Pitt as far as the New York border,

and destroying Mingo, Munsee, and Seneca villages and crops on the way, did not suffer a single casualty. The Sullivan-Clinton force, also unimpeded, was able to cut a swath of destruction through the heart of Iroquoia. It is estimated that 40 Indian villages were razed—hundreds of well-built homes along with many acres of crops and orchards. Most of the Iroquois warriors survived, however, and continued their resistance until October 1781 and the British surrender at Yorktown, and even for some time afterward. Joseph Brant, for one, would take part in further raids, many in the Ohio Valley.

The Northeast—that is, New England, New York, and Pennsylvania—was just one of several theaters of the war. Indians of the Old Northwest and the South were also involved in the Revolution, for the most part on the Loyalist side. Detroit was the northwestern headquarters for the British. Henry Hamilton, the lieuten-

ant-governor of Canada in command of this strategically located frontier post, came to be known among the Indians of the area as the "Hair Buyer" because of his reputed practice of paying bounties for rebel scalps.

In 1778, the American general Edward Hand led a force out of Fort Pitt against Shawnee and Delaware villages as far north as the Sandusky River, driving the Indians away and destroying their property. That same year, Major George Rogers Clark guided an army of Virginians and Kentuckians down the Ohio River as far as the Kaskaskia River, seized the Indian villages of Kaskaskia and Cahokia, then cut back and captured Fort Sackville at Vincennes on the Wabash River. During the summer of 1778, Clark did not lose a single man. That autumn, while Clark was at Kaskaskia, Hamilton marched from Detroit with 500 men and recaptured Vincennes for the British. But then, in a daring winter march through snow and icy waters, Clark and his rugged frontiersmen took Vincennes once more and even captured Hamilton, the "Hair Buyer." Clark had also hoped to advance on Detroit during his first-year campaign but, because of shortages of men and supplies, gave up the idea. Another autumn advance on Detroit on the part of 1,000 troops under Commandant Lachlan McIntosh out of Fort Pitt fell short because of cold weather. McIntosh succeeded only in building a frontier post, Fort McIntosh, and destroying several Indian villages.

Colonel Alexander McKee succeeded Hamilton at Detroit and, from 1780 to 1782, he sent out predominantly Indian armies against American settlements as far south as Kentucky. Kentucky had seen earlier action in the war, much of it involving Daniel Boone and the settlement of Boonesborough that he had founded. From 1775 on, American settlers had to ward off frequent Shawnee and Tory attacks. Boone himself had been captured in 1778 and held at the Shawnee village of Chillicothe for a time, but he managed to escape. In 1780, the Virginia Loyalist Colonel William Byrd led an Indian army of 1,000—mostly Wyandots and Shawnees—against Kentucky settlements at Ruddle's and Martin's stations. At Ruddle's Station, as many as 200 men, women, and children lost their lives. Byrd's force also defeated a force of Kentucky militia. And the following year, a Chickasaw and Tory force took Fort Jefferson in southwest Kentucky —built and manned by a detachment of Clark's men—after a protracted siege, also attacking the surrounding white settlements. In 1782, Colonel McKee and Simon Girty, leader of the western Tories, attacked but failed to take Bryan's Station near Lexington, Kentucky, defended by a garrison under Commandant John Craig. But soon afterward, at the Battle of Blue Licks, about half the Loyalist raiders routed a contingent of Kentuckians, killing 70.

Because of these rebel defeats, Major Clark traveled to Kentucky from his headquarters at Kaskaskia, mustered an army, and marched into Indian Country, destroying many

Shawnee and Delaware villages, including Chillicothe and Piqua. And his forces annihilated an Indian army under Simon Girty that was on its way to reinforce Piqua.

That same year, to the north, because of attacks on American settlements in western Pennsylvania by Shawnees, Delawares, and Senecas, a 300-man militia wreaked their vengeance on the peaceful Moravian Delaware Indians at the Gnaddenhutten mission. All but a few of the 90 Christian Indians—men, women, and children—were executed. Several months later, enraged Indians routed a rebel army out of Fort Pitt under Colonel William Crawford, a personal friend of George Washington, along the upper Sandusky. Crawford himself was captured and tortured to death. But this one-sided battle represented the last major victory for the Tories and their Indian allies on the western frontier during the Revolutionary years.

Meanwhile, over the course of the War of Independence, the Southeast also saw a certain amount of Indian activity. In May 1776, Shawnee, Delaware, and Mohawk emissaries traveled to the South to help British agents win the support of the Cherokees, Creeks, Choctaws, and Chickasaws. In July of that year, Cherokee warriors led by Dragging Canoe began raiding white forts and settlements in the trans-Appalachian region of Watauga as well as other isolated regions of Virginia, the Carolinas, and Georgia. The southern states organized militia armies which, after extended campaigns of destruction of Cherokee villages and crops, managed to force the tribe into treaties and land cessions by 1777.

But Dragging Canoe and his Chickamauga band of the Tennessee River Valley continued their attacks on settlers, with arms supplied by British agents out of Pensacola, until Colonel Evan Shelby, with an army of 600, invaded their territory in 1778. Thereafter, the Cherokee resistance was limited to rare and isolated attacks. Nonetheless, in 1780, North Carolina militiamen used these attacks as an excuse to once again invade Cherokee territory, raze villages, and demand more land cessions.

As for the other southern tribes, the long-time pro-British Chickasaws

The United States in 1783 after the American Revolution. Public Archives of Canada.

were active against American settlers as far north as Kentucky, and the Choctaws and Creeks helped the British in several engagements along the lower Mississippi. Yet, despite the money invested in them, they never wholeheartedly threw their backing to the Loyalist cause. For example, in early 1780, a Choctaw force of hundreds, disappointed in the supplies provided by the British, abandoned their station at Mobile, which enabled a Spanish fleet under Admiral Bernardo de Galvez to defeat the British garrison and take the town. The presence of 2,000 Creeks did, however, prevent Galvez from also attacking Pensacola as he had planned.

In the Treaty of Paris of 1783, which officially ended the American Revolution, the British made no provisions whatsoever for the many tribes who had supported their effort. Indians received no consideration as Loyalist allies or as proprietors of ceded land. Officials of both sides apparently considered them as incidental to both the past and future of the white race in America. The British, however, did extend some favors to those Indians who moved to Canada after the Revolution. Joseph Brant and his followers among others were granted parcels of land. His tract was on the Grand River in Ontario, whence he continued to play a key role in British-Indian relations.

But those Indians who stayed behind were left to fend completely for themselves with the new American nation, a nation made up mostly of people who thought of Indians as enemies. And, ironically, those Indians who had sided with the rebels were now lumped in the public's mind with all the pro-British Indians; consequently they would fare no better in terms of personal rights or land rights. The new nation and its Founding Fathers might at this time have been preoccupied with democracy, equality, liberty, and justice, but not with regard to the Indian. It is an interesting question to ponder whether the Indians, if they had uniformly fought with the rebels and

hastened American victory against the British, would have been extended the precepts of the Bill of Rights out of gratitude after the war. Probably not.

As it was, for their efforts in the American Revolution, the Indians suffered many casualties, experienced the devastation of villages and crops, lost much of their land in cessions, ended the unity of one of the oldest surviving Indian confederacies—the Iroquois League—and alienated the white population around them.

WARS FOR THE OLD NORTHWEST

What was once the Northwest of the fledgling United States—the Great Lakes region west of Pittsburgh and north of the Ohio River, and is now referred to by historians as the Old Northwest—was a fiercely contested area in the French and Indian Wars, Pontiac's Rebellion, and the American Revolution. It would be again in the Miami War, Tecumseh's Rebellion, the War of 1812, and the Black Hawk War, as well as the Kickapoo Resistance and the Winnebago Uprising.

The Old Northwest had become a melting pot of tribes after the Revolution. Northern and eastern tribes—Ottawa, Ojibway, Wyandot, Algonkin, Delaware, and remnants of the Iroquois League—now mingled here along with the Miami, Wea, Piankashaw, Potawatomi, Menominee, Kickapoo, Illinois, Peoria, Kaskaskia, Sauk, Fox, Winnebago, and, to the south, the Shawnees. And, as far as most of the tribes were concerned, although the British had declared peace with the American rebels, their war against intruding American settlers still continued. It is estimated that, during the years from 1783 to 1790, as many as 1,500 settlers died in isolated frontier Indian attacks. In 1787, the American Congress enacted the Northwest Ordinance to encourage development of the region. Major

clashes between Indians and whites were once again inevitable.

LITTLE TURTLE'S WAR

In 1790, President George Washington ordered an expedition outfitted, with the purpose of pacifying the hostile Indian tribes on the Northwest frontier. Brigadier General Josiah Harmar was given the command of a large force of about 1,100 Pennsylvania, Virginia, and Kentucky militia, plus 300 or so federal regulars, mustered at Fort Washington (Cincinnati). The troops headed north into Indian Country along the Maumee River Valley.

Yet Harmar, despite the size of his force, was no match for the brilliant and eloquent Indian leader commanding the loose confederacy of tribes—Little Turtle (Michikinikwa), a Miami chief. Little Turtle and his warriors, including Miamis, Shawnees, Ojibways, Delawares, Potawatomis, and Ottawas, sniping at their enemy and burning their own villages to feign panic, lured Harmar's men deeper into Indian Country. Then, in two surprise September ambushes, the Indians routed the enemy, killing 183 and wounding 31 more.

After this embarrassing defeat, Washington gave the command of the wilderness campaign to General Arthur St. Clair, governor of the Northwest territories. But St. Clair would fare no better than Harmar. His poorly equipped expedition of approximately 2,000 six-month enlistees marched northwestward out of Fort Washington and, building supply bases on the way—Fort Hamilton and Fort Jefferson—advanced on the Miami villages. By the time St. Clair's troops had taken up position on the high ground along the upper Wabash River (November 2, 1791), many of his men had deserted him because of short rations and no pay. The following morning at dawn, the Indians, hugging the ground, attacked. Their first foray routed the green recruits who flanked the main camp, driving them in confusion back inside, where the artillery had been stationed. When

St. Clair finally managed to organize a bayonet counterattack, the Indians retreated into the woods, picking off the soldiers who came at them. After three hours of fighting, the American troops were depleted by almost half and were surrounded by Little Turtle's warriors. St. Clair ordered a retreat. His men fought through enemy lines, then fled to Fort Jefferson, 29 miles away, many of them discarding weapons and equipment on the way. All in all, over 600 troops died in battle and nearly half again as many were wounded. The Indians had achieved one of their greatest victories in their many wars against the whites.

But with Washington's next choice of command—General "Mad" Anthony Wayne, the Revolutionary hero—the tide turned against Little Turtle and the warring Indians. During most of 1792 and the spring of 1793, the exacting disciplinarian Wayne built a formidable army of 3,000 well-equipped and well-trained men at Legionville and Fort Washington. In the summer of 1793, the United States made peace overtures to the Indians at the Sandusky Conference, but when the Indians insisted that the boundary of their lands extend as far east as the Ohio River, as in the Fort Stanwix agreement with the British in 1768, the talks broke down. Wayne's troops then followed St. Clair's old route and built Fort Greenville and a second outpost further north on the site of St. Clair's defeat, Fort Recovery. On June 29, 1794, Little Turtle ordered an attack on Fort Recovery, which was repelled.

Astute leader that he was, Little Turtle recognized the extent of the American military commitment and the inevitability of Indian defeat against an army such as Wayne's. Other than a small number of militiamen helping the Indians, the hoped-for British military involvement had not developed, despite recommendations to that effect by the Mohawk leader Joseph Brant, who had been granted lands in Canada north of Lake Erie and who provided intelligence to the British about the war. Hoping to save Indian lives and the confederacy of tribes, Little Turtle

therefore counseled peace. But his warriors spurned his advice and chose a new leader, Turkey Foot. The Indians withdrew northward. Wayne's army pursued them.

The two forces met in a decisive battle on August 20, 1794, at Fallen Timbers near the western shore of Lake Erie. When the American surprise attack came after a three-day delay, the disorganized, half-starved Indians fled in panic toward the British stockade, Fort Miami, on the Maumee River. But the British, fearing their own defeat by Wayne's men, refused to open their gates. Hundreds of Indians died in the fighting as compared to only 38 whites. After their resounding victory, "Mad" Anthony's troops put Indian villages and crops to the torch throughout the Old Northwest.

One year later, on August 3, 1795, at Fort Greenville, 1,100 chiefs and warriors agreed to a treaty that ceded Indian lands amounting to all of present-day Ohio and a good part of Indiana. Little Turtle was one of the signers. From that time on, he played a role as peacemaker between Indians and whites, and he became a celebrated hero among the people he had fought so masterfully. He died of a complication from gout—a white man's disease—in 1812.

It was Tecumseh's turn now to carry on the fight for Indian lands and rights.

TECUMSEH'S REBELLION AND THE WAR OF 1812

Tecumseh, the Shawnee chief, has often been referred to as the greatest Indian leader of all. Such a claim is of course subjective—there have been many great Indian leaders—but it does point up the practical ability, vision, compassion, and energy of the man. A great orator, he could inspire; a brilliant strategist, he was effective in battle; a visionary, he saw what it would take for his people to have an essential role in the future of North America; a man of compassion, he railed against torturing prisoners. And he pursued his goals with un-

flagging energy. But circumstances beyond his control conspired against him.

Tecumseh grew up at a critical time in American history—the post-Revolutionary period when the new nation was seeking its boundaries and identity. As a boy he had fought with the British in the Revolution, during which he lost his father, Puckeshinwa. Then, in his early 20s, he lost his brother, Cheeseekau, at Fallen Timbers in Little Turtle's War. Even this early in his military career, Tecumseh was gaining a reputation for opposing the torture of prisoners, a practice common among both Indians and whites. During this period too, Tecumseh took a stand against Indian land cessions, refusing to participate in the Treaty of Greenville of 1795, in which the Indians of the Old Northwest were forced to cede much of their territory.

In the years after Greenville, a friendship with Rebecca Galloway, a white woman, gave Tecumseh the opportunity to study American and world history and literature. He came to think of himself as an Indian first and a Shawnee second. He also reached the conclusion that no Indian tribe or individuals had the right to sell off land to whites without the consent of all the tribes. He saw the need for unified Indian action—a confederacy of tribes from Canada to the Gulf of Mexico, which one day could evolve into a separate Indian state centered in the Great Lakes and Ohio Valley region.

Meanwhile, Tecumseh's brother Tenskwatawa, who had led a dissolute life as a youth, came into his own as a prophet, claiming to have communicated directly with the Great Spirit. Rejecting white religion and customs, including the use of liquor, Tenskwatawa preached a return to traditional Indian ways. In 1808, the two brothers founded a town, Tippecanoe (later called Prophetstown), located near the confluence of the Tippecanoe and Wabash rivers in Indiana Territory, where Indians from different tribes could congregate free from white society.

As the Prophet and his disciples

5.11 WARS FOR THE OLD NORTHWEST, *including Little Turtle's War, 1790–94, Tecumseh's Rebellion, 1809–11, and the Black Hawk War, 1832 (with modern boundaries)*

spread word of the spiritual renaissance, Tecumseh set out on his own tireless travels from tribe to tribe with his message of Indian unity and a military alliance. Shawnees, Potawatomis, Sauks, Foxes, Menominees, Winnebagos, Kickapoos, Ottawas, Wyandots, Delawares, Weas, Ojibways, Miamis, Illinois, Piankashaws, Osages, Iowas, Senecas, Onondagas, Creeks, Seminoles, Choctaws, Cherokees, and others heard him. Some rallied to the cause; others rebuffed it; some wavered. Tecumseh persisted.

After his first trip south, Tecumseh returned to learn that William Henry Harrison, the governor of Indiana Territory, had tricked a group of nonrepresentative chiefs, through the use of alcohol and deceit, into signing away three million acres of land for $7,000 and a small annuity (the Treaty of Fort Wayne in 1809). Tecumseh protested vehemently and confronted Harrison personally, but he held his 1,000 warriors in check. Then again in 1811, when Harrison demanded that the Shawnees in Prophetstown turn over some Potawatomis, the al-

leged murderers of white settlers in Illinois, Tecumseh, although he refused to comply, contained his men and prevented war. As he had learned from the examples of others before him who had attempted tribal alliances—King Philip, Pontiac, Joseph Brant—proper timing was essential for political and military success.

Or failure. Immediately after the Potawatomi incident, Tecumseh embarked on a second trip south in order to increase his base of support; while Tecumseh was gone, Harrison managed to force the brother's hand prematurely. Using the excuse that a group of Indians had stolen an army dispatch rider's horses, Harrison marched on Prophetstown with a militia of 1,000. On the night of November 6, 1811, his troops set up camp three miles from the Indian village. Although Tecumseh had warned his brother against conflict at this stage, Tenskwatawa listened instead to the advice of a militant band of Winnebagos and ordered a nighttime attack. He assured his warriors they would be safe from injury because of his magic. For the last half mile, his men advanced on their stomachs under the cover of rain.

The attack came just before dawn. Harrison had wisely instructed his men to set up camp in a circular battle position and sleep on their weapons in case of a surprise attack. A sentry managed to get off a warning shot before being killed, and only an advance party of Indians managed to break through the circle of men into the center of camp. The main Indian force was repelled with each charge. By full light the fighting had ended. The militia had suffered 61 dead and twice as many wounded—more casualties, it is thought, than the Indians suffered—but that day the force found Prophetstown abandoned and burned it without opposition.

Tenskwatawa had lost more than a single, indecisive battle—he had lost his "magic," many of his followers, the emergency provisions in Prophetstown that were to be used during a unified uprising, and any momentum his brother had gained toward a confederacy. As Tecumseh had feared, tribes would now strike back at whites in a disorganized, piecemeal fashion. Harrison, in the meantime, made the most of the Battle of Tippecanoe, claiming a major military victory and turning it into a propagandistic and psychological one as well. (Thirty years later, Tippecanoe even helped him get elected to the presidency.) On returning from the south, Tecumseh was distraught at the turn of events and furious with his brother as well as Harrison, but he had not given up.

The Indian raids on settlers along the northern frontier after Tippecanoe—supposedly encouraged by Great Britain—became one of the main arguments of the American war hawks who wanted an attack on Canada. Other areas of dispute at the time were the questions of borders and ocean shipping rights. On June 18, 1812, the United States declared war on Great Britain. For three years after that, until the Treaty of Ghent, the two nations were involved in a costly standoff. The U.S. might very well have dominated the fighting from the start if it hadn't been for Tecumseh.

The Shawnee chief saw the War of 1812 as an opportunity to accomplish his goal of a new Indian homeland for all Indian tribes, and he joined the British in declaring war on the U.S. The British, recognizing his great talents as a leader, decided to make use of them for their own purposes and made him a brigadier general in their army. Following Tecumseh's example, many other Indians joined the British camp. And others took advantage of the situation to step up their raids on white settlers in an attempt to gain back their lands.

As a brigadier general, Tecumseh played a vital role in the war and was responsible for much of the early British success, especially in the taking of Detroit with his good friend, Major General Isaac Brock. Some of his Indians also participated in the capture of Fort Dearborn (Chicago). Tecumseh even found time in the fall of 1812 for one more trip south to seek the help of the powerful Creek tribe.

But other people's mistakes once again prevented Tecumseh from reaching his visionary goals. When General Brock was killed, Colonel Henry Proctor took his place. Proctor, unlike Tecumseh, allowed the butchering of prisoners, which served to arouse American anger and resolve, as happened after the Raisin River Massacre of 850 Kentuckians. Soon after Raisin River, Tecumseh's former nemesis, William Henry Harrison, and fresh troops built Fort Meigs on the Maumee River in northern Ohio. British and Indian forces came close to capturing it, but Proctor withdrew

his men too early out of unnecessary caution and allowed Harrison a further buildup of men.

Then, after a British naval defeat on Lake Erie by Americans under Commodore Oliver Hazard Perry, Proctor decided to pull all his men back to Canada. The dejected Tecumseh tried to dissuade Proctor from abandoning land the Indians had fought so hard to hold, but the Englishman stubbornly insisted on retreat. During the British retreat, which the Indians courageously protected, a major encounter took place on the Thames River. Proctor fled to eastern Ontario while Tecumseh stayed behind to fight—to his death, as it turned out. On October 5, 1813, the Shawnee chief reportedly took bullet after bullet while in the front lines, urging his men on. After the battle, a group of Kentuckians skinned the body of an Indian that they thought to be Tecumseh. But the actual body was never found. It is thought that some of Tecumseh's men hid his corpse in a hollow log to prevent its defilement.

And so one of the greatest Indian leaders died on the battlefield—a man who, if he had been commander in chief for the British, just might have won the war for them (in 1815, they agreed to many American terms in a peace treaty); or, if before the Battle of Tippecanoe he had had just a little more time, might have brought about a large-scale Indian confederacy and even a separate Indian state or nation.

THE KICKAPOO RESISTANCE

Turmoil continued in the Old Northwest as the white population increased and pressured the Indian tribes to cede their lands and relocate westward. Veterans of the War of 1812 who had been granted land warrants as payment for their service began to collect on them. Federal land agents were active on their behalf, negotiating for Indian lands, especially in the Illinois Country. Smaller tribes, such as the Peoria and Kaskaskia, agreed to federal terms, but some bands of the formerly pro-British Kickapoo tribe, with lands along the Wabash and Illinois rivers, resisted.

Mecina led one of these recalcitrant bands. He believed, as Tecumseh had, that no Indian land could be sold without the consent of all Indians. Some other Kickapoo bands yielded to white pressure and moved westward in 1819. Mecina and his followers, however, resisted by destroying and stealing white property. Troops in the region—both state and federal—were increased, and patrols were stepped up. Nonetheless, it took months of military pressure to drive Mecina's band across the Mississippi.

A second Kickapoo band held out even longer through passive resistance. Kennekuk, a chief and prophet who preached a return to traditional Indian ways, managed to stall white officials for years by expressing a willingness to depart westward, while at the same time coming up with one excuse after another to stay—the harvest, illness, or evil omens. It wasn't until after the Black Hawk War that Kennekuk and his band finally relocated.

THE WINNEBAGO UPRISING

The Winnebagos, like the Kickapoos and later the Sauks and Foxes, also resisted white intrusion onto their lands and the forced relocation westward. In their case, however, in addition to the usual farmers, the intruders were miners in quest of the rich lead deposits in the upper Mississippi country of northwest Illinois and southwest Wisconsin. With lead prices rising during the 1820s, more and more miners poured into the Galena area where the Fever (Galena) River branched off from the Mississippi, near the Illinois-Wisconsin border. When the Winnebagos began digging and selling lead to white traders, government officials became concerned they would never give up their profitable territory, and they ordered Indian agents to use their influence to prevent the practice.

In 1826, several Winnebagos, strik-

ing out at the whites in their midst, killed a family of maple-sugar farmers who lived near Prairie du Chien in Wisconsin, at the fork of the Mississippi and Wisconsin rivers. Soon afterward, again near Prairie du Chien, Chief Red Bird, who believed that his tribe's honor necessitated the spilling of white blood, led two of his braves in the arbitrary murder of a farmer and his hired man. Settlers and miners in the region, afraid of other Indian reprisals, pressured government officials into increasing the number of garrisoned troops.

Then, in June of 1827, there occurred the only actual engagement of the Winnebago Uprising. Two Mississippi keelboats, contracted to furnish provisions for troops stationed in the north country, stopped at a Winnebago village above Prairie du Chien. The boatmen drank rum with the Indian men, then kidnapped seven women, forced them onto the boats, and raped them. On realizing what had happened, the Winnebagos gathered a force of warriors and set out after the boats. Several nights after the incident, at a narrow stretch of water, the warriors, lying in their canoes, tried to approach and board one of the keelboats. The Indians failed in their attempt, but their women managed to escape during the melee. Several men on both sides died in the fighting.

White officials responded with federal troops and territorial militia under General Lewis Cass, General Henry Atkinson, General Samuel Whiteside, and Colonel Henry Dodge, whose various armies converged on the Winnebagos. A detachment caught up with Red Bird and his followers on the upper Wisconsin River. War was averted when the proud chief agreed to surrender himself in order to save the rest of his people. Broken in spirit, he died in the guardhouse while awaiting trial.

Other Winnebagos, notably White Cloud (Winnebago Prophet), would participate in the later Black Hawk War.

THE BLACK HAWK WAR

The Black Hawk War, the last in the numerous wars for the Old Northwest, had been long in coming. In 1803, the United States purchased the Louisiana Territory from France. In 1804, a group of Sauk Indians killed three settlers in a fight north of St. Louis. Soon afterward, Governor William Henry Harrison of the Indiana Territory received permission from Secretary of War Henry Dearborn to negotiate with the Sauks and Foxes for their lands (which they had shared ever since forming a confederacy in the 17th century); he decided to use the frontier incident to his advantage.

Harrison traveled from Vincennes to St. Louis and summoned tribal chiefs to a council, insisting they bring in the guilty party. A delegation of five chiefs under Quashquame arrived in St. Louis with one of the warriors involved in the killings. Harrison took the warrior prisoner, promising to free him as soon as the Sauks compensated the victims' families in material goods, as was the tribal custom. The Sauks agreed in principle. But then Harrison added a further stipulation: that the delegation sign an agreement ceding Indian lands. Harrison lavished gifts on the five chiefs along with a steady supply of liquor. Before the Sauks departed, they had relinquished all tribal lands east of the Mississippi, encompassing a large part of present-day Illinois, Missouri, and Wisconsin, in exchange for just over $2,000 plus an annuity in goods worth $1,000. The Indians would be allowed continued use of their territories until white settlement reached them. As for the warrior for whose life they had bargained, he never gained his freedom. Before his executive pardon came through, he was shot in the head with buckshot while trying to escape.

A Sauk chief by the name of Ma-ka-tai-me-she-kia-kiak, or Black Sparrow Hawk, who came to be known simply as Black Hawk, considered the Treaty of 1804 fraudulent. In his opinion, not only did the Sauk delegation who had met with Harrison lack tribal authority, but also, as he later wrote in his autobiography: "My reason teaches me that land cannot be sold. The Great Spirit gave it to his children to live upon. So long as they occupy and cultivate it they have the right to the soil. Nothing can be sold but such things as can be carried away."

Because of anger over the treaty, Black Hawk and his followers from the village of Saukenuk (Rock Island) at the junction of the Mississippi and Rock rivers participated in brief sieges on Fort Madison in the years 1808 and 1811, and they agreed to support Tecumseh's cause. After Tippecanoe, Black Hawk and some of his warriors fought along with Tecumseh on the Canadian side in the War of 1812. And, even after the Treaty of Ghent, Black Hawk led an attack on Fort Howard, killing 15 U.S. soldiers. Yet, when the British evacuated the Mississippi Valley, Black Hawk went along with an Indian delegation to sign a truce with the United States. In doing so, he unwittingly put his mark on a document reconfirming the Treaty of 1804 which he had contested so long. The agreement was also signed by Keokuk, another Sauk chief, who had been cultivated by the whites with gifts, flattery, a trip to Washington, D.C., and the promise of future power and influence if he cooperated with white plans for the region.

The unrest between Indians and whites continued over the years, as more and more settlers arrived in the region. In 1827, after a series of violent incidents, the federal government decided to remove all the Indians from Illinois during the next two years. Black Hawk and his followers, who had come to be known as the British Band because of frequent trading trips to Fort Malden in Ontario, steadfastly refused to relinquish their ancestral lands. Yet, on returning to Saukenuk in the spring of 1829 after their winter hunt, they found white squatters in some of their lodges. Keokuk and his pro-peace faction agreed to move to a new home

across the Mississippi on the Iowa River. The British Band, however, stayed on in lodges the squatters had left empty. The Indians and whites, despite frequent disputes, survived a planting season in these close quarters. And, when Black Hawk led his band away for the next winter's hunt, he promised to return again in the spring.

Animal hair roach (ceremonial headdress) of Great Lakes Indians

He kept his word. This time, however, when Black Hawk's band of 300 warriors along with their families occupied Saukenuk, Governor John Reynolds ordered up militia and requested additional federal troops to evict them. General Edmund Gaines was given the command. War seemed inevitable. But, on June 26, when the troops moved on Saukenuk, they found it empty. The British Band had disappeared across the Mississippi during the night. Four days later, Black Hawk and a small party of warriors appeared under a flag of truce and agreed to sign the Articles of Agreement and Capitulation. The conditions: The British Band must never return to Saukenuk, must submit to Keokuk's authority, must cease communication with the British, and must permit the building of roads over their Iowa lands. With this accord, it seemed, war had been prevented.

Yet, as it turned out, war had only been delayed. Black Hawk's support among other Indian bands grew. During this period, a Fox war party attacked a Menominee camp in retal-

iation for the killing of several of their chiefs. When the federal government demanded the surrender of the supposed aggressors, the Foxes went to Black Hawk for help and decided to join the British Band. Meanwhile, White Cloud, a Winnebago mystic and medicine man also called the Winnebago Prophet, preached against whites and fostered support for Black Hawk among Winnebagos, Potawatomis, and Kickapoos. When his force had grown to 600 with the hope of more to follow, Black Hawk again decided to cross the Mississippi and return to Saukenuk for another spring planting.

The whites received word of his intention and amassed an army—federal troops under General Henry Atkinson and state militia under General Samuel Whiteside. Serving among these troops were a number of notables: Colonel Zachary Taylor, Lieutenant Jefferson Davis, Captain Abraham Lincoln, and Daniel Boone's son, Nat. On April 12, 1832, both Indian and white forces reached the Rock River. The soldiers debarked from their boats at Fort Armstrong; the Indians continued overland past Saukenuk toward White Cloud's village. When a pro-peace Winnebago faction refused to give their support, Black Hawk and the Prophet led the faithful further up the Rock River to Potawatomi country. An advance detachment of calvary under Major Isaiah Stillman set out after them.

Black Hawk failed in council to gain full Potawatomi support and decided it was time to parley with the whites. He was some distance from his camp with about 40 warriors when Stillman's men approached. The date was May 14. Black Hawk sent out a three-man party under a flag of truce to arrange a meeting with Stillman and a second party of five to observe the proceedings. The American troops—jittery and anxious for a fight—attacked the Indians in both groups despite the truce flag and killed three. The remainder escaped to warn Black Hawk. He knew now there was no chance of peace and decided to make a military stand whatever the cost. To his surprise, his small force of forty warriors not only repelled Stillman's charge but thoroughly routed the larger force. The 275 militiamen panicked, threw down their arms, and ran 25 miles back to Whiteside's camp at Dixon Ferry. This one-sided battle came to be known as Stillman's Run. Afterward, Black Hawk and his band of men, women, and children headed northward into southern Wisconsin.

Encouraged by Black Hawk's victory, Potawatomis, Winnebagos, and Kickapoos, as well as other Sauk and Fox bands, began raiding white settlers and miners in the area. The Americans regrouped, and President Andrew Jackson gave General Winfield Scott overall command of the war. Scott organized another huge army in Chicago, while Atkinson's army was also reinforced and a Wisconsin militia was raised under the command of Colonel Henry Dodge.

The months of June and July were hard on both Indian and white forces. Atkinson's troops, following Black Hawk's trail northward, became bogged down in the swamplands of the Rock River headwaters. A cholera epidemic ravaged Scott's troops in Chicago. Meanwhile, Black Hawk's band suffered hunger and exhaustion in the wilderness.

On July 21, a combined force of Dodge's militiamen and an advance party of Atkinson's men under General James Henry, who had joined up in the field, overtook the British Band on the Wisconsin River. After a fierce fight during which many Indians and only one U.S. soldier were killed, the British Band managed to cross the river to safety on makeshift rafts and canoes. Black Hawk had hoped to descend the Wisconsin and the Mississippi to Keokuk's village where his people might be allowed to settle in peace. Nevertheless, because of the attack, he decided to lead his band overland northwestward through Wisconsin and across the upper Mississippi.

The ragged and starving British Band reached the Mississippi at its junction with the Bad Axe River on August 1. While his people were preparing rafts and canoes, they were confronted by the steamboat *Warrior*

which had been outfitted with cannon and troops. Black Hawk again tried to negotiate, sending a large party of warriors under a flag of truce to the water's edge. And again soldiers ignored the white flag, firing first. In the resulting battle, the Indians lost 23 men. The *Warrior*, however, running out of fuel, retreated downriver. After the encounter, Black Hawk tried to persuade his people to head northward to Ojibway country rather than attempt another crossing. Only 50 members of the British Band agreed to accompany him, one of them White Cloud.

Atkinson's force of 1,300 regulars and volunteers caught up with those who had stayed behind early in the morning of August 3 in the midst of their crossing. The troops fell on the Indians, killing women and children along with warriors. Many were shot while desperately swimming the river. Others who managed to reach islands were shelled with six-pounders and picked off by sharpshooters aboard the *Warrior*, which had returned upriver. Many of those who reached the west bank were killed by Sioux Indians. Probably as many as 300 Indians died in the Massacre at Bad Axe, as opposed to only 20 whites. The symbolism of the tragedy was all too evident. Here, at the last battle (if it can be called that) for the Old Northwest, just as the removal of the southern Indians was getting underway (see "The Trail of Tears" in chapter 6), Indians were mercilessly slaughtered as they tried to cross what was to become the boundary line between Indian and white—a fitting statement on the cruel relocation of eastern Indians and a precedent for what was to follow in the Wars for the West.

As for Black Hawk, he sought safety among the Winnebagos for several weeks; then he and White Cloud surrendered to whites at Prairie du Chien on August 27. He was held in jail at Fort Armstrong near his beloved village of Saukenuk, eventually being summoned to Washington by President Jackson and sent on a tour of eastern cities as if he were a trophy of war. The condition of Black Hawk's

release was that Keokuk be the sole chief of the Sauks. In the meantime, the government manipulated Keokuk into signing away all but 40 acres of land of the earlier Iowa grant.

Black Hawk dictated a powerful and moving autobiography in 1833. Embittered and depressed, he died in 1838, the year of the Cherokee Trail of Tears. In 1839, white vandals robbed his grave and removed his head for a tent show. Keokuk, a rich man from the sale of the Iowa lands, moved to Kansas, where he died in 1848. The United States, which had profited so much from his friendship, honored him with a statue. It took many years before history recognized Black Hawk as the true hero among his people.

THE CREEK WAR

Tecumseh's message was not lost on the Creek's of Alabama and Georgia. During his three trips south, the Shawnee leader had managed to inspire members of the Red Stick faction, or the Upper Creeks, the traditional warriors of the Creeks (as opposed to the White Sticks, or Lower Creeks, the People of the Peace). Two of Tecumseh's converts were half-breeds, Peter McQueen and William Weatherford, who became convinced that their people of choice, the Indians, had to make a stand against the whites.

A full-blooded Creek, Little Warrior, however, was the first to act, in 1813. He led a force of Creeks in the Raisin River Massacre during the War of 1812 and in the murder of settlers along the Ohio River during the trip home. His subsequent arrest and execution by the White Sticks under their leader Big Warrior further divided the Creek nation. Soon afterward, Peter McQueen led a detachment of Red Sticks to Pensacola to be outfitted by the Spanish; on their return trip they defeated a party of settlers at Burnt Corn Creek.

Yet it was the Creek action on August 20, 1813, under William Weatherford (Red Eagle), who eventually assumed command of all the Red Sticks, that brought about a major conflict and led to the involvement of Andrew Jackson. Red Eagle and a force of about 1,000 Creeks advanced on Fort Mims, located on the Alabama River, where a large group of settlers had taken refuge because of the earlier hostilities. The commanding officer, Major Daniel Beasley, ignored reports by black slaves of Indians hiding in the tall grass, and he didn't even order the gates closed. The attack came at noon during mess call. Beasley was killed at once outside the fort's walls. The survivors of the first onslaught fought from behind the second enclosure, the guns of the settlers holding the Red Sticks at bay for several hours. The Indians finally made use of flame-tipped arrows to rout the defenders and gain entrance to the stockade. It is reported that Red Eagle tried to stop the massacre that then took place. But his attempts failed, and about 400 settlers died. Only 36 whites escaped. However, most of the blacks were spared.

On learning of the Fort Mims massacre, the Tennessee legislature authorized $300,000 to outfit an army of 3,500 and called on General Andrew Jackson, commander of military forces south of the Ohio River, to head it. He rushed into action and quickly organized his men, despite severe wounds from a duel. An advance detachment under Colonel John Coffee (including Davy Crockett) fought the first engagement in early November 1813, at Tallasahatchee, drawing the Red Sticks into a trap and killing 186 warriors, while suffering only five dead and 41 wounded. A week later Jackson and his militiamen, plus regiments of Creeks, Chickasaws, Choctaws, and Cherokees, relieved the besieged Talladega, a Creek fort held by White Sticks. In this exchange, 290 Red Sticks supposedly died, with 15 whites killed and 85 wounded.

During the next two months Red Eagle regrouped his forces, while many of Jackson's soldiers deserted from Fort Strother or departed legally as their short-term enlistments expired. In December, a force under General William Claiborne nearly captured Red Eagle at his hometown, Econochaca, but the chief managed to escape by leaping astride his horse from a bluff into the river. In January 1814, soon after the arrival of 800 fresh recruits, Jackson's army was in the field again and fought two indecisive skirmishes with the Red Sticks at Emuckfaw and Enotachopco Creek.

Then in March, with 600 regulars from the 39th Infantry now reinforcing his army, Jackson moved on the latest Creek stronghold at Horseshoe Bend—a peninsula on the Tallapoosa River, across which Red Eagle's men had built a zigzag double-log barricade. This was the decisive battle of the Creek War. Jackson's men surrounded the Indian position on both sides of the river, removed the fleet of canoes the Indians had beached for their escape, then attacked. The battle lasted all day. Colonel Coffee was killed, and Ensign Sam Houston took command. Jackson's men finally succeeded in setting the barricade on fire and gaining the advantage, and by the end of the day, about 750 of 900 Red Sticks lay dead, most on the peninsula, others in the river, where they had been picked off by sharpshooters as they tried to escape. But Red Eagle was not among the dead. By chance, he had gone off before the surprise attack to inspect other fortifications.

However, the leader of the Red Sticks surrendered several days later by walking into the white camp and announcing, "I am Bill Weatherford." After a meeting with him, Jackson let him depart—whether out of magnanimity because the Creek leader had come of his own accord, or from political motives because Red Eagle had promised to enforce Jackson's terms of peace, or out of pride (legend

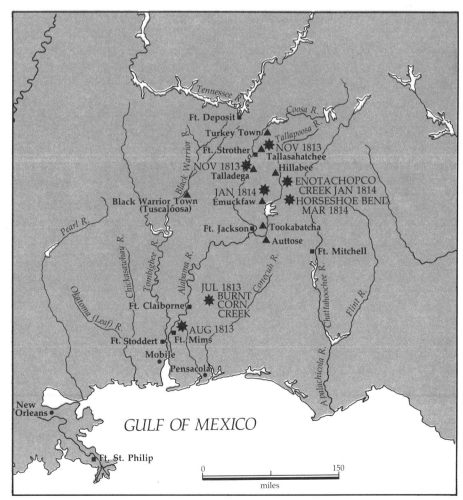

5.12 THE CREEK WAR, 1813–14

has it that Jackson dared Red Eagle to fight again), it isn't known. In any case, the next summer, in a follow-up series of coercive negotiations, Jackson was true to his form in later years and showed no magnanimity at all: In the infamous Treaty of Horseshoe Bend he demanded 23 million acres from the Creeks—from both the Red Sticks, and the White Sticks, his own supposed allies—to compensate the federal government for the war. Those Creeks who resisted these harsh terms eventually fled to Florida and joined relatives among the Seminoles and played a part in wars to follow.

THE SEMINOLE WARS

In 1817, Florida was a Spanish possession and the United States was in an expansionist mood. Moreover, there was growing ill-feeling between the Seminoles and whites along the Florida-Georgia border, the primary reason being the harboring of runaway black slaves by the Indians. Negotiations for the purchase of Florida from Spain had dragged on for years. Incidents involving the Seminoles, however, gave President James Monroe, Secretary of War John Calhoun, and their favorite general, Andrew Jackson, an excuse for making a move on territory they considered manifestly American.

During the period preceding major United States involvement, raids and counterraids occurred along the border. In 1816, a detachment of U.S. troops crossed the border in pursuit of runaway slaves and destroyed Negro Fort (which became Fort Gadsden). In 1817, troops from Fort Scott attacked the Seminole village of Fowltown in southwest Georgia when Chief Neamathla insisted that the soldiers stop trespassing on Indian hunting grounds. Both Indians and whites were killed, and the First Seminole War had begun.

In March of 1818, General Jackson, having had recent success in the Creek War, organized his forces at Fort Scott in Georgia—800 regulars,

900 Georgia militia, as well as a force of Lower Creeks under the half-breed William MacIntosh. Six days later, they crossed the border and marched on St. Marks, which was supposedly held by Seminoles. But, having learned of the army's approach, the Indians had abandoned the fort. Jackson's forces captured only an old Scottish trader, Alexander Arbuthnot, and two Creek chiefs—Peter McQueen and Francis—who had been active in the Creek War. Jackson had the Creeks executed at once and held Arbuthnot for trial.

Then his troops headed southward to the village of Chief Boleck on the Suwanee River. But again the Indians had been forewarned and had vanished into the Florida jungle. This time Jackson's men captured only two Englishmen who had been living among the Seminoles, Lieutenant Robert Ambrister of the Royal Marines and Peter Cook. The troops burned the village and then returned to St. Marks, where Arbuthnot and Ambrister were sentenced to death in a travesty of a trial and hung for aiding and abetting the Indians.

Seminole headdress

So much for the stated objective in Florida of controlling the Indians. Jackson next marched westward on the Spanish fort of Pensacola and, after a three-day siege, captured it, claiming West Florida for the United States. His actions, of course, were il-

legal under international law, and both Spain and England protested them. But the new administration of John Quincy Adams backed Jackson, sending an ultimatum to Spain either to control the Seminoles or to cede the territory. A treaty between the two countries in 1819 provided for the sale of East Florida to the U.S. Official occupation took place in 1821, and Florida was organized as a territory in 1822, after which settlers began pouring in and grabbing the good land. In 1823, the Seminoles were pressured into signing the Treaty of Tampa, in which they assented to move to a reservation inland from Tampa Bay. The first governor of the Florida Territory doing the pressuring was none other than Andrew Jackson; "Sharp Knife" was one step closer to the White House.

By 1829, Jackson had become president, and the next year, with the Removal Act, he was calling for the relocation of all eastern Indians to the Indian Territory west of the Mississippi River. (See "The Indian Territory" and "The Trail of Tears" in chapter 6.) The Treaty of Payne's Landing in 1832, forced upon the Seminoles by James Gadsden, a representative of Secretary of War Lewis Cass, required all Indians to evacuate Florida within three years in exchange for lands out west, a sum of money, plus blankets for the men and frocks for the women. It was also established that any Seminoles with black blood would be treated as runaway slaves, which meant the disintegration of many Seminole families. A delegation of seven Seminoles traveled west and in the Treaty of Fort Gibson of 1833 accepted an offer by Creeks for lands near them in the Indian Territory.

Yet, by the end of the appointed grace period, no Seminoles had moved west. In 1835, at Fort King on the Seminole reservation, the Indian agent General Wiley Thompson forced still another treaty, which reconfirmed the terms of removal, upon the Indians. One young Seminole by the name of Osceola (Black Drink Singer), who had risen to prominence within the tribe because of his stead-

5.13 THE SEMINOLE WARS *of the 19th century*

fast opposition to relocation, refused to sign. Thompson had him arrested. Finally, after a night of incarceration, Osceola capitulated, but only to gain his escape. A short time afterward Osceola killed one of the leaders of the pro-removal faction, Charley Emathla, and scattered the money whites had paid him for his cows to the wind as a symbolic gesture. With it, active Seminole resistance had begun. So had the Second Seminole War.

Seminole women and children hid out deep in the Florida jungles and swamps. The men formed small marauding parties, which would use the guerrilla tactics of small hit-and-run raids with great success. Three of the earliest Seminole victories took place within days of each other during the last week of 1835: Osceola and a small band of warriors ambushed and killed General Thompson and four other whites at Fort King. That same day, a larger contingent of 300 Indians under the chiefs Micanopy, Alligator, and Jumper attacked and massacred a column of 100 soldiers under Major Francis Dade on their way from Fort

Brooke on Tampa Bay to reinforce Fort King. Only three soldiers escaped by feigning death. Then, three days later on New Year's Eve, several hundred Seminoles under Osceola and Alligator surprised a force of 300 regulars and 500 Florida militia under General Clinch on the Withlacoochee River. In one of the few battles in which the Seminoles risked open conflict, the Indians managed to drive the much larger white force away.

The Second Seminole War lasted seven years. Many indecisive battles were fought and many commanders in chief were appointed and recalled by President Jackson. Generals Edmund Gaines, Duncan Clinch, Winfield Scott, Robert Call, Thomas Jesup, Colonel Zachary Taylor, generals Alexander McComb, Walker Armistead, and William Worth all failed in their efforts to conquer the Seminoles. General Jesup did manage to capture Osceola in 1837, but only through trickery at a supposed peace council near St. Augustine. The Seminole freedom fighter died in an army prison in South Carolina on January 30, 1838, almost exactly two years after

his victory at Withlacoochee, but the Indian resistance persisted under such leaders as Alligator and Billy Bowlegs. Also in 1837, the whites had one of their few military victories when Colonel Zachary Taylor surprised Alligator's warriors at Lake Okeechobee and won the ground. But even there the Indians suffered fewer dead and wounded than Taylor's men.

And so the war dragged on. With more and more troops sent against them, the Seminoles retreated farther and farther southward into the Everglades. Some warriors surrendered and some were captured. From 1835 to 1842, about 3,000 Seminoles were shipped to the Indian Territory. But for every two Seminoles transferred, one soldier died. And the war cost the federal government $20 million. In 1842, the government decided that the task of flushing the remaining Seminoles out of the Everglades was too costly and gave up trying. The Second Seminole War wound down with the Seminoles never formally conquered, a distinction their 20th-century descendants in Florida point out in claiming to have the rights of a sovereign nation.

A third Seminole uprising flared up in 1855, when a party of white engineers and surveyors in the Great Cypress Swamp stole some crops and destroyed others belonging to Indians in Billy Bowlegs' band, and then, when confronted, refused to give either an apology or compensation. Once again, the Seminoles went on a campaign of guerrilla warfare—attacking settlers, trappers, and traders in the region, then retreating into the wilds. And once again army regulars and militiamen couldn't contain them.

Finally, in 1858, when a group of Seminoles from the Indian Territory were brought to Florida to negotiate with their relatives, making an offer of peace and cash for the whites, Billy Bowlegs and his band agreed to emigrate west. In fact, the chief later fought valiantly for the Union in the Civil War. But many Seminoles who still refused to depart continued to inhabit the Florida Everglades.

THE ALEUT, TLINGIT, AND POMO RESISTANCE AGAINST THE RUSSIANS

The *promyshlenniki*—Russian fur traders and hunters—came to the Aleutian Islands and Alaskan mainland soon after Vitus Bering's voyage of exploration for Russia in 1741. They had already worked their way across Siberia in search of furs for their European markets and now were expanding their domain even further eastward. In North America they found not only a bountiful new harvest of furs—especially sea otter and seal—but also a people, the Aleuts, who possessed great hunting and fur preservation skills, and who could be bullied into free labor because they lacked firearms. As a result, while the English and French had impact from the east on native peoples, and the Spanish had impact from the south, the Russians impinged from the west. And, like the other colonial powers, they too were met with fierce native resistance.

During their first 20 years in the North American wilderness, the *promyshlenniki* had virtually no rules governing their treatment of natives. With regard to the New World, the primary concern of the court in St. Petersburg was the *yasak*, the 10 percent royal tax on furs. And, as was the case at other places and other times in Indian history, the Europeans at the edge of the advancing colonial frontier were often society's outcasts, with little respect for other peoples' life or property, especially when those people were of another race.

The typical early Russian method of acquiring furs was to sail to a native village, take hostages either by means of violence or with the threat of violence, pass out traps to the men, then demand furs in exchange for the lives of the women and children. And, while the native men were away on the hunt, the native women would be used as concubines. If the men failed to deliver the requisite number of furs, hostages would be executed. (On the island of Attu in 1745, the Russians executed 15 Aleuts to set an example; on Kanaga in 1757, they attacked, plundered, and razed an entire Aleut village.) Then, when the furs were collected, the Russians would depart until the next season.

The *promyshlenniki* worked their way eastward from island to island, exploiting the natives. By the early 1760s, they had reached the easternmost islands in the Aleutian chain—the Fox group—including the islands of Umnak, Unalaska, and Unimak—where they met the first organized

Tlingit iron and ivory war knife

native recalcitrance. Both Aleuts and Eskimos rebelled rather than work for the Russians or give over their women as hostages and concubines. On Umnak, in 1761, a native attack decimated a party of traders, only a few survivors escaping from the Aleut village to the mother ship. Then, the following year, in a series of small raids on landing parties and attacks on anchored ships, the Aleuts managed to destroy most of a fleet of five ships sailing out of Kamchatka. Aleut resistance was effective through 1765, during which time Russian traders and crews were in peril.

Then, in 1766, a Russian trader out of Okhotsk, Ivan Soloviof, organized and led an armada against the Aleuts with the purpose not only of crushing the rebellion but also of reducing the Aleut population. The fleet of ships, each with cannon and a force of heavily armed mercenaries, attacked island after island. The Russians bombarded the palisaded Aleut villages, overran resisters, and either executed prisoners—men, women, and children—or took them as slaves or concubines. As intended, the Aleut population declined drastically during this period, from both massacre and disease, to a level that the Russians could manage effectively without the continued threat of armed rebellion.

After 1765, businessmen in the trading center at Okhotsk across the Bering Sea began structuring the North American fur business, with investors buying shares in small companies organized for one-year ventures. The *promyshlenniki* found themselves with regulations for dealing with the surviving Aleut hunters. The natives were to work with the Russians on fur expeditions for half-shares. But, since the natives were charged by the traders for rations, protection, and all kinds of fabricated expenses, their supposed shares were meaningless.

By the 1780s, British and American traders were also working the region. To protect their territorial claims and economic interests, the Russians, under the impetus of the entrepreneur Gregory Shelikov, began establishing permanent colonies, the first at Three Saints on Kodiak Island in 1784. Because of Shelikov's efforts and those of another merchant-trader, Alexander Baranov, who worked for him, a trade monopoly developed. By the 1790s, the 40 or so ad hoc companies formed each year had become only three and then finally one, the United American Company. During the next several years, while Baranov ran the field operation, striving for new efficiency (entire Aleut villages became company employees in the acquisition and preparation of furs), Shelikov lobbied in St. Petersburg for a royal charter. He argued that with a royal-backed monopoly, the treatment of natives could be better supervised. He also pointed up the need of mission-

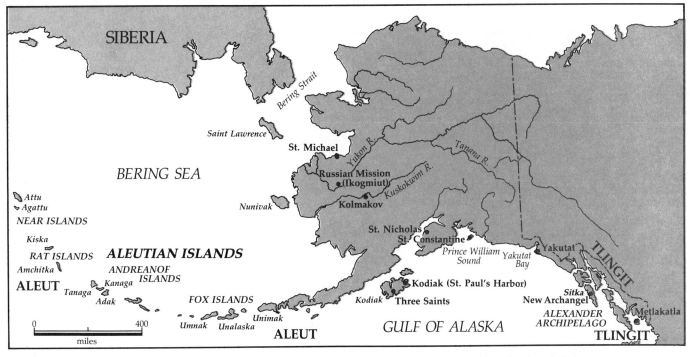

5.14 RUSSIAN ALASKA *and lands of the Aleuts and Tlingits during Russian tenure in North America (with modern boundaries). For Russian posts in California, see map 4.4.*

aries among the natives, a pleasing idea to the Russian Orthodox Church. The czar granted the charter in 1799, four years after Shelikov's death, authorizing the formation of the Russian American Company.

During the 19th century until the sale of Alaska to the United States in 1867, the Russian American Company would gather millions of furs in North America and, along with another huge monopoly, the Hudson's Bay Company (which had merged with the North West Company in 1821), would dominate the world market. But one proud, warlike people successfully resisted the *promyshlenniki* from first contact until the end of Russian tenure on the continent. In fact, these people had a great deal to do with Russia's abandoning its North American endeavor. They were known to the Russians as the Kolush. These were the Tlingits.

Early Russian-Tlingit encounters occurred in the 1790s on Yakutat Bay and the Alexander Archipelago. The Tlingits at first refused to trade with Baranov's men, claiming that Russian goods—metals and textiles—were more expensive but inferior to British and American goods. Yet they gave the Russians and their Aleut hunters

permission to use tribal lands in exchange for gifts. With further Russian activity in the region, however, the Tlingits became concerned that their own supply of furs would be depleted. At Prince William Sound, rather than grant permission, the Tlingits decided to attack and drive off the intruders. They did so at night, killing two Russians and nine Aleuts, wounding 15 more. The Indians wore animal masks to protect their faces as well as chest armor of wooden slats lashed together with rawhide strips, which actually repelled Russian bullets.

From that time until 1867, Tlingit insurgents continued to launch surprise raids on Russian hunting parties and trading posts. In 1802, a force of Tlingit warriors captured New Archangel on Sitka, killing 20 Russians and 130 Aleuts, and stealing thousands of pelts. Two years later, Baranov retaliated with an armada which, after long shelling of the island, managed to recapture the post. In 1805, Tlingit warriors raided the Russian outpost at Yakutat, again killing and capturing many. In 1806, the Tlinkits mounted another invasion of Sitka, consisting of 400 war canoes and 2,000 warriors. But the *promysh-*

lenniki, warned of the impending attack by Tlingit women living among them, bought off the warriors with a lavish feast and presents. Still other Tlingit assaults followed in 1809 and 1813. In 1818, Baranov requested help from the Russian Royal Navy, who sent in a warship to quiet the region.

Yet, year after year, the Russians had to contend with the bellicose Tlingit presence, which was made even more formidable by British and American firearms. Moreover, the Tlingit women living among the Russians as wives and concubines became a powerful political presence, playing both sides of the game.

Still another tribe resisted exploitation at the hands of the *promyshlenniki*. The Pomos lived in California near Bodega Bay, where the Russians founded Fort Ross in 1812 at the southern limits of their North American trading empire. As the Russians demanded more and more conscripted labor of them, the Pomos began committing acts of vandalism and violence. But, as in the case of the Aleuts, by the time the Russians abandoned this southern outpost (1841), the Pomo population had been reduced by murder, debilitating labor, and disease.

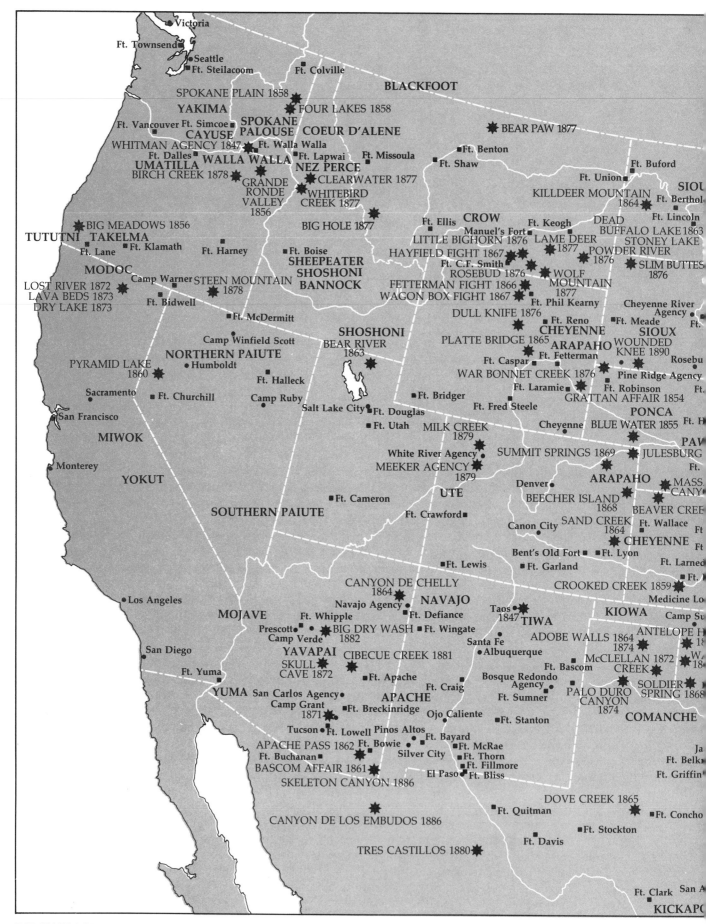

Victoria
Ft. Townsend
Seattle
Ft. Steilacoom
Ft. Colville
BLACKFOOT
SPOKANE PLAIN 1858
YAKIMA   SPOKANE   FOUR LAKES 1858
Ft. Vancouver Ft. Simcoe PALOUSE   COEUR D'ALENE   BEAR PAW 1877
CAYUSE
WHITMAN AGENCY 1847   Ft. Walla Walla   Ft. Benton   Ft. Buford
Ft. Dalles   WALLA WALLA   Ft. Lapwai   Ft. Missoula   Ft. Union
UMATILLA   NEZ PERCE   Ft. Shaw   SIOU
BIRCH CREEK 1878   GRANDE   CLEARWATER 1877   KILLDEER MOUNTAIN   Ft. Bertho
                   RONDE   WHITEBIRD   1864   Ft. Lincoln 1863
                   VALLEY   CREEK 1877   Ft. Ellis CROW   DEAD   BUFFALO LAKE 1863
BIG MEADOWS 1856   1856   Manuel's Fort Ft. Keogh   STONEY LAKE
TUTUTNI TAKELMA   BIG HOLE 1877   LITTLE BIGHORN 1876 LAME DEER POWDER RIVER
   Ft. Lane Ft. Klamath Ft. Harney   Ft. Boise   HAYFIELD FIGHT 1867 1877   1876   SLIM BUTTES
MODOC   SHEEPEATER   Ft. C.F. Smith   WOLF   1876
LOST RIVER 1872 Camp Warner STEEN MOUNTAIN SHOSHONI ROSEBUD 1876 MOUNTAIN
LAVA BEDS 1873   Ft. Bidwell   1878   BANNOCK   FETTERMAN FIGHT 1866 1877 Cheyenne River
DRY LAKE 1873   WAGON BOX FIGHT 1867 Ft. Phil Kearny   Agency
                   Ft. McDermitt   DULL KNIFE 1876   Ft. Reno Ft. Meade Ft.
                                        SHOSHONI   CHEYENNE SIOUX
              Camp Winfield Scott   BEAR RIVER PLATTE BRIDGE 1865 ARAPAHO WOUNDED
NORTHERN PAIUTE   1863   Ft. Caspar Ft. Fetterman KNEE 1890   Rosebu
PYRAMID LAKE   Humboldt   WAR BONNET CREEK 1876 Pine Ridge Agency
   1860   Ft. Laramie Ft. Robinson   Ft.
Sacramento   Ft. Churchill Ft. Halleck   GRATTAN AFFAIR 1854
                        Camp Ruby   Ft. Fred Steele   PONCA
San Francisco   Salt Lake City Ft. Douglas MILK CREEK Cheyenne BLUE WATER 1855 PAW
                          Ft. Utah   1879   White River Agency SUMMIT SPRINGS 1869 JULESBURG
MIWOK   MEEKER AGENCY Denver   ARAPAHO Ft.
                                      1879   BEECHER ISLAND MASS
Monterey   UTE   Canon City 1868 CANY
YOKUT   Ft. Cameron   SAND CREEK Ft. Wallace BEAVER CREE
                              Ft. Crawford   Bent's Old Fort 1864 Ft.
SOUTHERN PAIUTE   Ft. Lyon CHEYENNE
                                          Ft. Lewis   Ft. Larned
Los Angeles   Ft. Garland   Ft.
                    CANYON DE CHELLY   CROOKED CREEK 1859
           Navajo Agency 1864 NAVAJO   Taos   Medicine Lo
MOJAVE   Ft. Whipple Ft. Defiance 1847 TIWA KIOWA Camp Su
       Prescott BIG DRY WASH Ft. Wingate   Santa Fe ADOBE WALLS 1864 ANTELOPE H
       Camp Verde 1882   Albuquerque   1874   18
San Diego YAVAPAI CIBECUE CREEK 1881   McCLELLAN 1872 WA
       SKULL   Bosque Redondo CREEK   18
Ft. Yuma CAVE 1872 Ft. Apache   Ft. Craig Agency   PALO DURO SOLDIER
YUMA San Carlos Agency   APACHE   Ft. Sumner CANYON SPRING 1868
     Camp Grant Ft. Breckinridge Ojo Caliente   1874   COMANCHE
       1871   Tucson Ft. Lowell Pinos Altos Ft. Stanton
APACHE PASS 1862 Ft. Bowie Ft. Bayard   Ja
Ft. Buchanan   Silver City Ft. McRae   Ft. Belk
BASCOM AFFAIR 1861   El Paso Ft. Thorn   Ft. Griffin
SKELETON CANYON 1886   Ft. Fillmore
                    Ft. Bliss
                                DOVE CREEK 1865
CANYON DE LOS EMBUDOS 1886   Ft. Quitman   Ft. Concho
                              Ft. Stockton
TRES CASTILLOS 1880   Ft. Davis
                                      Ft. Clark San A
                                      KICKAPO

5.15 WARS FOR THE WEST *in the 19th century, showing major tribes, battles, settlements, and forts (with modern boundaries)*

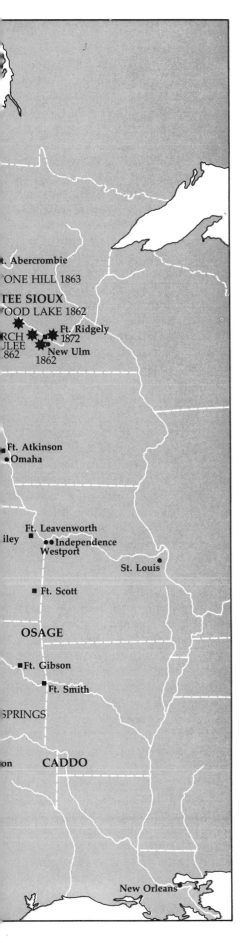

WARS FOR THE WEST

The various conflicts for the American West between Indians and whites are the most famous and best documented of all the Indian wars. The Great Plains warrior—his horsemanship, his tepees, his warbonnets—has even become the dominant Indian image in popular culture. Yet the Indian wars west of the Mississippi are the most difficult to sort out. Numerous tribes were involved—some independently and many in unison—in a vast theater of war that stretched from the prairies to the Pacific, and their resistance against the rapidly expanding white frontier lasted the better part of a century. There are any number of ways to organize the wars for purposes of study—by tribes, by geographical regions, by historical periods, by battles, by military campaigns, or by day-to-day accounts, as they were reported at the time in eastern newspapers. This book, to facilitate additional in-depth studies, will try to communicate a sense of all but the final approach by presenting, in this section, an overview of historical periods, and then, in lists of tribes organized alphabetically by regions—the Mountains and Far West, the Southwest, and the Great Plains—by summarizing tribal involvement. In the process, army campaigns and major battles will be touched upon. Battles and tribes are also represented visually on maps. It should be kept in mind that during the years of United States expansion westward, many of the wars did not have distinct beginnings and ends, as described for the sake of study, but were part of a continuous cycle of raids and counterraids.

Although widespread fighting did not occur until the later years of increased white expansion, it can be said that the Wars for the West began in the 1830s with the Indian Removal Act, the establishment of a so-called "Permanent Indian Frontier" west of the Mississippi, and the Trail of Tears. Even while federal and state governments were removing eastern Indians and assigning them lands in the West, more and more whites were turning their attention to the development of the same region—traders and trappers mainly, but some homesteaders as well. Most Indian and white clashes of this period took place on the southern plains and Southwest, part of Mexico's claim at the time. In 1835, when Texas declared itself an independent republic from Mexico, it also formed the Texas Rangers, in large part to contain the raids of the Comanches and their allies, the Kiowas. Indian raids persisted in Texas, however, as they were likely to wherever and whenever whites ventured through the homelands of territorial, warlike tribes.

Plains Indian warbonnet

The 1840s saw an increase in hostilities, much of it again involving the Comanches and Kiowas in Texas. And, during the Mexican War that broke out between the United States and Mexico largely because of the American annexation of Texas, the Navajos were drawn into their first conflict with Anglo-Americans, and the Tiwa Indians of the Taos Pueblo rebelled against the new American occupiers of their homeland, assassinating the first American governor of New Mexico. Moreover, in 1847, fighting broke out in the Pacific Northwest, when the Cayuses, blaming the missionaries for an outbreak of measles among the tribe, killed Marcus Whitman, his wife, and ten others. The Cayuse War lasted until 1850.

It was during the ensuing decade of the 1850s that white expansion dramatically increased and war spread to most parts of the American West, from the Great Plains to the Pacific. Two events account for the drastic rise in the white population and the resulting conflicts: the United States takeover of the Southwest from Mexico, following the resolution of the Mexican War in 1848, and the California Gold Rush, beginning the same year.

The Indians wars of this period, listed chronologically, were: 1) the Mariposa War in California (1850–51), involving Miwoks and Yokuts; 2) the Yuma and Mojave Uprising in Arizona and California (1851); 3) the Yakima War in Washington (1855–56), involving Yakimas, Walla Wallas, Umatillas, and Cayuses; 4) the Rogue River War in Oregon (1855–56), involving Takelmas and Tututnis; 5) the Coeur d'Alene War (or the Spokane War) in Washington (1858), involving Coeur d'Alenes, Spokanes, Palouses, Yakimas, and Northern Paiutes.

Meanwhile, on the southern plains, Comanches and Kiowas kept up their pattern of raiding. And in the central and northern plains, the Sioux, Cheyennes, and Arapahos had their first engagements with white military forces—in the Grattan Affair of 1854, and in the Battle of Solomon Fork of 1857.

It was also during these years that, along with the traders, trappers, miners, whiskey peddlers, and squatters, an increasing number of forts and military roads, built for their protection, began to appear. And with this added protection came even more whites—lumbermen to provide the wood to build the posts, traders to supply them with goods, steamboat crewmen to carry men and supplies to them, and homesteaders to

stake claims near them. The army meanwhile began to take on its new western character. In campaigning against the mounted and highly skilled Plains warriors, horse soldiers (at first called dragoons until after the Civil War, then cavalrymen) were more important than foot soldiers, having become the new army elite. Making up the new army were a certain number of veterans from eastern campaigns, continuing in their chosen profession; as well as some gentlemen officers, mostly of English descent, proving their courage and shaping their careers; some recent immigrants, especially Irish and German, looking for room, board, and regular pay; and some criminals, derelicts, and drunks, hiding out from the law back East or seeking new lives. These soldiers were outnumbered by the Indian warriors of the many tribes. But, other than some intertribal alliances, the Indians overall failed to present a united and organized front because of longstanding feuds.

Indian warriors outnumbered soldiers even to a greater extent in the early 1860s, as many of those mobilized in the West during the previous decade were pulled out of the frontier posts to fight in the Civil War. With the Pike's Peak Gold Rush in Colorado, starting in 1858, and mounting waves of trespassers on Indian lands, violence often erupted.

The major Indian-white conflicts during the first half of the 1860s were: 1) the Paiute War (or the Pyramid Lake War) in Nevada (1860), involving Southern Paiutes; 2) the Apache Uprising in Arizona and New Mexico (1861–63), surrounding the Bascom Affair and involving numerous Apache bands, with Mangas Colorado and Cochise the most important leaders (setting off 25 years of intermittent Apache unrest); 3) the Shoshoni War (or the Bear River Campaign) in Utah and Idaho (1863), involving Western Shoshonis under Bear Hunter; 4) the Minnesota Uprising of Santee Sioux under Little Crow (1862), which came to involve the Teton Sioux in North Dakota as well (1863–64); 5) the Navajo War in New

Mexico and Arizona (1863–66), culminating in the "Long Walk" of Navajo prisoners to Bosque Redondo in 1864 and the surrender of their principal leader, Manuelito, in 1866; 6) the Cheyenne-Arapaho War in Colorado and Kansas (1864–65), including the Sand Creek Massacre of Cheyenne innocents in 1864. Meanwhile, the Comanches and Kiowas, armed by the Confederates, continued their raiding activity on the southern plains. And the Mexican Kickapoos began striking at Texas settlements.

During this period, incidentally, some Indians fought alongside whites in the Civil War, especially recruits from the Indian Territory. Elements of Cherokees, Chickasaws, Choctaws, Creeks, and Seminoles fought on one side or another. Caddos, Wichitas, Osages, Shawnees, Delawares, Senecas, and Quapaws also participated, generally for the Confederacy.

The various conflicts during the 25 years from the end of the Civil War in 1865 up until the Wounded Knee incident in 1890, although scattered throughout the West, can be considered to have unity as the final and major stage of the struggle for the American West between Indians and whites. The pace of change was accelerating. The transcontinental railroad would be completed in 1869, with more and more lines soon to be added, able to bring migrants westward at a faster rate than ever—many of them unemployed veterans in quest of homesteads. The army now had thousands of war-tested troops free for service in the West, plus technologically advanced weapons to equip them and experienced officers to lead them—Civil War heroes such as William Tecumseh Sherman and Philip Henry Sheridan. The United States could mount a large and coordinated campaign, adding to their number of frontier posts, to conquer the resisting tribes, place them on reservations, and make the continent safe for the acting out of the Manifest Destiny doctrine. The Indians most involved at this stage were Sioux, Cheyennes, Arapahos, Comanches, Kiowas, and Apaches. But other tribes played a part as well—Nez Perces, Utes, Bannocks, Paiutes, and Modocs. The Indian leaders of this period are among the most famous—Red Cloud, Sitting Bull, Crazy Horse, Black Kettle, Little Raven, Quanah Parker, Satanta, Geronimo, Chief Joseph, Ouray, and Captain Jack, to name a few. It is from this post–Civil War period, in fact, that many of the themes and legends of the Old West have sprung.

It has been estimated that in the course of these years, the United States conducted over a dozen campaigns and took part in nearly 1,000 engagements with the Indians. By the end of the epic struggle, the great herds of buffalo, a distinct line of the frontier, and the aboriginal way of life had disappeared. Hostilities of the period can be organized into a number of wars and military campaigns. In a sense, the Sand Creek Massacre of Black Kettle's Cheyennes in the previously defined Civil War period can be considered the kickoff of the final intense stage, since the tragedy solidified Indian determination and resistance.

North American bison or buffalo

A summary of episodes is as follows: 1) the War for the Bozeman Trail in Wyoming and Montana (1866–68), involving primarily the Teton Sioux under Red Cloud, and their allies, the Northern Cheyennes and Northern Arapahos; 2) the Snake War in Oregon and Idaho (1866–68), involving the Yahuskin and Walpapi bands of Northern Paiutes; 3) Hancock's Campaign on the central plains (1867), primarily against the Southern Cheyennes, Southern Arapahos, and some Sioux allies; 4) Sheridan's Campaign on the southern and central plains (sometimes called the Southern Plains

War, 1868–69), against Cheyennes, Arapahos, Sioux, Comanches, and Kiowas; 5) the Modoc War in California (1872–73), involving the Modocs under Captain Jack; 6) the Red River War on the southern plains (1874–75), involving the Comanches, Kiowas, and Southern Cheyennes under Quanah Parker; 7) the Sioux War for the Black Hills in South Dakota, Montana, and Wyoming (1876–77), involving the Sioux, Cheyennes, and Arapahos under Sitting Bull and Crazy Horse, with the famous Battle of Little Bighorn; 8) the Flight of the Nez Perces through the Northwest (1877), involving the Nez Perces under Chief Joseph; 9) the Bannock War in Idaho and Oregon (1878), involving the Bannocks, Northern Paiutes, and Cayuses; 9) the Flight of the Northern Cheyennes through the central plains (1878), involving the Northern Cheyennes under Dull Knife; 10) the Sheepeater War in Idaho (1879), involving the Sheepeaters; 11) the Ute War (1879) in Colorado, involving the Utes; 12) the ongoing Apache Wars in the Southwest, including Crook's Tonto Basin Campaign against Apaches and Yavapais (1872–73), Victorio's Resistance (1877–80), and Geronimo's Resistance (1881–86).

Once again, the various lists of wars are an oversimplification. They have been handed down historically with an implicit white bias, since more often than not their time frames have been established from army campaigns. From the Indian point of view, the Wars for the West can perhaps best be organized by tribes and by individuals. For Indian peoples, the struggle did not start and stop with particular battles, army campaigns, or treaties. For most, the war became a way of life once the settlers and soldiers began arriving, and it wasn't just a war against armies but also against hunger—as squatters usurped the land and hunters practically exterminated the buffalo for its hide—and against the whites' diseases.

MOUNTAINS AND FAR WEST

BANNOCK

The conflict known as the Bannock War occurred in Oregon and Idaho in 1878, involving the Bannocks and Northern Paiutes, as well as a number of Cayuses and Umatillas. In previous years, especially during the early Civil War period, the Bannocks and other tribes of the Great Basin, such as the Paiutes, Utes, and Shoshonis, had raided travelers along the trails—migrants, prospecting parties, freight caravans, stagecoaches, etc. In 1860 and 1863, in the Pyramid Lake and Bear River campaigns, federal troops had pacified the tribes in the Basin and reopened trails (see "Paiute" and "Shoshoni"). Then again, in 1868, federal troops under the active General George Crook had moved against Northern Paiutes in the Snake War (see "Paiute"). Since that time, Bannocks and Paiutes had peacefully drawn their meager rations from the government agencies of the region, supplementing their diet through their traditional forms of hunting and gathering in the harsh environment.

It was the issue of digging camas roots on the Camas Prairie about 90 miles southeast of Fort Boise, Idaho, a right guaranteed by earlier treaty, that sparked the war of 1878 in the atmosphere of tension following the Nez Perce conflict of 1877 (see "Nez Perce"). Bannocks and Paiutes, furious at the despoilation of their camas staple by the hogs of white ranchers, began threatening settlers. The first incident was the wounding of two whites by a single Bannock in May. Afterward, a war party of about 200 Bannocks and Paiutes gathered under the Bannock leader Buffalo Horn. In June, Buffalo Horn was killed in a clash with volunteers; his warriors regrouped at Steen Mountain in Oregon with Paiutes from the Malheur agency. The Paiute medicine man Oyte, who had been proselytizing against whites, and the

Paiute chief Egan became the leaders of the combined force.

Regular troops under General Oliver O. Howard, who had fought in the Nez Perce War, and his cavalry commander, Captain Reuben F. Bernard, mobilized out of Fort Boise. A chase through the rugged terrain of southeastern Oregon and southern Idaho ensued. A major battle occurred at Birch Creek on July 8, with Howard's force dislodging the Indians from steep bluffs. On July 12, Captain Evan Miles and an infantry column cornered some of the insurgents at the Umatilla agency near Pendleton, Oregon, where a group of Umatillas had betrayed the rebels and murdered Chief Egan. After persistent tracking by white forces, Oyte surrendered on August 12 with a party of Paiutes. A final party of Bannocks were captured east of Yellowstone Park in Wyoming in September.

The Paiute reservation at Malheur was terminated and prisoners were settled at the Yakima reservation in Washington. After having been held prisoners in military posts for a time, the Bannock prisoners were allowed to return to their reservation on the upper Snake River in Idaho.

Another band of Indians, the Sheepeaters, with some Bannocks among them, fought a war of their own in 1878 and ended up among the other Bannocks (see "Sheepeater").

CAYUSE

The first significant outbreak of violence between Indians and whites in the Northwest—an area of traditionally peaceful relations since the Lewis and Clark Expedition of 1804—involved the Cayuses of the upper Columbia River; it is referred to as the Cayuse War. Trouble began at the Presbyterian mission at Waiilatpu in Oregon Country, founded by Marcus Whitman in the 1830s.

Whitman, like his associate in the region Henry Spalding—both Presbyterians competing bitterly with Catholic missionaries and both having fanatical approaches to the conversion of Indians—had never developed a strong rapport with the Cayuse tribe as a whole. In 1847, when Cayuse children enrolled at the mission school came down with measles and started an epidemic among the tribe, the Cayuses blamed the missionaries. On November 29, Chief Tilokaikt and a warrior by the name of Tomahas, while at the mission for medicine, tomahawked Whitman to death. Other Cayuses then raided the mission, killed Whitman's wife Narcissa and 10 others, and took about 50 men, women, and children hostages.

Oregon Country raised a volunteer militia, headed by Cornelius Gilliam, a fundamentalist clergyman who had fought Indians in the East and believed in the policies of extermination. A three-man peace commission was also established to meet with other tribes, headed by Joel Palmer. Meanwhile, Peter Skene Ogden of the Hudson's Bay Company managed, in the hope of protecting fur interests, to negotiate the release of the hostages.

Gilliam's troops, however, further aggravated the issue by attacking an encampment of innocent Cayuses, killing as many as 30. Indians who had previously disapproved of the Whitman murder now joined the cause. Palouse Indians attacked when some militiamen rustled their cattle, driving the force back to Waiilatpu. Gilliam himself was killed soon afterwards by his own gun in an accident. After an unsuccessful continuing campaign that threatened to unite all the Columbia Basin tribes, the troops retired. Tilokaikt and Tomahas, plus three other Cayuses, tired of hiding out, turned themselves in two years later. They were tried, convicted, and sentenced to hang. Before dying, they refused Presbyterian rites, accepting Catholic ones instead.

The Cayuse War had long-term repercussions. Cayuse lands were open to white settlement. The war also led Congress to establish a territorial government for Oregon and more military posts. And other tribes of the Columbia Basin, once peaceful, now distrusted the whites and feared for their own lands. More wars would follow. The Cayuses themselves would be involved in two of them: the Yakima War of 1855–59 and the Bannock War of 1878 (see "Yakima" and "Bannock").

COEUR D'ALENE

The Coeur d'Alene War of 1858 in Washington and Idaho territories can be thought of as the second phase of the Yakima War that had started three years before, as the conflict spread to more tribes, including the Coeur d'Alenes, Spokanes, Palouses, and Northern Paiutes. It is also sometimes referred to as the Spokane War because of that tribe's degree of involvement.

Chief Kamiakin of the Yakimas had been calling for a general alliance among the tribes on both sides of the Columbia River for some time, citing the inexorable growth of the mining frontier in the Colville region and the repeated pattern of forced treaties and land cessions. When a column of 164 federal troops under Major Edward Steptoe marched out of Fort Walla Walla and across the Snake River into Indian country, the tribes prepared for war.

The first engagement occurred in May 1858, at Pine Creek. A combined force of about 1,000 Coeur d'Alenes, Spokanes, and Palouses attacked and routed Steptoe's column. General Newman S. Clarke sent out another force, 600 strong, under Colonel George Wright, with instructions to persist in a severe defeat of the hostiles and to seek the capture of Kamiakin and other leaders, especially Owhi and his son, Qualchin, Kamiakin's relatives by marriage. Confident because of their earlier victory, the allied tribes made the mistake of meeting the enemy on an open field, the Spokane Plain. In that battle and the Battle of Four Lakes, both occurring the first week of September, the Indians suffered high casualties, whereupon they scattered to their villages.

The army column continued its trek through Indian lands, rounding up

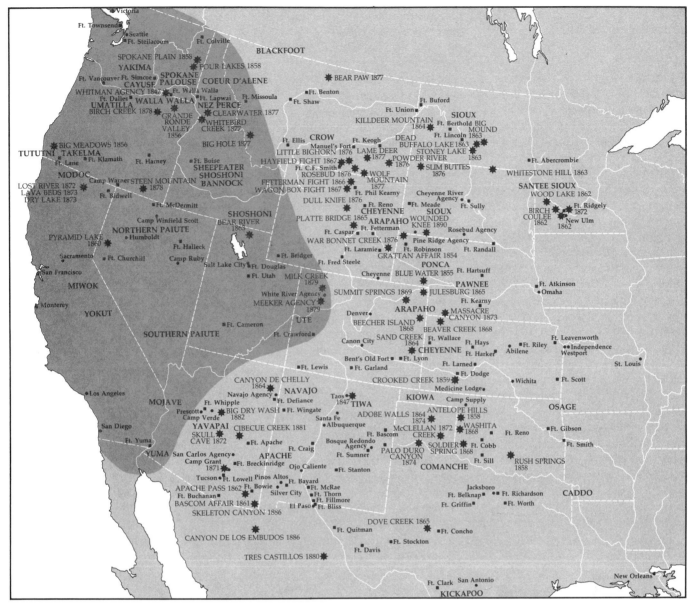

5.16 CONFLICTS IN THE MOUNTAINS AND FAR WEST (*with modern boundaries*)

dissidents. Fifteen were hanged; others jailed. Owhi gave himself up to Colonel Wright and was tricked into also surrendering his son, Qualchin. Qualchin was summarily hanged; Owhi was shot while trying to escape. Kamiakin, although wounded at Spokane Plain, managed to escape into Canada. He quietly returned three years later and lived out his life in peace on the Spokane reservation. The power of the Columbia Basin tribes had been broken. The next uprising in the region would occur to the south among the Nez Perces in 1877, the year Kamiakin died.

MIWOK

The discovery of gold in California in 1848 brought droves of settlers in search of the Mother Lode, leading to a drastic reduction in the number of California Indians. The disruption of their hunting and gathering patterns of subsistence by the rash of mining camps, the outbreak of European diseases among them, and policies of extermination, with many whites shooting Indians on sight, reduced the population by almost two-thirds within a few short years. The generally peaceful nature of the California Indians hastened their attrition since

most hostilities were one-sided against them.

In 1850, however, the Miwoks and Yokuts of the Sierra Nevada foothills and San Joaquin Valley mounted an uprising against the miners in their midst. Warriors under Chief Tenaya attacked prospectors and burned the trading posts of James D. Savage. Savage led a force of state militia, called the Mariposa Battalion, into the Sierra Nevada in 1851, to quell the insurgents; this resulted in only minor clashes. The resistance of the Miwoks and Yokuts, known historically as the Mariposa Indian War, faded gradually. A much larger rebellion, involving the Modocs, would occur 20 years later in the northern part of the state.

MODOC

As far as the whites were concerned, the Modocs had long been tamed together with the state in which they had formerly lived, California. The tribe had signed a treaty in which they ceded their lands and agreed to live on the Klamath reservation in southern Oregon. Many of them had even taken Anglo-American names. Nevertheless, while federal troops were concerned with Indian uprisings on the Great Plains and in the Southwest, and officials in Washington argued the merits of President Ulysses S. Grant's peace policy, the remnants of this once formidable tribe staged an uprising that shocked the nation.

Fed up with conditions on the Klamath reservation and their treatment at the hands of the Klamath Indians, a group of Modocs under a young leader by the name of Kintpuash, called Captain Jack, returned to their ancestral homelands just south of the California border, along the foothills of the Cascades in the northwest corner of the Great Basin. For several years, Kintpuash and his followers were allowed to live unmolested in their village on the Lost River just north of Tule Lake, where they had requested a permanent reservation. Yet, as the white population increased, so did complaints about the Indian presence. In November 1872, a force of cavalry under Captain James Jackson set forth from Fort Klamath with instructions to bring back the renegade Modocs. When the troops tried to persuade the Modocs to return to Oregon with them, a fight broke out with a fatality on each side. Kintpuash managed to lead his people out of the village to the cover of tules along the edge of the lake and then southward to the "Land of Burnt Out Fires," a volcanic highland of lava beds that served as natural fortifications. Another Modoc band under Hooker Jim resisted a posse of civilians trying to round them up, suffering the loss of an old woman and an infant. Hooker Jim's band retaliated with attacks on ranchers in the region,

killing about 15, then also took refuge in the Lava Beds.

Kintpuash had hoped that the army would not attempt to dislodge his people from their stronghold, and so he was dismayed to hear of Hooker Jim's actions, which made war inevitable. The feared attack came in mid-January 1873, after a buildup of regulars and Californian and Oregon volunteers under Lieutenant Colonel Frank Wheaton. Artillery rounds were fired into the dense fog enveloping the Lava Beds, but they dropped closer to the advancing bluecoats than to the Indians. Kintpuash recommended his people sue for peace. The militants under Hooker Jim prevailed in a democratic vote by 37 to 14, and they counterattacked. The Indians, protected behind their lava breastworks, triumphed in the ensuing fire fight. Wearing sagebrush in their headbands as camouflage, they moved about the lava trenches and caves and led the soldiers to believe they were a much larger force than 51. White casualties were high; the Indians did not lose a single man. Demoralized, Wheaton called for 1,000 reinforcements with mountain howitzers and mortars. The volunteers, who had had enough fighting, dispersed to their homes.

The military commander of the Northwest, Brigadier General Edward Canby, decided to take over the campaign personally. He built up his force to 1,000 but he also set a peace plan in motion. He managed to set up negotiations with the Modocs through the help of Kintpuash's cousin Winema—or Toby Riddle—the Modoc wife of the interpreter Frank Riddle, plus a rancher named John Fairchild, and President Grant's peace commissioners Alfred Meacham and Reverend Eleasar Thomas. A peace tent was erected on a neutral ground between the two forces and a series of talks were held. Kintpuash asked now only for the barren Lava Beds as a reservation. He also refused to turn over Hooker Jim and the other warriors involved in the attack on the settlers, pointing out that the whites were not prepared to turn over the killers of the Modoc innocents.

The militants, growing restless, taunted Kintpuash and called for action. A medicine man by the name of Curly Headed Doctor convinced Kintpuash that by killing the white leaders he would render the white troops helpless. At the next parley with Canby on April 11, Kintpuash drew a hidden revolver and killed the general, the only general killed in the Indian wars. Another warrior, Boston Charley, killed Eleasar Thomas. With these rash acts, any national sympathy for the Modoc's brave stand ended, as did any hope of a federal concession. Four days later, the new commander in the field, Colonel Alvan Gillem, launched an indecisive attack with minimal casualties on both sides. Because of the overwhelming firepower of the army, the Modocs moved further south to another lava formation. Then, on April 26, 22 Modocs under the war leader Scarfaced Charley ambushed a patrol of nearly 80 troops who had stopped in an indefensible hollow, killing 25, including all five officers.

Still, the Modoc resistance was coming to an end. The Modocs, torn by dissension, and without food and water, had scattered into small groups. The army, under a new commander, General Jeff Davis, began a mopping-up operation. They routed one group of warriors at Dry Lake. Another group under Hooker Jim turned themselves in, offering to track Kintpuash in exchange for their own freedom. Although Davis knew Hooker Jim was guilty in the death of the settlers, he agreed. After a chase over rugged and rocky terrain, Kintpuash was finally cornered in a cave on June 1. Three faithful warriors—Black Jim, Boston Charley, and Schonchin Jim—surrendered with him.

In a perfunctory trial, Hooker Jim served as a witness against Kintpuash and the others. Kintpuash claimed in his final statement that he had never been the one wanting to fight, but Hooker Jim had, and that he had been conquered by his own people, not by whites. The defendants were sentenced to be hanged. After the execution, grave robbers disinterred

Kintpuash's body, embalmed it, and displayed it in a carnival in eastern cities. Hooker Jim and the other Modocs were sent to the Indian Territory. In 1909, the surviving 51 Modocs were allowed to return to the Klamath reservation.

MOJAVE

The Mojaves of southwestern Arizona and southeastern California, like the Yumas of the same desert country, often raided travelers along southern trails westward, including the Spanish, Mexicans, and Mountain Men. In 1827, Mojaves had attacked and killed some members of a trapping expedition led by Jedediah Smith. Then, during the California Gold Rush, the Mojaves harassed voyagers along the Southern Overland Trail. In 1850, the army established Fort Yuma near the Yuma Crossing of the Colorado River to protect white migrants (see "Yuma").

NEZ PERCE

In 1855, when summoned along with other tribes of the Northwest to a council at Walla Walla in Washington Territory, the Nez Perces had been at peace with whites for half a century, since their contact with Lewis and Clark in 1805. They even proudly claimed that they had never killed a single white man. Governor Isaac Stevens's plan was to open up the majority of Indian lands to white settlement and mining, and to limit the various tribes on reservations. The Nez Perce bands agreed to Stevens's terms, in which they were to keep 10,000 square miles of their original domain, including the Wallowa Valley of northeastern Oregon. The Christianized chief Old Joseph of the Wallowa band was satisfied as long as his people could remain in their ancestral valley.

Yet, in the early 1860s, a gold rush to the region led to another wave of settlers, many of whom decided to stay in the rich Wallowa grazing country. In 1863, white officials called another council and proposed a revised treaty to further reduce the Nez Perce reservation from 10,000 to 1,000 square miles, all in western Idaho, which meant the cession of the entire Wallowa Valley. A pro-white faction of the tribe, led by Lawyer, signed the new agreement. However, Old Joseph and the Lower Nez Perces refused. On returning to the Wallowa Valley, he tore up his Bible out of disgust with the whites' ways. In the years that followed, the Lower Nez Perces stayed on in the valley, maintaining a policy of passive resistance. Many of them became involved with the Dreamer Cult, founded by the medicine man Smohalla, who preached that Indian lands had been bestowed by the Great Spirit and whites had no right to them.

In 1871, Old Joseph died. Leadership of his band passed to his two sons, one with the Christian name Joseph, the other known as Ollikut. Shortly after Old Joseph's death, a new group of white homesteaders moved into the Wallowa Valley and claimed a tract of Indian land. Young Joseph protested to the Indian agent in the region. An investigation followed. Based on the results, President Grant in 1873 formally set aside the Wallowa as a Nez Perce reservation. Nevertheless, the white land-grabbers ignored the presidential order, even threatening to exterminate the Indians if they stayed in the valley. In 1875, bowing to political pressure, the administration reversed its position to the earlier 1863 decision, declaring the valley open to white development. In May 1877, General Oliver Howard, following instructions from Washington, ordered the Lower Nez Perces to the Lapwai reservation in Idaho Territory. They had 30 days to relocate their possessions and livestock. Failure to comply would be regarded by the government as an act of war.

Joseph, fearing a major conflict and the loss of Indian life, argued for compliance in spite of taunts of cowardice from a militant faction. Ollikut, who had a reputation among the young warriors as a fearless hunter and fighter, backed his older brother,

and the issue was settled for the time being.

Yet, at dawn on June 12, while Joseph and Ollikut were south of the Salmon River tending to their cattle, a young man by the name of Wahlitits, publicly shamed for not avenging the earlier killing of his father by a white man and fueled by liquor, set out with two companions on a mission of redemption. By dark, they had attacked and killed four white men, every one known for his open hostility to Indians. Their act set in motion a chain reaction of random bloodletting. Over the next two days, other young braves joined the rampage, killing 14 or 15 more whites.

On returning home, Joseph was heartsick at the developments. But when he saw there was no stopping the other Nez Perce bands from heading south to a hiding place from where they could wage war on the whites, he decided to stand by them rather than abandon his people. He insisted on one condition, however. Joseph wanted no unnecessary violence—no slaying of women, children, and the wounded; no scalping. Two days later, with wife and newborn daughter, he joined the others at White Bird Canyon. In the meantime, General Howard at Lapwai sent a force of more than 100 mounted men into the field under Captain David Perry to round up the hostiles. The troops received word that the Indians were camped only 15 miles from Grangeville and closed in on them.

Several Indian boys, herding horses outside the camp, spotted the cavalry's approach. On the morning of June 17, the Nez Perces sent out a party of six under a flag of truce to parley. A trigger-happy bluecoat fired at them, however. The Indians fired back, killing two army buglers. There was no chance of a last-minute peace now. The remarkable flight of the Nez Perces—their running battle, against overwhelming numbers, that fell just miles short of the goal—would soon be launched.

The battle at White Bird Creek was a one-sided rout. The smaller force of Indians proved to be superior marksmen despite their old weapons, and

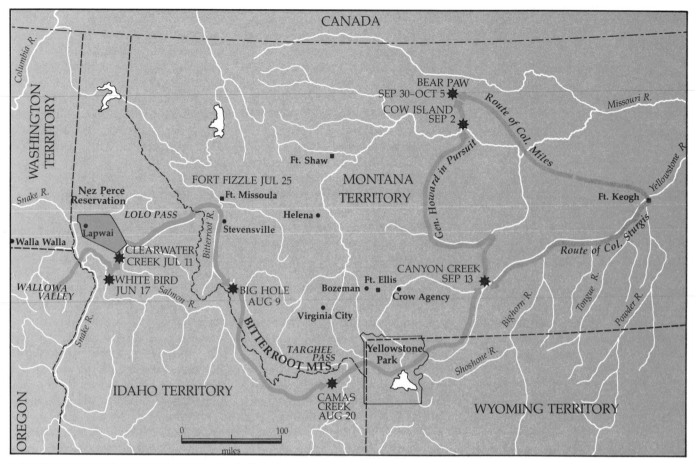

5.17 THE FLIGHT OF THE NEZ PERCE, 1877 *(with territorial boundaries)*

they outmaneuvered the soldiers on the rocky terrain. Thirty-four whites died and four were wounded. By contrast, no Indians died, with only two wounded. Moreover, the Indians captured a large number of newly issued firearms.

General Howard now led a much larger force into the field to track the renegade Nez Perce bands. For nearly a month, the warriors and their families evaded the troops along the banks of the rugged Salmon River. The Indians killed all the members of Lieutenant S.M. Rains' scouting party. Meanwhile, other Nez Perces were joining the breakaway bands, including one band under Looking Glass, whose people had been driven off their reservation in an unprovoked attack by a unit under Captain Stephen Whipple. The Nez Perces now counted about 700 among their ranks, but at least 550 of these were women, children, and men too old to fight. Leaders among them, in addition to Joseph, Ollikut, and Looking Glass, included Toohoolhoolzote, Red Echo,

Five Wounds, Rainbow, White Bird, and Lean Elk (a mixed-blood, known to the whites as Poker Joe).

On July 11, Howard's regulars, now some 600 strong, caught up with and attacked the rebels at their encampment on Clearwater Creek. But once again, the Nez Perce warriors outfought and outflanked the larger force, giving their families a chance to escape before finally, after a two-day battle, themselves retreating. Howard lost 13 men, with three times that number wounded; the Nez Perces suffered four dead and six wounded.

After the Battle of Clearwater, the various band leaders held a council on Weippe Prairie in which they decided to give up band autonomy and govern by democratic vote. Then they planned their next move. Joseph argued in favor of returning to the Wallowa Valley to fight for their ancestral homelands. The majority, however, chose to head east through the Bitterroot Mountains to seek a military alliance with the Crows. Looking

Glass was given overall command of the journey.

The ragtag force crossed into Montana through the treacherous Lolo Pass. On July 25, by guiding their horses along the face of a cliff, they bypassed a barricade hastily built by volunteers from Fort Missoula under Captain Charles Rawn. The failure of this operation led to the name Fort Fizzle for the temporary position. The Nez Perces outdistanced the volunteers and peacefully traded for desperately needed supplies at Stevensville. Then they cut south along the Bitterroot Valley. Unaware that Howard was telegraphing messages ahead to military posts in the region with instructions to intercept the fugitives, the Nez Perces stopped to rest in the Big Hole Valley. At this location, on August 9, about 200 troops under Colonel John Gibbon surprised the exhausted Indians, killing many. But the Indian sharpshooters in a fierce counterattack managed to extricate themselves and flee southeastward, crossing back into Idaho. It had been a costly stopover. Eighty-nine Indians had died, 77 of them women, children, and the elderly. The war leaders Red Echo, Five Wounds, and Rainbow were among the casualties. But Gibbon's men, with 33 wounded in addition to the 35 killed, were in no condition to follow. The colonel, who had been wounded himself, decided to dig in and wait for Howard's troops.

The pursuit continued. Howard's force closed ground on the battered Indian survivors, then commanded by Lean Elk because of Looking Glass's misjudgment at Big Hole. On the night of August 18, Ollikut and 28 others cut back for a raid on Howard's Camp at Camas Creek. The Indians managed to drive away 200 of the army's pack mules. During the delay, while the soldiers rounded up their beasts of burden, the Nez Perces angled through the Targhee Pass into Wyoming Territory and the recently established Yellowstone National Park. Parties of vacationing tourists were startled to see Indians passing through their midst. The Nez Perces pushed on through the Absaroka Mountains east of Yellowstone. Looking Glass forged ahead to seek out the help of the Crow Indians, but received nothing more than a pledge of neutrality from one band. To his dismay, he also learned that some Crows were scouting for the army. When the other leaders learned there would be no refuge among the Crows, they decided in council to head northward through Montana Territory to Canada. They now planned to seek the assistance of Sitting Bull, the famous Sioux leader, who had escaped across the border that same year (see "Sioux").

Colonel Samuel Sturgis and 350 troops of the Seventh Cavalry were now also in pursuit, approaching from the east out of Fort Keogh. The Nez Perces, having spotted their trackers, decoyed them towards the Shoshone River, then doubled back and headed north along Clark's Fork, a route the whites considered impassable. On September 13, Sturgis's men, driving their horses to their limit, caught up with the Indians at Canyon Creek, a dry, high-banked streambed. But once again, the Nez Perces outfoxed the formally trained American military. They fought a rearguard action from behind rocks and crevices in a slow retreat along the streambed, while their families hurried on ahead. Then the warriors blocked the canyon floor with boulders and brushwood. With three men dead and 11 wounded, plus a shortage of rations, Sturgis gave up the chase.

During the next two weeks, the trail-weary and battle-weary Nez Perces wound their way through the Montana wilderness toward the safety of the Canadian border. On several occasions, Crow scouts on fresh horses caught them and forayed against them before retreating. Many of the Nez Perce horses had gone lame by now, making travel even more difficult. Some of the old and wounded began dropping behind to whatever fate might come upon them. The main group crossed the Musselshell River and headed toward the northern reaches of the Missouri River. On September 25, they reached Cow Island on the river and, while a 13-man garrison hid out, they raided an army depot and obtained desperately needed supplies.

After a minor skirmish north of the river with a small detachment out of Fort Benton, the Nez Perces forged over a stretch of rolling plains and crossed the Bear Paw Mountains. Feeling more secure north of the range, convinced they had left behind all pursuers, they set up camp in a hollow next to Snake Creek, just 30 miles south of the Canadian border. Here they would regain some of their strength for the final leg of their monumental trek. What the Nez Perces did not know was that Howard, again via the telegraph, had ordered out still another force, from Fort Keogh to the southeast, under General Nelson Miles, including cavalry, infantry, and Cheyenne scouts—with orders to skirt the Bitterroot Mountains and block the escape route.

The fresh troops spotted the Indian camp on the biting cold morning of September 30. Wasting no time, Miles ordered an immediate charge. The cavalry units galloped forward across the plain, the infantry sprinting behind. In the course of a series of assaults from different directions, many warriors fell, including Joseph's brother Ollikut and Toohoolhoolzote. But Nez Perce marksmen took their toll, singling out enemy officers with deadly accuracy. Miles called off the assault and had his men dig in for a siege, rolling up the artillery. During the fray, a considerable number of warriors had managed to reach the remaining horses before the soldiers scattered them, escaping either to Canada or to wilderness hideouts; others escaped on foot. Many probably died in the days to come from exposure. Joseph, separated from the main body of Nez Perces during the early fighting, worked his way back, under rock cover, to center camp.

Howitzers and Gatling guns pounded the Nez Perce positions, but, sniping back with their small arms, the Indians stubbornly held out. Rain came on the second day, then snow. A party of six warriors slipped through enemy lines and headed north to seek help from Sitting Bull, only to die at the hands of Assiniboine Indians. Howard's troops reached the scene on October 5. Looking Glass, believing that Sioux reinforcements had arrived, moved forward to observe and took a sniper's bullet in the face. Of all the chiefs, only Joseph and White Bird remained. The time for surrender had come, they agreed. When White Bird successfully escaped through the ring of soldiers with warriors of his band, only Chief Joseph remained to speak for all the rest—about 350 women and children and 80 men.

Joseph mounted a horse and slowly rode across the battlefield toward the rows of bluecoats, several of his warriors following on foot. General Howard gave Miles the honor of accepting the surrender. It was at this time that Chief Joseph gave his speech, a translator and recording officer on hand: "Tell General Howard I know his heart. What he told me before, I have in my heart. I am tired of fighting. Our chiefs are killed. Looking Glass is dead. Toohoolhoolzote is dead. The old men are all dead. It is the young men who say yes or no. He who led the young men is dead [Joseph's brother]. It is cold and we have no blankets. The little children are freezing to death. My people, some of them, have run away to the hills, and have no blankets, no food. No one knows where they are—perhaps freezing to death. I want to have time to look for my children and see how many I can find. Maybe I shall find them among the dead. Hear me, my chiefs. I am tired. My heart is sick and sad. From where the sun now stands, I will fight no more forever."

With those words Chief Joseph carved a special place for himself in Indian history. Other chiefs had played a larger part in the strategy of the tribe's remarkable 1,700-mile flight, but by the end of the journey Joseph had become the tribe's soul; his anguish, so powerfully expressed, came to symbolize all Indian suffering. Yet, despite his national prominence and the sympathy generated by his words, he was never granted his desire to return to the Wallowa Valley. He was sent to Kansas by officials, then to the Indian Territory, and finally to the Colville reservation in Washington, where he died in 1904. The reservation doctor reported: "Joseph died of a broken heart."

PAIUTE

The Paiutes of the Great Basin, ranging within or just beyond the borders of Nevada, consisted of two major subgroups, the Northern and the Southern Paiutes. Both sets of peoples resented white intrusion into their territory, beginning in the 1850s with the influx of gold-seekers, and both were involved in conflicts with white troops.

The Northern Paiutes included a number of bands. The northernmost among them, ranging into Oregon and Idaho as well as Nevada, were the Walpapi and Yahuskin, also known collectively as the Snake Indians. Some of these Indians played

a prominent role in the Coeur d'Alene War of 1858 and the Bannock War 20 years later. But they also were the principal players in a war to which they gave one of their own names, the Snake War of 1866–68.

During the Civil War, with most federal troops drawn from the region, the rugged Paiutes had had a relatively free hand in their raids on miners and mining camps, stagecoaches and stage stations, ranches and farms, and freight caravans, especially in the drainage areas of the Malheur, John Day, and Owyhee rivers. Oregon and Nevada volunteers proved unequal to the task of taming them; in 1865, post-Civil War regulars were assigned to Fort Boise, Idaho, and other posts in the region.

The anti-Paiute campaign began unpromisingly for the army, with warriors under the chiefs Pauline and Old Weawa outmaneuvering patrols and suffering few casualties. But when Colonel George Crook took command of the operations in 1866, the tide turned. Crook began a relentless series of small tracking patrols that kept the insurgents on the run for a year and a half, forcing them into about 40 skirmishes in which, it is estimated, some 330 Paiutes were killed and 225 taken prisoner. Chief Pauline was killed in January 1867. In June the following year, Old Weawa surrendered to Crook with about 800 followers. The Paiutes remained in the region, drawing rations from Fort Harney. Some were later settled on the Malheur reservation in Oregon, and they became caught up in the Bannock War of 1878; others were settled on the Klamath reservation, also in Oregon.

Meanwhile, the Southern Paiutes of western Nevada had also engaged white forces in a conflict generally referred to as the Paiute War (also called the Pyramid Lake War) of 1860, the last major western Indian war before the Civil War. Two trading posts—Williams and Buckland—were situated in the Carson Valley, a relatively hospitable stretch of the California Trail running south of Pyramid Lake, and they served as Central Overland

Mail and Pony Express stations. War broke out with the Southern Paiutes when two Indian girls were abducted and raped by traders at Williams Station. Warriors attacked and burned the station, rescuing the girls and killing five whites.

Miners at Carson City, Virginia City, Gold Hill, and Genoa organized 105 Nevada volunteers under Major William M. Ormsby. In May, the force marched northward towards Pyramid Lake. Numaga, a Paiute chief, had fasted for peace but, in view of the recent occurrences, foresaw the inevitable; he set a trap at the Big Bend of the Truckee River Valley, his warriors hiding behind sagebrush on both sides of the pass. In the original ambush and panicked retreat through the Indian gauntlet, as many as 46 miners lost their lives.

Reinforcements out of California came to Carson Valley, as did a number of regulars, bringing the force to 800. A former Texas Ranger, Colonel Jack Hays, was given the command. At the beginning of June, the force encountered the Paiutes near the site of Ormsby's defeat. After an initial indecisive skirmish, Hays's men pursued the Indians to Pinnacle Mountain. Twenty-five warriors died in the fighting and survivors scattered into the hills. That summer, the army established Fort Churchill near Buckland Station to patrol the valley and keep the trail open.

Three decades later, a Paiute by the name of Wovoka, the founder of the Ghost Dance Religion, played an indirect role in the tragedy on the Plains that brought the Wars for the West to an end—at Wounded Knee (see "Sioux").

PALOUSE

The Palouse of the Columbia Plateau country in Washington played a significant role in both the Cayuse War of 1847–50 and the Coeur d'Alene War of 1858 (see "Cayuse" and "Coeur d'Alene").

SHEEPEATER

Sheepeater is a tribal name applied to a group of people who lived in the Salmon River Mountains of central Idaho and depended on mountain sheep for sustenance. It is not known with certainty from where these people came, but it is generally assumed they were predominantly renegade Shoshonis and Bannocks who had migrated to the highlands from the Great Basin to the south.

Whatever their blood affiliations, the Sheepeaters gave their name to an uprising the same year as the Bannock War, 1878 (see "Bannock"). On their rugged ground, the small force of Sheepeaters—perhaps only 50 in all—confounded the army, eluding a cavalry patrol under Captain Reuben F. Bernard and routing one under Lieutenant Henry Catley. Yet persistent tracking wore down the mountain Indians and brought about their surrender and the end of the so-called Sheepeater War by October, a month after the final surrender of the Bannocks in their uprising. The Sheepeaters were placed on a reservation with the Bannocks.

SHOSHONI

Because of Indian activity in the Great Basin during the Civil War, overland routes to California were often impeded. Mail carried along the road from Salt Lake City was often waylaid; telegraph lines were destroyed. In order to keep communication lines open to and from the East, California officials sent the Third California Infantry of volunteers under Colonel Patrick E. Connor across the Sierra Nevada, in what is called the Bear River Campaign.

In 1862, Connor founded Fort Douglas in the foothills of the Wasatch Mountains overlooking Salt Lake City. Out of this post, the California volunteers patroled the region, roaming into Idaho, Wyoming, and Nevada as well. Their presence, although serving to quell Indian

insurgency among the tribes of the region—the Shoshonis, Paiutes, and Bannocks—often irritated the Mormons, who resented outside interference. Yet the California volunteers enabled the Mormons to expand their land base at the expense of the Shoshonis.

The Western Shoshonis of the Great Basin saw Mormon settlements spreading northward from Salt Lake City, as well as increasing numbers of miners trespassing on their lands. Under the leadership of Chief Bear Hunter, they began fighting for their land through acts of violence against the intruders. Connor of course did not view the Shoshoni behavior as that of a desperate people defending what was rightfully theirs, but as an impediment to white progress, as well as an opportunity to prove himself to the Mormons and his superiors, and thus to further his career. In January 1863, he led a force of 300 men out of Fort Douglas northward toward the Shoshoni village on the Bear River that fed the Great Salt Lake.

The winter trek over snow-laden ground was 140 miles. By the time the Californians reached Bear River, many had severe cases of frostbite. Bear Hunter had ample warning of the invasion into Shoshoni territory. Preparing for a stand, he instructed his warriors to build barricades of rocks and earth in the hope of repelling the well-armed whites.

The attack came on January 27. The soldiers outflanked the Indian position and with their superior firepower poured round after round into the village. As many as 224 Indians, including Bear Hunter, died in the bitter fighting that lasted four hours; 164 women and children were taken prisoner. In comparison, only 21 whites were killed and 46 were wounded. Some Shoshonis managed to escape the white pincers, but afterwards they did not pose any threat to white encroachment.

As for the Northern Shoshonis of Wyoming and Montana, who lived the life of Plains hunters and were traditional enemies of the Sioux, some of them played a part in the Plains

wars, generally on the side of the whites. The famous Chief Washakie fought the Sioux on various occasions, including the Battle of the Rosebud, in which he allied himself with General George Crook's force in 1876 (see "Sioux").

SPOKANE

The Spokanes of the upper Columbia River region of eastern Washington and northern Idaho played a primary role in the Coeur d'Alene War, which is sometimes also called the Spokane War. The Yakima War of 1855, which had erupted among other Columbia Plateau tribes to the south, spread northward by 1858, leading to this second widespread uprising (see "Coeur d'Alene" and "Yakima").

TAKELMA AND TUTUTNI

The Takelma and Tututni Indians of Oregon's southern flank along the California border were called Rogue Indians by whites, because of their repeated attacks on travelers along the Siskiyou Trail. The river in their mountainous domain was also given the name Rogue, as was the war that broke out between them and white settlers in 1855–56.

With rumors of war and tensions mounting in the region because of the fighting that had broken out between Yakimas and whites east of the Cascade Mountains in September 1855, the commander of Fort Lane, Captain Andrew Jackson Smith, made a move to defuse the situation. He opened up the fort to the native population. The men arrived first; the women and children planned to follow shortly with possessions. Before they left their village, however, they were viciously attacked by Oregon volunteers not under Smith's command. Twenty-three women, children, and old men died in the massacre. The behavior of whites had made the rumors of war a self-fulfilling prophecy.

In retaliation for the murder of their families, warriors raided a settlement in the Rogue Valley, killing 27 whites.

Throughout the winter of 1855–56, Indians and whites of the valley raided and counterraided one another. Hostilities carried on until the resolution of the war the following spring, when regular troops, fresh from the Yakima War, arrived on the Rogue.

Rogue River chiefs, Old John, Limpy, and George, sent word to Captain Smith at Fort Lane that they were willing to surrender at Big Meadows. Smith set off into the field with a force of 50 dragoons and 30 infantrymen to take the Indians into custody.

Yet the Rogue River Indians, fed up with their treatment at the hands of whites, made plans for an ambush. Two Indian women warned Smith of the intended trap, however. He instructed his troops to dig in on a hilltop overlooking the Rogue. The attack came early on May 27, warriors advancing up the slopes while others fired from flanking hills. The soldiers held out against overwhelming numbers for a day, but with heavy casualties. Before the Indians could dislodge them on the second day, a company of regulars arrived under Captain Christopher Augur. In a spontaneous pincers operation, regulars attacked from the Indians' rear while militiamen charged from the hilltop, putting the Indians to flight.

Over the next several weeks, surviving Indians surrendered. Most were sent to the Siletz reservation to the north. Old John, however, was imprisoned at Fort Alcatraz in San Francisco Bay.

UMATILLA

Warriors among the Umatillas of Oregon and Washington joined other tribes of the region in the Yakima War of 1855–56. Others betrayed the Northern Paiute chief Egan in the Bannock War of 1878 (see "Yakima" and "Bannock").

UTE

With the growth of the mining frontier in eastern Utah and western Colorado beginning in the mid-19th century, the Utes had been forced by whites to cede more and more of their territory, their remaining tract in the White River region of Colorado. When Colorado joined the Union in 1876, white interests lobbied for rights to mine this last piece, calling for the removal of all the Utes to the Indian Territory. The phrase "The Utes must go" became a political slogan. The fact that the Utes had played a vital role as auxiliaries to white armies in Indian wars on the Great Plains and in the Southwest meant nothing to the expansionists who precipitated the Ute War.

The Ute leader Ouray, who had always been friendly to whites, encouraged his fellow tribesmen to increase their efforts at farming, as the Indian agent Nathan C. Meeker wanted, in order to protect their claims to land. The Utes were not natural farmers, however, and many among them, in particular bands under Douglas and Jack, resisted Meeker's uncompromising program of agriculturalization and assimilation into white culture. Meeker's solution was the calling in of federal troops to impose his will. Washington ignored his requests until a fight broke out in September 1879, between the agent and a medicine man named Johnson over the plowing of traditional grazing lands for Ute horses. A detachment of more than 150 cavalry and infantry under Major Thomas Thornburgh out of Fort Fred Steele in Wyoming was ordered to White River. When Meeker witnessed the heated reaction of the Utes, he became concerned for his own safety and sent word to Thornburgh to stop the march and continue in advance of his troops for a council. Thornburgh consented, but he ordered his troops to the edge of the reservation. One hundred warriors, believing Meeker had betrayed them, rode out under Chief Jack to block the column's path at Milk Creek, the reservation's boundary line.

Shots were exchanged before a parley could be arranged. The troops retreated to their wagon train across the creek. Major Thornburgh was felled by a Ute bullet early in the fighting. Captain J. Scott Payne took command and organized an effective defense from behind the wagons. The Utes patiently lay siege for almost a week. On the third day, a regiment of black cavalrymen arrived as reinforcements; on the seventh day, a much larger relief force arrived under Colonel Wesley Merritt. The Utes retreated. By the time the army had buried its 13 dead, tended to its 48 wounded, and reached the agency, Meeker and nine other whites had long been dead, killed by the Utes among whom he had lived for so long. Meeker's wife and daughter, along with another woman and two children, had been taken hostage.

Further violence was avoided through diplomacy. Secretary of the Interior Carl Schurz kept the militant generals Philip Henry Sheridan and William Tecumseh Sherman at bay, launching a peace mission under a former agent to the Utes, Charles Adams. Adams met with Ouray. The old and autocratic leader cajoled the hostile Utes into surrendering their hostages. Because of Ouray's mediating efforts, none of the insurgents came to trial.

Yet the push for Indian lands continued. In 1880, the same year Ouray died, the Utes were pressured into giving up their White River territory and moving to smaller parcels of land in Colorado and Utah.

WALLA WALLA

The Walla Wallas of Oregon and Washington were active in the Yakima War of 1855–56 (see "Yakima").

YAKIMA

At the Walla Walla Council in the Walla Walla Valley of Washington Territory in May 1855, Governor Isaac Stevens encouraged the tribes of the region—Nez Perce, Cayuse, Umatilla, Walla Walla, and Yakima—to relinquish the majority of their lands in exchange for reserved tracts, homes, schools, horses, cattle, and annuities. He also promised that the tribes would be able to remain in their ancestral homelands for two to three years after the ratification of the treaty. Tribal representatives disagreed on the best course of action. The majority, believing they could do no better at the hands of the whites, signed the agreement. Others, dubious of the offer, held out.

The dubious were proven right. Twelve days after the signing of the treaty, despite his promise of at least a two-year period before displacement, Stevens declared the Indian holdings open to white settlement. Because of this deception, war soon ensued. The Yakimas of the Columbia Basin were the first to erupt into violence and other tribes soon followed their example (see "Coeur d'Alene," and "Takelma and Tututni").

Kamiakin, the chief of the Yakimas, dismayed at the growing number of miners in the Colville region, advocated an alliance of tribes to contain white expansion, but he also feared direct confrontation with superior white forces. His nephew, Qualchin, plus five other young warriors, precipitated war by killing six prospectors in September 1855. When Indian agent A.J. Bolon tried to investigate the incident, he too was killed. Fort Dalles mobilized a reconnaissance force under Major Granville O. Haller. Five hundred warriors routed them, killing five, and drove them back to the fort. Subsequent expeditions under Major Gabriel Rains and Colonel James Kelly did little but arouse the hostility of other tribes. Kelly's volunteers murdered Chief Peo-peo-mox-mox of the Walla Wallas at a parley, and they displayed his scalp and ears to the settlers. Warriors among the Umatillas and Cayuses also took notice and raided some isolated settlements.

The situation had degenerated to a deadly cycle of raid and retaliation. General John E. Wool, the army commander of the Department of the Pacific, found himself at odds with Governor Stevens and his counterpart in Oregon, territorial governor George Curry, who wanted a military campaign of extermination against the Indians. In certain instances, army regulars had to defend innocent Indians from rampaging volunteers. A force of 500 regulars under George H. Wright marched through Indian lands in the spring of 1856, but found only villagers preoccupied with catching salmon. The warriors had taken refuge among sympathetic tribes to the east. The only significant encounter either that spring or summer involved a force of volunteers under Colonel B.F. Shaw against warriors of various tribes at Grande Ronde Valley in July.

The Yakima War gradually unwound to a period of inactivity by winter. Troops built Fort Walla Walla and Fort Simcoe to maintain the uneasy state of peace. The peace, however, was only temporary. The Coeur d'Alene War would follow soon.

YOKUTS

The Yokuts of central California, along with the Miwoks, were part of the uprising known as the Mariposa Indian War of 1850–51, which took place during the time of the California Gold Rush (see "Miwok").

YUMA

The Yumas and Mojaves of southwestern Arizona and southeastern California had preyed on travelers through their territory for years. In 1827, the Mojaves nearly wiped out a trapping expedition led by Jedediah Smith. Then, at the time of the California Gold Rush, the Yumas posed a special problem for gold-seekers taking the Southern Overland Trail (which later came to be called the Butterfield Southern Route), because they effectively controlled the Yuma Crossing, a natural crossing of the Colorado River located near the mouth of the Gila River in desert country.

In 1850, to keep the crossing open, the army built Fort Yuma on the California side of the river. Attacks by the Yumas and lack of supplies soon forced the abandonment of the fort, but the garrison returned after a year. The Irishman Thomas W. Sweeny, or "Fighting Tom," who had lost an arm in the Mexican War several years before, furthered his reputation as a lieutenant at the fort by raids on the Yumas. On one expedition into Baja California with 25 men, he razed villages and crops, and took 150 prisoners.

SOUTHWEST

APACHE

The first Athapascan peoples arrived in the Southwest about A.D. 850, nomadic hunters and gatherers from what is now western Canada. They spread throughout the arid tablelands of the Southwest, forming numerous bands, where they came to be known jointly among the region's original inhabitants as the Apaches—probably meaning "enemies." Even after having established their new homelands, the Apaches continued to wander over a wide range, raiding sedentary peoples for food and slaves. Fierce fighters and masters of survival in the wilderness, they were feared by other inhabitants of the Southwest—Pueblo Indians, Spanish, Mexicans, and Americans—until their ultimate conquest. Their presence and harassment checked Spanish and Mexican expansion northward. And, some years after the United States takeover of the Southwest in 1848, when they then had become enemies of the Anglo-American occupants, they proved themselves the most stubborn of the Indian guerrillas. General George Crook, who campaigned against the Apaches as well as against many other Indians, singled them out as the "tigers of the human species."

As masters of survival, the Apaches were wary of the American troops that began to arrive in great numbers after the 1848 Treaty of Guadalupe Hidalgo that ended the Mexican War. Therefore, during the 1850s, other than occasional attacks on Anglo-Americans traveling the Santa Fe Trail and Butterfield Southern Route, they preyed mostly on Mexicans south of the border. Mishandling of an incident by the army, however, shifted the pattern, providing the spark for 35 years of Apache unrest.

In 1861, a rancher by the name of John Ward wrongfully suspected Cochise, the chief of the Chiricahua Apaches, of having abducted his children and stolen his cattle. He reported the raid to the garrison at Fort Buchanan, about 40 miles south of Tucson. A lieutenant at the post, George Bascom, took it upon himself to organize a force of 54 men and ride to Apache Pass through the Chiricahua Mountains—the heart of Chiricahua Apache country, as well as the southern route westward. Bascom set up base at the Butterfield mail station, then sent word to Cochise requesting a meeting. On February 4, 1861, Cochise, suspecting no treachery, brought his brother, two nephews, a woman, and two children to the army tent. Bascom wasted no time in accusing Cochise of the raid. The chief claimed innocence, venturing a guess that the White Mountain Apaches—the Coyoteros—had enacted the raid, and offering to help recover the children. With his men surrounding the tent, Bascom informed the chief of his arrest. Cochise drew a knife, slashed through the tent, and escaped. Bascom took the other Apaches hostage.

Cochise and a war party soon began laying ambushes along the Butterfield Trail for their own hostages, killing Mexicans but taking Americans alive. Several attempts at negotiations between Cochise and Bascom failed. In one, Cochise and his men killed two Butterfield employees and seized another. The Chiricahuas were joined in further raids by White Mountain Apaches, as well as by Mimbreno Apaches led by Mangas Colorado, Cochise's father-in-law. They focused their attacks on stagecoaches on the trail. Bascom's men managed to capture three more hostages—White Mountain warriors. Two dragoon companies out of Fort Breckinridge finally drove the rampaging Apaches into Mexico. But before leaving, they killed their hostages. In retaliation, Bascom hanged all his male hostages, including Cochise's brother. The

Apaches, with bitter vengeance, swept down from their mountain hiding places in more attacks, killing, it is estimated, 150 whites and Mexicans during the next two months.

By the end of 1861, the troops had abandoned the forts in Chiricahua country because of the Civil War in the East. To fill the vacuum and protect the northern and southern routes to California, Governor John Downey organized two volunteer columns, sending one to Utah under Colonel Patrick Connor (see "Shoshoni"), and another into the Southwest under Colonel (soon to be General) James Carleton. Mimbrenos under Mangas Colorado and Chiricahuas under Cochise decided to lay a trap for the new troops invading their lands. They set up breastworks near the now abandoned mail station at Apache Pass. Carleton's advance company under Captain Thomas Roberts entered it on July 15, 1862, but, with two howitzers and repeater rifles, they were able to fend off the attackers. A private by the name of John Teal even managed to hold off the war party single-handedly with his carbine before his escape, striking Mangas Colorado in the chest.

The Apaches retreated into the wilderness. Some of the wounded chief's men took him all the way to Janos, Mexico, where they forced a Mexican doctor at gunpoint to remove the bullet in a successful operation. Meanwhile, Carleton's main column reached the mail station 10 days later. Realizing the importance of Apache Pass, the commander ordered the construction of Fort Bowie.

The following September, Carleton assumed leadership of the Department of New Mexico from General Edward Canby. General Joseph West became commander of the department's southern region. With Apache raids still occurring, West decided to use treachery to capture the most venerable of the Apache chiefs, Mangas Colorado. He had one of his captains request a parley with the chief. Mangas unwisely accepted and came to the army camp near Pinos Altos on January 17, 1863, where he was immediately seized. He was then im-

prisoned at Fort McLane on the Mimbres River. There, as it was later confirmed by a private, General West let it be known he wanted Mangas's death. That same night, as witnessed by a prospector at the post, two sentries heated their bayonets in a fire and pressed them against the sleeping Indian's feet. When he jumped up in pain, they emptied their guns into him. General West himself conducted the follow-up investigation and cleared all the soldiers involved, stating that the chief had tried to escape.

Meanwhile, to the east, the Mescalero Apaches were conducting their own raids near the El Paso end of the El Paso–Tucson link of the Butterfield Southern Route. General Carleton resolved to move against them and chose Christopher "Kit" Carson, the former trader, scout, Indian agent, and, as of late, Union soldier, to head up the operation. In early 1863, Carson set up base at Fort Stanton in southeast New Mexico, and from there he launched repeated strikes. One of his outfits, under Lieutenant William Graydon, managed to draw a war party into battle and kill two chiefs. By the end of spring, the Mescaleros, tired of the relentless pursuit, yielded and agreed to settle on a reservation near Fort Sumner in the Pecos River Valley—Bosque Redondo, as it was called, meaning "Round Grove of Trees," after a stand of cottonwoods on the parched flat. They would soon be joined at this location by Navajo prisoners captured in Carleton and Carson's next campaign (see "Navajo").

Ten years after the Bascom Affair, the Apaches were given further incentive for depredations against settlers. Chief Eskiminzin's band of Aravaipa Apaches (also called Western Apaches), desirous of peace, had moved to Camp Grant, a desert army outpost north of Tucson in what was now Arizona. (In 1863, Arizona had been organized as a separate territory from New Mexico.) The Indians turned in their weapons to Lieutenant Royal Whitman and his garrison. Citizens of Tucson, who feared and hated all Apaches, whether peaceful or not, organized a vigilante force of close to 150 Anglos, Mexicans, and Papago Indian mercenaries. On the morning of April 30, 1871, they moved on the Aravaipas and, sweeping through the sleeping camp, massacred from 86 to 150 of the innocents, mostly women and children. Of the survivors, women were raped and children carried into slavery.

President Ulysses Grant, who had devised his post–Civil War Peace Policy to avoid such massacres, was outraged and sent a peace commission to Arizona, led by General Oliver Howard and Vincent Coyler, with instructions to establish a reservation system for Apaches. By the fall of 1872, they had designated five agencies—four in Arizona and one in New Mexico—and contacted many of the bands, most of whom agreed to resettle in exchange for regular food and supplies. Howard also finally arranged a meeting with Cochise of the Chiricahuas that autumn, through the intercession of the frontiersman Thomas Jeffords. After 11 days of negotiations, the general granted Cochise's request for a reservation in the Chiricahua homeland, the Apache Pass, with Jeffords as the agent. Cochise, who promised Howard to keep order along the pass, proved good for his word, his people peaceful until his death in 1874.

In the meantime, however, other Apaches continued their marauding, many also drawing rations at the agencies. As a result of the public outcry, the military organized the Tonto Basin Campaign into the canyon and mountain country just to the south of the Mogollon Rim of central Arizona, where many of the guerrilla bands hid out. The commandant of the operation was General George Crook, recently assigned to the Southwest after establishing his reputation as an Indian-fighter in the Snake War in Idaho and Oregon (see

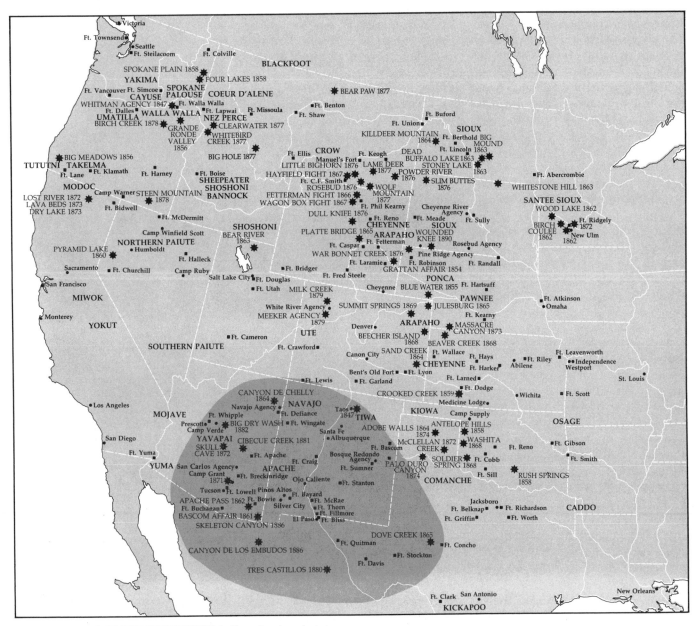

5.18 CONFLICTS IN THE SOUTHWEST (*with modern boundaries*)

"Paiute"). During the winter of 1872–73, nine small, mobile detachments, using Apache scouts recruited from the reservations, crisscrossed the basin and the surrounding tablelands in constant pursuit of the militants. They wore down their quarry, forcing as many as 20 clashes, during which they killed about 200. One outfit, under captains William Brown and James Burns, won a decisive battle at Salt River Canyon on December 28, the Battle of Skull Cave, against a band of Yavapai hostiles who had fled their reservation at Camp Verde and hid out with the Apaches (see "Yavapai"). And, on March 27, 1873, an outfit under Captain George Randall gained a decisive victory on Turret Peak which broke Indian resistance. The weary warriors and families began surrendering in April. By the following autumn, there were more than 6,000 Apaches and Yavapais, including those previously enrolled, on the reservation rolls in Arizona and New Mexico.

For the Apaches, reservation life proved an ordeal—scarce rations, disease, boredom. To escape the misery, many fled to the wilderness for a life of hunting, gathering, raiding, and plundering. In order to better control the many bands and at the same time open more territory to white settlement, officials ordered all Apaches west of the Rio Grande to the San Carlos reservation on the Gila River in Arizona in 1875. Yet some Apaches continued to resist. Two leaders became prominent—one from each of the two bands that in the 1860s had proved the most intractable. Victorio, who had grown up under the leadership of Mangas Colorado, led his Mimbreno Apaches and others in an uprising from 1877 to 1880. Geronimo, who had fought with Cochise, rallied his own band of Chiricahuas and others in the last major Indian stand, from 1881 to 1886. In doing so, his name became a war cry in the conquering culture.

The patterns of the two rebellions were similar. Both began on the San Carlos reservation and involved at least one breakout from it. Both took the guerrillas to the mountains, canyons, and deserts of the American Southwest and Mexico. And both necessitated a large number of troops on two sides of the border to win through the process of attrition.

On September 2, 1877, Victorio and more than 300 followers slipped away from San Carlos into the wilderness. Many gave themselves up within a month at Fort Wingate, New Mexico, but Victorio and 80 warriors remained in the mountains. Victorio hoped to settle his people at the Mescalero reservation at Ojo Caliente in western New Mexico, but negotiations failed. On September 4, 1879, his war party attacked a cavalry horse camp and killed the eight black guards. Joined by Mescaleros, Victorio led his force into Mexico, then Texas, then back into New Mexico, and into Arizona, carrying out a number of attacks. Both the United States and Mexico mobilized forces—under Colonel Edward Hatch in New Mexico, Colonel Benjamin Grierson in Texas, and General Geronimo Trevino in Chihuahua, Mexico. American troops regularly crossed the international border, this exception in policy made because of the Apache menace. Victorio and his men eluded them all, surviving a number of skirmishes. In the fall of 1882, while fleeing an American command of Colonel George Buell into the Chihuahua desert, Victorio let his guard down long enough to be attacked by 350 Mexican and Tarahumara Indians under Colonel Joaquin Terrazas. In the two-day Battle of Tres Castillos, meaning "Three Peaks," more than half the Apaches were killed, and all but a few of the rest were taken prisoner. Victorio turned up among the dead. It is not known whether he died fighting, or whether, as legend has it, he took his own life before the enemy could get to him.

Meanwhile, the Chiricahua Apache known as Geronimo had been living among Chief Juh's nomadic and predatory Nednhi band in the Sierra Madre, on Mexico's side of the border, ever since the dissolution of the Apache Pass reservation in 1875. In 1876, he and some others of the band appeared at the Mescalero agency at Ojo Caliente, where the San Carlos agent apprehended him along with Victorio's people and led him back to Arizona. After about a year, Geronimo had fled across the border again with Juh. And then, because of increased Mexican troop activity, the young warrior returned to San Carlos.

Increasingly, Geronimo was respected by the other warriors for his bravery and cunning, but he was still at this stage one of many leaders. He would soon prove to be the most tenacious. On August 30, 1881, the military at Fort Apache north of San Carlos made a move to arrest Nakaidoklini, a White Mountain Apache

Geronimo. New York Public Library.

who preached a new religion involving the return of dead warriors to rid native peoples of whites. Fighting erupted at Cibecue Creek. The mystic was killed. Some of his followers, including Apache army scouts in revolt, attacked Fort Apache but were driven back. Additional troops were called up to curb any more violence.

The Chiricahua leaders at San Carlos resented and feared the growing number of troops. One month after Cibecue Creek, Geronimo and Juh, along with Nachise (the son of Cochise), Chato (a Mescalero), and 74 followers, departed San Carlos for Mexico. They returned in April 1882, in a raid on the reservation in which they killed the chief of police and forced Loco and his Mimbreno Apaches to accompany them southward. Another attack followed that July by White Mountain warriors, still bitter over the death of Nakaidoklini, resulting in the Battle of the Big Dry Wash. Alarmed at the mounting level of violence, the military turned over the command to General George Crook, who had proven effective against Apaches in his Tonto Basin Campaign and had since been campaigning against the Sioux Indians. Crook organized a number of mobile units, including White Mountain Apache scouts, the only men who could track fellow Apaches.

With permission from Mexican authorities, Crook led units under Captain Emmet Crawford and Lieutenant Charles Gatewood into the Sierra Madre in May 1883. They used mules instead of horses since the former were better suited to desert campaigning. Crook managed an attack on Chato's camp on May 15. The skirmish proved inconclusive, but it was a way of announcing the military's presence and determination. In a follow-up parley, the Apache leaders agreed to return to the reservation. It took a year for all to comply, however. Juh had been killed earlier in an accident. But the others—Chato, Nachise, Loco, and Nana, who was the leader of the Mimbrenos since Victorio's death—trickled in with their followers. And finally in March 1884, the chief who had come to be revered

as the most effective of the war leaders also came in—Geronimo. Yet he was to burst forth from confinement two more times.

The next-to-last breakout in May 1885 resulted from a reservation ban on *tiswin*, the alcoholic beverage of the Apaches. Geronimo, Nachise, Nana, and almost 150 followers once again headed for the Sierra Madre. And once again, Crook's soldiers tracked them relentlessly until they finally agreed to a parley—this one at Canyon de los Embudos on March 25, 1886. Crook demanded unconditional surrender and imprisonment in the East for two years. Geronimo agreed. But while being led to Fort Bowie by Apache scouts, he, Nachise, and 24 others broke free once again.

The embarrassed army relieved Crook of his command, replacing him with General Nelson Miles, another proven Indian-fighter. In order to capture the 24 renegade Apaches, Miles put 5,000 soldiers in the field. Captain Henry Lawton led a unit into Mexico, which caught up with the fugitives on July 15. But Geronimo successfully eluded the troops.

Finally, after another month and a half of hiding out, Geronimo again agreed to surrender, but only to Miles. On September 4, 1886, at Skeleton Canyon, about 65 miles south of Apache Pass, where the Apache Wars had commenced 25 years before, the weary Geronimo and his faithful followers gave themselves up for the last time.

Soon afterward, Geronimo and nearly 500 other Apaches, including some who had served as scouts for the army, were sent by rail, in chains, to Fort Pickens in Pensacola, Florida. After a miserable one-year internment, they were relocated to Mount Vernon Barracks, Alabama, where about a quarter of them died from tuberculosis and other diseases. Although Eskiminzin's Aravaipas were finally allowed to return to San Carlos, the citizens of Arizona refused reentry to Geronimo and the Chiricahuas. Comanches and Kiowas in the Indian Territory offered to share their reservation with the Apache freedom fighters. They were led to

Fort Sill in 1894. Although already a legend to many white schoolboys throughout the United States, Geronimo was never granted permission by his former enemies to return to his homeland. He died a prisoner of war in 1909.

KICKAPOO

In the early 1850s, a large party of Kickapoos with some Potawatomis migrated to northern Mexico from the United States, having been granted land by the the Mexicans to provide a buffer between their settlements and Apache and Comanche raiders. These peoples became known as the Mexican Kickapoos. In the 1860s, because of unrest during the Civil War and efforts by both Confederate and Union armies to enlist them, some northern Kickapoos in Kansas and Texas decided to join the Mexican Kickapoos. On two different occasions, the migrants were attacked—in 1862, at Little Concho River, by a Confederate battalion; and in 1865, at Dove Creek, by an outfit of Texas Rangers. Survivors who escaped across the border reported the attacks. The Mexican Kickapoos, who had previously been content to stay south of the Rio Grande, launched a campaign of marauding and violence against Texas border communities.

In 1873, Colonel Ranald Mackenzie and his Fourth Cavalry, proven in actions against Comanches, crossed the Rio Grande for a retaliatory strike against the Mexican Kickapoos. On May 17, they razed the Kickapoo settlement near Nacimiento on the Remolino River, while most of the men were away on a hunt, and crossed back over into Texas with 50 or so women and children who were then taken to Fort Gibson in the Indian Territory. Mexico protested to Washington the violation of its border. More than 300 friends and relatives of the hostages, however—almost half the Mexican Kickapoo population—agreed to resettle in the Indian Territory. Those that stayed behind generally ceased their raids.

NAVAJO

Like the Apaches, who are thought to have preceded them by two centuries, the Navajos broke off from other Athapascan-speaking peoples in what is now western Canada and migrated to the Southwest. The approximate date given for the Navajo establishing a homeland between the three rivers—the Rio Grande, the San Juan, and the Colorado—is A.D. 1050. Also like the Apaches, the Navajos were originally a nomadic and predatory people who supplemented a hunting and gathering subsistence with raiding—at first on Pueblo peoples, and then on the Spanish. Unlike the Apaches, however, the Navajos, because of contact with the Pueblo Indians and the Spanish, experienced a revolution in life-style and economy. First of all, they adopted many of the customs—activities such as weaving, pottery making, and farming—of the villagers in their midst, many of whom fled to their sometime predators during times of warfare with the Spanish (see "The Pueblo Rebellion and Other Rebellions Against the Spanish" in this chapter). Second, the Navajos refrained from immediately eating the sheep they obtained in raids on the Spanish, as the Apaches were wont to do; instead they slowly built up their herds for both sustenance and wool, becoming in the process master sheepherders. The Navajos could now support themselves without raiding and pillaging. But they were still a rugged people. When Mexicans swept northward on one of their frequent slave raids for Navajo children, the Navajos fought back and then sought revenge through raids of their own on Mexican settlements. Continuing the common, deadly cycle, Mexican soldiers would then come to punish them, and they would have to leave their villages for the roaming and raiding life of their ancestors until the troops were gone. And, as the fledgling United States increasingly turned its attention westward in the first stirrings of Manifest Destiny in the early 19th

century, the Navajos sometimes attacked Anglo-American explorers and traders who intruded upon their domain via the Santa Fe and Gila trails. Then, during the American usurpation and occupation of the Southwest, the Dine, as the Navajos called themselves, meaning "The People," challenged the United States Army.

In 1846, during the Mexican War that was precipitated by the American annexation of Texas the year before, Colonel Stephen Kearny led a force of 1,600 men, including Missouri volunteers under Colonel Alexander Doniphan, from Fort Leavenworth, Kansas, along the Santa Fe Trail into the Mexican province of New Mexico. During his capture of Mexican towns, including Santa Fe which fell with no Mexican resistance, Kearny informed the inhabitants—Mexicans and Anglos alike—that henceforth as United States citizens they would be protected from the Indians, who would be punished for any raids upon them. The Navajos, who as Indians were not considered citizens, were given no such reassurances regarding the still-frequent Mexican slave raids to which they were subjected. As a result, because of a shortsighted lack of diplomacy, the new conquerors let the Indians know that they were outsiders, and that American rule would be no more fair than Mexican rule. The whites soon followed with a military campaign.

That winter, Colonel Doniphan organized his Missouri volunteers into three columns, totaling 330 men. The Navajos had not yet demonstrated hostility towards American troops. Doniphan's premise for the operation, however, was the continued marauding by Navajo bands stealing livestock from Mexicans and Pueblo Indians. Ironically, the very next year, Pueblo peoples and Mexicans joined together in a revolt against the American occupiers, even assassinating the new territorial governor, citing as their reason the appropriation of their livestock by the Missouri volunteers (see "Tiwa").

Doniphan's troops had a difficult time campaigning in the treacherous

high country of the lower Colorado Plateau in the winter months. Few Navajos were engaged in battle or even sighted, and Doniphan's operation became more of a wilderness exercise, with the harsh elements as the enemy. But the Navajos took notice, their scouts reporting back to the tribe's sacred stronghold, the deep and jagged Canyon de Chelly near the present-day Arizona–New Mexico border. They realized that the Americans were here to stay. They signed a treaty that year and another in 1849.

Navajo moccasins

The patterns of raids and counterraids continued, however, and, during the 1850s, the military launched a number of inconclusive campaigns against the Navajos. A point of contention between the army and the Indians was the pastureland around Fort Defiance, in a valley at the mouth of Canyon Bonito. The soldiers wanted the land for their horses. When Navajo herds continued to graze there, as their herds had been doing for generations, the soldiers shot them. The Navajos then raided army herds to recoup their losses, whereupon the soldiers attacked them. On April 30, 1860, the Navajos under Manuelito and his ally Barboncito stormed Fort Defiance itself and nearly captured the post before being forced back. In retaliation, Colonel Edward Canby led troops into the Chuska Mountains in search of Navajos. The Navajos harassed the column's flanks, but disappeared into the craggy terrain before the soldiers could counterattack. It was another standoff, but, wanting to tend their fields and herds, and feed their people, the Navajo leaders agreed to parley. A truce was reached at a council in January 1861.

It was short-lived. During the Civil War, with many soldiers heading east to fight in one army or another, an incident occurred on September 22, 1861, surrounding a horse race between Navajo and army mounts at Fort Fauntleroy (Fort Lyon since the war). Navajos claimed that a soldier had cut their horse's bridle rein, but the soldier-judges refused to run the race again; the Indians rioted and were fired upon with howitzers. Twelve Navajos died in the melee.

Meanwhile, Union and Confederate troops fought for New Mexico. By the spring of 1862, the graycoats had been driven eastward out of the region, and more bluecoats, the California column under General James Carleton, had arrived from the west to occupy the territory. Carleton, appointed as new commander of the Department of New Mexico, turned his attention to pacifying Indians. He chose Colonel Christopher (Kit) Carson, former trader, scout, Indian agent, and Union Soldier, as his commander in the field. Their solution to the persistent marauding of both Apaches and Navajos was the removal of the Indians from the areas of extensive Mexican and Anglo-American settlement along the valleys and trails. Bosque Redondo, meaning "Round Grove of Trees" and referring to a stand of cottonwoods on an otherwise barren flat of the Pecos River Valley, was chosen as the site of relocation for both Apaches and Navajos (see "Apache"). There, in the isolated eastern part of the territory, the Indians would be watched by the garrison of the heavily fortified Fort Sumner.

After contending with the Mescaleros in 1862 and early 1863, Carleton and Carson turned their attention to the Navajos. Carson sent overtures to his former friends. Some of the chiefs—Delgadito and Barboncito—having observed the effective army campaign against the Apaches, were in favor of peace, but not at the expense of trading their ancestral homelands for a piece of infertile soil on the Pecos lowlands, 300 miles to the east, at close quarters with their occasional enemies, the Mescaleros. They chose instead to follow the path of the militant Manuelito, who sought

no accommodation with the army since the horse race debacle. Carleton sent an ultimatum to the Navajos on June 23, 1863, giving them one month to report to army posts. The deadline passed. Kit Carson mobilized his force of New Mexico volunteers—Anglos, Mexicans, and a handful of Apache and Ute scouts.

Rather than attempt to track down the Navajo warrior bands in the tortuous canyon and arroyo country, forcing engagements as previous campaigns had tried to do, Carson launched a cruel but effective scorched-earth offensive against *Dinetah*, meaning "Navajo Land." His men relentlessly marched from the Continental Divide to the Colorado, destroying fields, orchards, and hogans, and confiscating livestock, the soldiers living off the Navajo produce when necessary. During the six-month sweep, Carson's soldiers reportedly killed only 78 of the estimated 12,000 Navajos, with few casualties themselves, but they thoroughly disrupted the Navajo way of life and crushed the Navajo spirit.

Then, in January 1864, Carson moved on the supposedly impregnable Canyon de Chelly itself, from where the Navajos had made successful stands against the Spanish in earlier times. Carson blocked the steep-walled canyon at one end, sending troops under Captain Albert Pfeiffer to work through it from the east. The Indians formed pockets of resistance, some throwing rocks on Pfeiffer's column from the canyon's rims. But before long, the soldiers had flushed out the defenders and taken the sacred Navajo stronghold.

By mid-March, nearly 6,000 half-starving, dejected Navajo people had surrendered to army bases. The removal began—the "Long Walk" of the Navajo—the Southwest's version of the Southeast's "Trail of Tears." Soldiers escorted 2,400 in the first forced march across 300 miles of New Mexico, about 200 of whom died en route. By the end of the year, 2,000 more Navajos had given themselves up, making 8,000 in all, the largest tribal surrender in all the Indian wars, and more were herded east. The re-

maining 4,000 under Manuelito fled towards the western limits of their domain. Manuelito himself, the most intransigent of all the Navajo chiefs, eventually succumbed to the war of attrition, surrendering at Fort Wingate on September 1, 1866.

Bosque Redondo proved a disaster for the Navajos—infertile soil, scarce supplies, disease, hostile Mescaleros. Finally, in 1868, after General Carleton had been transferred and a delegation of Navajo chiefs, including Manuelito and Barboncito, were allowed to travel to Washington to plead their case, officials finally relented and signed a new treaty with the Navajos, granting them a reservation in the Chuska mountains. The Navajos made their way back to their homeland over the trail of their Long Walk and, never making war on whites again, they began to rebuild their lives.

TIWA

During the Mexican War of 1845–48, three Indian peoples battled the new American occupiers of their homelands in the Southwest—the Apaches, the Navajos (see "Apache" and "Navajo"), and the generally peaceful Pueblo peoples of the Rio Grande Valley between Santa Fe and Taos. Although a number of other Pueblo peoples joined in the revolt, as well as some Mexican Americans, the Tiwa Indians of the Taos Pueblo were the major participants. All those involved were infuriated at the depredations of the occupying Missouri volunteers—the appropriation of crops and livestock, and the kidnapping of women. On January 19, 1847, they rose up against their occupiers, as Pope's followers had done almost two centuries before (see "The Pueblo Rebellion and Other Rebellions Against the Spanish" in this chapter), and in a series of raids killed Charles Bent, the first American territorial governor in New Mexico, and 20 other Anglo-Americans.

In rapid retaliation, Alexander Doniphan marshalled 500 militiamen in Santa Fe and sent them into the field under Colonel Sterling Price, along with Lieutenant Alexander Dwyer's artillery unit manning both six- and 12-pounder howitzers. At the village of La Canada on the road north, they were met by 800 rebels, who unsuccessfully tried to cut the advance troops off from the ammunition and supply wagons to the rear. After heavy shelling and casualties, the rebels retreated to Taos.

The troops pressed on through bitter winter weather and, three days later, reached the Taos Pueblo. The exhausted troops attacked almost immediately, bombarding the multistoried Indian dwelling and the Spanish mission church with the howitzers. The thick adobe brick, however, repelled repeated rounds of cannon shot. Then, under cover of another round, Price and Dwyer sent in the infantry, rolling up the artillery behind them. The overwhelming firepower routed the Indians, many of whom were shot while fleeing the church for the hills. Out of those taken alive, Price quickly tried and executed 15 as leaders of the insurrection. Probably more than 200 of an estimated 700 rebels lost their lives, with many more wounded.

YAVAPAI

The Yavapais, a Yuman-speaking people of central Arizona, came to be identified with the Apaches because of their activity with them in the Apache Wars, especially after 1871. During General George Crook's Tonto Basin Campaign of 1872–73 (see "Apache"), a detachment under captains William Brown and James Burns fought a band of Yavapai militants at Salt River Canyon in the Mazatzal Mountains, south of the Mogollon Rim, on December 28, 1872. In this so-called Battle of Skull Cave, the soldiers, when met with resistance, fired into the cave hideout high on the canyon wall, sending bullets ricocheting off the roof inside. Others fired from up above into the cave. Some Indians managed to surface and fight from behind rocks. Soldiers on the rim resolved the fight by rolling boul-

ders on them. About 75 Yavapais died at Skull Cave. Survivors were taken to the Apache reservation at San Carlos rather than to the Camp Verde reservation from where they had originally fled.

GREAT PLAINS

ARAPAHO

The Arapahos, like the Cheyennes and Sioux with whom they are closely associated in the Indian wars, were thought to have migrated onto the Great Plains sometime in the 17th or 18th century from the east, but probably from a region further north, perhaps the vicinity of the Red River of the North. Also, like the Cheyennes, they eventually separated into two groups. Those that came to be known as the Northern Arapahos settled just east of the Rocky Mountains, along the headwaters of the Platte River in present-day Wyoming; the Southern Arapahos settled further south, along the Arkansas River of Colorado.

The Northern Arapahos, along with the Northern Cheyennes, played a significant part in what have come to be known as the Sioux Wars (see "Sioux"). Important Northern Arapaho chiefs included Black Bear, Plenty Bear, and Sorrell Horse. The Southern Arapahos were active in Colorado and Kansas in wars involving the Cheyennes (see "Cheyenne"). Two of their important leaders in the Plains wars were Little Raven and Left Hand.

Black Bear and his northern band suffered the brunt of a campaign of three columns sent into the Powder River country of northern Wyoming and southern Montana against the allied northern tribes in August 1865, by General Patrick E. Connor. Although the 3,000 troops managed to engage the Sioux and Cheyennes in minor, inconclusive skirmishes, generally to their own disadvantage, they attacked and routed Black Bear's people, killing many men, women, and children; they then proceeded to burn their tepees and possessions. The in-

vading army was repelled from the Powder River country in September by hit-and-run Indian raids plus stormy weather. Yet the abortive campaign had a long-lasting effect: It further sealed the military alliance of the Northern Arapahos with the Sioux and Cheyennes. The massacre of Cheyenne innocents at Sand Creek one year earlier, in September 1864, witnessed by a number of Arapahos, had done the same for the southern group.

At the end of the wars (see "Cheyenne" and "Sioux") the Southern Arapahos were placed on a reservation with the Southern Cheyennes in the Indian Territory; the Northern Arapahos, however, ended up on the Wind River reservation in Wyoming with the Northern Shoshoni, once their enemies.

BLACKFOOT

The Blackfeet, also called the Siksika, along with their kinsmen, the Bloods and Piegans, probably migrated onto the northernmost plains from the northeast. Most of them settled in what is now part of Canada, but others reached as far south as present-day Montana. Although they persistently raided American whites who entered their domain—one of their victims was John Bozeman in 1867, whose trail sparked one of the Sioux uprisings (see "Sioux")—they did not confront the United States military as a tribe. They did, however, play a part in impeding the conquest of the Canadian West. (See "Canadian Indian Wars" in this chapter.)

CADDO

The Caddo of the southeastern plains in present-day Arkansas, Texas, and Louisiana were a farming people, at odds with the nomadic hunting tribes of the Plains. As a result, their Chief Guadalupe saw the war between Indians and whites as one between hunters and farmers and encouraged his people to serve as scouts in the United States Army.

CHEYENNE

The Cheyennes, who had once lived east of the Missouri River, came to be nomadic hunters on the Great Plains. In the 19th century, as white pressures increased, they also became allies of both the Sioux and the Arapahos. In the Fort Laramie Treaty of 1851, the Cheyennes living along the upper Arkansas were designated as the Southern Cheyennes, and those living along the North Platte were called the Northern Cheyennes. The northern group played a critical part in the so-called Sioux Wars of the northern plains in most of the major clashes with whites, during the period from 1865 to 1876; their important chiefs, such as Dull Knife, joined the Sioux leaders Red Cloud, Sitting Bull, and Crazy Horse (see "Sioux"). The Southern Cheyennes were also active in the Wars for the West, and many military campaigns were launched against them. The two Cheyenne groups of course were not mutually exclusive. During the war years, there was considerable movement among the various peoples, as there had always been among the hunting bands of the Plains, with some northern tribesmen fighting alongside their southern kinsmen and vice versa. The Cheyennes as a whole thought of themselves as the "Beautiful People."

An early engagement involving the Southern Cheyennes occurred in 1857, three years after the Grattan incident brought the whites' war to the Sioux. Because of raids on prospectors along the Smoky Hill Trail to the Rockies, the army sent in 300 cavalrymen under Colonel Edwin Sumner to punish the Cheyennes. In the Battle of Solomon Fork in western Kansas on July 29, Sumner routed an equivalent number of warriors in a sabre charge.

In the course of the next outbreak of violence—sometimes referred to as the Cheyenne-Arapaho War or the Colorado War of 1864–65—a tragedy occurred that served to unite many of the Plains tribes in their distrust and

Plains warriors. A crayon sketch by Howling Wolf, Cheyenne, while imprisoned at Fort Marion, Florida, 1876. New York State Library, Albany.

hatred of whites. Because of the rapid growth of mining interests in Colorado after the Pike's Peak Gold Rush of 1858, Governor John Evans sought to open up Cheyenne and Arapaho hunting grounds to white development. The tribes, however, refused to sell their lands and settle on reservations. Evans decided therefore to force the issue through war and, using isolated incidents of violence as a pretext, ordered troops into the field under the ambitious, Indian-hating territorial military commander Colonel John Chivington.

In the spring of 1864, while the Civil War raged in the east, Chivington launched a campaign of violence against the Cheyennes and their allies, his troops attacking any and all Indians and razing their villages. The Cheyennes, joined by neighboring Arapahos, Sioux, Comanches, and Kiowas in both Colorado and Kansas, went on the defensive warpath. Evans and Chivington reinforced their militia, raising the Third Colorado Cavalry of short-term volunteers who referred to themselves as "Hundred Dazers." After a summer of scattered small raids and clashes, Indian and white representatives met at Camp Weld outside Denver on September

28. No firm agreements were reached, but the Indians were led to believe that by reporting to and camping near army posts, they would be declaring peace and accepting sanctuary. A Cheyenne chief by the name of Black Kettle, long a proponent of peace, led his band of about 600 Cheyennes and some Arapahos to a camping place along Sand Creek, about 40 miles from Fort Lyon, and informed the garrison of their presence.

Shortly afterward, Chivington rode into the fort with a force of about 700, including the Third Cavalry, and gave the garrison notice of his plans for an attack on the Indian encampment. Although he was informed that Black Kettle had already surrendered, Chivington pressed on with what he considered a perfect opportunity to further the cause of Indian extinction. On November 29, he led his troops, many of them drinking heavily, to Sand Creek and positioned them, along with their four howitzers, around the Indian camp. Black Kettle, ever-trusting, raised both an American and a white flag over his tepee. In response, Chivington raised his arm for the attack. With army rifles and cannons pounding them, the Indians scattered in panic. Then the

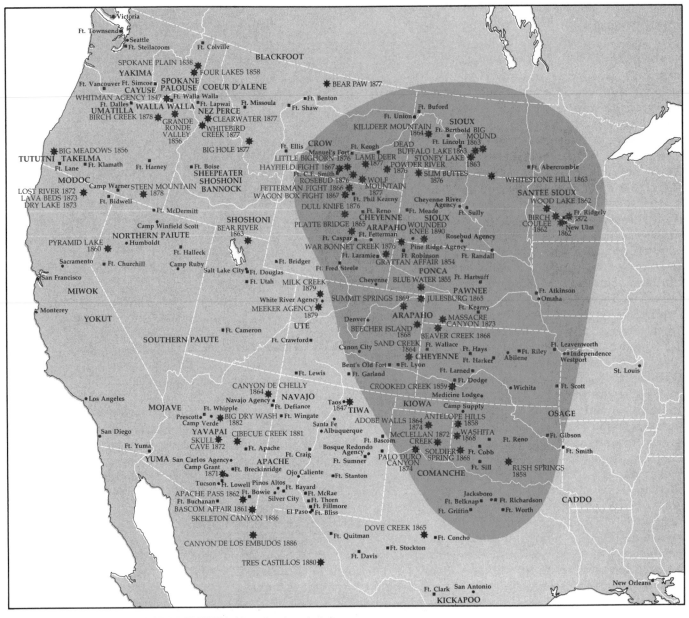

5.19 CONFLICTS ON THE GREAT PLAINS (*with modern boundaries*)

soldiers charged. A few warriors managed to fight back briefly from behind the high bank of the stream, and others, including Black Kettle, escaped over the plains. But by the end of the quick and brutal massacre, as many as 200 Indians, more than half of them women and children, had died. Chivington's policy was one of no prisoner taking, and his Colorado volunteers had been happy to oblige. Chivington was later denounced in a congressional investigation and forced to resign. Yet an after-the-fact reprimand of the colonel meant nothing to the Indians. As word of the massacre spread among them via refugees, Indians of the

southern and northern plains stiffened in their resolve to resist white encroachment. Cheyennes and Arapahos stepped up their raids and, on January 7 and again on February 18, they stormed the town and freight station at Julesburg along the South Platte River, on the overland route from the Oregon Trail to Denver, forcing its abandonment. The final and most intense phase of the war for the Plains had begun. It would take another massacre at Wounded Knee a quarter of a century later to end it.

Soon after the conclusion of the Civil War, the army organized an offensive against the Indians of the central

plains, which is known as the Hancock Campaign of 1867. General Winfield Scott Hancock set up his command at Fort Larned along the Santa Fe Trail in western Kansas. From there, after an unproductive parley with the Southern Cheyenne leaders Tall Bull and White Horse, Hancock launched a campaign that also turned out to be abortive. Hancock's chief commander in the field was the young cavalry officer George Armstrong Custer. Custer's career as an Indian-fighter would begin with frustration and end nine years later with disaster at Little Bighorn (see "Sioux").

During the summer of the Hancock

Campaign, Custer and his Seventh Cavalry chased the Cheyennes and their Sioux allies throughout western Kansas, northeastern Colorado, and southwestern Nebraska. He succeeded in burning an evacuated village on the Pawnee Fork but little else, as the Indians stayed one step ahead of his outfit and raided mail stations, stagecoaches, wagon trains, and railroad workers at will. The war parties even undertook forays against Fort Wallace on several occasions, where Custer's force ended up on July 13, with men and horses too exhausted to continue.

That autumn, peace advocates in the government, citing both the Hancock Campaign and the Bozeman Campaign to the north as failures and claiming that heavy-handed military policies, exemplified by Sand Creek, had only made matters worse, launched a peace commission that resulted in two treaties—the Medicine Lodge Treaty of 1867 in Kansas and the Fort Laramie Treaty of 1868 in Wyoming (see "Sioux"). In the former, the Sioux were granted a reservation in the northern plains, from the Powder River country to the Missouri; and in the latter, the Cheyennes and Arapahos were granted a combined reservation in the Indian Territory, as were the Comanches, Kiowas, and Kiowa-Apaches. Peace had not yet come to the Plains, however. As white encroachment on Indian lands continued, so did Indian raids.

It was General Philip Henry Sheridan's turn to try his hand against the Plains Indians. Appointed commander of the Division of the Missouri in September 1867, he set about organizing a campaign the following summer, because of continuing Indian unrest. The incident that sparked the new wave of violence was the refusal of officials to distribute arms and ammunition for hunting to the Southern Cheyennes because of an earlier raid on a Kaw Indian village. After a party of about 200 Cheyennes—many of them warriors in the tribe's Dog Soldier Society—unleashed their anger on settlements along the Sabine and Solomon rivers in Kansas, other militants joined

them, some southern Sioux as well, in frontier attacks.

Troops entered the field. On September 17, a force of about 50 men under Major George Forsyth picked up the trail of a war party. The much larger Indian force—probably 600-strong—led the soldiers as far as the Arikara Fork of the Republican River, then turned on them. The soldiers took refuge on a small island in the middle of the dry streambed. For a week they held off repeated attacks by Cheyenne warriors under Tall Bull, Bull Bear, White Horse, and Sioux warriors under Pawnee Killer, until help arrived and drove off the Indians. At least six were killed on each side and many more wounded. One of the dead was Lieutenant Frederick Beecher, for whom the island and the battle were named. Another killed was a much-revered Cheyenne warrior by the name of Roman Nose.

The following winter, Sheridan launched a major campaign of three converging columns on the insurgents—Major Andrew Evans leading out of Fort Bascom, New Mexico; Major Eugene Carr, out of Fort Lyon, Colorado; and Colonel Alfred Sully, out of Fort Dodge, Kansas. Custer's Seventh Cavalry was part of this third column. The most famous engagement of Sheridan's Campaign was the Battle of the Washita in late November. At Camp Supply in the northwestern part of the Indian Territory, Sheridan had transferred control of his main column from Sully to Custer. Custer, eager to prove himself after his frustration in Hancock's Campaign the year before, set out from the field base in a blizzard with his cavalry and some Osage scouts. The scouts picked up a fresh trail and led Custer's men to an Indian camp on the Washita River. Under the cover of darkness, Custer deployed his 800 men in four groups around the Indian camp for an attack at dawn.

Unknown to Custer, and probably irrelevant to him if he had known, opposite him were the people of Black Kettle's band. Even after witnessing the Sand Creek Massacre at Chivington's hands, Black Kettle had never gone to war with the white man. In

fact, he had led his people south into the Indian Territory, to avoid the subsequent fighting in Colorado and Kansas. Some of the younger warriors within the camp, those that had led the Osage scouts to it, had carried out raids on whites. But Black Kettle had tried to keep them in check; he had even traveled to Fort Cobb a week earlier to assure General William Hazen that he wanted peace. But, tragically, it was his destiny to die at the hands of whites.

At daybreak, the troops swept through the camp. The surprised Indians rallied as best they could and managed to kill five soldiers and wound 14. Another 15 were cut off from the main force and killed later. But the Indians lost their leader, Black Kettle, along with about 100 others and many more wounded. Although Custer claimed a major victory, he had only succeeded in decimating a largely peaceful band in what was essentially another Sand Creek, except for the presence of a few militants and the fact that women and children were not slaughtered but taken prisoner. On Christmas Day a few weeks later, Evans's column to the south engaged the Comanches at Soldier Spring.

The Sheridan Campaign continued into the following spring and summer, the Indians increasingly hounded by the white forces. By the Sweetwater Creek on the Staked Plain of the Texas Panhandle in March 1869, Custer, through threats and negotiations, effected the surrender of Southern Cheyenne bands under Little Robe and Medicine Arrows, who promised to return to the reservation. The Dog Soldiers under Tall Bull fled northward, however, with intentions to join their northern kinsmen in the Powder River country. They were cut off on their journey at Summit Springs in northeastern Colorado by a cavalry outfit under Major Carr. Scouting for him were Pawnees and Buffalo Bill Cody. In a surprise attack on the Cheyenne camp, Carr's men killed about 50 Indians and captured 117 more. Tall Bull had fought to his death along with other slain Dog Soldiers.

The Southern Cheyennes and Southern Arapahos had been virtually conquered. Some who escaped northward would join their northern kinsmen in an ongoing struggle, finally to be pacified along with the Sioux (see "Sioux"). Others would join the Comanches and Kiowas in an attack on buffalo hunters at Adobe Walls in Texas, during the Red River War of 1874–75 (see "Comanche"). But for the Cheyennes, the central plains would never be the same.

As has been stated, the Northern Cheyennes were involved in the Sioux Wars on the northern plains, and they triumphed with them in the battle over the Bozeman Trail of 1866–68 and at Little Bighorn during the Sioux Uprising of 1876–77. And, like the Sioux, they suffered a series of setbacks after Little Bighorn until ultimate defeat. For the Northern Cheyennes, the battles of War Bonnet Creek in Nebraska and the Battle of Dull Knife in Wyoming, in July and September 1876 respectively, were the most consequential, and the following spring their most influential leaders, Dull Knife and Little Wolf, surrendered at Fort Robinson, Nebraska (see "Sioux").

The Northern Cheyennes had expected to be assigned to the Sioux reservation in their former haunt, the Black Hills, but they were sent instead to the Indian Territory to join their southern kinsmen on the Cheyenne-Arapaho reservation near Fort Reno. Yet on these barren southern plains, difficult to farm, especially for a former hunting people, and with meager supplies from the government, there was not enough food for those already present. Moreover, the Northern Cheyennes soon experienced a devastating outbreak of malaria. Dull Knife, Little Wolf, and others resolved to return to the Tongue River country of Wyoming and Montana. They set out—297 men, women, and children—on the night of September 9, 1877, leaving their empty tepees behind.

In an epic and tragic six-week flight over lands now occupied and developed by whites—ranches, farms, roads, railroads—the Cheyennes eluded some 10,000 pursuing soldiers and an additional 3,000 civilians. They were cornered several times, some shot or taken, but the majority escaped. Two groups formed—the strong under Little Wolf would continue towards the Tongue River; the old, sick, and exhausted under Dull Knife would head to the Red Cloud's agency at Fort Robinson, Nebraska, to seek food and shelter from the Sioux leader. Dull Knife's followers were captured during a blizzard by a cavalry outfit under Captain John Johnson on October 23, and taken to the fort. The reservation lands surrounding it, however, had been taken away from the Sioux. Dull Knife expressed the desire of his people to be placed on Red Cloud's new agency in South Dakota. After a bureaucratic delay, he was told they would be sent back to the Indian Territory. White officials felt the whole reservation system would be threatened if the Cheyennes' wish were granted. The Cheyennes then staged a successful breakout. Yet in a bloody roundup operation by embarrassed troops, most of the Cheyennes were killed, including women and children, among them Dull Knife's daughter. Dull Knife, his wife, son, daughter-in-law, grandchild, and another boy made it to Red Cloud's reservation at Pine Ridge where they were taken prisoner. Meanwhile, Little Wolf and his group hid out for most of the winter at Chokecherry Creek, a tributary of the Niobrara, until discovered and induced to surrender by an outfit, under Captain William Clark, out of Fort Keogh, Montana, where they were then taken.

Finally, after more bureaucratic wrangling, the Northern Cheyennes were granted their original wish of a reservation on the Tongue River. By now, however, after all the warfare, disease, and reservation impoverishment, there were only about 80 Northern Cheyennes. And after the same hardship for the Southern Cheyennes, as well as Sand Creek and Washita, they too were a reduced and downtrodden people. The Beautiful People had been scarred by the force of an expanding and flexing nation.

COMANCHE

The Comanches, it is thought, separated from other Shoshonean-speaking peoples of the Great Basin and

Plains warriors. A crayon sketch by Howling Wolf, Cheyenne, while imprisoned at Fort Marion, Florida, 1876. New York State Library, Albany.

western Wyoming, migrating southeastward till they reached the southern plains, at least by the late 17th century. Their range, after they had evolved into horse-mounted Plains hunters, came to include what is now northern Texas, eastern Oklahoma, southwestern Kansas, southeastern Colorado, and eastern New Mexico. The Comanches on the whole were probably the most skilled of Indian horsemen—athletic riders, expert breeders and trainers, they maintained the largest herds. They were also among the most warlike people, a hazard to voyagers through their domain as well as to settlers beyond it, frequently mounting raids into northern Mexico for slaves, horses, and women. After 1790, they were often accompanied by their allies the Kiowas, who settled immediately to their north. As inveterate raiders, both tribes played a key role in halting Spanish expansion northward. In fact, European traders were happy to supply them with arms for this very purpose. Mexican Independence in 1821—the change in the political affiliation of their territory—proved irrelevant to Comanche power, at least for the time being.

The United States Army had an encounter with the Comanches as early as 1829, during Major Bennett Riley's reconnaissance of the Santa Fe Trail. Comanche warriors, along with some Kiowa allies, attacked Riley's wagon train and killed one soldier. Such attacks were common throughout the period, as more and more Anglo-Americans ventured into Comanche territory. The principal function of the Texas Rangers—from their formation during the Texas Revolution from Mexican rule in 1835, through the Republic of Texas period, and after American annexation in 1845 until 1875—was to contain the Comanches. In most early encounters, the Indians had the upper hand, as in 1837, when the Texas Rangers found themselves suddenly attacked by the very warriors they were pursuing and lost half their outfit. The next year, in the Council House Affair, the rangers managed to kill 35 of their nemeses,

but not in the field. The rangers seized as hostages a number of chiefs who had come to San Antonio to parley, in order to force the release of whites held by the Indians. After the resulting fight and Comanche loss of life, warriors swept down from their homeland north of the Red River along the Guadalupe Valley, all the way to the Gulf of Mexico, under

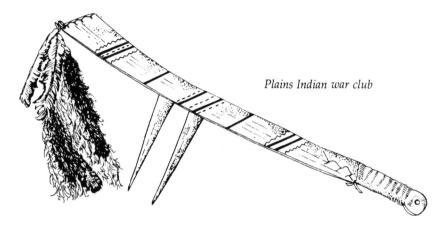

Plains Indian war club

Chief Buffalo Hump. Linnville was attacked and two dozen settlers who didn't reach their boats in time were killed; Victoria was burned. The rangers ambushed the Indians on their return northward at Plum Creek, near Lockhart, and managed to kill some more warriors, but their breaking the truce at the Council House had proven much more costly to whites than Indians.

The tide began to turn somewhat after 1840, when John Coffee Hays joined the Texas Rangers. He not only improved discipline and morale, but also armed his men with Walker Colt six-shooters instead of single-shot guns. During the Battle of Bandera Pass in 1841, the Indians came up against the "new rangers" and were repelled. But the contest between the Indians and whites was still basically a standoff, although more white settlers were arriving all the time. In 1848, Texas officials defined a boundary between the two groups, with Texas Rangers ordered to apprehend trespassers from both sides, but to no effect. Both groups violated the line. Army regulars moved in to help prevent Indian raids and, from 1849 to 1852, erected a chain of seven forts, from the Red River to the Rio Grande.

And in 1853, the same officials who had negotiated the Fort Laramie Treaty to protect the Oregon Trail from raids (see "Sioux")—David Mitchell and former Mountain Man Thomas Fitzpatrick—negotiated the Fort Atkinson Treaty in Kansas to protect the Santa Fe Trail, meeting with those chiefs of the Comanches, Kiowas, and other southern and central plains tribes willing to attend. The most damage the whites had inflicted on the Comanches had been indirectly, through a cholera epidemic beginning in 1849, at the time of the California Gold Rush and increased travel through their lands.

A new offensive was mounted against the Comanches in 1858 by both the Texas Rangers, reorganized by Governor Hardin Runnels who gave the command to Captain John "Rip" Ford, and the army, directed by General David Twiggs. On May 11, Ford's rangers, accompanied by Tonkawa, Kichai, Shawnee, and Anadarko scouts from the Brazos reserve in Texas, crossed the Red River into the Indian Territory, attacking a Comanche village in the Canadian River Valley flanked by the Antelope Hills. Suffering only four casualties, the force killed a reported 76 Comanches, including a chief by the name of Iron Jacket, took 18 prisoners, and captured 300 horses. Next, the army launched the Wichita Expedition, led by Major Earl Van Dorn, which struck at Buffalo Hump's encampment at Rush Springs on October 1, 1858, killing 58. Then they ambushed a band of Comanche warriors at Crooked

Creek further to the north, in Kansas, on May 13, 1859.

Yet the Comanches were not close to being pacified. During the Civil War years, with regulars and militiamen both pulled out of Texas, most of them fighting for the South, the various bands increased their activity. In fact, Confederate officials even armed some Comanche and Kiowa bands that had recently been their enemy, encouraging attacks on Union forces and sympathizers. In November 1864, just 19 weeks before the Confederate surrender at Appomattox, Colonel Christopher "Kit" Carson, who under the command of General James Carleton had recently defeated Apaches and Navajos (see "Apache" and "Navajo"), also led his New Mexico volunteers and the auxiliaries against a combined force of Comanches and Kiowas at Adobe Walls, a former trading post in the Canadian River Valley of the Texas Panhandle. Using 12-pounder howitzers, Carson's men managed to drive off the Indians and burn their winter stores. Ten years later, there would be another clash at this location.

After the Civil War, during General Sheridan's 1868–69 campaign against the tribes of the central and southern plains (see "Cheyenne"), Sheridan's southern column—under Major Andrew Evans out of Fort Bascom, New Mexico—located a combined Comanche-Kiowa encampment on the north fork of the Red River. In the Battle of Soldier Spring on Christmas Day, 1868, again white forces killed more men than they lost, driving the Indians away from their tepees and lodges, destroying their shelter and food, and serving notice that winter was not a time of security for raiding tribes. During his campaign, Sheridan established a combined Comanche-Kiowa reservation in the southern part of the Indian Territory, just north of the Red River, to be guarded by troops at Fort Sill. This period was the beginning of President Ulysses Grant's so-called Peace Policy toward the Indians, in which he appointed men of the church as Indian agents.

Yet raiding for the Comanches and Kiowas was a way of life and would persist, despite white attempts at acculturating, Christianizing, and pacifying the Indians.

The final showdown between the United States military and the Comanche-Kiowa warriors occurred in the so-called Red River War of 1874–75. However, the new phase of Indian hostilities and the subsequent army mobilization began in May 1871. While on a raiding expedition into Texas, one of the most influential of the militant Kiowa chiefs, Satanta, and his warriors set a trap along the Butterfield Southern Route (which led from St. Louis through the Southwest to California) on the Salt Creek Prairie near Jacksboro. The war party let a small army ambulance wagon train pass, then attacked a train of 10 army freight wagons following behind. The Indians killed eight of the 12 defenders, routed the rest, and plundered the wagons, which turned out to contain not arms or ammunition but corn. Seizing the mules, the Indians fled northward. As it turned out, General William Tecumseh Sherman, the commander of the army, had been riding in the ambulance train, and when he learned of the incident at Salt Creek—firsthand evidence that Grant's Peace Policy was not working—he resolved to make a move on Kiowa and Comanche militants. First, he sent Colonel Ranald Mackenzie and his Fourth Cavalry across the Red River onto the tribes' reservation, where they managed to scatter some bands, but little else. Then, with the help of Lawrie Tatum, the Quaker Indian agent at Fort Sill, he lured three of the known participants in the raid for a council—Satanta, Satank, and Big Tree—and proceeded to arrest them. Satank was killed in a fight that broke out; the other two were taken and later convicted of murder, sentenced to die by the Texas state court. Because of pressure from both the Quakers, who disapproved of Tatum's conspiracy, and federal proponents of the Peace Policy, the governor of Texas commuted the sentence; in 1873, he allowed the Kio-

was to return to their reservation. The action, it was hoped, would appease the agency bands and lead to the cessation of raids. But despite a large peace faction among the Kiowas, led by Kicking Bird, the militants still rode into Texas for booty.

Quanah Parker had by this time established himself as one of the foremost Comanche chiefs. He was a mixed-blood whose mother, Cynthia Parker, had been captured as a nine-year-old by Caddos who gained entrance, through trickery, into Parker's Fort near Mexia, Texas, in 1836. They sold her to the Comanches. As a teenager, she had become the wife of the Nocona Comanche chief Peta Nocona. She remained his only wife (although Comanche men were generally polygamous), bearing him three children. Content in her life as a Comanche, she had been recaptured unwillingly by white soldiers in 1860 and died four years later, broken-hearted. Quanah had lost his father in the same period from an infected wound inflicted by whites, and his brother died soon after that from a disease carried by whites. He had then joined the powerful Kwahadie band, who lived on the edge of the Staked Plain in the Texas Panhandle, and had grown up fighting whites with a vengeance, despite sharing their blood.

In September 1871, as a follow-up to the entrapment of the Kiowa chiefs, Mackenzie's Fourth Cavalry invaded the Staked Plain. In search of Kwahadies, they came up against the wily, fearless Comanche leader, who personally led two charges against the soldiers—the first right through their camp at Rock Station, stampeding and capturing many of their horses; and the second, attacking a scouting party in which Quanah himself killed and scalped the one casualty. Mackenzie continued his futile pursuit, finally ordering his men back to base with the first blizzard.

They returned in the spring of 1872. On this expedition into the Staked Plain, they traveled from waterhole to waterhole, as the Indians did, and managed two successes. They captured a number of so-called *Comanch-*

eros, New Mexican traders, thereby exposing the Comanche-Kiowa source of arms and ammunition. And they also defeated the Kotsoteka Comanche band camped near McClellan Creek, a tributary of the North Fork of the Red River, killing at least 30 and capturing 124. They also seized about 1,000 horses and burned all tepees and posessions. Quanah Parker and the Kwahadies were still at large, however, as were Satanta, Lone Wolf, and their militant Kiowa bands.

The ensuing Red River War of 1874–75 is sometimes referred to as the Buffalo War. The Indians had been witnessing the wholesale slaughter of the buffalo—their staple food—on the northern and central plains for some time. The white hunters previously had killed the animals during winter months, when their fur was long, skinning their hides mainly to sell for ruglike robes. By 1870, however, a new tanning process had been invented that made short-hair summer hides workable as well. Also by that year, the hunters carried high-powered telescopic Sharp rifles that could kill the massive animals at 600 yards. The rate of slaughter accelerated. The hunters soon depleted the Kansas plains and moved into the Staked Plain of Texas, setting up base with their skinners at the abandoned trading post of Adobe Walls, on the South Canadian River.

Their economy and whole way of life threatened, the Comanches and Kiowas talked in council of war. A Kwahadie mystic by the name of Isatai called for an alliance of tribes and a major offensive against the whites, promising to protect the warriors from bullets with magic paint. He urged Quanah to hold a Sun Dance, not a traditional Comanche custom, and invite other Plains tribes. Cheyenne and Arapaho warriors, recently defeated by Sheridan (see "Cheyenne" and "Arapaho"), came from their neighboring reservation. During the ceremony, a war party of 700 warriors from all four tribes was organized. Quanah Parker would lead it.

On June 26, 1874, the Indian force crept up under cover of darkness to Adobe Walls—the site of Kit Carson's fight with Comanches and Kiowas a decade before. The 28 buffalo hunters, aroused by a warning signal, managed to take shelter behind the adobe walls with their high-powered Sharp and Remington buffalo guns plus plenty of ammunition. The Indians charged repeatedly but, despite their overwhelming numbers, could not reach the hunters. Fifteen dead and many more wounded, they withdrew.

Afterward, in a state of frustration, perhaps now seeing the inevitable change of life-style in their near future, the Indians began a campaign of violence against the white settlers. Sherman gave Sheridan free rein for a massive offensive that July. Sheridan launched troops from a number of surrounding posts in Kansas, Texas, and New Mexico. In the field were Ranald Mackenzie and Nelson Miles. In the bitter heat of an extreme summer, they converged on the Staked Plain, forcing a number of inconclusive skirmishes and keeping the Indians on the run. Finally, on September 28, 1874, Mackenzie dealt a crushing blow to the Indians in an attack on their stronghold, the Palo Duro Canyon, where many had taken refuge. Although he killed only three braves, he captured or killed most of their horses—an estimated 1,500—and destroyed their tepees.

By the following October, demoralized and destitute refugees began surrendering to the garrisons at Fort Reno and Fort Sill. Of the Kiowas, Lone Wolf and 250 followers held out the longest—until February 25, 1875. Then, on June 2, the last of the Comanches, yielding to the pressures of relentless pursuit and the wilderness, also came in under a flag of truce, led by Quanah Parker. The so-called "Lords of the Southern Plains," as they are sometimes called—the Comanches and Kiowas—had been conquered once and for all.

The fates of the participants varied. Lone Wolf was among those sent to Fort Marion, in St. Augustine, Florida, where the military now deported warriors whom they considered dangerous. Kicking Bird of the Kiowa peace faction was given the unfortunate task of identifying those for deportation. He died mysteriously soon afterward, perhaps poisoned by a Kiowa medicine man, Mamanti, whom he had selected. Lone Wolf, having contracted malaria in Florida, was finally allowed to return to his homeland, where he soon died. Satanta was imprisoned in Huntsville, Texas, for violating his parole from the earlier Salt Creek incident. In 1878, in a state of depression, he killed himself by jumping headfirst from the second-story balcony of the prison hospital.

As for Quanah Parker, the stubborn Comanche war leader who, unlike the majority of the other militant chiefs, never once signed a treaty with the whites until his ultimate surrender, he quickly adapted to his new reality as a reservation Indian, continuing to play an important role as leader of his people. He never gave up his Indian identity, but he learned the ways of the whites, such as the leasing of lands and rights-of-way, to improve his tribe's lot. He also came to play a major part in spreading the pan-Indian religion that started up around the peyote ritual and came to be chartered as the Native American Church.

CROW

The Crow Indians, relatives of the Hidatsa peoples of the upper Missouri, migrated into the Great Plains from the east and settled in Montana, east of the Rockies, along the Yellowstone River. They were a menace to early white travelers along the Oregon Trail but, with time, came to be allies of the federal government against other tribes, serving as troops and scouts on various occasions. They fought with General George Crook at the Battle of Rosebud against Crazy Horse in 1876 (see "Sioux"), and helped track the Nez Perce during their attempted flight to Canada in 1877 (see "Nez Perce"). Chief Plenty Coups encouraged his warriors to help the army because, in his words, "When the war is over, the soldier-chiefs will not forget that the Crows came to their aid."

KIOWA AND KIOWA-APACHE

The Kiowas are thought to have migrated out of mountainous country of the upper Missouri, then southward along the plains just east of the Rocky Mountains, finally settling in the southern plains—in contiguous parts of present-day Oklahoma, Texas, New Mexico, Kansas, and Colorado. At some point early in their history, a number of Athapascan peoples joined up with them and shared their customs—the Kiowa-Apaches. In 1790, both these peoples became close allies of their neighbors to the south—the Comanches—and fought with them against common enemies. Like the Comanches, they were skillful horsemen and raiders, consistently preying on intruders in their domain, as well as on settlements in Mexico. In the 19th century, they also proved a formidable obstacle to United States expansion. The story of the Kiowa Wars is also the story of the Comanche Wars (see "Comanche").

OSAGE

The Osages of the lower Arkansas River region of the southeastern plains were traditional enemies of the Kiowas, Comanches, and other Plains tribes. As such, they regularly served as army scouts, notably during Sheridan's Campaign of 1868–69, in which they led Custer's Seventh Cavalry to Black Kettle's village on the Washita (see "Cheyenne").

PAWNEE

The Pawnees of the Platte River and the Republican Fork of the Kansas River in present-day Nebraska and northern Kansas were the most famous of all Indian scouts for the army in the Plains wars. Traditional enemies of the Sioux (one Sioux warrior even had the name Pawnee Killer), they were used especially in campaigns against them and their allies, the Cheyennes and Arapahos. Frank and Luther North organized a battalion of Pawnee scouts that was active from 1866 to 1870. And Sky Chief, the Pawnee leader, provided guards for railroad work crews.

In 1873, a large Sioux war party, seeking revenge, ambushed a smaller Pawnee hunting party in Nebraska. The army sent out a relief detachment that finally drove the Sioux away, but not until they had killed 150 Pawnees, including Sky Chief. The location and battle came to be known as Massacre Canyon.

PONCA

In the late 1870's, an incident with long-term consequences occurred among the Poncas; it defied the pattern of Indian and white interaction and hostility of the period. Some of the Ponca peoples, originally from Dakota Territory, had since migrated down the Missouri as far as the mouth of the Niobrara. In 1876, Congress passed an act to relocate them from Nebraska to the Indian Territory.

Not long after the forced relocation, the son of Chief Standing Bear died. The Ponca leader, who had also recently lost his daughter, wanted to bury the dead youth with his sister in the land of their ancestors and set out with an escort of 30 warriors. Settlers who spotted the party traveling through country they thought had been cleared of Indians notified the military of a potential uprising. General George Crook sent in a cavalry detachment that arrested the Indians and imprisoned them at Omaha.

The true purpose of Standing Bear's journey was learned. Some whites, including Crook himself, reacted with sympathy. Two lawyers, John L. Webster and Andrew Poppleton, volunteered their services and applied for a writ of habeas corpus in the United States district court on the Poncas' behalf. Federal attorneys argued that the writ be denied because Indians were not persons under the terms of the Constitution, therefore not entitled to the habeas corpus pro-

cess. Nevertheless, Judge Elmer S. Dundy ruled in favor of the Indians, arguing that they were indeed persons under the law, with inalienable rights. Standing Bear and his escort were permitted to proceed to and carry out the burial. Because of continuing white sympathy, some among the Poncas were even allowed to resettle in Nebraska permanently. Others were forcibly kept in the Indian Territory by federal officials. Yet, despite continuing federal unilateral policy with regard to Indians, a legal precedent had been set in the establishment of Indian rights.

SIOUX

During the late 17th and early 18th centuries, the Sioux peoples migrated from the lands their ancestors had settled, more than a century earlier, along the upper reaches of the Mississippi River. The fact that their traditional enemies, the Ojibways and other Algonquian-speaking peoples, had been given firearms by French traders impelled their move westward. The four major branches of Sioux established new territories—the easternmost Santee, still near the Mississippi River; the central Yankton along the Missouri; the Yanktonai, farther north also along the Missouri; and the westernmost Teton, in the Badlands and Black Hills. These various peoples, once the victims of French firepower, would in turn obtain deadly firearms themselves. Most would also mount what they called the "Sacred Dog," referring to the horse. They would expand their land base throughout much of the northern plains. And they would become among the most effective of Indian warriors, presenting a persistent defense against white expansion in the 19th century.

The Sioux War, or Wars, lasting almost half a century and comprising numerous engagements, can be organized into five phases, each a story in itself reflecting the subtleties of the period. Two episodes in the final two phases—Little Bighorn and Wounded Knee—are among the most famous in Indian history and carry special symbolic weight, one representing the once-great power of the Indian tribes, the other, their ultimate defeat.

Other incidents carry the same poignancy and drama. The first phase of the Sioux Wars occurred soon after the Fort Laramie Treaty of 1851, the primary purpose of which was to assure safe passage for whites along the Oregon Trail. It was whites, however, who broke the peace. In August 1854, a Mormon party was in transit along the North Platte River in Wyoming. A cow belonging to one of them escaped and wandered into a Brule Teton camp along the trail. The Mormon chased after it, became frightened at the sight of the Indians, departed, and reported to the army at Fort Laramie that the cow had been stolen. In the meantime, visiting Sioux from another band killed the cow.

The incident escalated. Although the Indians offered to make restitution for more than the cow was worth, Lieutenant John L. Grattan, fresh from West Point, insisted on the arrest of High Forehead, the man who had killed the cow. Grattan led a force of 30 infantrymen and two cannons to the Brule village to carry out his intention. When High Forehead refused to turn himself in, Grattan gave the order to fire. Chief Conquering Bear, the spokesman for all the Sioux, was mortally wounded in the first howitzer volley. Enraged, the Indians launched a counterattack in which they wiped out the detachment.

Alarmed whites dubbed the incident the Grattan Massacre and, in response, carried out a much more brutal act of their own. On September 3, 1855, 600 troops out of Fort Kearny in Nebraska, under General William S. Harney, swarmed over a Brule village at Blue Water, killing 85 of the scattering Sioux, and taking 70 women and children captive. Then Harney led his men on a march through Sioux country to demonstrate the army's strength to other Sioux bands. None rose up against the army for the time being. But they would remember the death of Conquering Bear and the attack at Blue Water. One young Oglala Teton who had been in the camp the

night Conquering Bear received his fatal blow would especially remember. His name was Crazy Horse and, in a vision soon after the incident, he would discover his purpose and destiny as a war chief in battles to come.

Yet before Crazy Horse came to play his part as a Sioux leader, war broke out to the east, in the territory of the Santee Sioux on the Minnesota River. By the Civil War years, the Santees were surrounded by whites who relentlessly sought more and more of their lands, repeatedly cheating and defrauding them. Factions within the tribe disagreed on how to best deal with the ongoing abuse, through accommodation or resistance. A group of four young braves forced the issue by killing five settlers. Little Crow, the Santee chief, had previously argued for peace. After the bold action by his young warriors, however, he too was persuaded that the only course of action was war. The words of a trader who had refused the Indians credit— "As far as I'm concerned, if they're hungry, let them eat grass"—became the rallying cry for all the Santee factions.

On August 18, 1862, the Santees opened their war with raids on trading posts and settlements. As many as 400 whites died the first day, including 23 from a detachment of volunteer infantry out of Fort Ridgely. On August 20 and 22, Little Crow led assaults on the fort itself where many more settlers had taken refuge. Three howitzers effectively cut down the attacking warriors, however. After losing as many as 100 men, Little Crow called off the siege. On August 23, another group of Santees stormed the village of New Ulm. But the village had prepared well and, after a day of bitter fighting, with heavy casualties on both sides and a third of the town destroyed, they drove the insurgents away. The next day, however, New Ulm was evacuated.

General Henry Hastings Sibley reached Fort Ridgely with 1,500 troops. On September 2, he sent out a burial party of 135 men and 20 wagons. Thirteen miles from the fort, at Birch Coulee, the detachment was set

upon by Little Crow's warriors. With their wagons in a defensive circle, the soldiers held out for 31 hours until a relief force from the fort arrived, but they had lost 23 of their number.

Sibley led his men into the field on September 18, following the Minnesota River northwestward into Santee country. The Santees, having decided in council to make a stand rather than flee westward, attacked the army camp at Wood Lake on September 23. Although 700-strong, they were no match for the whites' artillery; they scattered in defeat.

Many of the surviving Santees fled to Dakota Territory or Canada, Little Crow among them. Three hundred and three of those who stayed behind—although they had released their captives, surrendered willingly, and claimed innocence in the slayings of settlers—were sentenced to be hanged. President Abraham Lincoln, on examining the trial records, commuted the sentences for the large majority. But on December 26, 1862, at Mankato, Minnesota, the largest mass execution in American history took place as 38 Santee Sioux were simultaneously hanged.

Little Crow died in July of the following year on a horse-stealing expedition out of Canada to Minnesota, shot by settlers who now were being paid bounties for Sioux scalps. That same month, General Sibley, who had pushed on into North Dakota on a punitive expedition against the Sioux, defeated Santee remnants along with their Teton Sioux kinsmen at Big Mound, Dead Buffalo Lake, and Stoney Lake. Then, the following September and the spring of 1864, General Alfred Sully defeated the coalition of tribes at Whitestone Hill and Killdeer Mountain. The Santees, and the Tetons who had taken them in, had paid dearly for the Minnesota Uprising. In another rebellion, beginning the very next year, their western kinsmen in Wyoming and Montana would fare better.

At the heart of the Red Cloud War, which broke out in the years following the Civil War, was the question of the Bozeman Trail. With whites caught up in the mining fever and coming to Montana as well as California and Colorado, traffic increased over Indian lands guaranteed by treaty. John Bozeman, seeking a more direct route to Colorado other than circuitous eastern and western routes, cut west of the Bighorn Mountains through Wyoming via the North Platte River, thereby crossing the Teton domain. The various Sioux bands—among them Oglala Tetons under Red Cloud, including the teen-aged Crazy Horse; Hunkpapa Tetons under Sitting Bull; and Brule Tetons under Spotted Tail—resented the growing white traffic. They were joined in their concern by their allies on the northern plains—the Northern Cheyennes under Dull Knife and the Northern Arapahos under Black Bear. Beginning in 1865, these groups—sometimes on their own, but increasingly in united forces—stepped up their raids on white migrants and military patrols. In July 1865, for example, some of them attacked a cavalry detachment under Lieutenant Caspar Collins, riding out from Kansas to meet an eastwardbound army wagon train. Along the North Platte stretch of the Oregon Trail, just west of the point at which the Bozeman Trail branched off from it, the combined force of Sioux, Cheyennes, and Arapahos easily routed the cavalry and captured the wagon train. Three columns sent in that August, by General Patrick E. Connor, to the Powder River country from bases on the Platte River managed only to skirmish with the Sioux. They did, however, destroy Black Bear's Arapaho village (see "Arapaho").

One year later, in June 1866, Red Cloud and other chiefs arrived at Fort Laramie east of the Bozeman turnoff, to discuss the new trail. During the parley, an infantry column under Colonel Henry B. Carrington arrived with instructions to build forts in the Powder River country, to protect the Bozeman. Although some of the other chiefs signed a nonaggression treaty, Red Cloud rode off to make preparations for war.

Carrington's men proceeded up the Bozeman. While under ongoing ha-

Delegation of Sioux Indians to Washington, D.C., in 1875, including left to right, Rattling Ribs, Red Cloud, Mandan, Lone Horn, Spotted Tail, Little Wound, Black Bear, and Swan. New York State Library, Albany.

rassment from guerrilla strikes, they undertook to reinforce Fort Reno and build two more posts—Fort Phil Kearny and Fort C.F. Smith—in northern Wyoming and southern Montana. In addition to the numerous hit-and-run raids on work parties and supply convoys, the Indians also attacked army patrols. In December 1866, Crazy Horse used a decoy tactic in an attack by a few of his warriors on a wood train. Captain William Fetterman, in what has become known as the Fetterman Massacre, led an 80-man relief cavalry unit out of Fort Phil Kearny over Lodge Trail Ridge into a trap of 1,500 concealed Indians.

The army, realizing the extent of the Plains Indian threat, sent in fresh troops, with new breech-loading rifles, to the Bozeman posts. In August 1867, during a planned offensive by two separate war parties against workers out of Fort Smith and Fort Phil Kearny, the Indians went up against the modern weapons. Although they succeeded in chasing both the hay-cutting and wood-cutting parties back to their respective posts, the Indians suffered many casualties. The military declared the so-called Hayfield and Wagon Box Fights victories; nevertheless, with dogged Indian forays, and the transconti-

tal railroad south of the Platte near completion, the federal government yielded. In the Fort Laramie Treaty of 1868, officials granted Red Cloud's demands for the abandoning of the Bozeman posts in exchange for the cessation of raids. Immediately after the army's evacuation that summer, the Sioux in a victory celebration burned the posts down.

Meanwhile, in 1867, the army suffered another setback at the hands of the Southern Cheyennes, Southern Arapahos, and some Sioux also living on the central plains—the abortive Hancock Campaign. In that region too the whites made concessions, in the Medicine Lodge Treaty of 1867 (see "Cheyenne").

For the time being, anyway, the whites had been thwarted in the takeover of the Plains. But the railroad had come, carrying more and more settlers, and the Plains Indians staple—the buffalo—was slowly disappearing. In the next round, the whites, despite a major loss to the Indians at Little Bighorn, once more gained the upper hand.

By the 1870s, both whites and Indians had violated the terms of the Fort Laramie Treaty, with continued trespassing and continued raids. Surveys for a new railroad, the Northern Pacific, aggravated the situation. But it was the discovery of gold in the Black Hills, lands sacred to Sioux, by an 1874 expedition under Lieutenant Colonel George Armstrong Custer, and the subsequent potential onslaught of miners that again made war inevitable.

Red Cloud and Spotted Tail had opted for the life of the reservation Indian; the principal leaders of the allied nomadic hunting bands by this time were Sitting Bull and Crazy Horse. Opposing them were General William Tecumseh Sherman, who had become commander of the U.S. Army in 1869, and General Philip Henry Sheridan, commander of the Division of the Missouri since 1867, both Civil War heroes and both proponents of all-out war against resistive Indians. Sheridan is famous for the racist aphorism, "The only good Indian is a dead Indian."

War broke out when the military, in an effort to gain control of the Black Hills through coercive negotiation, sent word to the northern hunting bands to come in to an agency within two months or be classified as hostile. When the bands failed to report, General Sheridan organized two forces—one under the Paiute- and Apache-fighter General George Crook out of Fort Fetterman, Wyoming; and the other under Lieutenant Colonel George Armstrong Custer out of Fort Lincoln, North Dakota, a man who had fought Cheyennes and others on the central plains—for what he hoped would be preemptive winter strikes. The Custer force was delayed because of heavy snows. Colonel Joseph Reynolds of Crook's force led a cavalry attack against Tetons and Cheyennes at Powder River in Montana in March 1876, but it was quickly repelled by Crazy Horse's warriors, with heavy U.S. losses.

The next engagements came in the late spring during a new three-pronged army campaign—Crook from the south; Colonel John Gibbon, out of Forts Ellis and Shaw in Montana, from the west; and General Alfred Terry, now with Custer, from the east. The various bands had

united in a camp in southern Montana.

Crook's column approached from the south along the Rosebud Creek. On June 17, 1876, about 700 Sioux and Cheyennes under Crazy Horse moved against it. Although Crook's force was 1,000-strong, with almost 300 Crow and Shoshoni auxiliaries, it was hard pressed to defend against the repeated, well-organized assaults. By the time the attackers withdrew, Crook's men had suffered numerous casualties and were forced back to base. But the Battle of the Rosebud, although a significant Indian victory, was the preliminary to an even greater triumph.

The Indians regrouped at a new camp on a meadow they called the Greasy Grass along the Little Bighorn River. Indians who had spent the

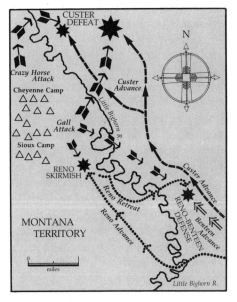

5.20 THE BATTLE OF LITTLE BIGHORN, 1876, *showing possible troop and Indian movement*

winter at agencies were arriving all the while—Teton Sioux, Santee Sioux, Northern Cheyennes, Northern Arapahos—making a total number of nearly 7,000, probably 1,800 of them warriors. Four days after Rosebud, Terry's and Gibbon's columns united on the Yellowstone River. When a scouting party under Major Marcus Reno reported the general location of the Indian force along the Little Bighorn, Terry sent Custer's Seventh Cavalry to cut them off from the south

while the rest of the troops approached from the north.

The operation did not go as planned. On June 25, when his scouts spotted the Indian encampment, the brash young cavalry officer whom the Indians called "Long Hair" organized for an immediate attack rather than wait another day for Terry and Gibbon. He organized his command into four sections—the pack train with an escort to stay behind; a detachment under Captain Frederick Benteen to block the Indians from the south; and detachments under Major Reno and himself to follow the river northward. On the way, he sent Reno's men westward across the river, in pursuit of a party of about 40 warriors, with instructions to strike the Indian camp from the valley to its south, while he proceeded along the rugged eastern bank of the river for an attack on the village at its northern end. The plan proved a disaster. In a series of separate actions against the divided force, the Indians managed to pin down and inflict severe damage on the outfits under Reno and Benteen—more than 50 dead and another 60 or so wounded, out of about 400—and wipe out to the last man Custer's detachment of about 200. Indian losses have been estimated at as few as 30 or as many as 300, but the low end is probably the more accurate guess. Custer's Last Stand would become legendary, as would the warriors who fought there, including Crazy Horse of the Oglalas, and Sitting Bull and Gall of the Hunkpapas. It would also serve to rally the whites in a stepped-up campaign of revenge and conquest against the Sioux and their allies.

The army triumphed in the next major encounters. In July 1876, soon after Little Bighorn, a force under Colonel Wesley Merritt out of Fort Laramie, Wyoming, intercepted and defeated about 1,000 Cheyennes who had left Nebraska agencies to join up with Sitting Bull and Crazy Horse, in the Battle of War Bonnet Creek in northwestern Nebraska. On September 8, General Crook's advance guard under Captain Miles captured American Horse's Teton band at Slim Buttes, South Dakota. On November

25, Crook's cavalry under Colonel Ranald Mackenzie routed Dull Knife's camp of Northern Cheyennes, along the Red Fork of the Powder River in Wyoming (the Battle of Dull Knife). In January 1877, General Nelson Miles, recently of the Red River War (see "Comanche"), with a force of nearly 500, defeated Crazy Horse's warriors in the Battle of Wolf Mountain, and in May 1877, he defeated Lame Deer's Miniconjou Tetons in Montana (the Battle of Lame Deer).

The end of the war trail had come for the great Sioux and Cheyenne leaders. Sitting Bull and his Hunkpapas took refuge in Canada. He returned in 1881 and surrendered at Fort Buford, Dakota Territory. His death in 1890 played a part in the tragedy at Wounded Knee. Dull Knife surrendered on May 6, 1877, at the Red Cloud agency near Fort Robinson, Nebraska; the next year he and his Northern Cheyennes made a desperate flight for freedom from there (see "Cheyenne"). But, for the time being, he and his people accompanied the Oglala Tetons under Crazy Horse—more than 1,000 Indians total—in the surrender party. Crazy Horse, one of the most effective guerrilla fighters in history, threw down his rifle. Although defeated, he was still considered a threat by officials who feared his ability to inspire an uprising. On September 5, 1877, while resisting orders from General Crook for his imprisonment, the freedom fighter was fatally wounded.

The last gasp for the Sioux and for all the Indian tribes in the Wars for the West occurred 13 years later at Wounded Knee Creek in South Dakota. In 1888, a Paiute Indian from Nevada by the name of Wovoka, son of the mystic Tavibo, drew on his father's teachings and his own vision during an eclipse of the sun, and began spreading a gospel that came to be known as the Ghost Dance Religion. He claimed that the earth would soon perish and then come alive again in a pure, aboriginal state, to be inherited by all Indians, including the dead, for an eternal existence free from suffering. To earn this new real-

ity, however, Indians had to live harmoniously and honestly, cleanse themselves often, and shun the ways of the whites, especially alcohol, the destroyer. He also discouraged the practice of mourning, because the dead would soon be resurrected, demanding instead the performance of prayers, meditation, chanting, and especially dancing through which one might briefly die and catch a glimpse of the paradise-to-come, replete with lush prairie grass, herds of buffalo, and Indian ancestors.

The new religion spread to the conquered, destitute, and despondent peoples of the Far West, Southwest, and Plains, most now living on reservations. Many of the Sioux, desperate in defeat for any glimmer of hope, took to the new religion after one of their own mystics, Kicking Bear, made his pilgrimage to Nevada to learn of it, and they began dancing the Ghost Dance. Kicking Bear and another mystic, Short Bull, both Miniconjou Tetons, gave the gospel their own interpretation, however, choosing to disregard Wovoka's anti-violence and emphasizing the possible elimination of whites. Special Ghost Dance Shirts, they claimed, could even stop the white man's bullets.

White officials became concerned at this religious fervor tinged with activism and insurgency and, in November 1890, banned the Ghost Dance on Sioux reservations. When the rites continued, officials called in troops to the Pine Ridge and Rosebud reservations in South Dakota. The military prepared for one more Indian campaign. General Nelson Miles was now the commander of the Division of the Missouri, having inherited the position from Crook who had died only two years after taking over. He set up headquarters at Rapid City, South Dakota.

The presence of troops exacerbated the situation. Kicking Bear and Short Bull led their followers to the northwest corner of the Pine Ridge reservation, to an escarpment known as the Stronghold. The dancers then sent word to Sitting Bull of the Hunkpapas to join them. Before he could set out from the Standing Rock reservation in

North Dakota, however, he was arrested by Indian police. In the scuffle that ensued, the once-great chief was slain, along with seven of his warriors. Six of the policemen, Indians who had followed the orders of the whites, were also fatally struck.

General Miles also ordered the arrest of Big Foot, a Miniconjou leader living along the Cheyenne River in South Dakota who had previously also advocated the Ghost Dance. But Big Foot and his followers had already departed southward for Pine Ridge, asked there not by the Ghost Dancers, as Miles assumed, but by Red Cloud and other reservation Indians supportive of whites in order to help restore tranquility. Miles sent out the Seventh Cavalry under Major S. M. Whitside to intercept them. The unit scoured the Badlands, finally locating them to the southwest at Porcupine Creek, about 30 miles east of Pine Ridge. The Indians offered no resistance. Big Foot, ill with pneumonia, rode in a wagon. The soldiers instructed the Indians to set up camp for the night about five miles westward, at Wounded Knee Creek. Colonel James Forsyth arrived to take command and ordered his guards to place four Hotchkiss cannons in position around the camp. The soldiers now numbered about 500; the Indians, 350, all but 120 of these women and children.

The following morning, December 29, 1890, the soldiers entered the Indian camp to gather all firearms. A medicine man by the name of Yellow Bird advocated resistance, claiming the Ghost Shirts would protect them. Big Foot, however, knew that a fight would be suicidal. But when one of the soldiers attempted to roughly disarm a deaf Indian by the name of Black Coyote, the rifle discharged. The silence of the morning was shattered, and other guns echoed the first shot. At first, the struggle was at close quarters, but when the Indians ran to take cover, the Hotchkiss artillery opened up on them, cutting down men, women, and children alike, the sick Big Foot among them. By the end of the brutal, unnecessary violence, which had lasted less than an hour, at least 150 Indians had been killed and 50 wounded. In comparison, army casualties were 25 killed and 39 wounded. Forsyth was later charged with the killing of innocents, but exonerated.

The spirit of the Sioux had once again been crushed. The next day, some warriors set a trap for the Seventh Cavalry at Drexel Mission Church north of the Pine Ridge agency and managed to kill two soldiers and wound five before retreating. Other Sioux fled the agency and joined Kicking Bear and Short Bull and their followers at White Clay. Yet, surrounded by a larger force of bluecoats and disagreeing among themselves on the course of action, the Sioux surrendered to Miles.

With Wounded Knee, the Indian wars had in effect ended. Appropriately, that same year, the Federal Census Bureau announced it could no longer designate a frontier of settlement on its map of the United States, as it had done in previous decades. Also appropriately, given the fact that Anglo-Americans had shaped a new nation out of Indian lands, starting in 1927 the federal government sponsored the carving of four presidents' faces on Mount Rushmore, in the Black Hills for which the Sioux had fought so hard. Wounded Knee itself, on the other hand, would become a catch phrase for all the wrongs inflicted on Native Americans by the descendants of Europeans. And, in 1973, Indian activists, drawing on the courage of their ancestors, would stage another uprising there.

Plains Indian rawhide shield with representation of elk in the Black Hills

CANADIAN INDIAN WARS

During all three stages of Canadian history—French colonial, British colonial and post–Confederation Dominion status—there was little warfare between Indian and white, as compared to events south of Canada in the region now comprising the United States. But the same long-term repercussions of white expansion—diseases, liquor, land cessions, and reservations—are as much a part of the Canadian Indian story as the U.S. one but without as many violent convulsions. A number of factors explain this historical difference.

With regard to the earliest stage, the French were more interested in furs than land (see "The Fur Trade" in chapter 4), with the white population growing at a much slower rate than in the British colonies. Moreover, white traders depended on Indian friendship and adopted Indian lifestyles. New France, of course, starting with Champlain, did make war with the pro-Dutch, then pro-English tribes of the Iroquois League during the 17th and 18th centuries; and various tribes did rebel against French dominance. But, except for the Iroquois invasions of Huron, Tobacco, Erie, and Neutral territory, plus later expeditions against settlements along the St. Lawrence, most of the hostilities occurred on what was to become U.S. soil. (See "The Beaver Wars," "The French and Indian Wars," and "Indian Rebellions against the French" in this chapter.)

An early exception to the pattern of peace between Indians and whites on what was to become Canadian soil involved the Beothuks of Newfoundland. Because of their failure to grasp the European concept of private property and their subsequent, related tendency toward stealing, the Beothuks came into conflict with both French and English fishermen who moored on the island. The fishermen organized punitive attacks. French officials placed bounties on Beothuk

scalps and provided arms for the Micmacs, who further decimated the tribe. By the mid-18th century, few Beothuks remained. The last known Beothuk, Nancy Shawanahdit, died in St. John's in 1829.

At the start of the British colonial stage of Canadian history in 1763, the new landlords experienced Indian unrest with Pontiac's Rebellion, but again most of the activity occurred south of the Canadian border. (See "Pontiac's Rebellion" in this chapter.) In the American Revolution the large majority of tribes sided with the British, many of them taking refuge in Canada at the end of the war. The Mohawk leader Joseph Brant, who founded Ohsweken on the Grand River (now Brantford, Ontario), is central to both Canadian and U.S. history. (See "Indians in the American Revolution" in this chapter.) In the same manner, the Shawnee leader Tecumseh, famous for his attempted alliance of tribes against the United States, as well as for his career as a British general in the War of 1812, has become a legendary figure in both countries. (See "Tecumseh's Rebellion and the War of 1812" in this chapter.)

Yet, within Canada's own boundaries, peace between the Indian and white populations remained the predominant pattern during England's tenure. As before, representatives of the fur companies—at this time the North West Company along with the Hudson's Bay Company—wanted to buy from, sell to, and employ Indians, not displace them. Even after Canada achieved Dominion status and began a period of accelerated expansion westward, the new government maintained the general pattern of peace with the Indians. The continuing low white population—about 10 percent of that of its neighbor to the south—was one factor. Another factor preserving the peace was the establishment of many of the western Indian reservations in advance of white settlement. (See "The Growth of Canada and Indian Land Cessions" in chapter 6.) Still another factor proved to be the levelheaded approach to Indian-white relations of the Northwest Mounted Police.

Organized in 1873, the Mounties used a combination of diplomacy, fairness, and saber-rattling to accomplish their goals on the frontier, as opposed to brute force. They fought most of their actual skirmishes against whites out of Montana—the whiskey traders who brought liquor onto the Canadian Plains; and the wolfers who hunted wolves with poisoned buffalo carcasses; both practices detrimental to the Plains Indian way of life. Fighting between Indians and Mounties as well as regular troops grew out of the so-called Riel rebellions. The Metis, mixed-blood descendants of the Cree Indians and French fur traders—the voyageurs and coureurs de bois (see "The Fur Trade" in chapter 4)—as well as to a lesser extent Indians of other tribes and Scotsmen, had settled the Red River Valley of the Canadian prairies and later the Saskatchewan River of the Plains. They were a true cultural mix, hunting buffalo and living in tepees part of the year, farming and living in frame houses the rest, and practicing both Indian and Catholic rituals.

THE
SELKIRK INCIDENT
AND THE
COURTHOUSE REBELLION

The first Metis incident occurred early in the 19th century. In 1811, the Hudson's Bay Company granted the Earl of Selkirk at his request a small part of Rupert's Land, in the Red River of the North area, for an agricultural community of dispossessed Scottish peasants. The first settlers arrived on the land patent in the summer of 1812. Their governor, Miles Macdonnell, fearing food shortages, gave the Metis notice that they were bound to sell their extra pemmican to his community rather than elsewhere. He also further meddled in Metis affairs by forbidding the running of buffalo on horseback. The Metis ignored both edicts. Tensions mounted. In the meantime, the North West Company, aggravated by this sponsoring of farmers in fur country by their rival, the Hudson's Bay Company, provid-

ed the Metis with arms and incited them to action.

Violence broke out in 1816. Robert Semple, who had replaced Macdonald as the colony's governor, sent 26 militiamen out of Fort Douglas to confront an armed party of Metis. Verbal insults led to violence in which all but three of the militiamen were killed. Although the opposing factions agreed to the compromise outlined in the Selkirk Treaty of 1817, ill feelings and harassment lasted until 1836, when the land, most of it abandoned by Selkirk's colonists (Selkirk himself had died in 1820), was given back to the Hudson's Bay Company.

A second incident involving the Metis erupted in 1849—the so-called Courthouse Rebellion. The Hudson's Bay Company, more powerful than ever since its merger with the North West Company in 1821, began trying to regulate the independent Metis hunters with strict trade regulations, one of which prohibited trading below the 49th parallel with Americans. Since southern trade with merchants in St. Paul, Minnesota, was integral to their economy, the Metis protested. And when the Hudson's Bay Company brought the part-Ojibway Metis Guillaume Sayer to trial for trying to smuggle his goods across the border, 300 armed Metis, led by the miller Louis Riel, assembled at Fort Garry and threatened violence. Although the nervous jury found Sayer nominally guilty, they recommended his release. For the next 20 years, Metis commerce remained relatively free of official restrictions. It is estimated that in one year alone—1867—more than 2,000 caravans of ox-drawn Red River carts made the trek to St. Paul.

THE FIRST RIEL REBELLION

It was Louis Riel's son of the same name who led the two Metis uprisings later in the century, the second of which also came to involve full-blooded Indians. After Confederation in 1867, the newly formed Dominion began taking an interest in its western lands, part of the motivation being

pressure from the expanding American frontier. The United States had just purchased Alaska from Russia. Moreover, 800,000 veterans of the U.S. Civil War were unemployed and hungry for land. In 1869, Canada purchased Rupert's Land from the Hudson's Bay Company and began encouraging settlement by Canadians to counter the threat from the U.S.

Settlers began streaming into the Red River of the North region. Among them were Canada Firsters, led by Dr. John Christian Schultz, annexationist members of the Canada Party. Being Protestant Orangemen prejudiced against Catholics, Frenchmen, and Indians—everything the Metis stood for—they were insensitive to Metis land rights. The confrontation known as the First Riel Rebellion (or the Red River Rebellion) flared up when the Dominion's first prime minister, John A. Macdonald, sent surveyors under Captain Adam Clark Webb to section off square townships of 800 acres apiece. Since the Red Riverites had always laid out their lands in strips along the water's edge, each lot extending back through stands of woods to fertile fields and then to community-held prairie for livestock grazing (referred to as the "hay privilege"), Macdonald's plan by definition disrupted the Metis way of life. The young, Montreal-educated Louis Riel and 16 other Metis faced off with the outsiders in October 1869, as his father had done 20 years earlier, and eventually drove them away.

In the meantime, Macdonald's choice as the new territorial governor, William McDougall, was approaching the Red River from Ottawa via Minnesota with a small retinue plus 300 rifles for arming a militia. Riel organized the *Comite National des Metis*, sent a force of 40 armed men to barricade the border, and led a force of 400 men in a bloodless takeover of Fort Garry (Winnipeg) from the aging Hudson's Bay governor, William Mactavish, and a small garrison. McDougall then crossed the border with his retinue and occupied an abandoned Hudson's Bay post. Riel advised their departure through his chief aide, Ambroise Lepine, a Metis

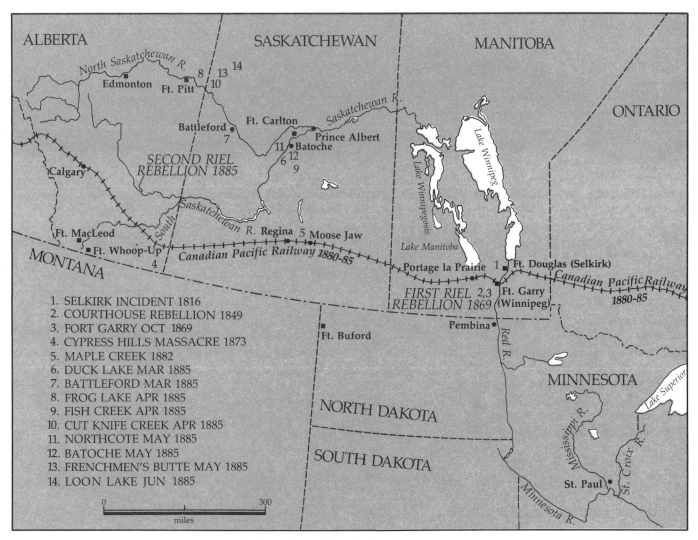

ALBERTA SASKATCHEWAN MANITOBA

North Saskatchewan R. 8 / 13 14

Edmonton Ft. Pitt 10 ONTARIO

Saskatchewan R.

Battleford Ft. Carlton
7 Prince Albert Lake Winnipeg

Calgary 11 • Batoche
SECOND RIEL 6 12 Lake Winnipegosis
REBELLION 1885 9

South Saskatchewan R. Lake Manitoba

Ft. MacLeod Regina 5 • Moose Jaw

Ft. Whoop-Up *Canadian Pacific Railway 1880-85* Portage la Prairie 1 Ft. Douglas (Selkirk)

MONTANA 4 *Canadian Pacific Railway*
1880-85

FIRST RIEL 2,3 Ft. Garry
REBELLION 1869 (Winnipeg)

Pembina

Ft. Buford *Red R.*

1. SELKIRK INCIDENT 1816 MINNESOTA
2. COURTHOUSE REBELLION 1849
3. FORT GARRY OCT 1869 *Lake Superior*
4. CYPRESS HILLS MASSACRE 1873
5. MAPLE CREEK 1882
6. DUCK LAKE MAR 1885
7. BATTLEFORD MAR 1885
8. FROG LAKE APR 1885 NORTH DAKOTA *Mississippi R.*
9. FISH CREEK APR 1885 *St. Croix R.*
10. CUT KNIFE CREEK APR 1885
11. NORTHCOTE MAY 1885
12. BATOCHE MAY 1885 SOUTH DAKOTA
13. FRENCHMEN'S BUTTE MAY 1885
14. LOON LAKE JUN 1885 St. Paul

0 300 *Minnesota R.*
miles

5.21 THE RIEL REBELLIONS OF CANADA *and other incidents (with modern boundaries)*

buffalo hunter. McDougall, without an army, had no choice but to comply, and he led his wagon train back to Pembina, Minnesota.

During the month of November, Riel presented a List of Rights to Ottawa, including the rights to land, rights to a voice on the Confederation government, rights to prior consultation for any decisions pertaining to the Red River country and the Red Riverites, and freedom of language and religion. Although McDougall lobbied for action, Prime Minister Macdonald's government, realizing how costly a military solution would be against the well-organized and highly skilled Metis frontiersmen, stalled for time. There were currently 6,000 French-speaking mixed-bloods, plus 4,000 English-speaking mixed-bloods. The latter group, however, had not yet completely thrown their

support behind Riel. Although they supported his list of rights, they condemned the ouster of McDougall and the seizure of Fort Garry.

In early December, McDougall gave the go-ahead to his aide, Lieutenant Colonel John Stoughton Dennis, to recruit a militia and to arm them with the 300 rifles they had carted from Ottawa in order to suppress the Metis insurrection. Dr. Schultz and his Canada Firsters agreed to help, as did a group of Saulteaux, motivated by the promise of rifles. But the English-speaking mixed-bloods refused to fight other Metis. With but 60 men, Dennis could achieve only the capture of an abandoned post and issue a meaningless proclamation calling for Metis submission to authority, whereupon he returned to Pembina.

The Firsters, however, returned to the settlement flanking Fort Garry,

occupied Schultz's storehouse, and waited for the Metis. When Riel arrived with a superior force of 200, a small cannon in tow, and surrounded the storehouse, the Firsters surrendered without a fight and were led off to the stockade. By the end of December, McDougall had left Pembina for Ottawa and the *Comite National des Metis* had proclaimed itself a provisional government.

Prime Minister Macdonald, now recognizing his options as either a massive invasion or a reconciliation, chose the latter course and sent in Donald Smith of the Hudson's Bay Company to meet with the Metis and convince them of the Dominion's fair intentions. After having met with Smith, the French and Scottish Metis organized a representative government and, on February 9, 1870, elected the 25-year-old Riel president. In this atmosphere of resolution and good will, Riel declared a state of amnesty and released all prisoners.

Some of them, he learned, had already escaped, including Dr. Schultz and an Irishman by the name of Thomas Scott. Scott and other Firsters traveled to Portage la Prairie, south of Fort Garry, with plans of a rebellion against Riel and an attack on the post, but their attempt was short-lived. Ambroise Lepine and a party of Metis intercepted the Firsters in the winter snows. Furious to be jailed again, the hot-tempered Scott attacked a guard and threatened to kill Riel. Riel, ever diplomatic, decided to meet with Scott to calm him. But at this stage, some action of Scott's—whether verbal abuse against Riel or an actual physical assault—led Riel to call for Scott's trial for the bearing of arms against the state.

A jury of seven, with Riel as one of three prosecution witnesses, sentenced Scott to death. Riel himself supported the decision, believing it necessary to gain the rest of Canada's respect for Metis authority and determination. The move proved to be a grave tactical error. Public sentiment turned against Riel; and warrant was sworn out for his arrest. Scott became a martyr to what was considered Metis injustice and cruelty. Although Macdonald's government passed the Manitoba Act in July 1870, granting the Red River area provincial status and guaranteeing many of the provisions of the List of Rights, it did not include amnesty for actions during the rebellion, and it ordered in a constabulary force of 1,200. Many of these men wanted nothing more than to avenge Thomas Scott's death. Riel had not only to relinquish the reigns of government but also to flee for his life. The Metis, still hopeful, elected him in absentia to the Canadian Parliament three times.

Yet, over the next years, the Red Riverites continued to be abused. Four members of the Scott jury were murdered. Protestant Ontarians squatted on Red River lands while the Metis were on their seasonal hunts. The provisions of the Manitoba Act were ignored. All that remained was provincial status. Many of the Metis, yielding to the mounting pressures, migrated westward to the Saskatchewan River, where the pattern of Metis displacement and rebellion would be played out again.

THE SECOND RIEL REBELLION

During the decade and a half after the First Riel Rebellion, the pace of change accelerated rapidly on the Canadian Plains. The presence of whiskey traders and wolfers out of Montana and related incidents of violence led to the formation of the North West Mounted Police in Ottawa in May 1873. That same month, a group of American wolfers and Canadian accomplices, angry over some stolen horses, attacked an Assiniboine village and killed 30. The Cypress Hills Massacre, as it came to be called, impelled the government to act quickly in recruiting and deploying the new force. The Mounties proceeded to move on the frontier strongholds, such as Fort Whoop-Up of the whiskey traders, taking many of them over as official outposts. By the beginning of 1875, the Mounties maintained garrisons in six widely distributed frontier posts, among them Fort Macleod in the heart of Indian country.

Life for the Canadian Plains Indians was undergoing transformation. In addition to the debilitating effects of alcohol, the native population suffered from outbreaks of white diseases. In 1869 and 1870, a smallpox epidemic killed more than 2,000 Blackfeet, Bloods, Piegans, Sarcees, and Plains Crees. Moreover, the once-great buffalo herds were dying out, victims of wholesale slaughter by American and Canadian hide hunters in conjunction with Indian subsistence hunting. In 1878, after a dry winter and spring, many of the remaining herds roamed southward across the border for better grazing. American hide hunters prevented their return into Canada by setting prairie fires north of them. By 1879, the buffalo was virtually extinct in Canada. Hunger and famine became the common condition for the once-great Plains hunters, who were ignorant in the ways of farming. Sioux Indians, Sitting Bull among them, who took refuge in Canada after their wars in the United States, put a further strain on food supplies. Having failed to receive enough rations from the Canadian government to survive, the Sioux drifted back across the border to their former homelands. Sitting Bull and his remaining small band of followers surrendered at Fort Buford, Dakota Territory, in 1881.

During the 1870s, as the Indians struggled to survive and as increasing numbers of whites entered their domain, tribal representatives agreed to

Plains Indian pipe

seven treaties, most of them negotiated by the Mounties, in which huge tracts of land were ceded. (See "The Growth of Canada and Indian Land Cessions" in chapter 6.) Although the Mounties themselves generally kept their word to the Indians, thereby avoiding unnecessary clashes, the system as a whole was taking advantage of the native peoples and compromising their future by leaving them little territory. And many of the Indians, encouraged in their ignorance by whites, failed to grasp the legal ramifications of such treaties and believed they were only leasing their lands to others, not irrevocably forfeiting their own rights of usage.

The building of the Canadian Pacific Railway also brought dramatic change to the Plains. The government had debated the value of such a monumental project for years—Prime Minister Macdonald was one of the foremost proponents—and finally, in 1881, Canada became committed to the idea of linking the nearly 3,000 miles of varying terrain between Montreal and Vancouver via railroad. By 1884, most of the track had been laid from Montreal to the Rockies, and it soon would link up with the track being laid eastward from Vancouver through the Coast Mountains. The work crews alone increased the white population. Extensive settlement along the tracks would follow. A Cree chief by the name of Piapot recognized the railroad's threat to the Indian way of life and, in 1882, led his braves in an act of nonviolent resistance, removing the survey stakes for a 30-mile stretch of track west of Moose Jaw. Then, several months later, at Maple Creek his band camped directly in the path of track-laying crews. However, the Mounties drove them away in a bloodless show of force.

Yet, before the completion of the Canadian Pacific Railway, the largest of all the Canadian Indian Wars broke out. And once again, the Metis were at the center of it. As formerly along the Red River, the Metis had arranged their homesteads in strips along the Saskatchewan River. And, true to form, the government sent surveyors to divide the land into square lots, the lines of which would intersect existing boundaries, disrupting farm, wood, and water use, even bisecting some houses. Moreover, to keep the rights to their own lands, the Metis were forced to apply for official ownership patents, a long and frustrating process. Metis leaders sent numerous documents to Ottawa, requesting surveys according to current land use, prompt drafting of deeds, and representative government. When ignored, the Metis decided to organize their opposition. They needed a leader for their cause—someone who would unite the Metis and could negotiate with the central government—and decided to send for Louis Riel. Gabriel Dumont—a renowned buffalo hunter, horseman, and sharpshooter who was to become Riel's general in the field—would lead the search for him.

In June 1884, Dumont's party tracked Riel down at a mission school in Judith Basin, Montana, where he lived with his mixed-blood wife and family, teaching Indian children. Still obsessed with Metis rights, but now having a spiritual bent, Riel agreed to

return to Canada and lead the resistance. On arrival, he began preaching to both Metis and white settlers, using on one occasion an eclipse of the sun to convince unbelievers of his divine purpose. He also drafted a bill of rights, formed the Provisional Government of the Saskatchewan, and had Dumont organize an army of 400 cavalrymen. When Metis appeals were still ignored, Riel gave the go-ahead for a campaign of sabotage—cutting telegraph lines, occupying government stores, and taking hostages. Riel also sent an ultimatum to the Mounties under Leif Crozier at Fort Carlton, demanding the surrender of the post in exchange for the garrison's safe conduct. The Second Riel Rebellion had begun.

Carlton with reinforcements, evacuated the post to take up position at the larger settlement of Prince Albert. Dumont and other Metis wanted to attack the force en route, but again Riel restrained them. Although the Metis leader wanted to demonstrate rebel strength and determination, he had little tolerance for unnecessary violence. After Duck Lake, Riel sent a communique to various Indian tribes, urging them to join in the uprising, but typically his rhetoric was mild, calling for the capture of the Mounties and not their death.

The majority of chiefs he contacted feared the consequences of war with government forces. Only two chose to participate: Poundmaker and Big Bear, both Crees, who had come to

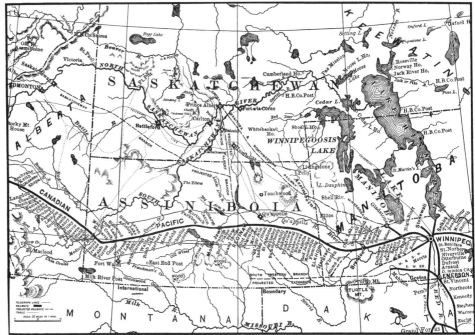

The Second Riel Rebellion of 1885. Public Archives of Canada.

Rather than submit, Crozier led a force of 55 Mounties and almost as many volunteers to retake an occupied trading post at Duck Lake. In the ensuing confrontation in the northern snows on March 26, 1885, 10 government troops were killed and 14 wounded before their retreat, compared to five rebels killed and three wounded. Riel, on hand to observe, called off any further massacre. The following day, the Mounties, now under the command of Commissioner A. G. Irvine, who had reached Fort

hate life on the reserve. Poundmaker and 200 warriors moved on the town of Battleford. The settlers took refuge in a fortified police stockade, holding out against a three-week siege, during which the Crees ransacked the Hudson's Bay store and other buildings, burned farmhouses, and killed one white. One hundred and fifty miles to the north, on the North Saskatchewan River, Big Bear led 200 warriors against the settlement of Frog Lake. They interrupted a Catholic mass where they captured 13 whites. When the Indian agent, Thomas Quinn, refused to be taken prisoner to the Cree camp, a fight broke out in which a warrior, by the name of Wandering Spirit, shot Quinn despite Big Bear's efforts to stop him. The other warriors joined in the violence and killed eight more. Two women and a Hudson's Bay clerk survived as captives. Another man escaped and reported the incident to the Mounties at Fort Pitt.

Word of these events reached Ottawa. Alarmed by the escalating violence, the government raised an army of 8,000, the North West Field Force. Unlike 15 years earlier, during the First Riel Rebellion, there now existed a railway to transport troops westward. The Canadian Pacific's general manager, William Van Horne, seizing on an opportunity of winning more funds for completion of the bogged-down, nearly bankrupt venture, promised to transport each troop shipment west in 11 days, with the railway providing wagon or sled transportation over the unfinished stretches of track. Although much of the trip was brutal on the troops, Van Horne kept his word. By mid-April 1885, all units had reached their staging points west of Winnipeg. Three battalions embarked: Major General Frederick Middleton, with overall command of the North West Field Force, would lead a force on Metis headquarters at Batoche; further west, Colonel William Otter would direct his men to Battleford; and Major General Thomas Strange would head a force via Calgary towards the Edmonton area. Middleton and Strange were to meet in the Fort Pitt region of Indian country.

On April 24, Dumont's rebel force took up position in rifle pits at the bottom of a depression at Fish Creek. By firing upward at the soldiers, who were silhouetted in plain view at the top of the rise and unable to use their artillery because of the steep angle, the Metis killed or wounded about 50 and suffered only 10 casualties in a rout of Middleton's men.

The same day, Otter's force relieved Battleford; then, after a stopover of several days, it moved to the Cree camp at Cut Knife Creek. But Poundmaker's warriors managed to slip away into the brush, then encircled and counterattacked the soldiers. After seven hours of fighting, Otter's troops had suffered 23 casualties and retreated to Battleford.

On May 9, the rebels gained still another victory against the riverboat *Northcote*, which Middleton had ordered outfitted to support his attack on Batoche. Dumont's men took the improvised gunboat out of commission by damaging it with a cable run across the South Saskatchewan River and raking it with gunfire from the banks. Middleton's first attack on Batoche that same day also ended in failure, with the Metis ambushing from a network of pits and trenches just inside the settlement. His men retreated behind a barricade of wagons at the edge of town.

The resulting stalemate at Batoche lasted three days, with both sides exchanging occasional sniper fire. The Metis, however, were running low on ammunition. Reinforcements arrived, increasing the government force to 900 men. With their superior numbers, more than four to one, many of Middleton's men wanted a bayonet charge, but the general wavered in his decision. Finally, a colonel of the Midland Battalion, A.T.H. Williams, forced Middleton's hand by launching his own attack. The general first ordered a recall, but when his troops ignored the signal, he had no choice but to send in more units. The Metis, firing nails, metal buttons, or stones when they ran out of bullets, retreated from trench to trench. By evening, after a stubborn resistance, they yielded. The soldiers suffered eight dead and 46 wounded; the rebels, 16 dead and 30 wounded. After the surrender, Metis women and children emerged from cellars and caves. Dumont, however, escaped through government lines and across the border into the United States. Riel hid in the nearby woods for three days,

pondering his future, then finally surrendered to a scouting party.

As for the Crees, Poundmaker and his warriors turned themselves in at Battleford. Big Bear and his men held out longer. Assiniboine Indians, scouting for Strange's battalion, picked up the war party's trail in the vicinity of Fort Pitt on May 26. Two days later, Strange launched an assault at Frenchmen's Butte. The Cree force repelled and outflanked the Canadian cavalry, then escaped northward. Middleton and 200 reinforcements united with Strange's men on June 3. A party of Mounties under Samuel Steele caught up with the Crees at Loon Lake but, after a brief firefight with several casualties on both sides, the Indians again escaped into the swampy wilderness. Several days later, on June 18, Big Bear released a group of white prisoners with a note asking for mercy. Many of the Crees then surrendered to the garrison at Fort Pitt. Big Bear remained at large until July 2, finally giving himself up 100 miles to the east, at Fort Carlton.

Both Cree chiefs, broken men, were released after two years of captivity and died soon afterward. Gabriel Dumont, in later years, became a member of Buffalo Bill Cody's Wild West Show. Louis Riel was taken to the territorial capital of Regina, where he was sentenced to death for the murder of Thomas Scott 15 years before, as well as crimes against the state. Riel's lawyers appealed to Ottawa for clemency. French Catholics voiced their support. Dumont organized relay stations for an escape that never came to pass. Riel probably could have saved himself up until the last, by claiming that his deeds were the result of insanity, but he refused to recant. The sentence was carried out on November 16. Nine days before he died, the Canadian Pacific Railroad, which had played a key role in suppressing the rebellion and which forever would change life on the Canadian Plains, was completed.

Chapter 6
INDIAN LAND CESSIONS

The question of land is central to the history of Indian and white relations. As whites came to dominate from ocean to ocean, the Indian domain dwindled—from all the Americas to a mere fraction. North American history is just as much the story of a displacement of a people as it is that of European expansion, although the Indian part of the story usually receives only marginal emphasis in historical accounts.

There are many different ways to depict Indian land cessions cartographically—by general geographic regions; by particular tribes; by historical periods or incidents; or in terms of varying aspects of white expansion, such as territorial acquisitions, the creation of states, or the development of roads, forts, and settlements. Much of the story of the white appropriation of Indian lands is contained within the previous chapter on Indian wars, because white encroachment was a root cause of strife and, by the same token, warfare served as a primary means for whites to achieve Indian removal.

This chapter will present a series of other overviews on the matter of Indian displacement from their ancestral lands.

In viewing the subject from any or all perspectives, it should be kept in mind that, for the Indians, land cessions were much more than just the loss of real estate. Indians did not see land as a source of profit as many European individuals and business concerns did, but rather as the direct source of life. The vast majority of native peoples had no concept of private ownership of land. Lands and the right to use them were held by entire communities or extended kin groups. Even in certain agricultural or fishing societies where particular fields or fishing stations were assigned to individuals, the entire community shared the produce or catch. And exclusive rights to specific territories were only for the use of lands, not for the nonuse or destruction of property as is inherent in the European notion of private ownership. Likewise, in most Indian societies, no one individual carried the authority to sign away tribal holdings. An exception to the general pattern were the Yuroks of California who individually owned land, measured wealth by it, and were able to sell it.

Yet, for the Yuroks as for all Native North Americans, in addtion to being a source of life, land also represented a way of life. Unlike Europeans who so often shaped their environment to fit their life-styles, building towns and cities, Indians generally adapted to the environment as they found it. And land was considered in Indian religions very much alive itself, sacred and filled with ghosts and animistic spirits. Therefore, by forcing Indians to cede their lands, whites not only displaced peoples, but also dispossessed cultures and disrupted faiths.

THE SPREAD OF EUROPEAN DISEASES

As devastating as warfare and forced removals were to Indian peoples, another result of contact with whites proved to be even more debilitating, demoralizing, and deadly—the spread of European diseases. It is estimated that, whereas many tribal populations declined by more than 10 percent from Indian-white conflicts, the average tribal loss of life from infectious diseases was 25–50 percent. For some tribes, these diseases meant near extinction. The Mandans of the upper Missouri, for example, are said to have declined from 1,600 to 131 during the smallpox epidemic of 1837.

Of all the diseases carried from Europe, smallpox was the principal destroyer of native peoples; it was especially deadly because it would return to the same populations in epidemic proportions time and again. From 1837 to 1870, at least four different epidemics struck the Plains tribes. Although a vaccination was

invented at the beginning of the 19th century, there were few doctors to vaccinate Indians and the Indians themselves resisted the process, depending rather on their shamans. But there were other killers besides smallpox against which the Indians, having lived in continental isolation, had no resistance—measles, scarlet fever, typhoid, typhus, influenza, tuberculosis, cholera, diphtheria, chicken pox, and venereal infections—all contributing to the rapid rate of depopulation and cultural dispossession.

It is of course impossible to thoroughly and accurately chart the

spread of such diseases. They occurred among all the tribes, keeping pace with or even preceding white expansion, as nomadic Indians or Indian traders carried them to tribes who had not yet come into contact with Europeans. It has even been theorized that the great Temple Mound Culture of the Mississippi Valley and Southeast (see "The Temple Mound Builders" in chapter 2) declined from a pandemic that started with the contact of a few Indians with the earliest European explorers of the late 15th or early 16th century. Nonetheless, specific historical outbreaks and epidemics are documented. The

6.1 EPIDEMICS AMONG INDIANS, *showing locations of certain among the worst outbreaks of European diseases within the native population*

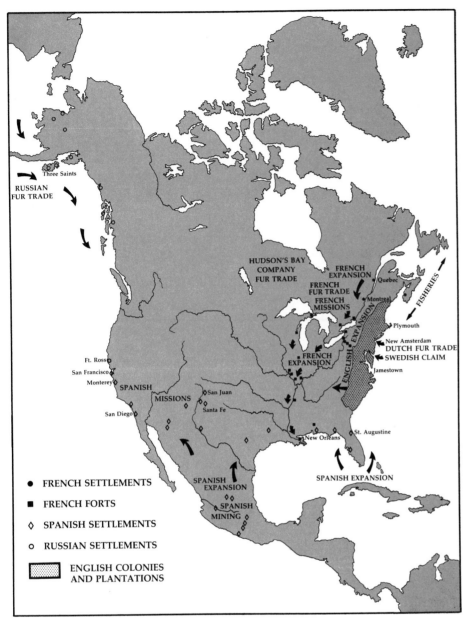

6.2 PATTERNS OF EARLY EUROPEAN SETTLEMENT

Map labels: Three Saints; RUSSIAN FUR TRADE; HUDSON'S BAY COMPANY FUR TRADE; FRENCH EXPANSION; FRENCH FUR TRADE; FRENCH MISSIONS; Quebec; Montreal; FISHERIES; Plymouth; New Amsterdam; DUTCH FUR TRADE; SWEDISH CLAIM; Jamestown; ENGLISH EXPANSION; FRENCH EXPANSION; Ft. Ross; San Francisco; Monterey; SPANISH; San Juan; Santa Fe; MISSIONS; San Diego; St. Augustine; New Orleans; SPANISH EXPANSION; SPANISH EXPANSION; SPANISH MINING

- ● FRENCH SETTLEMENTS
- ■ FRENCH FORTS
- ◇ SPANISH SETTLEMENTS
- ○ RUSSIAN SETTLEMENTS
- ENGLISH COLONIES AND PLANTATIONS

"I do not fear death . . . but to die with my face rotten, that even the wolves will shrink . . . at seeing me, and say to themselves, that is Four Bears, the friend of the whites.''

EUROPEAN USE OF INDIAN LANDS AND RESOURCES

For every European colonial power in North America, regardless of varying self-imposed stipulations and limitations, the concept of land discovery implied that of land title. And reinforcing the right of discovery was that of conquest. In fact, other than in the case of those Europeans of conscience who considered the Indians to have inherent rights, concessions to Indian wants and needs resulted from either a profit motive for trade, a defensive posture in the face of Indian military superiority, or relations with competing colonials. The sovereignty of Indian tribes was conveniently applied by Europeans to establish the credibility of their negotiated rights to previously held tribal tracts of land. Yet, in relations with the Indians, the Europeans at best treated tribal sovereignty as limited sovereignty—an often-used contradiction with an implicit notion of colonial self-interest. And the treaty-making process granting rights to Indians was usually one of forced concession or calculated deception on the part of whites for ulterior motives.

Of course, colonialism in North America, and the resulting Indian displacement and dispossession, was the natural outgrowth of an age-old process in Europe, Asia, and Africa— as well as among the Indians themselves—of a stronger people pushing aside a weaker one while expanding territorially. And, with no official controls whatsoever, treatment of the Indians might have been worse, as was often the case on the edge of the frontier. Yet the general pattern of European disregard for Indian rights—with exceptions usually for self-serving reasons—occurred in

accompanying map shows some of the more devastating ones.

The extent of the tragedy is staggering. The subject of infectious European diseases pervades every aspect of Indian studies. Disease was a principal disruptor of Indian culture, with shattering impact even on Indian faith and religion. The debilitating effects of these diseases also helped the whites win many of the Indian wars. Moreover, in some instances disease was even used as a weapon by whites who purposely passed out smallpox-infested blankets to the Indians. (See "Pontiac's Rebellion" in chapter 5.) For that matter, disease might be called another battleground for the

Indians where they were forced to make an impossible stand. As for land cessions, disease through depopulation played a large part in the ultimate displacement of tribes. And disease is still a problem for Indians today, who have higher illness and mortality rates than the general population. (See chapter 7, "CONTEMPORARY INDIANS.")

The words of Four Bears, a Mandan chief who at the time was dying from smallpox, help make the subject more human, rather than one of abstract demography and statistics:

"Four Bears never saw a white man hungry, but what he gave him to eat . . . and how have they repaid it! . . .

spite of nominally espoused Christian tenets and the supposed enlightenment of the Renaissance. It seems that Aristotle's doctrine of natural slavery—a classical rationalization for racial dominance and prejudice—had a greater hold on behavior. And because of European exploitation patterns, warfare between Indian and white became inevitable.

SPAIN

It is ironic that, of all the colonials, the Spanish first confronted the issue of aboriginal rights and set up the most detailed regulatory guidelines, with the Crown taking much of the initiative rather than private business, but arguably abused the Indians the most. In 1493, Pope Alexander VI divided the world outside Europe between Spain and Portugal, which supposedly gave Spain all of the Western Hemisphere except Brazil, and placed priority on the conversion of the native inhabitants to Catholicism and Spanish civilization. The means of carrying out this papal commission turned out to be the brute force of conquest cushioned only by the *requerimiento*, a royal decree read by conquistadors to tribes informing them of their duty to the Pope and the Crown, and their right to freedom if they submitted, along with the threat of war and enslavement if they did not. To achieve anything resembling freedom, however, the Indians also had to prove themselves "civilized" in terms of religion, language, shelter, and dress. In 1512, Pope Julius II issued a doctrine that the Indians were after all descended from Adam and Eve. Yet until Christianized and Hispanicized, they were considered inferior and wayward descendants—at best, pagan savages.

Because of reports by missionaries and theoreticians such as Bartolome de las Casas, Antonio de Montesinos, and Francisco de Vitoria of widespread abuses of the *requerimiento* (even if Indians managed to work out a translation of the decree and reacted peacefully, they were still often brutalized and taken as slaves for personal use or profit) and reports of the failure of forced acculturation, the

Mexico or New Spain in the 18th century by Emanuel Bowen. Public Archives of Canada.

Pope and the Crown further structured Indian policy. In 1512, the Laws of Burgos established the *encomienda* system, which required male Indians to work nine months out of each year in return for entry into Spanish society. The policy pleased, the clerical element of Spanish Christian society, who believed it would accomplish the desired Indian conversion and native cultural obliteration; it also pleased the lay, or *encomendero*, element—the conquistadors and officials—who would obtain labor for their various New World undertakings, such as mining, ranching, farming, or public works. In exchange, the *encomendero* would pay the Crown a head tax on each Indian, as well as finance the indoctrination. The Indians who achieved the so-called civilized status were known as *indios capaces*.

With continued criticism from missionaries—who claimed that, since the provisions for Hispanicization and training in the *encomienda* were being ignored, the program amounted to legalized enslavement—the Church and Crown shaped a new system. The *repartimiento*, official policy by the beginning of the 17th century, imposed on tribal populations an annual levy for labor and produce—more legal enslavement. In the Spanish colonies, in addition to disease and military aggression, forced labor was another debilitator and killer of Indian peoples.

Yet, since the Indians were a resource to be exploited as well as souls to be converted, they were not driven from their territories—although at times they were forced from particular sites. Spanish claims to their lands allowed for their presence. All three agencies of expansion—the Franciscan, Jesuit, and Dominican missions; the presidio military posts; and the civilian settlements of farmers, stock raisers, miners, traders, and trappers—had use for them.

With legal codes favoring colonial development at the expense of Indians, yet with a place for Indians in their society and among their settlements, Spain extended its territories throughout much of the Americas. After having developed and exploited Indian lands in the Caribbean, and Middle and South America during much of the 16th century—the colony of New Spain was founded in 1521 after the conquest of the Aztecs—Spain spread its dominion northward, eventually holding, at one time or another, Florida, the Gulf Coast, the Mississippi Valley, the Southwest, and California.

In 1565, Pedro Menendez de Aviles founded St. Augustine in Florida, the first permanent European settlement in North America. In 1763, with the reorganization of colonial territories after the French and Indian Wars, Spain ceded its Florida and Gulf Coast holdings to England, but it regained them in 1783 after the American Revolution. Florida became part of the United States in 1819. For a number of years during this period, Spain held the vast trans-Mississippi province of Louisiana—ceded by France in 1762—but without significant economic development of Indian lands. In 1800, the Louisiana Territory went back to France; then in 1803, with the Louisiana Purchase, it went to the United States.

In the Southwest in 1598, Juan de Onate founded the settlement of San Juan de Yunque (now San Juan Pueblo) in the Rio Grande country of what is now New Mexico. By the 1700s, the Spanish were also developing parts of Texas—San Antonio was founded in 1718—as well as the administrative district of Pimeria Alta, the northern district of which later became Arizona. Then, by the mid-18th century, Spain was establishing missions, presidios, and rancherias in Baja California. As for Alta California, Gaspar de Portola and Junipero Serra founded San Diego in 1769, and Juan Bautista de Anza founded San Francisco in 1776, with other centers of colonization developing between them. With Mexican Independence in 1821, these various western territories became part of Mexico. In 1848, after the Mexican War, between Mexico and the United States over the American annexation of Texas, most of the region was ceded to the United States. Yet it wasn't until the Gadsden Purchase of 1853—the American acqui-

sition of additional lands in New Mexico, Arizona, and California—that all the Indian peoples knew once and for all under whose imposed dominion they fell. (For further discussion of the absorption of Spanish lands by the United States, see "The Growth of the United States and Indian Land Cessions" in this chapter. For Spanish-Indian relations, see "The Pueblo Rebellion and Other Rebellions against the Spanish" in chapter 5.)

FRANCE

French use of Indian lands was relatively nondisruptive in comparison to that of the other colonial powers. Various factors account for this pattern of development. First, New France's economy revolved around the fur trade, not agriculture or mining. As such, most exploitation of land and resources involved Indian hunting grounds at a time when the hunting range was plentiful. Competition for choice village or agricultural sites, other than along the St. Lawrence Valley and the lower Mississippi Valley, was rare. And for the French, successful commerce depended on friendly relations with the Indians, who acted as hunters—either independently or in direct French employ—or as guides or as middlemen among other tribes. French traders and trappers, venturing into the wilderness and coming in close contact with Indians of many tribes, adopted a life-style compatible with that of the natives.

Perhaps even more significant than the fur trade, the slow rate of spillover from Europe and the subsequently low French colonial population contributed to the relative lack of Indian dispossession and cultural displacement by the French. Contrary to what was the case in other European colonies, settlements did not rapidly spring up around the trading and military posts. Rather, in French-held territory, the wilderness remained intact.

Yet these two factors alone—the fur trade and low population—do not entirely explain French relations with the Indians. (In Russian-held territory, a small number of traders practiced methods of virtual enslavement and had a disproportionate impact on the native population, all for the same goal—the acquisition of furs.) Scholars have looked for further explanation in French culture and character. Catholicism was not a determining factor in and of itself, since French and Spanish behavior toward the Indians varied significantly. Moreover, much of the French acceptance of the Indian way of life arose in spite of missionaries who advocated the transformation of Indian culture, as did many officials. And there were other exceptions to the generally permissive French attitudes toward the Indians. For example, the French readily made war on the Iroquois for their own ends, and they brazenly displaced the Natchez. French traders also often resorted to coercion, trickery, and liquor for better profits. The French even relocated certain Indian peoples, bullied some to fight in their armies, and punished or enslaved others who proved rebellious.

Yet basic racial acceptance of Indians within French character is proven by the common practice—even encouraged as official policy for purposes of acculturation—of intermarriage and miscegenation. The French also had the acumen to recognize the wide differences in culture among different tribes as well as the open-mindedness to participate in Indian rituals. They also perceived the special mystical relationship Indians had with their lands and generally made a point in seeking tribal approval of land use. Whatever the underlying cause or causes, perhaps the best evidence for the French acceptance of Indians is their acceptance by Indians. Through the fur trade many Indians came to regard the French as brothers in a shared enterprise. Relatively few tribes made war on the French. In the French and Indian Wars, the large majority sided with them against the English. When the French were finally defeated in 1763, many of the tribes of the Old Northwest showed their displeasure by rebelling under Pontiac against their new landlords.

(See chapter 5, "INDIAN WARS.")

Until that time, since the founding of trading settlements in Acadia and Quebec in the first part of the 17th century, France had come to hold claim to Indian lands along the St. Lawrence Valley, the Great Lakes and Ohio Valley, the upper Mississippi Valley, the upper Missouri Valley, and, by the 18th century, along the lower Mississippi as well. For a brief period after 1763, from 1800 to 1803, France again held land in North America, with the retrocession from Spain of the region stretching from the Mississippi to the Rockies, known as the Louisiana Territory. But Napoleon chose not to develop it but to sell it to the United States for $15 million. As usual, the Indians had no say in the transaction. (For further discussion of the French pattern of land use and the history of their land claims, see "The Fur Trade" in chapter 4 and the sections on the growth of the United States and Canada in this chapter. For French-Indian relations see chapter 5, "INDIAN WARS.")

ENGLAND

English colonials were land-hungry. They came to North America primar-ily as families and farmers, and they came to stake a claim and stay. The overflow from the British Isles was furious. Once colonies were established, boatload after boatload of hopeful settlers arrived in the busy harbors. They came for other purposes, too, and, as in the French-claimed territories, much expansion resulted from pioneering inroads of fur traders. But it was the English drive toward privately held land that pushed most Indians—those, that is, that survived European diseases, warfare, and in some instances enslavement—further and further back from the Atlantic seaboard, across the Appalachian Mountains and, eventually, after American Independence, across the Mississippi Valley as well.

In discussing British use of Indian lands, it is necessary to refer to three levels of policy and activity—the national, colonial, and local. Since the Crown left Indian policy to the various colonial governments (until 1755 and the creation of two departments or superintendencies for the centralization of Indian affairs), one colony's approach to Indians varied from another's. And since settlers on the edge of the frontier often ignored regulations no matter at what level they came from, local practice often varied from official policy. Moreover, as is

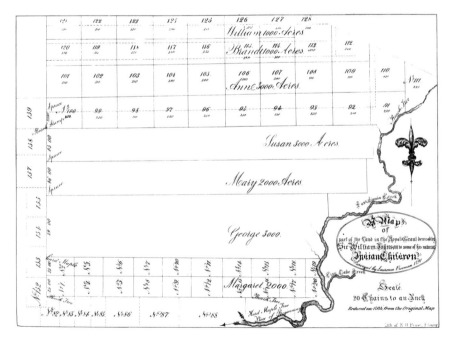

Land grants to William Johnson's Indian children. Chris Campbell Collection.

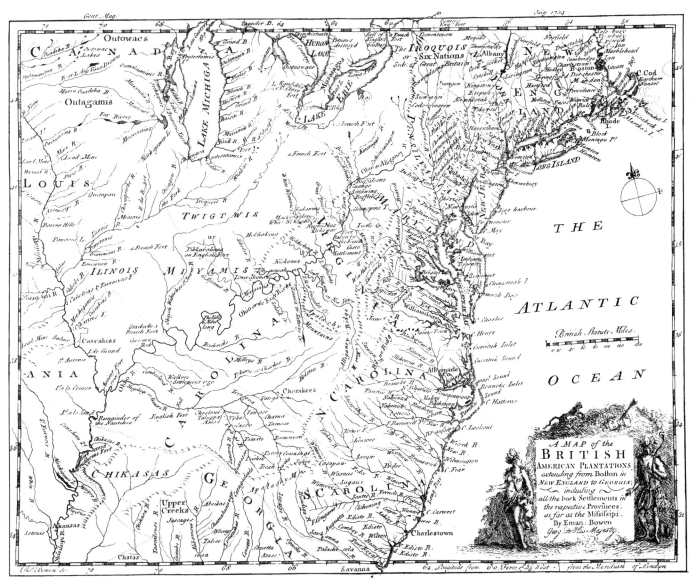

The English plantations by Emanuel Bowen, 1754. Chris Campbell Collection.

the case with all the colonial powers, it is difficult to analyze and make generalizations about a particular national character with regard to Indian relations. Farmers, traders, soldiers, officials, missionaries, and other elements of the colonial white population had different concerns and ambitions. And on all levels of activity and in all elements of society, Indian policy was not static but evolving with changing events. Yet, as a rule, the English throughout their tenure in North America showed only minimal respect for the Indian way of life and right to occupancy of ancestral lands.

Patterns of British land use can be analyzed in terms of four geographical areas—New England, the central colonies, and the southern colonies, as well as the wilderness areas of all three plus Canada. Of all, Pennsyl-

vania under the Quakers, after England had claimed the central colonies from the Dutch by right of conquest, had the most enlightened policy and saw the least warfare. In 1682, William Penn signed a treaty with Delaware tribal leaders acknowledging Indian title to land, and establishing strict and fair procedures for its purchase. With time, however, settlers managed to evade regulations—through leases of Indian lands, for example, or a combination of outright encroachment and official fraud.

In Virginia, tobacco was the major commodity and determinant. Because of the ever-increasing need for more farmland in a growing market, Indian lands were in perpetual demand. After early years of negotiated sales, uprisings among the Powhatans resulting from white encroachments

served as an excuse to confiscate additional Indian lands. In the less settled Carolinas and Georgia, two main kinds of trade—in furs and in slaves—shaped exploitation patterns. Barbaric and abusive practices such as forced labor and kidnapping led to Indian uprisings among the Yamasees and Tuscaroras. In the South, cotton and sugar cane also became important colonial crops.

New England also saw Indian rebellions because of the pressures of an expanding white population—in particular, the Pequot War and King Philip's War. Charters of land often ignored Indian rights altogether. When Indians were allowed to negotiate the sale of lands, they were often purposefully misled as to the true nature of the transaction. The entire concept of land ownership was

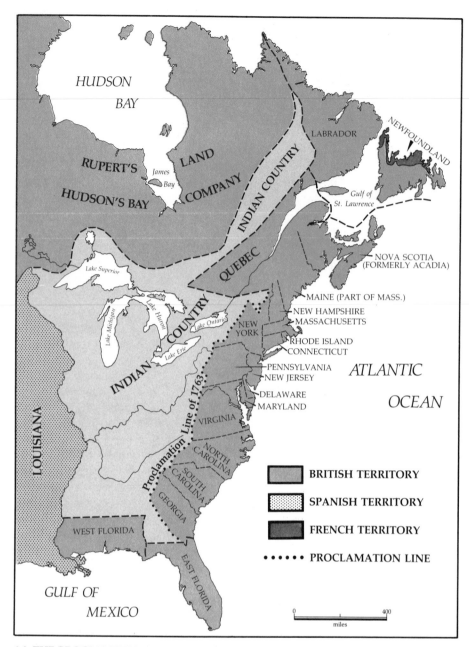

6.3 THE PROCLAMATION LINE OF 1763, *separating Indian lands from white lands*

became the northern superintendent, and Edmond Atkin, the southern.) After England gained control of France's claim in North America, a new Indian land policy was brought into effect. The Proclamation of 1763, which established boundaries for the colonies, also created a dividing line between white and Indian lands, with the intention of permanently separating the two populations. A pattern emerged, however, that when Indians crossed the boundary back onto ancestral lands, they were expelled by military force to their "Indian Country"; but that when whites violated the boundary to settle new lands, they were allowed to do so. Both British concepts—a centralized Indian office and a separate "Indian Country"—became part of American policy after Independence. Ironically, most Indian tribes supported the British, their former enemies, against the rebels in the American Revolution; to the Indians, the rebels represented the encroaching settlers. The Treaty of Paris of 1783 at the end of the war gave no consideration whatsoever to the Indians as allies or landholders. (For more on England's land claim and policy, see "The Growth of the United States and Indian Land Cessions" in this chapter, as well as chapter 5, "INDIAN WARS.")

HOLLAND AND SWEDEN

Dutch Indian policy was based on considerations of expediency needed to accomplish desired ends, which evolved from solely the fur trade to eventually agriculture as well. In order to establish to other European nations the credibility of their land claims, the Dutch recognized tribes as sovereign, with prior rights to land, and codified a legal process for purchase. To maintain the lucrative fur trade, they were responsive to Indian demands and practiced a policy of diplomacy and conciliation. Yet, as tribal lands became more important than trade, the Dutch readily resorted to cajolery and force to obtain new territory.

During the existence of New Neth-

alien to the Indians, who were allowed to believe they were selling the right to use land while keeping their own right of usage. And unlike the Quakers in Pennsylvania, who were more accepting of Indian ways, the paternalistic Puritans considered themselves to have divine justification in their jurisdication over Indians.

As for the wilderness areas under British claim, variations in exploitation patterns depended on types of development. In the South, as has been mentioned, small, independent fur traders took advantage of friendly tribes. In the Hudson Bay region of the far north, however, the Hudson's

Bay Company, with its monopoly, maintained fair trading practices. In New York as well, British traders who inherited their relationship with the Iroquois from the Dutch laid the foundations for a long-term political alliance between the Crown and the Iroquois League. And Iroquois lands remained inviolate until after the American Revolution.

It was one of these traders, William Johnson, close friend of the Mohawks, whose advice at the Albany Congress in 1754 led the following year to the establishment of a centralized Indian program with northern and southern departments. (Johnson

erland, which came to include territory stretching from the Hudson and Delaware river mouths westward over much of present-day Pennsylvania and New York, the thrust of Dutch policy evolved as follows: In the years of the United New Netherland Company charter from 1614 to 1617, the period of development by independent traders from 1617 to 1624, and the early years of the Dutch West India Company charter (although the charter was granted in 1621, commercial activity didn't begin until 1624, and lasted until 1664), there occurred little Indian displacement. The Dutch negotiated with the Indians for small tracts of land for isolated trading posts and village sites, and not large wilderness tracts. Yet, beginning in the 1630s, with the depletion of fur resources in coastal areas and the threat of British expansion, the Dutch embarked on a course of agricultural colonization that required more Indian lands. The patroon system was devised to expedite development. Like seigniors in New France and proprietors in the British colonies, patroons were colonial landlords who collected rent from tenant farmers. In return for purchasing available tracts of land from the Indians and settling at least 50 Europeans on each, patroons received deeded title from the Dutch West India Company. Among the most important land grants were Swaanendael on Delaware Bay, Pavonia on the west shore of the lower Hudson River, and Rensselaerwyck on the upper Hudson. During this period, too, the Dutch West India Company lost its trade monopoly. Independent *swanneken* (traders), whose activity on the frontier was more difficult to regulate, began taking greater advantage of and exerting greater pressures on Indian peoples. With increased friction on both accounts and the overtly racist William Kieft becoming governor-general in 1639, warfare resulted, with repeated outbreaks until England wrested control of New Netherland from the Dutch in 1664. (See "Rebellions against the Dutch" in chapter 5.)

In one area perhaps the Dutch were more enlightened than their colonial counterparts. Although the Dutch considered themselves superior to Indians and discouraged intermarriage, they were still liberal enough in their views to accept Indian culture in proximity to their own without an official policy of acculturation. The Dutch Reformed Church established a certain number of missions to convert Indians, but nowhere on the scale as that found in Spanish, French, or British territory.

During the Dutch presence in North America, Sweden, through the New Sweden Company, laid claim in 1638 to part of the original Dutch claim along Delaware Bay. Because of insufficient manpower in the area, the Dutch were unable to evict them. The Swedes established friendly relations with Delaware Indians for the purposes of trade, offering better prices than either the Dutch or English. There was also some missionary activity within their claim by Lutherans. Finally, in 1655, with a stepped-up military effort, the Dutch ousted them and reclaimed the territory which, nine years later, became British.

RUSSIA

Russia had few regulations governing the behavior of its nationals toward the native population within its North American claim along the North Pacific Coast, established in the 1740s. Other than the 10 percent royal tribute, known as the *yasak*, the *promyshlenniki*—fur traders—were left to shape their own policy, eventually imposing a certain number of restrictions on themselves and arguing in favor of Russian Orthodox missionary activity in order to obtain a royal-backed monopoly, which was granted by the czar in 1799. As a result, throughout Russia's tenure in North America, a small number of Russians, through particularly barbaric methods, had an extreme impact on many peoples they came into contact with, especially the Aleuts of Alaska and the Pomos of California. One tribe successfully resisted them and stymied even further expansion and exploitation—the Tlingits.

The Russians typically sailed to a native village, used force or the threat of force to take women and children hostages, and demanded labor and furs from the men. While the men hunted, the women were used as concubines. Every able member of a village was forced to help in the preparation of hides—men, women, and children. If the *promyshlenniki* were displeased, they carried out their threats with executions and torture. By the 1760s, when a system of ad hoc yearly companies was structured to develop the trade, some rules were established, with Aleuts working nominally for shares that were rarely granted. Starting in 1784, permanent year-round settlements were founded, the first at Three Saints on Kodiak Island, from where ongoing relations with particular groups of the native population could be overseen. By the 1790s, and the merger of the many Russian fur companies into one—the United American Company, the name of which, with the royal charter, became the Russian American Company—more rules were applied. Nevertheless, native inhabitants continued to be exploited through exacting discipline and outright cheating. From 1812 to 1841, the Russians maintained Fort Ross in Bodega Bay of California. With the sale of Alaska to the United States in 1864, Russian tenure in North America came to an end. The Aleuts, Eskimos, and other tribes had new landlords. (See also "The Aleut, Tlingit, and Pomo Resistance against the Russians" in chapter 5.)

THE GROWTH OF THE UNITED STATES AND INDIAN LAND CESSIONS

United States territorial expansion meant Indian territorial reduction. Every white territorial thrust had its own set of consequences among differing elements of the native population, changing lives and history, the end result being the diminishing of the vast aboriginal land base to a present-day size of a mere 52 million acres, less than the state of Minnesota. As a result, the story of Indian land cessions within what has evolved into the continental United States is immense and intricate, each region of the country, each tribe, and each period of history having its own chronicle.

In order to make the complex subject of United States growth and the resulting tribal displacement manageable, this section will summarize the material, in conjuction with a series of maps, from several points of view—a summary of the general forces at play and recurring patterns of displacement; the acquisition of territories by the federal government and formation of states along with white settlement patterns; a review of the important dates and historical periods affecting Indians and tribal locations; and a survey of regional displacement patterns. The list of tribes in the Appendix, showing historical and contemporary tribal locations also

presents a view of Indian displacement and migrations. Most tribes ended up far from their original homes. (See also other sections in this chapter for different aspects of Indian land cessions. See chapter 7, "CONTEMPORARY INDIANS," for further discussion of United States Indian policy.)

The typical cycle of Indian displacement can be summarized as follows: 1) The first period was one of acceptance, peace making, and treaty making, even mutual aid and trade, between the first white settlers in a region and the local Indians. Often the Indians willingly ceded land in exchange for goods or the promise of annuities. Boundary lines between Indians and whites were assumed by the limits of white settlement or determined by natural boundaries, with degrees of segregation depending primarily on trade activity. Peace generally lasted several years; 2) after

a period of time, white settlers from a rapidly expanding, land-hungry population trespassed into Indian country and appropriated territory. The violation of earlier agreements led to reprisals by the Indians against the settlers, which in turn fostered a great deal of publicity and fear mongering in the white centers of political power, about the Indian presence on the frontier; 3) white leaders called up a military action, usually involving both regulars and volunteer militia, against the Indians. The invading troops often built wilderness forts, which in turn attracted more settlers; 4) the Indians, overwhelmed by superior numbers and arms, with many of their villages and crops destroyed, sued for peace and were forced to negotiate new territorial cessions and withdraw further into the wilderness.

This compendium is of course an oversimplification and does not address various other factors involved in Indian land cessions besides the

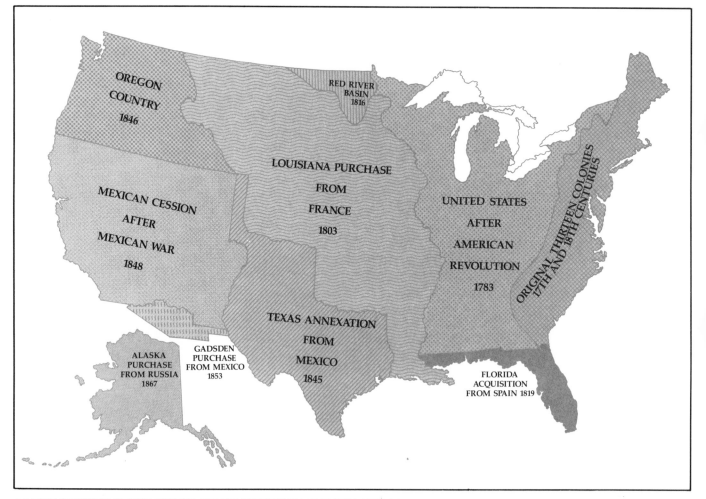

6.4 THE GROWTH OF THE UNITED STATES BY REGION AND THE APPROPRIATION OF INDIAN LANDS

pressures of the expanding white frontier. It does not take into account, for example, the role of white economic interests, with their desire for cheap land and resources, from the early colonial chartered joint-stock companies that developed the fur trade and agriculture to later corporate enterprises, such as the railroads, lumber and mining concerns, and cattle barons. Many of these interests received huge land grants from respective governments that gave no consideration to Indian rights. Nor does the summary take into account the competition over land among various white factions, with the Indians often considered incidental players, as in the French and Indian Wars, the American Revolution, the War of 1812, and the Civil War. Nor does it address the question of Manifest Destiny and the calculated governmental policy of Indian removal.

There are other concepts to keep in mind—five general patterns of Indian displacement—when studying Indian land cessions and migrating: 1) drift, in which tribes migrated away from white settlements by choice, or sometimes toward them; 2) banishment, in which tribes were prevented from entering certain areas; 3) relocation, in which tribes were forcibly moved to a new region; 4) concentration, in which tribes were forced to live in a smaller part of their existing territory; and 4) extinction, in which tribes were either obliterated through disease and warfare, or assimilated within the white population.

The event normally cited as marking the beginning of American history is the voyage of Christopher Columbus, although Columbus did not actually land in North America and although the United States did not form for another three centuries. In any case, his journey set off a period of intense European exploration along the eastern coastline of North America; however, other than perhaps the spread of some European diseases and a certain amount of slave raiding, this had minimal impact on native peoples north of Mexico and the Caribbean.

Most of the early attempts at settlement within the area now comprising the continental United States were failures, such as French Huguenot colonies in South Carolina and Florida, headed by Jean Ribault and Rene de Laudonniere, during the years 1562 to 1565, and British colonies on Roanoke Island, North Carolina, backed by Walter Raleigh, from 1585 to 1590. The first permanent European settlement in North America was St. Augustine in Florida, founded by the Spanish under Pedro Menenedez de Aviles in 1565, who drove away the French Huguenots. Then, in 1607 (two years after the French established the permanent settlement of Port Royal in what is now Canada), the English founded their first permanent settlement at Jamestown,

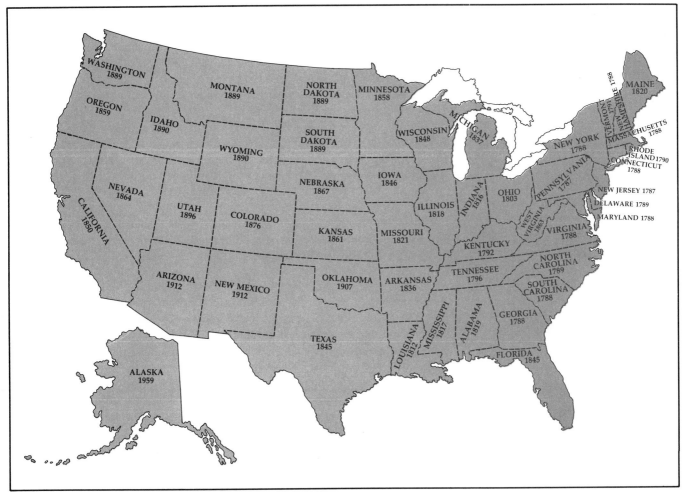

6.5 THE GROWTH OF THE UNITED STATES BY STATEHOOD

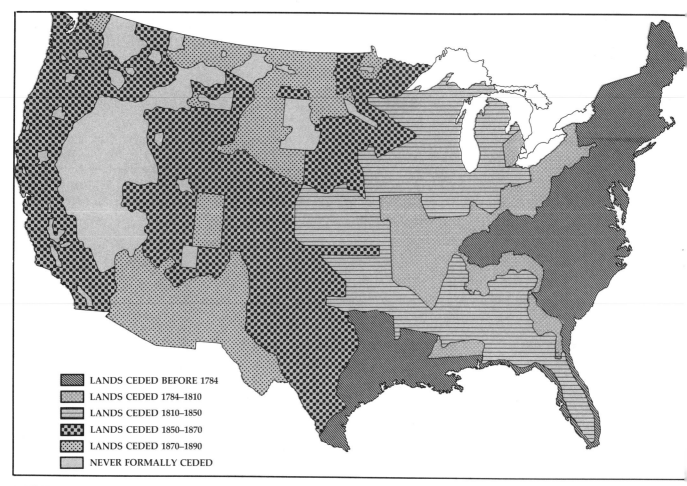

LANDS CEDED BEFORE 1784
LANDS CEDED 1784–1810
LANDS CEDED 1810–1850
LANDS CEDED 1850–1870
LANDS CEDED 1870–1890
NEVER FORMALLY CEDED

6.6 INDIAN LAND CESSIONS IN THE UNITED STATES BY REGION AND DATE

Virginia, under John Smith, and in 1620, the Pilgrims arrived at Plymouth, Massachusetts. Meanwhile, in the Southwest, the Spanish founded Santa Fe, New Mexico, in 1609. And the Dutch gained a foothold in North America along the Hudson River during the 1620s—Fort Orange (Albany) and New Amsterdam (Manhattan).

These permanent settlements effected the first Indian land cessions, through early trade, territorial purchases and agreements, disease, and eventual warfare: the Powhatan Wars of 1622 and 1644 in Virginia; the Pequot War of 1636–37 and King Philip's War of 1675–76 in New England; the Wappinger and Delaware Uprisings against the Dutch from 1643 to 1664 in New Netherland; and the Pueblo Rebellion against the Spanish in New Mexico in 1680. (See chapter 5, "INDIAN WARS".)

Most Indian displacement during the 17th century occurred at the hands of the British and the Dutch, whose patterns of colonization necessitated extensive cultivable homesteads (see previous section) and whose presence dramatically reduced the number of Algonquian-speaking peoples along the eastern seaboard. In the 18th century, the French expanded their sphere of activity into the Mississippi and Ohio valleys, appropriating some Indian lands, such as that of the Natchez; the Spanish spread out from the Rio Grande into Texas, Arizona, and California, where they established many missions and brought about the phenomenon of Mission Indians, dispossessed of land and culture; and the Russians gained dominance over and had great impact on the Aleuts of Alaska. Yet, although the Indians who came into contact with the traders, missionaries, and settlers of France, Spain, and Russia suffered a certain degree of cultural attrition, with European diseases and forced labor exacting a toll, trans-Appalachian tribal locations remained fairly constant during this period. A greater impact on the western Indian territorial patterns during the 17th century was the advent of the horse, which brought many formerly sedentary peoples from other regions onto the Great Plains. (See "The Great Plains Culture Area" and "The Indian and the Horse" in chapter 3.)

The beginning of the new order for Native Americans, as well as the beginning of the end of the colonial period, came about in 1763, with the Treaty of Paris in which France ceded New France to England; Pontiac then led the tribes of the Great Lakes region in the rebellion against the English; and England issued a Royal Proclamation which established the Appalachian watershed as the dividing line between Indians and whites, prohibiting white settlement on Indian lands and the displacement of Indian peoples without tribal and Crown consent. During the next 10 years, a series of treaties and purchases further defined the Proclamation Line that came to stretch from

Canada to Florida. The lasting consequence of the Proclamation of 1763, however, was not the preservation of Indian lands, because white settlers violated its provisions from the start, but rather the policy-making precedent of separate and segregated Indian lands.

After the American Revolution and the new Treaty of Paris of 1783, the Royal Proclamation of course was no longer in effect within the United States. The Northwest Ordinance of 1787, formulated under the Articles of Confederation and defining a North-west Territory in the region of the Great Lakes (the Old Northwest), echoed the same concept of Indian land rights but also, adversely, set up guidelines for political and economic development, thereby encouraging white settlement. It was during this entire period that many of the tribes of the region came to be conquered and displaced. The American Revolution saw the destruction of much of the Iroquois homeland as well as the migration of many Iroquois peoples to Canada. New York established reservations in the western part of the state for some of the Iroquois who remained. Then, after the Revolution, a series of wars for the Old Northwest occurred, starting with Little Turtle's War of 1790–95 and, in the following century, Tecumseh's Rebellion of 1809–11 and the Black Hawk War of 1832.

Even while the Old Northwest was being disputed, the new nation was beginning to expand its domain into other Indian lands through various territorial acquisitions. In 1790, Spain signed the Nootka Convention, ceding territory in the Pacific Northwest

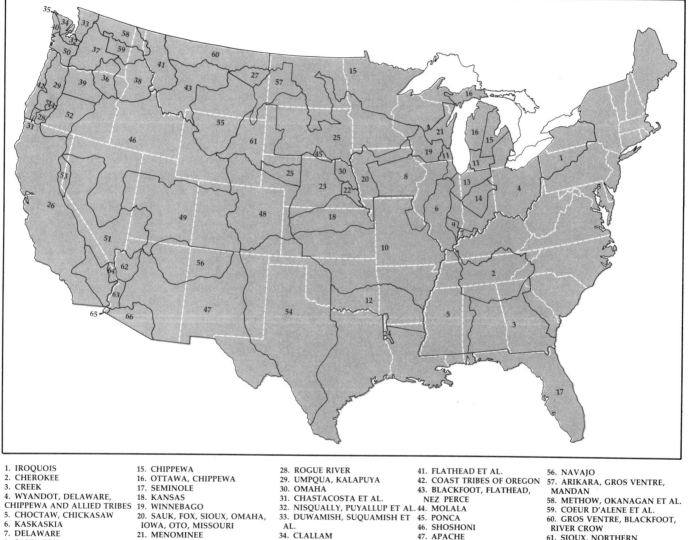

1. IROQUOIS	15. CHIPPEWA	28. ROGUE RIVER	41. FLATHEAD ET AL.	56. NAVAJO
2. CHEROKEE	16. OTTAWA, CHIPPEWA	29. UMPQUA, KALAPUYA	42. COAST TRIBES OF OREGON	57. ARIKARA, GROS VENTRE,
3. CREEK	17. SEMINOLE	30. OMAHA	43. BLACKFOOT, FLATHEAD,	MANDAN
4. WYANDOT, DELAWARE,	18. KANSAS	31. CHASTACOSTA ET AL.	NEZ PERCE	58. METHOW, OKANAGAN ET AL.
CHIPPEWA AND ALLIED TRIBES	19. WINNEBAGO	32. NISQUALLY, PUYALLUP ET AL.	44. MOLALA	59. COEUR D'ALENE ET AL.
5. CHOCTAW, CHICKASAW	20. SAUK, FOX, SIOUX, OMAHA,	33. DUWAMISH, SUQUAMISH ET	45. PONCA	60. GROS VENTRE, BLACKFOOT,
6. KASKASKIA	IOWA, OTO, MISSOURI	AL.	46. SHOSHONI	RIVER CROW
7. DELAWARE	21. MENOMINEE	34. CLALLAM	47. APACHE	61. SIOUX, NORTHERN
8. SAUK, FOX	22. OTO, MISSOURI	35. MAKAH	48. ARAPAHO AND CHEYENNE	CHEYENNE, ARAPAHO
9. PIANKASHAW	23. PAWNEE	36. WALLA WALLA, CAYUSE,	49. UTE	62. HUALAPAI
10. OSAGE	24. CADDO	UMATILLA	50. CHEHALIS, CHINOOK ET AL.	63. YUMA
11. OTTAWA, CHIPPEWA,	25. SIOUX	37. YAKIMA	51. PAIUTE	64. MOJAVE
POTAWATOMI	26. CALIFORNIA INDIANS	38. NEZ PERCE	52. KLAMATH ET AL.	65. COCOPA
12. QUAPAW	27. SIOUX, CHEYENNE, ARAPAHO,	39. CONFEDERATED TRIBES OF	53. WASHO	66. PAPAGO, PIMA, MARICOPA
13. POTAWATOMI	CROW, ASSINIBOINE, GROS	MIDDLE OREGON	54. COMANCHE, KIOWA	
14. MIAMI	VENTRE, MANDAN, ARIKARA	40. QUINAULT, QUILEUTE	55. CROW	

6.7 INDIAN LAND CESSIONS IN THE UNITED STATES BY TRIBE, 1776–1945 (with modern boundaries). For lands never ceded by or returned to the Indians, see map 7.2 showing present-day reservations. After Royce.

to the United States and England. Then, with the Louisiana Purchase of 1803, the United States purchased a hugh tract of land west of the Mississippi, extending from New Orleans to Canada, and, with the ensuing Lewis and Clark Expedition, initiated a new era of western exploration. In 1816, after the War of 1812, the Red River of the North area of present-day Minnesota became part of the United States; the border between the United States and Canada was defined as the 49th parallel two years later. (To the east, the border between Maine and Canada was resolved in 1842; and to the west, the border between Oregon and Canada was finally resolved in 1846.) In 1819, Spain ceded Florida to the United States, enlarging the American domain in the East to the Gulf of Mexico. Other territorial expansion in the 19th century included the Texas Annexation of 1845, which led to the Mexican War, leading in turn to the Mexican Cession of 1848. The policies of Manifest Destiny had taken the United States all the way to the Pacific. The Gadsden Purchase in 1853 of additional Spanish territory in the Southwest, plus the Alaska Purchase, of 1867, from Russia, filled out the United States to its present continental shape.

With each stage of growth, vast new reaches of territory, and the Indian peoples within them, came under United States dominion. In the process of admitting territories and states to the Union, Indians were considered incidental and were given no voice. White settlement previous to official American procurement of territories had varying degrees of impact on native populations at the local level. After official acquisition, however, the pace of change inevitably accelerated. Pioneers claimed the land; politicians instituted policies to remove the Indian obstacle from the land; merchants, bankers, speculators, and other business tycoons invested in it; and soldiers patrolled it.

Within this framework of the territorial acquisitions of an expanding nation, other factors and policies related to Indian displacement and led to the following key events and dates:

A separate Indian Country west of the Mississippi was first defined in 1825, between the Red and Missouri rivers. The Indian Removal Act, signed into effect in 1830, called for the relocation of eastern Indians to the Indian Country or the Indian Territory, as it came to be called. The Trade and Intercourse Act of 1834 further defined the Indian Territory and the "Permanent Indian Frontier." During these and ensuing years, tribes of the Southeast, the Old Northwest, the Prairies, and the Plains were relocated to the Indian Territory, which was gradually reduced in size and evolved into the state of Oklahoma by 1907. The experience of the Cherokees, removed from their homeland in the Southeast, as well as that of others of the Five Civilized Tribes, has come to be known as the Trail of Tears. (See "The Indian Territory" and "The Trail of Tears" in this chapter.)

Midway through the century—starting with the California Gold Rush of 1848–49 and continuing with the Colorado Gold Rush of 1858–59—the settlement on Indian lands by whites dramatically increased. The 1850s also saw a series of hostilities in the Far West between Indians and whites, the signing of numerous treaties, and the creation of reservations. By the end of the decade, the Indians were virtually surrounded on the Great Plains by an expanding white population and a string of forts. The Civil War from 1861 to 1865 slowed down the repeated pattern of warfare, treaty making, and the creation of reservations, although the Homestead Act of 1862 opened up Indian lands in Kansas and Nebraska to white homesteaders, who were deeded plots of land after inhabiting them for five years.

After the Civil War, the pace of white development again picked up, leading to the most intense period of warfare on the Plains until Wounded Knee in 1890, as well as the most active period in the formation of reservations until the start of the breakup of reservations through allotment in 1887. The Railroad Enabling Act of 1866, and the subsequent completion of the transcontinental railroad in

1869, facilitated white travel westward. And the end of treaty making with Indian tribes as federal policy in 1871 facilitated unilateral action against Indians on the part of officials. Another gold rush, to the Black Hills of South Dakota and Wyoming, starting in 1874, precipitated another invasion of miners onto Indian lands. (See also "Wars for the West" in chapter 5, "Indian Trails and White Inroads" in this chapter, and "United States Indian Policy and the Indian Condition" in chapter 7.)

Yet forced land cessions for Indian peoples did not cease after the period of warfare and reservations. Under the federal allotment policy that began with the General Allotment Act of 1887—which broke up and allotted tribally held lands to individual Indians in small parcels, opening up the surplus to whites—and bolstered by the Curtis Act of 1898 and various inheritance laws, the Indian land base shrunk from about 150 million acres to 60 million acres. The Oklahoma Land Run in 1889, with settlers lining up for a race to the best property and with "sooners" already illegally having staked their claims, can be viewed as symbolic of the white hunger for land at the expense of Indian peoples.

Additional Indian displacement occurred during the 20th century, through the building of dams and other public works by the Army Corps of Engineers and private contractors, under the concept of eminent domain, as well as various methods of extortion—such as the invalidation of wills, the appropriation of land in exchange for social services, the declaration of landowners as incompetent, and the manipulation and intimidation of Indians, forcing sales. And, as can be seen in chapter 7, "CONTEMPORARY INDIANS," some Indian lands and resources are still threatened.

INDIAN TRAILS AND WHITE INROADS

Indians were the first trailblazers in North America. Once trails were established, repeated use kept undergrowth at a minimum. Some paths were open to whoever happened to pass that way; others were sacred to and guarded by territorial bands or tribes. Knowledge of a people's favored route was passed down from generation to generation.

White explorers, traders, and trappers in turn learned of these trodden paths, a man's width in size, from helpful Indians or discovered them on their own. Various armies also used these trails and passes to interconnect their frontier outposts, broadening and smoothing them if necessary to accommodate artillery and supply trains. These military roads then often became the migratory wagon roads for settlers and miners. Once communities were established, these same frequently traveled routes became commercial roads for trade. And many of these commerical roads became the paved roads and highways of today, following the same logical contours of land instinctively engineered by Indians.

Of course, there were exceptions to this typical progression of Indian trails to modern roads, with one or several stages being skipped. In some parts of the continent, especially from the Great Lakes northward, Indians and the white traders traveled the rivers and lakes, leaving them only when necessary to haul their canoes along overland portage routes. Also, Indian hunters often left their favored trails to track game, and warriors left the trails to surprise an enemy.

Because of the insufficient historical documentation, as well as the great number of routes involved over the centuries, it is impossible to depict Indian trails on a continental scale. Yet, to a certain extent, because so many modern roads were originally important Indian paths of transportation, one can get a sense of the intricate network of historical Indian trails crisscrossing the continent by looking at current road maps. And one can assume with near certainty, when taking a walk in any part of North America, that native peoples previously walked the same path.

For Postcontact Indians, some early roads, passes, and waterways, whether formerly exact Indian routes or not, had special significance in that they carried the waves of white settlers onto tribal lands during the periods of European, American, and Canadian expansion, usually in a westward direction. The building of canals and railroads further contributed to white settlement and Indian displacement. The following are represented visually on the accompanying map.

CUMBERLAND GAP AND WILDERNESS ROAD: The Cumberland Gap in the Cumberland Mountains of the Appalachian chain, a natural passage carved by the erosive action of an earlier stream as well as a commonly used Indian trail, was mapped and named by Dr. Thomas Walker during his expedition out of Virginia in 1750. In 1775, the Transylvania Land Company hired Daniel Boone and 30 others to open the Wilderness Road, from Fort Chiswell in the Shenandoah Valley through the Cumberland Gap, as a route to the Ohio Valley. In 1792, after Kentucky became a state, the road was widened for travel by wagon.

BRADDOCKS'S ROAD: In 1749 and 1750, Nemacolin, a Delaware Indian, and Thomas Cresap, a Maryland frontiersman, cleared a trail between the Potomac and Monongahela rivers that came to be known as Nemacolin's Path. In 1755, during the French and Indian Wars, the British General Edward Braddock expanded this trail to transport his troops from Fort Cumberland (Cumberland, Maryland) across the Allegheny Mountains to the French Fort Duquesne (Pittsburgh).

FORBES ROAD: In 1758, during the French and Indian Wars, the British general John Forbes built another road north of Braddocks's Road, to advance on Fort Duquesne through the Alleghenies. A postwar extension joined the eastern end of the road with Philadelphia.

NATIONAL ROAD: Braddock's Road westward from Cumberland, Maryland, became the first leg of the National (or Cumberland) Road, built in 1818, to Wheeling, West Virginia, the most ambitious road-building project in the United States to that point, with a surface of crushed stone. In 1825, an extension was undertaken to Vandalia, Illinois, eventually reaching St. Louis.

NATCHEZ TRACE: The Natchez Trace from Natchez, Mississippi, to Nashville, Tennessee, was used successively by the French, English, and Spanish in colonial times, and then by Americans after the Revolution. At first, Americans traveled only northward on it because, on the southward trip, they could float their goods downriver by boat. With expansion, however, it came to be traveled both ways. In the War of 1812 and later Indian campaigns, Andrew Jackson used the Trace as a military road.

SANTE FE TRAIL: During the early 19th century, small trapping parties used the Santa Fe Trail—originally an Indian trail—between Independence, Missouri, and Santa Fe, New Mexico, but they were not permitted to trade in Spanish territory. It wasn't until after Mexican Independence in 1821 and the deregulation of trade that the trail assumed its importance. William Becknell led a caravan over the route in 1822. In addition to the original northern wagon road, the southern cutoff known as the Cimarron came to be established. By 1850, a monthly stage line provided passenger and freight service along the northern division.

OLD SPANISH TRAIL: The Old Spanish Trail, used by the Spanish in the 18th century to travel from Santa Fe to Los Angeles, regained its importance after William Wolfskill and

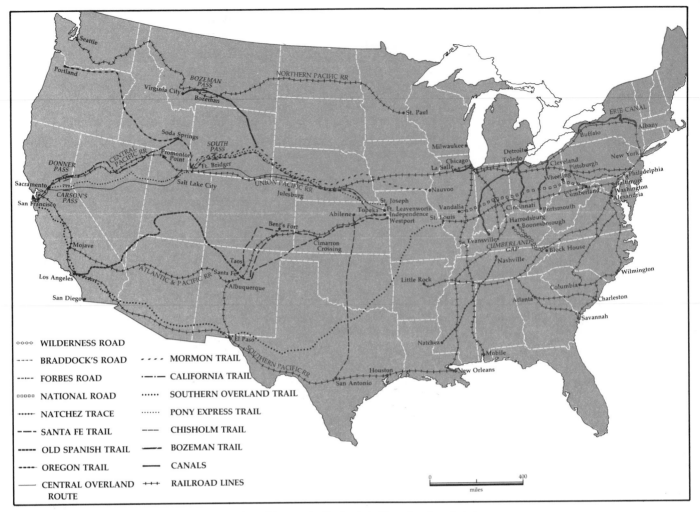

6.8 WAGON ROADS AND RAILROADS, *carrying whites onto Indian lands (with modern boundaries)*

George Yount led an expedition retracing its path in 1830 and 1831.

OREGON TRAIL: The Oregon Trail and its various offshoots—including the Central Overland, Mormon, and California trails—carried most white traffic westward during the period of accelerated settlement in the mid-1800s, as it had carried Indian traffic for numerous generations before. Mountain Men thoroughly explored this region in the years following the Lewis and Clark Expedition of 1803–06. They established a route from Independence and Westport (both now part of Kansas City, Missouri) all the way to the Columbia River region in Oregon, crossing the Continental Divide through the 7,750-foot-high South Pass in the Rocky Mountains. In open prairie country, the abundant wagon trains of the ensuing years did not follow one roadbed as such, but spread out over a wide region, con-

verging again for river crossings and mountain passes. The roughly 21,000-mile journey took, on the average, six months.

CENTRAL OVERLAND ROUTE: This southern alternate route of the Oregon Trail branched southward from its parent trail at the junction of the North Platte and South Platte rivers, then joined up with the Mormon Trail to Great Salt Lake, continuing west through Carson's Pass in the Sierra Nevada Range to California.

MORMON TRAIL: In 1847, the Mormons reached their new settlement on the Great Salt Lake (now Salt Lake City, Utah) via a route from Illinois that came to be known as the Mormon Trail. For some stretches, the trail paralleled the Oregon Trail and also passed through the Rockies by the South Pass.

CALIFORNIA TRAIL: The California Trail, the gateway to California during the Gold Rush of 1848–49, branched off from the Oregon Trail at Soda Springs, followed the Humboldt River, crossed the Nevada Desert, and traversed the Sierra Nevada along the Donner Pass. The Donner Pass took its name from the leader of a party trapped there in blizzards of the winter of 1846.

BUTTERFIELD SOUTHERN ROUTE (or Southern Overland Trail): In 1857, John Butterfield and his American Express Company were awarded the contract for an overland mail route from St. Louis to Los Angeles and San Francisco, over what was also called the Southern Overland Trail, providing service until 1861, when stages began traveling the Central Overland Route.

PONY EXPRESS TRAIL: The Pony Express—founded in 1860 by the firm of Russell, Majors, and Waddell—carried mail westward from the western limit of the telegraph in St. Joseph, Missouri, as far as Sacramento, California. A series of relay riders, who changed horses every 10–15 miles, could complete the approximately 2,000-mile trip in about eight days. The trail they followed paralleled part of the Oregon Trail and part of the Central Overland Route, using both South Pass and Carson's Pass.

CHISHOLM TRAIL: In 1866, the part-Cherokee fur trader Jesse Chisholm drove a wagonload of buffalo hides, its wheels forming deep ruts in the prairie, from Texas northward through the Indian Territory to his trading post in Kansas. The resulting trail became a preferred route for cowboys who drove Texas longhorn cattle to railheads in Kansas, and it was used into the 1880s. Other cattle trails were the Goodnight-Loving Trail and the Western Cattle Trail west of the Chisholm, and the Shawnee Trail to the east.

BOZEMAN TRAIL: After having traveled to Montana's gold fields in 1862, John Bozeman followed a direct route through Indian treaty lands west of the Bighorn Mountains back to Colorado, rather than following more circuitous eastern or western routes. The army tried to maintain posts along the Bozeman after 1865 but, after a successful Indian uprising under the Sioux leader Red Cloud, abandoned both the forts and the trail.

ERIE CANAL: The Erie Canal, a man-made waterway connecting Lake Erie and the Hudson Rver, was completed in 1825. Henceforth, it facilitated economic development in the East throughout the 19th century. Subsequent canals were the Ohio and Erie, the Miami and Erie, and the Wabash and Erie, all connecting Lake Erie with various points on the Ohio River, as well as the Illinois and Michigan, connecting Lake Michigan with the Illinois River.

THE RAILROADS: Railways began to expand rapidly in the East after 1830. By 1850, they connected the Atlantic Coast with the Great Lakes; by 1853, with Chicago; and, by 1856, with the west side of the Mississippi. In 1862 and 1864, two acts of Congress initiated the building of a transcontinental line. In 1869, the Union Pacific and the Central Pacific met at Promontory Point, Utah, linking the coasts by rail. The 1880s saw another burst of railroad building. The Southern Pacific from San Francisco and Los Angeles reached New Orleans in 1883; and the Northern Pacific between Seattle and Minnesota opened in 1884. Also, during the 1880s, the gauge of track was standardized. With the establishment of railways, the steady stream of white settlers onto Indian lands became a flood.

THE INDIAN TERRITORY

Boundaries were the way of the whites, and the Indians had to learn to cope with them. It wasn't easy,

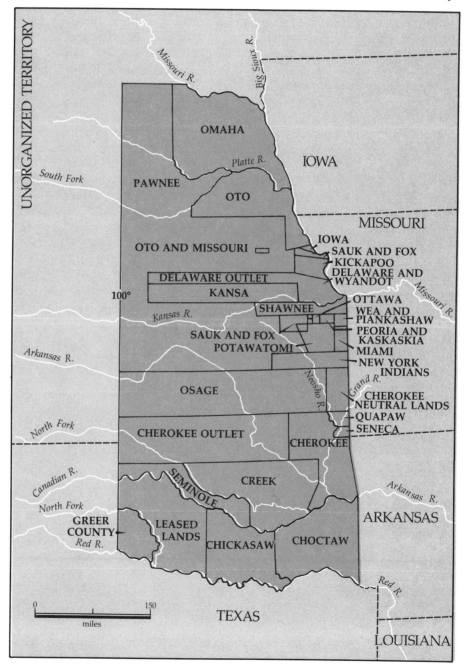

6.9 THE INDIAN TERRITORY IN 1854

even for the law abiding. Because of the ever-expanding white population, the boundaries kept changing. Time and again, the whites violated treaties, and eastern Indians were pushed further westward.

In the 1820s, it was thought that the formation of an extensive Indian colonization zone in the wilderness area west of the Mississippi would stop, once and for all, the clash of cultures over land. The idea appealed to those on both sides of the Indian question: For the sympathetic, a permanent Indian homeland closed to white settlement would prevent further cruel uprooting; for the uncaring, it would open new lands to white settlement in the East and confine Indians to one area.

With the support of Congress, Secretary of War John Calhoun of the Monroe Administration delineated a new Indian Country in 1825, which by the 1830s and the Jackson Administration came to be called the Indian Territory. The Trade and Intercourse Act of 1834 redefined it and gave the federal government the right to quarantine Indians for the purpose of "civilizing" them. During this period, the Stokes Commission was created

to work out disputes between the various tribes—immigrant and native—and military expeditions, such as the Dragoon Expedition, were sent in for pacification. At its largest size, in the years before 1854, the Indian Territory extended from the Red River to the Missouri, and from the state lines of Arkansas, Missouri, and Iowa to the 100th meridian, at that time the United States' western boundary.

The name Indian Territory is misleading. The zone never possessed an integrated territorial government but, rather, a collection of independent tribal governments. Nor did the tribes have a unified life-style, since they came from different regions. Local tribes of the eastern Great Plains, such as Pawnee, Missouri, Iowa, Omaha, and Oto, were located near tribes of the Old Northwest, such as Miami, Potawatomi, Kickapoo, Ottawa, Shawnee, Sauk, and Fox. South of them were the Five Civilized Tribes of the Southeast. (See "The Trail of Tears" in this chapter.) Western Plains tribes, such as Sioux, Cheyenne, Arapaho, and Comanche, ranged near the territory, at times even coming into conflict with the immigrant tribes. Homogeneity and

6.11 THE INDIAN TERRITORY IN 1896

stability were further disrupted within the territory by the steady stream of white settlers passing through along the Santa Fe, Oregon, and Mormon trails, especially during the California Gold Rush starting in 1848.

Reduction of the supposedly inviolate Indian Territory began in the 1850s, as a result of pressure from railroad interests seeking transcontinental routes. The Indians in the northern portion, impoverished and disorganized, were persuaded by federal agents to sign away tribal rights. In 1854, by an act of Congress, the northern part of the Indian Territory became Kansas and Nebraska territories. And in 1862, the Homestead Act opened up Indian lands in the territories to white homesteaders, who were deeded 160-acre plots after inhabiting them for five years. Similar moves were made on the southern portion of the Indian Territory, which was also coveted by developers, but the bill was defeated.

Nevertheless, further shrinkage occurred in 1866 after the Civil War. Because of their involvement with the Confederacy, the Five Civilized Tribes were forced to accept the terms of Reconstruction, which gave the federal government the right to appropriate Indian lands and relocate tribes from Kansas (now a state) within the current Indian Territory.

Each modification of the Indian Territory and relocation of tribes was presented as final. Yet during the 1880s, the Indians had to endure even

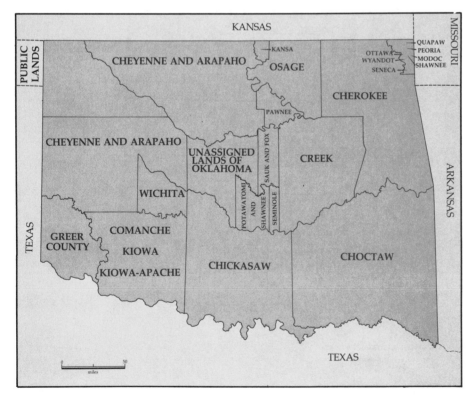

6.10 THE INDIAN TERRITORY IN 1876

more change and displacement. This was the age of the Boomers—bands of white home seekers squatting on Indian reservations. Backing the Boomer cause for their own self-interests, railroads, banks, and other commercial developers lobbied Congress for the opening of Indian lands to settlement. Congress succumbed and, in 1887, passed the General Allotment Act (or the Dawes Severalty Act), which broke up certain tribal landholdings into tracts and allotted them to individual Indians who could then sell them to whites. By 1889, two million acres had been bought from the Indians, usually at ridiculously low prices, and thrown open to white settlement in the Land Run. In 1890, Oklahoma Territory was formed from these lands. Eight years later, the Curtis Act dissolved tribal governments, with the purpose of extending the effects of allotment policy to the Five Civilized Tribes.

The treaties of removal signed by the Five Civilized Tribes had prom- ised perpetuity for the lands within the Indian Territory. The Choctaw treaty had stated: "No part of the land granted them shall ever be embraced in a territory (non-Indian) or state." In 1907, their remaining western lands became part of the state of Oklahoma, as did the rest of the now much reduced Indian Territory.

THE TRAIL OF TEARS

In 1830, President Andrew Jackson, the former Indian-fighter ("Sharp Knife" to the Indians), signed the Indian Removal Act to relocate eastern tribes to a designated Indian Territory west of the Mississippi River—a swift and final solution, it was thought, to the persistent tension between Indians and land-hungry whites. Thus began a decade of torment and tragedy for the tribes of the Southeast.

The Five Civilized Tribes, especially the Cherokees, had adapted to the ways of the whites, educating themselves, establishing an efficient agriculture-based economy, and finding a new, vital cultural mix of tradition and progress. Working within the American legal system, the Cherokees under John Ross resisted the Removal Act in the courts, finally winning their case before the Supreme Court. However, their efforts were to no avail. Sharp Knife ignored the decision and ordered the army to evict the tribe anyway, along with the Choctaws, Creeks, Chickasaws, and Seminoles, from their ancestral lands.

The Choctaws were the first to go. A nonrepresentative minority of leaders, bribed by governmental agents, signed the Treaty of Dancing Rabbit Creek in 1830, ceding all Choctaw land in Mississippi in exchange for western lands. Some Choctaws refused to depart and escaped into the backwoods of Mississippi and Louisiana. But from 1831 to 1834, most members of the tribe were herded westward, in groups of 500 to

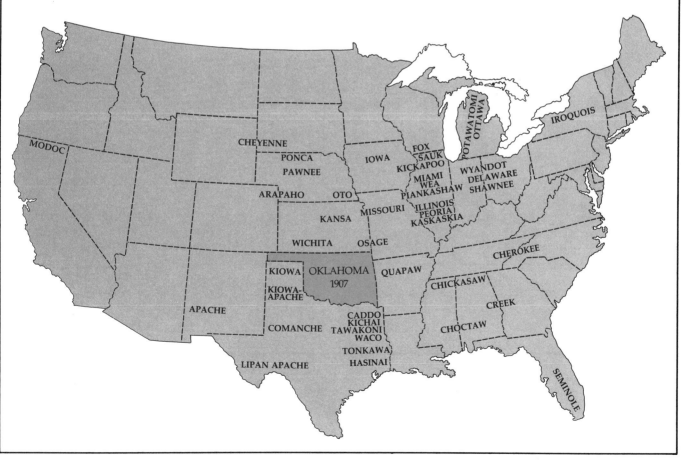

6.12 THE STATE OF OKLAHOMA, 1907, AND EARLIER LOCATIONS OF ITS INDIAN PEOPLES

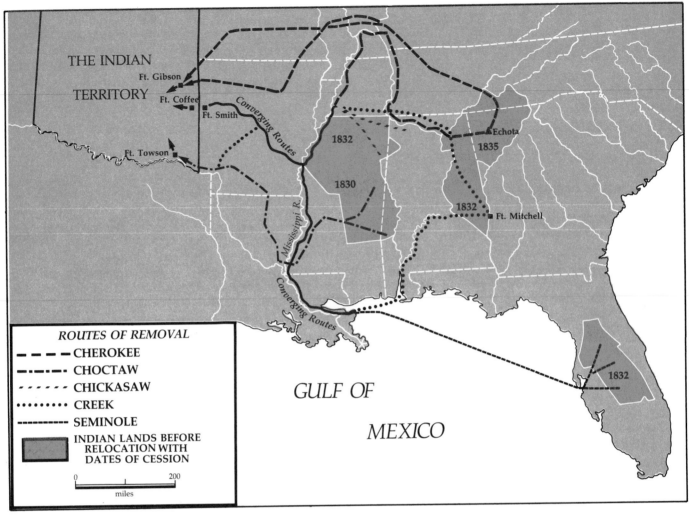

ROUTES OF REMOVAL

- – – – CHEROKEE
- ·–·–· CHOCTAW
- ······ CHICKASAW
- •••••• CREEK
- –––––– SEMINOLE

INDIAN LANDS BEFORE RELOCATION WITH DATES OF CESSION

0 ___ 200
miles

THE INDIAN TERRITORY

Ft. Gibson
Ft. Coffee
Ft. Smith
Ft. Towson
Converging Routes
Mississippi R.
Converging Routes
1832
1830
Echota
1835
1832
Ft. Mitchell
1832

GULF OF MEXICO

6.13 THE TRAIL OF TEARS *(with modern boundaries)*

1,000, by bluecoats. Conditions were miserable. Because of the inadequate federal funds for the removal, there were shortages of food, blankets, wagons, and horses. Roadside merchants charged exorbitant prices for supplies. Bandits preyed upon the weak and exhausted migrants. Disease ran rampant. At least a quarter of the Indians died before even reaching the Indian Territory. And many more died afterward, as they struggled to build new lives in the rugged terrain, with meager supplies and surrounded by hostile western Indians.

The other tribes also endured maltreatment, hardship, and death in similar stories of forced exodus. After a period of near civil war among the divided Creeks, with some bought out by the government and some resisting removal, tribal representatives signed a treaty giving individuals the choice of remaining in Alabama with land allotments or leaving for new lands in the West. White settlers and developers proceeded to take advantage of this new private Indian ownership of land, resulting in increased tensions. Finally, in 1836, the federal government and the government of Alabama used a unified Creek resistance under Eneah Emothla as justification for the tribe's complete relocation. Approximately 3,500 of 15,000 men, women, and children died of disease and exposure during and shortly after the ensuing removal.

The Chickasaws, having already ceded lands in western Kentucky and Tennessee in 1818, were again pressured in the 1830s by federal and state governments to give up their remaining lands, now mostly in northern Mississippi and northwestern Arkansas. Since they managed to hold out for the best possible deal, and since their journey to the Indian Territory was shorter than that of the other

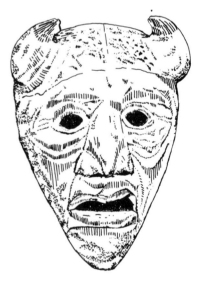

Cherokee buffalo dance mask

tribes, they suffered less during their removal, begun in 1837. But disease, especially the dreaded cholera, and food poisoning ravaged the tribe after their arrival.

The Seminoles of Florida, southern

Alabama, and southern Georgia resisted removal more than any of the other tribes. Their bravery and tenacity forced the United States into a protracted war from 1835 to 1842 in the jungles and swamps of Florida. (See "The Seminole Wars" in chapter 5.) Approximately 3,000 Seminoles were eventually relocated, some willingly and some by coercion, but for every two Indians transferred to the Indian Territory, one white soldier died. And today many Seminoles continue to live in Florida.

The most famous removal of all and the one that has come to symbolize all the others is that of the Cherokees. The fact that their great suffering followed a successful legal battle to save their lands makes their story all the more poignant. After the Cherokees' futile attempt, the state of Georgia, with President Jackson's blessing, ruthlessly began liquidating Indian lands for paltry prices and promises of land in the west. Cherokee homes and possessions were plundered by opportunistic whites. Spring Place Mission, the cultural and learning center of the Cherokees, was grabbed up in the lottery of Indian lands and converted into a tavern for whites. Using resistance to removal as an excuse, the Georgia militia moved upon

the Cherokee capital of Echota and destroyed the printing press of the *Cherokee Phoenix*, the newspaper written in the Cherokee syllabary created by Sequoyah. The Georgia militia, with the help of the United States Army, also built stockades and rounded up Cherokee families to hold in preparation for removal.

During this time, some Cherokees did manage to escape the dragnet and hide out in the mountains of North Carolina, where their descendants still live today. But for the rest, the first exodus came in the spring of 1838 and lasted into part of the summer, with intense heat and thirst the result. That same year, a fall-winter migration began first with rain and mud, then freezing temperatures, snow, and ice. And there was starvation because of inadequate food rations; and disease; and bandits. Goaded on at a cruel pace by the bluecoats, the Indians were not even allowed to bury their dead. An approximate total of 4,000 Cherokees died during confinement in the stockades and/or the 800-mile trek westward.

The final Cherokee migration of 1838–39 came to be called the "Trail of Tears." The name now stands for the forced removals and suffering of all the Five Civilized Tribes, and by

extension the forced relocation of tribes of the Old Northwest and all other displaced Indians.

A final fact: Because of charges of fraud and the misappropriation of funds and supplies promised to the Indians in their treaties of removal, the federal government ordered an inquiry by Major Ethan Allen Hitchcock. His thorough and honest investigation, begun in 1841, reported that before, during, and after removal "bribery, perjury, and forgery, short weights, issues of spoiled meat and grain, and every conceivable subterfuge was employed by designing white men." The federal government decided not to release the Hitchcock report to the public.

THE GROWTH OF CANADA AND INDIAN LAND CESSIONS

The first permanent white settlement within the area now comprising Canada was founded in 1605 by Samuel de Champlain and the Sieur de Monts at Port Royal, Acadia (now Annapolis Royal, Nova Scotia) on the Bay of Fundy. Then, in 1608, Champlain, who is known as the "Founder of Canada," established a fur-trading post at the Huron village of Stadacona, now Quebec City. In 1642, the Sieur de Maisonneuve and Paul de Chomedy founded the Ville Marie de Montreal at the site of the Huron village Hochelaga.

During these formative years of New France, the fur trade determined European use of the land and white settlement was minimal. (See "The Fur Trade" in chapter 4.) Even after 1663, when the charter of the Company of New France (the Company of One Hundred Associates) was withdrawn and New France became a Crown colony ruled by a royal governor, an intendant, and a bishop, the white population grew at a much slower pace than those of New England and Virginia. In that year, it is estimated that the colonial population

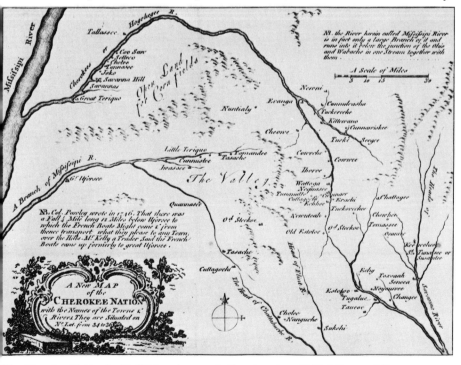

The Cherokee Nation by T. Kitchen from an Indian drawing, 1760. Library of Congress.

of New France was only 2,500 as compared to 80,000 in the British colonies to the south. Nevertheless, New France continued to expand, with Acadia, Quebec, and Newfoundland taking shape as the economic and political subdivisions.

Because of the relative low numbers of the white settlers and their dependency on the Indians as suppliers of furs, the impact on the Algonquian and Iroquoian tribes of New France was gradual. Disease and alcohol proved the most disruptive elements. (See "The Spread of European Diseases" in this chapter.) Intermarriage between Indians and whites, a common practice in New France, unlike in the English colonies, also contributed to cultural metamorphosis. Yet it also helped keep the peace.

There were exceptions to the general harmony and slow rate of change. For example, the French indirectly played a part in the rapid disintegration of the Huron culture in the mid-17th century, by alienating the powerful Iroquois League to the south and seeking a trade monopoly. The Hurons and the smaller Tobacco, Erie, and Neutral tribes of the Great Lakes region never recovered from the ensuing Iroquois invasion. Survivors migrated to the Saint Lawrence and southwest of the Great Lakes. (See "The Beaver Wars" in chapter 5.) And the Beothuks of Newfoundland were the victims of harsh reprisals after they repeatedly stole property belonging to French and English fishermen mooring on their island. Bounties were placed on their scalps,

the Micmacs were armed against them, and attacks were mounted on their villages, resulting in their displacement and, by the 19th century, their extinction. (See "Canadian Indian Wars" in chapter 5.)

As for the tribes in what was to become central, northern, and western Canada, they experienced minimal contact with whites and minimal disruption during France's tenure in North America. The thrust of France's expansion was southwestward from the Great Lakes along the Ohio and Mississippi river valleys onto what is now U.S. soil. (See "The White Penetration of North America" in chapter 4.) After the formation of the Hudson's Bay Company in 1670, some of the tribes of the Canadian Shield became trading partners with whites. A

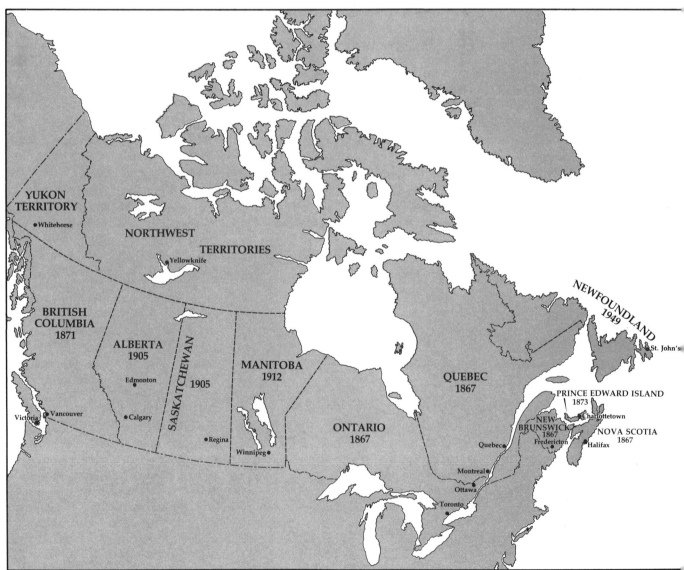

6.14 THE GROWTH OF CANADA, *showing dates of provincial status*

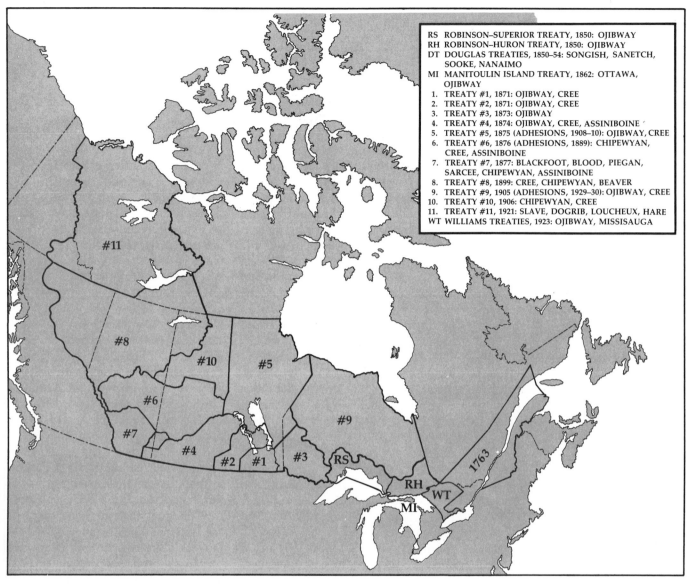

6.15 INDIAN LAND CESSIONS IN CANADA *(with modern boundaries)*

RS ROBINSON–SUPERIOR TREATY, 1850: OJIBWAY
RH ROBINSON–HURON TREATY, 1850: OJIBWAY
DT DOUGLAS TREATIES, 1850–54: SONGISH, SANETCH,
    SOOKE, NANAIMO
MI MANITOULIN ISLAND TREATY, 1862: OTTAWA,
    OJIBWAY
1. TREATY #1, 1871: OJIBWAY, CREE
2. TREATY #2, 1871: OJIBWAY, CREE
3. TREATY #3, 1873: OJIBWAY
4. TREATY #4, 1874: OJIBWAY, CREE, ASSINIBOINE
5. TREATY #5, 1875 (ADHESIONS, 1908–10): OJIBWAY, CREE
6. TREATY #6, 1876 (ADHESIONS, 1889): CHIPEWYAN,
    CREE, ASSINIBOINE
7. TREATY #7, 1877: BLACKFOOT, BLOOD, PIEGAN,
    SARCEE, CHIPEWYAN, ASSINIBOINE
8. TREATY #8, 1899: CREE, CHIPEWYAN, BEAVER
9. TREATY #9, 1905 (ADHESIONS, 1929–30): OJIBWAY, CREE
10. TREATY #10, 1906: CHIPEWYAN, CREE
11. TREATY #11, 1921: SLAVE, DOGRIB, LOUCHEUX, HARE
WT WILLIAMS TREATIES, 1923: OJIBWAY, MISSISAUGA

certain amount of depopulation resulted because of the Indian vulnerability to European diseases. Yet, other than isolated frontier trading posts and a number of fur traders living in the wilderness, there was virtually no white settlement and no resulting tribal displacement.

With England's ultimate victory over France in 1763, modern Canada began to take shape and white population levels began to rise. The first dramatic increase came at the time of the American Revolution and the flight of Loyalists northward. Waves of Scottish and Irish immigrants also began arriving in great numbers. For these differing elements as well as the descendants of earlier settlers, Canada as a unified entity rather than a collection of European colonies and territories was increasingly a public concept. As early as 1651, the *habitants* had referred to themselves as "Canadois" (and later "Canadiens") instead of French. And now certain British elements also considered themselves as "Canadians" first and foremost. The Indians of course were excluded from any such concept and were considered incidental to Canadian destiny. And, accordingly, as Canada grew, the Indians were increasingly pushed from their homelands.

The various provinces and territories of Canada developed as follows, with opposing factions competing for political and economic power and independence; Nova Scota (formerly Acadia) and Prince Edward Island, united in 1763 with England's victory over France, became separate colonies again in 1784. Also in 1784, New Brunswick and Cape Breton were carved out of Nova Scotia. Cape Breton, however, rejoined Nova Scotia in 1820. As for Newfoundland, merchants in England who controlled trans-Atlantic fishing and whose fishermen used the island as their North American base of operations, lobbied against granting it political status. A system of nongovernment existed until a representative system was introduced in 1832 and a parliamentary system in 1855.

In the Quebec Act of 1774, Quebec was allowed to retain its language, religion, customs, and courts of law as a compromise to the French citizens. But, as a result of the increase in Loyalists, the Canada Act of 1791 divided Quebec into two colonies, Lower Canada (present-day Quebec) and Upper Canada (present-day Ontario) with the Ottawa River as the dividing line. The struggle for representative government among various factions in these colonies led to the Rebellions of 1837. Farmers who desired agrarian reforms in Upper Canada under William Mackenzie joined forces in a revolt with French-speaking radicals who desired self-determination in Lower Canada under Louis Papineau. Opposing them were the Conservative Anglicans of Upper Canada and the English merchants and Roman Catholic hierarchy of Lower Canada. When the rebellions in both colonies failed, Mackenzie and Papineau fled to the United States. England reunited the two colonies in 1841, when they became known as Canada East (Quebec) and Canada West (Ontario). The reunion proved unworkable, and the two became separate provinces with Canadian Confederation in 1867.

In the meantime, the Hudson's Bay Company controlled the vast region to the north and west of the eastern colonies, known as Rupert's Land, and exploited it for furs. Also in the meantime, despite specific claims by representative officials, Canadian-American boundaries remained uncertain for many years. In 1818, after the War of 1812, the border extending westward from the Great Lakes was defined as the 49th parallel. To the east, however, the border between Quebec–New Brunswick and Maine was not resolved until 1842, after the Aroostook War. And to the far west, rival British and American claims were not settled until 1846, when the 49th parallel was also accepted as the dividing line between Canada and Oregon. Soon afterward, in 1849, Vancouver Island became a Crown colony, followed by British Columbia in 1858. The two united in 1866 under the name of the latter.

The British North America Act of 1867 brought about the Confederation of four of the colonies (now provinces)—Nova Scotia, New Brunswick, Quebec, and Ontario—into the Dominion of Canada, with a centralized government in the capital city of Ottawa. A primary incentive for Confederation was common defense and unity in the face of an expanding land-hungry American population. This same pressure helped spur the development of the Canadian West and the building of a transcontinental railway. In 1869, two years after the United States' purchase of Alaska from Russia, the Dominion purchased Rupert's Land from the Hudson's Bay Company. In 1870, part of this holding now known as the Northwest Territories was delineated as Manitoba Province, the course of events shaped by the First Riel Rebellion of the Metis in 1869 and 1870. (See "Canadian Indian Wars" in chapter 5.) The next year, because of the promise of financial aid, British Columbia voted to join the Dominion. And in 1873, Prince Edward Island, which had held out for equal representation, also joined.

The Klondike Gold Rush of 1897 and 1898 brought increased numbers of whites to the Canadian north country. In the course of the late 19th and early 20th centuries, the Klondike region and other parts of the huge Northwest Territory came to be sectioned off into various administrative districts. Some of these, namely Alberta and Saskatchewan, gained provincial status in 1905. Another, Ungava, became part of Quebec. Ontario and Manitoba were expanded to include parts of others. And some regions maintained their territorial status, such as Yukon Territory east of Alaska, and the remaining part of the Northwest Territories west of Hudson Bay, both on the Arctic Ocean. In 1949, Newfoundland, now comprising Labrador as well, voted to join the Dominion and became Canada's 10th province.

In the process of growth and formation, from 1850 to 1923, Canada negotiated a series of treaties with various Indian tribes to obtain their lands. In exchange for conveyances of huge tracts of territory, the Indians were to receive reserve lands, the legal title of which would be held in trust by the Crown, and generally based on the formula of one square mile per family of five. Along with reserves, the Indians were to receive, in varying combinations, one-time cash payments and supplies, much of it farm equipment; as well as annuities, again in cash and supplies, especially ammunition and clothing. The government also agreed to provide schooling on the reserves, by Indian request, and permit the use of the ceded lands by the Indians for hunting and fishing, except for tracts taken up for settlement, mining, lumbering, trading, or other purposes. This final agreement led many of the Indians to believe they would retain use of a large part of their former territory—which, with time and extensive white settlement and development, proved not to be the case. Many claims to lands, by tribes involved in the treaties as well as by other tribes—claims based both on the treaty agreements and on the concept of aboriginal title—are only now being worked out since the establishment, by the Canadian government in 1974, of the Office of Native Claims. (See "Canada's Indian Policy and the Indian Condition" in chapter 7.)

Chapter 7
CONTEMPORARY INDIANS

The subject matter of Indian studies is not remote and fixed in time but, rather, relevant and current. As those people living near reservations or other Indian communities realize, as do those interested in Indian art or minority sociology and politics, there is a sizable and vital Native North American population with contemporary concerns and aspirations. The Indian story of course did not end in the 19th century, after the Wars for the West, but continues right up to the present. The previous chapters of this book therefore have significance, not only as they relate to general American history, but also as they lead up to the present Indian situation.

This chapter will give an overview of contemporary Indian issues, showing where pertinent the historical stages of government policy toward Indians.

UNITED STATES INDIAN POLICY AND THE INDIAN CONDITION

The route to the current Indian policy of the United States government has been a long and tortuous one, beginning with England's colonial policy, then evolving from Revolutionary times to the present through various stages and reversals. Some of the relevant and often contradictory concepts have already been touched upon in previous chapters, with regard to Indian wars and land cessions: tribal sovereignty, treaties, federal trust responsibility, federal bureaucracy, Indian removal and concentration, boundaries and reservations, assimilation, and land allotment. Since these concepts are also essential to the contemporary Indian situation, they will be summarized here along with past governmental programs of the 20th century. Then the present-day federal and Indian relationship will be defined, along with contemporary Indian demographics and social conditions.

CENTRALIZATION AND BUREAUCRATIZATION

Each British colony was originally responsible for its own Indian policy. As it turned out, a majority of tribes came to support the French, and, at the Albany Congress in 1754, in an effort to gain more consistent and better relations with the Indians, the English decided to unify Indian affairs, with northern and southern departments directly under the royal government. In the following years, the English implemented this policy, appointing superintendents for both regions.

In 1775, the Continental Congress of the American rebels organized a Committee on Indian Affairs to decide on policy. Using the British system as a model, the rebels maintained a centralized Indian program because of the advantages of collective bargaining, with authority vested in the federal congress rather than the states. Instead of two departments, however, as in the British system, three departments were established—northern, central, and southern. The northern was responsible for the tribes of the Iroquois League and all Indians to their north; the southern was responsible for the Cherokees and all Indians to their south; and the central covered the Indians between them.

In 1778, the Continental Congress enacted its first treaty with Indians—the Delawares. The practice of treaty making was also based on colonial policy. The English, French, and Dutch all recognized the sovereignty of Indian tribes, and they negotiated treaties with them in order to establish the credibility of their own land purchases and claims to the other colonial powers, as well as to establish trade agreements with the Indians. For the United States, however, as had been the case for the colonial powers, treaties came to serve, on some occasions, as a legalization of the right of conquest and might just as well have been unilateral. Indian sovereignty was treated as limited sovereignty by the federal government and as nonexistent by many settlers, land speculators, and even state governments, which often forced the federal government's hand.

These various questions—tribal sovereignty, right of conquest versus right of purchase, federal versus state authority—were dealt with under the Articles of Confederation in effect from 1781 to 1789, along with other ordinances of the same period, which accepted in principle that the central government should regulate Indian affairs and trade, and that Indian lands and property should not be taken from them without their consent. Nevertheless, because of violations by settlers on the frontier and Indian uprisings, the secretary of war was made responsible for all Indian affairs in 1786, with superintendents under him. The following year, the Northwest Ordinance reaffirmed the provisions of the British Royal Proclamation of 1763, maintaining the rights of Indians to lands west of the Appalachian Divide. The Federal Constitution, drawn up in 1787, ratified by the required number of states in 1788, and enacted in 1789, adopted and refined the same principles of Indian policy.

During the period from 1790 to 1799, the American Congress enacted four Trade and Intercourse Acts relating to Indian affairs and commerce. The acts licensed traders and established government trading houses (the "factory system") to sell American supplies to Indians on credit; provided for the appointment of Indian agents by the president, and authorized expenditures for farm implements and domestic animals for the Indians; determined boundaries for Indian lands; and required federal approval and public treaty for the purchase of Indian lands by states. In 1802, a new Trade and Intercourse Act that codified the four previous ones was put into effect. And in 1806, an Office of Indian Trade was created within the War Department—with a superintendent of Indian Trade under the secretary of war—to administer the federal trading houses. The "factory system" lasted until 1822, when the inefficient trading houses and the Office of Indian Trade were abolished. Provisions were made at the time for the licensing of independent traders, better able to meet the great demand for furs.

In 1824, to fill the void created by the abolition of the Office of Indian Trade, the secretary of war created an Office of Indian Affairs, with a staff within the War Department. It was at this time that the appellation Bureau of Indian Affairs first came into usage. In 1832, the new system was formally recognized by an act of Congress, which gave the president the right to appoint a commissioner of Indian Affairs. In 1834, Indian policy was further codified with a new Trade and Intercourse Act. And in 1849, the Bureau of Indian Affairs was transferred from the War Department to the Department of the Interior.

REMOVAL
AND RESERVATIONS

The concept of a separate Indian Country and a boundary line separating Indians from whites originated with the British Royal Proclamation of 1763, which reserved territory and prevented white settlement west of the Appalachian watershed. With the Northwest Ordinance of 1787, the United States government reaffirmed this policy. Yet it followed through with only partial support, using troops to keep Indians in but rarely to keep whites out. Whites therefore pushed on toward the next natural boundary—the Mississippi River.

After the U.S. acquisition, with the Louisiana Purchase of 1803, of vast new reaches of territory, a new dimension was added to the concept of a separate Indian Country—that of tribes exchanging their lands east of the Mississippi for lands to the west (under threat of loss of federal protection against state and local elements, and other forms of coercion). The concept became policy in 1825, with the creation of an Indian Country between the Red and Missouri rivers (which was further defined and referred to as the Indian Territory in the Trade and Intercourse Act of 1834), and with the Removal Act of 1830 leading to the subsequent relocation of many eastern tribes. Continuing white expansion, however, caused the so-called "permanent" Indian Territory to dwindle in size. (See "The Indian Territory" and "The Trail of Tears" in chapter 6.)

Throughout the period of extensive Indian removal, United States policy was often at odds with itself. For example, in 1833, Chief Justice John Marshall ruled in favor of the Cherokees keeping their ancestral lands, but President Andrew Jackson ignored this decision. Similarly, eastern politicians did not always approve of the methods of negotiation or coercion employed by territorial governors who assumed the responsibilities of Indian superintendents.

In general, however, despite opposing voices, the trend was toward unilateral action on the part of the federal government. During the 1850s, a great number of treaties were negotiated with Indian tribes—52 from 1853 to 1856 alone—in which the United States acquired 174 million acres of land. In many instances, methods of deceit and duress were employed by federal agents, but at least the process honored the treaty-making principle. Treaty making as policy ended with a negotiated agreement between the federal government and the Nez Perce in 1867, the last of some 370 treaties. A landmark decision in the Cherokee Tobacco Case of 1870 ruled that the Cherokees were subject to federal revenue laws and not the special exemption granted four years earlier by the Cherokee Reconstruction Treaty. Then in 1871, an act of congress officially impeded further treaties. Although past treaty obligations were not invalidated, Indians henceforth would be subject to unilateral laws of Congress and presidential rulings.

It was during this same post-Civil War period—the 20 years from 1867 until the inception of the allotment policy in 1887—that the greatest number of reservations were created. The reservation policy was consistent with that of the earlier removal policy, in that it attempted to segregate Indians from whites. The difference was that instead of one large Indian Country, lands were divided up piecemeal, with tribes confined to separate parcels with specific boundaries.

The reservation idea extended back to early missionary activities in the colonies—the Quinnipiac reservation in New Haven, established by the Puritans in 1638, and the Caughnawaga reservation for the Mohawks in Quebec, founded by the Jesuits in 1676, are two early examples. But early reservations were designed more for separation from other Indians, for the purposes of acculturation, rather than separation from whites. Two centuries later, in the years following the Revolution, the Iroquois were granted reservations in western New York with the latter concept more in mind.

Then, during the 1850s, after the California Gold Rush, California, Oregon and Washington served as testing grounds for the reservation system, with the double purpose of preventing conflicts between Indians and whites, and creating places where Indians might be instructed in white customs and technology. After the Civil War, the policy became widely applied throughout the West, with reservations serving as holding and prison camps in a period of considerable strife. For the Plains warriors whose territory had been drastically reduced and who had to adapt to an alien farming life-style, the reservation experience proved an immeasurable ordeal. And, even if a tribe did make progress in adapting to the new order, it might be subject to further federal unilateral policies, such as the consolidation of lands caused by bringing additional tribes to the reservation for the express purpose of detribalization, or outright compression of lands in order to open more territory to white settlement. Then there came allotment.

ASSIMILATION
AND ALLOTMENT

The white policy toward Indians of assimilation was not new. Missionaries and educators had been practicing it since the earliest colonial times, striving to Christianize and "civilize" Indians, assuming they were bestowing upon them a better life. During the late 19th century, after the period of separation as governmental policy, in which the primary objective was the removal of Indians from lands desired by whites, acculturation under duress, detribalization, and Americanization followed. The stated official goal was the self-sufficiency of Indian peoples, but it was self-sufficiency through terms dictated by whites—i.e., the suppression of Indian culture and the adoption by Indians of white traditions and technologies. The means to the end became allotment.

In 1887, the United States Congress passed the General Allotment Act (or the Dawes Severalty Act), under which Indian reservations were to be broken up and allotted to the heads of Indian families in 160-acre pieces, with the rationale that the lands would then be developed and farmed by economically motivated landholders. After the assignment of plots to Indians, any surplus territory would be distributed to non-Indians with the idea of bringing about the maximum utilization of tillable lands. In 1891, because of the continuing disuse of many of the parcels by Indians, followup legislation provided for the leasing of their allotted lands to whites. And when the Cherokees and Choctaws of the Indian Territory refused allotment, taking their case to federal courts, Congress passed the Curtis Act of 1898, which dissolved their tribal governments and extended land allotment policy to them. (See "The Indian Territory" in chapter 6.) In terms of individual rights under the law, nonallotted Indians were under the jurisdiction of the Court of Indian Offences, established in 1884, with tribal units administering justice in all but major crimes. (The Major Crimes Act of 1885 formally gave jurisdiction of major crimes to United States courts.) Allotted Indians, however, were to be subject to state civil and criminal jurisdiction.

Thus, coming into the 20th century, Indians were subject to a federal policy that sought to eliminate tribal landholdings and political organizations, suppress communal customs, and terminate trust status. At the end of the trust period, when so-called Indian "competency" was established—a 25-year schedule had originally been projected in 1887—Indians were to be granted citizenship. To expedite the process, the Burke Act of 1906 further amended the General Allotment Act, giving the secretary of the interior authority to release allotees from federal supervison ahead of schedule and remove any remaining restrictions on allotted lands. From 1917 to 1920, the Department of the Interior's Competency Commission issued thousands of patents discontinuing federal guardianship of Indian lands (the "forced patent" period).

Other legislation of the period encouraged Indian acculturation, such as the imposed cutting of traditionally long Indian hair and the outlawing of the Plains Indian Sun Dance. Meanwhile, federally administered schools strived to educate Indians in the ways of white society. Federal funds also went to private schools, sponsored by various church denominations or by the so-called "Friends of the Indian" societies. The most successful of these in easing the cultural transition was the Carlisle School in Pennsylvania, founded in 1879 by Richard Pratt, which set the precedent for the many Indian boarding schools of the early 20th century.

In 1924, after the projected 25-year period but before the large majority of Indians had proven "competency," Congress passed the Citizenship Act, granting all Indians citizenship (although some states still withheld the right to vote; New Mexico, Arizona, and Maine did not grant it until after World War II). The impetus for citizenship resulted in part from the Indian contribution in World War I. But an additional motive was the hope for more rapid assimilation.

Yet, by the 1920s, the concepts of both assimilation and allotment were being widely questioned. Coercive acculturation had created a cultureless generation, caught between two worlds. Tribal governments had been replaced by a paternalistic and unresponsive federal bureaucracy. And many Indians in the allotted tribes had lost not only their cultural and tribal identity but also their potential economic base—their land. During the entire period of allotment, Indians were dispossessed of millions of acres, nearly two-thirds of the total held in 1887. The original redistribution of tribal holdings accounted for much of the loss, with surplus lands going to whites. But without tribal or federal protection, individual allottees lost many more parcels. Unscrupulous land speculators used whatever means possible to separate the Indians from their lands. If they were unable to purchase lands directly at an unfair price, they might purchase inheritance rights or secure guardian-

ship over Indian children who were heirs. Tribal heirship customs no longer applied, but state and local laws did. State policy also helped drive Indians from their lands because, if an Indian did make progress in farming his allotted parcel, he was heavily taxed. And under the concept of eminent domain, federal and state governments granted rights of way to railroads and telegraph lines. Another side effect of allotment was the corruption of government officials. In the greed over land, bribery and graft became common. Some executives in the Interior Department, for example, became stockholders in companies dealing in Indian real estate.

A series of reform commissions during the 1920s culminated in the Meriam Commission undertaken by the private Brookings Institution which, in 1928 after a two-year study, released its report on Indian conditions—the *Problem of Indian Administration*—declaring the allotment system a dismal failure. The lasting policies of the period would not be assimilation or allotment but, rather, those that fostered greater protection of Indian rights, resources, and health, such as the Citizenship Act of 1924; or the Winters Doctrine of 1908, which defined Indian water rights; or the creation within the Bureau of Indian Affairs of a Division of Medical Assistance in 1910, which evolved into the Division of Indian Health in 1924; or the Snyder Act of 1921 which made the Department of the Interior responsible for Indian social, educational, and medical services. By the 1930s, the stage was set for the Indian "New Deal."

TRIBAL RESTORATION AND REORGANIZATION

In 1934, under socially progressive President Franklin D. Roosevelt and his commissioner of Indian Affairs, John Collier, who had founded the American Indian Defense Association, Congress passed the Indian Reorganization Act (or the Wheeler-Howard Act). Reversing the policies of assimilation and allotment, this act

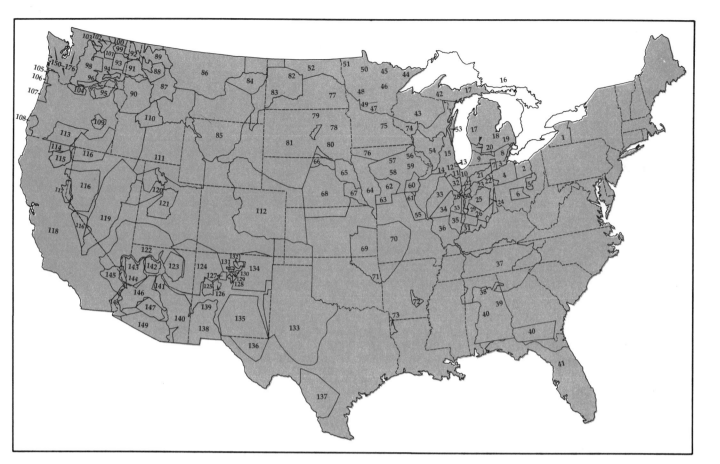

1. SENECA, 1797
2. DELAWARE, WYANDOT, POTAWATOMI, OTTAWA, CHIPPEWA, 1805
3. OTTAWA, 1808
4. DELAWARE, OTTAWA, SHAWNEE, WYANDOT, 1819
5. DELAWARE, 1795
6. SHAWNEE, 1795
7. POTAWATOMI, OTTAWA, CHIPPEWA, 1819
8. POTAWATOMI, 1807
9. POTAWATOMI, 1821
10. POTAWATOMI, 1827
11. POTAWATOMI, 1832
12. POTAWATOMI, 1816
13. POTAWATOMI, 1795
14. POTAWATOMI, 1829
15. POTAWATOMI, 1833
16. SAULT ST. MARIE BAND OF CHIPPEWA, 1821
17. OTTAWA, CHIPPEWA, 1820
18. SAGINAW, CHIPPEWA, 1820
19. SAGINAW, CHIPPEWA, 1808
20. GRAND RIVER BAND OF OTTAWA, 1821
21. MIAMI, POTAWATOMI, 1818
22. MIAMI, POTAWATOMI, 1827
23. MIAMI, 1818
24. MIAMI, EEL RIVER, 1809
25. MIAMI, DELAWARE, 1818
26. MIAMI, WEA, 1809
27. POTAWATOMI, WEA, 1818
28. POTAWATOMI, WEA, KICKAPOO, 1818
29. WEA, KICKAPOO, 1810
30. WEA, 1818
31. DELAWARE, PIANKESHAW, 1804
32. POTAWATOMI, KICKAPOO, 1819
33. KICKAPOO, 1819
34. KASKASKIA, KICKAPOO, 1803
35. PIANKESHAW (PEORIA), 1805
36. KASKASKIA (PEORIA), 1803

37. CHEROKEE, 1785–1835
38. CREEK, 1816
39. CREEK, 1832
40. CREEK, 1814
41. SEMINOLE, 1823
42. LAKE SUPERIOR BANDS, MISSISSIPPI BANDS (CHIPPEWA), 1843
43. LAKE SUPERIOR BANDS, MISSISSIPPI BANDS (CHIPPEWA), 1838
44. LAKE SUPERIOR BANDS (CHIPPEWA), 1851
45. BOIS FORTE BAND (CHIPPEWA), 1866
46. MISSISSIPPI BANDS (CHIPPEWA), 1855
47. LAKE SUPERIOR BANDS, MISSISSIPPI BANDS (CHIPPEWA), 1848
48. PILLAGER AND LAKE WINNIBIGOSHISH BANDS (CHIPPEWA), 1855
49. PILLAGER BAND (CHIPPEWA), 1848
50. RED LAKE BAND (CHIPPEWA), 1863
51. RED LAKE BAND, PEMBINA BAND (CHIPPEWA), 1863
52. PEMBINA BAND (CHIPPEWA), 1905
53. POTAWATOMI, 1833
54. WINNEBAGO, 1829
55. SAC AND FOX, 1805
56. SAC AND FOX, 1832
57. SAC AND FOX, 1831
58. SAC AND FOX, 1842
59. SAC AND FOX, 1837
60. IOWA, SAC AND FOX, 1838,1832
61. SAC AND FOX, 1824
62. IOWA, 1838
63. IOWA, 1824
64. OTOE AND MISSOURIA, IOWA, OMAHA, SAC AND FOX, 1825

65. OMAHA, 1854
66. PONCA, 1858
67. OTOE AND MISSOURIA, 1833
68. PAWNEE, 1833
69. OSAGE, 1825
70. OSAGE, 1810
71. OSAGE, 1819
72. QUAPAW, 1824
73. CADDO, 1835
74. MEDAWAKANTON BAND (SIOUX), 1837
75. EASTERN OR MISSISSIPPI SIOUX, 1851
76. YANKTON (SIOUX), 1825
77. SISSETON AND WAHPETON BANDS (SIOUX), 1851
78. SISSETON (SIOUX), 1872
79. TETON AND YANKTONAI (SIOUX), 1869
80. YANKTON (SIOUX), 1859
81. SIOUX (DAHCOTAH) NATION, 1851
82. ARIKARA, MANDAN, HIDATSA (FORT BERTHOLD RESERVATION), 1870
83. ARIKARA, MANDAN, HIDATSA, 1851
84. ASSINIBOINE, 1851
85. CROW, 1868
86. BLACKFEET AND GROS VENTRE, 1855
87. FLATHEAD, 1855
88. UPPER PEND D'OREILLE, 1855
89. KOOTENAI, 1855
90. NEZ PERCE, 1859
91. COEUR D'ALENE, 1887
92. KALISPEL, 1887
93. SPOKANE, 1892
94. PALUS, 1859
95. CAYUSE (UMATILLA), 1859
96. WALLA WALLA (UMATILLA), 1859
97. UMATILLA, 1859
98. YAKIMA, 1859
99. COLVILLE, 1872

100. LAKE TRIBE (COLVILLE), 1872
101. SANPOIL-NESPELEM (COLVILLE), 1872
102. OKANOGAN (COLVILLE), 1872
103. METHOW (COLVILLE), 1872
104. WARM SPRINGS, 1859
105. CLATSOP, 1851
106. TILLAMOOK, 1851
107. TILLAMOOK (ALCEA), 1855
108. COQUILLE, CHETCO, TOO-TOO-TO-NEY (TILLAMOOK), 1855
109. SNAKE, 1879
110. LEMHI (SHOSHONI), 1875
111. SHOSHONE, 1869
112. CHEYENNE AND ARAPAHO, NORTHERN CHEYENNE, NORTHERN ARAPAHO, 1865
113. KLAMATH, 1870
114. MODOC, 1870
115. PITT RIVER, 1853
116. NORTHERN PAIUTE, 1853
117. WASHOE, 1853
118. INDIANS OF CALIFORNIA, 1851
119. WESTERN SHOSHONE, 1869
120. GOSHUTE, 1875
121. UINTAH UTE, 1865
122. SOUTHERN PAIUTE, 1880
123. HOPI, 1882
124. NAVAJO, 1868
125. ACOMA (KERES), 1858
126. LAGUNA (KERES), 1858
127. ZIA (KERES), SANTA ANA (KERES), JEMEZ, 1912
128. SANTO DOMINGO (KERES), 1905
129. SAN IDLEFONSO (TEWA), 1905
130. NAMBE (TEWA),1905
131. SANTA CLARA (TEWA), 1905
132. TAOS (TIWA), 1905
133. KIOWA, COMANCHE, AND APACHE, 1865–1900
134. JICARILLA APACHE, 1883
135. MESCALERO APACHE, 1873
136. MESCALERO APACHE, 1873

137. LIPAN APACHE, 1856
138. CHIRICAHUA APACHE, 1886
139. CHIRICAHUA APACHE, 1886
140. WESTERN APACHE, 1873
141. TONTO APACHE, 1873
142. HAVASUPAI, 1882
143. HUALAPAI, 1883
144. MOJAVE, 1853, 1865
145. CHEMEHUEVI, 1853
146. YAVAPAI, 1873
147. PIMA-MARICOPA, 1883
148. QUECHAN, 1853, 1884
149. PAPAGO, 1916
150. NOOKSACK, 1855
151. LUMNI, 1859
152. SAMISH, 1859
153. UPPER SKAGIT, 1859
154. SWINOMISH, 1859
155. LOWER SKAGIT, 1859
156. KIKIALLUS, 1859
157. STILLAGUAMISH, 1859
158. MAKAH, 1859
159. CLALLAM, 1859
160. SNOHOMISH, 1855
161. QUILEUTE, 1859
162. SKOKOMISH, 1859
163. SKYKOMISH, 1859
164. SNOQUALMIE, 1859
165. SUQUAMISH, 1859
166. DUWAMISH, 1859
167. QUINAIELT, 1859
168. SQUAXIN, 1855
169. MUCKLESHOOT, 1859
170. PUYALLUP, 1855
171. STEILACOOM, 1855
172. NISQUALLY, 1855
173. LOWER CHEHALIS, 1855
174. UPPER CHEHALIS, 1855
175. COWLITZ, 1855
176. CHINOOK, 1851

7.1 INDIAN LAND CLAIMS IN THE UNITED STATES, *showing tribal title and dates of established ownership, as determined by the federal government's Indian Claims Commission from 1946 to 1978 (with modern tribal spellings)*

gave legal sanction to tribal landholdings; returned unsold allotted lands to tribes, made provisions for the purchase of new lands; encouraged tribal constitutions, systems of justice, and business corporations; expanded educational opportunities through new facilities and loans, with an emphasis on reservation day schools instead of off-reservation boarding schools; advocated the hiring of Indians by the Bureau of Indian Affairs and Indian involvement in management and policy making at national and tribal levels; extended the Indian trust status; and granted Indians religious freedom. Earlier that same year, Congress had also passed the Johnson-O'Malley Act, which authorized federal contracts with states or private agencies for the provision of additional social, educational, medical, and agricultural services in order to help raise Indian standards of living.

In addition to tribal restoration and reorganization, Collier and his supporters encouraged intertribal activity. In 1944, with a newfound sense of pan-Indianism, Indian leaders, many of them employees of the BIA, founded the National Congress of American Indians. (See "Indian Activism" in this chapter.) Also under the impetus of Collier and Indian leaders, Congress created the Indian Claims Commission, an independent federal agency, in 1946. Tribal land claims had been handled since 1881 by the Court of Claims, which had proven inadequate to the heavy Indian case load. The Indian Claims Commission, designed to expedite the process and provide financial compensation for treaty violations, would last until 1978 and grant awards of $800 million on 60 percent of the cases brought before it (the Court of Claims would reassume any unheard claims). Indian bravery and sacrifice in World War II helped foster a new sense of fairness toward Indians among politicians and the general public, and it helped bring about the Indian Claims Commission.

Nonetheless, Collier's enlightened policies, as pared down by Congress, did not redress all past injustices. Al-

lotted holdings were not all consolidated and much of the Indian economic base remained fractionalized. The federal government still held a unilateral power over the policies and fate of Indians; BIA agents still managed many Indian activities. Moreover, both the relief funds of the New Deal, which improved the financial status and increased the options of individuals, and World War II, which took individuals off the reservations, countered the reawakened drive toward tribalization.

During and after Collier's administration, which lasted until 1945, bills to abolish Indian reservations were introduced in most sessions of Congress. As time went on and anti-Communist sentiment grew during the Cold War, Collier's policies came under increasing fire because they encouraged a communal life-style. In the passion and ignorance of the time, it was no matter that Indians had lived tribally for centuries, long before *communal* was even a word. During the 1950s, the federal government would reverse its approach to Indians once again with a renewed coercive assimilationist policy.

TERMINATION
AND URBANIZATION

Proponents of the termination of the federal–Indian trust relationship and Indian assimilation into the cultural mainstream, notably commissioners of Indian Affairs Dillon Myer and Glenn Emmons plus Senator Arthur Watkins of Utah, came to shape the United States Indian policies of the 1950s and early 1960s. To achieve Indian acculturation, they also advocated the relocation of Indians to urban centers. The report of the Hoover Commission on the Reorganization of Government in 1949, recommending termination, became the basis for the series of governmental resolutions.

In 1952, Congress established a Voluntary Relocation Program, which offered counseling and guidance before relocation as well as assistance in finding residence and employment in the new community. In 1953, Con-

gress passed the Termination Resolution (House Concurrent Resolution 108), which called for Indian equality under the law as well as the release of certain tribes from federal supervision. That same year, Public Law 280 gave certain states civil and criminal jurisdiction over Indian reservations without the consent of tribes. Also that year, Congress repealed the special prohibition laws regarding Indians. In 1955, the Public Health Service of the Department of Health, Education, and Welfare assumed responsibility for Indian health and medical care from the BIA. And, in 1956, the BIA instituted off-reservation educational programs, including the Adult Vocational Training Program.

Meanwhile, from 1954 to 1962, Congress terminated the federal relationship with 61 tribes, bands, and communities. Among the largest were the Menominees of Wisconsin. Although termination was presented to them as freedom from further federal intervention, an underlying motive for various private white interests and their allies in Congress centered around the acquisition of timber on Indian lands. After termination, the new Menominee corporation, Menominee Enterprises, Inc., encountered economic setbacks in the lumber business. Many tribal members lost their lands because of an inability to pay the new property taxes. And without federally sponsored social, educatonal, and health services and facilities, the tribe sunk deeper and deeper into poverty. As a result, a coalition of Menominee factions along with non-Indian supporters lobbied for restoration of trust status for the tribe and reservation status for remaining lands. In 1974, Congress finally complied, passing the Menominee Restoration Act. Four years later, Congress also restored the federal government's trust relationship with the Ottawas, Wyandots, Peorias, and Modocs.

The Indian Claims Commission, created in 1946 for tribes to present their long-standing claims concerning stolen lands and broken treaties and to receive monetary compensation, indirectly served as another instrument of termination, in that settlement of claims finalized the process, ruling out the procurement of former lands for all compensated tribes—lands that in the long run would have been more valuable than the cash awards. In terms of having actual lands returned, Indians have been successful in only a number of cases brought before federal agencies or courts. In 1971, for example, the federal government agreed to return 48,000 acres of the Blue Wilderness Area in New Mexico to the Taos Pueblo, and in 1972, the government returned 21,000 acres to the Yakima tribe in Washington.

The positive results of the Indian Claims Commission and those results consistent with the concept of tribal restoration, as instituted under Collier's earlier tenure, as well as with the next phase of governmental policy—self-determination for Indian peoples—are as follows: the $800 million in cash awards has aided tribal economies; tribal legal consciousness has been raised, with many tribes continuing to maintain legal counsel even after the settlements; Indians have received publicity concerning past injustices and present low standards of living; valuable ethno-historical research concerning Indian-white relations has been conducted; and tribes have found pan-Indian unity of cause.

SELF-DETERMINATION

Termination as official federal policy came to an end during the 1960s, although various programs from the termination period carried over even to the 1970s. The catchall phrase used to describe United States Indian policy from the 1960s to the present is "Indian Self-Determination," which embraces a variety of concepts, including tribal restoration, self-government, cultural renewal, development of reservation resources, and self-sufficiency, as well as the ongoing special Indian and federal trust relationship for the protection of the trust assets and the provision of economic and social programs needed to raise the stan-

dard of living of Indian peoples to a level comparable to the rest of society. The thrust of the policy of course has varied with changing federal administrations. And Indian leaders themselves have advocated varying aspects of it, as consistent with the meaning of the phrase itself, which expresses Indian involvement and choice.

A number of governmental studies and commissions were pivotal in the trend away from termination and towards self-determination: In 1961, three commissions—the Keeler Commission on Indian Affairs; the Brophy Commission on Rights, Liberties, and Responsibilities of the American Indian; and the United States Commission on Civil Rights—recommended more constructive Indian programs supporting Indian self-determination and fostering Indian economic and social equality. In 1964, the Council on Indian Affairs sponsored the Capital Conference on Indian Poverty, calling attention to the plight of modern Indians. In 1966, the Coleman Report criticized the BIA for its handling of Indian education. Also in 1966, a White House Task Force on Indian Health condemned medical and sanitation conditions on reservations. In 1969, two reports—the Josephy Report on Federal Indian Policy and the Kennedy Report on Indian Education—called for greater Indian involvement in both political and educational processes. In 1977, the American Indian Policy Review Commission opposed forced assimilation of Indian peoples and advocated tribal self-determination and self-government.

Just as these various studies and commissions increased society's awareness of the Indian condition, so did the work of Indian activists who, in a mood of growing militancy, founded many new pan-Indian groups and staged many political events and demonstrations. (See "Indian Activism" in this chapter.) Out of the new public and congressional awareness came numerous social relief and reform measures, such as the Public Housing Act (1961), offering assistance to Indians in housing improvement; the Area Redevelopment

Act (1961), granting reservations federal funds for economic development; the Manpower Development and Training Act (1962), offering vocational training to Indians; the Economic Opportunity Act (1964), creating an Indian Desk in the Office of Economic Opportunity through which tribes could receive Head Start, Upward Bound, Vista, and Community Action Funds, breaking the BIA monopoly over funding of services to Indians; the Civil Rights Act (1964) and the Voting Rights Act (1965), applying to all minorities; the Elementary and Secondary Education Act (1966), providing special programs for Indian children; the Small Business Administration's "Project Own" (1968), guaranteeing loans for small businesses on reservations; the Civil Rights Act (1968), extending provisions of the Bill of Rights to reservation Indians; the Environmental Policy Act (1969), protecting Indian resources; the Indian Education Act (1972), establishing compensatory educational programs for Indian students; the State and Local Fiscal Assistance Act (1972), establishing revenue-sharing among federal, state, and local governments; the Indian Financing Act (1974), establishing a program for the financing of Indian businesses; the Housing and Community Development Act (1974), providing funds for Indian housing; the Indian Self-Determination Act (1975), permitting tribes to participate in federal social programs and services, and providing mechanisms for tribes to contract and administer federal funds; the Indian Child Welfare Act (1978), establishing standards for federal foster programs and providing assistance to tribal child and family programs; and the American Indian Freedom of Religion Act (1978), stating that Indian religion is protected by the First Amendment.

Although federal programs for Indian self-betterment and tribal development have declined in number during the 1980s because of cutbacks in funds, the federal government continues to nominally back the principles of Indian self-determination. Another dramatic shift to a new pol-

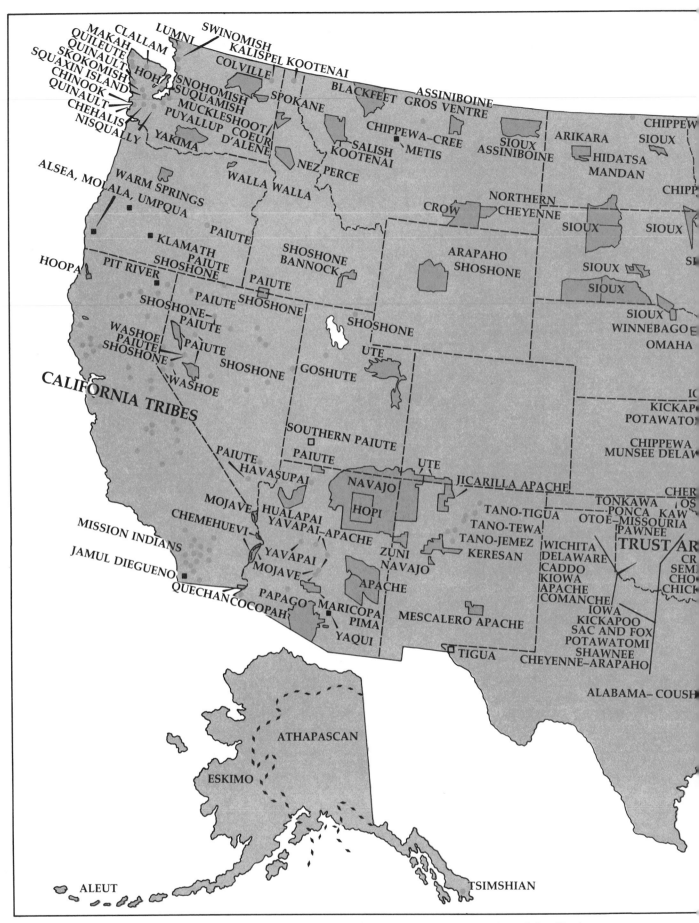

MAKAH
QUILEUTE
QUINAULT
SKOKOMISH
SQUAXIN ISLAND
CHINOOK
QUINAULT
CHEHALIS
NISQUALLY

CLALLAM LUMNI SWINOMISH
HOH? KALISPEL KOOTENAI
COLVILLE
SNOHOMISH
SUQUAMISH SPOKANE
MUCKLESHOOT
PUYALLUP COEUR
YAKIMA D'ALENE
NEZ PERCE
SALISH
KOOTENAI
METIS

ASSINIBOINE
BLACKFEET GROS VENTRE
CHIPPEWA–CREE
SIOUX
ASSINIBOINE

CHIPPEW
ARIKARA
HIDATSA
MANDAN

SIOUX

ALSEA, MOLALA, UMPQUA
WARM SPRINGS
WALLA WALLA

NORTHERN
CROW CHEYENNE
CHIPP

ARAPAHO
SHOSHONE

SIOUX SIOUX

HOOPA
PIT RIVER
KLAMATH
PAIUTE
SHOSHONE
PAIUTE

PAIUTE
SHOSHONE
BANNOCK

SHOSHONE

PAIUTE
SHOSHONE

SHOSHONE

SIOUX

SIOUX
WINNEBAGO
OMAHA

SHOSHONE–
PAIUTE
WASHOE
PAIUTE
SHOSHONE
PAIUTE

UTE

SHOSHONE

CALIFORNIA TRIBES
WASHOE
SHOSHONE
GOSHUTE

SOUTHERN PAIUTE
PAIUTE

IO
KICKAP
POTAWATO

CHIPPEWA
MUNSEE DELAW

PAIUTE
HAVASUPAI
UTE
NAVAJO
HOPI
JICARILLA APACHE

CHER
TONKAWA OS
PONCA KAW
OTOE–MISSOURIA
PAWNEE

MOJAVE
CHEMEHUEVI
HUALAPAI
YAVAPAI–APACHE

TANO-TIGUA
TANO-TEWA
TANO-JEMEZ
KERESAN

TRUST AR

MISSION INDIANS
YAVAPAI
MOJAVE
ZUNI
NAVAJO
WICHITA
DELAWARE
CADDO
KIOWA
APACHE
COMANCHE

CR
SEMI
CHO
CHICK

JAMUL DIEGUENO
QUECHANCOCOPAH
PAPAGO
MARICOPA
PIMA
YAQUI
APACHE
MESCALERO APACHE
IOWA
KICKAPOO
SAC AND FOX
POTAWATOMI
SHAWNEE

TIGUA
CHEYENNE–ARAPAHO

ALABAMA– COUSH

ATHAPASCAN

ESKIMO

ALEUT
TSIMSHIAN

7.2 CONTEMPORARY INDIAN LANDS AND COMMUNITIES IN THE UNITED STATES (*with modern tribal spellings*)

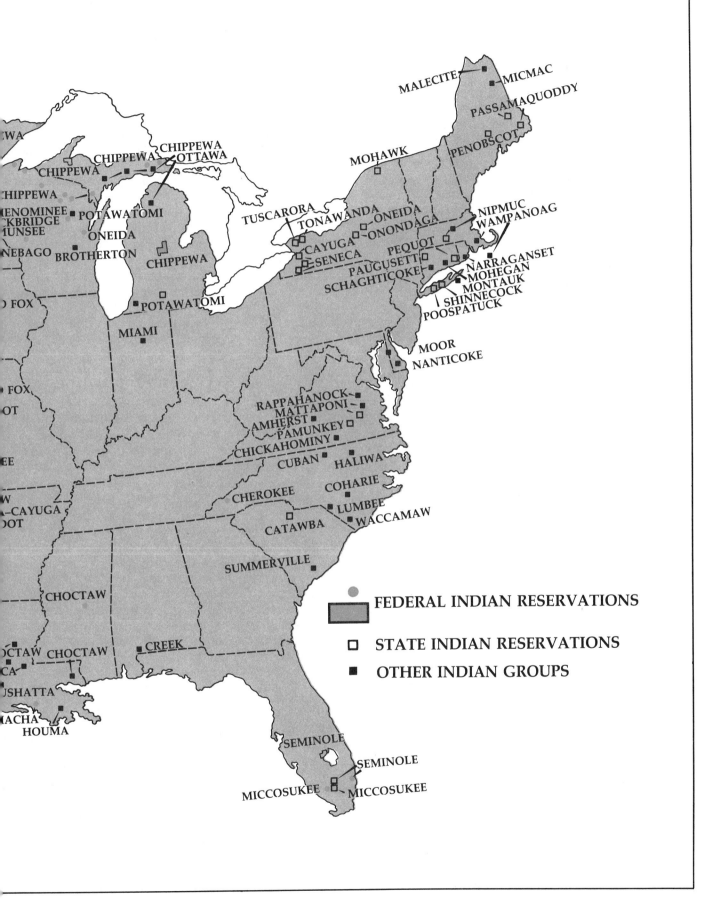

MALECITE · MICMAC
PASSAMAQUODDY
PENOBSCOT

CHIPPEWA
CHIPPEWA · OTTAWA
CHIPPEWA
CHIPPEWA
MENOMINEE
CKBRIDGE
MUNSEE
POTAWATOMI
NEBAGO
ONEIDA
BROTHERTON
CHIPPEWA

MOHAWK
TUSCARORA
TONAWANDA   ONEIDA
ONONDAGA
CAYUGA
SENECA
NIPMUC
WAMPANOAG
NARRAGANSET
PEQUOT
MOHEGAN
PAUGUSETT
MONTAUK
SCHAGHTICOKE
SHINNECOCK
POOSPATUCK

FOX
POTAWATOMI
MIAMI

FOX
OT

MOOR
NANTICOKE

EE

RAPPAHANOCK
MATTAPONI
AMHERST
PAMUNKEY
CHICKAHOMINY

CAYUGA
OT

CUBAN   HALIWA

CHEROKEE   COHARIE
LUMBEE
CATAWBA   WACCAMAW

SUMMERVILLE

CHOCTAW

● FEDERAL INDIAN RESERVATIONS

CTAW   CHOCTAW
CA
SHATTA
CREEK

□ STATE INDIAN RESERVATIONS

■ OTHER INDIAN GROUPS

ACHA
HOUMA

SEMINOLE
SEMINOLE
MICCOSUKEE   MICCOSUKEE

See also reservation list in the Appendix.

icy—some new version of forced assimilation, for example—seems unlikely. United States Indian policy seems to have finally found itself.

THE FEDERAL AND INDIAN TRUST RELATIONSHIP AND THE RESERVATION SYSTEM

In the contemporary relationship between the federal government and federally chartered tribes, as it has reached the present through a number of historical stages, the United States Congress with its powers to ratify treaties and regulate commerce is the trustee of the special Indian status. The trusteeship involves protection of Indian property; protection of Indian right to self-government; and the provision of services necessary for survival and advancement. Since the relationship exists at the tribal level, Congress does not act as the guardian of individual Indians any more than of other citizens, and Indians are not "wards" of the federal government.

In the commission of its trusteeship, Congress has placed the major responsibility for Indian matters in the Department of the Interior and its subdivision the Bureau of Indian Affairs. In addition to the central office in Washington, D.C., the BIA maintains regional offices in 12 states, mostly in the West, with agencies on particular reservations as well. At the top of the organization, there is a commissioner of Indian Affairs and a deputy commissioner, with various staffs; at the regional level, area directors; and at the agency level, superintendents. Many Native Americans have positions in the BIA, but relatively few are at the highest positions. Other governmental agencies are involved in Indian affairs through the provision of special programs and activities, including the Departments of Agriculture, Commerce, Education, Energy, Health and Human Services, Housing and Urban Development, Justice, Labor, Transportation, and the Community Services Administration. Under the policy of self-deter-

mination, the tribes themselves have assumed a large share of management responsibilities for Indian-related services.

In the federal–Indian trust relationship, specific treaties can be cited as the source of the federal obligation to some tribes; executive orders, congressional legislation, and judiciary decisions are the basis of obligation to other tribes. A treaty is by definition a binding agreement between two sovereign nations, covering governmental rights, human rights, and property rights. By signing treaties, the federal government by implication recognized the sovereignty of Indian tribes. In exchange for the promises made by the government, the United States received millions of acres of land. The abrogation of treaties therefore by extension represents a violation of the principles of the American Constitution.

Sovereignty, as it has been applied to Indian tribes, is a relative term. Unilateral action on the part of the federal government has eroded the original concept as inherent in the treaty-making process. The limited sovereignty of tribes as it exists today is comparable to that held by the states. The tribes have powers to govern themselves, but only under federally imposed regulations. Tribes receive assistance for services in the same way that states receive subsidies for social programs, education, transportation, etc. Tribes also receive further federal aid as many private corporations do, in the form of tax relief and funds for research and development or job training.

As governments, tribes have the right to regulate tribal membership; make laws; establish courts and tribal police; enforce laws and administer justice (except major crimes which are under the jurisdiction of federal courts, as set forth by the Major Crimes Act of 1885); remove nonmembers from tribal property; levy taxes on tribal members; and regulate land use, including resource development, environmental protection, and hunting and fishing. Some tribes have written constitutions and legal codes; others maintain traditional unwritten systems. Most govern by some form of council—some representative and others general for all adults—with an elected chief or president.

There were, in 1984, 283 federally recognized tribes in the United States and nearly 200 Alaskan villages, all existing as unique political entities. Many other tribes exist with their own governmental and legal structures, some of them incorporated under the laws of the state, but without federal charters and without trust status. There exist about 300 federal reservations, with a total of 52,017,551 acres held in trust by the federal government, the large majority west of the Mississippi (some reservations in California are called rancherias). There are also 21 state reservations, most of these in the East. Some reservations are restricted to one tribe; others are jointly held. Some reservation land is owned, rented, and occupied by non-Indians. Some reservations are solid blocks of land; other pieces are interspersed with nonres-

Cherokee Indian Reservation, North Carolina. Photo by Molly Braun.

Indian Island, Penobscot Reservation, Maine. Photo by Molly Braun.

ervation lands. The largest reservation is held by the Navajo tribe, with 14 million acres; other reservations are only a few acres. (See the list of U.S. reservations in the Appendix).

Only federal and tribal laws apply on federal trust reservations unless Congress has determined otherwise, by granting state and local governments a certain degree of jurisdiction as well (as is the case in 13 states under Public Law 280, enacted in 1953 during the termination era). Full-fledged state reservations are subject to state regulations, with federal Indian policy in an ancillary role. Whereas the BIA operates about 225 elementary and secondary schools on federal reservations, state bureaucracies are responsible for the provision of education, through school or tuition subsidies on state reservations.

A distinction is made between those tribes that once held federal acknowledgement—terminated tribes—and those that never did. Since the treaty-making period ended in 1871, the way to achieve federal acknowledgment is by an act of Congress or an Executive Order. Various tribes are now under petition for acknowledgment. A Federal Acknowledgment Project in the Division of Tribal Government Services of the BIA judges several criteria of tribal identity, in-

cluding history, genealogy, territoriality and community, and political structure.

Although Indians are the only ethnic group specifically mentioned in the Constitution, the designation is not relevant at the individual level but rather at the tribal—Indian tribes are distinct political entities with executive, legislative, and judicial powers. That is to say, Indians as individuals have the same rights and are subject to the same laws as all other American citizens—right to vote; right to travel freely; right to buy and sell off-reservation property; right to buy alcoholic beverages; subject to federal,

state, and local taxes, etc. Indians as tribal members, however, have a special relationship with the government—inability to sell trust lands without tribal and BIA approval; special reservation nondrinking laws (dry reservations as opposed to wet); special exemptions to federal, state, and local taxes, etc. And each tribe has its unique infrastructure and regulations. Under United States law, therefore, Indians might be citizens of four different governments—federal, state, county or city, and tribal, with complex overlapping jurisdictions. And, contrary to popular belief, individual Indians do not automatically receive federal funds simply because they are Indians. Types and sources of funds vary from tribe to tribe—income from leasing or development of tribal property and resources; federal compensation for treaty violations, encroachments on Indian lands, and mismanagement of trust property and funds; or subsidies from special governmental programs.

As to the question of Indian ethnicity, tribes determine membership and naturalization proceedings, and standards of acceptance. It generally holds that to be accepted into a tribe, at least one parent has to qualify as a tribal member. But because of low populations, some tribes accept members with only one qualifying grandparent. Tribal recognition is necessary for federal recognition (although not for a census count).

Hollywood Seminole Reservation, Florida. Photo by Molly Braun.

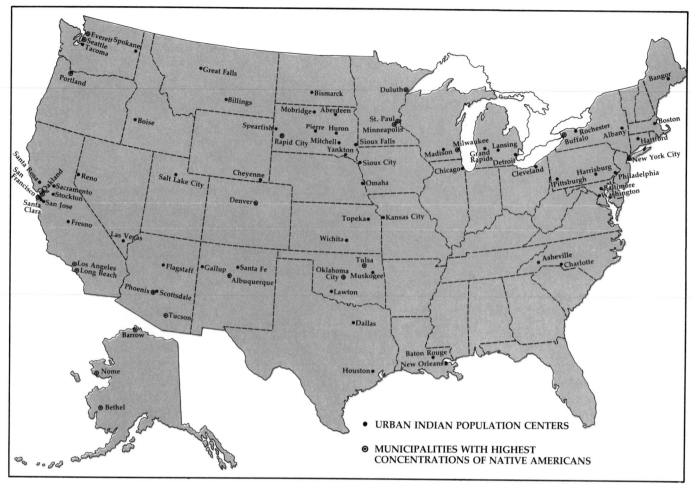

• URBAN INDIAN POPULATION CENTERS

◉ MUNICIPALITIES WITH HIGHEST
   CONCENTRATIONS OF NATIVE AMERICANS

7.3 URBAN INDIAN CENTERS

URBAN INDIANS

It is estimated that one-third to one-half the Indian population in the United States now lives in cities. From 1900 to 1940, the percentage of the urban Indian population fluctuated within the range of 1–10 percent. Urbanization began to accelerate during World War II, however, when great numbers of Indians joined the armed services or worked at off-reservation wartime jobs, breaking traditional ties. With the federal government's termination and relocation policies of the 1950s and 1960s, migration towards the cities continued at a fast rate. In fact, at every 10-year census from 1940 to 1970, the urban percentage has close to doubled, from seven to 13 to 28 to 45 percent, before leveling off. Some Native Americans have made the move as a result of government-sponsored counseling and training, and others have moved

on their own in search of economic opportunity.

But few in both groups have been able to break out of the cycle of poverty, unemployment, and societal discrimination or indifference. The newfound cultural isolation of the cities has led many to opt for the poverty of the reservations. Those that do stay in urban centers fall into at least three recognizable patterns: first, skilled laborers, often living on the edges of cities in Indian enclaves; second, those remaining oriented to their home reservations or rural communities, journeying back and forth depending on seasonal jobs; and third, an Indian middle class interspersed in white neighborhoods. Many of this third group remain active in Indian cultural and political affairs and, like the others, can be called bicultural. The Mohawks of the Caughnawaga reserve outside of Montreal in Canada and other Iroquois high-steel workers fit into the first two categories, some living year-round in a Brooklyn col-

ony and others traveling seasonally to jobs in various cities.

Because of difficult social conditions and detachment from direct tribal affiliations, the urban setting has fostered a new brand of Indian social and political activity—numerous urban centers with programs and services designed to ease the transition to city life and encourage a sense of "Indianness" and belonging, as well as political groups, such as the American Indian Movement (AIM), founded in Minneapolis in 1968. (See "Indian Activism" in this chapter.) Another outcome of Indian urbanization has been a certain amount of "brain drain" on the reservations, with many of the more successful and upwardly mobile individuals siphoned off.

The greatest concentration of urban Indians, about 60,000, are found in the Los Angeles–Long Beach area of California. Other cities with large Indian populations are San Francisco–Oakland in California; Tulsa and Oklahoma City in Oklahoma; New

York City and Buffalo in New York; Phoenix and Tucson in Arizona; Minneapolis–St. Paul and Duluth in Minnesota; Seattle–Everett in Washington; Rapid City in South Dakota; Denver in Colorado; Milwaukee in Wisconsin; Portland in Oregon; Albuquerque in New Mexico; and Nome, Bethel, and Barrow in Alaska.

NONRESERVATION RURAL INDIANS

In the discussion of contemporary Native Americans, quite often a third category besides reservation Indians and urban Indians is overlooked—those Indians living in cohesive rural communities without federal or state acknowledgment or trust status. As is the case with some urban Indian communities, many of these groups are just as culturally and politically integrated and organized as the legally defined tribes.

Nonreservation Indian communities evolved out of three differing sets of circumstances. In the East, where the majority of such groups exist, the fact that many Indian peoples were defeated and displaced by whites long before American Independence meant a minimum of reservations. In the West, the federal allotment policy beginning in 1887 meant the breakup of many reservations, as did termination 60 years later. Some of these groups have sought federal acknowledgment (or reacknowledgement) in order to protect their culture and resources.

INDIAN SOCIAL CONDITIONS

The United States Indian population has been growing since its lowpoint of less than 250,000 at the turn of the century. According to the 1980 census, there are almost one-and-one-half million Native Americans, or just over one-half of one percent of the total population. In analyzing the results of any census, the systems of collection and classification have to be taken into consideration, with a plus

or minus margin assumed. In recent censuses, the method of self-identification is employed, along with the gathering of tribal lists; respondents are asked to enumerate the ethnic groups with which they identify, leading to the inclusion of a certain number of mixed-bloods and the exclusion of others. The large increase in the Indian population since 1970—from a total of 827,108 to 1,418,195—is attibuted to better census-taking methods and greater Indian cultural identification, in addition to a climbing birth rate.

The accompanying table gives a state-by-state breakdown. In a regional comparison, 49 percent of the native population lives in the West, 27 percent in the South, 18 percent in the North Central states, and six percent in the East, the same general ratios as found in 1970. Not quite half of all Native Americans (628,409 according to the 1980 census) reside in just four western states: California, Oklahoma, Arizona, and New Mexico. California, which had the third highest count in 1970, now heads the list, largely due to migration to urban areas.

Yet, despite the fact of a growing population, a positive sign for the future, Indian social conditions on and off reservations remain problematic. Native Americans, on a national average, have the shortest life span of any ethnic group; the highest infant mortality rate; the highest suicide rate; the lowest per capita income; the highest unemployment; the highest school dropout rate; the poorest housing; and the most inadequate health care, with extensive diabetes, tuberculosis, high blood pressure, respiratory disease, and alcoholism. Many factors account for these conditions: unproductive land; lack of capital; lack of education; a cycle of poverty difficult to escape; and cultural dislocation and depression caused from an existence as a conquered people within a historically alien culture.

Indian leaders charge that by not bringing Native Americans up to the national standard of living, the federal government has failed to live up to its agreements of the past and its moral obligations. And, they point out, progress in alleviating the socioeconomic plight of Native Americans has

1980 UNITED STATES CENSUS COUNT OF NATIVE AMERICANS

California	201,311	Idaho	10,521
Oklahoma	169,464	Pennsylvania	9,459
Arizona	152,857	Arkansas	9,411
New Mexico	104,777	Virginia	9,336
North Carolina	64,635	Nebraska	9,197
Alaska	64,047	New Jersey	8,394
Washington	60,771	Maryland	8,021
South Dakota	45,101	Indiana	7,835
Texas	40,074	Massachusetts	7,743
Michigan	40,038	Georgia	7,619
New York	38,732	Alabama	7,561
Montana	37,270	Wyoming	7,125
Minnesota	35,026	Mississippi	6,180
Wisconsin	29,497	South Carolina	5,758
Oregon	27,309	Iowa	5,453
North Dakota	20,157	Tennessee	5,103
Florida	19,316	Connecticut	4,533
Utah	19,256	Maine	4,087
Colorado	18,059	Kentucky	3,610
Illinois	16,271	Rhode Island	2,898
Kansas	15,371	Hawaii	2,778
Nevada	13,304	West Virginia	1,610
Missouri	12,319	New Hampshire	1,352
Ohio	12,240	Delaware	1,330
Louisiana	12,064	District of Columbia	1,031
		Vermont	984

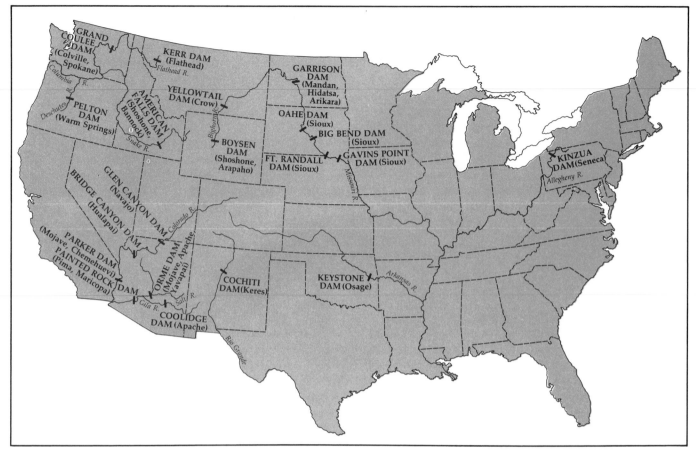

7.4 SOME DAMS ON INDIAN LANDS

slowed with the Reagan administration, which has cut back 40 percent of its federal funds for Indian social programs. They cite the fact that inhabitants of the continent who were forced to give up the vast majority of their ancestral homelands are now assigned less than one-half of one percent of the federal budget. The only time the federal government spent what would seem proportionate funds on the people it displaced was to make war on them.

Moreover, they claim, despite supposed official policies of self-determination and protection of Indian resources, certain federal policies as well as governmental laissez-faire attitudes toward the private business sector have encouraged continuing threats to the Indian cultural and economic base. Some federal agencies have projected a bureaucratic indifference; others have been guilty of paternalism, assuming they know what is best for Native Americans. Some programs have encouraged too much dependency on the federal bu-

reaucracy; others—relocation to cities, for example—have caused disruption of kin-based systems of familial interdependence.

Meanwhile, federal and state policies of eminent domain can still take away Indian lands, supposedly protected by treaty, for dams and other

energy projects, as well as for national parks. It is an established fact that, in the West, Indian water rights, although supposedly guaranteed under the Winters Doctrine of 1908—which gave tribes "first rights" to any sources touching their reservations— are being increasingly ignored by

Caughnawaga Iroquois Reserve, Quebec. Photo by Molly Braun.

white interests caught up in rapid development. And Indian leaders complain that, although tribes nominally own their resources, they do not necesarily control them because of a lack of capital for investment and development. Many tribes, in order to have any income from their land or mineral resources, are forced to lease them to agricultural, timber, and mining monopolies. And many of the leases, signed years ago, do not reflect current economics. Increased profits usually have gone to the petrochemical companies, not the tribes, despite large coal, oil, gas, or uranium deposits. And, Indian leaders point out, some of these private concerns, insensitive to the needs and aspirations of Indians and improperly regulated by the federal government, are destroying Indian lands while they profit from them, through water and air pollution, strip-mining, road-gouging, and over-lumbering. The environmental crisis threatening Indian peoples results not just from development of leased Indian lands, but also from industrial growth closing in on their remaining holdings.

Indian activists have said that the American dream is the Native American nightmare. It would seem that, tragically, this often has been the case. And, other than in regions directly flanking concentrations of Indian peoples, there seems to be little public awareness of the Indian situation. The media devotes little attention to it, unless Indian activists generate a story through some dramatic action. The situation is not all bleak, of course. There has been progress on many fronts, in addition to the already mentioned Indian population growth.

Books that discuss the contemporary Indian situation tend to end on one of two notes: in sadness and anger over the plight of the Indian and with a call to action aimed at both Indians and society at large; or in awe of the Indian cultural contribution and the Indian cultural persistence, with a declaration of hope for the future. The former sentiment has been expressed here. After a discussion of Indian activism in the 20th century and a look at the contemporary Indian

situation in Canada, the final section will undertake a view of the positive side of the Indian condition.

INDIAN ACTIVISM

Although Indian military power ended in the 19th century, resistance to white domination and exploitation has continued to the present. Tactics have varied with the times, as has the degree of militancy. Political action, rather than violence, has become the primary means in the 20th century. Yet continuity of cause exists from earlier centuries, with Indians still struggling for their ancestral lands

Caughnawaga Iroquois Reserve, Quebec. Photo by Molly Braun.

and an economic base, tribal self-government and self-determination, and cultural freedom and expression.

As for Indian activism at the turn of the century, a Creek by the name of Chitto Harjo (Crazy Snake) led a rebellion against allotment in the Indian Territory, which came to be known as the Snake Uprising of 1901. His followers harassed white settlers, as well as Indians who accepted allotment, with beatings and destruction of property. Federal marshals and columns of cavalry moved in on the insurgents, arresting them. Choctaws and Cherokees also showed overt resistance to allotment. In 1912, federal posses rounded up Cherokees who

refused to live on allotted parcels. That same year, anti-allotment Creeks, Choctaws, Cherokees, and Chickasaws formed the Four Mothers Society for collective political action, and they sent various delegations to Congress to argue their cause.

The year before, in 1911, the Society of American Indians, also committed to the idea of collective tribal action, had been formed. It evolved into the most important of the early pan-Indian organizations, playing a critical role as an advocate for Indian citizenship, which was finally granted in 1924. (See "United States Indian Policy and the Indian Condition in this chapter.) Other intertribal groups came together during these years, such as the Alaskan Native Brotherhood and Sisterhood, formed in 1912 to protect native resources, and the All Pueblo Council, formed in 1922, which successfully opposed the proposed Bursum Bill legislating rights for squatters on Indian lands along the Rio Grande. Then, in 1944, Indian employees of the BIA founded the National Congress of American Indians (NCAI) in Denver, with representatives from a majority of federally chartered tribes. The still-active organization has played an important part, since its inception, in lobbying for Indian rights.

Throughout the years preceding World War II and through the 1940s and 1950s, Indian activism was non-violent, with an emphasis on legal remedies. In 1922, as a symbolic gesture, Deskaheh, a Cayuga chief, traveled to the League of Nations in Geneva, Switzerland, to obtain recognition of his tribe's sovereignty, which was denied. Again symbolically, in 1939, the Seneca Nation at Tonawanda issued a "Declaration of Independence" to the state of New York. During World War II, whereas many Indians fought and died for the United States, and the Iroquois League even went so far as to independently declare war on Germany, others resisted selective service laws and were jailed, among them Iroquois, Utes, Papagos, Hopis, and Seminoles.

After the war, many tribes and organizations resisted the new federal termination policy. DRUMS, or Determination of Rights and Unity for Menominee Shareholders, helped bring about restoration of the tribe's trust status. During this period, many tribes also offered resistance to various reclamation projects forced on

them by the governmental concept of eminent domain. For example, the Senecas sought legal grounds to prevent the building of Kinzua Dam in Pennsylvania (1958); the Tuscaroras resisted the Tuscarora Power Project of the New York State Power Authority (1957–58); and the Miccosukees fought the Everglades Reclamation Project in Florida (1958). Most federal and state reclamation projects did in fact go through, despite tribal efforts and treaties protecting Indian lands, with the tribes receiving only minimal compensation, if any. Further acts of Indian resistance in the 1950s included the symbolic recognition of the revolutionary government of Cuba by various tribes in 1958; the breakup of a Ku Klux Klan rally in Robeson County, North Carolina, by 3,000 Lumbees in 1958; and the symbolic attempt to arrest the commissioner of Indian Affairs during a demonstration by Indian leaders in Washington, D.C., in 1959.

In the 1960s and 1970s, however, Native American resistance took on a

new dimension. Many of the new activist leaders were college-educated and radicalized youth influenced by the civil rights and counterculture movements in other segments of society. Many also lived in urban areas, their parents having resettled there as a result of federal relocation programs. Many were at odds with the generally older, more politically conservative tribal leaders, some of whom they believed to be, in effect, dupes of an interventionist, colonialist government and exploitative corporate interests. As far as the new activists were concerned, not only had the federal government failed to fulfill the promises of its treaties, acts, and agreements in correcting the miserable Indian socioeconomic conditions, but federal officials continued to act bureaucratically and presumptively in Indian affairs, as if they alone knew what was best for Indian peoples. Activists were also concerned with continuing racial discrimination in housing and employment, as well as police brutality against Indians. The

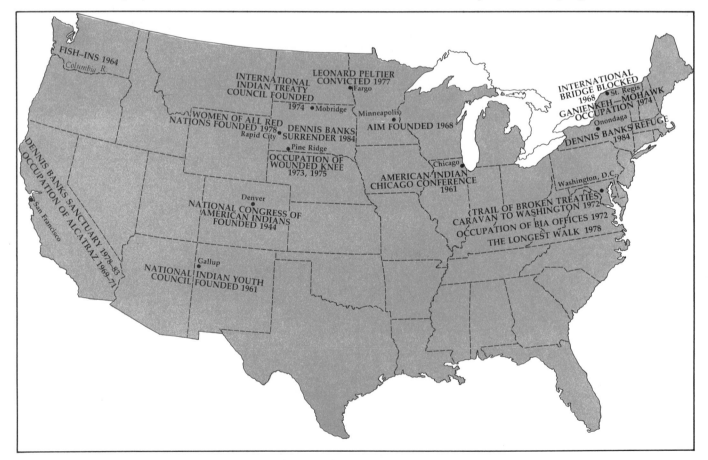

7.5 INDIAN ACTIVISM *in the 20th century, showing the formation of important organizations, and major incidents*

only hope for true social reform, they believed, was not surrogate action by whites but direct Native American political action, including wide-based pan-Indian organization and lobbying, plus occasional demonstrations, vandalism, and acts of violence to draw public attention to the Indian plight from an otherwise somnolent, uncaring society.

The history of the Indian movement since the 1960s—the struggle for "Red Power"—involves many incidents, individuals, organizations, and publications on both the tribal and national level (and the international as well, with activists extending their coalition into Canada, and Central and South America). Here is a brief summary of key dates and events that correspond to changes in United States Indian policy as presented in that section of this chapter:

In 1961, the American Indian Chicago Conference convened in Chicago—almost 500 delegates from 67 tribes, most with close ties to the National Congress of American Indians (NCAI)—to review pan-Indian policies and plan for the future. The conference, which came to define itself as the American Indian Charter Convention, issued a Declaration of Indian Purpose, calling for greater Indian involvement in the decision-making process of all governmental programs affecting Indians.

Some of the younger participants at the convention wanted more direct political action than called for by the tribal elders of the NCAI, and soon after in Gallup, New Mexico, they founded the National Indian Youth Council (NIYC). NIYC founders and leaders were Clyde Warrior, a Ponca, and Melvin Thom, a Paiute. Out of their efforts came an action program and a newspaper, *ABC: Americans Before Columbus*. In 1964, the NIYC sponsored a number of "fish-ins" along rivers in the state of Washington, in support of aboriginal fishing rights nullified by a state supreme court decision. Out of this action came the Survival of the American Indians Association.

Pan-Indian political action also effected the "Resolution of the Thirty Tribes" against an omnibus bill, the Indian Resources Development Act, which would have given more power to the federal government in Indian land transactions, but which was defeated in Congress in 1967. And in 1968, in a successful joint American and Canadian effort, Mohawks at St. Regis blocked the St. Lawrence Seaway International Bridge to protest the failure of the Canadian government to honor the Jay Treaty of 1795, guaranteeing tribal members the right to unrestricted travel between Canada and the United States. The Indian activist movement of the period led to many other national and regional organizations—political, legal, and cultural—such as AMERIND, United Native Americans, the Alaskan Federation of Natives, the Indian Land Rights Association, the American Indian Civil Rights Council, and the American Indian Culture Research Center.

The most important organization, in terms of recent activism, turned out to be the American Indian Movement (AIM), founded in Minneapolis in 1968 by the Chippewas Dennis Banks, George Mitchell, and Clyde Bellecourt, as well as the Sioux Russell Means, who became spokesmen for urban Indians. AIM more than any other group was responsible for the upsurge in militant political action in the late 1960s and early 1970s, especially the occupation of federally held property to dramatize the Native American cause. The takeover of the abandoned island of Alcatraz in 1969 gained worldwide attention and support. But when public interest waned by 1971, federal marshalls made their move and dislodged the dissidents. In less-publicized events, Indian activists occupied the federal building in Littleton, Colorado; Ft. Lawton in Washington; Mt. Rushmore; Stanley Island; Ellis Island; and the Coast Guard Station on Lake Michigan. Another dramatic action of the period was the Trail of Broken Treaties Caravan in 1972, consisting of a march on Washington, D.C., and the subsequent six-day demonstration during which dissidents occupied BIA offices and destroyed public files.

Then, the following year, 1973, AIM members and supporters occupied the Sioux Pine Ridge reservation in South Dakota, the site of the Wounded Knee Massacre of 1890. The occupation grew out of a dispute among the Indians themselves. Young activists demonstrated against what they considered to be the autocratic and sometimes corrupt practices of the elder Sioux leaders. But the occupation evolved into a state of siege, with the dissidents holding out behind roadblocks and barriers against federal agents. One of the Indian demands was a review of the

Preparing for the Great Jim Thorpe Longest Run, Onondaga Reservation, New York. Photo by Molly Braun.

historical treaties, between the federal government and the tribes, that AIM alleged had been broken. By the time a settlement had been reached, after 71 days of alternate shootings, negotiations, and inactivity, two Indians, Frank Clearwater and Buddy Lamont, had been killed and a federal marshall wounded. AIM leaders were subsequently indicted, but the case was dismissed on grounds of misconduct by the prosecution.

A second shootout on the Pine Ridge reservation in 1975 led to the death of two FBI agents and the conviction of Leonard Peltier, who is still in jail and whose situation has come to be a rallying point for Indian activists.

Another prominent Indian activist, one of AIM's co-founders, Dennis Banks, was convicted in 1975 of riot and assault in a demonstration two years earlier at Custer, South Dakota (just before the occupation of Wounded Knee), in protest over the judicial handling of a case involving an Indian's death. Banks fled before sentencing to Oregon and then, in 1978, he took refuge in California. California's governor at the time, Jerry Brown, was sympathetic to the Native American cause and protected Banks from extradition, allowing him free movement within the state to earn a living as a college administrator and

Dennis Banks speaking at the Great Jim Thorpe Longest Run, Onondaga Reservation, New York. Photo by Molly Braun.

lecturer. Just before Brown's term expired in 1983, Banks asked and received sanctuary among the Onondagas of New York, in the hope that New York's newly elected governor, Mario Cuomo, would also prove supportive. Cuomo refused to grant sanctuary to the AIM leader, but he agreed not to make any legal move on him if Banks stayed on the Onondaga reservation. Indian activists claimed that the fact Banks had participated in a trial of the Tribal Court of the Rosebud reservation in 1973, which found William Janklow, who later became governor of South Dakota, guilty in the rape of an Indian

girl, had turned the pursuit of Banks by state officials into a personal vendetta. (The rape charge was never brought before federal courts and Janklow denies the incident.)

In any case, while at Onondaga, Banks used his organizational skills to help arrange the Great Jim Thorpe Longest Run, in which Native American individuals and teams of various tribes carried medicine bundles from the Onondaga reservation through 14 states to Los Angeles, the location of the Jim Thorpe Memorial Pow-Wow and Games, sponsored by the Native American Fine Arts Society. Both events, the run and games, were staged in 1984, the year of the Los Angeles Olympics, to honor the great Olympic and Carlisle School Indian athlete Jim Thorpe, who won both the decathlon and pentathlon at the 1912 Stockholm Olympics, then had his medals stripped the next year because he had played a season of semi-professional baseball. (In 1983, the International Olympic Committee reinstated the medals.)

Yet, on September 13, 1984, stating that he wanted to "get on with his life," Dennis Banks surrendered to state and local law-enforcement officials in Rapid City, South Dakota. On October 8, he was sentenced to three years in prison.

Other milestones in the Indian movement have been the formation in 1974 of a grass-roots coalition, the International Indian Treaty Council, and its recognition three years later as a non-governmental organization by the United Nations; "Ganienkeh," the Mohawk occupation of state lands in the Adirondacks beginning in 1974; the presentation in 1977 of a resolution to the International Human Rights Conference in Geneva, Switzerland, calling for United Nations recognition of Indian tribes as sovereign nations; the formation of the Council of Energy Resource Tribes (CERT) in 1975, to protect resources on reservations and develop them for greater Indian profit; the formulation in 1978 of the Women of All Red Nations (WARN), an activist women's organization; and the Longest Walk to Washington, D.C., in 1978

CANADA'S INDIAN POLICY AND THE INDIAN CONDITION

Canada's Indian policy, like that of the United States, evolved out of colonial England's policy, but it remained closer to it over the ensuing years. The Royal Proclamation of 1763, prohibiting the displacement of native population without both tribal and Crown consent, became the basis for later Indian policy. And a centralized Indian department, structured earlier in 1754 by colonial representatives at the Albany Congress, became the bureaucracy for administering that policy.

During the following century, starting in the 1830s, England adopted as common practice the setting aside of Indian reserve lands, the titles of which were to be vested in the Crown, with the idea of establishing locations where Indians might be Christianized and "civilized"—a dual policy of protection and assimilation. Lands that France had earlier set aside for Indians remained in Indian hands, and new reservations were formed. In 1850, the government signed the first in a series of treaties with tribes, gaining control of the majority of Indian territory in exchange for guaranteed reserve lands and perpetual trusteeship under the British Crown, plus one-time payments and annuities in cash and goods, and the promise of schools and services. (See "Canadian Indian Wars" in chapter 5 and "The Growth of Canada and Indian Land Cessions" in chapter 6.)

In the years just before Confederation, England transferred control of Indian affairs to Canada and its provinces. With the British North America Act of 1867 and the Indian Act of 1868, the new Dominion's Indian policy and its administrative machinery, the Department of Indian Affairs, were redefined and structured, drawing heavily on the earlier British model. The Indian Act of 1876 further shaped

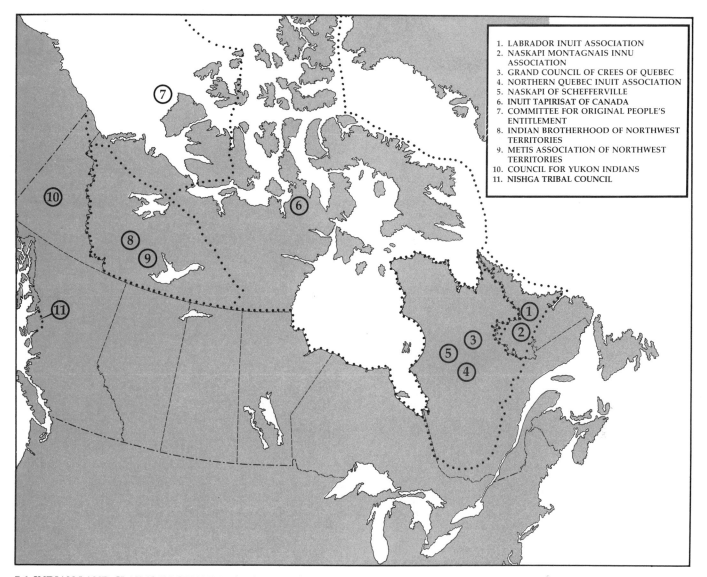

7.6 INDIAN LAND CLAIMS IN CANADA, *showing comprehensive claims to traditional land use and occupancy by native associations to be negotiated by the Office of Native Claims*

1. LABRADOR INUIT ASSOCIATION
2. NASKAPI MONTAGNAIS INNU ASSOCIATION
3. GRAND COUNCIL OF CREES OF QUEBEC
4. NORTHERN QUEBEC INUIT ASSOCIATION
5. NASKAPI OF SCHEFFERVILLE
6. INUIT TAPIRISAT OF CANADA
7. COMMITTEE FOR ORIGINAL PEOPLE'S ENTITLEMENT
8. INDIAN BROTHERHOOD OF NORTHWEST TERRITORIES
9. METIS ASSOCIATION OF NORTHWEST TERRITORIES
10. COUNCIL FOR YUKON INDIANS
11. NISHGA TRIBAL COUNCIL

Canada's Indian policy, granting individual Indians, or bands by majority vote, the right to request enfranchisement as Canadian citizens, thereby renouncing rights and privileges as "status" natives to become "non-status" natives. Status women who married citizens were automatically to become enfranchised.

Canada's Indian policy stayed on this same course into the 20th century. Additional treaties were negotiated and additional reserves established until 1923. The Confederation government continued to encourage acculturation. By mid-century, the government instituted a revised policy under the Indian Act of 1951, which gave Indians the right to vote in national (although not provincial)

elections and made them generally subject to the same laws as other Canadians. The system of enfranchisement was maintained in combination with the Department of Indian Affairs' Band Lists of status Indians, plus the General List of status Indians not registered as part of a band.

In 1969, because of criticism concerning the paternalistic nature of Indian policy, Jean Chretien, the minister of Indian Affairs, offered the *Statement of the Government of Canada on Indian Policy,* popularly known as the White Paper, which called for the repeal of the Indian Act, the abolition of the Indian Department, the transfer of Indian affairs to provincial governments, and the transfer of Indian land management to the bands them-

selves—in effect, termination of the special trust relationship. Yet the plan was never implemented. The White Paper met with almost unanimous opposition from the Indian population, who feared the loss of lands, loss of governmental treaty obligations, and loss of tribal identity and culture. Similarly, most Canadian Indians have resisted assimilation and enfranchisement in order to preserve lands, rights, and heritage.

Since the rejection of the White Paper, the government, with a new awareness of Indian needs and aspirations, has shifted its policy away from assimilation to Indian self-determination and cultural expression, along with continuing protection. Antiquated legislation and adminis-

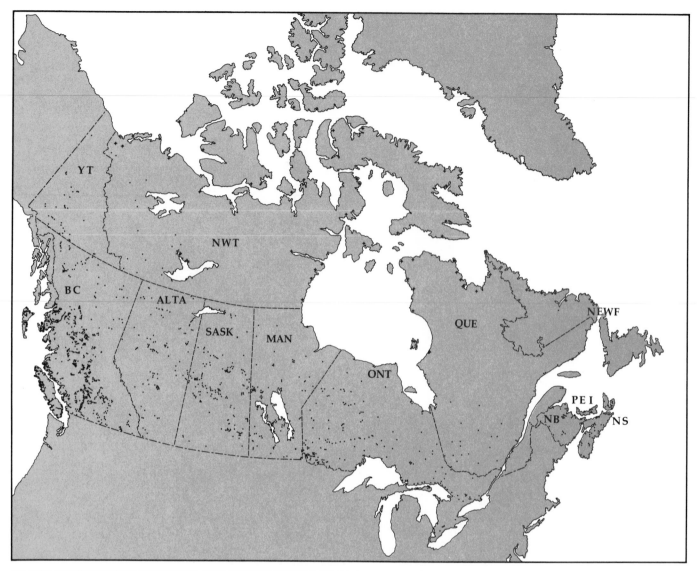

7.7 THE DISTRIBUTION OF INDIAN AND INUIT RESERVES IN CANADA. *Dots show the general locations of 2,242 tracts of land held by 573 recognized bands, with no indication of size or shape. In certain cases, a single dot represents more than one tract. (See also band list in the Appendix.)*

Caughnawaga Iroquois Reserve, Quebec. Photo by Molly Braun.

trative practices suppressing Indian language and culture have been ferreted out. The abolition of the last of the Indian agents from the reserves the same year as the White Paper has also helped counter a paternalistic federal bureaucracy. Moreover, with the *Statement on Claims of Indian and Inuit People* in 1973, and the establishment of the Office of Native Claims in 1974, the government has set up the machinery to hear and act on Indian claims—both "comprehensive claims," based on the notion of aboriginal title to land, and "specific claims," based on lawful treaty obligations and government mismanagement of band assets.

The stated current mandate of the Department of Indian Affairs and Northern Department (DIAND) is "initiating, encouraging, and supporting measures that will respond to the needs and aspirations of Indian and Inuit people and improve their social, cultural, and economic well-being." DIAND oversees Indian social services, including education, housing, medical care, loans, and job placement, and administers trust monies from the sale and lease of reserve lands. Nevertheless, in spite of the overall greater consistency in Canada's Indian policy, without periods of forced allotment and termination as in the United States, as well as the fact that Canada historically did not war with its Indians to the same degree, violate as many treaties, or experience the same degree of corruption in its Indian service, the present-day Canadian Indian condition is similar to that of fellow Indians across the border, with the same persistent problems and obstacles. Likewise, Indian activists view the challenge in both countries as one and the same.

The following statistics are a barometer of the difficult social, health, economic, and educational conditions facing Indians in Canada. There are roughly 300,000 Indians and 25,000 Eskimos in Canada, only two percent of the national population, but the number has been climbing rapidly. And among these Indians of 10 distinct language families and 58 dialects, there are 573 bands—the political unit recognized by the government—with an average membership of 525 people, and with each band having an elected chief and representative band council. The various bands hold 2,242 separate parcels of land, with a total area of 10,021 square miles. Just less than 30 percent of the total native population lives off-reserve, although a certain number travel back and forth periodically. For Indians in Canada, overall life expectancy is 10 years less than the national average. Perinatal and neonatal Indian mortality is almost twice as high. Violent deaths are three times as high. Suicides occur among Indians at more than six times the national rate. Indians are jailed at more than three times the national rate. Over 50 percent of Indian health problems are alcohol-related. One out of three Indian families lives in crowded conditions. Only 50–60 percent of Indian housing has running water and sewage disposal. Although participation in elementary schools has recently approached the national level, secondary school participation is still 12 percent lower, with a com-

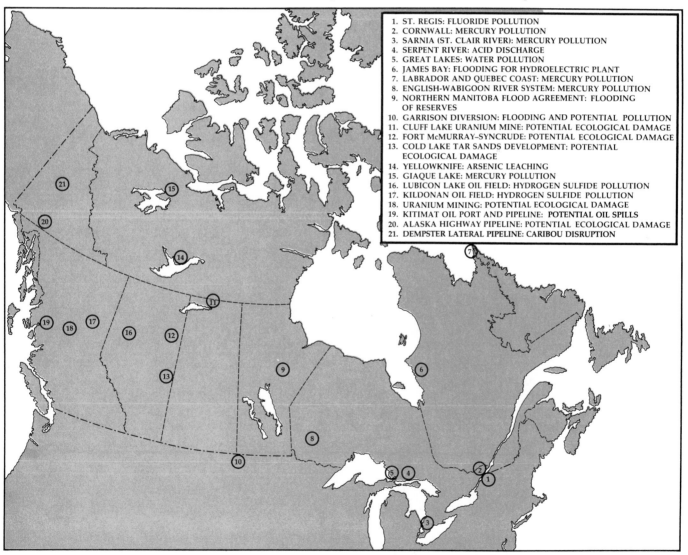

1. ST. REGIS: FLUORIDE POLLUTION
2. CORNWALL: MERCURY POLLUTION
3. SARNIA (ST. CLAIR RIVER): MERCURY POLLUTION
4. SERPENT RIVER: ACID DISCHARGE
5. GREAT LAKES: WATER POLLUTION
6. JAMES BAY: FLOODING FOR HYDROELECTRIC PLANT
7. LABRADOR AND QUEBEC COAST: MERCURY POLLUTION
8. ENGLISH-WABIGOON RIVER SYSTEM: MERCURY POLLUTION
9. NORTHERN MANITOBA FLOOD AGREEMENT: FLOODING OF RESERVES
10. GARRISON DIVERSION: FLOODING AND POTENTIAL POLLUTION
11. CLUFF LAKE URANIUM MINE: POTENTIAL ECOLOGICAL DAMAGE
12. FORT McMURRAY–SYNCRUDE: POTENTIAL ECOLOGICAL DAMAGE
13. COLD LAKE TAR SANDS DEVELOPMENT: POTENTIAL ECOLOGICAL DAMAGE
14. YELLOWKNIFE: ARSENIC LEACHING
15. GIAQUE LAKE: MERCURY POLLUTION
16. LUBICON LAKE OIL FIELD: HYDROGEN SULFIDE POLLUTION
17. KILDONAN OIL FIELD: HYDROGEN SULFIDE POLLUTION
18. URANIUM MINING: POTENTIAL ECOLOGICAL DAMAGE
19. KITIMAT OIL PORT AND PIPELINE: POTENTIAL OIL SPILLS
20. ALASKA HIGHWAY PIPELINE: POTENTIAL ECOLOGICAL DAMAGE
21. DEMPSTER LATERAL PIPELINE: CARIBOU DISRUPTION

7.8 ENVIRONMENTAL HAZARDS TO INDIANS IN CANADA, *showing selected sites of industrial pollution*

pletion rate of about 20 percent, as compared to a national rate of 75 percent. University participation is less than half the national level. Participation in the labor force is less than 40 percent. And with employment at only about 30 percent of the working-age group, and average income well below national levels, about 50 percent of the Indian population has to resort to governmental social assistance. Even for off-reserve Indians who have attempted to enter the economic mainstream, the levels of unemployment and governmental dependency stand at about 25–30 percent.

Among the reasons cited by DIAND for these conditions are the lack of an independent economic base in Indian communities, government programs that have reinforced a sense of dependency among Indians, too rapid development after years of isolation, minimal education, and a rapid increase since 1950 of the Indian population. For Indians who have left the reserves, these problems have been compounded by the lack of social and cultural linkage.

Moreover, in addition to the challenges facing Indians, as reflected in these statistics, another area of difficulty has escalated in recent years. Increased industrial activity and resource development projects in remote wilderness areas has meant new environmental damage, erosion of the Indian land base, and disruption of Indian ways of life. New health hazards have been created through industrial and chemical pollution; fish and game populations have been depleted; native peoples and communities have been displaced; traditional ways of life have been disrupted by the incursion of a large outside population, along with the loss of their own band members into the wage economy. In some instances, the agent of dispossession is private industry; in others, the provincial or federal government through public works. Whichever, Indian activists claim that, in not adequately protecting Indian interests, the national government is not fulfilling its side of the trust relationship. In fact, they point

out, the very concerns of the Department of Indian Affairs would seem to be in conflict with those of its branch department, Northern Development.

With regard to the issue of northern development, Canada has recently taken a positive step toward greater native control of policies and resources. A new Canadian territory might be carved out of northern and eastern sections of the Northwest Territories—Nunavut. It would be predominantly Inuit, bringing many native peoples into the political process; Frobisher Bay would be the capital. The proposed territory has been approved in a territorial plebiscite and has the endorsement of the national government. But before Nunavut can become a reality, various land claims have to be negotiated and boundaries finalized.

INDIAN CULTURAL RENEWAL

As has been expressed earlier in this chapter, the contemporary Indian socioeconomic condition in both the United States and Canada is a difficult one, with many problems carried over from the past and many challenges for the future. Concern and urgency are called for because of old social injustices and new environmental threats. Yet, some aspects of the contemporary Indian question leave room for celebration. Although many Indians as individuals suffer in poverty and cultural alienation, with relatively few able to break out of the cycle of deprivation to higher standards of living, Indian culture as a whole is in a vital, creative, and politically involved stage. And although society at large is stubbornly indifferent to the interests of particular subgroups within it, many non-Indian individuals are attuned to the Indian presence and are interested in Indian history and culture.

On the positive side of the Native North American situation, Indian art is enjoying a renaissance: first, in the realm of fine arts, where Indian

painters and sculptures, in a burst of new esthetics that blend the traditional with the modern, have developed international reputations; and second, in the realm of Indian arts and crafts, where many Indians, using traditional techniques and forms, have found reliable markets among both tourists and serious collectors. The same vitality is found in the dramatic arts, many Indians having established reputations in ballet, theater, and film; and others have been successful working in traditional forms of music, dance, and storytelling. Likewise, many Indians have established themselves in the field of literature, drawing on the rich and challenging Indian experience in novels and poetry. Indian artists have continuity with the past through both old and new forms.

Another positive development since the days of coercive assimilation earlier in the century is tribal restoration. Cohesive in nature, tribes serve as large extended families for members. Although reservations often reveal a shocking degree of poverty, they all manifest a degree of social integration and community rarely found in other parts of American and Canadian society. Moreover, tribes function as business concerns or corporations, protecting and serving individual interests. There is widespread Indian participation at the tribal level, more than found at most other local levels of society. Tribes have increasingly taken control of their destiny from the federal bureaucracy and, when possible, from outside exploitative interests. And there are tribal economic success stories— solid incomes or, in some instances, even fortunes made through tourism, industrial development, and wise investment of land-claim awards.

Along with tribal restoration comes newfound Indian identity. A growing number of pan-Indian coalitions, organizations, publications, and powwows have contributed to this sense of common purpose, even at the international level. Differences between various factions—one tribe and others; reservation Indians and urban Indians; elders and youth; as-

Jim Skye Musicians at the Iroquois Indian Festival, Cobleskill, New York. Photo by Molly Braun.

similationists and traditionalists; conservatives and activists; whatever the breakdown—increasingly have been resolved since the political catharsis of the 1960s and 1970s, and common threats to Indian progress have been recognized. Practically all the tribes and factions have grown in political and legal awareness. Indians are less likely than ever to be exploited by bureaucrats and businessmen. Religion plays a large part in this pan-Indian revitalization, organizations such as the Native American Church having a large intertribal membership. The Indian Religion Freedom Act of 1978 has given Indian groups new legal ammunition in the protection of sacred lands.

Self-betterment for some Indians has meant integration into the American mainstream. Educated and trained individuals are found in fields other than the arts—civil service, academia, medicine, law—as well as in blue-collar professions, such as high-steel construction. Some stay in close cultural contact with other Indians, choosing to live or work among them. For those who do not, their "Indianness" fosters a greater sense of pride than ever before in this century. And whites now often brag about any Indian ancestry they have.

Indian pride is well founded. Contributions to American and Canadian civilization are apparent for anyone who takes the time to look. Historically, Indian assistance and knowledge helped explorers and settlers survive in the North American wilderness. Indian hunters revolutionized European markets through the fur trade. Indian trails evolved into modern roads and highways. Cultur-

Fancy Dancer, Onondaga Reservation, New York. Photo by Molly Braun.

ally, Indians also changed the world through the diffusion of new staple food crops—corn, potato, tomato, sunflower, and squash, to name a few. In the healing arts, Indian knowledge of herbs and animal derivatives has contributed to modern medicine. Indian military techniques have been adapted by many modern armies. Indian forms of government—confederations, such as the Iroquois League, with emphasis on individual rights—have influenced modern democracies. Also, both the United States and Canada have thousands of Indian place-names, and the English and French languages contain many Indian loan words. Many originally Indian objects and technologies are widespread in the world—canoes, kayaks, moccasins, parkas, tents, cotton, rubber, etc.—and Indian esthetics have influenced world art and design.

There is another aspect to the Indian contribution that is more difficult to measure and that can be called the philosophical or the spiritual element in the Indian example. Indians represent heroic and romantic historical figures who held out, through skill and courage, against overwhelming forces. They also represent beings who were in tune with themselves, one another, and nature. Balance and harmony are concepts often applied to Indian ways of life, as well as to Indian inner life. For societies alarmed by ecological damage from modern technologies, Indian coexistence with the natural environment serves as a model for survival. And Indian humor, stoicism, and focus serve as inspiration. The Indian world view continues to have relevance.

For civilizations based on cultural pluralism, native peoples should hold symbolic places of honor as the first North Americans. And, for having been deprived of most of what was once all their land by the people who came after them, they should be granted the necessary means to achieve their social and cultural goals. Native North American culture in both the United States and Canada is a national treasure. Its renewal is everyone's renewal.

Appendix

CHRONOLOGY OF NORTH AMERICAN INDIAN HISTORY

circa 50,000–11,000 B.C.
Waves of Paleo-Siberians arrive in the New World from Asia, across the Bering Strait Land Bridge (Beringia), and disperse throughout the Americas.

c. 50,000—5,000 B.C.
So called-Lithic (or Paleo-Indian) period, characterized by migratory big-game hunting and chipped-stone artifacts.
   c. 50,000–25,000 B.C.: Pre-Projectile-Point stage.
   c. 25,000–10,000 B.C.: Sandia Spear-Point culture.
   c. 15,000–8,000 B.C.: Clovis (or Llano) Spear-Point culture.
   c. 8,000–7,000 B.C.: Folsom Spear-Point culture. Development of atlatl spear-throwing device.
   c. 7,500–4,500 B.C.: Plano (Plainview) Spear-Point culture.

c. 10,000–8,000 B.C.
Pleistocene epoch (Ice Age) ends with final retreat of northern glaciers.

c. 9,000–5,000 B.C.
Big-game species become extinct, including mastodons, wooly mammoths, lions, saber-toothed tigers, tapirs, ground sloths, bighorn bisons, camels, giant armadillos, and native horses.
   c. 8,000 B.C.: Climate is warm enough to support cone-bearing trees.
   c. 6,000 B.C.: Climate is warm enough to support deciduous trees.

c. 9,000 B.C.
Old Cordilleran culture (Cascade) established on the Columbian Plateau. (Protoarchaic forerunner of later Archaic period.)

c. 9,000 B.C.
Desert culture established in Great Basin. (Protoarchaic forerunner of later Archaic period.)
   c. 7,500 B.C.: Early twined baskets at Danger Cave.
   c.7,000–1,000 B.C.: Cochise culture (branch of Desert culture) in Southwest.

c. 8,000 (or 5,000)–1,000 B.C.
So-called Archaic (or Foraging) period, characterized by migratory hunting and gathering of a wide assortment of fauna and flora, as well as by the use of a wide assortment of tools and utensils.

c. 7,000–2,000 B.C.
While Archaic cultures are dominant in North America, the Mesoindian phase occurs in Middle America, characterized by beginnings of food production and pottery, setting stage for later Formative period (or Preclassic period).
   c. 7,000–5,000 B.C.: Many wild plants, including maize, are collected. Squash, pumpkins, gourds, beans, and peppers are first cultivated.
   c. 5,000–3,500 B.C.: Cultivated strain of maize is introduced.
   c. 4,500 B.C.: Chalco-style pottery is developed.
   c. 3,500 B.C.: Cultivated maize as far north as New Mexico is found among Cochise people.
   c. 2,500 B.C.: Improved hybrid strain of maize is introduced.
   c. 2,500–1,500 B.C.: Permanent villages established in Middle America, with agriculture-based economics. Irrigation is developed.
   c. 2,000 B.C.: Agriculture and pottery spread into much of North America.

c. 4,000–1,500 B.C.
Old Copper culture active around Great Lakes.

c. 3,000–500 B.C.
Red Paint People active in Northeast.

c. 3,000–1,000 B.C.
Aleuts and Eskimos migrate from Siberia to New World.

c. 2,000–1,500 B.C.
Indians of Southeast first make pottery. Pottery culture spreads throughout North America.

c. 1,500 B.C.
Dog domesticated in North and Middle America.

c. 1,500 (or 1,000) B.C.–A.D. 1000 (or 1500)
So-called Formative period, characterized by village life, use of agriculture, pottery making, weaving, stone carving, ceremonial structures, and trade. (Referred to as Preclassic period in reference to Middle America: 1,500 B.C.–A.D. 300.)

c. 1,500 B.C.–A.D. 300
Olmec civilization in Middle America.
   c. 1,200–900 B.C.: City of San Lorenzo flourishes.
   c. 800–400 B.C.: La Venta flourishes.
   c. 100 B.C.: Tres Zapotes flourishes.

c. 1,400 B.C.–A.D. 1500
Woodland cultures in East. (Comprehensive term used to describe a variety of Formative cultures and stages in East, including Adena, Hopewell, Mississippian, and others.)

c. 1,000 B.C.–A.D. 200
Adena (Mound Building) culture in and around Ohio Valley.

c. 300 B.C.–A.D. 700
Hopewell (Mound Building) culture in East.

c. 300 B.C.–A.D. 1300
Mogollon culture in Southwest.
   c. A.D. 900: Mimbres-style painted pottery.

c. 100 B.C.–A.D. 1500
Hohokam culture in Southwest. Extensive canal systems developed to irrigate desert.
   c. A.D. 1000: Hohokam people develop acid etching of shells.

100 B.C.–A.D. 1500
Patayan or Hakataya culture in Southwest (sometimes considered Pioneer stage of Hohokam culture).

c. 100 B.C.–A.D. 1300
Anasazi culture in Southwest.
  c. 100 B.C.–A.D. 750: Basket Maker period.
  c. A.D. 750–1300: Pueblo period.
  c. A.D. 1150: Pueblo of Oraibi founded, oldest continuously occupied town in U.S.

A.D. c. 300–900
So-called Classic period in Middle America, characterized by highly developed civilizations with hieroglyphic writing systems, elaborate calendars, and ceremonial centers containing large temples.
  c. 300–700: City of Teotihuacan flourishes in Central America. (Unidentified people and culture founded city.)
  c. 300–900: Mayan civilization dominant in Central America.
  c. 600: Zapotecs inhabit Monte Alban at Oaxaca.
  c. 700: Chichimecs invade Tehuacan Valley from north.
  c. 900: Mixtecs inhabit Monte Alban at Oaxaca.

c. 500
Bow and arrow widely used in North America, generally replacing atlatl. By **c. 1,000,** use of the bow and arrow has also spread to Middle America.

c. 700–1700
Mississippian (Temple Mound Building) culture in Mississippi Basin and Southeast.
  c. 1500: Southern Death Cult at cultural zenith.

c. 825
Ancestral Apache bands break from northern Athapascan groups and migrate into Southwest.

c. 900–1500
So-called Postclassic period in Middle America.
  c. 900–1200: Toltecs (a Chichimec people) invade from north and become dominant in Middle America. **c. 987:** Toltecs make Tula their capital.
  c. 900–1200: Mayas on Yucatan Peninsula.
  c. 900: Mixtecs use Monte Alban at Oaxaca as cemetery.
  c. 1200–1500: Aztec civilization dominant. **c. 1325:** Aztecs build Tenochtitlan (site of present-day Mexico City).

c. 1000
Indians of Middle America begin using "lost wax" process to cast copper bells, as metallurgy spreads throughout region from South America.

c. 985–1014
Norsemen, including Eric the Red and Leif Ericson, establish settlements in Greenland and North America and encounter Eskimos, Beothuks, or Micmacs.

c. 1025
Ancestral Navajo bands break from northern Athapascans and migrate into Southwest.

c. 1275
Drought and raiding Athapascans cause abandonment of many pueblo cities in Southwest.

1492
Christopher Columbus (backed by Spain) reaches the island of San Salvador (Guanahani to the natives) in the Caribbean and encounters Arawaks. Believing he has reached India, Columbus refers to the inhabitants as "Indians," a name that endures. At this time in the Americas, there are millions of Native Americans, speaking thousands of distinct languages.

1497–98
John and Sebastian Cabot (backed by England) explore eastern coastline of North America. They kidnap three Micmac Indians.

1497–1503
Amerigo Vespucci (backed by Spain) explores West Indies and South America.

c. 1500
European diseases begin ravaging North American Indians.

1501
Gaspar Corte Real (backed by Portugal) explores East Coast and kidnaps more than 50 Indians.

1512
Spanish "Law of Burgos" gives right to Spanish land grantees to make slaves of Indians on granted lands under the *encomienda* system.

1512
Bartholome de las Casas becomes missionary to Indians of Cuba, and he writes tracts defending Indians against Spanish misrule.

1512
Pope Julius II decrees that Indians are descended from Adam and Eve.

1513
Vasco Nunez de Balboa crosses Middle America and sights Pacific Ocean.

1513–21
Ponce de Leon (backed by Spain) reaches Florida and has extensive

contact with Indians. Calusa Indians in 80 war canoes drive his ships away from the coast. On a second expedition in 1521, he is wounded by a Seminole arrow and later dies in Havana.

1517–21
Spanish conquest of Middle America. Hernando Cortes conquers Aztecs. The Aztec emperor Montezuma is killed. In **1521,** the colony of New Spain is founded.

1523
A Spanish expedition to America's southern coast returns to Spain with Chicora, a captured Indian. The historian Peter Martyr uses Chicora as a historical source, making him the first Indian informant.

1523–24
Giovanni da Verrazano (backed by France) explores the Atlantic Coast, encountering Wampanoag, Narraganset, and Delaware Indians.

1528–36
Men of the Panfilo de Narvaez Expedition (Spain), including Alvar Nunez Cabeza de Vaca and Estevan the Moor, trek through the Southeast into the Southwest, encountering many tribes.

1534–41
Jacques Cartier (France) explores the St. Lawrence River system in three voyages, making contact with Algonquian- and Iroquoian-speaking tribes of the Northeast. On a second voyage, he reaches the Huron settlements of Stadacona and Hochelaga (present sites of Quebec City and Montreal).

1539
Marcos de Niza and Estevan the Moor (Spain) explore the Southwest.

1539
Lectures of Francisco de Vitoria in Spain advocate that Indians are free men and exempt from slavery.

1539–43
Hernando de Soto claims Florida for Spain and explores the Southeast, encountering and alienating Creek, Hitchiti, Chickasaw, Chakchiuma, Choctaw, Tunica, Yuchi, Cherokee, and Alabama tribes. In **1541,** De Sota dies on the Mississippi River and Luis de Moscoso assumes command.

1540–42
Francisco Vasquez de Coronado (Spain) explores the Southwest in search of the Seven Cities of Cibola, encountering Hopi, Apache, Pawnee, Zuni, and Wichita Indians.

1542
Juan Rodriguez Cabrillo and Bartolome Ferrelo explore the Pacific Coast, encountering numerous California tribes.

c. 1560–70
Iroquois League of Five Nations, including the Mohawk, Oneida, Onondaga, Cayuga, and Seneca tribes, is formed by Deganawida, a Huron Iroquois prophet, and his Mohawk disciple Hiawatha.

1562–64
Jean Ribault establishes a short-lived French Huguenot colony on Parris Island, South Carolina, until the Spanish drive them out.

1564–65
Rene de Laudonniere establishes a French Huguenot colony on the St. Johns River in Florida until the Spanish drive them out. Among the French is the artist Jacques le Moyne, who creates the first-known European pictorial representations of Indians.

1565
Spanish under Pedro Menendez de Aviles found St. Augustine in Florida, the first permanent European settlement in North America.

1568
Jesuits organize a school in Havana for Indian children brought from Florida, thus forming the first missionary school for North American Indians.

1576–78
Martin Frobisher (England) seeks the Northwest Passage, encountering Eskimos.

1578–79
Francis Drake (England) explores the California Coast, encountering Miwoks.

1585–86
First British settlement in North America is founded on Roanoke Island, North Carolina, headed by Richard Grenville and backed by his cousin, Sir Walter Raleigh. It lasts only one year.

1586–90
Sir Walter Raleigh's second attempt at a colony on Roanoke. Governor John White returns to England with paintings of Indians. Potato crop also brought back to England from Indians. Roanoke colony fails when settlers disappear.

1598
Mexico's first effective Indian insurrection occurs among Tepic miners against Spanish.

1598
Juan de Onate founds Spanish colony of San Gabriel del Yunque in northern New Mexico, known today as San Juan Indian Pueblo.

1598–99
Indians of Acoma Pueblo in New Mexico attack a group of visiting Spanish. A year later, a Spanish retaliatory force under Juan de Onate kills as many as 800 Indians.

c. 1600
Sheep brought into the Southwest by Spanish. Use of wool and loom introduced to Indians.

c. 1600–1770
Use of horse spreads from Mexico through the Southwest into the Great Plains.

1603–15
Samuel de Champlain's voyages in the Northeast leads to extensive contact with various Algonquian and Iroquois tribes.
   1603: Visits site of present-day Montreal.
   1605: Founds Port Royal (now Annapolis Royal) with Sieur de Monts in Micmac country.
   1608: Founds Quebec City.
   1609: Discovers lake, which now bears his name.
   1615: Explores Lake Huron and Lake Ontario with Etienne Brule and a party of Hurons.
   1615: Attacks Onondaga villages with Huron war party and turns Iroquois League against French.

1607
English establish their first permanent settlement in North America at Jamestown, Virginia, under John Smith, leading to extensive contact with the Tidewater tribes of the Powhatan Confederacy. In **1609**, John Smith's capture by the Indians gives rise to the story of the intercession by Pocahontas, the daughter of Chief Powhatan, on Smith's behalf. In **1613**, Pocahontas is captured by the settlers and eventually converts to Christianity, marries John Rolfe, and travels to England, where she dies from an illness.

1609
Spanish found Santa Fe in New Mexico.

1609–10
Henry Hudson (Holland) explores river now bearing his name. Two canoes of Manhattan Indians attack his ship. Mahican Indians make peaceful contact.

1613
In response to a shooting attempt on their tribesmen by a Frenchman, the Beothuk Indians in Newfoundland kill 37 fishermen. In retaliation, the French arm the Micmacs, the traditional enemies of the Beothuks, and offer them bounties for scalps, leading to the virtual extinction of the Beothuk tribe.

1614
United New Netherland Company begins developing the Dutch fur trade in North America.

1615
Squanto (or Tisquantum), a Wampanoag, is kidnapped and taken to England. In **1619**, he returns to North America and aids settlers.

1616–20
Smallpox epidemic among the New England Indians living between Narragansett Bay and Penobscot River.

1619
Virginia Company establishes schools for Indians. They are abandoned in **1622**.

1620
Pilgrims arrive in Plymouth. Squanto shows the Pilgrims how to plant corn and how to use fish as fertilizer. In **1621**, with Squanto acting as an interpreter, they make a pact of peace and mutual assistance with Chief Massasoit of the Wampanoags, the first treaty between Indians and whites. The Pilgrims first celebrate Thanksgiving in tribute to a plentiful harvest and peace with the Indians.

1621
Dutch West Indian Company is chartered on the principles of opening trade routes by means of treaties with the Indians.

1622
Powhatan Confederacy of 32 Tidewater tribes under Opechancanough attacks settlers at Jamestown.

1624
Dutch settlers found Fort Orange (Albany) in New Netherland.

1626
Canarsee Indians sell Manhattan Island to Peter Minuit, governor of New Netherlands, for 60 guilders worth of trade goods. Later Dutch have to clear deal with Manhattan Indians, who actually hold the territory.

1627
Company of New France chartered by French to colonize New France and develop the fur trade with Indians.

1629–33
Spanish found Christian missions among Acoma, Hopi, and Zuni tribes.

1631
Thomas James and Luke Fox (England) explore James Bay.

1631
Roger Williams contends that the royal charter for the Massachusetts colony illegally expropriates tribal lands. He urges a humane policy toward Indians. In **1636**, Williams founds Rhode Island, insisting that settlers there must buy land from Indians. In **1642**, Williams's Indian-English dictionary is published in London.

1633
General Court of Massachusetts colony sets precedent of land allotment to Indians and of central rather than local governments handling Indian affairs.

1633–35
Smallpox epidemics among Indians of New England, New France, and New Netherland.

1636–37
Pequot War in New England. The colonists kill more than 600 men, women, and children in a surprise attack on the main stockaded Pequot village.

1638
Reservation is established in New Haven for the Quinnipiacs.

1638
Sweden lays claim to land along the Delaware Bay and maintains a trading post until **1655**.

c. 1640–85
Beaver and otter nearly exterminated in Iroquois country. During the years that follow, until about **1685**, the Iroquois League of Five Nations wages war on and defeats the Hurons, Tobaccos, Neutrals, Eries, Mahicans, and Susquehannocks. In **1650**, 300 Hurons settled at Lorette under the protection of the French.

1641
In reaction to the killing of a Staten Island farmer by a group of Raritans, the Dutch offer bounties for Raritan scalps or heads.

1642
Montreal founded by Sieur de Maisonneuve and Paul de Chomedey.

1643
Mohawks and Dutch sign a treaty. That same year, Dutch settlers attack a group of Wappingers in the Pavonia Massacre.

1644
Powhatan Confederacy mounts a second uprising against Jamestown settlers. Opechancanough dies in captivity.

1644–75
John Eliot converts many New England Indians (the "Praying Indians"). He establishes villages, schools, and a church for them. In **1653**, he publishes *Catechism in the Indian Language* in an Algonquian dialect. In **1681**, he publishes his translation of the Bible into the Algonquian language.

1655
Peach Wars sparks a period of violence between Dutch and Hudson River Indians, which lasts until **1664**.

1661
Spanish raid the sacred kivas of the Pueblo Indians and destroy hundreds of *kachina* masks in an effort to suppress Indian religion.

1663
Company of the New France disbanded, and New France becomes a colony with a royal governor.

1664
English gain control of New Netherland from the Dutch and become allies and trade partners with the Iroquois League. New Amsterdam on Manhattan Island becomes New York.

1668–69
Pierre Esprit Radisson and Sieur de Groseilliers explore west of the St. Lawrence River as far as Lake Superior, plus the Hudson Bay region, for England.

1669–73
Louis Jolliet and Jacques Marquette (France) explore the Great Lakes and the Mississippi River.

1670
Hudson's Bay Company is chartered.

1672
Colonial postal clerks use Indian couriers to carry mail between New York City and Albany

because winter weather is too severe for white couriers.

c. 1675
Use of European glass beads to decorate apparel spreads among eastern Indians, replacing porcupine quillwork.

1675
The English establish a Board of Commissioners and a secretary of Indian Affairs in Albany.

1675–76
King Philip's War between the Wampanoags, Narragansets, and Nipmucs, and the New England Confederation of colonies. Metacom (King Philip) is killed in **1676.**

1676
Bacon's Rebellion against royal authority in Virginia leads to the defeat of the Susquehannocks and Virginia Tidewater tribes by settlers.

1676
Caughnawaga is founded in Quebec for Iroquois converts to Christianity.

1678–79
Daniel Greysolon Duluth (France) explores Great Lakes and negotiates treaties between the warring Ojibway (Chippewa) and Sioux.

1680
Pueblo Indians stage the Pueblo Rebellion under Pope, a Tewa medicine man, against Spanish rule and religion, and manage to drive out the occupiers. In **1689,** the Spanish begin reconquest of the Pueblo Indians.

1682
Rene Cavalier de la Salle claims the Mississippi Valley (Louisiana) for France. In **1685,** he establishes a settlement on Matagorda Bay on the Gulf of Mexico.

1682
William Penn's treaty with the Delawares begins a period of friendly relations between the Quakers and Indians.

1689
Nicholas Perrot formally claims upper Mississippi region for France.

1689–92
Henry Kelsey (England) explores the Canadian Plains.

1689–97
King William's War, the first in a series of colonial wars between England and France, and their respective Indian allies. The period of warfare lasts almost 75 years, to **1763** (referred to as the French and Indian Wars). During these wars, generally speaking, the Iroquois League sides with the British, and the Algonquian tribes side with the French.

1691
College of William and Mary chartered in Virginia. In the years to come, it is attended by many Indian students.

1695
First Pima Uprising against the Spanish in the Southwest.

1702–13
Queen Anne's War—between England and France in the Northeast, and between England and Spain in the Southeast, and their various Indian allies.

1703–04
The English and their Indian auxiliaries attack Spanish missions among the Apalachees of Florida and practically annihilate the tribe.

1710
Three Mohawk chiefs and one Mahican are received in Queen Anne's court as "The Four Kings" of the New World.

1711–13
Tuscarora War on the North Carolina frontier, between British settlers and Tuscarora Indians. Remnants of the tribe migrate north. In **1722,** they are formally recognized as part of the Iroquois League.

1715–28
Yamasee War in South Carolina, between the British and Yamasees.

1720–35
Fox Resistance against the French in the Great Lakes country.

1720–52
Chickasaws fight French and Choctaws in the Southeast.

1723
First permanent Indian school created in Williamsburg, Virginia, with funds provided by the British scientist Robert Boyle.

1727–43
Sieur de la Verendrye and his sons (France) explore the Great Plains.

1729
French governor of Louisiana orders Natchez Indians to evacuate their main village, to use it as his plantation site. In response, the Natchez kill 200 Frenchmen at Fort Rosalie. The French retaliate in force, defeating the Natchez.

1730
Seven Cherokee Indian chiefs visit London and form an alliance, "The Articles of Agreement," with King George II.

1738
Smallpox epidemic among Cherokees of Southeast. Smallpox also reaches tribes in western Canada.

1739–41
War of Jenkins's Ear, between England and Spain in the Caribbean.

1739–41
Paul and Pierre Mallet (France) explore the Missouri, Platte, and Canadian rivers.

1741
Vitus Bering (Russia) reaches Alaska.

1744–48
King George's War, between the French and British, and their respective Indian allies.

1746
Typhoid fever epidemic among Micmacs of Nova Scotia.

1750
Moor's Indian Charity School founded in Connecticut. In **1769,** it moves to New Hampshire and becomes Dartmouth College, where Indian enrollment is encouraged.

1751
Benjamin Franklin cites Iroquois League as a model for his Albany Plan of Union.

1751
Second Pima Uprising against the Spanish in the Southwest.

1754
Albany Congress of English Colonies, in which officials discuss colonial Indian policy and establish a framework for an Indian Department.

1754–55
Anthony Henday (England) explores the Canadian Plains.

1754–63
French and Indian War (the colonial phase of the European Seven Years War). In **1763,** with the Treaty of Paris, France cedes New France to England, and Louisiana to Spain.

1755–62
British Government appoints superintendents of Indian Affairs for northern and southern departments.

1755–56
William Johnson, superintendent of Indian Affairs for the northern department (appointed in **1756**), persuades the Iroquois League to break their neutrality and ally with England against France.

1755
British officials proclaim each Indian scalp of enemy tribes worth 40 pounds.

1760–61
Cherokee War on Carolina frontier, between colonists and Cherokees.

1760–75
Daniel Boone explores wilderness areas of Tennessee and Kentucky, including the Cumberland Gap.

1761–66
Aleuts revolt against Russians in Alaska.

1763
Proclamation of King George III, prohibiting displacement of Indians without both tribal and Crown consent, attempts to keep settlers east of the Appalachian Divide and establish an Indian Country of protected lands to the west. From **1763–73,** the north-south line is further defined through new treaties and Indian land cessions. White settlers, however, ignore the supposed boundary lines.

1763–64
Pontiac's Rebellion against the British in the Great Lakes region. Pontiac, a chief of the Ottawas, is assassinated in **1769.** In **1763,** because of frontier attacks by Indians, the Paxton Riots occur in Pennsylvania; peaceful Conestoga Mission Indians are massacred by settlers.

1765
Reserve system of Canada begins with provision of a tract of land for Malecite tribe.

1767
Spanish royal decree expels Jesuits from all of New Spain. In **1769,** Gaspar de Portola claims California for Spain and establishes first missions under Juanipero Serra, a Franciscan, including San Diego.

1769–72
Samuel Hearne (England) discovers the Coppermine river and is the first European to reach the Arctic Ocean from the North American continent. During his voyages he encounters Chipewyan Indians.

1773
Mexican Indians find ruins of ancient Mayan city of Palenque.

1774
Lord Dunmore's War in Virginia, between settlers and Shawnees.

1775–83
American Revolution. In **1776**, the Declaration of Independence is signed.

1775
Continental Congress of the American Revolutionary Government formulates Indian policy and names commissioners for northern, middle, and southern departments.

1776
Juan Bautista de Anza founds San Francisco.

1776–78
James Cook (England) explores the Pacific Northwest.

1778
Treaty between United States and Delaware Indians, the first United States and Indian treaty, is negotiated in which Delaware tribe is offered the prospect of statehood.

1778
Iroquois Indians under Joseph Brant and British regulars attack American settlers on the western New York and Pennsylvania frontiers (Cherry Valley and Wyoming Valley massacres). In **1779**, the Americans launch a counteroffensive under Generals Sullivan and Clinton, and Colonel Brodhead that lays waste to Indian towns and crops, and breaks the power of the Iroquois League.

1778
Peter Pond (Canada) explores the Canadian Plains and Rockies.

c. 1780
Great Lakes Indians develop ribbonwork style of dress, using European materials. The craft spreads south and westward.

1780–1800
Smallpox and measles among Indians in Texas and New Mexico. In **1782–83**, a smallpox epidemic among Sanpoils of Washington.

1781–89
Under the Articles of Confederation defining federal and state relationships, it is accepted in principle that the central government should regulate Indian affairs and trade.

1782
Christian Delaware Indians massacred in Ohio at Gnadenhutten.

1783
Continental Congress issues a proclamation warning against squatting on Indian lands.

1784
Congress orders the War Office to provide militia troops to assist commissioners in their negotiations with Indians. In **1786**, the secretary of War is made responsible for Indian affairs. In **1789**, Congress establishes a Department of War and formally grants the secretary of War authority over Indian affairs.

1784
Russians found Three Saints, first permanent Russian settlement in North America, on Kodiak Island, one of the centers of Russian fur trading.

1784
North West Company is chartered in Montreal, to compete with the Hudson's Bay Company.

1787
Northwest Ordinance calls for Indian rights, the establishment of reservations, and sanctity of tribal lands, echoing the British Proclamation of 1763, but it also sets guidelines for the development of the Old Northwest, leading to increased white settlement.

1787–89
In the Constitution drawn up in **1787**, ratified by the required number of states (nine) by **1788**, and put into effect in **1789**, the federal government alone is given the power to regulate commerce with foreign nations, among the states, and with Indian tribes.

1789–93
Alexander Mackenzie (Canada), seeking northern river route to the Pacific Ocean, discovers the river now bearing his name and travels to Arctic Ocean. On a second expedition he completes first overland journey across North America north of Mexico, making contact with many tribes.

1790
Spain signs the Nootka Convention, ceding the Pacific Northwest to England and the United States.

1790–94
Little Turtle's War, involving many tribes of the Old Northwest. In **1794**, the Battle of Fallen Timbers.

1790–99
Four Trade and Intercourse Acts regulate Indian commerce and create the "factory system" of government trading houses. An informal Indian Department within the War Department is responsible for enforcing these regulations. In **1802**, a new Trade and Intercourse Act, a continuation of the four earlier acts, becomes federal law.

1791–93
George Vancouver (England) explores the Pacific Northwest.

1792
Robert Gray and William Broughton (U.S.) sails up the Columbia River.

1794
Canadian Jay Treaty guarantees Mohawk Indians the right to travel unrestrictedly between the United States and Canada.

1797
Smallpox epidemic among Indians of Mexico.

1791–1811
David Thompson (Canada) explores the Canadian and American West.

1799
Russian American Fur Company chartered under impetus of the traders Gregory Shelikov and Alexander Baranov.

1799
Handsome Lake, a Seneca chief, founds the Longhouse religion.

c. 1800
Silverwork becomes widespread among Indians of the Northeast, eventually reaching the Indians of the Southwest.

1802
Federal law prohibits the sale of liquor to Indians.

1802
Congress appropriates funds to "civilize and educate" the Indians.

1802–67
Tlingits resist Russian incursions into their territory.

1803
Louisiana Purchase by the United States from France (who had gained the territory back from Spain two years before) adds a large Indian population to the United States. In **1804**, the Louisiana Territory Act shows the intent of the United States to move eastern Indians west of the Mississippi.

1803–06
Meriwether Lewis and William Clark Expedition opens the American West.

1805–06
Zebulon Pike (U.S.) expeditions to source of the Mississippi River and the Rockies.

1805–20
Simon Fraser (Canada) explores river now bearing his name, and he becomes the first white man to visit the Carrier tribe.

1806
Office of Superintendent of Indian Trade is established in the War Department under the secretary of War, to administer federal Indian trading houses.

1808
American Fur Company is chartered by John Astor to compete with Canadian fur trade. In **1810–12**, an Astorian overland western expedition established trade relations with Indians.

1809
The St. Louis Missouri Fur Company is chartered by the Chouteau family.

1809
Treaty of Fort Wayne. General William Henry Harrison obtains 2½ million acres from Indians in Ohio and Indiana.

1809–11
Tecumseh's Rebellion. Tecumseh, a Shawnee chief, endeavors to unite tribes of the Old Northwest, South, and the Mississippi Valley against the United States. His brother, Tenskwatawa, is defeated at Tippecanoe in **1811**.

1809–21
Sequoyah single-handedly creates a Cherokee syllabic alphabet so that his people's language can be written.

1812–15
War of 1812 between the United States and England. Tecumseh, brigadier general for British, is killed in **1813**.

1812–41
Russians maintain Fort Ross in northwestern California, Pomo Indian country.

1813–14
Creek War in the Southeast. In the Treaty of Fort Jackson, Andrew Jackson strips Creeks of their land.

1816
The Selkirk incident between the Metis and settlers in the Red River Valley of Canada over farmland.

1817–18
First Seminole war in Southeast. Andrew Jackson invades Florida in a punitive expedition against the Indians. In **1819**, Spain cedes Florida to the United States.

1819–24
Kickapoo Resistance to removal from the Illinois Country.

1821
Hudson's Bay Company and North West Company merge.

1821
Mexican Independence from Spain. In **1824**, Mexico becomes a federal republic.

1822
Office of Indian Trade and Indian trading houses (the "factory system") are abolished by Congress.

1822
Henry Rowe Schoolcraft is appointed Indian agent and begins his ethnological research of Indians.

1824
Bureau of Indian Affairs is organized as part of the War Department. In **1832**, it is formally recognized by a law of Congress.

1825
Separate Indian Country west of the Mississippi is first defined.

1825–26
Expeditions backed by William Henry Ashley explore the Missouri, Platte, and Green rivers, and develop the American fur trade.

1825–30
Peter Skene Ogden explores the Canadian and American West for the Hudson's Bay Company.

1827
Winnebago Uprising in Wisconsin.

1827
Cherokees adopt a constitution patterned on that of the United States but it is nullified by the Georgia legislature.

1828–35
Cherokee Phoenix, a weekly newspaper, is published, using Sequoyah's syllabary.

1829
Last known Beothuk, Nancy Shawanahdit, dies in Newfoundland.

1830
Indian Removal Act passes Congress, calling for relocation of eastern Indians to an Indian Territory west of the Mississippi River. Cherokees contest it in court, and in **1832** the Supreme Court decides in their favor, but Andrew Jackson ignores decision. From **1831–39**, the Five Civilized tribes of the Southeast are relocated to the Indian Territory. The Cherokee "Trail of Tears" takes place in **1838–39**.

1830
Influenza epidemic among tribes of British Columbia. In **1830–33**, there are outbreaks of European diseases in California and Oregon.

1830–36
George Catlin travels among and paints the Plains Indians.

1832
Black Hawk War in Illinois and Wisconsin between combined Sauk and Fox tribes and the United States.

1833–34
Missouri River Expedition of two Europeans, Prince Maximilian and the painter, Karl Bodmer.

1834
Congress reorganizes the Indian Offices, creating the U.S. Department of Indian Affairs (still within the War Department). The Trade and Intercourse Act redefines the Indian Territory and Permanent Indian Frontier, and gives the army the right to quarantine Indians.

1835
Texas declares itself a republic independent from Mexico. The Texas Rangers are organized to compaign against the Comanches.

1835–37
Toledo War among the whites (also called the Ohio and Michigan Boundary Dispute).

1835–42
Second Seminole War. Osceola dies in prison in **1838**.

1837
Smallpox epidemic among Mandan, Hidatsa, and Arikara tribes of the upper Missouri. From **1837–70**, at least four different smallpox epidemics ravage western tribes.

1839–42
Mayan ruins rediscovered in Central America by John Lloyd Stephens and Frederick Catherwood.

1841–42
John Charles Fremont (U.S.) explores the Far West with Kit Carson as a guide.

1843
Russian–Greek Orthodox Church establishes the first mission school for Eskimos in Alaska.

1844
The first issues of the *Cherokee Advocate* are published in Oklahoma. Federal soldiers confiscate the press.

1845–48
War between the United States and Mexico over the American annexation of Texas. With the Treaty of Guadalupe Hidalgo in **1848**, the Spanish Southwest and its many Indian tribes become part of the United States.

1846
Oregon Country becomes part of the United States as a result of a settlement with England.

1846
Paul Kane travels among and paints Indians of southern Canada and the American Northwest.

1847
Mormon settlers reach site of present-day Salt Lake City.

1847
Outbreak of measles among the Cayuses.

1847–50
Cayuse Indian War in Oregon.

1848
Commercial whalers first arrive in Alaska.

1848–49
Gold discovered in California, starting the California Gold Rush and attrition of California and Plains Indians.

1849
Bureau of Indian Affairs transferred from the War Department to the Department of Interior.

1849
The Courthouse Rebellion in Canada, involving the Metis of the Red River.

1850
The first of a series of treaties between Canada and Canadian tribes are enacted, a policy continuing until **1923**.

1850–51
Mariposa War in California between miners, and Miwoks and Yokuts.

1850–60
Cholera epidemic among Indians of the Great Basin and southern plains.

1851
Yuma and Mojave Uprising in California and Arizona.

1851
Treaty of Fort Laramie between whites and tribes of the northern plains.

1853
Gadsden Purchase. American acquistion from Mexico of lands in New Mexico, Arizona, and California.

1853–54
Liquidation of northern portion of the Indian Territory, with creation of the state of Kansas and Nebraska Territory.

1853–56
United States acquires 174 million acres of Indian lands through 52 treaties, all of which are subsequently broken by whites.

1854
Commissioner of Indian Affairs calls for end of the Indian removal policy.

1854
Grattan Affair in Wyoming, involving the Sioux.

1855
Walla Walla Council in Washington between white officials and tribes of the Columbia Plateau.

1855–56
Yakima War in Washington, involving the Yakimas, Walla Wallas, Umatillas, and Cayuses,.

1855–56
Rogue River War in Oregon, involving the Takelmas and Tututnis.

1855–58
Third Seminole Uprising in Florida.

1857
Battle of Solomon Fork in Kansas, involving the Cheyennes.

1858
Coeur d'Alene War or Spokane War in Washington involving the Coeur d'Alenes, Spokanes, Palouses, Yakimas, and Northern Paiutes.

1858–59
Colorado Gold Rush (Pike's Peak Gold Rush).

1860
British government transfers control of Indian affairs to the Canadian provinces.

1860
Paiute War (also called the Pyramid Lake War) in Nevada, involving the Southern Paiutes.

1861–65
Civil War. In **1861,** the Confederate government organizes a Bureau of Indian Affairs. Most tribes remain neutral. The South, however, makes promises to Indians concerning the return of their tribal lands to encourage their support. After the war, as punishment for their support of the Confederacy, the Five Civilized Tribes are compelled to accept a treaty relinquishing the western half of the Indian Territory to 20 tribes from Kansas and Nebraska.

1861–63
Apache uprisings under chiefs Cochise and Mangas Colorado in the Southwest, resulting from the Bascom Affair.

1862
Homestead Act opens up Indian land in Kansas and Nebraska to white homesteaders, who are deeded 160-acre plots after inhabiting them for five years.

1862–63
Santee Sioux stage an uprising in Minnesota under Chief Little Crow. In **1863–64,** it spreads to North Dakota and involves the Teton Sioux as well. Thirty-eight Indians are sentenced and hanged.

1863
Shoshoni War (also called the Bear River Campaign) in Utah and Idaho, involving the Western Shoshonis.

1863–66
Navajo War in New Mexico and Arizona. In **1864,** Navajo prisoners are forced on the "Long Walk" to Bosque Redondo. Manuelito surrenders in **1866.**

1864–65
Cheyenne-Arapaho War in Colorado and Kansas. In **1864,** Chivington's Colorado Volunteers kill more than 300 Indians in the Sand Creek Massacre.

1864
Indians regarded as competent witnesses under federal law and allowed to testify in trials.

1865
United States gives contract to Protestant missionary societies to operate Indian schools.

1865–66
Jesse Chisholm, a mixed-blood, opens the Chisholm Trail.

1865–73
Mexican Kickapoo Uprising in the Southwest.

1866
Railroad Enabling Act appropriates Indian lands for railway use.

1866–68
War for the Bozeman Trail in Wyoming and Montana, involving the Sioux, Cheyennes, and Arapahos under Chief Red Cloud. A second Fort Laramie Treaty resolves the conflict in **1868.**

1866–68
Snake War in Oregon and Idaho, involving Northern Paiute bands of Yakuskins and Walpapis.

1867
British North American Act establishes Confederation of Canada. First Dominion Parliament assembled. In **1868,** an Indian Act shapes new administrative machinery for Indian affairs.

1867
United States purchases Alaska from Russia, adding Eskimo and Aleut population to its own.

1867
Hancock Campaign against the Cheyennes and Arapahos on the central plains.

1867
Treaty of Medicine Lodge in which Plains tribal leaders accept permanent lands within the Indian Territory.

1867
"Peace Commission" makes a survey of Indian affairs and recommends that the current treaty process be abandoned. This commission and the Nez Perce Indians negotiate the last of 370 treaties between the federal government and tribes.

1868
Commissioner of Indian Affairs estimates that Indian Wars in the West are costing the government $1 million per Indian killed.

1868
Indians are denied the right to vote as a result of the 14th Amendment.

1868–69
Southern Plains War (also called the Sheridan Campaign), involving the Cheyennes, Sioux, Arapahos, Kiowas, and Comanches.

1869
President Grant's so-called "Peace Policy" is inaugurated and lasts until 1874.

1869
Brigadier General Ely Parker (Donehogawa), a Seneca, becomes the first Indian commissioner of Indian Affairs, serving until **1871.**

1869
Transcontinental railroad completed: the Union Pacific and Central Pacific join up at Promontory Point, Utah.

1869
Hudson's Bay Company sells its vast holdings of land (Rupert's Land) to the Dominion of Canada.

1869
First Riel Rebellion in Canada of Red River Metis.

1869–70
Smallpox epidemic among Canadian Plains Indians including Blackfeet, Piegans, and Bloods.

1869–72
John Wesley Powell, geologist and ethnologist, explores the Colorado River and Grand Canyon.

c. 1870–90
Use of peyote spreads from Mexican Indians to Comanches, Kiowas, and other tribes.

1870
President Grant gives control of Indian agencies to 12 different Christian denominations instead of army officers.

1871
Treaty-making period formally ends as Congress passes law forbidding further negotiations of treaties with Indian tribes. The Cherokee Tobacco Case of 1870, ruling that the Cherokees are not exempt from taxes on produce (as established in an earlier treaty), sets the stage for the new law. Indians are now to be subject to acts of Congress and executive orders.

1871
General Sheridan issues orders forbidding western Indians to leave reservations without permission of civilian agents.

1871
White hunters begin wholesale killing of buffalo.

1871
Indian burial grounds invaded by whites seeking bones for manufacture of buttons.

1872–73
Modoc War in California and Oregon. Indian leader Captain Jack hanged in **1873.**

1872–73
Crook's Tonto Basin Campaign against the Apaches and Yavapais in the Southwest.

1873
First International Indian Fair held in Oklahoma.

1874
North West Mounted Police organized in Canada.

1874
Gold discovered in the Black Hills of South Dakota. Treaties protecting Indian lands ignored by miners.

1874–75
Red River War on the southern Plains, involving the Comanches, Kiowas, and Cheyennes, under Quanah Parker.

1876
Canada enacts Canadian Indian Act which defines Indian policy and gives individual Indians the right to seek enfranchisement as Canadian citizens by renouncing their rights and privileges as Indians.

1876–77
Sioux War for the Black Hills, involving the Sioux, Cheyennes, and Arapahos, under Sitting Bull and Crazy Horse. In **1876,** the Battle of Little Bighorn.

1877
Blackfeet cede land to the Dominion of Canada.

1877
Flight of the Nez Perces under Chief Joseph in the Northwest.

1877–80
Apache Resistance in the Southwest under Victorio.

1878
Bannock War in Idaho and Oregon, involving the Bannocks, Northern Paiutes, and Cayuses.

1878
Congress makes appropriation to provide for Indian Police, a policy which in **1883** brings about the Court of Indian Offenses with authorization for tribal units to administer justice in all but major crimes. In the Major Crimes Act of **1885,** federal courts are formally given jurisdiction over Indian cases involving major crimes.

1878–79
Flight of the Northern Cheyennes under Dull Knife on the plains.

1879
Sheepeater War in Idaho.

1879
Ute War in Colorado.

1879
Richard Pratt founds the Carlisle Indian School in Pennsylvania, with the philosophy of assimilating Indians into white culture.

1879
Bureau of American Ethnology, a branch of the Smithsonian, is founded for anthropological studies.

1879
Federal Court at Omaha, Nebraska, responding to a habeas corpus trial brought by Standing Bear, a Ponca, gives Indians the right to sue.

1879–85
Many "Friends of the Indian" organizations are founded, including Indian Protection Committee, Indian Rights Association, Women's National Indian Association, and National Indian Defense Association.

1881
Sitting Bull and his band of 187 surrender to officials at Fort Buford, North Dakota.

1881
Court of Claims is opened to Indians when the Choctaws are granted access to it.

1881–86
Apache Resistance under Geronimo in the Southwest. Geronimo surrenders in **1886.**

1884
Canadian Parliament passes the Indian Advancement Act, encouraging "democratic" election of chiefs by Indian bands. The Mohawks at St. Regis, Ontario, resist the provision, wanting to keep their traditional method of choosing leaders.

1884
Canada outlaws the Potlatch Ceremony among Northwest Coast Indians.

1884
Congress acknowledges the rights of Eskimos to Alaskan territorial lands.

1885
Last great herd of buffalo exterminated.

1885
Second Riel Rebellion of Metis living along the Saskatchewan River in Canada. Cree Indians surrender to Dominion troops.

1885
Canadian Pacific transcontinental railroad is completed.

1886
Mohawk Indians of the Caughnawaga Reserve in Quebec are trained in high-steel construction to work on a bridge across the St. Lawrence River. This starts a tradition among Iroquois.

1887
Congress passes the General Allotment Act (the Dawes Act) in which reservation lands are given to individual Indians in parcels. Indians lose millions of acres of land.

1889
Two million acres of the Indian Territory are bought from Indians and given to white settlers for the Land Run.

1890
Ghost Dance Movement led by the Paiute prophet Wovoka gains influence among western Indians. At Wounded Knee, United States troops massacre 350 Sioux Indians en route to a Ghost Dance celebration.

1890–1910
Lowpoint of United States Indian population. Less than 250,000.

1891
Provision is made for the leasing by whites of allotted Indian lands.

1891–1901
Sixty-five Sarcees die of tuberculosis in Alberta.

1893
Indian Appropriations Act contains provision to eliminate Indian agents, transferring their responsibilities on reservations to superintendents of schools.

1896–98
Klondike Gold Rush to the Yukon Territory and Alaska.

1898
Curtis Act dissolves tribal governments, requires Indians of abolished Indian nations to submit to allotment, and institutes civil government for the Indian Territory, with purpose of extending the effects of allotment policy to the Five Civilized Tribes.

1901
Snake uprising in Oklahoma Territory in which Creek Indians under Chitto Harjo resist allotment.

1902
Entire Eskimo population of Southampton Island in Hudson Bay is wiped out by typhus.

1902
Secretary of the Interior makes first oil and gas leases on Indian lands in Oklahoma.

1902
Reclamation Act encourages settlement of the West by whites through subsidies for water development.

1906
Burke Act amends the General Allotment Act, giving the secretary of the Interior authority to remove restrictions on allotted Indian lands.

1906
Federal government seizes 50,000 acres of wilderness land, the Blue Lake region in the mountains of New Mexico, sacred to Taos Pueblo Indians, and makes it part of a national park.

1907
Oklahoma Territory, including the Indian Territory, is admitted as a state. Its citizens seek to have Indian lands on the market and subject to taxation.

1907
Seventy high-steel construction workers of the Iroquois Caughnawaga Band killed while working on the Quebec Bridge.

1908
In the Winters Doctrine, the Supreme Court defines rights of the federal government to reserve water for the use of Indian tribes.

1909
Teddy Roosevelt, two days before leaving the presidency, issues eight executive orders transferring 2½ million acres of timbered Indian reservation lands to national forests.

1910
Division of Medical Assistance established within the Bureau of Indian Affairs, beginning a regular Indian medical service.

1910
Federal government forbids the Sun Dance among Plains Indians, giving the use of self-torture as reason.

1911
Society of American Indians, committed to Pan-Indianism and citizenship for Indians, is founded.

1912
Alaskan Native Brotherhood and Sisterhood are founded.

1912
Anti-allotment Cherokees, Creeks, Choctaws, and Chickasaws form the Four Mothers Society to argue their case before Congress.

1912
Jim Thorpe, a Sauk athlete of the Carlisle School, participates in the Olympic Games in Stockholm, Sweden, winning the pentathlon and decathlon. In **1913,** however, he is forced to surrender his medals to the Olympic committee because he had played one season of semi-professional baseball. In **1983,** his awards are reinstated.

1913
Federal government issues "Buffalo Head" nickel with composite portrait of three Indian chiefs, a Cheyenne, a Seneca, and a Sioux, on one side, and a buffalo on the reverse side.

1914–18
World War I. Many American Indians enlist, fight, and die.

1915
Congress passes appropriation act authorizing Bureau of Indian Affairs to buy land for landless Indians in California.

1917
For the first time in 50 years, Indian births exceed Indian deaths.

1917
Papago Indian Reservation in Arizona is the last to be established by executive order.

1917
Congress abolishes practice of payment of subsidies to religious groups for Indian education.

1917–20
Department of the Interior's Competency Commission removes restrictions on allotments, and the "Forced Patent" period begins. Thousands of patents are issued, discontinuing federal guardianship of Indian lands. As a result, many Indians lose their lands to corrupt whites.

1918
Native American Church with ritual surrounding the use of peyote is incorporated in Oklahoma by members of Kiowa, Comanche, Apache, Cheyenne, Ponca, and Oto tribes. By **1930,** it is estimated that half the nation's Indians are Native American Church members.

1921
The Snyder Act makes the Department of the Interior responsible for Indian education, medical, and social services.

1922
Rio Grande Pueblo Indians unite for the first time since **1680,** forming the All Pueblo Council to contest the proposed Bursum Bill that legislates rights for white squatters on Indian lands. The Bursum Bill is defeated.

1922
Deskaheh, a Cayuga chief, travels to Geneva, Switzerland, in an effort to seek recognition of his tribe from the League of Nations.

1923
Department of the Interior forms the Committee of One Hundred to review Indian policy.

1923
American Indian Defense Association formed by John Collier. At this time, the only 19th-century "Friends of the Indian" organization still active is the Indian Rights Association.

1924
With the Citizenship Act, Congress bestows American citizenship on all native-born Indians who have not yet obtained it. This ruling results in part from gratitude for the Indian contribution to the American effort in World War I.

1924
Division of Indian Health created within the BIA.

1926
National Council of American Indians is founded.

1928
Charles Curtis, a Kaw Indian and U.S. senator, is elected vice-president under Hoover.

1928
The Meriam Report, after a two-year commission, deplores Indian living conditions and declares the allotment system a failure.

1930
Senate Investigating Committee on Indian Affairs conducts a survey of Indian policy. One finding discloses the use of kidnapping techniques by BIA school officials trying to educate Navajo children.

1930
Northern Cheyenne Reservation becomes last communally owned tract to be allotted.

1932
Leavitt Act frees liens totalling millions of dollars on Indian lands.

1933
John Collier is appointed

commissioner of Indian Affairs by President Roosevelt, to administer the "New Deal" for Indians.

1934
Wheeler-Howard Act (or Indian Reorganization Act), the work of Commissioner John Collier, reverses the policy of breaking up tribal governments and landholdings through allotment, provides for tribal ownership of land and tribal self-government, and launches an Indian credit program. The Johnson-O'Malley Act allows the secretary of the Interior to contract with state and territory agencies to provide social, education, agricultural, and medical services to Indians.

c. 1935–40
Navajo system of writing known as the Harrington–La Farge alphabet is devised.

1936
Congress extends provisions of the Indian Reorganization Act to Alaskan Natives.

1936
Congress passes the Oklahoma Indian Welfare Act for the organization of now tribeless Indians whose lands have been allotted.

1936
Congress establishes the Indian Arts and Crafts Board, giving official recognition to Indian culture.

1939
The Senecas of Tonawanda, New York, issue a "Declaration of Independence" from the state of New York.

1940
First Inter-American Conference on Indian life is held in Patzcuaro, Mexico.

1941–45
World War II. More than 25,000 Indians on active duty and thousands more in war-related industries. Navajo Marines become famous for the use of their language as a battlefield code which the enemy is unable to decipher. Some Indians are jailed as draft resisters.

1943
Kateri Takakwitha, a Mohawk of the 17th century, is declared venerable by the Roman Catholic Church. In **1980,** she is declared blessed, one step closer to sainthood.

1944
National Congress of American Indians is organized in Denver, Colorado.

1944
House Indian Affairs Committee conducts an investigation of federal Indian policy.

1946
Indian Claims Commission created by Congress to settle tribal land claims against the United States (which formerly had been handled by the Court of Claims) and to provide financial compensation.

1946
John Collier's BIA administration ends. The termination policy, in which federal government seeks to end special Indian trust status, begins to take hold.

1948
Arizona is forced by court decree to give Indians the right to vote as in other states; this results from a trial brought by a Tewa Indian who claimed citizenship because he paid taxes on cigarettes.

1948
Assimilative Crimes Act holds that offenses committed on reservations, not covered under a specific federal statute but punishable under state law, are to be tried in federal courts.

1948
Congress gives the secretary of the Interior the power to grant rights-of-way on Indian lands with consent of tribal authorities.

1949
The Hoover Commission on the Reorganization of Government recommends termination of the federal-Indian trust relationship. In **1950,** Dillon Myer becomes the commissioner of Indian Affairs. He supports termination as well as a relocation-and-urbanization program for reservation Indians, encouraging migration to cities and cultural assimilation.

1950
Navajo Rehabilitation Act calls for appropriations to benefit tribes.

1951
Canadian Indian Act grants Indians the right to vote and makes them generally subject to the same laws as other Canadians.

1952
Division of Program is established within the BIA, to work with individual tribes to achieve standards of living comparable to the rest of society, and to transfer certain BIA functions to Indians themselves or the appropriate local, state, or federal agencies.

1952
BIA establishes Voluntary Relocation Program.

1953
Congress repeals special Indian prohibition laws.

1953
With the Termination Resolution (House Concurrent Resolution 108), Congress calls for the end of the special federal relationship with certain tribes in certain states. That same year, with Public Law 280, Congress empowers certain states to take over civil and criminal jurisdiction of Indian reservations without consent of tribes.

1954
Indians in Maine, previously barred from voting on the grounds that they are not under federal jurisdiction, are given the right to vote.

1954
Legislation to secure transfer of BIA agricultural extension to Department of Agriculture fails enactment, but this transfer is later accomplished by executive action.

1954–62
Congress strips 61 tribes, bands, and communities of federal services and protection. In **1973,** the Menominee Restoration Act reestablishes that tribe's trust status. In **1978,** Congress restores four Oklahoma tribes—Ottawas, Modocs, Wyandots, and Peorias—to trust status.

1955
The Public Health Service of the Department of Health, Education, and Welfare assumes responsibility for Indian health and medical care from the BIA.

1956
BIA's Adult Vocational Training Program is established for Indians, with an emphasis on service, trade, and clerical jobs.

1957
Iroquois activism in New York State. Senecas oppose the building of the Kinzua Dam. Tuscaroras fight the New York State Power Authority. Mohawks reoccupy lands taken by white squatters.

1958
Department of the Interior agrees to some modifications of termination policy.

1958
Three Thousand Lumbees drive off Ku Klux Klansmen who attempt to hold a rally in Robeson County, North Carolina.

1958
Miccosukees of Florida resist the Everglades Reclamation Project.

1958
Several tribes recognize the new revolutionary government of Cuba.

1959
Alaska becomes a state.

1959
Congress authorizes the surgeon general to provide and maintain essential sanitation facilities for Indian communities.

1960
First American Indian ballet, *Koshare*, by Louis W. Ballard, a Cherokee-Sioux, is performed.

1961
Department of the Interior changes federal land sales policy to allow Indian tribes the first opportunity to purchase lands offered for sale by individual Indians, countering the termination policy.

1961
Beginnings of modern Indian movement. The American Indian Charter Convention in Chicago and the National Indian Youth Conference in New Mexico define new goals. In the following years, many activist organizations are founded.

1961
Keeler Commission on Rights, Liberties, and Responsibilities of the American Indian recommends tribal self-determination and the development of tribal resources.

1961
Public Housing Act assists Indians in improving homes, and the Area Redevelopment Act gives grants to communities.

1961
U.S. Commission on Civil Rights reports on injustices in Indian living conditions.

1962
New Mexico is forced by the federal government to give Indians voting rights.

1962
Manpower Development and Training Act provides vocational facilities and programs for Indians.

1962
Department of the Interior names Task Force to study and make recommendations on Alaskan Natives.

1964
National Indian Youth Council sponsors ''fish-ins'' along the

rivers of the state of Washington, in support of the fishing rights of the Pacific Northwest tribes. Out of the action, the Survival of American Indians Association is founded.

1964
Capital Conference on Indian Poverty is held in Washington, D.C., with Indian delegates reporting on the extent of poverty among their tribes. The same year, the Office of Economic Opportunity is created with an Indian Desk that sponsors antipoverty programs.

1964
Civil Rights Act prohibits discrimination for reason of color, race, religion, or national origin.

1965
Voting Rights Act ensures equal voting rights.

1966
The Alaska Federation of Natives is founded, representing Eskimos, Aleuts, and Indians.

1966
Coleman Report on Indian Education. White House Task Force on Indian Health. Elementary and Secondary Education Act provides special programs for Indian children. A trachoma program for Indians is signed into law, as well as a mental health program for Eskimos.

1967
The Indian Resources Development Act, which would have vested final authority over Indian land transactions in the Department of the Interior, is countered by the ''Resolution of the Thirty Tribes'' and subsequently defeated in Congress.

1968
Civil Rights Act extends provisions of the Bill of Rights to reservation Indians; decrees that states cannot assume law and order jurisdiction on reservations without the consent of tribes; and restricts tribal governments in the same way federal and state governments are restricted.

1968
American Indian Movement (AIM) is founded in Minneapolis to deal with the many problems faced by relocated urban Indians. It has since come to be involved in struggles of reservation Indians as well.

1968
In a special message to Congress on the ''Forgotten American,''

President Johnson calls for the establishment of a National Council on Indian Opportunity, to be chaired by the vice-president, and to include a cross section of Indian leaders and directors of departments and agencies involved with Indian programs. He suggests also that termination should be replaced by Indian self-determination.

1968
''Project Own'' is launched by the Small Business Administration, guaranteeing loans to enable Indians to open their own small businesses on reservations.

1968
Navajo Community College, the first four-year college on a reservation, is chartered in Arizona.

1968
Mohawks of St. Regis, Ontario, attempt to block the St. Lawrence Seaway International Bridge to protest the Canadian government's failure to honor the Jay Treaty of **1795** that guarantees the Mohawks the right to travel unrestricted between Canada and United States. After this action, border-crossing rights are honored.

1969
Indians occupy Alcatraz Island in San Francisco Bay to call attention to the plight of contemporary Indians. The occupation lasts until **1971**.

1969
AMERIND is founded to protect Indian rights and improve Indian working conditions.

1969
Indian Task Force of 36 tribes makes a statement opposing federal termination policy in reaction to Department of the Interior statements that Indians are overprotected by trust status of reservations.

1969
Josephy Report on federal Indian policy argues against termination.

1969
Kennedy Report on Indian education recommends greater Indian self-determination.

1969
Environmental Policy Act protects Indian resources.

1969
National Council on Indian Opportunity created in office of vice-president to oversee Indian programs, including a cross

section of Indian leaders within departments and agencies involved with Indian programs.

1969
Court upholds land ''freeze'' order of the secretary of the Interior on behalf of Indians.

1969
Dr. N. Scott Momaday, a Kiowa, is awarded the Pulitzer Prize for literature.

1969
''White Paper'' on Indian affairs is issued in Canada, calling for the repeal of the Indian Act and for termination of special Indian status and benefits as derived from treaties. Indians reject proposal, and it is never implemented.

1970
A federal policy of Indian self-determination is formulated.

1970
Pit River Indians of California resist development plans of Pacific Gas and Electric.

1970
Blue Lake Wilderness Area in New Mexico, taken from Taos Pueblo in 1906, is returned.

1971
Alaska Native Claims Settlement Act reaches a money-land settlement with Alaskan natives.

1971
Model Urban Indian Center Program created by federal government to provide essential services for urban Indians.

1972
Trail of Broken Treaties Caravan, organized by AIM, formulates a 20-point position paper concerning the plight of Indians, then marches on Washington. Demonstrators occupy and destroy offices of the BIA.

1972
White vigilantes beat Raymond Yellow Thunder to death in Gordon, Nebraska. Court ruling of death by suicide causes protest of more than 1,000 Sioux from Pine Ridge Reservation. Officials forced to perform autopsy. The verdict is changed to manslaughter, and two of the killers are convicted.

1972
Indian Education Act provides educational programs for Indians.

1972
State and Local Fiscal Assistance Act provides loans for Indians.

1972
Yakima tribe is returned 21,000 acres in the state of Washington.

1973
Canadian Supreme Court upholds the aboriginal land claim of British Columbia's Niska Indians.

1973
Members of AIM and about 200 armed Oglala Sioux occupy the site of the Wounded Knee massacre of 1890, on the Pine Ridge reservation in South Dakota, for 71 days, demanding a change of tribal leaders, a review of all Indian treaties, and an investigation into the treatment of Indians. A state of siege results with alternate negotiation and gunfire, and the eventual death of two Indians.

1973
Marlon Brando rejects an Academy Award for Best Actor in protest of Hollywood's depiction of Indians.

1974
A group of Mohawks occupy Eagle Bay at Moss Lake in the Adirondacks, claiming original title to it, and found Ganienkeh, the "Land of Flintstone."

1974
Canada establishes the Office of Native Claims to resolve Indian land and treaty claims.

1974
In Minnesota the first trial stemming from the occupation of Wounded Knee takes place. In **1975**, the AIM leaders, Dennis Banks and Russell Means, are convicted on assault and riot charges. In **1978**, Governor Jerry Brown gives Dennis Banks sanctuary in California.

1974
Indian Financing Act provides loans to Indians for business projects.

1974
Navajo-Hopi Land Settlement Act tries to resolve dispute between two tribes.

1974
Housing and Community Development Act provides Indian housing.

1974
International Treaty Council, a grass-roots Indian coalition, is organized.

1975
Shootout on the Pine Ridge reservation in South Dakota between AIM members and FBI agents results in the death of two agents. Leonard Peltier is later convicted.

1975
American Indian Policy Review Commission analyzes the unique relationship of Indians with the federal government. In **1977**, the commission makes Final Report which opposes forced assimilation and supports Indian self-determination.

1975
Indian Self-Determination Act permits tribes to participate in all federal social programs and services relating to Indians.

1975
Council of Energy Resource Tribes (CERT) is formed as a cartel to protect and manage energy resources on reservations.

1975
Eighteen tribes are granted 346,000 acres of land held by the federal government since the Submarginal Lands Act of **1933.**

1976
Anna Mae Aquash, an AIM leader, is found shot to death on the Pine Ridge reservation in South Dakota.

1977
Indian activists present resolution to International Human Rights Conference in Geneva, Switzerland, calling on the United Nations to recognize Indian tribes as sovereign nations. The International Treaty Council is recognized as a nongovernmental organization of the United Nations.

1977
Oklahoma Human Rights Commission reports on racial bias against Indians.

1978
Indian Education Act gives greater decision-making powers to Indian school boards.

1978
Indian Child Welfare Act establishes standards for federal foster programs and provides assistance to tribes for child and family service programs.

1978
Indian activists stage the "Longest Walk" to Washington, D.C.

1978
Women of All Red Nations (WARN) is organized.

1978
Wampanoags of Massachusetts are denied claims to land because, when their suit was filed in 1976, they did not comprise a legal tribe.

1978
Congress passes the American Indian Freedom of Religion Act which states that Indian religion is protected by the First Amendment.

1978
Indian Claims Commission ends. In all, $800 million has been granted to Indian tribes since formation of commission in **1946,** with tribes winning awards on 60 percent of the claims. The Court of Claims assumes the remaining claims.

1980
Federal Census reports that the Native American population in the U.S. exceeds the 1 million mark at 1,418,195.

1980
Maine Indian Claims Settlement Act is reached in which the Passamaquoddy and Penobscot Indians agree to abandon land claims in Maine in exchange for a $27 million federal trust fund and $54 million in federal land acquisition fund.

1981
Reagan administration initiates a policy of cutbacks of funds for Indian social programs. Eventually, as much as 40 percent of funds cut.

1982
President Reagan vetoes $112 million congressional settlement of a water-rights suit brought by Papago Indians against Arizona. A settlement is eventually reached, with the federal government to pay the Papagos $40 million and local government, $5¼ million.

1982
Territorial plebiscite in Canada's Northwest Territories approves the idea of establishing a new territory, Nanavut, in Canadian Eskimo country, with Eskimo leaders.

1983
President Reagan vetoes $900,000 congressional land-claim suit brought by Pequot tribe against the state of Connecticut.

1983
Dennis Banks, the AIM leader, still under indictment by the state of South Dakota, leaves California and takes refuge on the Onondaga Reservation in New York.

1984
Great Jim Thorpe Longest Run, in which Indian runners cross the country, and the Jim Thorpe Memorial Pow Wow and Games in Los Angeles honor the memory of the Indian athlete and Olympian during the summer of the Los Angeles Olympics.

1984
Dennis Banks surrenders to state and local officials in Rapid City, South Dakota. He is sentenced to three years in prison.

1984
President Reagan's Commission on Indian Reservation Economies accuses the BIA of excessive regulation and incompetent management, with the agency consuming more than two-thirds of its budget on itself, and recommends assigning the agency's programs to other federal agencies. The Commission also recommends a shift away from tribal goals toward increased private ownership and individual profit motive, as well as the waiving of tribal immunity from certain lawsuits.

1985
National Tribal Chairmen's Association, meeting in Reno, Nevada, votes to reject the proposals of Reagan's Commission, fearing a new attempt by the federal government to terminate tribal sovereign status and gain control of tribal resources.

1986
Dispute over 1974 Navajo-Hopi Land settlement Act is still unresolved as Navajos continue to legally battle forced relocation from Big Mountain in Arizona.

THE INDIAN TRIBES OF THE UNITED STATES AND CANADA WITH HISTORICAL AND CONTEMPORARY LOCATIONS

No list of Indian tribes can be all-inclusive or absolute. The use of the term "tribe" creates an immediate problem for the researcher, because, like other often used terms, such as "band" or "nation," it has no uniform application. Anthropologists disagree on these and other terms applied to varying degrees of sociopolitical organization, such as "village," "town," "tribelet," "chiefdom," "confederacy," and "city-state." Many contemporary Indians prefer the term "nation" over all the others because it implies the concept of political sovereignty.

In any case, in the following list that limits itself to groups in the area consisting of the United States and Canada, the concept of

reek

Algonkin

ki, Wabanaki)
clude:
nobscot,
ly, and

Maine
ne

(Pit River)
n (Hokan)
—California

ja
an
st—Louisiana,
ppi
with **Bayogoula** and

uan
east—Florida

two names
historically interchangeable,
the former is generally used by
Indians in Canada and the latter
by Indians in the United States.
In some instances, the subtle
historical distinctions are
especially relevant to
contemporary Indians.

The following alphabetically
arranged list is not exhaustive
with regard to either subdivisions
or alternate names. There are
thousands more of both. Rather,
it presents those mentioned in
the text, plus others likely to be
encountered in further general
Indian readings. For a more
thorough accounting, see John R.
Swanton's *The Indian Tribes of
North America* and Frederick W.
Hodge's *Handbook of American
Indians North of Mexico* (see
bibliography), plus other sources.
For modern-day groups and
favored spellings, see also the
lists of Indian reservations and
bands following the tribal list.

Under each entry in the tribal
list appear the following:

(I) Language family (see also
"Indian Languages" in chapter 3).

(II) Historical locations by
culture area (see also "The Indian
Culture Areas" in chapter 3), as
well as by state, or, in the case of
Canadian tribes, by province.
When more than one state or
province is given, that which is
most closely associated with the
tribe is mentioned first.

(III) Contemporary location by

Subdivision of **Caddo**
I. Caddoan
II. Southeast—Louisiana

Ahantchuyuk
I. Kalapuyan (Penutian)
II. Northwest—Oregon

Ahtena (Atna, Copper)
I. Athapascan
II. Subarctic—Alaska, Yukon Territory
III. Alaska

Ais
I. Probably Muskogean
II. Southeast—Florida

Akokisa
See **Atakapa**

Alabama (Alibamu)
I. Muskogean
II. Southeast—Alabama, Florida, Louisiana
III. Texas, Oklahoma, Louisiana

Aleut
Subdivisions include: **Atka Aleut** and **Unalaska Aleut**
I. Eskimo-Aleut
II. Arctic—Alaska
III. Alaska

Algonkin
I. Algonquian
II. Northeast/Subarctic—Ontario, Quebec
III. Quebec, Ontario

Alibamu
See **Alabama**

Alliklik
I. Uto-Aztecan

II. California—California
III. California

Alsea (Alcea)
I. Yakonan (Penutian)
II. Northwest—Oregon

Altamaha
Subdivision of **Yamasee**

Amacano
Associated with **Caparaz** and **Chine**
I. Probably Muskogean
II. Southeast—Florida

Amacapiras
See **Macapiras**

Amikwa (Otter)
I. Algonquian
II. Northeast—Ontario

Anadarko
Member of **Hasinai Confederacy**

Andaste
See **Susquehannock**

Apache
Subdivisions include:
**Aravaipa (Western),
Chiricahua, Jicarilla, Kiowa-Apache, Lipan, Mescalero,
Mimbreno, Tonto, White
Mountain (Coyotera)**
I. Athapascan
II. Southwest—New Mexico, Arizona, Texas, Oklahoma, Colorado, Mexico
III. Arizona, New Mexico, Oklahoma

Apalachee
I. Muskogean
II. Southeast—Florida, Louisiana

Apalachicola
I. Muskogean
II. Southeast—Georgia, Alabama, Florida, Oklahoma

Aranama
I. Probably Coahuiltecan (Hokan)
II. Southwest—Texas

Arapaho
I. Algonquian
II. Great Plains—Wyoming, Colorado, Nebraska, Montana, Kansas, Oklahoma, Minnesota, North Dakota, South Dakota, Canada
III. Wyoming, Oklahoma, Montana

Aravaipa
Subdivision of **Apache**

Arikara (Ricaree)
I. Caddoan
II. Great Plains—North Dakota, South Dakota, Montana, Nebraska
III. North Dakota

Arkansa
See **Quapaw**

Assiniboine (Stoney)
I. Siouan
II. Great Plains— Saskatchewan, Montana, North Dakota, Manitoba

III. Alberta , Saskatchewan, Montana

Atakapa (Akokisa)
I. Atakapan (Macro-Algonquian)
II. Southeast—Louisiana, Texas

Atasi
Subdivision of Creek

Atfalati
I. Kalapuyan (Penutian)
II. Northwest—Oregon

Athapascan
Language family name also used in reference to particular tribes in Subarctic and Southwest

Atna
See **Ahtena**

Atsina
See **Gros Ventre**

Atsugewi
I. Palaihnihan (Hokan)
II. California—California

Attikamek
Subdivision of **Montagnais**

Avogel
I. Muskogean
II. Southeast—Louisiana

B

Bannock
I. Uto-Aztecan
II. Great Basin—Idaho, Wyoming, Montana, Colorado, Oregon, Utah
III. Idaho

Bayogoula
I. Muskogean
II. Southeast—Louisiana
III. Merged with **Houma**

Bear Lake
See **Saschutkenne**

Bear River
I. Athapascan
II. California—California

Beaver (Tsattine)
I. Athapascan
II. Subarctic—Alberta
III. Alberta, British Columbia

Bella Bella
I. Wakashan
II. Northwest—British Columbia
III. British Columbia

Bella Coola
I. Salishan
II. Northwest—British Columbia
III. British Columbia

Beothuk
I. Beothukan
II. Subarctic—Newfoundland

Bidai
I. Tunican (Macro-Algonquian)
II. Southeast—Texas

Biloxi
I. Siouan
II. Southeast—Mississippi, Louisiana, Oklahoma, Texas
III. Louisiana

Blackfoot (Siksika)
See also **Blood** and **Piegan**
I. Algonquian
II. Great Plains—Montana, Saskatchewan, Alberta
III. Alberta, Montana

Black Minqua
See **Honniasont**

Blood (Kainah)
Subdivision of **Blackfoot**
I. Algonquian
II. Great Plains—Montana, Saskatchewan, Alberta
III. Alberta

Bois Brules
See **Metis**

Brotherton
Name used by various tribes who settled together on land granted by whites
I. Algonquian
II. Northeast—New York, New Jersey

Brule
Subdivision of **Teton Sioux**

Bungee
Subdivision of **Ojibway**

C

Caddo
See also **Kadohadacho Confederacy, Hasinai Confederacy, Natchitoches Confederacy, Adai,** and **Eyeish**
I. Caddoan
II. Southeast/Great Plains—Texas, Arkansas, Louisiana
III. Oklahoma

Cahokia
Subdivision of **Illinois**

Cahuilla (Kawia)
I. Uto-Aztecan
II. California—California
III. California

Calapooya
See **Kalapuya**

Calusa
I. Probably Muskogean
II. Southeast—Florida

Canarsee
Subdivision of **Delaware**

Caparaz
Associated with **Chine** and **Amacano**
I. Probably Muskogean
II. Southeast—Florida

Cape Fear
I. Siouan
II. Southeast—North Carolina

Carrier
I. Athapascan
II. Subarctic—British Columbia
III. British Columbia

Catawba
I. Catawba (Macro-Siouan)
II. Southeast—South Carolina,

North Carolina, Tennessee
III. South Carolina

Cathlamet
I. Chinookan (Penutian)
II. Northwest—Washington, Oregon

Cathlapotle
I. Chinookan (Penutian)
II. Northwest—Washington

Cayuga
Member of **Iroquois Confederacy**
I. Iroquoian
II. Northeast—New York
III. New York, Ontario, Oklahoma

Cayuse
I. Cayuse (Penutian)
II. Plateau—Oregon, Washington
III. Oregon

Cenis
See **Hasinai Confederacy**

Chakchiuma
I. Muskogean
II. Southeast—Mississippi

Chastacosta (Chasta)
I. Athapascan
II. Northwest—Oregon

Chatot
I. Muskogean
II. Southeast—Florida, Georgia, Alabama, Louisiana

Chawasha
I. Tunican (Macro-Algonquian)
II. Southeast—Louisiana

Chehalis
I. Salishan
II. Northwest—Washington
III. Washington

Chehaw
See **Chiaha**

Chelamela
I. Kalapuyan (Penutian)
II. Northwest—Oregon

Chelan
I. Salishan
II. Plateau—Washington

Chemehuevi
Offshoot of **Paiute**
I. Uto-Aztecan
II. Great Basin—California
III. California

Chepenafa
I. Kalapuyan (Penutian)
II. Northwest—Oregon

Cheraw
I. Probably Siouan
II. Southeast—North Carolina, South Carolina

Cherokee
I. Iroquoian
II. Southeast—Tennessee, North Carolina, South Carolina, Georgia, Alabama, Virginia, Arkansas, Kansas, Oklahoma
III. Oklahoma, North Carolina

Chetco
I. Athapascan
II. Northwest—Oregon, California

Cheyenne
I. Algonquian
II. Great Plains—South Dakota, North Dakota, Colorado, Kansas, Minnesota, Montana, Nebraska, Oklahoma, Wyoming
III. Montana, Oklahoma

Chiaha (Chehaw)
I. Muskogean
II. Southeast—Georgia, Tennessee, South Carolina, Florida

Chickahominy
Member of **Powhatan Confederacy**

Chickamauga
Subdivision of **Cherokee**

Chickasaw
I. Muskogean
II. Southeast—Mississippi, Alabama, Arkansas, Tennessee, Georgia, Kentucky, South Carolina, Oklahoma
III. Oklahoma

Chilcotin
I. Athapascan
II. Subarctic—British Columbia
III. British Columbia

Chilkat
Subdivision of **Tlingit**

Chilliwack
I. Salish
II. Northwest—British Columbia

Chilluckittequaw
I. Chinookan (Penutian)
II. Northwest—Washington

Chilucan
I. Possibly Timucuan
II. Southeast—Florida

Chilula
I. Athapascan
II. California—California

Chimakum
I. Chimakuan
II. Northwest—Washington

Chimariko
I. Chimariko (Hokan)
II. California—California

Chine
Associated with **Amacano** and **Caparaz**
I. Probably Muskogean
II. Southeast—Florida

Chinook
I. Chinookan (Penutian)
II. Northwest—Washington
III. Washington

Chipewyan
I. Athapascan
II. Subarctic—Saskatchewan, Alberta, Manitoba, Northwest Territories
III. Northwest Territories,

Saskatchewan, Alberta, Manitoba

Chippewa
See **Ojibway**

Chiricahua
Subdivision of **Apache**

Chitimacha
I. Chitimacha (Macro-Algonquian)
II. Southeast—Louisiana
III. Louisiana

Choctaw
I. Muskogean
II. Southeast—Mississippi, Alabama, Louisiana, Arkansas, Texas, Oklahoma
III. Oklahoma, Mississippi

Chopunnish
See **Nez Perce**

Choula
Possible offshoot of **Ibitoupa**
I. Probably Muskogean
II. Southeast—Mississippi

Chowanoc
I. Algonquian
II. Northeast—North Carolina

Chowchilla
Name used for both **Miwok** and **Yokut**

Chumash
I. Chumashan (Hokan)
II. California—California

Clackamus
I. Chinookan (Penutian)
II. Northwest—Oregon, Washington
III. Oregon

Clallam (Skallam, Tlallam)
I. Salishan
II. Northwest—Washington
III. Washington

Clatskanie (Tlatskanai)
I. Athapascan
II. Northwest—Oregon, Washington

Clatsop
I. Chinookan (Penutian)
II. Northwest—Oregon

Clayoquot
Subdivision of **Nootka**

Clear Lake
Subdivision of **Pomo**

Clowwewalla
I. Chinookan (Penutian)
II. Northwest—Oregon

Coahuiltec (tribes)
I. Coahuiltecan (Hokan)
II. Southwest—Texas, Mexico
III. Mexico

Cocopa
I. Yuman (Hokan)
II. Southwest—Arizona, Mexico

Coeur d'Alene (Skitswish)
I. Salishan
II. Plateau—Idaho
III. Idaho, Washington

Columbia (Sinkiuse-Columbia)

I. Salishan
II. Plateau—Washington
III. Washington

Colville
I. Salishan
II. Plateau—Washington
III. Washington

Comanche (Padoucah)
I. Uto-Aztecan
II. Great Plains—Texas, Oklahoma, Colorado, New Mexico, Kansas, Nebraska, Wyoming
III. Oklahoma

Comox
I. Salishan
II. Northwest—British Columbia
III. British Columbia

Conestoga
See **Susquahannock**

Congaree
I. Siouan
II. Southeast—South Carolina

Conoy
I. Algonquian
II. Northeast—Maryland, District of Columbia, Pennsylvania, New York

Coos
I. Coos (Penutian)
II. Northwest—Oregon

Copalis
I. Salishan
II. Northwest—Washington

Copper
See **Ahtena, Yellowknife**

Coquille, Lower
See **Miluk**

Coquille, Upper (Mishikhwutmetunne)
I. Athapascan
II. Northwest—Oregon

Corree
I. Iroquoian or Algonquian
II. Southeast—North Carolina

Costano
I. Miwok-Costanoan (Penutian)
II. California—California

Coushatta
See **Koasati**

Coweta
Subdivision of **Creek**

Cowichan (Halkomelem)
I. Salishan
II. Northwest—British Columbia
III. British Columbia

Cowlitz
See also **Taidnapam**
I. Salishan
II. Northwest—Washington, Oregon
III. Washington

Coyotera
See **White Mountain**

Cree
Subdivided into **Plains Cree, Western Wood Cree, Swampy Cree** (Maskegon), **Mistassini Cree,** and **Tete de Boule Cree**

I. Algonquian
II. Subarctic—Saskatchewan, Manitoba, Ontario, Quebec
III. Saskatchewan, Alberta, Manitoba, Ontario, Quebec, Montana

Creek (Muskogee)
I. Muskogean
II. Southeast— Georgia, Alabama, Florida, Louisiana, Tennessee, Texas, Oklahoma
III. Oklahoma, Alabama

Crow (Absaroka, Kite)
I. Siouan
II. Great Plains—Montana, Wyoming
III. Montana

Cuitoa
Possible subdivision of **Kansa**

Cupeno
I. Uto-Aztecan
II. California—California

Cusabo
I. Muskogean
II. Southeast—South Carolina, Florida

D

Dakota
See **Sioux**

Dakubetede
I. Athapascan
II. Northwest—Oregon

Deadose
Subdivision of **Atakapa**

Delaware (Lenni Lenape)
I. Algonquian
II. Northeast—New Jersey, New York, Pennsylvania, Delaware, Ohio, Indiana, Kansas, Missouri
III. Oklahoma, Wisconsin (**Munsee** tribe), Kansas (**Munsee**), Ontario (**Munsee** and **Moravian**)

Diegueno
I. Yuman (Hokan)
II. California—California
III. California

Diggers
Name used for various Great Basin tribes

Dogrib (Thlingchadinne)
I. Athapascan
II. Subarctic—Northwest Territories
III. Northwest Territories

Duwamish
I. Salishan
II. Northwest—Washington

E

Eno
I. Possibly Siouan
II. Southeast—North Carolina, South Carolina

Erie
I. Iroquoian
II. New York—Ohio, New York, Pennsylvania, Indiana

Eskimo (Inuit)
Subdivisions include North Alaskan, Labrador, West Alaskan, South Alaskan, Saint Lawrence Island, Siberian (Yuit), Netsilik, Iglulik, Caribou, Copper, Southampton, Baffinland, East Greenland, West Greenland, Polar, Mackenzie
I. Eskimo-Aleut
II. Arctic—Alaska, Northern Canada
III. Alaska, Northern Canada

Esophus
Subdivision of **Delaware**

Esselen
I. Esselen (Hokan)
II. California—California

Etchaottine
See **Slave**

Etchemin
See **Malecite**

Eufala
Subdivision of **Creek**

Eyak
I. Athapascan
II. Northwest Subarctic—Alaska, Yukon Territory, British Columbia

Eyeish (Aiz)
I. Caddoan
II. Southeast—Texas
III. Merged with **Caddo**

F

Fernandeno
I. Uto-Aztecan
II. California—California

Flathead (Salish)
I. Salishan
II. Plateau—Montana, Idaho
III. Montana

(**Chinook** and **Choctaw** were also formerly called **Flathead** but are not referred to here)

Fox (Mesquaki, Outagami)
Allied with **Sauk**
I. Algonquian
II. Northeast—Wisconsin, Illinois, Iowa, Michigan, Minnesota, Missouri, Kansas, Nebraska, Oklahoma
III. Iowa, Kansas, Oklahoma

Freshwater (Agua Dulce)
I. Timucuan
II. Southeast—Florida

Fus-hatchee
Subdivision of **Creek**

G

Gabrielino
I. Uto-Aztecan

II. California—California

Galice
See **Taltushtuntude**

Gitksan (Kitksan)
I. Tsimshian (Penutian)
II. Northwest—British Columbia
III. British Columbia

Gosiute (Goshute)
I. Uto-Aztecan
II. Great Basin—Utah
III. Utah

Griga
I. Tunican (Macro-Algonquian)
II. Southeast—Mississippi

Gros Ventre (Atsina)
I. Algonquian
II. Great Plains—Montana, Saskatchewan
III. Montana

Guacata
I. Muskogean
II. Southeast—Florida

Guaicura
I. Yuman (Hokan)
II. California—California

Guale
I. Muskogean
II. Southeast—Georgia, Florida
III. Merged with **Yamasee**

Guasco
Member of **Hasinai Confederacy**

H

Hackensack
Subdivision of **Delaware**

Haida
I. Haida (Na-Dene)
II. Northwest—British Columbia, Alaska
III. British Columbia, Alaska

Hainai
See **Hasinai Confederacy**

Haisla
I. Wakashan
II. Northwest—British Columbia
III. British Columbia

Halchidhoma
I. Yuman (Hokan)
II. Southwest—Arizona, California
III. Absorbed by **Maricopa**

Halkomelem
See **Cowichan**

Halyikwamai (Kikima)
I. Yuman (Hokan)
II. Southwest—Arizona, Mexico

Hammonasset
Subdivision of **Quinnipiac**

Han
I. Athapascan
II. Subarctic—Alaska, Yukon Territory

Hanis
I. Probably Yukonan (Penutian)
II. Northwest—Oregon

Hare (Kawchottine)
I. Athapascan
II. Subarctic—Northwest Territories
III. Northwest Territories

Hasinai Confederacy (Texas, Cenis)
Subdivision of **Caddo**
I. Caddoan
II. Southeast—Texas

Hassanamisco
Subdivision of **Nipmuc**

Hatteras
I. Algonquian
II. Northeast—North Carolina

Havasupai
I. Yuman (Hokan)
II. Southwest—Arizona
III. Arizona

Heiltsuk
I. Wakashan
II. Northwest—British Columbia
III. British Columbia

Hidatsa (Minitari)
I. Siouan
II. Great Plains—North Dakota, Montana
III. North Dakota

Hilibi
Subdivision of **Creek**

Hitchiti
I. Muskogean
II. Southeast—Georgia, Florida, Oklahoma
III. Merged with **Creek**

Hoh
I. Chimakuan
II. Northwest—Washington
III. Washington

Honniasont (Black Minqua)
Possible subdivision of **Erie**
I. Iroquoian
II. Northeast—Pennsylvania, Ohio, West Virginia

Hoopa
See **Hupa**

Hopi (Pueblos)
I. Uto-Aztecan
II. Southwest—Arizona
III. Arizona, New Mexico

Houma
I. Muskogean
II. Southeast—Mississippi, Louisiana
III. Louisiana

Housatonic
See **Stockbridge**

Hualapai (Walapai)
I. Yuman (Hokan)
II. Southwest—Arizona
III. Arizona

Huchnom
I. Yukian
II. California—California

Huliwahli
Subdivision of **Creek**

Humptulips
I. Salishan
II. Northwest—Washington

Hunkpapa
Subdivision of **Teton Sioux**

Hupa (Hoopa)
I. Athapascan
II. California—California
III. California

Huron
See also **Wyandot**, the name used by Huron descendants
I. Iroquoian
II. Northeast—Ontario, Quebec

I

Ibitoupa
I. Probably Muskogean
II. Southeast—Mississippi

Icafui
I. Probably Timucuan
II. Southeast—Florida, Georgia

Illinois
I. Algonquian
II. Northeast—Illinois, Indiana, Ohio, Wisconsin, Iowa, Missouri, Kansas, Oklahoma
III. Oklahoma

Ingalik
I. Athapascan
II. Subarctic—Alaska
III. Alaska

Inuit
Self-chosen name of **Eskimo**

Iowa
I. Siouan
II. Great Plains—Iowa, Wisconsin, Minnesota, Nebraska, Kansas, Missouri, and Oklahoma
III. Kansas, Oklahoma

Iroquois (Confederacy)
See also **Mohawk, Oneida, Onondaga, Cayuga, Seneca, Tuscarora**
I. Iroquoian
II. Northeast—New York, Ontario, Quebec, Pennsylvania, Ohio, Indiana, Wisconsin, Kansas, Oklahoma
III. New York, Ontario, Quebec, Oklahoma, Wisconsin

J

Jeaga
I. Muskogean
II. Southeast—Florida

Jemez (Towa Pueblo)
I. Kiowa-Tanoan
II. Southwest—New Mexico
III. New Mexico

Jicarilla
Subdivision of **Apache**

Juaneno
I. Uto-Aztecan
II. California—California

Jumano (Shuman)
I. Uto-Aztecan
II. Southwest—Texas, Mexico

K

Kadohadacho Confederacy
Subdivision of **Caddo**
I. Caddoan
II. Southeast—Texas, Arkansas, Louisiana
III. Oklahoma

Kaibab
Subdivision of **Paiute**

Kainah
See **Blood**

Kalapuya (Calapooya)
I. Kalapuyan (Penutian)
II. Northwest—Oregon

Kalispel (Pend d'Oreille)
I. Salishan
II. Plateau—Idaho, Montana, Washington
III. Washington

Kamia (Tipai)
I. Yuman (Hokan)
II. California—California, Mexico

Kan-hatki
Subdivision of **Creek**

Kansa (Kaw)
I. Siouan
II. Great Plains—Kansas, Nebraska, Oklahoma
III. Oklahoma

Karankawa
I. Karankawan
II. Southwest—Texas

Karok
I. Karok (Hokan)
II. California—California
III. California

Kasihta
Subdivision of **Creek**

Kaska
Subdivision of **Nahane**
I. Athapascan
II. Subarctic—British Columbia, Yukon
III. Yukon

Kaskaskia
Subdivision of **Illinois**
I. Algonquian
II. Northeast—Illinois, Indiana, Ohio, Wisconsin, Iowa, Missouri, Kansas, Oklahoma
III. Oklahoma

Kaskinampo
I. Muskogean
II. Southeast—Tennessee, Arkansas

Kato
I. Athapascan
II. California—California

Kavelchadoma
Subdivision of **Yuma**

Kaw
See **Kansa**

Kawaiisu
I. Uto-Aztecan
II. Great Basin—California
III. California

Kawchottine
See **Hare**

Kawia
See **Cahuilla**

Kawita
Subdivision of **Creek**

Kealedji
Subdivision of **Creek**

Keres (Pueblos) (Keresan)
I. Keresan
II. Southwest—New Mexico
III. New Mexico

Keyauwee
I. Siouan
II. Southeast—North Carolina, South Carolina

Kichai (Kitsei)
I. Caddo
II. Great Plains—Texas, Oklahoma
III. Joined **Wichita** in Oklahoma

Kickapoo
I. Algonquian
II. Northeast—Wisconsin, Michigan, Illinois, Indiana, Ohio, Missouri, Kansas, Oklahoma, Mexico
III. Kansas, Oklahoma, Mexico

Kikiallus
Subdivision of **Swinomish**

Kikima
See **Halyikwamai**

Kiowa
I. Kiowa-Tanoan
II. Great Plains—Oklahoma, Kansas, Colorado, New Mexico, Texas
III. Oklahoma

Kiowa-Apache
I. Athapascan
II. Great Plains—Oklahoma, Kansas, Colorado, New Mexico, Wyoming
III. Oklahoma

Kitamat
Subdivision of **Kwakiutl**

Kitanemuk
I. Uto-Aztecan
II. California—California

Kitchigami
I. Algonquian
II. Northeast—Wisconsin
III. Probably absorbed by **Kickapoo** or **Peoria**

Kite
See **Crow**

Kitksan
See **Gitskan**

Klallam
See **Clallam**

Klamath
I. Klamath-Modoc (Penutian)
II. Plateau—Oregon, California
III. Oregon

Klickitat
I. Sahaptin-Nez Perce
II. Plateau—Washington, Oregon
III. Merged with **Yakima**

Koasati (Coushatta)
I. Muskogean
II. Southeast—Alabama, Mississippi, Florida, Louisiana, Texas, Oklahoma
III. Texas

Kohuana
I. Yuman (Hokan)
II. Southwest—Arizona, Mexico

Kolomi
Subdivision of **Creek**

Konkow
Subdivision of **Maidu**

Konomihu
I. Shastan (Hokan)
II. California

Kootenay (Kootenai, Kutenai)
I. Kutenai
II. Plateau—British Columbia, Alberta, Montana, Washington, Idaho
III. British Columbia, Idaho, Montana

Koroa
I. Tunican (Macro-Algonquian)
II. Southeast—Mississippi, Louisiana

Koso
See **Panamint**

Koyukon
I. Athapascan
II. Subarctic—Alaska
III. Alaska

Kuitsh (Lower Umpqua)
I. Yakonan (Penutian)
II. Northwest—Oregon

Kutchin
Subdivisions include **Dihai, Kutcha, Loucheux, Natsit, Tennuth, Tranjik, Vunta-Kutchin**
I. Athapascan
II. Subarctic—Alaska, Yukon
III. Yukon, Northwest Territories

Kutenai
See **Kootenay**

Kwahadie
Subdivision of **Comanche**

Kwaiailk
I. Salishan
II. Northwest—Washington

Kwakiutl
I. Wakashan
II. Northwest—British Columbia
III. British Columbia

Kwalhioqua
I. Athapascan
II. Northwest—Washington, Oregon

L

Lake (Senijextee)
I. Salishan
II. Plateau—Washington, British Columbia
III. Washington

Lakmiut (Luckiamute)
I. Kalapuyan (Penutian)
II. Northwest—Oregon

Lakota
See **Sioux**

Lassik
I. Athapascan
II. California—California

Latgawa
I. Takelma (Penutian)
II. Northwest—Oregon

Lenni Lanape
See **Delaware**

Lillooet
I. Salishan
II. Plateau—British Columbia
III. British Columbia

Lipan
Subdivision of **Apache**
I. Athapascan
II. Great Plains/Southwest—Texas, New Mexico, Oklahoma
III. New Mexico

Loucheux
Subdivision of **Kutchin**

Luiseno
I. Uto-Aztecan
II. California—California
III. California

Lumbee
I. Tribe of mixed ancestry
II. Northeast—North Carolina, South Carolina
III. North Carolina, South Carolina

Lumni
I. Salishan
II. Northwest—Washington, British Columbia
III. Washington

M

Macapiras (Amacapiras)
I. Probably Muskogean
II. Southeast—Florida

Macaw
See **Makah**

Machapunga
I. Algonquian
II. Northeast—North Carolina

Mahican
I. Algonquian
II. Northeast—New York, Connecticut, Massachusetts, Vermont, Wisconsin
III. Wisconsin, Connecticut

Maidu
I. Maidu (Penutian)
II. California—California
III. California

Makah (Macaw)
I. Wakashan
II. Northwest—Washington
III. Washington

Malecite (Maliset, Etchemin)
Subdivision of **Abnaki**
I. Algonquian
II. Northeast—New Brunswick, Maine
III. New Brunswick, Quebec

Manahoac (Mahock)
I. Siouan
II. Southeast—Virginia

Manakin
See **Monacan**

Mandan
I. Siouan
II. Great Plains—North Dakota
III. North Dakota

Manhattan
Subdivision of **Delaware** or **Wappinger**

Manso
I. Kiowa-Tanoan
II. Southwest—New Mexico

Maricopa
I. Yuman (Hokan)
II. Southwest—Arizona
III. Arizona

Mariposa
See **Yokuts**

Mascouten
See **Peoria**

Maskegon (Swampy Cree)
Subdivision of **Cree**

Massachuset
I. Algonquian
II. Northeast—Massachusetts

Mattabesec
I. Algonquian
II. Northeast—Connecticut

Mattaponi
Member of **Powhatan** Confederacy

Mattole
I. Athapascan
II. California—California

Mdawakanton
Subdivision of **Santee Sioux**

Meherrin
I. Iroquoian
II. Northeast—Virginia, North Carolina

Menominee (Rice)
I. Algonquian
II. Northeast—Wisconsin, Michigan
III. Wisconsin

Mescalero
Subdivision of **Apache**

Mesquaki
See **Fox**

Methow
I. Salishan
II. Plateau—Washington

Metis (Bois Brules)
Indian-French or Indian-Scottish mixed-bloods
I. Algonquian, French, English
II. Manitoba, Saskatchewan
III. Canada, Montana

Miami
I. Algonquian
II. Northeast—Indiana, Illinois, Ohio, Michigan, Wisconsin, Kansas, Oklahoma
III. Oklahoma, Indiana

Mical
I. Sahaptin-Nez Perce
II. Plateau—Washington

Miccosukee (Mikasuki)
I. Muskogean
II. Southeast—Florida, Oklahoma
III. Florida

Micmac
I. Algonquian
II. Northeast—New Brunswick, Nova Scotia, Prince Edward Island, Newfoundland
III. Nova Scotia, New Brunswick, Quebec, Prince Edward Island, Maine

Mikasuki
See **Miccosukee**

Miluk (Lower Coquille)
I. Probably Yakonen (Penutian)
II. Northwest—Oregon

Mimbreno
Subdivision of **Apache**

Miniconjou
Subdivision of **Teton Sioux**

Minitari
See **Hidatsa**

Mingo
Subdivision of **Iroquois**

Mishikhwutmetunne
See **Coquille, Upper**

Mission
Term used in reference to various California tribes living at Spanish missions

Missisauga (Mississauga)
See **Ojibway**

Missouri (Missouria)
I. Siouan
II. Great Plains—Missouri, Iowa, Minnesota, Nebraska, Wisconsin, Oklahoma
III. Oklahoma

Mistassini
Subdivision of **Cree**

Miwok (Me-Wuk)
Subdivided into **Lake, Coast,** and **Valley Miwok**
I. Miwok-Costanoan (Penutian)
II. California—California
III. California

Moache
Subdivision of **Ute**

Mobile
I. Muskogean
II. Southeast—Alabama, Florida

Mococo (Mucoco)
I. Timucuan
II. Southeast—Florida

Moctobi
Possible subdivision of **Biloxi**
I. Possibly Siouan
II. Mississippi

Modoc
I. Klamath-Modoc (Penutian)
II. Plateau—Oregon, California, Oklahoma
III. Oregon, Oklahoma

Mohave
See **Mojave**

Mohawk
Member of **Iroquois Confederacy**
I. Iroquoian
II. Northeast—New York, Ontario, Quebec
III. New York, Ontario, Quebec

Mohegan (Mohican)
I. Algonquian
II. Northeast—Connecticut
III. Connecticut

Mohican
See **Mohegan**

Mojave (Mohave)
I. Yuman (Hokan)
II. Southwest—Arizona, California
III. Arizona, California

Molala
I. Molale (Penutian)
II. Plateau—Oregon
III. Oregon

Monacan (Manakin)
I. Siouan
II. Southeast—Virginia

Monache
See **Mono**

Moneton
I. Siouan
II. Northeast—West Virginia

Mono (Monache)
I. Uto-Aztecan
II. Great Basin—Nevada, California
III. California

Montagnais
Southern branch of **Montagnais-Naskapi**
I. Algonquian
II. Subarctic—Quebec, Labrador
III. Quebec

Montauk
See also **Shinnecock** and **Poospatuck**
I. Algonquian
II. Northeast—New York
III. New York

Moratok
I. Algonquian
II. Northeast—North Carolina

Moravian
Subdivision of **Delaware**

Mosopelea
See **Ofo**

Mosquito
I. Probably Timucuan
II. Southeast—Florida

Mountain (Tsethaottine)
I. Athapascan
II. Subarctic—Yukon Territory, Northwest Territories

Muckleshoot
I. Salishan
II. Northwest—Washington
III. Washington

Mugulasha
Probably same tribe as **Quinipissa**

Muklasa
I. Muskogean
II. Southeast—Alabama, Florida

Multomah
I. Chinookan (Penutian)
II. Northwest—Oregon

Munsee (Muncie)
Subdivision of **Delaware**

Muskogee
See **Creek**

N

Nabedache
Member of **Hasinai Confederacy**

Nabesna
I. Athapascan
II. Subarctic—Alaska, Yukon
III. Alaska

Nahane (Nahani)
See **Kaska, Tagish,** and **Tahltan**

Nahyssan
I. Siouan
II. Southeast—Virginia, West Virginia

Nanaimo
I. Salishan
II. Northwest—British Columbia

Naniaba
Subdivision of **Choctaw**

Nansemond
Member of **Powhatan Confederacy**

Nanticoke
I. Algonquian
II. Northeast—Maryland, Delaware, Pennsylvania

Napochi
I. Muskogean
II. Southeast—Alabama

Narraganset
I. Algonquian
II. Northeast—Rhode Island, Massachusetts, Connecticut
III. Rhode Island

Nashua
I. Algonquian
II. Northeast—Massachusetts

Naskapi
Northern branch of **Montagnais-Naskapi**
I. Algonquian
II. Subarctic—Quebec, Labrador
III. Quebec

Natchez
I. Natchez (Macro-Algonquian)
II. Southeast—Mississippi, Louisiana, Alabama, Tennessee, North Carolina, South Carolina, Oklahoma

Natchitoches Confederacy
Subdivision of **Caddo**
I. Caddoan
II. Southeast—Louisiana

Natick
Subdivision of **Massachuset**

Nauset
I. Algonquian
II. Northeast—Massachusetts

Navajo (Navaho)
I. Athapascan
II. Southwest—New Mexico, Arizona, Colorado, Utah
III. Arizona, New Mexico, Utah

Nawunena (Nawathinehena)
Subdivision of **Arapaho**

Nehelem
I. Salishan
II. Northwest—Oregon·

Nespelem
See **Sanpoil**

Neusiok
I. Algonquian or Iroquoian
II. Northeast—North Carolina

Neutral
I. Iroquoian
II. Northeast—Ontario, New York, Ohio, Michigan, Indiana

Nez Perce (Chopunnish, Sahaptin)
I. Sahaptin-Nez Perce
II. Plateau—Idaho, Washington, Oregon
III. Idaho, Washington

Niantic
I. Algonquian
II. Northeast—Rhode Island, Connecticut
III. Connecticut

Nicola
Subdivision of **Ntlakyapamuk**

Nicoleno
I. Uto-Aztecan
II. California—California

Nipissing
I. Algonquian
II. Northeast—Ontario

Nipmuc
I. Algonquian
II. Northeast—Massachusetts, Rhode Island, Connecticut
III. Massachusetts

Niska (Nishga)
I. Tsimshian (Penutian)
II. Northwest—British Columbia, Alaska
III. British Columbia

Nisqually
I. Salishan
II. Northwest—Washington
III. Washington

Nitinat
Subdivision of **Nootka**

Nomlaki (Nom-laka)
Subdivision of **Wintun**

Nongatl
I. Athapascan
II. California—California

Nooksack
I. Salishan
II. Northwest—Washington
III. Washington

Nootka
I. Wakashan
II. Northwest—British Columbia
III. British Columbia

Noquet
I. Algonquian
II. Northeast—Michigan, Wisconsin

Nottaway
I. Iroquoian
II. Northeast—Virginia

Ntlakyapamuk (Thompson)
I. Salishan
II. Plateau—British Columbia, Washington
III. British Columbia

O

Ocale (Etocale)
I. Timucuan
II. Southeast—Florida

Ocaneechi
I. Siouan
II. Southeast—Virginia, North Carolina

Ocita
See **Pohoy**

Oconee
I. Muskogean
II. Southeast—Georgia, Florida

Ofo (Mosopelea)
I. Siouan
II. Southeast—Mississippi, Arkansas, Tennessee, Kentucky, Indiana, Oklahoma

Oglala
Subdivision of **Teton Sioux**

Ohlone
Subdivision of **Costano**

Ojibway (Chippewa)
Subdivisions include **Missisauga, Bungee, Plains Ojibway, Saulteaux**
I. Algonquian
II. Subarctic/Northeast/Great Plains—Minnesota, Michigan, Wisconsin, Ontario, Manitoba, Ohio, Indiana, Illinois, Iowa, North Dakota, Montana, Saskatchewan
III. Ontario, Manitoba, Saskatchewan, Michigan, Minnesota, North Dakota, Wisconsin, British Columbia, Montana

Okanagan (Okanogan)
I. Salishan
II. Plateau—Washington, British Columbia
III. British Columbia

Okchai
Subdivision of **Creek**

Okelousa
I. Muskogean
II. Southeast—Louisiana, Mississippi

Okmulgee
I. Muskogean
II. Southeast—Georgia, Alabama, Oklahoma

Okwanuchu
I. Shastan (Hokan)
II. California—California

Omaha
I. Siouan
II. Great Plains—Nebraska, Iowa, South Dakota, Minnesota, Missouri
III. Nebraska

Onatheaqua
I. Timucuan
II. Southeast—Florida

Oneida
Member of **Iroquois Confederacy**
I. Iroquoian
II. Northeast—New York
III. New York, Ontario, Wisconsin

Onondaga
Member of **Iroquois Confederacy**
I. Iroquoian
II. Northeast—New York
III. New York, Ontario

Opelousa
I. Atakapan (Macro-Algonquian)
II. Southeast—Louisiana

Osage
I. Siouan
II. Great Plains—Missouri, Kansas, Arkansas, Oklahoma
III. Oklahoma

Osochi
Subdivision of **Creek**

Oto (Otoe)
I. Siouan
II. Great Plains—Nebraska, Missouri, Iowa, Kansas, Minnesota, Wisconsin, Oklahoma
III. Oklahoma

Ottawa
I. Algonquian
II. Northeast—Ontario, Michigan, Minnesota, Wisconsin, Illinois, Indiana, Iowa, Ohio, Kansas, Oklahoma
III. Ontario, Michigan, Kansas, Oklahoma

Otter
See **Amikwa**

Ouachita
Member of **Natchitoches Confederacy**

Outagami
See **Fox**

Owens Valley
Subdivision of **Paiute**

Ozette
Southern branch of **Makah**
I. Wakashan
II. Northwest—Washington

P

Padoucah
See **Comanche**

Pahvant
Subdivision of **Ute**

Paiute, Northern (Paviotso)
I. Uto-Aztecan
II. Great Basin—Nevada, Idaho, California, Oregon
III. Nevada, Oregon

Paiute, Southern
I. Uto-Aztecan
II. Great Basin—Nevada, Utah, Arizona, California
III. Arizona, California, Nevada, Utah

Pakana
Subdivision of **Creek**

Palouse (Palus)
I. Sahaptin-Nez Perce
II. Plateau—Washington, Idaho
III. Washington

Pamlico
I. Algonquian
II. Northeast—North Carolina

Pamunkey
Member of **Powhatan Confederacy**

Panamint (Koso)
I. Uto-Aztecan
II. Great Basin—California, Nevada

Papago
I. Uto-Aztecan
II. Southwest—Arizona, Mexico
III. Arizona

Pascagoula
I. Probably Muskogean
II. Southeast—Mississippi, Louisiana, Texas

Passamaquoddy
Subdivision of **Abnaki**
I. Algonquian
II. Northeast—Maine, New Brunswick
III. Maine

Patiri
I. Atakapan (Macro-Algonquian)
II. Southeast—Texas

Patwin
I. Wintun (Penutian)
II. California—California

Paugusset
Subdivision of **Wappinger**

Paviotso
See **Paiute, Northern**

Pavonia
Subdivision of **Delaware**

Pawnee
I. Caddoan
II. Great Plains—Nebraska, Kansas, Oklahoma
III. Oklahoma

Pawokti
I. Muskogean
II. Southeast—Florida, Alabama

Pecos (Pueblo)
I. Kiowa-Tanoan
II. Southwest—New Mexico

Pedee
I. Siouan
II. Southeast—South Carolina

Pend d'Oreille
See **Kalispel**

Pennacook
Subdivision of **Abnaki**
I. Algonquian
II. Northeast—New Hampshire, Maine, Massachusetts, Vermont, Quebec

Penobscot
Subdivision of **Abnaki**
I. Algonquian
II. Northeast—Maine
III. Maine

Pensacola
I. Muskogean
II. Southeast—Florida

Peoria (Mascouten)
Subdivision of **Illinois**
I. Algonquian
II. Northeast—Illinois, Indiana, Ohio, Wisconsin, Iowa, Missouri, Kansas, Oklahoma
III. Oklahoma

Pequawket
Subdivision of **Abnaki**
I. Algonquian
II. Northeast—Connecticut, Rhode Island
III. Connecticut

Pequot
I. Algonquian
II. Northeast—Connecticut, Rhode Island
III. Connecticut

Petun
See **Tobacco**

Piankashaw (Piankeshaw)
Subdivision of **Miami**
I. Algonquian
II. Northeast—Indiana, Illinois, Michigan, Kansas, Oklahoma
III. Oklahoma

Piegan
Subdivision of **Blackfoot**
I. Algonquian
II. Great Plains—Alberta, Montana
III. Alberta, Montana

Pilalt
Subdivision of **Cowichan**

Pima
I. Uto-Aztecan
II. Southwest—Arizona, Mexico
III. Arizona

Piro (Pueblos)
I. Kiowa-Tanoan
II. Southwest—New Mexico

Pithlako
Subdivision of **Creek**

Pit River
See **Achomawi**

Pocasset
Subdivision of **Wampanoag**

Pocomtuc (Pocutuc)
I. Algonquian
II. Northeast—Massachusetts, Connecticut, Vermont

Podunk
I. Algonquian
II. Northeast—Connecticut

Pohoy (Posoy, Ocita)
I. Timucuan
II. Southeast—Florida

Pomo
I. Pomo (Hokan)
II. California—California
III. California

Ponca
I. Siouan
II. Great Plains—South Dakota, Nebraska
III. Oklahoma, Nebraska

Poospatuck
Member of **Montauk Confederacy**
I. Algonquian
II. Northeast—New York

Potano
I. Timucuan
II. Southeast—Florida

Potawatomi
I. Algonquian
II. Northeast—Michigan, Illinois, Indiana, Iowa, Kansas, Ohio, Missouri, Wisconsin, Oklahoma
III. Oklahoma, Kansas, Michigan, Wisconsin , Ontario

Potomac
Member of **Powhatan Confederacy**

Powhatan (Confederacy)
I. Algonquian
II. Northeast–Virginia, Maryland, District of Columbia
III. Virginia **(Mattaponi, Pamunkey, Potomac,** and **Chickahominy** tribes)

Pshwanwapam
I. Sahaptin-Nez Perce (Penutian)
II. Plateau—Washington

Pueblo
See **Hopi, Jemez, Keres, Pecos, Piro, Tewa, Tiwa, Zuni**

Puntlatch (Pentlatch)
I. Salishan
II. Northwest—British Columbia
III. British Columbia

Puyallup
I. Salishan
II. Northwest—Washington
III. Washington

Q

Quahatica
I. Uto-Aztecan
II. California—California

Quaitso (Queets)
I. Salishan
II. Northwest—Washington

Quapaw (Arkansa)
I. Siouan
II. Great Plains—Arkansas, Louisiana, Mississippi, Kansas, Oklahoma, Texas
III. Oklahoma

Quechan
I. Yuman (Hokan)
II. California—Arizona, California
III. California

Quileute
I. Chimakuan
II. Northwest—Washington
III. Washington

Quinault (Quinaielt)
I. Salishan
II. Northwest—Washington
III. Washington

Quinipissa
I. Muskogean
II. Southeast—Louisiana

Quinnipiac
I. Algonquian
II. Northeast—Connecticut

R

Rappahannock
Member of **Powhatan Confederacy**

Raritan
Subdivision of **Delaware**

Redwood
See **Whilkut**

Ricaree
See **Arikara**

Rice
See **Menominee**

Rogue River
See **Takelma** and **Tututni**

S

Sac
See **Sauk**

Sahaptin
See **Nez Perce**

Sahehwamish
I. Salishan
II. Northwest—Washington

Sakonnet
I. Algonquian
II. Northeast—Rhode Island

Salina
I. Salinan (Hokan)
II. California—California

Salish, Coast
See **Flathead** for Inland **Salish**
I. Salishan
II. Northwest—Washington

Saluda
I. Algonquian
II. Southeast—South Carolina

Samish
I. Salishan
II. Northwest—Washington

Sanetch
Subdivision of **Songish**

Sanpoil (Nespelem)
I. Salishan
II. Plateau—Washington
III. Washington

Santee
Subdivision of **Sioux**

Santee
I. Siouan
II. Southeast—South Carolina

Santiam
I. Kalapuyan
II. Northwest—Oregon

Saponi
I. Siouan
II. Southeast—Virginia

Sara
See **Cheraw**

Sarcee (Sarsi)
I. Athapascan
II. Great Plains—Alberta
III. Alberta

Saschutkenne
I. Athapascan
II. Subarctic—British Columbia

Satsop
I. Salishan
II. Northwest—Washington

Saturiwa
I. Timucuan
II. Southeast—Florida

Sauk (Sac)
Allied with **Fox**
I. Algonquian
II. Northeast—Wisconsin, Illinois, Iowa, Kansas, Michigan, Minnesota, Missouri, Oklahoma
III. Iowa, Kansas, Oklahoma

Saulteaux
Subdivision of **Ojibway**

Sawokli
I. Muskogean
II. Southeast—Alabama, Georgia, Florida

Scaticook (Schaghticoke)
Subdivision of **Pequot**

Secotan
I. Algonquian
II. Northeast—North Carolina
III. Merged with **Machapunga**

Seechelt (Sishiatl)
I. Salishan
II. Northwest—British Columbia
III. British Columbia

Sekani
I. Athapascan
II. Subarctic—British Columbia
III. British Columbia

Sematuse
I. Salishan
II. Plateau—Montana

Semiahmoo
I. Salishan
II. Northwest—Washington, British Columbia
III. British Columbia

Seminole
I. Muskogean
II. Southeast—Florida
III. Florida—Oklahoma

Seneca
Member of **Iroquois Confederacy**
I. Iroquoian

II. Northeast—New York, Ontario, Ohio, Pennsylvania, Indiana, Wisconsin, Oklahoma
III. New York, Ontario, Oklahoma

Senijextee
See **Lake**

Serrano
I. Uto-Aztecan
II. California—California

Sewee
I. Siouan
II. Southeast—South Carolina

Shakori (Shoccoree)
I. Siouan
II. Southeast—North Carolina, South Carolina, Virginia

Shasta
I. Shastan (Hokan)
II. California—California
III. California

Shawnee
I. Algonquian
II. Northeast—Ohio, Indiana, Pennsylvania, Tennessee, Missouri, Kansas, Kentucky, Virginia, Alabama, Georgia, Maryland, District of Columbia, South Carolina, Illinois, Texas
III. Oklahoma, Kansas, Texas

Sheepeater
Name used for **Shoshonis** and **Bannocks**

Shinnecock
Member of **Montauk Confederacy**
I. Algonquian
II. Northeast—New York
III. New York

Shivwits
Subdivision of **Paiute**

Shoshoni, Northern (Wind River Shoshone)
I. Uto-Aztecan
II. Great Basin/Great Plains—Wyoming, Montana, Utah, Idaho
III. Wyoming, Idaho

Shoshoni, Western (Shoshone)
I. Uto-Aztecan
II. Great Basin—Nevada, Utah, Idaho, California
III. Nevada, California, Idaho

Shuman
See **Jumano**

Shuswap
I. Salishan
II. Plateau—British Columbia
III. British Columbia

Siksika
See **Blackfoot**

Siletz
I. Salishan
II. Northwest—Oregon

Sinanoy
Subdivision of **Wappinger**

Sinkakaius
I. Salishan
II. Plateau—Washington

Sinkiuse
See **Columbia**

Sinkyone
I. Athapascan
II. California—California

Sioux (Dakota, Lakota)
Subdivisions include **Santee, Teton, Yankton, Yanktonai**
I. Siouan
II. Great Plains—South Dakota, North Dakota, Nebraska, Montana, Wyoming, Minnesota, Iowa, Wisconsin, Missouri
III. South Dakota, North Dakota, Minnesota, Nebraska, Alberta, Saskatchewan, Manitoba

Sishiatl
See **Seechelt**

Sisseton
Subdivision of **Santee Sioux**

Sissipahaw
I. Siouan
II. Southeast—North Carolina, South Carolina

Siuslaw
I. Yakonan (Penutian)
II. Northwest—Oregon

Skagit
I. Salishan
II. Northwest—Washington

Sklallam
See **Clallam**

Skidi
Subdivision of **Pawnee**

Skilloot
I. Chinookan (Penutian)
II. Northwest—Washington

Skin
I. Sahaptin-Nez Perce (Penutian)
II. Plateau—Washington

Skitswish
See **Coeur d'Alene**

Skokomish
Branch of **Twana**
I. Salishan
II. Northwest—Washington
III. Washington

Skykomish
Subdivision of **Snoqualmie**

Slave (Etchaottine)
I. Athapascan
II. Subarctic—Alberta, British Columbia, Yukon
III. British Columbia, Northwest Territories

Snake
Name formerly used for **Northern Paiute, Walpapi, Yahuskin, Bannock, Northern Shoshoni, Commanche**

Snohomish
I. Salishan

II. Northwest—Washington
III. Washington

Snoqualmie
I. Salishan
II. Northwest—Washington

Sobaipuri
I. Uto-Aztecan
II. Southwest—Arizona
III. Merged with **Papago**

Socatino
I. Probably Caddoan
II. Southeast—Texas, Louisiana

Songish
I. Salishan
II. Northwest—British Columbia, Washington
III. British Columbia

Sooke
Subdivision of **Songish**

Spokane
I. Salishan
II. Plateau—Washington, Idaho, Montana
III. Washington

Squamish (Squawmish)
I. Salishan
II. Northwest—British Columbia
III. British Columbia

Squaxin (Squakson)
I. Salishan
II. Northwest—Washington
III. Washington

Stalo
I. Salishan
II. Northwest—British Columbia, Washington

Steilacoom
Subdivision of **Puyallup**

Stillaguamish
Subdivision of **Skagit**

Stockbridge (Housatonic)
Subdivision of **Mahican**

Stoney
See **Assiniboine**

Stuwihamuk
I. Athapascan
II. Plateau—British Columbia
III. Absorbed by **Ntlakyapamuk**

Sugeree
I. Probably Siouan
II. Southeast—North Carolina

Sumass
Subdivision of **Cowichan**

Suquamish
I. Salishan
II. Northeast—Washington
III. Washington

Surruque
I. Timucuan
II. Southeast—Florida

Susquehannock
(Susquehanna, Conestoga)
I. Iroquoian
II. Northeast— Pennsylvania, New York, Maryland

Sutaio
Possible branch **Cheyenne**

I. Algonquian
II. Great Plains—South Dakota

Swallah
I. Salishan
II. Northwest—Washington

Swinomish
Possible offshoot of **Skagit**
I. Salishan
II. Northwest—Washington
III. Washington

T

Tacatacura
I. Timucuan
II. Southeast—Florida

Tachi
Subdivision of **Yokut**

Taensa
I. Muskogean
II. Southeast—Louisiana, Alabama

Tagish
Subdivision of **Nahane**
I. Athapascan
II. Subarctic—Yukon, British Columbia
III. Yukon

Tahltan
Subdivision of **Nahane**
I. Athapascan
II. Subarctic— Alberta, British Columbia

Taidnapam (Upper Cowlitz)
I. Sahaptin-Nez Perce (Penutian)
II. Northwest—Washington

Takelma (Rogue River)
I. Takelma (Penutian)
II. Northwest—Oregon

Tali
Probable subdivision of **Creek**

Taltushtuntude (Galice)
I. Athapascan
II. Northwest—Oregon

Tamaroa
Subdivision of **Illinois**

Tamathli
I. Muskogean
II. Southeast—Georgia, Florida

Tanaina
I. Athapascan
II. Subarctic—Alaska
III. Alaska

Tanana
I. Athapascan
II. Subarctic—Alaska
III. Alaska

Tangipahoa
I. Muskogean
II. Southeast—Louisiana

Tanoan Pueblos
See **Tewa, Tiwa, Jemez, Pecos**

Taovayas
French name for **Wichita** and **Caddo** fur traders

Taposa
I. Muskogean
II. Southeast—Mississippi

Tappan
Subdivision of **Delaware**

Tatsanottine
See **Yellowknife**

Tawakoni
I. Caddoan
II. Great Plains—Oklahoma, Texas
III. Merged with **Wichita**

Tawasa
I. Timucuan
II. Southeast—Florida, Louisiana

Tawehash
See **Taovayas**

Tegua or **Tehua**
See **Tewa**

Tekesta (Tequesta)
I. Probably Muskogean
II. Southeast—Florida

Tenino (Warm Springs)
I. Sahaptin-Nez Perce (Penutian)
II. Plateau—Oregon
III. Washington

Tete de Boule
Subdivision of **Cree**

Teton
Subdivision of **Sioux**

Tewa (Pueblos) (Tegua, Tehua)
I. Kiowa-Tanoan
II. Southwest—New Mexico
III. New Mexico

Texas
See **Hasinai Confederacy**

Thlingchadinne
See **Dogrib**

Thompson
See **Ntlakyapamuk**

Tigua or **Tihua**
See **Tiwa**

Tillamook
I. Salishan
II. Northwest—Oregon

Timucua (Utina)
I. Timucuan
II. Southeast—Florida

Tionontati
See **Tobacco**

Tiou
I. Tunica (Macro-Algonquian)
II. Southeast—Mississippi

Tipai
See **Kamia**

Tiwa (Pueblos) (Tigua, Tihua)
I. Kiowa-Tanoan
II. Southwest—New Mexico
III. New Mexico

Tlallam
See **Clallam**

Tlatskanai
See **Clatskanie**

Tlingit
I. Tlingit (Na-Dene)
II. Northwest—Alaska
III. Alaska

Toanho
See **Twana**

Tobacco (Petun, Tionontati)
I. Iroquoian
II. Northeast—Ontario, Wisconsin
III. Descendants among **Wyandot**

Tocobaga
I. Timucuan
II. Southeast—Florida

Tohome
I. Muskogean
II. Southeast—Alabama

Tolowa
I. Athapascan
II. California—California, Oregon
III. Oregon

Tongass
Subdivision of **Tlingit**

Tonkawa
I. Tonkawan (Macro-Algonquian)
II. Great Plains—Texas, Oklahoma
III. Oklahoma

Tonto
Subdivision of **Apache**

Towa
See **Jemez**

Tsattine
See **Beaver**

Tsetsaut
I. Athapascan
II. Subarctic—British Columbia

Tsethaottine
See **Mountain**

Tsimshian
I. Tsimshian (Penutian)
II. Northwest—British Columbia, Alaska
III. British Columbia, Alaska

Tubatulabal
I. Uto-Aztecan
II. California—California

Tukabahchee
Subdivision of **Creek**

Tukuarika
Subdivision of **Shoshoni**

Tule Lake
Subdivision of **Modoc**

Tunica
I. Tunica (Macro-Algonquian)
II. Southeast—Mississippi, Arkansas
III. Louisiana

Tuscarora
Member of **Iroquois Confederacy**
I. Iroquoian
II. Northeast—North Carolina, Pennsylvania, New York
III. New York, Ontario

Tuskegee
I. Muskogean
II. Southeast—Alabama, Tennessee, Oklahoma

Tutchone
I. Athapascan
II. Subarctic—Yukon
III. Yukon

Tutelo
I. Siouan
II. Southeast—Virginia, North Carolina, Pennsylvania, New York

Tututni (Rogue River)
I. Athapascan
II. Northwest—Oregon

Twana (Toanho)
I. Salishan
II. Northwest—Washington
III. Washington

Tyigh
I. Sahaptin-Nez Perce
II. Plateau—Oregon

U

Uinkarets
Subdivision of **Paiute**

Uintah
Subdivision of **Ute**

Umatilla
I. Sahaptin-Nez Perce
II. Plateau—Oregon, Washington
III. Oregon

Umpqua, Lower
See **Kuitsh**

Umpqua, Upper
I. Athapascan
II. Northwest—Oregon

Unalachtigo
Subdivision of **Delaware**

Unami
Subdivision of **Delaware**

Ute
I. Uto-Aztecan
II. Great Basin—Utah, Colorado, New Mexico, Nevada, Wyoming
III. Colorado, Utah

Utina
See **Timucua**

V

Vanyume
I. Uto-Aztecan
II. California—California

W

Wabanaki
See **Abnaki**

Waccamaw
I. Siouan
II. Southeast—South Carolina, North Carolina
III. South Carolina

Waco
I. Caddoan
II. Great Plains—Texas, Oklahoma

Wahpeton
Subdivision of **Santee Sioux**

Wailaki
I. Athapascan
II. California—California

Wakokai
Subdivision of **Creek**

Walapai
See **Hualapai**

Walla Walla (Wallawalla)
I. Sahaptin-Nez Perce (Penutian)
II. Plateau—Oregon, Washington
III. Oregon

Walpapi
Subdivision of **Paiute, Northern**

Wampanoag
I. Algonquian
II. Northeast—Rhode Island, Massachusetts
III. Rhode Island, Massachusetts

Wanapam
I. Sahaptin-Nez Perce (Penutian)
II. Plateau—Washington

Wappinger
I. Algonquian
II. Northeast—New York, Connecticut
III. Connecticut

Wappo
I. Yukian
II. California—California
III. California

Warm Springs
See **Tenino**

Wasco
I. Chinookan (Penutian)
II. Northwest—Oregon
III. Oregon

Washa
I. Tunican (Macro-Algonquian)
II. Southeast—Louisiana

Washo (Washoe)
I. Washo (Hokan)
II. Great Basin—Nevada
III. Nevada, California

Watteree
I. Siouan
II. Southeast—South Carolina, North Carolina

Watlala
I. Chinookan (Penutian)
II. Northwest—Oregon

Wauyukma
I. Sahaptin-Nez Perce
II. Plateau—Washington

Waxhaw
I. Siouan
II. Southeast—South Carolina, North Carolina

Wea
Subdivision of **Miami**
I. Algonquian
II. Northeast— Indiana, Wisconsin, Illinois, Missouri, Kansas, Oklahoma

III. Oklahoma

Weapemeoc (Yeopim)
I. Algonquian
II. Northeast—North Carolina

Wenatchee
I. Salishan
II. Plateau—Washington
III. Washington

Wenro (Wenrohronon)
I. Iroquoian
II. Northeast—New York, Pennsylvania

Western Apache
See **Aravaipa**

Westo
See **Yuchi**

Whilkut (Redwood)
I. Athapascan
II. California—California
III. California

White Mountain (Coyotera)
Subdivision of **Apache**

Wichita (Pict)
I. Caddoan
II. Great Plains—Kansas, Texas, Oklahoma
III. Oklahoma

Winnebago
I. Siouan
II. Northeast—Wisconsin, Illinois, Iowa, Minnesota, South Dakota
III. Nebraska, Wisconsin, Minnesota

Winnemucca
Subdivision of **Paiute, Northern**

Wintun
I. Wintun (Penutian)
II. California—California
III. California

Wishram
I. Chinookan (Penutian)
II. Plateau—Oregon, Washington
III. Washington

Wiwohka
Subdivision of **Creek**

Wiyot
I. Wiyot (Macro-Algonquian)
II. California—California
III. California

Woccon
Possible subdivision of **Waccamaw**
I. Siouan
II. Southeast—North Carolina

Wokokai
Subdivision of **Creek**

Wongunk
Subdivision of **Mattabesec**

Wyandot
Descendants of **Huron** and **Tobacco**
I. Iroquoian
II. Northeast—Ontario, Quebec, Ohio, Illinois, Indiana, Kansas, Michigan, Minnesota,

Wisconsin
III. Oklahoma, Kansas

Wynoochie
I. Salishan
II. Northwest—Washington

Y

Yadkin
I. Siouan
II. Southeast—North Carolina

Yahi
I. Yanan (Hokan)
II. California—California

Yahuskin
Subdivision of **Paiute, Northern**
I. Uto-Aztecan
II. Great Basin—Oregon

Yakima
I. Sahaptin-Nez Perce
II. Plateau—Washington
III. Washington

Yakutat
Subdivision of **Tlingit**

Yamasee
I. Muskogean
II. Southeast—Georgia, Florida, Alabama, South Carolina

Yamel
I. Kalapuyan
II. Northwest—Oregon

Yana
I. Yanan (Hokan)
II. California—California

Yankton
Subdivision of **Sioux**

Yanktonai
Subdivision of **Sioux**

Yaqui
I. Uto-Aztecan
II. Southwest—Mexico
III. Arizona, Mexico

Yaquina
I. Yakanan (Penutian)
II. Northwest—Oregon

Yavapai
I. Yuman (Hokan)
II. Southwest—Arizona
III. Arizona

Yazoo
I. Tunican (Macro-Algonquian)
II. Southeast—Mississippi, Arkansas, Louisiana

Yellowknife (Tatsanottine, Copper)
I. Athapascan
II. Subarctic—Northwest Territories
III. Northwest Territories

Yeopim
See **Weapemeoc**

Yokuts (Mariposa)
I. Yokuts (Penutian)
II. California—California
III. California

Yoncalla
I. Kalapuyan
II. Northwest—Oregon

Yskani
I. Caddoan
II. Great Plains—Kansas

Yuchi (Westo)
I. Yuchi (Macro-Siouan)
II. Southeast—Georgia, Florida, South Carolina, Tennessee
III. Oklahoma,

Yui
I. Timucuan
II. Southeast—Florida, Georgia

Yuki
I. Yukian
II. California—California
III. California

Yuma (Quechan)
I. Yuman (Hokan)
II. Southwest—Arizona, California
III. Arizona

Yurok
I. Yurok (Macro-Algonquian)
II. California—California
III. California

Z

Zuni (Pueblos)
I. Zuni (Penutian)
II. Southwest—New Mexico, Arizona
III. New Mexico

FEDERAL AND STATE INDIAN RESERVATIONS, TRUST AREAS, AND NATIVE VILLAGES IN THE UNITED STATES

ALASKA

AHTNA, INCORPORATED
Copper Center
Copper River Native Association
2 Native Villages (Athapascan): Copper Center, Gulkana

ALEUT CORPORATION
Anchorage
Aleut League
13 Native Villages (Aleut): Akutan, Atka, Belkofsky, False Pass, King Cove, Nelson Lagoon, Nikolski, Pauloff Harbor, St. George, St. Paul, Sand Point, Squaw Harbor, Unalaska

ARCTIC SLOPE REGIONAL CORPORATION
Barrow
Arctic Slope Native Association
5 Native Villages (Eskimo): Anaktuvak Pass, Barrow, Kaktovik (Barter Island), Point Hope, Wainwright

BERING STRAITS NATIVE CORPORATION
Nome
Bering Straits Native Association

16 Native Villages (Eskimo): Brevig Mission, Diomede (Inalik), Elim, Gambell, Golovin, Koyuk, Nome, St. Michael, Savoonga, Shaktoolik, Shishmaref, Stebbins, Teller, Unalakleet, Wales, White Mountain

BRISTOL BAY NATIVE CORPORATION
Dillingham
Bristol Bay Native Association
24 Native Villages (Eskimo and Aleut): Chignik, Chignik Lagoon, Chignik Lake, Clark's Point, Dillingham, Egegik, Ekuk, Ekwok, Igiugig, Ivanof Bay, Koliganek, Lake Aleknagik, Levelock, Manokotak, Newhalen, New Stuyahok, Nondalton, Pedro Bay, Perryville, Pilot Point, Port Heiden (Meshik), South Naknek, Togiak, Twin Hills

CALISTA CORPORATION
Anchorage
Yupiktak Bista Association
44 Native Villages (Eskimo and Athapascan): Akiachak, Akiak, Akolmuit (Nunapitchuk and Kasigluk), Alakanuk, Aniak, Bethel, Chefornak, Chevak, Crooked Creek, Eek, Emmonak, Goodnews Bay, Holy Cross, Hooper Bay, Kipnuk, Kongiganak, Kotlik, Kwethluk, Kwigillingok, Kwinhagek (Quinhagek), Lime Village, Lower Kalskag, Marshall (Fortuna Ledge), Mekoryuk, Mountain Village, Napakiak, Napaskiak, Newtok, Nightmute (Nightmuit), Oscarville, Pilot Station, Pitkas Point, Platinum, Russian Mission (Yukon), St. Mary's, Scammon Bay, Sheldon's Point, Sleetmute, Stony River, Tanunak, Toksook Bay, Tuluksak, Tuntutuliak, Upper Kalskag (Kalskag)

CHUGACH NATIVES, INCORPORATED
Anchorage
Chugach Native Association
4 Native Villages (Aleut and Athapascan): English Bay, Port Graham, Seldovia (Indian Possessions), Tatitlek

COOK INLET REGION, INCORPORATED
Anchorage
Cook Inlet Native Association
3 Native Villages (Athapascan): Eklutna, Ninilchik, Tyonek

DOYON, LIMITED
Fairbanks
Tanana Chiefs Conference
32 Native Villages (Athapascan and Eskimo): Alatna, Allakaket, Anvik, Arctic Village, Beaver, Cantwell, Chalkyitsik, Circle, Dot Lake, Eagle Village (Eagle), Fort Yukon, Galena, Grayling, Hughes, Huslia, Kaltag, Koyukuk, McGrath (McGrath Native Village), Mentasta Lake (Mentasta), Minto, Nenana Addition (Nenana), Nikolai,

Northway, Nulato, Rampart, Ruby, Shageluk, Stevens Village, Tanacross, Tanana, Tetlin, Venetie

KONIAG, INCORPORATED
Kodiak
Kodiak Area Native Association
7 Native Villages (Aleut): Akhiok, Karluk, Kodiak, Larsen Bay, Old Harbor, Ouzinkie, Port Lions

NANA REGIONAL CORPORATION
Kotzebue
Northwest Alaska Native Association
10 Native Villages (Eskimo): Ambler, Buckland, Deering, Kiana, Kivalina, Kotzebue, Noatak, Noorvik, Selawik, Shungnak

SEALASKA CORPORATION
Juneau
Tlingit-Haida Central Council
11 Native Villages (Tlingit and Haida): Angoon, Craig, Hoonah, Hydaburg, Juneau (Juneau Indian Village), Kake, Klawock, Klukwan, Saxman, Sitka Village, Yakutat

ANNETTE ISLAND RESERVE (Federal)
Southeast Region
Tribal Headquarters: Metlakatla
Tsimshian Tribe

ARIZONA

AK CHIN RESERVATION (Federal)
Pinal County
Tribal Headquarters: Ak Chin Community
Papago Tribe

CAMP VERDE RESERVATION (Federal)
Yavapai County
Tribal Headquarters: Middle Verde
Yavapai-Apache Tribe

COCOPAH RESERVATION (Federal)
Yuma County
Tribal Headquarters: Somerton
Yuma Tribe

COLORADO RIVER RESERVATION (Federal)
Yuma County, Arizona
San Bernardino and Riverside counties, California
Tribal Headquarters: Parker, Arizona
Mojave and Chemehuevi Tribes

FORT APACHE RESERVATION (Federal)
Apache, Gila, and Navajo counties
Tribal Headquarters: Whiteriver
White Mountain Apache Tribe

FORT MCDOWELL RESERVATION (Federal)
Maricopa County
Tribal Headquarters: Scottsdale
Mojave, Apache, and Yavapai Tribes

GILA RIVER INDIAN COMMUNITY (Federal)
Maricopa and Pinal counties
Tribal Headquarters: Sacaton
Pima and Maricopa Tribes

HAVASUPAI RESERVATION (Federal)
Coconino County
Tribal Headquarters: Supai
Havasupai Tribe

HOPI RESERVATION (Federal)
Coconino and Navajo counties
Tribal Headquarters: Oraibi
Hopi Tribe

HUALAPAI RESERVATION (Federal)
Mohave, Coconino, and Yavapai counties
Tribal Headquarters: Peach Springs
Hualapai Tribe

KAIBAB RESERVATION (Federal)
Mohave County
Tribal Headquarters: Tribal Affairs Building, Fredonia
Paiute Tribe

NAVAJO RESERVATION (Federal)
Apache, Navajo, and Coconino counties, Arizona
San Juan and McKinley counties, New Mexico
San Juan County, Utah
Tribal Headquarters: Window Rock, Arizona
Navajo Tribe

PAPAGO RESERVATION (Federal)
Maricopa, Pima, and Pinal counties
Tribal Headquarters: Sells
Papago Tribe

PAYSON COMMUNITY OF YAVAPAI-APACHE INDIANS (Federal)
Gila County
Tribal Headquarters: Payson
Yavapai-Apache Tribe

SALT RIVER RESERVATION (Federal)
Maricopa County
Tribal Headquarters: Scottsdale
Pima and Maricopa Tribes

SAN CARLOS RESERVATION (Federal)
Gila and Graham counties
Tribal Headquarters: San Carlos
Apache Tribe

YAVAPAI RESERVATION (Federal)
Yavapai County
Tribal Headquarters: Prescott
Yavapai Tribe

CALIFORNIA

AGUA CALIENTE RESERVATION (Federal)
Riverside County
Tribal Headquarters: Palm Springs
Agua Caliente Band of Mission Indians

ALTURAS RANCHERIA (Federal)
Modoc County
Tribal Headquarters: Alturas
Pit River Tribe

AUGUSTINE RESERVATION
(Federal)
Riverside County
Tribal Headquarters: Thermal
Augustine Band of Mission
Indians

BARONA RESERVATION
(Federal)
San Diego County
Tribal Headquarters: Lakeside
Barona Group of Capitan Grande
Band of Mission Indians

BERRY CREEK RANCHERIA
(Federal)
Butte County
Tribal Headquarters: Berry Creek
Maidu Tribe

BIG BEND RANCHERIA
(Federal)
Shasta County
Tribal Headquarters: Big Bend
Pit River Tribe

BIG LAGOON RANCHERIA
(Federal)
Humboldt County
Tribal Headquarters: Orick
Yurok Tribe

BIG PINE RESERVATION
(Federal)
Inyo County
Tribal Headquarters: Big Pine
Paiute and Shoshone Tribes

BIG SANDY RANCHERIA
(Federal)
Fresno County
Tribal Headquarters: Auberry
Mono Tribe

BISHOP RESERVATION (Federal)
Inyo County
Tribal Headquarters: Bishop
Paiute and Shoshone Tribes

CABAZON RESERVATION
(Federal)
Riverside County
Tribal Headquarters: Indio
Cabazon Band of Mission Indians

CAHUILLA RESERVATION
(Federal)
Riverside County
Tribal Headquarters: Hemet
Cahuilla Band of Mission Indians

CAMPO RESERVATION
(Federal)
San Diego County
Tribal Headquarters: Campo
Campo Community Band of
Mission Indians

CAPITAN GRANDE
RESERVATION (Federal)
San Diego County
Tribal Headquarters: Alpine
Capitan Grande Band of Mission
Indians

CEDARVILLE RANCHERIA
(Federal)
Modoc County
Tribal Headquarters: Cedarville
Paiute Tribe

CHEMEHUEVI RESERVATION
(Federal)
San Bernardino County
Tribal Headquarters: Havasu Lake
Chemehuevi Tribe

COLD SPRINGS RANCHERIA
(Federal)
Fresno County
Tribal Headquarters: Tollhouse
Mono Tribe

COLUSA RANCHERIA (Federal)
Colusa County
Tribal Headquarters: Colusa
Cachil Dehe Band of Wintun
Indians

CORTINA RANCHERIA (Federal)
Colusa County
Tribal Headquarters: Williams
Me-Wuk Tribe

CUYAPAIPE RESERVATION
(Federal)
San Diego County
Tribal Headquarters: Mount
Laguna
Cuyapaipe Band of Mission
Indians

DRY CREEK RANCHERIA
(Federal)
Sonoma County
Tribal Headquarters: Geyserville
Pomo Tribe

ENTERPRISE RANCHERIA
(Federal)
Butte County
Tribal Headquarters: Oroville
Maidu Tribe

FORT BIDWELL RESERVATION
(Federal)
Modoc County
Tribal Headquarters: Fort Bidwell
Paiute Tribe

FORT INDEPENDENCE
RESERVATION (Federal)
Inyo County
Tribal Headquarters:
Independence
Paiute Tribe

FORT MOJAVE RESERVATION
(Federal)
Clark County, Nevada
San Bernardino County,
California
Mohave County, Arizona
Tribal Headquarters: Needles,
California
Mojave Tribe

FORT YUMA RESERVATION
(Federal)
Imperial County, California
Mohave County, Arizona
Tribal Headquarters: Fort Yuma,
California
Quechan Tribe

GRINDSTONE CREEK
RANCHERIA (Federal)
Glenn County
Tribal Headquarters: Elk Creek
Wintun Tribe

HOOPA EXTENSION
RESERVATION (Federal)
Humboldt County
Tribal Headquarters: Hoopa
Yurok Tribe

HOOPA VALLEY
RESERVATION (Federal)
Humboldt County
Tribal Headquarters: Hoopa
Hoopa Tribe

HOPLAND RANCHERIA
(Federal)
Mendocino County
Tribal Headquarters: Hopland
Pomo Tribe

INAJA-COSMIT RESERVATION
(Federal)
San Diego County
Tribal Headquarters: Julian
Inaja-Cosmit Band of Mission
Indians

JACKSON RANCHERIA (Federal)
Amador County
Tribal Headquarters: Jackson
Me-Wuk Tribe

LA JOLLA RESERVATION
(Federal)
San Diego County
Tribal Headquarters: Escondido
La Jolla Band of Mission Indians

LA POSTA RESERVATION
(Federal)
San Diego County
Tribal Headquarters: c/o Southern
California Agency, Bureau of
Indian Affairs, Riverside
La Posta Band of Mission Indians

LAYTONVILLE RESERVATION
(Federal)
Mendocino County
Tribal Headquarters: Laytonville
Cahto Tribe

LIKELY RESERVATION (Federal)
Modoc County
Tribal Headquarters: Likely
Pit River Tribe

LONE PINE RESERVATION
(Federal)
Inyo County
Tribal Headquarters: Lone Pine
Paiute and Shoshone Tribes

LOOKOUT RANCHERIA
(Federal)
Modoc County
Tribal Headquarters: Lookout
Pit River Tribe

LOS COYOTES RESERVATION
(Federal)
San Diego County
Tribal Headquarters: Warner
Springs
Los Coyotes Band of Mission
Indians

MANCHESTER–POINT ARENA
RANCHERIA (Federal)
Mendocino County
Tribal Headquarters: Manchester
Pomo Tribe

MANZANITA RESERVATION
(Federal)
San Diego County
Tribal Headquarters: Boulevard
Manzanita Band of Mission
Indians

MESA GRANDE RESERVATION
(Federal)
San Diego County

Tribal Headquarters: Pala
Mesa Grande Band of Mission
Indians

MIDDLETOWN RANCHERIA
(Federal)
Lake County
Tribal Headquarters: Middletown
Pomo Tribe

MONTGOMERY CREEK
RANCHERIA (Federal)
Shasta County
Tribal Headquarters: Montgomery
Creek
Pit River Tribe

MORONGO RESERVATION
(Federal)
Riverside County
Tribal Headquarters: Banning
Morongo Band of Mission Indians

PALA RESERVATION (Federal)
San Diego County
Tribal Headquarters: Pala
Pala Band of Mission Indians

PAUMA AND YUIMA
RESERVATION (Federal)
San Diego County
Tribal Headquarters: Pauma
Valley
Pauma Band of Mission Indians

PECHANGA RESERVATION
(Federal)
Riverside County
Tribal Headquarters: Temecula
Pechanga Band of Mission
Indians

RAMONA RESERVATION
(Federal)
Riverside County
Tribal Headquarters: c/o Southern
California Agency, Bureau of
Indians Affairs, Riverside
Cahuilla Band of Mission Indians

RESIGHINI RANCHERIA
(Federal)
Del Norte County
Tribal Headquarters: Klamath
Coast Indian Community

RINCON RESERVATION
(Federal)
San Diego County
Tribal Headquarters: Valley
Center
San Luiseno Band of Mission
Indians

ROARING CREEK RANCHERIA
(Federal)
Shasta County
Tribal Headquarters: Montgomery
Creek
Pit River Tribe

ROUND VALLEY
RESERVATION (Federal)
Mendocino County
Tribal Headquarters: Covelo
Yuki, Pit River, Little Lake,
Konkau, Wailaki, Pomo, Nom-
laka, and Wintun Tribes

RUMSEY RANCHERIA (Federal)
Yolo County
Tribal Headquarters: Brooks
Wintun Tribe

SAN MANUEL RESERVATION
(Federal)
San Bernardino County
Tribal Headquarters: San
Bernardino
San Manuel Band of Mission
Indians

SAN PASQUAL RESERVATION
(Federal)
San Diego County
Tribal Headquarters: Valley
Center
San Pasqual Band of Mission
Indians

SANTA ROSA RANCHERIA
(Federal)
Kings County
Tribal Headquarters: Lemoore
Tachi Tribe

SANTA ROSA RESERVATION
(Federal)
Riverside County
Tribal Headquarters: Hemet
Santa Rosa Band of Mission
Indians

SANTA YNEZ RESERVATION
(Federal)
Santa Barbara County
Tribal Headquarters: Santa Ynez
Santa Ynez Band of Mission
Indians

SANTA YSABEL RESERVATION
(Federal)
San Diego County
Tribal Headquarters: Santa Ysabel
Santa Ysabel Band of Mission
Indians

SHEEP RANCH RANCHERIA
(Federal)
Calaveras County
Tribal Headquarters: Sheepranch
Me-Wuk Tribe

SHERWOOD VALLEY
RANCHERIA (Federal)
Mendocino County
Tribal Headquarters: Willits
No tribal designation

SOBOBA RESERVATION
(Federal)
Riverside County
Tribal Headquarters: San Jacinto
Soboba Band of Mission Indians

STEWARTS POINT RANCHERIA
(Federal)
Sonoma County
Tribal Headquarters: Stewarts
Point
Kashia Band of Pomo Indians

SULPHUR BAND RANCHERIA
(Federal)
(El-Em Indian Colony)
Lake County
Tribal Headquarters: Clearlake
Oaks
Pomo Tribe

SUSANVILLE RANCHERIA
(Federal)
Lassen County
Tribal Headquarters: Susanville
Paiute, Maidu, Pit River, and
Washoe Tribes

SYCUAN RESERVATION
(Federal)
San Diego County
Tribal Headquarters: El Cajon
Sycuan Band of Mission Indians

TORRES MARTINEZ
RESERVATION (Federal)
Imperial and Riverside Counties
Tribal Headquarters: Thermal
Torres Martinez Band of Mission
Indians

TRINIDAD RANCHERIA
(Federal)
Humboldt County
Tribal Headquarters: Trinidad
Yurok Tribe

TULE RIVER RESERVATION
(Federal)
Tulare County
Tribal Headquarters: Porterville
Tule River Tribe

TUOLUMNE RANCHERIA
(Federal)
Tuolumne County
Tribal Headquarters: Tuolumne
Tuolumne Band of Me-Wuk
Indians

TWENTYNINE PALMS
RESERVATION (Federal)
San Bernardino County
Tribal Headquarters: North Palm
Springs
Twentynine Palms Band of
Mission Indians

UPPER LAKE RANCHERIA
(Federal)
Lake County
Tribal Headquarters: Upper Lake
Pomo Tribe

VIEJAS RESERVATION (Federal)
San Diego County
Tribal Headquarters: Alpine
Viejas Group of Capitan Grande
Band of Mission Indians

X L RANCH RESERVATION
(Federal)
Modoc County
Tribal Headquarters: Alturas
Pit River and Paiute Tribes

COLORADO

SOUTHERN UTE RESERVATION
(Federal)
La Plata, Archuleta, and
Montezuma counties
Tribal Headquarters: Ignacio
Mouache and Capote Ute Tribes

UTE MOUNTAIN
RESERVATION (Federal)
Montezuma and La Plata
counties, Colorado
San Juan County, New Mexico
San Juan County, Utah
Tribal Headquarters: Towaoc,
Colorado
Wiminuche Ute Tribe

CONNECTICUT

EASTERN PEQUOT & WESTERN
PEQUOT RESERVATIONS (State)
New London County
Tribal Headquarters: Eastern

Pequot Reservation: North
Stonington Western Pequot
Reservation: Ledyard
Pequot and Mohegan Tribes

GOLDEN HILL RESERVATION
(State)
Fairfield County
Tribal Headquarters: Trumbull
Pequot and Mohegan Tribes

SCHAGHTICOKE
RESERVATION (State)
Litchfield County
Tribal Headquarters: Kent
Schaghticoke Tribe

FLORIDA

BIG CYPRESS RESERVATION
(Federal)
Hendry County
Tribal Headquarters: Hollywood
Seminole Tribe

BRIGHTON RESERVATION
(Federal)
Glades County
Tribal Headquarters: Hollywood
Seminole Tribe

FLORIDA STATE RESERVATION
(State)
Broward County
Tribal Headquarters: Hollywood
Miccosukee and Seminole Tribes

HOLLYWOOD RESERVATION
(Federal)
Broward County
Tribal Headquarters: Hollywood
Seminole Tribe

MICCOSUKEE RESERVATION
(Federal)
Dade County
Tribal Headquarters: Homestead
Miccosukee Tribe

IDAHO

COEUR D'ALENE
RESERVATION (Federal)
Benewah and Kootenai counties
Tribal Headquarters: Plummer
Coeur d'Alene Tribe

FORT HALL RESERVATION
(Federal)
Bannock, Bingham, Caribou, and
Power counties
Tribal Headquarters: Fort Hall
Shoshone and Bannock Tribes

KOOTENAI RESERVATION
(Federal)
Boundary County
Tribal Headquarters: Bonners
Ferry
Kootenai Tribe

NEZ PERCE RESERVATION
(Federal)
Nez Perce, Lewis, Clearwater,
and Idaho counties
Tribal Headquarters: Lapwai
Nez Perce Tribe

IOWA

SAC AND FOX RESERVATION
(Federal)
Tama County
Tribal Headquarters: Bureau of

Indian Affairs School, Tama
Sac and Fox (Mesquakie) Tribes

KANSAS

IOWA RESERVATION (Federal)
Richardson County, Nebraska
Brown County, Kansas
Tribal Headquarters: Horton,
Kansas
Iowa Tribe

KICKAPOO RESERVATION
(Federal)
Brown County
Tribal Headquarters: Horton
Kickapoo Tribe

POTAWATOMI RESERVATION
(Federal)
Jackson County
Tribal Headquarters: Horton
Potawatomi Tribe

SAC AND FOX RESERVATION
(Federal)
Brown County, Kansas
Richardson County, Nebraska
Tribal Headquarters: Horton,
Kansas
Sac and Fox Tribes

LOUISIANA

CHITIMACHA RESERVATION
(Federal)
Saint Mary Parish
Tribal Headquarters: Charenton
Chitimacha Tribe

MAINE

PENOBSCOT RESERVATION
(State)
Penobscot County
Tribal Headquarters: Indian
Island, Old Town
Penobscot Tribe

PLEASANT POINT AND
INDIAN TOWNSHIP
RESERVATIONS (State)
Washington County
Tribal Headquarters: Peter Dana
Point
Passamaquoddy Tribe

MASSACHUSETTS

HASSANAMISCO
RESERVATION (State)
Worcester County
Tribal Headquarters: Grafton
Hassanamisco-Nipmuc Tribe

MICHIGAN

BAY MILLS RESERVATION
(Federal)
Chippewa County
Tribal Headquarters: Brimley
Chippewa Tribe

HANNAHVILLE RESERVATION
(Federal)
Menominee County
Tribal Headquarters: Wilson
Potawatomi Tribe

HURON POTAWATOMI BAND,
INC. (State)
Calhoun County
Tribal Headquarters: Athens

Township
Potawatomi Tribe

ISABELLA RESERVATION
(Federal)
Isabella County
Tribal Headquarters: Mount
Pleasant
Saginaw Chippewa Tribe

KEWEENAW BAY
RESERVATION (Federal)
Baraga County
Tribal Headquarters: Baraga
Lake Superior Band, Chippewa
Tribe

MINNESOTA

FOND DU LAC RESERVATION
(Federal)
Carlton and Saint Louis Counties
Tribal Headquarters: Cloquet
Mississippi Band of Chippewa

GRAND PORTAGE
RESERVATION (Federal)
Cook County
Tribal Headquarters: Grand
Portage
Chippewa Tribe

LEECH LAKE RESERVATION
(Federal)
Beltrami, Cass, Hubbard, and
Itasca counties
Tribal Headquarters: Cass Lake
Chippewa Tribe

LOWER SIOUX RESERVATION
(Federal)
Redwood County
Tribal Headquarters: Morton
Eastern or Mississippi Sioux Tribe

MILLE LACS RESERVATION
(Federal)
Mille Lacs, Aitkin, and Pine
counties
Tribal Headquarters: Onamia
Chippewa Tribe

NETT LAKE RESERVATION
(Federal)
Koochiching and St. Louis
counties
Tribal Headquarters: Nett Lake
Chippewa Tribe

PRAIRIE ISLAND
RESERVATION (Federal)
Goodhue County
Tribal Headquarters: Welch
Eastern or Mississippi Sioux Tribe

PRIOR LAKE RESERVATION
(Federal)
Carver County
Tribal Headquarters: Prior Lake
Shakopee Mdewakanton Sioux
Tribe

RED LAKE RESERVATION
(Federal)
Beltrami and Clearwater counties
Tribal Headquarters: Redlake
Chippewa Tribe

UPPER SIOUX RESERVATION
(Federal)
Yellow Medicine County
Tribal Headquarters: Granite Falls
Eastern or Mississippi Sioux Tribe

WHITE EARTH RESERVATION
(Federal)
Mahnomen, Becker, and
Clearwater counties
Tribal Headquarters: White Earth
Chippewa Tribe

MISSISSIPPI

CHOCTAW RESERVATION
(Federal)
Neshoba, Newton, Leake, Scott,
Jones, Attala, Kemper, and
Winston counties
Tribal Headquarters: Pearl River,
Neshoba County
Choctaw Tribe

MONTANA

BLACKFEET RESERVATION
(Federal)
Glacier and Pondera counties
Tribal Headquarters: Browning
Blackfeet Tribe

CROW RESERVATION (Federal)
Big Horn, Yellowstone, and
Treasure counties
Tribal Headquarters: Crow
Agency
Crow Tribe

FLATHEAD RESERVATION
(Federal)
Flathead, Lake, Missoula, and
Sanders counties
Tribal Headquarters: Dixon
Salish and Kootenai Tribes

FORT BELKNAP RESERVATION
(Federal)
Blaine and Phillips counties
Tribal Headquarters: Harlem
Gros Ventre and Assiniboine
Tribes

FORT PECK RESERVATION
(Federal)
Valley, Roosevelt, Daniels, and
Sheridan counties
Tribal Headquarters: Poplar
Assiniboine and Sioux Tribes

NORTHERN CHEYENNE
RESERVATION (Federal)
Big Horn and Rosebud counties
Tribal Headquarters: Lame Deer
Northern Cheyenne Tribe

ROCKY BOY'S RESERVATION
(Federal)
Chouteau and Hill counties
Tribal Headquarters: Box Elder
Chippewa-Cree Tribe

NEBRASKA

OMAHA RESERVATION
(Federal)
Thurston County
Tribal Headquarters: Macy
Omaha Tribe

SANTEE RESERVATION
(Federal)
Knox County
Tribal Headquarters: Niobrara
Santee Sioux Tribe

WINNEBAGO RESERVATION
(Federal)
Thurston County

Tribal Headquarters: Winnebago
Winnebago Tribe

NEVADA

ALPINE COLONY (Federal)
Alpine County, California
Tribal Headquarters: Nevada
Agency, Bureau of Indian Affairs,
Stewart, Nevada
Washoe Tribe

BATTLE MOUNTAIN COLONY
(Federal)
Lander County
Tribal Headquarters: Battle
Mountain
Shoshone Tribe

CARSON COLONY (Federal)
Ormsby County
Tribal Headquarters: Carson City
Washoe Tribe

DRESSLERVILLE COLONY
(Federal)
Douglas County
Tribal Headquarters: Dresslerville
Washoe Tribe

DUCK VALLEY RESERVATION
(Federal)
Elko County, Nevada
Owyhee County, Idaho
Tribal Headquarters: Owyhee,
Nevada
Shoshone and Paiute Tribes

DUCKWATER RESERVATION
(Federal)
Nye County
Tribal Headquarters: Duckwater
Shoshone Tribe

ELKO COLONY (Federal)
Elko County
Tribal Headquarters: Elko
Shoshone Tribe

ELY COLONY (Federal)
White Pine County
Tribal Headquarters: Ely
Shoshone Tribe

FALLON COLONY AND
RESERVATION (Federal)
Churchill County
Tribal Headquarters: Fallon
Paiute and Shoshone Tribes

FORT MCDERMITT
RESERVATION (Federal)
Humboldt County, Nevada
Malheur County, Oregon
Tribal Headquarters: McDermitt,
Nevada
Paiute and Shoshone Tribes

LAS VEGAS COLONY (Federal)
Clark County
Tribal Headquarters: Las Vegas
Paiute Tribe

LOVELOCK COLONY (Federal)
Pershing County
Tribal Headquarters: Lovelock
Paiute Tribe

MOAPA RIVER RESERVATION
(Federal)
Clark County
Tribal Headquarters: Moapa
Paiute Tribe

PYRAMID LAKE RESERVATION
(Federal)
Washoe County
Tribal Headquarters: Nixon
Paiute Tribe

RENO-SPARKS COLONY
(Federal)
Washoe County
Tribal Headquarters: Reno-Sparks
Washoe and Paiute Tribes

RUBY VALLEY RESERVATION
(Federal)
Elko County
Tribal Headquarters: c/o Nevada
Indian Agency, Bureau of Indian
Affairs, Stewart
Shoshone Tribe

SOUTH FORK AND ODGERS
RANCH RESERVATIONS
(Federal)
Elko County
Tribal Headquarters: Lee
Shoshone Tribe

SUMMIT LAKE RESERVATION
(Federal)
Humboldt County
Tribal Headquarters: c/o Nevada
Indian Agency, Bureau of Indian
Affairs, Stewart
Paiute Tribe

WALKER RIVER RESERVATION
(Federal)
Churchill, Lyon, and Mineral
counties
Tribal Headquarters: Schurz
Paiute Tribe

WINNEMUCCA COLONY
(Federal)
Humboldt County
Tribal Headquarters: Winnemucca
Paiute and Shoshone Tribes

WOODSFORD COLONY
(Federal)
Alpine County, California
Tribal Headquarters: c/o Nevada
Indian Agency, Bureau of Indian
Affairs, Stewart, Nevada
Washoe Tribe

YERINGTON COLONY AND
RESERVATION (Federal)
Lyon County
Tribal Headquarters: Campbell
Ranch
Paiute Tribe

YOMBA RESERVATION (Federal)
Lander County
Tribal Headquarters: Austin
Shoshone Tribe

NEW MEXICO

ACOMA PUEBLO (Federal)
Valencia County
Tribal Headquarters: Acoma
Pueblo
Keresan Tribe

ALAMO RESERVATION
(Federal)
McKinley and Valencia counties
Tribal Headquarters: Alamo
Navajo Tribe

CANONCITO RESERVATION
(Federal)
Bernalillo and Valencia counties
Tribal Headquarters: Canoncito
Navajo Tribe

COCHITI PUEBLO (Federal)
Sandoval County
Tribal Headquarters: Cochiti
Pueblo
Keresan Tribe

ISLETA PUEBLO (Federal)
Bernalillo and Valencia counties
Tribal Headquarters: Isleta
Tano-Tigua Tribe

JEMEZ PUEBLO (Federal)
Sandoval County
Tribal Headquarters: Jemez
Pueblo
Tano-Jemez Tribe

JICARILLA RESERVATION
(Federal)
Rio Arriba and Sandoval counties
Tribal Headquarters: Dulce
Jicarilla Apache Tribe

LAGUNA PUEBLO (Federal)
Valencia, Bernalillo, and Sandoval
counties
Tribal Headquarters: Laguna
Keresan Tribe

MESCALERO RESERVATION
(Federal)
Otero County
Tribal Headquarters: Mescalero
Mescalero Apache Tribe

NAMBE PUEBLO (Federal)
Santa Fe County
Tribal Headquarters: Nambe
Pueblo
Tano-Tewa Tribe

PICURIS PUEBLO (Federal)
Taos County
Tribal Headquarters: Picuris
Pueblo
Tano-Tigua Tribe

POJOAQUE PUEBLO (Federal)
Santa Fe County
Tribal Headquarters: Pojoaque
Pueblo
Tano-Tewa Tribe

RAMAH RESERVATION
(Federal)
McKinley and Valencia counties
Tribal Headquarters: Ramah
Navajo Tribe

SANDIA PUEBLO (Federal)
Sandoval County
Tribal Headquarters: Sandia
Pueblo
Tano-Tigua Tribe

SAN FELIPE PUEBLO (Federal)
Sandoval County
Tribal Headquarters: San Felipe
Pueblo
Keresan Tribe

SAN ILDEFONSO PUEBLO
(Federal)
Santa Fe County
Tribal Headquarters: San
Ildefonso Pueblo
Tano-Tewa Tribe

SAN JUAN PUEBLO (Federal)
Rio Arriba County
Tribal Headquarters: San Juan
Tano-Tewa Tribe

SANTA ANA PUEBLO (Federal)
Sandoval County
Tribal Headquarters: Santa Ana
Pueblo
Keresan Tribe

SANTA CLARA PUEBLO
(Federal)
Rio Arriba and Sandoval counties
Tribal Headquarters: Santa Clara
Pueblo
Tano-Tewa Tribe

SANTO DOMINGO PUEBLO
(Federal)
Sandoval County
Tribal Headquarters: Santo
Domingo Pueblo
Keresan Tribe

TAOS PUEBLO (Federal)
Taos County
Tribal Headquarters: Taos Pueblo
Tano-Tigua Tribe

TESUQUE PUEBLO (Federal)
Santa Fe County
Tribal Headquarters: Tesuque
Pueblo
Tano-Tewa Tribe

ZIA PUEBLO (Federal)
Sandoval County
Tribal Headquarters: Zia Pueblo
Keresan Tribe

ZUNI PUEBLO (Federal)
McKinley and Valencia counties
Tribal Headquarters: Zuni
Zuni Tribe

NEW YORK

ALLEGANY RESERVATION
(State)
Cattaraugus County
Tribal Headquarters: Saylor
Building, Irving
Seneca Nation of Indians

CATTARAUGUS RESERVATION
(State)
Cattaraugus, Erie, and
Chautauqua counties
Tribal Headquarters: Irving
Seneca Nation of Indians

OIL SPRINGS RESERVATION
(State)
Cattaraugus and Allegany
counties
Tribal Headquarters: Irving
Seneca Tribe

ONONDAGA RESERVATION
(State)
Onondaga County
Tribal Headquarters: Nedrow
Onondaga and Oneida Tribes

POOSPATUCK RESERVATION
(State)
Suffolk County
Tribal Headquarters: Mastic, Long
Island
Poospatuck Tribe

ST. REGIS MOHAWK
RESERVATION (State)

Franklin County
Tribal Headquarters: Hogansburg
St. Regis Mohawk Tribe

SHINNECOCK RESERVATION
(State)
Suffolk County
Tribal Headquarters:
Southampton, Long Island
Shinnecock Tribe

TONAWANDA RESERVATION
(State)
Niagara, Erie, and Genesee
counties
Tribal Headquarters: Tonawanda
Indian Community
Tonawanda Band of Seneca Tribe

TUSCARORA RESERVATION
(State)
Niagara County
Tribal Headquarters: Tuscarora
Rural Community, Niagara
County
Tuscarora Tribe

NORTH CAROLINA

CHEROKEE RESERVATION
(Federal)
Cherokee, Graham, Jackson,
Macon, and Swain counties
Tribal Headquarters: Cherokee
Eastern Band of Cherokee

NORTH DAKOTA

FORT BERTHOLD
RESERVATION (Federal)
Dunn, McLean, McKenzie,
Mountrail, and Mercer counties
Tribal Headquarters: New Town
Mandan, Hidatsa, and Arikara
Tribes

FORT TOTTEN RESERVATION
(Federal)
Benson, Nelson, and Eddy
counties
Tribal Headquarters: Fort Totten
Devils Lake Sioux Tribe

STANDING ROCK
RESERVATION (Federal)
Sioux County, North Dakota
Corson, Dewey, and Ziebach
counties, South Dakota
Tribal Headquarters: Fort Yates,
North Dakota
Sioux Tribe

TURTLE MOUNTAIN
RESERVATION (Federal)
Rolette County
Tribal Headquarters: Belcourt
Chippewa Tribe

OKLAHOMA

ABSENTEE SHAWNEE TRIBE
(Federal Trust Area)
Pottawatomi and Cleveland
counties
Tribal Headquarters: Shawnee
Agency, Shawnee

CADDO TRIBE (Federal Trust
Area)
Caddo, Canadian, and Grady
counties
Tribal Headquarters: Anadarko

CHEROKEE TRIBE (Federal Trust
Area)
Adair, Cherokee, Delaware,
Mayes, and Sequoyah counties
Tribal Headquarters: Tahlequah

CHEYENNE AND ARAPAHO
TRIBES (Federal Trust Area)
Canadian, Blaine, Roger Mills,
Washita, Kingfisher, Dewey, and
Custer counties
Tribal Headquarters: Concho

CHICKASAW TRIBE (Federal
Trust Area)
Pontotoc, Carter, Murray, Love,
Johnston, Marshall, Grady,
Garvin, and McClain counties
Tribal Headquarters: Ardmore

CHOCTAW TRIBE (Federal Trust
Area)
Latimer and Pushmataha counties
Tribal Headquarters: Durant

CITIZEN BAND OF
POTAWATOMI TRIBE (Federal
Trust Area)
Pottawatomi and Cleveland
counties
Tribal Headquarters: Community
House, Shawnee

COMANCHE TRIBE (Federal
Trust Area)
Caddo, Comanche, Cotton,
Grady, Kiowa, Tillman, and
Washita counties
Tribal Headquarters: Andarko

CREEK TRIBE (Federal Trust
Area)
Creek, Okmulgee, Wagoner,
Okfuskee, McIntosh, Muskogee,
Hughes, and Tulsa counties
Tribal Headquarters: Okmulgee

DELAWARE INDIAN TRIBE OF
WESTERN OKLAHOMA (Federal
Trust Area)
Caddo, Canadian, and Grady
counties
Tribal Headquarters: Anadarko

EASTERN SHAWNEE TRIBE
(Federal Trust Area)
Ottawa County
Tribal Headquarters: Quapaw

FORT SILL APACHE TRIBE
(Federal Trust Area)
Caddo, Comanche, and Stephens
counties
Tribal Headquarters: Anadarko

IOWA TRIBE OF OKLAHOMA
(Federal Trust Area)
Lincoln, Payne, and Logan
counties
Tribal Headquarters: Shawnee
Agency, Shawnee

KAW TRIBE (Federal Trust Area)
Osage County
Tribal Headquarters: Pawnee
Agency, Pawnee

KICKAPOO TRIBE OF
OKLAHOMA (Federal Trust
Area)
Oklahoma, Lincoln, and
Pottawatomi counties
Tribal Headquarters: Community
House, McLoud

KIOWA TRIBE (Federal Trust Area)
Caddo, Comanche, Cotton, Grady, Kiowa, Tillman, and Washita counties
Tribal Headquarters: Anadarko

KIOWA-APACHE TRIBE (Federal Trust Area)
Caddo, Comanche, Cotton, Grady, Kiowa, Tillman, and Washita counties
Tribal Headquarters: Anadarko

OSAGE TRIBE (Federal Trust Area)
Osage County
Tribal Headquarters: Pawhuska

OTOE-MISSOURIA TRIBE (Federal Trust Area)
Noble County
Tribal Headquarters: Pawnee Agency, Pawnee

PAWNEE TRIBE (Federal Trust Area)
Pawnee County
Tribal Headquarters: Pawnee

PONCA TRIBE (Federal Trust Area)
Kay and Noble counties
Tribal Headquarters: White Eagle

QUAPAW TRIBE (Federal Trust Area)
Ottawa County
Tribal Headquarters: Miami

SAC AND FOX TRIBE (Federal Trust Area)
Lincoln, Payne, and Pottawatomi counties
Tribal Headquarters: Shawnee Agency, Shawnee

SEMINOLE TRIBE (Federal Trust Area)
Seminole County
Tribal Headquarters: Wewoka

SENECA-CAYUGA TRIBE (Federal Trust Area)
Ottawa County
Tribal Headquarters: Miami Agency, Miami

TONKAWA TRIBE OF OKLAHOMA (Federal Trust Area)
Kay County
Tribal Headquarters: Pawnee Agency, Pawnee

WICHITA TRIBE (Federal Trust Area)
Caddo, Canadian, and Grady counties
Tribal Headquarters: Anadarko

OREGON

BURNS PAIUTE RESERVATION (Federal)
Harney County
Tribal Headquarters: Burns Paiute Tribe

CELILO VILLAGE (Federal)
Wasco County
Tribal Headquarters: c/o Portland Area Office, Bureau of Indian Affairs, Portland
Fishing site for various Columbia River tribes

UMATILLA RESERVATION (Federal)
Umatilla County
Tribal Headquarters: Pendleton
Cayuse, Wallawalla, and Umatilla Tribes

WARM SPRINGS RESERVATION (Federal)
Jefferson, Wasco, Linn, Marion, and Clackamas counties
Tribal Headquarters: Warm Springs
Warm Springs, Northern Paiute, and Wasco Confederated Tribes

SOUTH DAKOTA

CHEYENNE RIVER RESERVATION (Federal)
Perkins, Dewey, and Ziebach counties
Tribal Headquarters: Eagle Butte
Sioux Tribe

CROW CREEK RESERVATION (Federal)
Buffalo, Hyde, and Hughes counties
Tribal Headquarters: Fort Thompson
Sioux Tribe

FLANDREAU RESERVATION (Federal)
Moody County
Tribal Headquarters: Flandreau
Flandreau Santee Sioux Tribe

LOWER BRULE RESERVATION (Federal)
Lyman and Stanley counties
Tribal Headquarters: Lower Brule
Sioux Tribe

PINE RIDGE RESERVATION (Federal)
Sheridan County, Nebraska
Bennett, Shannon, and Washabaugh counties, South Dakota
Tribal Headquarters: Pine Ridge, South Dakota
Oglala Sioux Tribe

ROSEBUD RESERVATION (Federal)
Mellette, Todd, and Tripp counties
Tribal Headquarters: Rosebud
Sioux Tribe

SISSETON RESERVATION (Federal)
Roberts, Day, Codington, Marshall, and Grant counties, South Dakota
Sargent and Richland counties, North Dakota
Tribal Headquarters: Sisseton, South Dakota
Sisseton-Wahpeton Sioux Tribe

YANKTON RESERVATION (Federal)
Charles Mix County
Tribal Headquarters: Wagner
Yankton Sioux Tribe

TEXAS

ALABAMA-COUSHATTA RESERVATION (State)
Polk County
Tribal Headquarters: Livingston
Alabama and Coushatta Tribes

TIGUA RESERVATION (State)
El Paso County
Tribal Headquarters: Ysleta del Sur Pueblo, El Paso
Tigua Tribe

UTAH

GOSHUTE RESERVATION (Federal)
White Pine County, Nevada
Juab County, Utah
Tribal Headquarters: Ibapah, Utah
Goshute Tribe

SKULL VALLEY RESERVATION (Federal)
Tooele County
Tribal Headquarters: Grantsville
Goshute Tribe

SOUTHERN PAIUTE RESERVATION (State)
Iron, Millard, and Sevier counties
Tribal Headquarters: Cedar City
Southern Paiute Tribe

UNINTAH AND OURAY RESERVATION (Federal)
Uintah, Duchesne, and Grand counties
Tribal Headquarters: Fort Duchesne
Ute Tribe

VIRGINIA

MATTAPONI RESERVATION (State)
King William County
Tribal Headquarters: West Point
Mattaponi Indians (Powhatan)

PAMUNKEY RESERVATION (State)
King William County
Tribal Headquarters: Pamunkey
Pamunkey Indians (Powhatan)

WASHINGTON

CHEHALIS RESERVATION (Federal)
Grays Harbor and Thurston counties
Tribal Headquarters: Oakville
Chehalis Tribe

COLVILLE RESERVATION (Federal)
Ferry and Okanogan counties
Tribal Headquarters: Nespelem
Confederated Tribes

HOH RESERVATION (Federal)
Jefferson County
Tribal Headquarters: Forks
Hoh Tribe

KALISPEL RESERVATION (Federal)
Pend Oreille County
Tribal Headquarters: Usk
Kalispel Tribe

LOWER ELWHA RESERVATION (Federal)
Clallam County
Tribal Headquarters: Port Angeles
Clallam Tribe

LUMMI RESERVATION (Federal)
Whatcom County
Tribal Headquarters: Bellingham
Lummi and Nooksack Tribes

MAKAH RESERVATION (Federal)
Clallam County
Tribal Headquarters: Neah Bay
Makah Tribe

MUCKLESHOOT RESERVATION (Federal)
King County
Tribal Headquarters: Auburn
Muckleshoot Tribe

NISQUALLY RESERVATION (Federal)
Thurston County
Tribal Headquarters: Yelm
Nisqually Tribe

OZETTE RESERVATION (Federal)
Clallam County
Tribal Headquarters: Bureau of Indian Affairs, Everett
Makah Tribe seeking use

PORT GAMBLE RESERVATION (Federal)
Kitsap County
Tribal Headquarters: Little Boston
Clallam Tribe

PORT MADISON RESERVATION (Federal)
Kitsap County
Tribal Headquarters: Bremerton
Suquamish Tribe

PUYALLUP RESERVATION (Federal)
Pierce County
Tribal Headquarters: Puyallup
Puyallup Tribe

QUILEUTE RESERVATION (Federal)
Clallam County
Tribal Headquarters: La Push
Quileute Tribe

QUINAULT RESERVATION (Federal)
Grays Harbor and Jefferson counties
Tribal Headquarters: Taholah
Quinault Tribe

SHOALWATER RESERVATION (Federal)
Pacific County
Tribal Headquarters: Tokeland
Quinault, Chinook, and Chehalis Tribes

SKOKOMISH RESERVATION (Federal)
Mason County
Tribal Headquarters: Shelton
Skokomish Tribe

SPOKANE RESERVATION (Federal)
Stevens County
Tribal Headquarters: Wellpinit
Spokane Tribe

SQUAXIN ISLAND
RESERVATION (Federal)
Mason County
Tribal Headquarters: Shelton
Squaxin Island Tribe

SWINOMISH INDIAN TRIBAL
COMMUNITY (Federal)
Skagit County
Tribal Headquarters: La Conner
Swinomish Tribe

TULALIP RESERVATION
(Federal)
Snohomish County
Tribal Headquarters: Marysville
Snohomish Tribe

YAKIMA RESERVATION
(Federal)
Yakima and Klickitat counties
Tribal Headquarters: Toppenish
Confederated Tribes and Bands of
the Yakima Indian Nation

WISCONSIN

BAD RIVER RESERVATION
(Federal)
Ashland and Iron counties
Tribal Headquarters: Odanah
Bad River Band of Chippewa
Indians

LAC COURTE OREILLES
RESERVATION (Federal)
Sawyer County
Tribal Headquarters: Reserve
Lac Courte Oreilles Band of
Chippewa Indians

LAC DU FLAMBEAU
RESERVATION (Federal)
Iron and Vilas counties
Tribal Headquarters: Lac du
Flambeau
Lac du Flambeau Band of
Chippewa Indians

MOLE LAKE RESERVATION
(Federal)
Forest County
Tribal Headquarters: Mole Lake
Mole Lake Band of Chippewa
Indians

ONEIDA RESERVATION
(Federal)
Brown, Oneida, and Outagamie
counties
Tribal Headquarters: Oneida
Oneida Tribe

POTAWATOMI RESERVATION
(Federal)
Forest County
Tribal Headquarters: Potawatomi
Potawatomi Tribe

RED CLIFF RESERVATION
(Federal)
Bayfield County
Tribal Headquarters: Red Cliff
Red Cliff Band of Chippewa
Indians

ST. CROIX RESERVATION
(Federal)
Burnett, Barron, and Polk
counties
Tribal Headquarters: Danbury
St. Croix Band of Chippewa
Indians

STOCKBRIDGE-MUNSEE
RESERVATION (Federal)
Shawano County
Tribal Headquarters: Bowler
Stockbridge (Mahican) and
Munsee Tribes

WINNEBAGO RESERVATION
(Federal)
Parts of 10 counties in Wisconsin
Tribal Headquarters: Wisconsin
Dells
Winnebago Tribe

WYOMING

WIND RIVER RESERVATION
(Federal)
Fremont and Hot Springs
counties
Tribal Headquarters: Riverton
Shoshone and Arapaho Tribes

INDIAN BANDS IN CANADA

(Band names are listed
alphabetically by province or
territory, with tribal names
included parenthetically. Postal
locations of band headquarters—
or in some cases the nearest
towns—are also given. Most
Canadian bands have rights to
more than one reserve—many of
them tracts of only several
acres—which are not listed here.)

ALBERTA

ALEXANDER (Cree)
Morinville

ALEXIS (Dakota)
Glenevis

BEAVER LAKE (Cree)
Lac La Biche

BIGSTONE CREE (Cree)
Desmarais

BLACKFOOT (Blackfoot)
Gleichen

BLOOD (Blackfoot)
Standoff

BOYER RIVER (Beaver)
High Level

COLD LAKE (Chipewyan, Cree)
Cold Lake

CREE (Cree)
Fort Chipewyan

DENE THA' TRIBE (Slave)
High Level

DRIFTPILE (Cree)
Driftpile

DUNCAN'S (Cree)
Brownvale

ENOCH (Cree)
Winterburn

ERMINESKIN (Cree)
Hobbema

FORT CHIPEWYAN (Chipewyan)
Fort Chipewyan

FORT MCKAY (Chipewyan)
Fort McMurray

FORT MCMURRAY (Cree,
Chipewyan)
Clearwater Station
Fort McMurray

FROG LAKE (Cree)
Frog Lake

GROUARD (Cree) Grouard

HEART LAKE (Beaver)
Lac La Biche

HORSE LAKE (Beaver)
Hythe

JANVIER (Chipewyan)
Chard

KEHEWIN (Cree)
Bonnyville

LITTLE RED RIVER (Cree)
High Level

LOUIS BULL (Cree)
Hobbema

LUBICON (Cree)
Peace River

MONTANA (Cree)
Hobbema

O'CHIESE (Cree)
Rocky Mountain House

PAUL (Dakota, Cree)
Duffield

PIEGAN (Blackfoot)
Brocket

SADDLE LAKE (Cree)
Goodfish Lake Group
Goodfish Lake

SADDLE LAKE (Cree)
Saddle Lake Group
Saddle Lake

SAMSON (Cree)
Hobbema

SARCEE (Sarcee)
Calgary

SAWRIDGE (Cree)
Slave Lake

STONEY (Dakota)
Bearspaw Group
Morley

STONEY (Dakota)
Chiniki Group
Morley

STONEY (Dakota)
Wesley Group
Morley

STURGEON LAKE (Cree)
Valleyview

SUCKER CREEK (Cree)
Enilda

SUNCHILD CREE (Cree)
Rocky Mountain House

SWAN RIVER (Cree)
Kinuso

TALLCREE (Cree)
Fort Vermilion

WHITEFISH LAKE (Cree)
Atikameg

BRITISH COLUMBIA

ADAMS LAKE (Shuswap)
Chase

AHOUSAHT (Nootka)
Ahousaht

AITCHELITZ (Cowichan)
Sardis

ALEXANDRIA (Chilcotin)
Quesnel

ALEXIS CREEK (Chilcotin)
Chilanko Forks

ALKALI (Shuswap)
Alkali

ANAHAM (Chilcotin)
Alexis Creek

ANDERSON LAKE (Lillooet)
D'Arcy

ASHCROFT (Shuswap)
Ashcroft

BEECHER BAY (Songish)
Sooke

BELLA COOLA (Bella Coola)
Bella Coola

BLUEBERRY RIVER (Beaver)
Buick

BONAPARTE (Shuswap)
Cache Creek

BOOTHROYD (Ntlakyapamuk)
Boston Bar

BOSTON BAR (Ntlakyapamuk)
North Bend

BRIDGE RIVER (Lillooet)
Lillooet

BURNS LAKE (Carrier)
Burns Lake

BURRARD (Squamish)
North Vancouver

CAMPBELL RIVER (Kwakiutl)
Campbell River

CANIM LAKE (Shuswap)
Canim Lake

CANOE CREEK (Shuswap)
Dog Creek

CANYON CITY (Niska)
Canyon City

CAPE MUDGE (Kwakiutl)
Quathiaski Cove

CAYOOSE CREEK (Lillooet)
Lillooet

CHEAM (Cowichan) Rosedale

CHEHALIS (Cowichan)
Agassiz

CHEMAINUS (Cowichan)
Ladysmith

CHESLATTA (Carrier)
Burns Lake

CLAYOQUOT (Nootka)
Tofino

CLINTON (Shuswap)
Kamloops

COLDWATER (Ntlakyapamuk)
Merritt

COLUMBIA LAKE (Kootenay)
Windermere

COMOX (Comox)
Courtenay

COOK'S FERRY (Ntlakyapamuk)
Merritt

COQUITLAM (Cowichan)
Port Coquitlam

COWICHAN (Cowichan)
Duncan

DEADMAN'S CREEK (Shuswap)
Savona

DOIG RIVER (Beaver)
Rose Prairie

DOUGLAS (Lillooet)
Mission

EHATTESAHT (Nootka)
Vancouver

ESQUIMALT (Songish)
Victoria

FORT GEORGE (Carrier)
Shelley

FORT NELSON (Slave)
Fort Nelson

FORT WARE (Sekani)
Fort Ware
via Mackenzie

FOUNTAIN (Lillooet)
Lillooet

FRASER LAKE (Carrier)
Fort Fraser

GITANMAAX (Gitksan)
Hazelton

GITLAKDAMIX (Niska)
New Aiyansh

GITWANGAK (Gitksan)
Kitwanga

GLEN VOWELL (Gitksan)
Hazelton

HAGWILGET (Gitksan)
New Hazelton

HALALT (Cowichan)
Chemainus

HALFWAY RIVER (Beaver)
Wonowon

HARTLEY BAY (Tsimshian)
Hartley Bay

HEILTSUK (Heiltsuk)
Bella Bella Band Office
Waglisla

HESQUIAHT (Nootka)
Tofino

HIGH BAR (Shuswap)
Clinton

HOMALCO (Comox)
Powell River

HOPE (Cowichan)
Hope

INGENIKA (Sekani)
Ingenika Point
via MacKenzie

ISKUT (Tahltan)
Iskut

KAMLOOPS (Shuswap)
Kamloops

KANAKA BAR (Ntlakyapamuk)
Lytton

KATZIE (Cowichan)
Pitt Meadows

KINCOLITH (Niska)
Kincolith

KISPIOX (Gitksan)
Hazelton

KITAMAAT (Haisla)
Haisla
Kitamaat Village

KITASOO (Tsimshian)
Klemtu

KITKATLA (Tsimshian)
Kitkatla

KITSEGUKLA (Gitksan)
South Hazelton

KITSELAS (Tsimshian)
Terrace

KITSUMKALUM (Tsimshian)
Terrace

KITWANCOOL (Gitksan)
Kitwanga

KLAHOOSE (Comox)
Powell River

KLUSKUS (Carrier)
Quesnel

KWAKIUTL (Kwakiutl)
Port Hardy

KWA-WA-AINEUK (Kwakiutl)
Sullivan Bay

KWAW-KWAW-A-PILT
(Cowichan)
Chilliwack

KWICKSUTAINEUK (Kwakiutl)
Gilford Island Village
Simoon Sound

KYUQUOT (Nootka)
Kyuquot

LAKAHAHMEN (Cowichan)
Deroche

LAKALZAP (Niska)
Greenville

LAKE BABINE (Carrier)
Burns Lake

LAKE COWICHAN (Nootka)
Lake Cowichan

LANGLEY (Cowichan)
Fort Langley

LILLOOET (Lillooet)
Lillooet

LITTLE SHUSWAP (Shuswap)
Chase

LOWER KOOTENAY (Kootenay)
Creston

LOWER NICOLA
(Ntlakyapamuk)
Merritt

LOWER SIMILKAMEEN
(Okanagan)
Keremeos

LYACKSON (Cowichan)
Chemainus

LYTTON (Ntlakyapamuk)
Lytton

MALAHAT (Cowichan)
Mill Bay

MAMALILLIKULLA (Kwakiutl)
Campbell River

MASSET (Haida) Masset

MATSQUI (Cowichan)
Matsqui

MCLEOD LAKE (Sekani)
McLeod Lake

METLAKATLA (Tsimshian)
Prince Rupert

MORICETOWN (Carrier)
Smithers

MOUNT CURRIE (Lillooet)
Mount Currie

MOWACHAHT (Nootka)
Gold River

MUSQUEAM (Cowichan)
Vancouver

NANAIMO (Cowichan)
Nanaimo

NANOOSE (Cowichan)
Lantzville

NAZKO (Carrier)
Quesnel

NECOSLIE (Carrier)
Fort St. James

NEMAIAH VALLEY (Chilcotin)
Nemaiah Valley

NESKAINLITH (Shuswap)
Chase

NICOMEN (Ntlukyapamuk)
Lytton

NIMPKISH (Kwakiutl)
Alert Bay

NITINAHT (Nootka)
Port Alberni

NOOAITCH (Ntlakyapamuk)
Merritt

NORTH THOMPSON (Shuswap)
Barriere

NUCHATLAHT (Nootka)
Tahsis

NUWITTI (Kwakiutl)
Vancouver

OHIAHT (Nootka)
Bamfield

OKANAGAN (Okanagan)
Vernon

OMINECA (Carrier)
Burns Lake

OPETCHESAHT (Nootka)
Port Alberni

OREGON JACK CREEK
(Ntlakyapamuk)
Ashcroft

OSOYOOS (Okanagan)
Oliver

OWEEKANO (Heiltsuk)
Rivers Inlet

PACHEENAHT (Nootka)
Port Renfrew

PAUQUACHIN (Songish)
Sidney

PAVILION (Shuswap)
Lillooet

PENELAKUT (Cowichan)
Chemainus

PENTICTON (Okanagan)
Penticton

PETERS (Cowichan)
Hope

POPKUM (Cowichan)
Rosedale

PORT SIMPSON (Tsimshian)
Port Simpson

PROPHET RIVER (Slave)
Alaska Highway

QUALICUM (Puntlatch)
Qualicum Beach

QUATSINO (Kwakiutl)
Coal Harbour

QUESNEL (Carrier)
Quesnel

ST. MARY'S (Kootenay)
Cranbrook

SAMAHQUAM (Lillooet)
Mission

SCOWLITZ (Cowichan)
Lake Errock

SEABIRD ISLAND (Cowichan)
Agassiz

SECHELT (Seechelt)
Sechelt

SEMIAHMOO (Semiahmoo)
Surrey

SETON LAKE (Lillooet)
Shalalt

SHACKAN (Ntlakyapamuk)
Merritt

SHESHAHT (Nootka)
Port Alberni

SISKA (Ntlakyapamuk)
Lytton

SKAWAHLOOK (Cowichan)
Hope

SKIDEGATE (Haida)
Queen Charlotte City

SKOOKUMCHUCK (Lillooet)
Mission

SKOWKALE (Cowichan)
Sardis

SKUPPAH (Ntlakyapamuk)
Lytton

SKWAH (Cowichan)
Chilliwack

SKWAY (Cowichan)
Chilliwack

SLIAMMON (Comox)
Powell River

SODA CREEK (Shusway)
Williams Lake

SONGHEES (Songish)
Victoria

SOOKE (Songish)
Sooke

SOOWAHLIE (Cowichan)
Chilliwack

SPALLUMCHEEN (Shuswap)
Enderby

SPUZZUM (Ntlakyapamuk)
Spuzzum

SQUAMISH (3 bands) (Squamish)
North Vancouver

SQUAMISH (Squamish)
Squamish

SQUIALA (Cowichan)
Chilliwack

STELLAQUO (Carrier)
Fraser Lake

STONE (Chilcotin)
Hanceville

STONEY CREEK (Carrier)
Vanderhoof

STUART–TREMBLEUR LAKE
(Carrier)
Fort St. James

SUMAS (Cowichan)
Abbotsford

TAHLTAN (Tahltan)
Telegraph Creek

TAKLA LAKE (Carrier)
Takla Landing
via Fort St. James

TANAKTEUK (Kwakiutl)
Campbell River

TOBACCO PLAINS (Kootenay)
Grasmere

TOOSEY (Chilcotin)
Williams Lake

TOQUAHT (Nootka)
Ucluelet

TSARTLIP (Songish)
Brentwood Bay

TSAWATAINEUK (Kwakiutl)
Kingcome Inlet

TSAWOUT (Songish)
Saanichton

TSAWWASSEN (Cowichan)
Ladner

TSEYCUM (Songish)
Sidney

TSULQUATE
Port Hardy

TURNOUR ISLAND (Kwakiutl)
Coquitlam

TZEACHTEN (Cowichan)
Sardis

UCHUCKLESAHT (Nootka)
Port Alberni

UCLUELET (Nootka)
Port Alberni

ULKATCHO (Carrier)
Anahim Lake

UNION BAR (Cowichan)
Hope

UPPER NICOLA (Ntlakyapamuk)
Merritt

UPPER SIMILKAMEEN
(Okanagan)
Keremeos

WEST MOBERLY (Beaver)
Chetwynd

WESTBANK (Okanagan)
Westbank

WILLIAMS LAKE (Shuswap)
Sugarcane
Williams Lake

YAKWEAKWIOOSE (Cowichan)
Sardis

YALE (Cowichan)
Hope

MANITOBA

BARREN LANDS (Chipewyan)
Brocket

BERENS RIVER (Ojibway)
Berens River

BIRDTAIL SIOUX (Dakota)
Beulah

BLOODVEIN (Cree)
Bloodvein

BROKENHEAD (Ojibway)
Scanterbury

BUFFALO POINT (Ojibway)
Middlebro

CHEMAHAWIN (Cree)
Easterville

CHURCHILL (Chipewyan)
Lynn Lake

CRANE RIVER (Ojibway)
Crane River

CROSS LAKE (Cree)
Cross Lake

DAKOTA PLAINS (Dakota)
Edwin

DAKOTA TIPI (Dakota)
Portage La Prairie

DAUPHIN RIVER (Ojibway)
Gypsumville

EBB AND FLOW (Ojibway)
Ebb and Flow

FAIRFORD (Ojibway)
Fairford

FISHER RIVER (Ojibway, Cree)
Koostatak

FORT ALEXANDER (Ojibway)
Pine Falls

FOX LAKE (Cree)
Gillam

GAMBLERS (Ojibway)
Binscarth

GARDEN HILL (Cree)
Island Lake

GOD'S LAKE (Cree)
God's Lake

GOD'S RIVER (Cree)
God's River

GRAND RAPIDS (Cree)
Grand Rapids

HOLLOW WATER (Ojibway)
Wanipegow

INDIAN BIRCH (Ojibway, Cree)
Birch River

JACKHEAD (Ojibway)
Dallas

KEESEEKOOWENIN (Ojibway)
Elphinstone

LAKE MANITOBA (Ojibway)
Vogar

LAKE ST. MARTIN (Ojibway)
Gypsumville

LITTLE BLACK RIVER (Ojibway)
O'Hanley

LITTLE GRAND RAPIDS
(Ojibway)
Little Grand Rapids

LITTLE SASKATCHEWAN
(Ojibway)
Gypsumville

LONG PLAIN (Ojibway)
Edwin

MATHIAS COLOMB (Cree)
Pukatawagan

MOOSE LAKE (Cree)
Moose Lake

NELSON HOUSE (Cree)
Nelson House

NORTHLANDS (Chipewyan)
Lac Brochet

NORWAY HOUSE (Cree)
Norway House

OAK LAKE SIOUX (Dakota)
Pipestone

OXFORD HOUSE (Cree)
Oxford House

PEGUIS (Ojibway, Cree)
Hodgson

PINE CREEK (Ojibway)
Camperville

POPLAR RIVER (Cree, Ojibway)
Negginan

RED SUCKER LAKE (Cree)
Red Sucker Lake

ROLLING RIVER (Ojibway)
Erickson

ROSEAU RIVER (Ojibway)
Ginew

ST. THERESA POINT (Cree)
St. Theresa Point

SANDY BAY (Ojibway)
Marius

SHAMATTAWA (Cree)
Shamattawa

SHOAL RIVER (Ojibway)
Shola River Reserve
Pelican Rapids

SIOUX VALLEY (Dakota)
Griswold

SPLIT LAKE (Cree)
Split Lake

SWAN LAKE (Ojibway)
Swan Lake

THE PAS (Cree)
The Pas

VALLEY RIVER (Ojibway)
Shortdale

WAR LAKE (Ojibway, Cree)
Ilford

WASAGAMACK (Cree)
Wasagamack

WATERHEN (Ojibway)
Skownan

WAYWAYSEECAPPO (Ojibway)
Rossburn

YORK FACTORY (Cree)
via Ilford

NEW BRUNSWICK

BIG COVE (Micmac)
Big Cove Reserve
Rexton

BUCTOUCHE (Micmac)
Buctouche

BURNT CHURCH (Micmac)
Burnt Church Indian Reserve
Lagaceville

EDMUNDSTON (Malecite)
St. Basile Indian Reserve
Edmundston

EEL GROUND (Micmac)
Newcastle

EEL RIVER (Micmac)
Dalhousie

FORT FOLLY (Micmac)
Dorchester

INDIAN ISLAND (Micmac)
Rexton

KINGSCLEAR (Malecite)
Kingsclear Indian Reserve
Fredericton

OROMOCTO (Malecite)
Oromocto

PABINEAU (Micmac)
Bathurst

RED BANK (Micmac)
Red Bank Indian Reserve
Red Bank

ST. MARY'S (Malecite)
Fredericton

TOBIQUE (Malecite)
Tobique Indian Reserve
Perth Andover

WOODSTOCK (Malecite)
Woodstock

NORTHWEST TERRITORIES

AKLAVIK (Loucheux)
Aklavik

ARCTIC RED RIVER (Loucheux)
Arctic Red River

DOG RIB RAE (Dogrib)
Fort Rae

FITZGERALD–SMITH
(Chipewyan)
Fort Smith

FORT FRANKLIN (Hare)
Fort Franklin

FORT GOOD HOPE (Hare)
Fort Good Hope

FORT LIARD (Slave)
Fort Liard

FORT MCPHERSON (Loucheux)
Fort McPherson

FORT NORMAN (Slave)
Fort Norman

FORT PROVIDENCE (Slave)
Fort Providence

FORT RESOLUTION
(Chipewyan)
Fort Resolution

FORT SIMPSON (Slave)
Fort Simpson

FORT WRIGLEY (Slave)
Fort Wrigley

HAY RIVER (Slave)
Hay River

SNOWDRIFT (Chipewyan)
Snowdrift

YELLOWKNIFE "B"
(Yellowknife)
Yellowknife

NOVA SCOTIA

ACADIA (Micmac)
Yarmouth Indian Reserve
Yarmouth

AFTON (Micmac)
Afton Reserve
Antigonish County

ANNAPOLIS VALLEY (Micmac)
Cambridge Indian Reserve
King's County

BEAR RIVER (Micmac)
Bear River Indian Reserve
Digby County

CHAPEL ISLAND (Micmac)
St. Peters
Richmond County

ESKASONI (Micmac)
Eskasoni

PICTOU LANDING (Micmac)
Trenton

SHUBENACADIE (Micmac)
Micmac Post Office
Hants County

SYDNEY (Micmac)
Sydney

TRURO (Micmac)
Truro

WAGMATCOOK (Micmac)
Baddeck

WHYCOCOMAGH (Micmac)
Whycocomagh

ONTARIO

ABITIBI–ONTARIO (Ojibway,
Cree)
Matheson

ALBANY (Ojibway, Cree)
Sinclair Island
Fort Albany

ALBANY (Ojibway, Cree)
Village of Kashechewan
Kashechewan

ALDERVILLE (Ojibway)
Roseneath

ALGONQUIN OF GOLDEN
LAKE (Algonkin)
Golden Lake

ANGLING LAKE (Cree)
Angling Lake

ATTAWAPISKAT (Cree)
Attawapiskat

BATCHEWANA (Ojibway)
Sault Ste Marie

BEARSKIN LAKE (Cree)
Bearskin Lake

BEAUSOLEIL (Ojibway)
Christian Island

BIG GRASSY (Ojibway)
Morson

BIG ISLAND (Ojibway)
Morson

BIG TROUT LAKE (Cree)
Big Trout Lake

BRUNSWICK HOUSE (Ojibway,
Cree)
Chapleau

CALDWELL (Potawatomi)
Kingsville

CARIBOU LAKE (Cree)
Patricia

CAT LAKE (Ojibway)
Cat Lake

CHAPLEAU CREE (Cree)
Sault Ste Marie

CHAPLEAU OJIBWAY (Ojibway)
Chapleau

CHIPPEWAS OF GEORGINA
ISLAND (Ojibway)
Sutton West

CHIPPEWAS OF NAWASH
(Ojibway)
Wiarton

CHIPPEWAS OF RAMA
(Ojibway) Rama

CHIPPEWAS OF SARNIA
(Ojibway)
Sarnia

CHIPPEWAS OF THE THAMES
(Ojibway)
Muncey

COCKBURN ISLAND (Ojibway)
Sault Ste Marie

CONSTANCE LAKE (Cree)
Calstock via Hearst

COUCHICHING (Ojibway)
Fort Frances

CURVE LAKE (Ojibway)
Curve Lake

DALLES (Ojibway)
Keewatin

DEER LAKE (Cree)
Sandy Lake via Favourable Lake

DEER LAKE (Cree)
Deer Lake Band Office
Via Pickle Lake

DEER LAKE (Cree)
North Spirit Lake
Cochenour

DOKIS (Ojibway)
Dokis Bay
Monetville

EAGLE LAKE (Ojibway)
Eagle River

FORT HOPE (Ojibway)
Eabamet Lake via Nakina

FORT SEVERN (Cree)
Fort Severn via Pickle Lake

FORT WILLIAM (Ojibway)
Thunder Bay

GARDEN RIVER (Ojibway)
Sault Ste Marie

GIBSON (Mohawk)
Bala

GRASSY NARROWS (Ojibway)
Grassy Narrows

GULL BAY (Ojibway)
Gull Bay Reserve
Gull Bay via Armstrong

HENVEY INLET (Ojibway)
Pickerel

HIAWATHA (Ojibway)
Keene

IROQUOIS OF ST. REGIS
(Mohawk)
Cornwall

ISLINGTON (Ojibway)
Whitedog

KASABONIKA (Cree)
Kasabonika Lake
via Central Patricia

KINGFISHER LAKE (Cree)
Kingfisher Lake
via Central Patricia

LAC LA CROIX (Ojibway)
Fort Frances

LAC DES MILLES LACS
(Ojibway) Upsala

LAC SEUL (Ojibway)
Lac Seul

LANSDOWNE HOUSE (Ojibway)
Lansdowne House Settlement
via Pickle Lake

LONG LAKE NO. 58 (Ojibway)
Longlac

LONG LAKE NO. 77 (Ojibway)
Longlac

MAGNETAWAN (Ojibway)
Britt

MARTIN FALLS (Ojibway)
Marten Falls   via Nakina

MATACHEWAN (Ojibway, Cree)
Matachewan

MATTAGAMI (Ojibway)
Mattagami Reserve
Gogama

MICHIPICOTEN (Ojibway)
Wawa

MISSISSAUGA (Ojibway)
Blind River

MISSISSAUGAS CREDIT
(Ojibway)
Hagersville

MOHAWKS OF THE BAY OF
QUINTE (Mohawk)
Deseronto

MOOSE DEER POINT (Ojibway)
Mactier

MOOSE FACTORY (Cree)
Moose Factory

MORAVIAN OF THE THAMES
(Delaware)
Bothwell

MUNCEY OF THE THAMES
(Delaware)
Muncey

MUSKRAT DAM (Cree)
Muskrat Dam
via Central Patricia

NAICATCHEWENIN (Ojibway)
Devlin

NEW POST (Cree)
Cochrane

NICIKOUSEMENECANING
(Ojibway)
Fort Frances

NIPISSING (Ojibway)
Sturgeon Falls

NORTHWEST ANGLE NO. 33
(Ojibway)
Angle Inlet, Min. (U.S.A.)

NORTHWEST ANGLE NO. 37
(Ojibway)
Sioux Narrows

OJIBWAYS OF ONEGAMING
(Ojibway)
Nestor Falls

ONEIDA OF THE THAMES
(Oneida)
Southwold

OSNABURG (Ojibway)
New Osnaburg

PARRY ISLAND (Ojibway)
Parry Sound

PAYS PLAT (Ojibway)
Pays Plat Indian Reserve
Pays Plat via Rossport

PIC HERON BAY (Ojibway)
Heron Bay

PIC MOBERT (Ojibway)
Mobert

PIKANGIKUM (Ojibway)
Pikangikum

POPLAR HILL (Ojibway)
Red Lake

RAINY RIVER (Ojibway)
Emo

RAT PORTAGE (Ojibway)
Kenora

RED ROCK (Ojibway)
Nipigon

ROCKY BAY (Ojibway)
Macdiarmid

SACHIGO (Cree)
Sachigo Lake

SANDY LAKE (Ojibway, Cree)
Sandy Lake

SAUGEEN (Ojibway)
Southampton

SCUGOG (Ojibway)
Port Perry

SEINE RIVER (Ojibway)
Administration Bldg.
via Mine Centre

SERPENT RIVER (Ojibway)
Serpent River Reserve
Cutler

SHAWANAGA (Ojibway)
Nobel

SHEGUIANDAH (Ojibway,
Ottawa)
Sheguiandah

SHESHEGWANING (Ojibway)
Sheshegwaning

SHOAL LAKE NO. 39 (Ojibway)
Kejick

SHOAL LAKE NO. 40 (Ojibway)
Kejick

SIX NATIONS OF THE GRAND
RIVER (Iroquois)
Oshweken

SPANISH RIVER (Ojibway)
Massey

STANGECOMING (Ojibway)
Fort Frances

SUCKER CREEK (Ojibway,
Ottawa)
Little Current

SUMMER BEAVER (Ojibway)
Summer Beaver
via Pickle Lake

TEMAGAMI (Ojibway, Cree)
Bear Island
Temagami

THESSALON (Ojibway)
Thessalon

WABAUSKANG (Ojibway)
Kenora

WABIGOON (Ojibway)
Dinorwic

WAHNAPITAE (Ojibway)
Wahnapitae

WALPOLE ISLAND (Ojibway,
Potawatomi)
Wallaceburg

WASHAGAMIS (Ojibway)
Keewatin

WEBEQUI INDIAN
SETTLEMENT (Ojibway)

Webequi
via Nakina

WEENUSK (Ojibway, Cree)
Weenusk Band Office
Winisk

WEST BAY (Ojibway)
Excelsior

WHITEFISH BAY (Ojibway)
Pawitik

WHITEFISH LAKE (Ojibway,
Ottawa)
Whitefish Lake Reserve no. 6
Naughton

WHITEFISH RIVER (Ojibway)
Birch Island

WHITESAND (Ojibway)
Armstrong

WIKWEMIKONG (Ojibway,
Ottawa)
Wikwemikong

WUNNUMIN (Cree)
Wunnumin Lake
via Central Patricia

PRINCE EDWARD ISLAND

ABEGWEIT (Micmac)
Cornwall

LENNOX ISLAND (Micmac)
Lennox Island

QUEBEC

ABENAKIS OF BECANCOUR
(Abnaki)
Becancour

ABITIBI DOMINION (Ojibway,
Cree)
Pikogan Indian Reserve
Amos

BARRIERE LAKE (Algonkin)
Rapid Lake

BERSIMIS (Montagnais)
Saguenay

CHISASIBI (Cree)
Fort George

EASTMAIN (Cree)
Eastmain

ESCOUMAINS (Montagnais)
Les Escoumains

GASPE (Micmac)
Gaspe

GRAND LAC VICTORIA
(Algonkin)
Louvicourt

GREAT WHALE RIVER (Cree)
Nouveau Quebec

HURONS OF LORETTE (Huron)
Village Huron

IROQUOIS OF
CAUGHNAWAGA (Mohawk)
Caughnawaga

KIPAWA (Algonkin)
Kebaoweck Indian Reserve
Timiscaming

LAC ST. JEAN (Montagnais)
Pointe-Bleue

LAC SIMON (Algonkin)
Lac Simon via Louvicourt

LONG POINT (Algonkin)
Winneway River via LaForce

MANOWAN (Cree)
Manowan Indian Reserve
via St.-Michel-des-Saints

MICMACS OF MARIA (Micmac)
Maria Indian Reserve
Maria

MINGAN (Montagnais)
Mingan

MISTASSINI (Cree)
Mistassini Lake
via Chibougamu

MONTAGNAIS OF
SCHEFFERVILLE (Montagnais)
Schefferville

NASKAPIS OF SCHEFFERVILLE
(Naskapi)
Schefferville

NATASHQUAM (Montagnais)
Natashquam Indian Reserve
Natashquam

NEMASKA (Cree)
Nemaska

OBEDJIWAN (Algonkin)
Obedjiwan Indian Reserve
via Roberval

ODANAK (Abnaki)
Odanak
Yemaska County

OKA (Mohawk)
Oka

OLD FACTORY (Cree)
Paint Hills

RESTIGOUCHE (Micmac)
Restigouche

RIVER DESERT (Algonkin)
Maniwaki

ROMAINE (Montagnais)
La Romaine

RUPERT HOUSE (Cree)
Rupert House

ST. AUGUSTIN (Montagnais)
Duplessis County

SEPT-ILES (Montagnais)
Sept-Iles

TIMISKAMING (Algonkin)
Timiskaming

WASWANIPI (Cree)
Desmaraisville

WEYMONTACHIE (Cree)
Laviolette via Sanmaur

WOLF LAKE (Algonkin)
L'Etang via Timiskaming

SASKATCHEWAN

BEARDY & OKEMASIS (Cree)
Duck Lake

BIG RIVER (Cree)
Debden

BUFFALO RIVER (Chipewyan)
Dillon

CANOE LAKE (Cree)
Canoe Lake

CARRY THE KETTLE
(Assiniboine, Dakota)
Sintaluta

COTE (Ojibway)
Kamsack

COWESSESS (Cree)
Broadview

CUMBERLAND HOUSE (Cree)
Cumberland House

DAY STAR (Cree)
Wynyard

ENGLISH RIVER (Chipewyan)
Patuanak

FISHING LAKE (Ojibway)
Kylemore

FLYING DUST (Cree)
Meadow Lake

FOND DU LAC (Chipewyan)
Fond Du Lac

GORDON (Ojibway, Cree)
Punnichy

ISLAND LAKE (Cree)
Loon Lake

JAMES SMITH (Cree)
Kinistino

JOHN SMITH (Cree)
Birch Hills

JOSEPH BIGHEAD (Cree)
Pierceland

KAHKEWISTAHAW (Cree)
Broadview

KEESEEKOOSE (Ojibway)
Kamsack

KEY (Ojibway)
Norquay

KINISTINO (Ojibway)
Chagoness

LAC LA HACHE (Chipewyan)
Wollaston Lake

LAC LA RONGE (Cree)
La Ronge

LITTLE BLACK BEAR (Cree)
Goodeve

LITTLE PINE (Cree)
Paynton

LUCKY MAN (Cree)
North Battleford

MAKWA SAHGAIEHCAN (Cree)
Loon Lake

MISTAWASIS (Cree)
Leask

MONTREAL LAKE (Cree)
Montreal Lake

MOOSEWOODS (Dakota)
Saskatoon

MOOSOMIN (Cree)
Cochin

MOSQUITO GRIZZLY BEAR'S
HEAD (Assiniboine)
Cando

MUSKEG LAKE (Cree)
Leask

MUSKOWEKWAN (Ojibway)
Lestock

NIKANEET (Cree)
Maple Creek

NUT LAKE (Ojibway)
Langham

OCHAPOWACE (Cree)
Broadview

OKANESE (Cree, Ojibway)
Balcarres

ONE ARROW (Cree)
Batoche

ONION LAKE (Cree)
Onion Lake

PASQUA (Ojibway, Cree)
Fort Qu'Appelle

PEEPEEKISIS (Cree)
Balcarres

PELICAN LAKE (Cree)
Leoville

PETER BALLANTYNE (Cree)
Pelican Narrows

PIAPOT (Cree)
Craven

POORMAN (Cree)
Quinton

PORTAGE LA LOCHE
(Chipewyan)
La Loche

POUNDMAKER (Cree)
Paynton

RED EARTH (Cree)
Red Earth

RED PHEASANT (Cree)
Cando

SAKIMAY (Cree)
Grenfell

SANDY LAKE (Cree)
Shell Lake

SAULTEAUX (Ojibway)
Cochin

SHOAL LAKE (Cree)
Pakwaw Lake

STANDING BUFFALO (Dakota)
Fort Qu'Appelle

STARBLANKET (Cree)
Balcarres

STONEY RAPIDS (Chipewyan)
Black Lake

STURGEON LAKE (Cree)
Spruce Home

SWEETGRASS (Cree)
Gallivan

THUNDERCHILD (Cree)
Turtleford

TURNOR LAKE (Chipewyan)
Turnor Lake

WAHPETON (Dakota)
Prince Albert

WATERHEN LAKE (Cree)
Waterhen Lake

WHITE BEAR (Cree, Ojibway,
Assiniboine)
Carlyle

WITCHEKAN LAKE (Cree)
Spiritwood

WOOD MOUNTAIN (Dakota)
Wood Mountain

YUKON TERRITORY

ATLIN (Tagish)
Atlin (British Columbia)

CARCROSS–TAGISH (Tagish)
Carcross

CHAMPAGNE–AISHIHIK
(Kutchin)
Haines Junction

DAWSON (Kutchin)
Dawson City

KLUANE (Kutchin)
Beaver Creek

KWANLIN DUN (Nahani)
Whitehorse

LIARD RIVER (Nahani)
Watson Lake

LITTLE SALMON–CARMACKS
(Kutchin)
Carmacks

MAYO (Kutchin)
Mayo

OLD CROW (Loucheux)
Old Crow

ROSS RIVER (Nahani)
Ross River

SELKIRK (Kutchin)
Pelly Crossing

TESLIN (Tagish)
Teslin

INUIT (Eskimo) COMMUNITIES IN CANADA

LABRADOR (Newfoundland)

HOPEDALE
MAKKOVIK
NAIN
RIGOLET

NORTHWEST TERRITORIES

AKLAVIK (also Loucheux tribe)
ARCTIC BAY
BAKER LAKE
BATHURST INLET
BROUGHTON ISLAND
CAMBRIDGE BAY
CAPE DORSET
CHESTERFIELD INLET
CLYDE RIVER
COPPERMINE
CORAL HARBOUR
ESKIMO POINT
FROBISHER BAY
GJOA HAVEN
GRISE FIORD
HALL BEACH
HOLMAN ISLAND
IGLOOLIK

INUVIK
LAKE HARBOUR
PANGNIRTUNG
PAULATUK
PELLY BAY
POND INLET
RANKIN INLET
REPULSE BAY
RESOLUTE BAY
SACHS HARBOUR
SANIKILUAN (Belcher Islands)
SPENCE BAY
TUKTOYAKTUK
UMINGMATOK
WHALE COVE

QUEBEC

AKULVIK
AUPALUK
BETTIN (Payne)
FORT-CHIMO
INOUCDJOUAL (Port Harrison)
IVUJIVIK
KOARTAC
MARICOURT (Wakeham)
PORT BURWELL
PORT-NOUVEAU-QUEBEC
POSTE-DE-LA-BALEINE (also
Cree tribe)
POVUNGNITUK
SAGLOUC
TASIUJAQ

MAJOR INDIAN PLACE NAMES IN THE UNITED STATES AND CANADA

A vast number of Americans and Canadians unwittingly speak in Indian tongues every day. When they declare they are residents of Massachusetts or Ontario, or are visiting Alaska or Manitoba, they are using Indian phonemes. In fact, counting Indiana, the name of which although not from an Indian language is Indian-inspired, over half the names of the American states are Indian-derived. And four out of ten Canadian provinces have Indian names, plus the Yukon territory and Canada itself. Yet the names of these large political entities are only a small part of the rich Indian linguistic legacy. Multitudinous cities, towns, villages, counties, mountains, plateaus, mesas, buttes, hills, lakes, ponds, rivers, streams, bays, and other geographical locations and features have Indian-related place names. It is estimated that New England alone has 5,000 Indian place names.

The etymology of Indian place names takes various forms. Some place names are English spellings of spoken Indian words or word-phrases—the original Indian names for geographical features, altered over the centuries through usage. Others are Indian tribal

names. Some are personal names, after celebrated Indian individuals or even mythical and fictional characters. Others are named after Indian-related events. Still others are English translations of Indian concepts or objects. Obviously then, some of these places names were bestowed by Indians and adopted by whites, and others were applied by whites with some Indian connection in mind. Whichever, they offer a perspective on Indian history and culture, especially with regard to tribal and language locations and the profound Indian relationship with the natural environment. Indian-derived place names also provide a poetic and poignant reminder of the once formidable and still inspirational Indian presence, so central to the history of both the United States and Canada—signposts of earlier times and of the displacement and dispossession of peoples and cultures.

The following alphabetical list (and a following separate list for Canada), as extensive as it is, is far from all-inclusive, limiting itself for the most part to political and geographical entities included in the National Atlas, published by the United States Department of the Interior. Many more Indian place names exist—physical features as well as municipalities. Streams, hills, and ponds are not included here, except in some cases when they happen also to be the name of some other larger landform or geographical entity. Many small towns and villages have also been omitted. And Indian place names are not cited here when pertaining to a reservation or pueblo. Nevertheless, from this list one still gets a sense of the enormous linguistic debt owed to Indians.

It should also be pointed out that in many cases the etymologies or definitions of place names are unknown or in dispute. Many Indian place names were adopted by whites centuries before scholars began researching these Indians or their root languages. And identical sounds occur in different Indian language families and dialects.

In this list the amount of information accompanying each entry varies significantly. Sometimes the specific tribal dialect, the original Indian word-phrase or name, and the English translation are all known. Sometimes only the larger language family is known (see "Indian Languages" in chapter 3), and sometimes just the fact of Indian derivation. In terms of usage within the list, the phrase "Indian derivation" is used to convey any kind of Indian-related derivation, whether originally applied by Indians or whites. The word "tribal" also is given broad usage—much broader in fact than in this book's list of tribes—including in the place name list what might be considered a subtribe or band in the tribal list, or an alternate name rarely used historically, or a French or Spanish name for the tribe. With regard to the present-day geographical information cited after each entry, if the place name refers to a municipality—either a city, town, or village—the state or states where it is located are listed afterwards (e.g., *Oneonta:* NY, KY, AL). If the place name refers to some other kind of geographic entity or landform, its specific nature is also identified (e.g., *Otsego:* MI, OH. Also counties and lakes in NY and MI).

UNITED STATES

Abiquiu: NM. Also reservoir in NM. Probably village name from Tewa *abay:* "chokecherry."

Absaroka: Mountains in WY and MT. From native name for Crow Indians.

Acadia: ME, VA. Also park in ME; parish in LA. Probably from Micmac *acada:* "place of plenty" or "village."

Accokeek: MD. Delaware.

Accomac: VA. Also county. Tribal name: "the other side."

Acomita: NM. After Indian pueblo and people *Acoma:* "white-rock people."

Adak: Strait and island in AK. Aleut: possibly "father."

Adirondacks: NY. Also mountains and park. Tribal name, from Iroquoian *ratirontacks:* "bark eaters."

Agawam: MA, MT, OK. Also river in MA. Algonquian: "overflowed land" or "lowland."

Ahloso: OK. Muskogean: "there black," probably referring to a burned place.

Ajo: AZ. Also mountains. From Papago *auauho:* "paint."

Akaska: SD. Siouan.

Akiak: AK. Eskimo: probably "crossing."

Akutan: Bay, island, and mountain in AK. Aleut: possibly from *hakuta:* "I made a mistake."

Alabama: State and river. Also township in CA. Tribal name, also *Alibamu.* From Choctaw *alba:* "thickets" or "plants," and *amo:* "reapers.'"

Alachua: FL. Also county. Possibly Creek: "grassy, marshy plain."

Alamance: County and creek in NC. Possibly Siouan: "noisy stream."

Alamota: KS. Probably after Osage chief.

Alapaha: GA. Also river in FL. Seminole village name.

Alarka: Mountains in NC. Cherokee.

Alaska: State. Also gulf and peninsula. Aleut word, variously spelled *alaeksu, alachschak, alaschka,* and *alaxa:* "mainland" as opposed to islands.

Alcona: County in MI. Pseudo-Indian derivative. Coined by Henry Rowe Schoolcraft, explorer and ethnologist, from Indian roots.

Aleutian: Islands, and national wildlife refuge in AK. From tribal name *Aleut,* possibly a derivation of the Russian word *aleaut:* "bald rock."

Algoma: WI, ID, MS. Coined by Schoolcraft from *Algonquian:* the Indian tribal and linguistic name, and *goma:* "water."

Algona: IA, WA. Coined from *Algonquian.*

Algonac: MI. Coined by Schoolcraft from *Algonquian,* and *auke:* "land of."

Ali Chukson: AZ. Papago: "little black hills foot."

Aliquippa: Borough in PA. After Seneca woman reputed to be a queen.

Allagash: River in ME. Abnaki: "bark shelter."

Allatoona: GA. Also lake. Probably Cherokee.

Allegany: NY, OR. Also counties in NY and MD. See **Allegheny.**

Alleghany: County and town in VA; county in NC; town in CA. See **Allegheny.**

Allegheny: Plateau in NY, OH, and WV; mountains in PA, VA, and WV; river and reservoir in PA and NY; national forest and county in PA. Probably from Delaware name for Allegheny and Ohio rivers.

Alloway: Township and creek in NJ. After Indian chief whose name means "beautiful tail" or "fox."

Alluwe: OK. Delaware: probably "better."

Almota: WA. Nez Perce: "torchlight fishery."

Alpena: SD, MI. Also county in MI. Devised by Schoolcraft from Algonquian and Ojibway.

Amagansett: NY. Algonquian; "well at."

Amawalk: NY. Algonquian.

Amboy: IL, and many other places. Algonquian; "hollow inside" or "like a bowl," describing a valley.

Anadarko: OK. Tribal name.

Anahuac: TX. Also national wildlife refuge. Probably after Indian chief *Anahaw;* or possibly Aztec: "waterland."

Anaktuvuk: River in AK. Eskimo: "dung everywhere," referring to a pass frequented by caribou.

Anamoose: ND. Ojibway: "dog."

Anamosa: IA. Possibly after Sauk Indian girl whose name means "white fawn."

Anatone: WA. Probably after Indian woman.

Anchorage: AK. For *Knik Anchorage. Kinik* or *Kinnick:* the name of a Tanaina village, meaning "fire."

Androscoggin: County, lake, and river in ME and NH. From *Amasagunticook:* tribal name, meaning "fish spearing" or "fish-curing place."

Aniwa: WI. From Ojibway *aniwi:* "those," a prefix signifying superiority.

Annawan: IL. Also township. After Massachuset Indian chief.

Annona: TX. After Indian girl.

Anoka: MN, IN, NY. Also county in MN. Siouan: "on both sides."

Antietam: MD. Algonquian.

Antigo: WI. From Ojibway *neequee-antigo-sebi:* "place where evergreens grow."

Apache: AZ, OK. Also county, pass, lake, and peak in AZ; river in NM; national forest in AZ and NM; mountains in TX. Zuni tribal name for Athapascan people, meaning "enemy" or "alien."

Apalachee: GA. Also river in GA: bay in FL. Tribal name, either Hitchiti: "on the other side"; or Choctaw: "helper."

Apalachicola: FL. Also river, bay, and national forest. Probably from Hitchiti *apalachi:* "on the other side," and *okli:* "people."

Apishapa: River in CO. Ute: "standing water."

Apopka: FL. Also lake. From Seminole *aha:* "potato," and *papka:* "eating place."

Appalachian: Mountains in eastern North America, extending from AL to Quebec. See **Apalachee.**

Appanoose: KS. Also county in IA. After Sauk chief whose name means "a chief when a child."

Appomattox: VA. Also county and river. From *Appomattoc,* tribal name, probably derived from village name *Appamatuck:* "tobacco plant country" or "curving tidal estuary." *Apumetec* is also the name of an Indian queen.

Aptakisic: IL. After Potawatomi chief whose name means "half-day."

Aptos: CA. Probably from village name *Owatos:* "meeting of the waters."

Arapaho: OK. Also national forest in CO. Tribal name, probably from *tirapihu:* "trader."

Arapahoe: NE, NC, WY. Also county, peak, and national wildlife refuge in CO. See **Arapaho.**

Arcata: CA. Indian derivation: probably "place where the boats land," or "union," or "sunny spot."

Arenac: MI. Also county. Coined by Schoolcraft from Algonquian *auke:* "place"; and Latin *arena.*

Arikaree: CO. Also river. Tribal name: "horns" or "elk," in reference to hair style.

Aripeka: FL. After Indian chief.

Arivaca: AZ. Probably Pima: "little reeds."

Arizona: State. Probably from Pima or Papago *ali:* "small," and *shonak:* "place of the spring"; or possibly from Spanish *arida* and *zona:* "dry zone"; or from Aztec *arizuma:* "silver-bearing."

Arkansas: State, county, and township. Also river in several states and city in KS. After French name *Alkansas* or *Akamsea,* for Indian tribe later known as Quapaw.

Arlee: MT. After Indian chief.

Armonk: NY. Algonquian: probably "beaver" or "fishing place."

Aroostook: River and county in ME. Algonquian (probably Malecite): "good, beautiful, or clear river."

Arrow Rock: MO. Also Arrowrock Reservoir in ID. The Indians in the area used the local rock for their arrowheads.

Ascutney: VT. Also mountain. Abnaki: probably "end of river fork," or "fire mountain."

Ashippun: WI. Algonquian: probably "raccoon."

Ashkum: IL. After Potawatomi chief whose name means "more and more."

Ashokan: NY. Also reservoir. Algonquian: "small mouth" or "outlet."

Ashtabula: OH, ND. Also county and river in OH; lake in ND. Algonquian: "fish river."

Asotin: WA. Also county. Nez Perce: "eel creek."

Assinippi: MA. Algonquian: "rock water."

Astatula: FL. Probably Seminole.

Atchafalaya: Bay and river in LA. Choctaw: "long river."

Atoka: OK, TN. Also county in OK. In OK, named after the Choctaw athlete, *Captain Atoka*. Elsewhere, Muskogean: "ball ground."

Atsion: NJ. Algonquian: "stone at."

Attala: AL. Also county in MS. From Cherokee *otale*: "mountain."

Attapulgus: GA. Indian derivation: "boring holes in wood to make a fire."

Aucilla: River in FL and GA. Timucuan.

Autauga: County and creek in AL. Village name: probably "border."

Aztec: NM, AZ. Tribal name: "place of the heron," or "land of flamingos," or "shallow land where vapors rise."

Azusa: CA. From Gabrielino *azuncsbit*: "skunk hill," possibly after a chief's daughter.

Bally (Bolly, Bully, Baily): Generic name in northern CA, as in Hayfork Bally or Bully Choop Mountain, usually meaning "high." From Wintun *buli*: "peak."

Bannock: County and peak in ID: peak in WY. Shoshonean tribal name: "hair in backward motion," referring to scalp locks.

Bedias: TX. From *Bidai*: tribal name.

Bejou: MN. Ojibway adaptation of French *bonjour*.

Bemidji: MN. Also lake. After Ojibway chief whose name probably means "river crossing lake."

Beowawe: NV. Probably Shoshonean: "pass" or "gateway."

Biloxi: MS. Also bay. Tribal name: "broken pot."

Bithlo: FL. Seminole: "canoe."

Biwabik: MN. Ojibway: "iron."

Blackfoot: River and reservoir in ID; river in MT. Tribal name.

Black Hawk: IA, Co. Also county and lake in IA. After chief of Sauk and Fox tribes.

Black Hills: Mountain range in SD: national forest in SD and WY. Translation of Siouan *paha sapa*.

Black Warrior: River in AL. Translation of *Tuscaloosa*: tribal name.

Bly: OR. From Klamath *p'lai*: "high."

Bodcaw: River in AR and LA. Probably Caddo.

Bogalusa: LA. Choctaw: "black stream."

Bogue Chitto: MS. Plus river in MS and LA. Choctaw: "big stream."

Bokhoma: OK. Choctaw: "red stream."

Bokoshe: OK. Choctaw: "little stream."

Boligee: AL. Probably Choctaw.

Bolinas: CA. Probably from *Baulenes*: tribal name.

Botna: IA. From Siouan *Nishnabotna*: the name of a nearby river.

Broken Arrow: OK. From a Creek Indian ceremony symbolizing peace after the Civil War.

Brule: WI, NE. Also county in SD, river in WI and MI; lake in MN. Siouan tribal name, a translation into French of *sicangu*: "burned thighs."

Burgaw: NC. Tribal name.

Byhalia: MS. Choctaw: "white oaks standing."

Bylas: AZ. After Indian chief.

Caddo: TX, OK, AR. Also county in OK; parish and lake in LA: river in AK: reservoir in CO. Tribal name.

Cahokia: IL. Tribal name.

Cahuilla: CA. Also valley. Tribal name: probably "master."

Calcasieu: Parish, lake, and river in LA. After Indian chief whose name in Atakapan probably means "crying eagle."

Caloosahatchee: River in FL. From tribal name *Calusa*: possibly "fierce people," and Seminole *hachi*: "stream."

Calpella: CA. Tribal name.

Calumet: IL, IA, OK, MI, MN, PA. Also county, lake, river, and harbor in WI; rivers in IN. Adaptation of French *chalemel*: "little reed," used to refer to Indian ceremonial pipes.

Canajoharie: NY. Iroquoian: "pot that washes itself," referring to a pothole in the bed of the creek.

Canandaigua: NY. Also lake. From Iroquoian *gandundagwa*: probably "town set off" or "townsite."

Canaseraga: NY. Iroquoian: "among milkweeds."

Canastota: NY. From Iroquoian

kniste: "cluster of pines," and *stota*: "still."

Caneadea: NY. Iroquoian: "where the heavens rest upon the earth."

Canisteo: NY. Also river. From Seneca *kanestie*: "board on water," or "head of navigation."

Canoochee: GA. Also river. From Creek *Canosi*: name of ancient Indian region.

Canutillo: TX. Possibly from Indian: "alkali flat," or Spanish: "small pipe."

Capac: MI. After *Manco Capac*, founder of Inca dynasty.

Casco: ME, WI. Also bay in ME. Micmac: "muddy."

Cassadaga: NY. Also lakes and creek. Iroquoian: "under the rocks."

Cataula: GA. Creek: "dead mulberry."

Catawba: NC, SC, OH, VA. Also county and river in NC; Island in OH. Tribal name.

Cathlamet: WA. Tribal name.

Catoosa: County in GA. Probably after Cherokee chief whose name means "high place."

Cattaraugus: NY. Also county and creek. Iroquoian: "bad smelling shore."

Cayuga: NY, IN, ND. Also canal, county, and lake in NY. Tribal name, possibly from Irouquoian *gaw ugwck*: "where they take the boats out."

Cayuse: OR. Tribal name.

Chanhassen: MN. Also river. From Siouan *chan* and *hasan*: "tree with sweet juice" or " maple."

Chappaqua: NY. Algonquian: possibly for an edible root.

Chappaquiddick: Island in MA. From Wampanoag *cheppiaquidne*: "separated island."

Chaska: MN. Also lake and creek. Siouan: "first-born son."

Chassahowitzka: River in FL. Seminole: "pumpkins hanging."

Chatawa: MS. Probably from *Choctaw*: tribal name.

Chateaugay: NY. Also river and lake. Probably Iroquoian.

Chattahoochee: FL. Also county, river, and park in GA: river in AL. Muskogean: "marked rock."

Chattanooga: TN, OK, OH. Creek: "rock rising to a point," probably in reference to Lookout Mountain.

Chattaroy: WV. Tribal name.

Chattooga: County in GA: river in GA, AL, and SC. Cherokee: probably "has crossed the river," or "drank by sips."

Chautauqua: NY. Also county and lake in NY; county in KS. Iroquoian: "place where one was lost," or "foggy place," or "bag tied in the middle," or "where the fish was taken out," or "place of early death," or "place where a child was washed away."

Chebanse: IL. After Potawatomi chief whose name means "little duck."

Cheboygan: MI. Also county and river. Algonquian: probably "pipe" or "funnel."

Checotah: OK. After Creek chief *Samuel Checote*.

Cheektowaga: NY. Iroquoian: "crabapple place."

Chehalis: WA. Also county and river. Tribal name: "sand."

Chemult: OR. After Klamath chief.

Chemung: NY. Also county and river. Seneca: "big horn."

Chenango: County and river in NY. Onondaga: "bull thistle."

Chenoa: IL. Cherokee name.

Cheraw: CO, SC. Tribal name.

Cherokee: NC, KY, IA, KS, OK, AL. Also counties in AL, GA, IA, KS, NC, SC, OK, and TX; lakes in TN and OK; national forest in NC and TN. Tribal name, possibly from Creek *tciloki*: "people of a different speech."

Chesaning: MI. Algonquian: "big rock."

Chesapeake: VA, WV, MD. Also bay in MD and VA. Algonquian: possibly "on the big bay."

Chetek: WI. After Ojibway chief.

Chetopa: KS. After Osage chief.

Chewelah: WA. Possibly Spokane for a kind of snake.

Cheyenne: OK, WY, TX. Also counties in CO, KS, and NE; river in SD. Tribal name, given by Sioux: "red talkers."

Chicago: IL. Also river. Algonquian: "onion place" or "garlic place."

Chickalah: AR. After Indian.

Chickaloon: AK. Also bay and river. Athapascan name.

Chickamauga: GA. Also lake in TN. Cherokee tribal name: possibly "sluggish water" or "whirlpool."

Chickasaw: AL. Also counties in IA and MS. Tribal name.

Chickasawhay: River in MS. From a Choctaw village name plus *hay* or *ahe*: "potato."

Chicopee: MA, GA, KS. Also river in MA. Algonquian: possibly "swift water."

Chilchinbito: AZ. Navajo: "sumac water."

Chilhowee: MO. Cherokee village name.

Chillicothe: IL, IA, OH, MO, and TX. Tribal name, possibly Shawnee: "village."

Chilocco: OK. Probably Muskogean: "big deer."

Chiloquin: OR. After Klamath chief.

Chimacum: WA. Tribal name.

Chinle: AZ. Navajo: "mouth of canyon."

Chinook: MT, WA. Tribal name. In MT, derived from chinook wind, also named after Indians.

Chippewa: Counties in MI, MN, and WI; lake in WI; rivers in MI and WI; national forest in MN. Tribal name; also *Ojibway.* From *adji:* "voice," and *bwa:* "gathering up" or "puckered."

Chiricahua: Mountains, peak, and national monument in AZ. Tribal name from Apache *tsil:* "mountain," and *kawa:* "great."

Chisago: County in MN. From Ojibway *kichi-sago:* "large and beautiful."

Chittenango: NY. Iroquoian: probably "waters divide and run north."

Chocowinity: NC. Probably Algonquian.

Choctaw: Counties in AL, MS, and OK. Tribal name.

Chokio: MN. Siouan: "middle."

Chokoloskee: FL. Seminole: "old house."

Choptank: River in MD. Adaptation of Nanticoke tribal name: possibly "tidal stream" or "tidal change."

Chowan: County and river in NC. From the tribal name *Chowanoc.*

Chowchilla: CA. Tribal name.

Chuichu: AZ. Pima: "caves."

Chula: GA, MO, and VA. Probably Muskogean: "fox."

Chulitna: Rivers in AK. Tanaina.

Chuluota: FL. Probably Seminole: "fox den."

Chunchula: AL. Probably Muskogean: "alligator."

Chuska: Mountains in AZ and NM. Probably Navajo: "white spruce."

Clackamas: County in OR. Tribal name.

Clallam: County and bay in WA. Tribal name: "big brave nation."

Claremore: OK. After Kiowa chief *Grah-mah.*

Clatskanie: OR. Tribal name.

Clatsop: County in OR. Tribal name.

Coahoma: TX. Also county in MS. After *Sweet Coahoma,* daughter of the last Choctaw in the area, whose name means "red panther."

Cochise: County in AZ. After Apache chief.

Coconino: County, plateau, and national forest in AZ. Tribal name, either Zuni: "pinyon people"; or Havasupai: "little water."

Cohasset: MA. Algonquian: "fishing promontory."

Cohocton: NY. Also river. From Iroquoian: "trees in the water."

Cohoes: NY. Algonquian: "pine tree."

Cokato: MN. Siouan: "at the middle."

Colusa: CA. Also county and national wildlife refuge. Village name.

Comanche: Counties in KS, OK, and TX. Tribal name.

Commack: NY. From Algonquian *winne-comac:* "pleasant land, field, or house."

Comobabi: AZ. Papago: "hackberry well."

Conasauga: River in GA and TN. Cherokee.

Conata: SD. Siouan.

Concho: River and county in TX; lake in AZ. Tribal name.

Conconully: WA. Indian derivation: probably "cloudy."

Conecuh: County and national forest in Al; river in AL and FL. Probably Muskogean.

Conehatta: MS. Choctaw: "white skunk."

Congaree: River in SC. Tribal name.

Conneaut: OH. Also lake in PA. Possible adaptation of Indian *gunniate:* "it is a long time since he is gone"; or possibly Iroquoian: "mud" or "many fish."

Connecticut: State and river. From Mohican *quonehtacut* or *quinnehtukguet* or *connittecock:* "the long river."

Conshohocken: PA. Delaware: "pleasant valley," or "roaring land."

Coos: County in NH: county and bay in OR. In NH, Pennacook: "pine tree." In OR, tribal name.

Coosa: GA. Also county and river in AL. Tribal name: "reed."

Coosada: AL. From *Koasati:* tribal name.

Coosawhatchie: SC. Also river. Muskogean: "stream with cane."

Copalis: WA. Also national wildlife refuge. Tribal name.

Copiah: County in MS. Choctaw, probably from *koi:* "panther," or possibly from word for "clear water."

Coram: NY, MT. Algonquian: "valley."

Coshocton: OH. Also county. From Delaware *goschachgunk:* "black bear town," or "river crossing," or "ford."

Cotati: CA. Miwok village name.

Council: GA, ID. For Indian meeting places.

Council Bluffs: IA. For a meeting held between the Oto Indians and members of the Lewis and Clark Expedition.

Council Grove: KS. Also reservoir. For a site where a treaty was signed with the Osage Indians.

Coushatta: LA. Choctaw: "canebrake white." Tribal name.

Coweta: OK. Also county in GA. In honor of William McIntosh, Coweta Indian.

Cowlic: AZ. Papago: "hill."

Cowlitz: River and county in WA. Tribal name: "power" or "catch the spirit."

Coxsackie: NY. Algonquian, probably from *sack:* "stream outlet"; derivation of the rest is uncertain.

Creek: County in OK. For the Creek Indians.

Croatoan: NC. Also national forest. Probably Algonquian: possibly "talk town."

Crosswicks: NJ. Algonquian: idea of separation inherent in name.

Croton: NY, IA. After Indian chief *Cnoten.*

Crow Wing: County in MN. A translation of Ojibway *gagagiwigwuni.*

Cucamonga: CA. Shoshoni: "sandy place."

Currituck: NC. Also county and sound. Tribal name: probably "wild geese."

Cusseta: AL, GA. From *Kasihta:* tribal name.

Cuyahoga: River, county, and falls in OH. Probably Iroquoian: "important river."

Dacoma: OK. Coined from *Dakota* and *Oklahoma.*

Dahlonega: GA. From Cherokee *talonega:* "place of yellow money," the site where gold was first discovered in the United States (1818).

Dakota: States, North and South. Also, county and city in NE: county in MN: city in IA. Tribal name for people also known as *Sioux.*

Decorah: IA. Also peak in WI. After one among several Winnebago chiefs. Also *Decorra* in IL, and *Decoria* in MN.

Dishna: River in AK. Ingalik.

Dowagiac: MI. From Potawatomi *ndowagayuk:* "subsistence area."

Eastanollee: GA. From Cherokee *oostanaula:* "place of rocks across stream."

Econfina: River in FL. Creek: "natural bridge."

Edisto: Island and river in SC. Tribal name.

Eek: River and lake in AK. Eskimo.

Ekalaka: MT. After Siouan woman *Ijkalaka.*

Elkatawa: KY. After Indian prophet *Ellskwatawa.*

Ellijay: GA. From Cherokee village name *Elatseyi.*

Elloree: SC. Indian derivation: probably "home I love."

Encampment: WY. For a regular yearly Indian camping place during the fur-trading period.

Enoree: River in SC. Tribal name.

Entiat: River in WA. Indian derivation: "rapid water."

Erie: ND, PA, CO, IL, KS. Also lake and canal in NY: counties in NY, OH, and PA; national wildlife refuge in PA. Tribal name. From Iroquoian *erie* or *erike* or *eriga:* "long tail," in reference to the wildcat, or simply "cat."

Escambia: Counties and river in AL and FL. Spanish translation of Choctaw or Chickasaw word: possibly cane-cutting place," or "killer," or "rain maker."

Escanaba: MI. Also river. Ojibway: possibly "flat rock."

Escatawpa: MS. Also river in MS and AL. Choctaw: "cane cut there."

Ethete: WY. Arapaho: "good."

Etowah: NC, TN. Also county in AL and river in GA. For Etowah Indian mound. Possibly Cherokee or Creek: "high tower" or "village."

Eufaula: AL, OK. Also natural wildlife refuge in AL and GA; reservoir in OK. Creek village name.

Eutaw: AL. Tribal name.

Eyota: MN. Siouan: "greatest" or "most."

Fenholloway: FL. Also river. Seminole: "high footlog (bridge)."

Flathead: County, river, lake, and national forest in MT. Tribal name.

Gagen: WI. Probably Algonquian: "no."

Gakona: AK. Also glacier and river. Athapascan: "rabbit river."

Geauga: County in OH. Iroquoian, possibly from *sheauga*: "raccoon"; or possibly from *cageauga*: "dogs around the fire"; or possibly a variant of *cuyahoga*: "important river."

Genesee: ID, MI, PA, WI. Also counties in NY and MI; river in NY and PA. Iroquoian: "beautiful valley."

Geneseo: NY, KS, IL. See **Genesee.**

Gila: NM, AZ. Also river, mountains, and county in AZ; national forest in NM. Tribal name.

Gogebic: Lake and county in MI. From Ojibway *bic*: "lake"; and rest probably means "high."

Goshute: UT. Also lake in NV. Tribal name: "dust people." Also *Gosiute* and *Goshiute*.

Gotebo: OK. After Kiowa chief.

Gowanda: NY. Shortened form of Iroquoian phrase: "almost surrounded by a hill."

Gros Ventre: Mountain range in WY. Tribal name: French for "big bellies."

Gu Achi: AZ. Papago: "big ridge."

Gu Komelik: AZ. Papago: "big flats."

Gu Oidak: AZ. Papago: "big ridge."

Gualala: CA. From Indian village name *hawalali*: "river mouth."

Gulkana: AK. Also river. From Athapascan *na*: "river"; derivation of the rest is uncertain.

Hackensack: NJ. Also river. Tribal name: possibly "hook mouth," "confluence of streams," "big snake land," or "low ground."

Haiwee: CA. Also reservoir. Probably Shoshonean: "dove."

Hatchie: River in MS and TN. Also national wildlife refuge. Choctaw: "stream."

Hatteras: NC. Also cape and island. Tribal name.

Hauppauge: NY. Algonquian: "overflowed land."

Hemet: CA. Probably Shoshonean.

Hialeah: FL. Probably Seminole: "beautiful prairie."

Hiawassee: GA. From Cherokee *ayuhwasi*: "meadow."

Hiawatha: CO, UT, KS. Also

national forest in MI. After character in Longfellow's poem, a name he took from Iroquoian mythological figure who helped organize Iroquois League. The name means "river maker."

Higganum: CT. Algonquian: "a quarry for stone tomahawks."

Hiko: NV. Probably Shoshonean: "white man."

Hoboken: NJ, GA. From Delaware *hobocan hackingh*: "land of the tobacco pipe."

Hohokus: NJ. Probably tribal name.

Hoholitna: River in AK. Probably Athapascan: "sudden river."

Hokah: MN. Siouan: "root," name of chief.

Holitna: River in AK. Athapascan.

Holopaw: FL. Seminole: probably "haul" or "draw."

Homochitto: River and national forest in MS. Choctaw: "big red."

Homosassa: FL. Village name: probably "pepper is there."

Honeoye: Lake in NY. From Iroquoian *hayeayah*: "finger lying," based on a legend of a snake biting off a brave's finger.

Hoonah: AK. Tribal name.

Hoopa: CA. Klamath.

Hopatcong: NJ. Also lake. Algonquian: probably "hill above a body of still water having an outlet."

Horicon: WI. Also national wildlife refuge. Originally tribal name: possibly "silver water." Applied by James Fenimore Cooper in *The Last of the Mohicans* to Lake George.

Houma: LA. From Choctaw *humma*: "red."

Housatonic: MA. Also river in MA and CT. Mahican: "at the place beyond the mountain."

Hulah: OK. Also river and reservoir. Osage: "eagle."

Huron: CA, IN, KS, OH, SD, MI. Also counties in MI and OH; mountains, river, bay, and national forest in MI. Tribal name for people also known as *Wyandot*.

Hyak: WA. Chinook: "hurry."

Hyampom: CA. From Wintun *pom*: "land"; derivation of the rest is uncertain.

Hyannis: NE, MA. After Indian chief *Hianna*.

Hypoluxo: FL. Seminole: probably "round heap."

Iatan: TX, MO. Probably after Indian chief.

Idaho: State. Also city and county. From Shoshonean *ee*: "coming down"; *dah*: "sun" or "mountain"; and *how*: an exclamatory phrase; i.e., "Behold, the sun coming down the mountain." Or possibly "sun up" or "gem of the mountains."

Iditarod: River in AK. Village name.

Igloo: SD. Eskimo: "snowhouse."

Ikpikpuk: River in AK. From Eskimo *ikpikpak*: "big cliff."

Iliamna: AK. Also lake and volcano. Probably Eskimo: the name of a mythical fish said to bite holes in boats.

Illinois: State. Also river in AR and OK; river in CA and OR; river in IL. Tribal name: "men."

Ilwaco: WA. After Indian named *El-wah-ko Jim*.

Immokalee: FL. Cherokee: "tumbling water."

Imnaha: River in OR. Probably from *Imna*: the name of an Indian chief, and *ha*: his region.

Indian: A common place name for many rivers, and lakes, etc., commemorating the Indians in the area.

Indiana: State. Also county. Latinized form of Indian.

Inola: OK. Probably Cherokee: "black fox."

Inyo: Mountains, county, and national forest in CA. Probably Shoshonean: "dwelling place of a great spirit."

Iosco: County in MI. A pseudo-Indian name, coined by Schoolcraft: probably intended to mean "spring water."

Iowa: State. Also city, county, river, and falls in IA; counties in IA and WI; town in LA. Tribal name.

Irondequoit: NY. Iroquoian: "bay."

Iroquois: IL, SD. Also peak and national wildlife refuge in NY; county in IL; river in IL and IN. Tribal name: "real adders"; given by Algonquians, with French spelling.

Isanti: MN. Also county. From tribal name *Santee*.

Ishpeming: MI. Ojibway: "high place."

Issaquena: County in MS. Choctaw: "deer's head."

Istachatta: FL. Seminole: "red man."

Itawamba: County in MS. Muskogean: a personal name.

Itkillik: River in AK. Eskimo: "Indian."

Itta Bena: MS. From Choctaw *bina*: "camp," and *ita*: "together."

Iuka: IL, KS, MS. After Chickasaw chief.

Ivishak: River in AK. From Eskimo *ivishaq*: "red paint," in reference to iron oxide.

Jacumba: CA. Probably Dieguено, with *aha*: "water"; derivation of the rest is uncertain.

Jadito: AZ. Navajo: "antelope water."

Jamul: CA. Dieguено: probably "foaming water."

Jelloway: OH. After Indian named *John Jelloway*.

Jemez: NM. Also mountains in NM. Tribal name: Spanish adaptation of *hay mish*; "people."

Jocassee: SC. After Indian woman.

Joseph: OR, UT. Also peak in WY; creek in OR and WA. After *Chief Joseph* of the Nez Perce.

Juab: County in UT. Gosiute: probably "level," "valley," or "plain."

Juniata: NE. Also county in PA. Iroquoian.

Kadoka: SD. Siouan: "opening" or "hole."

Kahiltna: River and glacier in AK. Athapascan, with *na*: "river."

Kahlotus: WA. Indian derivation: "hole in the ground."

Kahoka: MO. Variant of *Cahokia*: tribal name.

Kaibab: AZ. Also plateau and national forest in AZ. Paiute: "mountain lying down."

Kalamazoo: MI. Also county. From Algonquian *Ke-kala-mazoo*: probably "it smokes," or "he is troubled with smoke."

Kalispell: MT. From tribal name *Kalispel*: "camas," a type of lily.

Kalkaska: MI. Also county. Ojibway.

Kamela: OR. Probably Nez Perce: "tamarack."

Kamiah: ID. Probably Nez Perce: "hemp."

Kanab: UT. Paiute: "willows."

Kanabec: County in MN. Ojibway: "snake."

Kanaga: Island, pass, sound, and volcano in AK. Aleut.

Kanawha: IA. River and county in WV. Tribal name: possibly "hurricane."

Kandiyohi: County in MN. Siouan: "buffalo fish come."

Kankakee: IL. Also county in IL; river in IL and IN. Mohegan: "wolf" or "wolf land."

Kansas: State. Also city and river. Tribal name: "people of the south wind."

Kaskaskia: River in IL. Tribal name.

Kasota: MN. Siouan: "clear," in reference to a treeless ridge in the area.

Katonah: NY. After Indian chief.

Kaukauna: WI. From Ojibway *okakaning:* possibly for "pike fishing place."

Kaweah: CA. Also lake. Tribal name.

Kawkawlin: MI. Algonquian: probably "pickerel river."

Kayenta: AZ. From Navajo *tyende:* "where they fell into a creek."

Keatchie: LA. Caddoan: "panther," probably tribal name.

Keewatin: MN. Algonquian: "north wind."

Kenai: AK. Also lake, mountains, and peninsula. Tribal name.

Kennebec: SD. Also county and river in ME. Algonquian: "long lake."

Kennebunk: ME. Also river. Algonquian: "long cut bank."

Kenosha: WI. Also county. Potawatomi: "pickerel."

Kentucky: State, lake, and river. From Wyandot *ken-tah-teh:* "land of tomorrow"; or from Iroquoian *kentake:* "meadow land."

Keokuk: IA. Also county. After Fox chief, whose name, originally *Kiyokaga,* means "he who moves around alert."

Keosauqua: IA. Probably from *Keosauk:* Algonquian name for the Des Moines River.

Keshena: WI. After Menominee chief.

Ketchikan: AK. Probably from Tlingit *kitschkhin:* either "eagle wing river" or "city under the eagle."

Keuka: NY. Also lake. Iroquoian: "place for landing canoes."

Kewanee: IL, MO. Potawatomi: "prairie hen."

Kewaskum: WI. After Indian chief.

Kewaunee: WI. Also county. Ojibway: "to cross a point," or "prairie hen," or "wild duck."

Keweenaw: MI. Also bay, county, peninsula, and point in MI. See **Kewaunee.**

Kiamichi: River in OK. Possibly Caddoan: village name.

Kickapoo: River in WI: creek in IL. Tribal name: "he moves about."

Killdeer: ND. Translation from Siouan: "where they kill deer."

Killik: River in AK. Eskimo: probably tribal name.

Kinta: OK. Choctaw: "beaver."

Kiowa: CO, KS, MT, OK. Also counties in CO, KS, and OK. Tribal name: "principal people."

Kisatchie: LA. Also national forest. Choctaw: "reed river."

Kissimmee: FL. Also lake and river. Possibly from Seminole *ki:* "mulberry," and *asima:* "yonder."

Kitchawan: NY. Algonquian: "strong running," applied first to Croton River.

Kitsap: County and lake in WA. After Indian chief.

Kittanning: PA. Delaware: "on the big stream."

Kittitas: WA. Also county in WA. Probably tribal name: either "shoal people," "clay-gravel valley," or "land of bread."

Kitty Hawk: NC. Adaptation by folk etymology of Algonquian *chickahauk.*

Klamath: CA. Also county, mountains, river, lake, falls, and national wildlife refuge in OR; mountains, lake, river, and national forest in CA. Tribal name: probably from Chinook *tlamatl.*

Klawock: AK. After Indian chief.

Klickitat: River and county in WA. Tribal name: "beyond," given by Chinooks.

Klondike: IL, WI, TX. Adaptation of Indian *throndiuk:* "river full of fish." The river in Canada was the first to have this name, which then became associated with the discovery of gold.

Klukwan: AK. Tlingit: probably "old town."

Klutina: River and lake in AK. Athapascan: "glacier river."

Knik: AK. Also river and glacier. Probably Eskimo: "fire."

Kodiak: AK. Also island and national wildlife refuge. Probably from Eskimo *kikhtak:* "island."

Kokadjo: ME. Algonquian: "kettle mountain," from the legend of a giant who, in pursuit of a moose, threw his kettle down.

Kokechik: Bay and river in AK. Eskimo: "has wood."

Kokomo: CO, IN, MS. After Miami chief whose name means "black walnut."

Koochiching: County in MN. Cree: probably "rainy lake."

Koosharem: UT. From a tuber eaten by the local Indians.

Kooskia: ID. From Nez Perce *kooskooskia:* probably "clear water."

Kootenai: ID. Also river, county, and national wildlife refuge in ID: river and national forest in MT. Tribal name: "water people."

Koshkonong: MO. Also lake in WI. Ojibway: "closed in by fog," or "hog place," or "place for shaving."

Koyuk: AK. Also river in AK. Eskimo: "big river," probably a tribal name.

Kuna: ID. Probably Shoshonean: "fire."

Kuskokwim: Bay, river, and mountains in AK. Eskimo, with *kwim:* "stream": derivation of the rest is uncertain.

Kvichak: AK. Also bay and river. Eskimo.

Kwethluk: AK. Also river. Eskimo: "little river" or "bad river."

Kwiguk: AK. Eskimo: "big river."

Lackawanna: NY. Also river and county in PA. Delaware: "the stream that forks." Also *Lackawannock.*

Lacoochee: FL. Creek: "little river."

Lakota: IA, WA, ND. Also peak in SD. Variant of *Dakota:* tribal name.

Lapwai: ID. Nez Perce: probably "butterfly stream."

Latah: WA. Also county in ID. From Nez Perce *lakah:* "place of the pines;" and *tah-ol:* "pestle."

Leech: Lake in MN. Translation of Ojibway word, from the legend of a giant leech in the lake.

Lehigh: IA, KS, AL, OK. Also river and county in PA. An adaptation of Delaware *lechauweking:* "where there are forks."

Lenape: PA. Tribal name.

Lenawee: County in MI. Either from Shawnee *lenawaii:* "man," or coined by Schoolcraft.

Leota: MN. Said to be an Indian maiden from a story.

Letohatchee: AL. Creek: "arrow-wood stream."

Lilliwaup: WA. Twana: "inlet."

Lochloosa: FL. Adaptation of Choctaw: "black turtle," with Scottish influence.

Lochsa: River in ID. Nez Perce: probably "rough water."

Lolo: MT. Also national forest and pass. Probably the result of Flathead attempt to pronounce an English or French name.

Lompoc: CA. Chumash: probably "where the waters break through."

Loxahatchee: FL. Also river. Seminole: "turtle river."

Lycoming: County in PA. Delaware: "sandy creek."

Machias: ME. Also lakes, rivers, bay, and falls. Algonquian: "bad little falls."

Mackinac: MT. Also county, island, and straits in MI. From Ojibway *michilimackinak:* "island of the large turtle."

Mackinaw: MI, IL. Also river in IL. See **Mackinac.**

Macopin: NJ. Algonquian: "potato."

Macoupin: County in IL. See **Macopin.**

Macwahoc: ME. Algonquian: "bog."

Mad: River in VT. Adaptation of Abnaki *maditegon:* "bad river."

Madawaska: ME. Algonquian.

Mahaska: KS. Also county in IA. After Iowa chief whose name means "white cloud."

Mahnomen: MN. Also county. Ojibway: "wild rice."

Mahomet: IL. After Indian prophet.

Mahoning: County in OH: river in PA. From Delaware *mahonoi* or *m'hoani;* "salt lick."

Mahtomedi: MN. Siouan: "white bear lake."

Mahtowa: MN. Coined from Siouan *mahto* and the last syllable of Ojibway *makwa,* both meaning "bear."

Mahwah: NJ. Algonquian: possibly "beautiful" or "meeting place."

Majenica: IN. After Miami chief *Man-ji-ni-ka.*

Makanda: IL. Possibly after Indian chief.

Makoti: ND. Mandan: "earthlodge."

Malibu: CA. Probably Chumash village name.

Mamaroneck: NY. After Indian chief.

Manakin: VA. Tribal name.

Manalapan: NJ, FL. Algonquian.

Manasquan: NJ. Algonquian, with *mana:* "island."

Manawa: WI. Ojibway; probably personal name.

Mandan: ND. Tribal name: "those who live along the bank of the river."

Mandaree: ND. Coined from tribal names *Mandan, Hidatsa,* and *Arickaree,* as a town site for the three tribes.

Manhasset: NY. Tribal name.

Manhattan: Island (borough) in NY; towns elsewhere; beach in CA. Tribal name: possibly "island-mountain."

Manistee: MI. Also county, national forest, and river. Ojibway: probably "crooked river," or possibly "lost river," or "red river."

Manistique: MI. Also lake and river in MI. From Ojibway *tique*: "river," and the rest probably "crooked."

Manitou: Islands in MI; springs in CO. Algonquian: "spirit."

Manitowish: WI. Algonquian: "bad spirit."

Manitowoc: WI. Also county. Algonquian: "land of the spirit."

Mankato: MN, KS. Siouan: "blue earth."

Manteno: IL. After Indian woman *Maw-te-no*.

Manteo: NC. After Indian taken to England.

Maquoketa: IA. Also river. Algonquian: "bear river."

Maquon: IL. From Algonquian *a-ma-quon*: "mussel."

Maricopa: AZ, CA. Also county in AZ. Tribal name.

Marinette: AZ, WI. Also county in WI. From French name of Indian woman.

Maroa: IL. From *Tamaroa*: tribal name.

Masardis: ME. Algonquian.

Mascoutah: IL. Algonquian: "prairie."

Mashulaville: MS. After Choctaw chief *Mashulatubbee*.

Massachusetts: State and bay. From Algonquian *massa*: "great," and *wachusett*: "hill." The English originally used it as a tribal name.

Massapequa: NY. Tribal name.

Mastic: NY. Algonquian: "big tidal stream," a variant of *Mystic*.

Matawan: MN, NJ. Algonquian: "where two rivers come together."

Mattituck: NY. Algonquian: probably "no timber."

Maumee: OH. Also river in OH and IN. Tribal name, variant of *Miami*, from Ojibway *Omaumeg*: "people of the peninsula."

Maza: ND. After Sioux chief *Maza Chante*.

Mazomanie: WI. After Winnebago Indian *Manzemoneka*.

Mazon: IL. Algonquian: "nettle."

Mecosta: MI. Also county in MI.

After Potawatomi chief whose name means "bear cub."

Medicine: A common place name given to areas used by Indians for medicinal and ritualistic purposes.

Meherrin: VA. Also river in VA and NC. Tribal name.

Mekinock: ND. After Ojibway chief *Mickinock*.

Menahga: MN. Ojibway: "blueberry."

Menasha: WI. Algonquian: probably "island."

Menominee: MI, NE. Also county, mountains, and river in MI; mountains and river in WI. Tribal name: "wild rice people."

Mentasta: AK. Also mountains. Athapascan.

Mequon: WI. From Ojibway *miquan*: "ladle," for the shape of the stream.

Meramec: River in MO. Tribal name: "catfish."

Mermentau: LA. Adaptation of chief's name *Nementou*.

Merrimack: NH. Also county in NH and river in NH and MA. Algonquian: probably "deep place."

Mesabi: Mountains in MN. Ojibway: "giant."

Mescalero: NM. Tribal name.

Metea: IN. After Potawatomi chief *Mitia*.

Methow: WA. Also river. Tribal name.

Metlakatla: AK. Tsimshian: a village name, transferred from British Columbia.

Metolius: OR. Also river. From Indian *mpto-ly-as*: "light-colored fish."

Mettawa: IL. After Potawatomi chief.

Metuchen: NJ. After Indian chief *Metochshaning*.

Mexico: State (New Mexico), gulf. Municipalities in ME, MO, KY, NY, OH, and PA. Aztec: "place of the war god."

Miami: Common place name with diversity of origin. In FL, from Muskogean tribal name *Mayaimi*. In midwest and southwest, a tribal name as *Miami*, probably from Ojibway *oumaumeg*: "people of the peninsula"; or possibly from Delaware *we-mi-a-mik*: "all friends." In OR, from Chinook *me-mie*: "downstream."

Micanopy: FL. Seminole: "head chief."

Micco: FL. Seminole: "chief."

Miccosukee: FL. Tribal name.

Michigan: State. One of the Great Lakes. Also municipalities in ND, IN, MS; island in WI; river in CO. Ojibway: "big lake."

Millinocket: ME. Also lake. Algonquian.

Milwaukee: WI. Also river, county, and bay. Algonquian: probably "good land."

Minatare: NE. Tribal name.

Minco: OK. Choctaw: "chief."

Mineola: NY, IA, TX. From Algonquian *meniolagamika*: "pleasant village" or "palisaded village."

Mingo: County in WV; national wildlife refuge in MO. From Algonquian *mingwe*: "stealthy" or "treacherous." Iroquoian tribal name.

Minidoka: ID. Also county and national wildlife refuge. Possibly Shoshonean: "broad expanse."

Minneapolis: MN, KS. From Siouan *minnehaha*: "waterfall" (also the heroine of Longfellow's *Hiawatha*), and the Greek *polis*: "city."

Minnehaha: WA, WV. Also county and falls in SD. Siouan: "waterfall" (also the heroine of Longfellow's *Hiawatha*).

Minneiska: MN. Siouan: "white water."

Minneola: MN, KS, FL. Siouan: "much water."

Minnesota: State. Also municipality, lake, and river. From Siouan *minne*: "water," and *sota*: probably "reflection of sky on water" or "cloudy."

Minnetonka: MN. Also lake. Coined from Siouan *minne*: "water," and *tonka*: "big."

Minnewaukan: ND. From Siouan *mini-waukon-chante*: "water of the bad spirit."

Minonk: IL. Algonquian: probably "good place."

Minooka: IL. Delaware: probably "good land."

Minquadale: DE. Tribal name.

Mishawaka: IN. Potawatomi: possibly "place of dead trees" or "thick trees."

Mishicot: WI. Algonquian: probably after chief.

Missaukee: County and lake in MI. After Ottawa chief whose name means "big outlet at."

Mississinewa: River in OH and IN. Algonquian: "river of big stones."

Mississippi: State and river. Also city in state of same name; counties in AR and MO; and sound in LA and MS. From Algonquian *messipi*: "big river."

Missoula: MT. Also county. Flathead: "feared water."

Missouri: State and river. Also municipalities in TX, MO, and IA. Tribal name: "muddy water."

Moapa: NV. Paiute: "mosquito spring."

Mobile: AL, AZ. Also bay and county in AL. Tribal name.

Moccasin: AZ, CA, MT, VA. Also lake in OR. Because it resembles the outline of a moccasin.

Moclips: WA. Quinault: indicates a place where girls were sent during puberty rites.

Modoc: SC, GA, OR. Also county and national forest in CA. Tribal name, from *moatokni*: "southerners."

Moenkopi: AZ. Hopi: "place of running water."

Mohave: County in AZ; mountains in AZ and CA; lake in AZ and NV. Tribal name: "three mountains."

Mohawk: NY, AZ, MI. Also river in NY and valley in AZ. Tribal name given by Algonquian neighbors: "cannibals."

Moiese: MT. After Flathead chief.

Moingona: IA. Tribal name.

Mojave: CA. Also desert and river. Tribal name: "three mountains."

Mokelumne: CA. Also river. Miwok tribal name, with *umne*: "people."

Mokena: IL. Algonquian: "turtle."

Molalla: OR. Tribal name.

Momence: IL. Probably after Indian *Isidore Momence*.

Monches: WI. After Potawatomi chief.

Mondamin: IA. Algonquian: "corn."

Monee: IL. After Indian woman.

Moniteau: County in MO. A French rendering of *Manitou*: "spirit."

Monon: IN. Probably Potawatomi.

Monona: WI. Also lake in WI; county in IA. Algonquian: after either an Indian divinity or a legendary Indian girl who leaped into the Mississippi River when she believed her lover had been killed.

Monongahela: PA. Also river in PA and WV; national forest in WV. From Delaware *menaungehilla*: "river with the sliding banks."

Monsey: NY. From tribal name *Munsee*.

Montauk: NY. Also point. Algonquian: possibly "fort at."

Montezuma: CO, GA, IA, KS. Also county in CO; peak and river in UT; national wildlife refuge in NY. After the Aztec ruler of Mexico.

Moquah: WI. Algonquian: "bear."

Moshannon: PA. Also creek. Algonquian: "moose stream."

Mosinee: WI. Algonquian: "moose."

Mound: The name is often associated with the "mound builders" of the central Mississippi Valley (e.g., *Mound City,* Missouri).

Moweaqua: IL. Potawatomi: "wolf-woman."

Moyock: NC. Algonquian: "place of oaks by trail."

Mukwonago: WI. Algonquian: "bear-lair."

Multnomah: County and falls in OR. Tribal name.

Muncie: IN, KS. Tribal name: "people of the stone country."

Munising: MI. From Algonquian *minissing:* "island in a lake."

Munuscong: Lake and river in MI. Algonquian: "the place of reeds."

Muscatatuck: River and national wildlife refuge in IN. Algonquian: "clear river."

Muscatine: IA. Also county and island. From *Mascouten:* tribal name.

Muscoda: WI. Algonquian: "prairie."

Muscogee: County in GA. Tribal name.

Muskegel: Channel and island in MA. Wampanoag: "grassy place."

Muskegon: MI. Also county and river in MI. Ojibway: "swampy."

Muskingum: County and river in OH. Algonquian village name: probably "at the river."

Muskogee: OK. Also county. Tribal name.

Myakka: FL. Also river in FL. Timucuan village name.

Mystic: CT, IA. Algonquian: "great tidal river."

Nabesna: AK. Also river and glacier. Athapascan, with *na:* "river."

Naches: WA. Also river. Possibly from *nahchess:* "plenty of water."

Nacogdoches: TX. Also county. Tribal name.

Nahant: MA. Also bay. Algonquian: probably from the name of a chief *Nahantum.*

Nahunta: GA. Also river and swamp in NC. Tuscarora: "tall trees" or "black creek."

Namekagon: WI. Also lake and river. Ojibway: "place for sturgeon."

Nampa: ID. After Shoshoni chief: possibly "big foot."

Nansemond: County in VA. Tribal name, or from *neunschimend:* "whence we were driven off."

Nantahala: Mountains, gorge, lake, river, national forest in NC. Cherokee: "place of the middle sun."

Nanticoke: MD, PA. Also river in DE and MD. Tribal name from Delaware *nentego:* "tidewater people."

Nantucket: MA. Also county, island, sound. Algonquian: probably "narrow tidal river at."

Nanuet: NY. After Indian chief.

Napa: CA. Also county. Probably Patwin: "house."

Napavine: WA. Indian derivation: "small prairie."

Nappanee: IN. Probably from Ojibway *nah-pah-nah:* "flour."

Narcoossee: FL. From Seminole *nokosi:* "bear."

Narragansett: RI. Also bay. Tribal name.

Naselle: WA. Tribal name.

Nashoba: OK. Choctaw: "wolf."

Nashotah: WI. Algonquian: "twins."

Nashua: NH, IA, MN, MT. Also river in NH and MA. Tribal name: "beautiful river with pebbly bottom."

Nassawadox: VA. Algonquian: "between streams."

Natchez: MS, LA. Tribal name.

Natchitoches: LA. Also Parish. Caddoan tribal name: "chestnut eaters" or "pawpaws."

Natick: MA, RI. Tribal name: "a place of hills," "a clear place," or "my land."

Naubinway: MI. After an Indian.

Naugatuck: CT. Also river. Algonquian: "long tree."

Navajo: AZ. Also county in AZ; mountain in UT; reservoir in NM. Tribal name.

Navasota: TX. Also river. Probably from Indian *nabototo:* "muddy water."

Navesink: NJ. Also river. Algonquian: "point at."

Nebraska: State, city, and national forest. From Siouan *ni:* "water," and *bthaska:* "flat," in reference to a wide river.

Necedah: WI. Also national wildlife refuge. Winnebago: "yellow."

Neche: ND. Ojibway: "friend."

Neches: TX. Also river. Tribal name.

Neenah: WI. Winnebago: "running water."

Negaunee: MI. Ojibway: "he walks ahead."

Nehalem: River in OR. Tribal name.

Nehawka: NE. Adaptation of an Omaha-Oto name: "murmuring water."

Nekoma: KS, ND. Possibly Algonquian.

Nekoosa: WI. Winnebago: "running water."

Nelagoney: OK. Probably Osage: "good water."

Nemaha: IA, NE. Also counties in KS and NE. Oto: "muddy water."

Nenana: AK. Also river. Athapascan, with *na:* "river."

Neodesha: KS. Pseudo-Indian coinage, with Siouan *ne:* "water," meaning "meeting of the waters."

Neoga: IL. Possibly Iroquoian: "dirty place."

Neopit: WI. After Menominee chief.

Neosho: MO, WI. Also county in KS; river in KS and OK. Osage: "cold, clear water" or "main river."

Nesconset: NY. After Indian chief *Nassiconset* whose name means "at the second crossing."

Neshanic Station: NJ. Algonquian tribal name: "at the double stream."

Neshkoro: WI. Winnebago, with *ne:* "water."

Neshoba: MS. Also county. Choctaw: possibly "wolf."

Nespelem: WA. Tribal name.

Nesquehoning: PA. Algonquian.

Netarts: OR. Tribal name.

Netawaka: KS. Possibly Potawatomi: "fine view."

Netcong: NJ. From Algonquian *musconetcong:* "rapid stream."

Neuse: NC. Also river. From *Neusiok:* tribal name.

Newaygo: MI. Also county. After Ojibway chief.

Newcomerstown: OH. After the second wife of Chief *Eagle Feather,* known as the *newcomer,* who supposedly murdered him.

Nez Perce (Nezperce): ID. Also county and national forest in ID; mountain in WY. Tribal name.

Niagara: NY, KY, ND. Also river, falls, and county in NY. Possibly Iroquoian: "point of land cut in two" or "thunder of waters resounding with a great noise."

Niangua: MO. Also river in MO. Probably Siouan, with *ni:* "river."

Niantic: CT. Also river. Tribal name: "at the point of land on a tidal river."

Niobrara: NE. River in NE and WY; county in WY. From Omaha and Ponca, *ni obthantha ko:* "spreading water river."

Niota: TN. Probably a pseudo-Indian coined name, with *ni:* "river."

Nipomo: CA. Chumash: village name.

Niskayuna: NY. Iroquoian: probably "big cornfields."

Nisqually: WA. Also river. Tribal name.

Nissequogue: NY. Tribal name.

Nitta Yuma: MS. Choctaw: "bear there."

Niwot: CO. After Arapaho chief, whose name means "left hand."

Noatak: AK. Also river. Eskimo: probably "inland river" or "new land."

Nobscot: OK, MA. Algonquian: "rocky place."

Nocatee: FL. From Seminole *nakiti:* "What is it?"

Nodaway: IA. Also county and river in MO. Probably Siouan.

Nokomis: IL. Also lake in WI. Ojibway: "grandmother." Also a character in Longfellow's *Hiawatha.*

North Dakota: See **Dakota.**

Notasulga: AL. Probably Muskogean.

Nottoway: VA. Also county and river. Tribal name: "rattlesnake."

Novato: CA. After Indian chief with a Spanish name.

Nowata: OK. Also county. Delaware: "welcome."

Nowitna: River in AK. Indian derivation.

Noxubee: River and county in MS. Choctaw: "stinking water."

Nunda: NY, SD. Iroquoian: probably "hilly."

Nunivak: Island and national wildlife refuge in AK. Eskimo: probably "big land."

Nushagak: AK. Also bay, river, and peninsula in AK. Eskimo.

Nuyaka: OK. Probably a Creek rendering of "New Yorker."

Nyack: NY. Algonquian: "point land."

Oacoma: SD. Siouan: "place between."

Obion: TN. Also county and river. Possible Indian derivation: "many forks."

Ocala: FL. Also national forest. Timucuan village name.

Occoquan: VA. Also creek. Algonquian: "hooked inlet."

Ochelata: OK. The Indian name of Cherokee chief *Charles Thompson*.

Ocheyedan: IA. Also river in IA and MN. Siouan: "mourning."

Ochlockonee: River in FL and GA. Hitchiti: "yellow water."

Ochopee: FL. Probably Seminole: "hickory tree."

Ocmulgee: River and national monument in GA. Hitchiti tribal name: "where water bubbles up."

Ocoee: FL, TN. Cherokee: "apricot-vine place."

Oconee: GA, IL. Also county, river, and national forest in GA; county in SC. Muskogean, with *oc*: "water."

Oconomowoc: WI. Also lake. Probably Algonquian: "beaver dam."

Oconto: WI, NE. Also county, falls, and river in WI. Menominee: "pickerel place."

Ocracoke: NC. Also inlet and island. From Algonquian *wocokon*: "curve" or "bend." Or possibly Algonquian: "enclosed place."

Odanah: WI. Ojibway: "village."

Ogallala: NE. Tribal name: "to scatter one's own."

Ogemaw: AR. Also county in MI. Probably Algonquian: "chief."

Ohatchee: AL. Creek, with *hatchee*: "stream," and *o*: probably "upper."

Ohio: State and river. Also counties in IN, KY, and WV; municipalities in OH, CO, and IL. From Iroquoian *oheo*: "beautiful."

Ojai: CA. From Chumash *ahwai*: "moon."

Ojibway: WI. Tribal name.

Ojus: FL. Probably Seminole: "plentiful."

Okahumpka: FL. Muskogean: possibly "water-biter."

Okaloosa: County in FL. Choctaw: "black water."

Okanogan: WA. Also county, river, and national forest. Tribal name: possibly "meeting place."

Okarche: OK. Coined from first syllables of *Oklahoma, Arapaho,* and *Cheyenne.*

Okaton: SD. Siouan.

Okauchee: WI. Also lake. Algonquian: possibly "pipe stem."

Okeana: OH. If not pseudo-Indian coinage, probably named after an Indian princess.

Okeechobee: FL. Also lake and county. Hitchiti: "big water."

Okeelanta: FL. Coined from Muskogean *oka*: "water," and *lanta*: from Atlantic.

Okeene: OK. From *Oklahoma* and the final letters of *Cherokee* and *Cheyenne.*

Okefenokee: Swamp and national wildlife refuge in GA. From Hitchiti *oke*: "water," and *finoke*: "trembling."

Okemos: MI. After Ojibway chief: "little chief."

Oketo: KS. After Oto chief *Arkaketah.*

Okfuskee: County in OK. Creek: "promontory."

Oklahoma: State, city, and county. Also municipality in PA. Muskogean: "red people," coined by Allen Wright, a Choctaw chief, to designate the Indian Territory.

Okmulgee: OK. Also county. Hitchiti tribal name: "where water boils up."

Okolona: OH, AR, MI, KY. Choctaw, with *oka*: "water."

Oktaha: OK. After Creek chief *Oktahasars.*

Oktibbeha: County in MS. Choctaw: "pure water."

Olamon: ME. Algonquian: "vermilion."

Olancha: CA. Tribal name.

Olathe: KS, CO. Shawnee: "beautiful."

Olustee: FL, OK. Muskogean: "black water."

Oma: AR, MS. Probably from Muskogean *homa*: "red."

Omaha: NE, TX, AR. Tribal name: possibly "those who live upstream beyond others."

Omak: WA. Also lake and mountain. Indian derivation.

Omemee: ND. Ojibway: "pigeon" or "dove."

Onaga: KS. After Potawatomi Indian.

Onaka: SD. Siouan.

Onamia: MN. Ojibway.

Onancock: VA. Algonquian: tribal or village name.

Onarga: IL. Possible adaptation of an Indian name.

Onaway: MI, ID. From Ojibway *onaiwah*: "awake."

Oneida: NY, OH, IL, WI, TN, IA, AR, KS. Also lake in NY; counties in NY, WI, and ID. Tribal name: "stone people."

Onekama: MI. Algonquian: "arm."

Oneonta: NY, KY, AL. Iroquoian: probably "stony place," "hills," or "cliffs."

Onondaga: County in NY. Tribal name: "hill people."

Ontario: One of the Great Lakes. Also municipality in NY; municipalities in CA and OR. From Iroquoian *oniatario*: "sparkling or beautiful water."

Ontonagon: MI. Also county and river. Ojibway: possibly "a place where game was shot by luck"; or from Ojibway *onagan*: "dish" or "bowl."

Oologah: OK. Also reservoir. After Cherokee chief whose name means "dark cloud."

Opa-locka: FL. Seminole: "big swamp."

Opelika: AL. Creek: "big swamp," village name.

Opelousas: LA. Tribal name: "black hair" or "black legs."

Oquawka: IL. Probably Sauk: "yellow banks."

Oradell: NJ. Also reservoir. After *Oratam*, a Delaware chief, and *Delford*, the former name of the area.

Oregon: State and city. Also municipalities in IL, MO, OH, and WI; county in MO; butte in WA. Origin disputed. Possibly from Shoshonean *oyer-un-gon*: "place of plenty"; or from Shoshonean *ogwa*: "river," and *pe-on*: "of the west"; or possibly from Siouan *ourigan*: referring to a great western river.

Orick: CA. Village or tribal name.

Oriska: ND. After an Indian princess in a poem by Lydia Sigourney.

Oriskany: NY, VA. Iroquoian: "nettles."

Osage: KS, IA, WV, AR, MN, WY, MO. Also counties in KS, MO, and OK; river in KS and MO. Tribal name.

Osawatomie: KS. From *Osage* and *Potawatomi*: tribal names.

Osceola: AR, IA, MO, NE, SD, WI, PA. Also counties in FL, IA, and MI; national forest in FL; mountain in NH. After Seminole chief whose name means "black drink hallower."

Oscoda: MI. Also county. Coined by Schoolcraft from Algonquian *ossin*: "pebble," and *muscoda*: "prairie."

Oshkosh: WI, NE. After Menominee chief.

Oshoto: WY. Arapaho: "stormy day."

Oskaloosa: IA, KS, MO. After one of Osceola's wives. Choctaw: "black water."

Osseo: MN, WI, MI. After "Son of the Evening Star" in Longfellow's *Hiawatha.*

Ossineke: MI. Ojibway: "he gathers stones."

Ossipee: NH. Also lake and mountains. Abnaki: "beyond the water" or "river of the pines."

Oswego: NY, KS, IL, MO. Also county, lake, and river in NY; lake in OR. From Iroquoian *osh-we-ge*: "the outpouring" or "the place where the valley widens."

Osyka: MS. Chocatw: "eagle."

Otay: CA. Diegueno: "brushy."

Otego: NY. Iroquoian: "to have fire there."

Oto: IA. Tribal name: "lechers."

Otoe: NE. Also county. See Oto.

Otsego: MI, OH. Also counties and lakes in NY and MI. Iroquoian: "rock place," from a particular rock at the outlet of the lake.

Ottawa: IL, KS, OH, MN. Also counties in KS, OH, MI, and OK; national forest in MI; national wildlife refuge in OH. Tribal name. Probably from Algonquian *adawe*: "to trade."

Ottumwa: IA, KS, SD. Probably Algonquian: "swift water" or "place of the lone chief."

Ouachita: AR. Also county and lake in AR; mountains and national forest in AR and OK; river in AR and LA; parish in LA. Tribal name: possibly "big hunt," "county of large buffaloes," or "sparkling water."

Ouray: CO, UT. Also county and peak in CO; national wildlife refuge in UT. After Ute chief: possibly "the arrow."

Outagamie: County in WI. From Ojibway *o-dug-am-eeg*: "dwellers on the other side," for the Fox Indians.

Owaneco: IL. Indian derivation.

Owanka: SD. Siouan: "camping place."

Owasso: OK. Probably Cherokee: "end of the trail."

Owatonna: MN. Siouan: "straight."

Owego: NY, TX. Also river in NY. Iroquoian: probably "the place that widens."

Owosso: MI. After Ojibway chief Wasso.

Ozark: AR, MO, AL. Also county and lake in MO; plateau in MO and AR; national forest in AR.

From French *aux Arks*: "at the Arks" or "at the Arkansas," the tribal name.

Ozaukee: County in WI. Tribal name: "river-mouth people" or "yellow earth." Also *Sauk*.

Pacolet: SC. Also river. Tribal name.

Paducah: KY, TX. After Chickasaw chief. Also tribal name.

Pahokee: FL. Hitchiti: "grass-water," for the Everglades.

Pahranagat: NV. Tribal name.

Pahrump: NV. Also valley in CA. Paiute: "water stone."

Paicines: CA. Costanoan: village name.

Pala: CA. Luiseno: probably "water."

Palatka: FL. From Seminole *pilotaikita*: "ferry crossing."

Palouse: WA. Also river in ID and WA. Tribal name: originally *palloatpallah*, "grassy expanse."

Pana: IL. Also lake. After Cahokia chief whose name means "partridge" or "slave."

Panaca: NV. After local Paiute who discovered an ore ledge.

Panguitch: UT. Also lake. Paiute: tribal name derived from the lake, meaning "fish people" or "place where fish can be found."

Panola: AL. Also counties in MS and TX. Choctaw: "cotton."

Paragonah: UT. Tribal name.

Paramus: NJ. Algonquian: "turkey river."

Paria: River in AZ and UT; plateau in AZ. Paiute: "elk water."

Parowan: UT. Tribal name: "marsh people."

Parsippany: NJ. Probably tribal name.

Pascagoula: MS. Also river. Tribal name: "bread people."

Pascoag: RI. Also reservoir. Algonquian: "forking place."

Paskenta: CA. Wintun: "under the bank."

Pasquotank: County in NC. Weapemeoc tribal name: probably "divided tidal river."

Passadumkeag: ME. Also mountain. Abnaki: "rapids over sandy places."

Passaic: NJ. Also county and river. Delaware: "valley" or "peace."

Patchogue: NY. Probably tribal name: "turning place" or "boundary."

Patoka: IL, IN. Also river in IN. After a Kickapoo chief.

Paulina: OR. Also lake and marsh. After chief, who was also known as *Paunina*.

Pawcatuck: River in CT. Algonquian: probably "open divided stream."

Pawhuska: OK. After Osage chief *Paw-hiu-skah*: "white hair."

Pawnee: NE, OK. Also county and river in KS; counties in NE and OK; creek in CO. Tribal name: possibly "horn" for their style of hair lock.

Pawtucket: RI. Algonquian: "at the falls in the river."

Paxico: KS. After Indian chief *Pashqua*.

Pecatonica: IL. Also river in IL. From Algonquian *pekitanoui*: "muddy."

Pecos: TX, NM. Also county in TX; river in NM and TX. Spanish adaptation of Keresan: "watering place."

Pembina: ND. Also county and river. From Ojibway *anepeminan*: "summer berry," a kind of cranberry.

Pemiscot: County in MO. Possibly Fox: "place of the long rock."

Pend Oreille: Lake in ID; county in WA; river in ID and WA. French: "ear pendants," name given to the Kalispel Indians.

Penobscot: County, bay, lake, and river in ME. From Algonquian *penobskeag*: "rocky place" or "river of rocks."

Pensacola: FL, OK. Tribal name, from Choctaw *panshi*: "hair," and *okla*, "people"; i.e., "long-haired people."

Pensaukee: WI. Menominee: probably "goose place."

Peoa: UT. Probably Ute.

Peoria: IL, AZ, KS, MS, OH. Also county in IL. Tribal name, from *peouarea*: "carriers."

Pequannock: NJ. Also river. Algonquian: "open field."

Pequop: NV. Also mountain. Probably tribal name.

Perkasie: PA. Delaware: "hickory nuts cracked."

Perquimans: County and river in NC. Weapemeoc tribal name.

Peshtigo: WI. Also river. Algonquian: possibly "snapping turtle" or "wild goose."

Pesotum: IL. After Potawatomi Indian.

Petaluma: CA. Village and tribal name, from Miwok *peta*: "flat," and *luma*: "back."

Petoskey: MI. Algonquian: "between two swamps."

Pewaukee: WI. Also lake. Algonquian: "swampy place."

Picabo: ID. Coined from the Shoshonean word for "friend."

Pickaway: WV. Also county in OH. Tribal name: possibly "ashes" or "bear." Also *Piqua*.

Pima: AZ. Also county. Tribal name.

Pinconning: MI. From Algonquian *o-pin-a-kan-ning*: "potato place."

Pinole: CA. From Aztec *pinolli*: "parched or toasted grain."

Pipestone: MN. Also county. For the catlinite used by the Indians to make pipe bowls.

Piqua: KS, OH. Tribal name: possibly "ashes" or "bear."

Piru: CA. Also lake. Shoshonean: probably a plant's name.

Piscataquis: County and river in ME. Abnaki: "at the fork of the river."

Pisinimo: AZ. Papago: "brown-bear head."

Pismo (Beach): CA. Probably from Chumash *pismu*: "tar."

Pistakee: IL. Illinois: "buffalo."

Piute: County and reservoir in UT. Tribal name, also *Paiute*: "Ute of the water."

Pluckemin: NJ. Possibly Algonquian.

Poca: WV. From *Pocatalico*: probably tribal or village name.

Pocahontas: IA, AR, IL, MS. Also counties in IA and WV. After the Indian princess, daughter of Powhatan: "radiant" or "playful."

Pocasset: OK. Algonquian: "where the stream narrows or widens."

Pocatalico: WV. Also river in SC and WV. Probably tribal or village name.

Pocatello: ID. After Bannock chief: "the wayward one."

Pocomoke: MD. Also sound in MD and VA. Algonquian: probably "small field" or "dark water."

Pocono: Mountains, lake, and creek in PA. Delaware: probably "valley stream."

Pocopson: PA. Algonquian.

Pohick: VA. Algonquian: "hickory."

Pojoaque: NM. Tewa: "drinking place."

Ponca: AR, OK, NE. Tribal name.

Ponchatoula: LA. Choctaw: "hair-hanging," probably in reference to Spanish moss.

Pontiac: MI, IL. After Ottawa chief.

Pontotoc: MS, TX. Also counties in MS and OK. Chickasaw: "cattails on the prairie."

Poquoson: VA. Algonquian: "swamp."

Potlatch: ID, WA. Chumash: "give," name of Indian ceremony.

Potomac: MD, IL. Also river in WV, VA, and MD. Tribal name, possibly mixture of Iroquoian, Delaware, and Powhatan forms: "where the goods are brought in."

Pottawatomie: Counties in KS and OK. Tribal name: "people of the place of the fire."

Poughkeepsie: NY. Algonquian: "little rock at water."

Poway: CA. Village name: possibly "end of the valley."

Poweshiek: County in IA. After Fox chief *Pawishika* whose name means "he who shakes something off."

Powhatan: VA, AR, LA. Also county in VA. After the chief also known as *Wahunsonacock*: possibly "at the falls."

Poy Sippi: WI. Adaptation of Algonquian: "Sioux river."

Prophetstown: IL. After Winnebago medicine man White Cloud.

Punxsutawney: PA. From Delaware *ponsetunik*: "place of the gnats."

Puposky: MN. Ojibway: "end of shaking lands (marshes)."

Pushmataha: County in OK. After Choctaw chief.

Puxico: MO. Probably after Indian chief.

Puyallup: WA. Also river. Tribal name: "generous people."

Quanah: TX. After Comanche chief *Quanah Parker*. *Quanah*: "perfume," for the fragrance of prairie flowers.

Quantico: VA. Algonquian: "long reach at."

Quapaw: OK. Tribal name.

Quasqueton: IA. Probably Algonquian: "rapids."

Queets: WA. Tribal name.

Quenemo: KS. After Sauk chief.

Quilcene: WA. Tribal name.

Quillayute: River in WA. Tribal name.

Quinault: WA. Also lake and river. Tribal name.

Quitaque: TX. Probably Indian derivation: "horse manure."

Rahway: NJ. Also river. Named by Indian *Rawhawhack*, either after himself or from *na-wak-na*: "in the middle of the woods."

Ramapo: NY. Also river and mountain in NJ. Delaware: possibly "round pond."

Rancocas: NJ. Tribal name.

Rappahannock: River and county in VA. Algonquian: "back-and-forth stream" or "river of quick-rising water."

Raritan: NJ. Also river and bay. Tribal name: possibly "stream overflows" or "forked river."

Red Cloud: NE. After Teton Sioux chief.

Repaupo: NJ. Algonquian.

Requa: CA. Tribal or village name: probably "creek mouth."

Roanoke: VA, AL, IL, IN, TX, NC. Also county and river in VA; island, lake, and river in NC. Probably Algonquian: possibly "white-shell place," "northern people," or "wampum." *Roanoke* is the first recorded Indian name or word adopted by the English.

Rockaway: NJ, OR. Also river in NJ. Tribal name: "sandy place."

Romancoke: MD. Algonquian: "low ground there."

Sabetha: KS. After Ute woman, the wife of *Ouray.*

Sac: IA. Also county in IA; river in MO. Tribal name: "outlet." Also *Sauk.*

Sacajawea: Peak in OR. After the Shoshoni woman who was part of the Lewis and Clark Expedition; her name means "bird woman."

Sacandaga: Lake, river, and park in NY. Iroquoian: probably "swampy" or "drowned land."

Saco: ME. Also rivers in ME and NH. Algonquian: "mouth of river."

Sagadahoc: County in ME. Algonquian: with "mouth of river."

Sagamore: PA, OH. Algonquian: "chief."

Sagavanirktok: River in AK. Eskimo: probably "strong current."

Saginaw: MN, AL, TX. Also county, bay, and river in MI. Ojibway: "place of Sauks."

Saguache: CO. Also county and creek. From Ute *sa-gua-gua-chi-pa:* "blue-earth spring," in reference to blue clay.

Saluda: SC, NC, VA. Also river and county in SC. Possibly from Cherokee *selu:* "corn," and *tah:* "river."

Sandusky: OH, MI. Also county, bay, and river in OH. From Wyandot *ot-san-doos-ke:* "source of pure water."

Sangamon: County and river in IL. Ojibway, probably with *sag:* "outlet."

Sanilac: County in MI. After Wyandot chief.

Sanpete: County in UT. From Ute *sampitches:* "homelands."

Sanpoil: River in WA. Tribal name.

Santaquin: UT. After Ute chief.

Santee: NE, SC, CA. Also river and national wildlife refuge in SC. Tribal name.

Sapulpa: OK. After Creek Indian whose name means "sweet potato."

Saranac: NY, MI. Lakes and river in NY. Iroquoian.

Sarasota: FL. Also county and bay in FL. Probably a Spanish adaptation of Indian name: "point of rocks."

Saratoga: NY, CA, IN, IA, NC, TX, WY. Also county and lake in NY. Possibly Mohawk: "springs from the hillside"; or possibly Mahican: "beaver place."

Sarcoxie: MO. After Delaware chief.

Sasakwa: OK. Probably Creek: "brant goose."

Satanta: KS. After Kiowa chief.

Satartia: MS. Choctaw: "pumpkins are there."

Saticoy: CA. Chumash village name.

Satolah: GA. Also battlefield. Cherokee: "six."

Saugatuck: CT, MI. Also river and reservoir in CT. Paugusett: "tidal outlet."

Sauk: IL, MN, WI. Also county in WI; river in WA. Tribal name.

Saunemin: IL. After Kickapoo chief.

Sauquoit: NY. Iroquoian.

Saxapahaw: NC. Tribal name. Also *Sissipahaw.*

Schenectady: NY. Also county. From Mohawk village name *Schaaunactoda:* probably "beyond the pines."

Schenevus: NY. Iroquoian, possibly after local Indian: "hoeing of corn."

Schoharie: NY. County, creek, and reservoir in NY. Iroquoian: "driftwood."

Schroon: NY. Also lake. Possibly from Iroquoian *sknoo-na-pus:* "the largest lake."

Scioto: OH. Also county and river. Iroquoian: probably "deer."

Scituate: MA. Also reservoir in RI. Algonquian: "cold stream" or "at the salt stream."

Seattle: WA. After Indian chief, also known as *See-yat* and *Sealth.*

Sebec: ME. Also lake in ME. Algonquian: "big lake."

Sebeka: MN. Ojibway: "river town."

Sebewaing: MI. Algonquian: "small river at."

Seboeis: ME. Also lake and river. Abnaki: "small lake."

Secaucus: NJ. Algonquian: "salt marsh" or "snake land."

Selah: WA. Indian derivation: "still water."

Selawik: AK. Also lake and river. Eskimo tribal name.

Seminole: FL, AL, OK, TX. Also lake in FL and GA; counties in FL, OK, and GA. Tribal name.

Senatobia: MS. From Choctaw *sen-ato-ho-ba:* "white sycamore," possibly a chief's name.

Seneca: PA, KS, IL, MD, MO, NE, OR, SC, SD, WI. Also county, lake, river, and falls in NY; county and lake in OH. Tribal name given by Mohegans: possibly "stony place," shaped by folk etymology into classical form.

Sequatchie: County and river in TN. After Cherokee chief whose name means "hog river."

Sequim: WA. Clallam: probably "quiet water."

Sequoyah: County in OK, mountain in TN. After the Indian who devised the Cherokee written syllabary.

Sespe: CA. Chumash: village name.

Setauket: NY. Algonquian: probably "river-mouth at."

Sewickley: PA. Tribal name.

Shakopee: MN. Siouan: "six," a hereditary name of chieftains.

Shamokin: PA. Delaware: probably "eel place."

Shasta: CA. Also county, lake, mountain, dam, and national forest in CA. Tribal name.

Shawano: WI. Also county, lake, and point. Algonquian: probably "south at." Point named after Ojibway chief.

Shawnee: KS, OK, OH, NY, GA, WY, IL. Also county in KS; national forest in IL. Tribal name: "southerner."

Shawsheen: MA. Also river. Algonquian: probably the name of a chief, *Shoshanim* or *Sagamore Sam.*

Sheboygan: WI. Also county, river, and falls in WI. Algonquian: possibly "reedlike" or "pipe stem."

Shenandoah: VA, PA, IA. Also county and national park in VA; river and mountains in VA and WV. From Algonquian *schind-han-do-wi:* "spruce stream," "great plains," or "beautiful daughter of the stars."

Shenango: River and reservoir in PA. Probably Algonquian: "beautiful one," from village named *Shaningo.*

Sheyenne: ND. Also river. Variant of *Cheyenne:* tribal name.

Shiawassee: County and national wildlife refuge in MI. Algonquian: "straight ahead water."

Shinnecock: NY. Algonquian tribal name: "level land at."

Shiocton: WI. Algonquian: "to float upstream."

Shipshewana: IN. After Potawatomi Indian *Cup-ci-wa-no.*

Shobonier: IL. After Potawatomi chief.

Shongaloo: LA. Choctaw: "cypress tree."

Shoshone: ID, CA. Also county and falls in ID; lake, river, plateau, and national forest in WY; mountains in NV. Tribal name. Also *Shoshoni.*

Shoshoni: WY. Also peak in CO. Tribal name.

Shubuta: MS. Choctaw: "smoky."

Shuqualak: MS. Choctaw.

Siasconset: MA. Algonquian: "big bones at."

Siletz: OR. Also river. Tribal name.

Simcoe: ND. Also mountain in WA. Indian derivation: "waist spine."

Simi: CA. Chumash: probably "valley of the wind" or "village."

Similk: WA. Also bay. Indian derivation.

Sioux: IA, SD, MT. Also counties in IA, ND, and NE; rivers in IA and SD. Tribal name, from Ojibway *nadouessioux:* "snakes" or "enemies."

Sipsey: River in AL. Chickasaw-Choctaw: "poplar tree."

Siskiyou: OR. Also county in CA; mountains and national forest in CA and OR. Possibly Cree: "bobtail horse."

Sisseton: SD. Siouan: tribal name.

Sitka: AK, KS, KY. Tlingit: possibly "by the sea."

Siuslaw: River and national forest in OR. Tribal name.

Skagit: County, bay, and river in WA. Tribal name.

Skagway: AK. From Tlingit *schkague:* probably "a place exposed to the north wind."

Skamania: County in WA. Indian derivation: probably "swift water."

Skamokawa: WA. After Indian chief.

Skaneateles: NY. Also lake. From Iroquoian *skahneghties:* "long lake."

Skedee: OK. Tribal name.

Skiatook: OK. After Osage Indian.

Skokie: IL. Also river. Potawatomi: "marsh."

Skowhegan: ME. Algonquian: "waiting and watching place."

Skykomish: River in WA. Tribal name, with *skaikh:* "inland," and *mish:* "people."

Sleepy Eye: MN. After Sisseton Sioux chief.

Snohomish: WA. Also county and river. Tribal name.

Snoqualmie: WA. Also river, pass, and national forest. Tribal name: "moon."

Somis: CA. Chumash: village name.

Sonoma: CA, TX. Also county. Tribal name.

South Dakota: See **Dakota.**

Spokane: WA, MO. Also county, mountain, and river in WA. From Indian *spo-kan-ee:* "sun." Possibly after Indian *Illim-spokanee:* "chief of the sun." Also tribal name.

Spoon: River in IL. Algonquian: "mussel shell."

Squaw: Common place name, in reference to Indian women.

Stehekin: WA. Also river. Skagit: "pass."

Steilacoom: WA. After Indian chief *Tail-a-koom.*

Steinhatchee: FL. Also river. From Seminole *isti-in-hachi:* "man-his-river."

Stikine: River and strait in AK. Tlingit: "big river."

Suamico: WI. Menominee: "sand bar."

Succasunna: NJ. Algonquian: "black stone."

Sultan: WA. Also river. After Indian chief *Tseul-tud,* by folk etymology.

Suncook: NH. Also lakes and river. Algonquian: "at the rocks."

Sundance: WY. Also mountain. For the Indian sun-worshiping ceremony.

Suquamish: WA. Tribal name.

Susitna: AK. Also mountain, lake, river, and glacier. From Tanaina *sushitna:* "sandy river."

Susquehanna: River in NY and

PA; county in PA; national wildlife refuge in MD. Tribal name.

Suwannee: FL. Also sound and county in FL; river in FL and GA. Possibly from Seminole *sawni:* "echo."

Swampscott: MA. From Algonquian *muski-ompsk-ut:* "at the red rocks" or "broken waters."

Swannanoa: NC. Cherokee: "Suwali (tribal name) trail."

Sylacauga: AL. From Creek *suli:* "buzzards," and *kagi:* "roost"; or for the Shawnee town *Chalakagay.*

Syosset: NY. Algonquian.

Tabiona: UT. After Ute chief.

Tacoma: WA. Also lake in ME. Algonquian: possibly "mountain" or "gods."

Taconic: CT. Also mountains in NY, VT, MA, and CT. Possibly Algonquian, with *tugk:* "tree" or "forest"; or possibly "steep ascent" or "small field."

Tahlequah: OK. Cherokee, possibly from village or tribal name *Tallegawi:* possibly "two are enough."

Tahoe: CA. Also lake in CA and NV. National forest in CA. Washo: "big water."

Tahoka: TX. Indian derivation: possibly "deep, clear, or fresh water."

Tahquamenon: River and falls in MI. Ojibway: "dark-colored water."

Talala: OK. After Cherokee Indian.

Talihina: OK. Choctaw.

Talkeetna: AK. Also mountains. Tanaina, with *na:* "river."

Talladega: AL. Also county and national forest. Creek village name: "town on the border" (between Creek and Natchez tribes).

Tallahassee: FL. From Creek *talwa:* "town," and *hasi:* "old."

Tallahatchie: River and county in MS. From Creek *Talwa:* "town," and *hachi:* "river."

Tallapoosa: GA. Also county in AL; river in GA and AL. Possibly from Choctaw *tali:* "rock," and *pushi:* "crushed"; or possibly "golden water."

Tallassee: AL, TN. From Indian *talise:* "beautiful water."

Tallulah: LA. Cherokee village name.

Taloga: OK. Probably Creek: "rock place" or "beautiful place."

Tama: IA. Also county. After either Fox chief or wife of Chief

Poweshiek: possibly "bear with a voice that makes the rocks tremble" or "beautiful."

Tamaqua: PA. Delaware: probably "beaver."

Tampa: FL, KS. Also bay in FL. Village name, probably from Creek *itimpi:* "near it."

Tanaga: AK. Also bay, island, lake, pass, and volcano. Aleut: "big land."

Tanana: AK. Also river. Athapascan tribal name: "mountain river."

Tangipahoa: LA. Also parish and river. Tribal name, probably from Choctaw *tanchapi:* "corn," and *ayua:* "gather."

Taos: NM. Also county. From Tewa *tuota:* "red willow place," or *tuatah:* "at the village."

Tappahannock: VA. Algonquian: "back and forth stream."

Tappan: NY, ND. Also lake in OH. Tribal name: "cold stream."

Targhee: Pass and national forest in ID. After Shoshoni chief.

Tarkio: MO. Also River. Indian derivation.

Tawas: MI. Also point. After Ojibway chief; or shortened form of *Ottawa:* tribal name.

Tazlina: AK. Also glacier, lake, and river. From Athapascan *taslintna:* "swift river."

Tchula: MS. Also river. Choctaw: probably "marked."

Tecopa: CA. After Paiute chief.

Tecumseh: MI, OK, KS, NE, MO. Also mountain in NH. After Shawnee chief: "one who springs" or "panther."

Tehachapi: CA. Also mountains. Paiute: "frozen."

Tehama: CA. Also county. Probably Indian derivation: village or tribal name.

Tekamah: NE. Indian derivation: possibly "cottonwood trees" or "field of battle."

Tekonsha: MI. Algonquian: "little caribou."

Telico: TN. Cherokee village name. Also *Talequah.*

Telocaset: OR. Nez Perce: "something on the top."

Telogi: FL. Probably Creek: "rock place" or "beautiful place."

Ten Sleep: WY. Indian derivation.

Tenakee: AK. Also inlet. Tlingit: "copper shield."

Tendoy: ID. After Indian chief.

Tenino: WA. Tribal name.

Tennessee: State. Also river and

municipalities. Cherokee village name. Also *Tanasi.*

Tensaw: AL. Also river. From *Taensa:* tribal name.

Tepee: Mountains in MT and OK; buttes in ND. Siouan: Indian tent.

Teshekpuk: Lake in AK. Eskimo: "big coastal lake."

Tesuque: NM. Spanish adaptation of Tewa: "spotted dry place."

Tetlin: AK. Also lake. After Indian chief *Tetling.*

Teton: Counties in ID, MT, WY; pass, range, and national forest in WY; river in MT. Siouan tribal name.

Texas: State and city. Also counties in MO and OK. Indian adaptation of Spanish tribal name *Tejas:* "allies."

Thonotosassa: FL. Seminole: "flint is there."

Tickfaw: LA. Also river in LA and MS. Choctaw: probably "pine rest."

Ticonderoga: NY. Iroquoian: probably "between lakes."

Tieton: WA. Also river. Indian derivation: "roaring water."

Tillamook: OR. Also county, bay, and cape. Chinook tribal name.

Tillatoba: MS. Choctaw: "gray rock."

Timpahute: Range in NV. Tribal name: "rock spring people."

Timpas: CO. Probably from Ute *timpa:* "rock."

Timpie: UT. Gosiute: "rock."

Tintah: MN. Siouan: "prairie."

Tioga: PA, LA, ND, TX, WV. Also counties and river in NY and PA; pass in CA. Iroquoian: "at the forks."

Tionesta: PA. From Iroquoian *tiyohwenoisto:* "it penetrates the island."

Tioughnioga: River in NY. Iroquoian: "fork of river."

Tippah: County in MS. Either tribal name, or named after the wife of the Chickasaw chief *Pontotoc.*

Tippecanoe: OH. Also county and river in IN. From Potawatomi *kith-ti-pe-ca-numk:* "buffalo fish."

Tishomingo: MS, OK. Also county in MS. After Chickasaw chief whose name means "assistant chief."

Tiskilwa: IL. Probably Algonquian.

Titicus: CT. Algonquian: "without trees."

Titonka: IA. Probably Siouan.

Tittabawassee: River in MI. Algonquian: probably "river following the line of the shore."

Tlingit: AK. Tribal name.

Toana: Range in NV. Indian derivation: "black hill."

Toccoa: GA. Indian derivation: "Tagwa place," in reference to the Catawba tribe.

Togiak: AK. Also river and bay. Eskimo.

Tohatchi: NM. Navajo, with *to*: "water."

Tomah: WI. Also in ME. In WI, after Menominee chief *Thomas Carron*. In ME, probably after an earlier chief.

Tomahawk: WI. Also lake and river. Algonquian: "war hatchet."

Tomales: CA. Also bay and point. Spanish adaptation of *Tamal*: tribal name.

Tombigbee: River and national forest in MS and AL. From Choctaw *itombi*: "coffin," plus *ikbi*: "makers," for the tribesmen who prepared the bones of the dead. Shaped by folk etymology.

Tonawanda: NY. Iroquoian: "swift water."

Tonganoxie: KS. After Delaware chief.

Tonica: IL. Probably from Algonquian *pekitanoui*: "muddy."

Tonkawa: OK. Tribal name, probably from Waco *tonkaweya*: "they all stay together."

Tonopah: NV, AZ. Paiute: probably "greasewood spring" or "thorny bush."

Tooele: UT. Also county. Possibly Gosiute for a plant, or after Indian chief *Tuilla*.

Topanga: CA. Shoshonean.

Topawa: AZ. Papago: "it is a bean," in reference to a game.

Topeka: KS, IN, IL. Kansa: "good potato place."

Topinabee: MI. After Potawatomi chief.

Topock: AZ. Mojave: "bridge."

Toponas: CO. Ute.

Toppenish: WA. Tribal name.

Toquerville: UT. After Paiute chief *Toker*.

Toquima: Range in NV. Tribal name: "black backs."

Totogatic: Lake and river in WI. Ojibway: "boggy river."

Totowa: NJ. Algonquian.

Touchet: WA. Also river. French adaptation of Indian *toosha*: possibly "fire-cured salmon."

Tougaloo: MS. From Cherokee *tugulu*: "fork of a stream."

Toughkenamon: PA. Probably Algonquian: "firebrand," because of a hill the Indians used for signaling.

Toutle: River in WA. From tribal name *Hullooetell*.

Towaco: NJ. Probably tribal name.

Towalaga: River in GA. Creek: "scalp place" or "place of sumac trees."

Towanda: PA, KS. Delaware: "burial ground," in reference to a burial site used by the Nanticokes.

Towaoc: CO. Ute: "all right."

Toyah: TX. Also lake. Probably Indian derivation: "much water."

Truckee: CA. Also river in CA and NV. After Indian guide.

Tucannon: River in WA. Nez Perce: "bread-root."

Tuckahoe: NY, NJ. Also River in NJ. From Algonquian *tuckahog*: probably "round," in reference to an edible root.

Tuckaseigee: River in NC. From Cherokee village name *tsiksitsi*: possibly "crawling turtle."

Tucson: AZ. Spanish adaptation of Papago *chuk shon*: "black base," in reference to a mountain.

Tucumcari: NM. Also mountain. From Comanche *tukamukaru*: "to lie in ambush" or "signal peak."

Tukwila: WA. From Indian *tuck-will-la*: "land of hazelnuts."

Tula: MS. Choctaw: probably "peak."

Tulalip: WA. Also bay. Indian derivation: probably "bay with a small mouth."

Tulamdie: River in ME. Algonquian: "canoe sandbar."

Tullahoma: TN. From Muskogean *homa*: "red," and *tulla*: probably "town."

Tulsa: OK. Also county. Probably from Creek *talwa*: "town," and *hasi*: "old."

Tumwater: WA. From Chinook *tumtum*: "heart."

Tunica: MS, LA. Also county in MS. Tribal name: "the people."

Tunkhannock: PA. Algonquian: "small stream" or "forest."

Tuolumne: CA. Also county and river. Miwok and Yokut tribal names, with *yomi*: "people."

Tuscaloosa: AL. Also county. From Choctaw *tashka*: "warrior," and *lusa*: "black." "Black warrior" was the tribal name for their chief.

Tuscarawas: OH. Also county. Indian derivation: "open mouth."

Tuscarora: NY, NV. Also mountain in PA; mountain in NV. Tribal name: "hemp gatherers."

Tuscola: IL, MI, TX. Also county in MI. Coined by Schoolcraft to mean "level lands" or "warrior prairie." In MS, it is probably a genuine Indian name.

Tuscumbia: AL, MO. After Cherokee chief whose name means "warrior rain maker."

Tushka: OK. Muskogean: "warrior."

Tuskegee: AL, OK. Also national forest in AL. Muskogean tribal name: "warrior."

Twisp: WA. Also river. Indian derivation.

Uinta: River and national forest in UT; county in WY; mountains in UT and WY. Tribal name: "pine land."

Umatilla: OR, FL. Also county, river, and dam in OR. national forest in WA. Tribal name: possibly "water rippling over sand."

Umnak: AK. Also island. Aleut: "fish line."

Umpqua: OR. Also river. Athapascan tribal name.

Unadilla: NY, MI, GA. Also river in NY. Iroquoian: "place of meeting."

Unalakleet: AK. Eskimo.

Unalaska: AK. Also island. Aleut: "this mainland," probably tribal name.

Uncasville: CT. After Mohegan chief.

Uncompahgre: Mountains, peak, plateau, river, and national forest in CO. Ute: "red water canyon."

Unga: AK. Also island. Aleut.

Unicoi: TN. Also county and pass. Cherokee: "white."

Unimak: Island, bay, and pass in AK. Eskimo.

Utah: State, lake, and county. From tribal name *Ute* or *Eutaw*: "high up," "the land of the sun," "the land of plenty," or "in the mountaintops."

Ute: IA, NM. Tribal name.

Venango: PA, NE. Also county in PA. Probably from Iroquoian *in-nun-gah*: in reference to an erotic carving in a tree.

Villisca: IA. Indian derivation.

Viroqua: WI. Probably Algonquian: the personal name of an Indian maiden.

Wabash: IN, AR, OH, WA. Also river in IN and IL; counties in IN and IL. From Miami *wahba*: "white," and *skik-ki*: "bright color." Translated as "white water."

Wabasha: MN. Also county. A Siouan personal name for hereditary chiefs: "red leaf," "red hat," or "red battle-standard."

Wabasso: MN, FL. Ojibway: "rabbit." Also from Longfellow's *Hiawatha*.

Wabaunsee: County in KS. After Potawatomi chief.

Wabeno: WI. Ojibway and Potawatomi: part of the medicine lodge ritual.

Wabuska: NV. Paiute.

Waccamaw: Lake in NC; river in NC and SC. Tribal name.

Wacissa: FL. Timucuan.

Waco: TX, NE, GA, MO, KY, TN. Also lake in TX. In TX, tribal name, also *Hueco*. In NE, Muskogean: "heron."

Waconia: MN. Latinized form of Siouan: "fountain."

Wadena: MN, IN, IA, OK. Also county in MN. Ojibway: "little round hill."

Wahkiakum: County in WA. After Chinook chief. Also tribal name.

Wahkon: MN. From Siouan *wakan*: "spirit."

Wahpeton: ND. Tribal name.

Wah Wah: Mountains in UT. Paiute: probably "juniper."

Waka: TX. Indian derivation.

Wakonda: SD. From Siouan *wakan*: "spirit."

Wakpala: SD. Siouan: "creek."

Wakulla: FL. Also river, springs, and county. Seminole: "loon."

Walla Walla: WA. Also county in WA; river in WA and OR. Tribal name: "little swift river."

Walloomsac: River in NY and VT. Algonquian: "paint at the rocks."

Wallowa: OR. Also county, lake, river, mountains, and national forest. Nez Perce: "triangular stakes," a kind of fish trap.

Wallum: RI. Also lake in RI and MA. Nipmuc: "dog."

Wanakah: NY. Possibly Algonquian: "good land."

Wanaque: NJ. Also reservoir. Algonquian: probably "sassafras place."

Wando: SC. Also river. Probably tribal name.

Wannaska: MN. Ojibway: "deep place in river."

Wantagh: NY. After Indian chief.

Wapakoneta: OH. Shawnee village and personal name.

Wapato: WA. Also lake in OR. Probably Algonquian: "wild potato" or "arrowhead."

Wapella: IL. After Fox chief: "light," "dawn," or "he of the morning."

Wapello: IA. Also county. See **Wapella.**

Wapsipinicon: River in IA. Algonquian: "white potato," or possibly after legendary Indian lovers, *Wapsie* and *Pinicon*, who drowned in the river.

Wartrace: TN. Because of location on an Indian trail.

Wasatch: County and national forest in UT; range in UT and ID. Ute: possibly "mountain pass." Possibly after Ute chief.

Wasco: OR, CA. Also county in OR. Tribal name.

Waseca: MN. Also county. Siouan: "fertile."

Washakie: WY. Also county, lake, mountain, creek, and national forest. After Snake chief.

Washita: OK. Also river and county. River in OK and TX. See **Wichita.**

Washoe: NV, MT. Also county, lake, and range in NV. Tribal name: probably "person."

Washta: IA. Siouan: "good."

Washtenaw: County in MI. From Ojibway *wash-ten-ong:* "on the river" or "far off."

Washtucna: WA. After Palouse chief.

Wasta: SD. Siouan: "good."

Watauga: SD, TN, TX. Also lake in TN; county in NC; river in NC and TN. Cherokee: probably village name.

Wateree: River and lake in SC. Tribal name.

Wathena: KS. After Kickapoo chief.

Watonga: OK. After Arapaho chief whose name means "black coyote."

Watonwan: County and river in MN. Probably Siouan: "where fish bait can be found."

Watova: OK. After Osage chief.

Watseka: IL. After a Potawatomi woman: possibly "pretty woman."

Waubay: SD. Also lake. Siouan: "nesting place for wild fowl."

Waubun: MN. Ojibway: "east" or "morning."

Wauchula: FL. Muskogean: "crane"; or from Creek *wiwa:* "water," and *achuli:* "stale."

Waucoma: IA. Algonquian.

Wauconda: IL, WA. Siouan: "spirit."

Waukau: WI. Algonquian: "sweet flag," a kind of plant.

Waukegan: IL. Algonquian: "trading post," "fort," or "house."

Waukesha: WI. Also county. From Potawatomi *Wakusheg,* name of tribe most commonly called Fox in English.

Waukomis: OK. Probably pseudo-Indian: "walk home."

Waukon: IA, WA. After Winnebago chief *Waukon-Decorah:* "white crow."

Waumandee: WI. Algonquian.

Wauna: WA. Probably Klickitat: a spirit creature.

Waunakee: WI. Algonquian: "he has peace."

Waupaca: WI. Also county. Indian derivation: possibly "place of clear water."

Waupun: WI. From Algonquian *wabun:* "east" or "dawn."

Waurika: OK. Indian derivation: possibly "pure water."

Wausau: WI, FL. Algonquian: probably "far away."

Wausaukee: WI. Algonquian: "far away land."

Wauseon: OH. After Potawatomi chief, half-brother of *Ottokee.*

Waushara: County in WI. After Winnebago chief.

Wautoma: WI. Probably coined from Algonquian *waugh:* "good," and *Tomah:* the name of a chief.

Wauwatosa: WI. From Algonquian *wauwautaesie:* "firefly."

Wawona: CA. Probably Miwok: "big tree."

Waxahachie: TX. Probably from Creek *waka:* "cow," and *hachi:* "stream."

Waxhaw: NC. Tribal name.

Waynoka: OK. Cheyenne: "sweet water."

Wayzata: MN. Siouan: "north at the pines."

Wedowee: AL. After Creek chief, with *wiwa:* "water," and *tawa:* "sumac."

Weehawken: NJ. Algonquian, shaped by folk etymology into a pseudo-Dutch form.

Wenatchee: WA. Also mountains, river, and national forest in WA. Tribal name: "river issuing from canyon" or "those who live at the source."

Wetonka: SD. Probably Siouan: "big."

Wetumpka: AL. From Creek *we-wau:* "water," and *tumcau:* "rumbling."

Wewahitchka: FL. From Creek *wiwa:* "water," and either

ahichkita: "to obtain," or *ahichka:* "view."

Weweantic: River in MA. Algonquian: "crooked river."

Wewela: SD. Siouan: "small spring."

Wewoka: OK. Also creek. Creek village name: "water roaring."

Weyauwega: WI. Ojibway: "he embodies it."

Whatcom: County and lake in WA. After Indian chief.

Whippany: NJ. Also river. Delaware: probably "arrow stream."

Wichita: KS, OR, TX. Also counties in KS and TX; county, river, and lake in TX; mountains in OK. Tribal name: "man."

Wicomico: County in MD. Delaware tribal name: "pleasant village."

Willamette: River and national forest in OR. Probable Indian derivation with French influence.

Willapa: Bay and river in WA. Tribal name.

Willimantic: CT. Also river and reservoir. Nipmuc: "good cedar swamp" or "land of swift-running waters."

Wilmette: IL. After *Archange Ouilmette,* the Potawatomi wife of a French trader.

Winamac: IN. After Potawatomi chief *Wi-na-mak.*

Winnabow: NC. Probably Indian personal name.

Winnebago: WI, NE, IL, NE. Also county and lake in WI; counties in IL and IA; river in MN and IA. Tribal name: probably "fish eaters."

Winneconne: WI. Algonquian: "skull."

Winnemucca: NV. Also lake. A hereditary name of Paiute chiefs.

Winneshiek: County in IA. After Winnebago chief whose father had the same name.

Winnisquam: NH. Also lake. Algonquian, with *squam:* "salmon."

Winona: AZ, IN, MO, KS, WA, MI, MS. Also county in MN; lake in IN. Siouan personal name given to the first-born daughter.

Winooski: VT. Also river. Abnaki: "onion land."

Wiota: WI, IA. Probably Algonquian.

Wisacky: SC. Tribal name.

Wiscasset: ME. Algonquian: probably "hidden outlet at."

Wisconsin: State, river, lake, and rapids. French version of Ojibway

wees-kon-san: "the gathering of the waters" or "grassy place."

Withlacoochee: River in GA and FL. Creek: "little river."

Woonsocket: RI, SD. Algonquian: probably "at a steep spot."

Wyaconda: MO. Also river. Siouan: "spirit."

Wyalusing: PA, WI. Algonquian: "old warrior's home."

Wyandanch: NY. After Indian chief.

Wyandot: County in OH. Tribal name: possibly "islanders."

Wyandotte: OK, MI. Also county in KS. See *Wyandot.*

Wyocena: WI. Potawatomi: "something else."

Wyoming: State, range, and peak. Also counties in NY, PA, and WV; municipalities in DE, IL, IA, MI, NY, PA, RI, OH, and WY. From Delaware *maughwauwame:* "large meadows."

Wyomissing: PA. Indian derivation: "place of flats."

Wytopitlock: ME. Algonquian: "alder place."

Yachats: OR. Tribal name.

Yacolt: WA. Indian derivation: for a prairie known as the "haunted place."

Yadkin: County and river in NC. Indian derivation, shaped by folk etymology.

Yakima: WA. Also county and river. Tribal name: possibly "runaway."

Yakutat: AK. Also bay. Tribal name.

Yalobusha: County and river in MS. Choctaw: "little tadpole."

Yamhill: OR. Also county and river. From tribal name *Yamhela.*

Yampa: CO. Also river. Tribal name and kind of root.

Yankton: SD. Also county. Tribal name, from Siouan *ihanktonwan:* "end village."

Yantic: CT. Also river. Mohegan: "tidal limit."

Yazoo: MS. Also county and river. Tribal name: possibly "waters of the dead."

Yentna: River and glacier in AK. Tanaina.

Yocono: River in MS. Choctaw: possibly "far reach."

Yolo: CA. Also county. From Patwin tribal name *Yodoi:* "place where rushes grow."

Yoncalla: OR. Indian derivation: "haunt of eagles."

Yosemite: CA, KY. Also national park in CA. Tribal name: "grizzly bear."

Yukon: AK, PA, OK, MO, FL. Also river in AK. From Athapascan *yukon-na*: "big river."

Yuma: AZ, CO, MI. Also county and desert in AZ; county in CO. Tribal name: possibly "sons of the river."

Zewapeta: MO. Probably Shawnee: "place of no return."

Zitziana: River in AK. Athapascan, with *na*: "river."

Zuni: NM, VA. Also mountains in NM; river in NM and AZ. Village and tribal name.

CANADA

Abitibi: Lake and river in Ontario; territory in Quebec. Algonquian *abitah*: "halfway," and *nipi*: "water." Tribal name.

Antigonish: County, town, and harbor in Nova Scotia. Micmac: "broken branches."

Arichat: Island, town, and village in Nova Scotia. From Micmac *nerichat*: "the camping ground."

Aroostook: Village and river in Nova Scotia. Possibly from Malecite *woolastook*: "beautiful or clear river."

Arthabaska: County and cantons in Quebec. Iroquoian: "a place obstructed by reeds and grass."

Assiniboine: River in Saskatchewan and Manitoba. Mountain in British Columbia. Tribal name: "stone roasters," in reference to a method of cooking.

Athabaska: River in Alberta; mountain in Alberta and British Columbia. Cree: "where there are reeds."

Belly: River in Alberta. Named after the Atsina Indians whose tribal sign was incorrectly translated by whites as "belly people" or "big bellies."

Bobcaygeon: Town in Ontario. Missisauga: "rocky portal."

Bow: Lake, river, and glacier in Alberta. The Indians used timber in this area for bow making.

Brant and **Brantford:** County and city in Ontario. Named after *Joseph Brant (Thayendanegea)*, the Mohawk chief.

Canada: Country. Probably from Iroquoian *kanata* or *kanada*: "cabin" or "lodge."

Cataraqui: River in Ontario. Iroquoian: "where river and lake meet."

Cayuga: County and town in Ontario. Tribal name, possibly from Iroquois *gwa ugwck*: "here they take the boats out."

Chibougamau: River, lake, and settlement in Quebec. Indian derivation: "the water is stopped."

Chicoutimi: River, county, and city in Quebec. From Montagnais *shkoutimeou*: "end of the deep water."

Chignecto: Bay in Nova Scotia and New Brunswick. Micmac: "foot cloth."

Chilliwack: City in British Columbia. From Indian word *chill-a-whaak*: "valley of many rivers."

Chinguacousy: Township in Ontario. From Ojibway *shing-wark-ous-e-ka*: "where young pines grow."

Chipewyan: Lakes, river, and Hudson's Bay Company post in Alberta. Tribal name: "pointed skins."

Consecon: Lake and village in Ontario. Missisauga: "pickerel."

Coquitlam: Lake, mountain, river, and port in British Columbia. Tribal name: "small red salmon."

Cowichan: Bay, river, and village in British Columbia. Tribal name: "between streams."

Crow's Nest: Village, lake, river, and mountain pass in Alberta. Possible English translation of Indian word; or possibly a name commemorating slaughter of Crow Indians by Blackfeet, Bloods, and Piegans.

Delaware: Township in Ontario. Named after Indian tribe which moved to Canada from United States. The name originally comes from *Lord De la Warre*, governor of Virginia in early 17th century.

Esquimalt: City in British Columbia. Indian derivation: "place gradually shoaling."

Etobicoke: River and township in Ontario. From Indian word *wah-do-be-kaung*: "the place where the alders grow."

Gaspe: County in Quebec. Possibly Micmac: "the extremity"; or else after Portuguese explorer *Gaspar Contereal*, or Basque village of *Caspe*.

Grand Manan: Island in New Brunswick. *Manan* possibly derived from Algonquian *mun-aa-nook*, "the island."

Hamiota: Village and municipality in Manitoba. The name is contracted from English name Hamilton and Siouan *otah*: "much too many," i.e., "too many Hamiltons."

Hochelaga: County in Quebec. Originally an Indian village where Montreal is now located. Possibly from Iroquoian *oshelaga*: "where one is surprised and attacked"; or

possibly from Iroquoian *Oserake*: "the way to the beavers," or "where they make hatchets," or "where they pass the winter."

Huron: One of the Great Lakes; a township in Ontario; and name of river in Quebec. Tribal name. On seeing a party of Indians, a French soldier is supposed to have exclaimed, *"Quelle hures!"*: "What boar-heads!" because of their style of plucked hair. Or possibly French: "rough."

Illecillewaet: River, village, glacier, and mining district in British Columbia. Indian derivation: "swift water."

Iroquois: Town in Ontario. Possibly from Indian *hiro*: "I have spoken," and *koue* an exclamation of joy; or possibly from *ierokwa*: "they who smoke."

Kaministikwia: River in Ontario. Indian derivation: "the river with short bends and many islands"; or possible adaptation of *kaw-maw-naw-taw-quaw*: "the place where there is always plenty of game."

Kamloops: City in British Columbia. From Indian *cumeloups*: "the meeting of the waters."

Kamouraska: County in Quebec. Indian derivation: "where there are rushes on the side of the river."

Kapuskasing: Town and river in Ontario. Cree: "branch river" or "divided waters."

Keewatin: District in Northwest Territories; river in Manitoba; town in Ontario. Cree: "north wind."

Kelowna: City in British Columbia. Indian derivation: "grizzly bear."

Kennebec: Township in Ontario. Possibly Abnaki: "snake" or "deep river," or from *kanibeseck*: "the path which leads to the lake," or from *kinibeki*: "long-reach" or "long lake."

Kennebecasis: River in New Brunswick. Probably from Malecite *ken-a-bee-kay-sis*: a diminutive of *Kennebec*.

Kenogami: Town, lake, and river in Quebec. Indian derivation: "long lake."

Klondike: Village and river in Yukon Territory. Derived from Indian *throndiuk*: "river full of fish."

Kootenay: River and national park in British Columbia. Tribal name: "water people."

Lillooet: Town, district, lake, and river in British Columbia. Tribal name: "wild onion."

Mackinac: Strait connecting Lake Huron with Lake Michigan, and islands in both lakes. Algonquian; "tortoise" or "turtle."

Maganatawan: Town and river in Ontario. Indian derivation: "long channel."

Malagash: Town and point in Nova Scotia. Possibly Micmac: "the end of smooth waters," or from *malegawate*: "the mocking place," or from *meligech*: "milk."

Manitoba: Province of Canada and lake in province. Either from Cree *manito-wapow* or Ojibway *manito-baw*: both meaning "the strait of the manito or spirit"; or possibly from Assiniboine or Sioux *mine*: "lake," and *toba*: "prairie," i.e., "the water or lake of the prairie."

Manitoulin: Island in Lake Huron. Algonquian: "the home of the spirit."

Maniwaki: Town in Quebec. Algonquian: "Mary's land."

Maskinonge: County in Quebec. Algonquian *mac* or *mask*: "large," and *kinonge*: "pike," for a species of fish.

Matane: Lakes, river, and canton in Quebec. From Micmac *mtctan*: "beaver ponds."

Matapedia: Town, lake, and river in Quebec. Micmac: "a volume of water which descends into a great sea," or "roughly flowing waters."

Mattagami: Lake and river in Ontario and lake in Quebec. Possibly from Montagnais *mitta gamii*: "a lake where one may find wood for fuel."

Medicine Hat: City in Alberta. Indian name is *Saamis*, referring to the headdress of a medicine man. Possibly resulting from Cree and Blackfoot fight when a Cree medicine man lost his hat in river; or from the rescue of a squaw by a brave, on which occasion he received a medicine hat; or from a hill east of the town, which resembles a medicine man's hat.

Megantic: County and lake in Quebec. Either from Abnaki *namesokanjik*: "the place where they preserve fish"; or from Cree *miatick*: "great forest."

Michipicoten: Island in Lake Superior; village, river, and harbor in Ontario. Algonquian: "the great bluff."

Mimico: Town in Ontario. Missisauga: "the place of the wild pigeon."

Minnedosa: Town and river in Manitoba. From Siouan *minne*: "water," and *duza*: "rapid."

Miramichi: River in New Brunswick. Possible adaptation of

Indian word *megumagee*: "the land of the Micmacs," or "happy retreat."

Missisquoi: County, bay, and river in Quebec. Abnaki: possibly "much water fowl," "much flint," "big woman," "big rattlesnake," or "great grassy meadows."

Mississauga: River in Ontario. Tribal name, derived from *michi* or *missi*: "much" or "many," and *saki* or *saga*: "outlet," i.e., "a river with many outlets."

Mistassini: Town, lake, and river in Quebec. Tribal name: "great rock."

Moose Jaw: City in Saskatchewan. Possible English translation of Indian word: "the place where the white man mended the cart wheel with the jaw bone of the moose."

Muskoka: District, lake, river, and bay in Ontario. Probably after Ojibway chief *Misquuckkey*.

Naas: River and bay in British Columbia. Tlingit: "satisfier of the stomach."

Nanaimo: City, river, and harbor on Vancouver Island, British Columbia. Indian derivation: "strong, big, great," after a confederacy of tribes called *Esta Nanaimo*.

Napanee: Town and river in Ontario. Possibly from Missisauga *nan-pan-nay*: "flour."

Nassagaweya: Township, village, and river in Ontario. From Missisauga *na-zhe-sah-ge-way-yong*: "a river with two outlets."

Neebing: Township and river in Ontario. Ojibway: "summer."

Nepigon (Nipigon): Lake, river, and bay in Ontario. Possible adaptation of Indian word *annimigon*: "the lake that you cannot see the end of"; or possibly from Algonquian: "a deep lake of clear water"; or from *aweenipigo*: "the water which stretches far."

Niagara: Township in Ontario. River between Lake Erie and Lake Ontario, and the falls on the river. Possibly Huron: "thunderer of waters, resounding with a great noise"; or possibly Iroquois: "connecting water," "divided waterfalls," or "point of land cut in two."

Nipissing: District, township, village, and lake in Ontario. Tribal name: "the little body of water."

Nootawasaga: Township, river, and bay in Ontario. From Algonquian *Nahdoway*: "the Iroquois," and *saga*: "the outlet of the river," in reference to a route Iroquois warriors used.

Okanagan: Town, lake, river, and valley in British Columbia. Salish tribal name, possibly from *kana*: "place of," and *gan*: "water."

Okotoks: Town and mountains in Alberta. Blackfoot: "many stones."

Oneida: Township in Ontario. Tribal name, from compound of *onenhia*: "stone," and *kaniote*: "upright," in reference to a large boulder near the Oneidas' chief village.

Ontario: Province of Canada and one of the Great Lakes. From Iroquoian *oniatario*: "sparkling or beautiful water."

Oromocto: Village, island, lake, and river in New Brunswick. Malecite: "good river."

Oshawa: City in Ontario. Seneca: "the carrying place" or "the portage."

Otonabee: Township and river in Ontario. Indian derivation: "water at the mouth of a river."

Ottawa: City in Ontario; river in Ontario and Quebec; islands in Northwest Territories. Tribal name: possibly from Algonquian *adawe*: "to trade."

Pembina: County, river, and mountains in Manitoba; river in Alberta; and two lakes in Quebec. From Ojibway *anepeminan*: "summer berry" (a kind of cranberry).

Penetanguishene: Town in Ontario. Abnaki: "place of white falling sands."

Penticton: Town in British Columbia. Indian derivation: "meeting of the ways."

Petawawa: River in Ontario. Adaptation of Algonquian *pitwewe*: "where one hears a noise like this," referring to the sound of the waters.

Petitcodiac: River and village in New Brunswick. Micmac: "the bend in a bow fitted to an arrow," referring to the river's winding course.

Pictou: Village, county, and strait in Nova Scotia. Possible French adaptation of Micmac *mickeak bucto*: "great fire," in reference to the destruction by fire of a Micmac encampment. Or from Micmac *piktook*: "bubbling water."

Pilot Mound: Town in Manitoba. Name taken from old Indian mound used as a reference point by pioneers on the Emerson Trail in the 1880s.

Ponoka: Town in Alberta. Cree: "black elk."

Pontiac: County in Quebec. After the Ottawa chief.

Port Coquitlam: City in British Columbia. *Coquitlam*: tribal name.

Pugwash: Village, river, and bay in Nova Scotia. Micmac: "a bank of sand."

Quebec: Province of Canada. Also, city and county. Algonquian: "where the river narrows," referring to the St. Lawrence River. Legend also has it that when Champlain arrived opposite what is now the city of Quebec, Indians yelled, "Kabec! Kabec!" to him, encouraging him to "Debark! Debark!"

Restigouche: River and county in New Brunswick. Possibly from Micmac *listogotig*: "the scene of the great quarrel about the squirrel," referring to a quarrel between the Micmacs and Mohawks; or possible adaptation of Micmac *lustegooch*: "dead and decaying trees"; or possibly from Micmac *lust-a-gooch*: "river with five branches."

Richebucto: Town and river in New Brunswick. Possibly from Micmac *lichibouktouck*: "river which enters the woods," or from *booktaoo*: "fire."

Rimouski: County and town in Quebec. Malecite or Micmac: "the home of the dogs" or "where there are moose."

Saguenay: County and river in Quebec. Possibly from Cree *sake*: "to emerge," and *nipi*: "water," i.e., "water which emerges." Or possible French derivation.

Saskatchewan: Province of Canada and river. From Cree *saskadjiwan*: "running of the thaw" or "swift current."

Saskatoon: City in Saskatchewan. Indian name for a wild berry, used in making buffalo pemmican.

Saugeen: River and township in Ontario. Huron: "river mouth."

Scubenacadie: River and village in Nova Scotia. From Micmac *segubun*: "ground nut," and *akade*: "place of."

Shawinigan: Lake and river in Quebec. Possibly from Cree *shabonigan*: "a portage shaped like a beech-nut," "the eye of a needle," or "crest."

Shippigan: Village, island, and harbor in New Brunswick. Micmac: "duck road."

Shubenacadie: River, lake, and village, in Nova Scotia. From Micmac *segubunaakade*: "where nuts grow in abundance."

Skeena: River in British Columbia. From Indian words *iksh*: "out of," and *shean* or *shyen*: "the clouds."

Slave: Great Slave is a lake in the Northwest Territories and a river in Northwest Territories and Alberta. Lesser Slave is a lake and river in Alberta. The Cree Indians referred to the Indians of the region as *Awokanak*: "Slaves."

Stadacona: One of the wards of Quebec City and the original name of the city's site. Possibly from Algonquian *statakwan*: "wing," referring to the angle formed by the St. Lawrence and St. Charles rivers. Or from Montagnais *statakosnen*: "the place where they pass on a collection of logs as on a bridge."

Stikine: River in British Columbia. Indian derivation: "great river."

Tadoussac: Town in Quebec. From Montagnais *tutushits*: "breasts."

Tecumseh: Township and town in Ontario. After the Shawnee chief whose name supposedly means "a panther crouching for its prey."

Temiscouata: Lake and county in Quebec. From Malecite *temig*: "deep," and *esgoateg*: "lake forming the source of a river."

Tignish: Village, river, and pond on Prince Edward Island. From Micmac *mtagunich*: "a paddle."

Toronto: City in Ontario. Iroquois, possibly from *thoron-to-hen*: "fallen trees in the water"; or from *de-on-do*: "the logs floating on water"; or from *kanitare*: "lake," and *onto*: "to open," i.e., the opening from Lake Ontario to the country of the Hurons. Or possibly from words with following meanings: "much or many," "a place of plenty," or "trees rising out of the water."

Tracadie: Village in New Brunswick, and bay and settlement on Prince Edward Island. From Micmac *tulakadik*: "camping ground."

Ungava: Bay in Quebec. Eskimo: "an unknown, faraway land."

Wabigoon: Lake, river, and village in Ontario. Algonquian: "white feather."

Wetaskiwin: City in Alberta. Indian derivation: "hills of peace."

Windigo: Bay, islands, lake, and river in Ontario. River in Quebec. Algonquian: "devil" or "monster." According to legend, this giant cannibal, the dweller of certain lakes, devoured Indian hunters.

Winnipeg: City and lake in Manitoba; river in Manitoba and Ontario. From Cree *win*: "dirty," and *nipi*: "water."

Yamaska: County, village, and river in Quebec. From Cree *igamaska*: "where the grass and rushes are high"; or possibly "where there is grass under water."

Yoho: River, lake, pass, peak, glacier, and park in British Columbia. Cree: "How wonderful!"

Yukon: Territory and river in northwestern Canada. From Athapascan *yukon-na*: "big river."

MUSEUMS, HISTORICAL SOCIETIES, RECONSTRUCTED VILLAGES, AND ARCHAEOLOGICAL SITES PERTAINING TO INDIANS IN THE UNITED STATES AND CANADA (located by town or nearest town)

UNITED STATES

ALABAMA

Alabama Department of Archives and History Museum, Montgomery
Alabama Museum of Natural History, University
Birmingham Museum of Art, Birmingham
Fort Toulouse Park, Wetumpka
Indian Mound and Museum, Florence
Kinlock Knob Petroglyphs, Bandhead National Forest, Haleyville
Mound State Monument, Moundville
Red Mountain Museum, Birmingham
Russell Cave National Monument, Bridgeport

ALASKA

Alaska Indian Arts, Haines
Alaska Native Village, Fairbanks
Alaska State Museum, Juneau
Anchorage Historical and Fine Arts Museum, Anchorage
Carrie Mclain Museum, Nome
Circle District Historical Society Museum, Central
Dinjii Zhuu Museum, Fort Yukon
Duncan Cottage Museum, Annette Island Reserve Metlakatla
Hoonah Cultural Center, Hoonah
Inupiat University of the Arctic, Barrow
Katmai National Museum, King Salmon
Kenai Historical Society and Museum, Kenai
Kotzebue Museum, Kotzebue
Museum of the Arctic, Kotzebue
Pratt Museum, Homer

Sheldon Jackson Museum, Sitka
Sitka National Historical Park Museum, Sitka
Southeast Alaska Indian Cultural Center, Sitka
Tongass Historical Society Museum, Ketchikan
Totem Heritage Center, Ketchikan
University of Alaska Museum, Fairbanks
Wrangell Museum, Wrangell
Yugartik Regional Museum, Bethel

ARIZONA

Amerind Foundation, Dragoon
Arizona Archaeological and Historical Society, Tucson
Arizona State Museum, University of Arizona, Tucson
Besh-Ba-Gowah, Globe
Canyon de Chelly National Monument, Chinle
Casa Grande Ruins National Monument, Coolidge
Chiricahua National Monument, Dos Cabezas
Clara T. Woody Museum of Gila County, Globe
Colorado River Indian Tribes Museum, Parker
Eastern Arizona Museum and Historical Society, Pima
Gila River Indian Museum, Sacaton
Grand Canyon National Park, Tusayan and Yavapai museums, Grand Canyon
Havasu Canyon, Supai
Heard Museum of Anthropology and Primitive Art, Phoenix
Hopi Cultural Center, Second Mesa
Hopi Tribal Museum, Second Mesa
Hubbell Trading Post National Historic Site, Ganado
Kinishba Pueblo Ruins, Whiteriver
Kinlichee Tribal Park, Ganado
Mohave Museum, Kingman
Montezumu Castle National Monument, Clarkdale
Museum of Northern Arizona, Flagstaff
Navajo National Monument, Tonalea
Navajo Tribal Museum, Window Rock
Ned A. Hatathali Cultural Center, Navajo Community College, Tsaile
Oraibi Pueblo, Tuba City
Painted Rocks State Historic Park, Holbrook
Pimeria Alta Historical Society, Nogales
Pueblo Grande Museum, Phoenix
State Museum, Tempe
Strading Museum of the Horse, Globe
Tonto National Monument, Roosevelt
Tubac Presidio State Historic Park, Tubac
Tuzigoot National Monument, Clarkdale

Walnut Canyon National Monument, Flagstaff
Walpi Pueblo, Tuba City
Western Archaeological Center, Ephrata
Wupatki National Monument, Flagstaff

ARKANSAS

Arkansas State Museum, Conway
Arkansas State University Museum, Jonesboro
Caddo Burial Grounds, Murphreesboro
Hampson State Museum, Wilson
Henderson State University Museum, Arkadelphia
Ka-Do-Ha Discovery Museum, Murphreesboro
Museum of Science and History, Little Rock
Nodena Site, Wilson
Siloam Springs Museum, Siloam Springs
Toltec Indian Mound State Park, England
University of Arkansas Museum, Fayetteville

CALIFORNIA

Antelope Valley Indian Research Museum, Lancaster
Assistencia de San Gabriel, Redlands
Big and Little Petroglyph Canyons, China Lake
Bowers Memorial Museum, Santa Ana
Cabot's Old Pueblo Museum, Desert Hot Springs
Calico Mountains Archaeological Project, Barstow
California State Indian Museum, Sacramento
Catalina Island Museum, Avalon
Chaw-se Indian Grinding Rocks State Park, Jackson
Clarke Memorial Museum, Eureka
Clear Lake State Park, Kelseyville
Coyote Hills Regional Park, Fremont
Death Valley National Monument Museum, Death Valley
Diablo Valley College Museum, Pleasant Hill
Giant Desert Intaglios, Blythe
Indian Grinding Rock State Historical Park, Pine Grove
Inscription Canyon, Barstow
Jesse Peter Memorial Museum, Santa Rosa
Joshua Tree National Monument, Twentynine Palms
Kern County Museum, Bakersfield
Lake Country Museum, Lakeport
Lompoc Museum, Lompoc
Los Angeles County Museum of History and Science, Los Angeles
Lowie Museum of Anthropology, Berkeley
Malki Museum, Morongo Indian Reservation, Banning
Marin Museum of the American Indian, Novato

Maturango Museum, China Lake
Merritt College Anthropology Museum, Oakland
Mexican Museum, San Francisco
M.H. DeYoung Memorial Museum, San Francisco
Museum of Cultural History, Los Angeles
Natural History Museum of Los Angeles County, Los Angeles
Oakland Museum, History Division, Oakland
Old Indian Pueblo, Desert Hot Springs
Palm Springs Desert Museum, Palm Springs
Porterville Museum, Porterville
Pioneer Museum and Haggin Galleries, Stockton
Rancho Los Alamitos, Long Beach
Randall Junior Museum, San Francisco
Redding Museum and Art Center, Redding
Renegade Canyon Petroglyphs, China Lake
Riverside Municipal Museum, Riverside
Robert H. Lowie Museum of Anthropology, University of California, Berkeley
San Bernadino County Museum, Redlands
San Diego Museum of Man, San Diego
San Luis Rey Historical Society, Carlsbad
Santa Barbara Museum of Natural History, Santa Barbara
Southwest Museum, Los Angeles
Stagecoach Inn Museum, Newbury Park
Sun House, Ukiah
Treganza Anthropology Museum, San Francisco State University, San Francisco
Tulare County Museum, Visalia

COLORADO

Adams State College Museum, Alamosa
Arapahoe Community College Museum of Anthropology, Littleton
Canon City Municipal Museum, Canon City
Clarence T. Hurst Museum, Gunnison
Cliff Dwellings Museum, Colorado Springs
Colorado Springs Fine Art Center, Taylor Museum, Colorado Springs
Colorado State Museum, Denver
Denver Art Museum, Denver
Denver Museum of Natural History, Denver
Escalante Ruin, Dolores
Gem Village Museum, Bayfield
Grand Sand Dunes National Monument, Alamosa
Hovenweep National Monument, Pleasant View
Koshare Indian Kiva Museum, La Junta
Lowry Pueblo Ruins, Cortez
Mesa Verde National Park Museum, Cortez

Moffat County Museum, Craig
Pioneers Museum, Colorado Springs
University of Colorado Museum, Boulder
Ute Indian Museum, Montrose
Ute Mountain Tribal Park, Towaoc

CONNECTICUT

American Indian Archaeological Institute, Washington
Bruce Museum, Greenwich
Children's Museum of Hartford, West Hartford
New Britain Youth Museum, New Britain
New Milford Historical Society Museum, New Milford
Peabody Museum of Natural History, Yale University, New Haven
Slater Memorial Museum, Norwich
Stamford Museum and Nature Center, Stamford
Tantaquidgeon Indian Museum, Uncasville

DELAWARE

Delaware State Museum, Dover
Island Field Site and Museum, South Bowers

DISTRICT OF COLUMBIA

Explorers Hall, National Geographic Society, Washington
Indian Crafts Board, Department of the Interior, Washington
National Museum of Natural History, Smithsonian Institution, Washington

FLORIDA

Crystal River State Archaeological Site, Crystal River
Florida Anthropological Society, Panama City
Florida Junior College, Kent Campus Museum, Jacksonville
Florida State Museum, University of Florida, Gainesville
Gulf Islands Visitors' Center, Gulf Breeze
Historical Museum of Southern Florida, Miami
Indian Temple Mound Museum, Fort Walton Beach
Jacksonville Museum of Arts and Sciences, Jacksonville
Kingdom of the Sun, Ocala
Lake Jackson Mounds, Tallahassee
Madira Bickel Mount State Archaeological Site, Bradenton
Miccosukee Cultural Center, Tamiami Trail
Museum of Archaeology Broward County Archaeological Society, Fort Lauderdale
Museum of Florida History, Tallahassee
Museum of Science, Miami
Peninsular Archaeological Society, Holiday

Pensacola Historical Museum, Pensacola
Safety Harbor Museum of History and Fine Arts, Safety Harbor
St. Petersburg Historical Museum, St. Petersburg
Seminole Native Village, West Hollywood (Dania)
Southeast Museum of the North American Indian, Marathon
South Florida Museum, Bradenton
Temple Mound Museum and Park, Fort Walton Beach
Tiger's Miccosukee Indian Village, Miami
T.T. Wentworth, Jr., Museum, Pensacola
Turtle Mound State Archaeological Site, New Smyrna Beach
University Museum, Tallahassee
West Museum of History, Pensacola

GEORGIA

Chief McIntosh Home, Indian Springs
Chief Vann House, Spring Place
Columbus Museum of Arts and Sciences, Columbus
Creek Museum, Indian Springs
Emory University Museum, Atlanta
Etowah Mounds Archaeological Area, Cartersville
Kolomoki Mounds State Park, Blakely
New Echota Historic Site, Calhoun
Ocmulgee National Monument, Macon
Rock Eagle Effigy Mound, Eatonton
Thronateeska Heritage Foundation, Albany
Track Rock Archaeological Area, Blairsville
Wormsloe Historic Site, Savannah

IDAHO

Alpha Rockshelter, Salmon
Appaloosa Museum, Moscow
Clearwater Historical Society Museum, Orofino
Herrett Museum, Twin Falls
Idaho Museum of Natural History, Idaho State University, Pocatello
Nee Mee Poo Museum, Kooskia
Nez Perce National Historical Park, Spalding
University of Idaho Museum, Moscow

ILLINOIS

Andrew Cook Museum, Wauconda
Anthropology Laboratories and Museum, DeKalb
Cahokia Mounds State Historic Site and Museum, East St. Louis
Chicago Museum of Natural History, Chicago
Dickson Mounds Museum, Lewiston

Field Museum of Natural History, Chicago
Ford County Historical Society, Paxton
Illinois State Museum, Springfield
Kampsville Archaeological Museum, Kampsville
Lakeview Museum of Arts and Sciences, Peoria
Madison County Historical Museum, Edwardsville
Mississippi Palisades State Park, Savanna
Newberry Library Center, Chicago
Old Time Village, Morris
Pere Marquette State Park, Grafton
Quincy and Adams County Museum, Quincy
Southern Illinois University Museum, Carbondale
University of Illinois Museum of Natural History, Urbana

INDIANA

Angel Mounds State Memorial, Evansville
Children's Museum, Indianapolis
Crawford County Indian Museum, Alton
Indiana Historical Society, Indianapolis
Indiana State Museum, Bloomington
Indiana University Museums, Bloomington
Miami County Historical Museum, Peru
Mounds State Park, Anderson
Museum of Indian Heritage, Indianapolis
Puterbaugh Museum, Peru
Sonotabac Prehistoric Indian Mound and Museum, Vincennes

IOWA

Audubon County Historical Society, Exira
Davenport Public Museum, Davenport
Effigy Mounds National Monument, McGregor
Fish Farms Mounds, New Albin
Mills County Historical Society and Museum, Glenwood
Museum of Natural History, Iowa City
North Lee County Historical Society, Fort Madison
Putnam Museum, Davenport
Sanford Museum, Cherokee
Sioux City Public Museum, Sioux City
Toolesboro National Historic Landmark, Wapello

KANSAS

Ellsworth County Museum, Ellsworth
El Quartelejo Indian Kiva Museum, Scott City
Fort Larned National Historic Landmark, Larned
Indian Burial Pits, Salina

Indian Museum, Wichita
Inscription Rock, Lake Kanapolis State Park, Ellsworth
Kansas City Museum, Kansas City
Kansas Sac and Fox Museum, Highland
Kansas State Historical Society, Topeka
Kansas State Museum, Topeka
Kaw Indian Mission, Council Grove
Larned Historical Society Museum, Larned
Last Indian Raid Museum, Oberlin
Museum of Anthropology, Lawrence
Pawnee Indian Village Museum, Republic
Rice County Historical Museum, Lyons
Sternberg Memorial Museum, Hays
Wyandotte County Historical Society Museum, Kansas City

KENTUCKY

Adena Park, Lexington
Ancient Buried City, Wickliffe
Blue Licks Museum, Mount Olivet
Filson Club, Louisville
J.B. Speed Art Museum, Louisville
Kentucky Museum, Western Kentucky University, Bowling Green
Mammoth Cave National Park, Mammoth Cave
Museum of Anthropology, Highland Heights
Museum of Anthropology, University of Kentucky, Lexington
Owensboro Area Museum, Owensboro

LOUISIANA

Grindstone Bluff Museum and Environmental Education Center, Shreveport
Lafayette Natural History Museum, Lafayette
Louisiana State Exhibit Museum, Shreveport
Marksville State Commemorative Area and Prehistoric Museum, Marksville
Middle American Research Institute, Tulane University, New Orleans
Museum of Geoscience, Louisiana State University, Baton Rouge
Williamson Museum, Natchitoches

MAINE

Anthropology Museum, University of Maine, Orono
Damariscotta River Shell Mounds, Damariscotta
Indian Island National Historical Society, Old Town
L.C. Bates Museum, Hinckley
Maine Archaeological Society, Orono

Maine State Museum, Augusta
Maine Tribal Unity Museum, Unity
Robert Abbe Museum of Stone Age Antiquities, Mount Desert Island
Wilson Museum, Castine

MARYLAND

Archaeological Society of Maryland, Silver Spring
Baltimore Museum of Art, Baltimore
Walters Art Gallery, Baltimore

MASSACHUSETTS

Aptucxet Trading Post, Bourne
Bronson Museum, Attleboro
Children's Museum, Dartmouth
Fruitlands Museum, Harvard University, Cambridge
Howland House, Plymouth
Indian House Museum, Deerfield
Longhouse Museum, Grafton
Mashpee Wampanoag Indian Tribal Council, Mashpee
Massachusetts Archaeological, Attleboro
Memorial Hall Museum, Deerfield
Minute Man National Historical Park, Concord
Peabody Museum of Archaeology and Ethnology, Harvard University, Cambridge
Peabody Museum of Salem, Salem
Pratt Museum of Natural History, Amherst
Robert S. Peabody Foundation for Archaeology, Andover
Springfield Science Museum, Springfield
Wampanoag Indian Program of Plymouth Plantation, Plymouth
Wistariahurst Museum, Holyoke

MICHIGAN

Armstrong Museum of Art and Archaeology, Olivet
Chief Andrew J. Blackbird Museum, Harbor Springs
Chippewa Nature Center, Midland
Cranbook Institute of Science, Bloomfield Hills
Detroit Historical Museum, Detroit
Fort De Buade Museum, St. Ignace
Fort St. Joseph Museum, Niles
Fort Wayne Military Museum, Detroit
Grand Rapids Public Museum, Grand Rapids
Great Lakes Indian Museum, Cross Village
Indian Drum Lodge Museum, Traverse City
Isle Royale National Park, Houghton
Jesse Besser Museum, Alpena
Kalamazoo Public Museum, Kalamazoo
Kingman Museum of Natural History, Battle Creek
Mackinac Island State Park, Mackinac Island

Norton Mounds, Grand Rapids
Oakwoods Metropark Nature Center, Flat Rock
Sanilac Petroglyphs, Grand Rapids
University of Michigan Exhibit Museums, Ann Arbor
Wayne State University Museum of Anthropology, Detroit

MINNESOTA

Crow Wing County Historical Society, Brainerd
Jeffers Petroglyphs, Jeffers
Mille Lacs State Indian Museum, Onamia
Minnesota Historical Society Museum, St. Paul
Mound Group, International Falls
Pipestone National Monument, Pipestone
St. Louis County Historical Society, Duluth
The Science Museum of Minnesota, St. Paul
Voyageurs National Park, International Falls

MISSISSIPPI

Amory Regional Museum, Amory
Cobb Institute of Archaeology, Mississippi State University, Mississippi State
Cottonlandia Museum, Greenwood
Grand Village of the Natchez, Natchez
Jp Museum of Indian Artifacts, Lyman
Nanih Waiya Historic Site, Louisville
Natchez Trace Visitors' Center, Tupelo; and sites, including Bear Creek Mound, Boyd Mounds, Bynum Mounds, Chickasaw Village, Emerald Mound, Mangum Mound, Owl Creek Mound, Pharr Mounds, Pocahontas Mound
North Delta Museum, Friars Point
Winterville Mounds, Historic Site

MISSOURI

Cherokee Museum, St. Louis
E.M. Violette Museum, Kirksville
Fort Osage, Sibley
Graham Cave State Park, Montgomery City
Hickory County Historical Society, Hermitage
Kansas City Museum of History and Science, Kansas City
Lyman Archaeological Research Center and Hamilton Field School, Miami
Missouri Historical Society, St. Louis
Missouri Resources Museum, Jefferson City
Missouri State Museum, Jefferson City
Museum of Anthropology, University of Missouri, Columbia
Museum of Science and Natural History, St. Louis

Ralph Foster Museum, School of the Ozarks, Point Lookout
St. Joseph Museum, St. Joseph
Towosahgy Archaeological Site, East Prairie
Van Meter State Park, Miami
William Rockhill Nelson Gallery and Atkins Museum of Fine Arts, Kansas City

MONTANA

Chief Plenty Coups State Monument, Pryor
Crow Tribe Historical and Cultural Commission, Crow Agency
Custer–Sitting Bull Battlefield Museum, Crow Agency
Flathead Indian Museum, St. Ignatius
H. Earl Clark Memorial Museum, Havre
Madison Buffalo Run, Logan
Museum of the Plains Indian and Crafts Center, Browning
Museum of the Rockies, Bozeman
Northern Montana College Collections, Havre
Pictograph Cave State Monument, Billings
Poplar Indian Arts and Crafts Museum, Poplar

NEBRASKA

Ash Hollow State Park, Lewellen
Fort Atkinson State Historical Park, Fort Calhoun
Fort Robinson State Historic Site, Crawford
Fur Trade Museum, Chadron
Hastings Museum, Hastings
Historical Society of Garden County, Oshkosh
Nebraska State Historical Society, Ft. Robinson
Nebraska State Historical Society Museum, Lincoln
Oregon Trail Museum, Scotts Bluff National Monument, Gering
Turtle Mound Museum, Murray
University of Nebraska State Museum, Lincoln
Weeping Water Valley Historical Society, Weeping Water

NEVADA

Churchill County Museum and Archive, Fallon
Gypsum Cave, Las Vegas
Lake Mead National Recreation Area, Boulder City
Lost City Museum of Archaeology, Overton
Museum of Natural History, Las Vegas
Nevada State Historical Society, University of Nevada, Reno
Nevada State Museum, Carson City
Rocky Gap Site, Las Vegas
Valley of Fire State Park, Boulder City

NEW HAMPSHIRE

Dartmouth College Museum and Galleries, Hanover

Hood Museum, Hanover
Libby Museum, Wolfeboro
Manchester Historic Association, Manchester
Woodman Institute, Dover

NEW JERSEY

Archaeological Society of New Jersey, South Orange
Bergen Community Museum, Paramus
Hopewell Museum, Hopewell
Montclair Art Museum, Montclair
Morris Museum of Arts and Sciences, Morristown
Museum of Natural History, Princeton University, Princeton
Newark Museum, Newark
New Jersey State Museum, Trenton
Peterson Museum, Peterson
Seton Hall University Museum, South Orange
Sussex County Historical Society, Newton
Van Ripper–Hopper House Museum, Wayne

NEW MEXICO

Abo State Monument, Mountainair
Aeoma Museum, Pueblo of Acoma
Albuquerque Archaeological Society, Albuquerque
Anthropology Museum, Eastern New Mexico University, Portales
Aztec Ruins National Monument, Aztec
Bandelier National Monument, Los Alamos
Blackwater Draw Museum, Portales
Carlsbad Municipal Fine Arts and Museum, Carlsbad
Chaco Culture National Monument, Bloomfield
Church Rock Museum of Indian Art, Gallup
Coronado State Park and Monument, Bernalillo
El Morro National Monument, Ramah
Ernest Thompson Seton Memorial Library and Museum, Gimarron
Folsom Museum, Folsom
Gadsen Museum, Mesilla
Gallup Museum of Indian Arts, Gallup
Gila Cliff Dwellings National Monument, Silver City
Gran Quivira National Monument, Mountainair
Hall of the Modern Indian, Santa Fe
Indian Petroglyph State Park, Albuquerque
Indian Pueblo Cultural Center, Albuquerque
Institute of American Indian Arts Museum, Santa Fe
Jemez State Monument, Jemez Springs
Jicarilla Apache Tribal Museum, Dulce
Kit Carson Museum, Taos

Kwilleylekia Ruins Monument, Cliff
Laboratory of Anthropology, Santa Fe
Laguna Pueblo, Alburquerque
Los Alamos County Historical Museum, Los Alamos
Maxwell Museum of Anthropology, University of New Mexico, Alburquerque
Mescalero Apache Cultural Center, Mescalero
Miles Museum, Portales
Millicent Rogers Museum, Taos
Museum of Navajo Ceremonial Art, Santa Fe
Museum of New Mexico, Hall of Ethnology and Anthropology, Santa Fe
New Mexico State University Museum, Las Cruces
Palace of the Governors, Santa Fe
Paleo Indian Institute and Museum, Portales
Pecos National Monument, Pecos
Picuris Pueblo Tribal Museum, Picuris Pueblo
Puye Cliff Ruins, Santa Clara Indian Reservation, Espanola
Quarai State Monument, Mountainair
Red Rock Museum, Church Rock
Roswell Museum and Art Center, Roswell
Salinas National Monument, Mountainair
Salmon Ruins, Farmington
Sandia Man Cave, Albuquerque
San Ildefonso Pueblo Museum, Santa Fe
San Juan County Archaeological Research Center and Library at Salmon Ruins, Farmington
Santa Clara Pueblo, Santa Fe
Santa Fe Fine Arts Museum, Santa Fe
School of American Research, Santa Fe
Silver City Museum, Silver City
Society for Historical Archaeology, Albuquerque
Taos Pueblo, Taos
Three Rivers Rock Art, Carrizozo
Tularosa Basin Historical Societies, Alamogordo
Wheelwright Museum of the American Indian, Santa Fe
Zia Pueblo, Santa Ana
Zuni Pueblo, Gallup

NEW YORK

Akwesasne Museum, St. Regis Mohawk Reservation, Hogansburg
Albany Institute of History and Art, Albany
American Museum of Natural History, New York
Archaeological Field Museum, New York Institute of Anthropology, West Fulton
Archaeological Society of Staten Island, Staten Island
Brooklyn Museum, Brooklyn
Buffalo and Erie County Historical Society, Buffalo
Buffalo Historical Museum, Buffalo

Buffalo Museum of Science, Buffalo
Canandaigua Historical Society Museum, Canandaigua
Castile Historical Society Museum, Castile
Cayuga Museum of History and Art and the Archaeological Society of Central New York, Auburn
Chautauqua County Historical Society, Westfield
Chemung County Historical Museum, Elmira
Chenango County Historical Society Museum, Norwich
Cherry Valley Museum and Historical Society, Cherry Valley
Fort Edward Historical Association, Fort Edward
Fort Johnson, Amsterdam
Fort Plain Museum, Fort Plain
Fort William Henry Restoration and Museum, Lake George
Gallery of American Art, New York
Garvies Point Museum and Preserve, Glen Cove
Gravesend Historical Society, Gravesend
History Center and Museum, Westfield
Kateri Galleries, The National Shrine of the North American Martyrs, Auriesville
Mohawk-Caughnawaga Museum, Fonda
Museum of Archaeology of Staten Island, Wagner College, Staten Island
Museum of Primitive Art, New York
Museum of the American Indian, Heye Foundation, New York
Nassau County Museum, Syosset
Native American Center for the Living Arts, Niagara Falls
New York Historical Society, New York
New York State Archaeological Association, Rochester
New York State Historical Association, Cooperstown
New York State Museum, Albany
Old Stone Fort, Schoharie
Ontario County Historical Society, Canandaigua
Owasco Stockaded Indian Village, Auburn
Oysterponds Historical Society, Orient
Rochester Museum of Arts and Sciences, Rochester
Rockwell Museum, Corning
Sainte Marie de Gannentaha, Liverpool
Schoharie Museum of the Iroquois Indian, Schoharie
Seneca-Iroquois National Museum, Salamanca
Sidney Historical Association, Sidney
Six Nations Indian Museum, Onchiota
Staten Island Institute of Arts and Sciences, Staten Island
Suffolk County Indian and

Archaeological Museum, Huntington
Tioga County Historical Society Museum, Owego
Tonawanda-Seneca Museum, Basom
Trailside Nature Museum, Cross River
Yager Museum, Hartwick College, Oneonta

NORTH CAROLINA

Archaeological Society of North Carolina, Chapel Hill
Catawba Museum of Anthropology, Salisbury
Cliffs of the Neuse State Park, Seven Springs
Discovery Place, Charlotte
Indian Museum of the Carolinas, Laurinburg
Lake Waccamaw Depot Museum, Lake Waccamaw
Morrow Mountain State Park, Albemarle
Mountain Heritage Center, Cullowhee
Museum of Man, Wake-Forest University, Winston-Salem
Museum of the American Indian, Boone
Museum of the Cherokee Indian, Cherokee
Oconaluftee Indian Village, Cherokee
Research Laboratories of Anthropology, University of North Carolina, Chapel Hill
Roanoke Indian Village, Manteo
Town Creek Indian Mound State Historic Site, Mt. Gilead
Weymouth Woods–Sandhill Nature Preserve Museum, Southern Pines

NORTH DAKOTA

Affiliated Tribes Museum, New Town
Department of Anthropology, University of North Dakota, Grand Forks
Double Ditch Indian Village, Bismarck
Fort Buford Historic Site, Buford
Fort Clark Historic Site, Stanton
Fort Lincoln Museum, Mandan
Four Bears Museum, Fort Berthold, Newtown
Huff Indian Village Historic Site, Mandan
Knife River Indian Villages National Historic Site, Stanton
Lewis and Clark Trail Museum, Alexander
Menoken Indian Village Historic Site, Bismarck
Mollander Indian Village, Washburn
Slant Indian Villages, Fort Lincoln State Park, Mandan
State Historical Society Museum, Bismark
Three Tribes Museum, Fort Berthold Indian Reservation, New Town
Writing Rock Historic Site, Fortuna

OHIO

Allen County Museum, Lima
Butler Institute of American Art, Youngstown
Campbell Mound, Columbus
Cincinnati Museum of Natural History, Cincinnati
Cleveland Museum of Art, Cleveland
Cleveland Museum of Natural History, Cleveland
Dayton Museum of Natural History, Dayton
Firelands Museum, Norwalk
Flint Ridge Memorial, Glenford
Fort Ancient Memorial and Museum, Lebanon
Fort Hill Memorial, Hillsboro
Fort Recovery Museum, Fort Recovery
Greater Cleveland Ethnographic Museum, Cleveland
Horseshoe Mound, Portsmouth
Inscription Rock, Kelleys Island
Johnson-Humrickhouse Memorial Museum, Coshocton
Leo Petroglyph, Chillicothe
Licking County Historical Society Museum, Newark
Mercer County Historical Museum, Celina
Miamisburg Mound, Miamisburg
Mound Cemetary, Marietta
Mound City Group National Monument, Chillicothe
Newark Earthworks State Memorials, Newark
Ohio Historical Center, Columbus
Ohio Prehistoric Indian Art Museum, Newark
Ohio State Museum, Columbus
Piqua Historical Area, Piqua
Ray Beatson's Indian Ridge Museum, Elyria
Seip Mound State Memorial, Bainbridge
Serpent Mound State Memorial, Peebles
Story Mound, Chillicothe
Tarlton Cross Mound, Tarlton
Tremper Mound, Portsmouth
Warren County Historical Society Museum, Lebanon
Western Reserve Historical Society, Cleveland

OKLAHOMA

Anadarko Museum, Anadarko
Bacone College Museum, Ataloa Art Lodge, Muskogee
Cherokee Center, Tahlequah
Cherokee National Museum, Tahlequah
Chickasaw Council House Museum, Tishomingo
Comanche Cultural Center, Walters
Five Civilized Tribes Museum, Muskogee
Heavener Runestone, Heavener
Indian City, Anadarko
Kerr Museum, Poteau
Memorial Indian Museum, Broken Bow
Museum of the Great Plains, Lawton

Museum of the Red River, Idabel
Muskogee Creek National Museum, Okmulgee
National Hall of Fame for Famous American Indians, Anadarko
No Man's Land Historical Museum, Panhandle State College, Goodwell
Oklahoma Historical Society Museum, Oklahoma City
Osage Tribal Museum, Pawhuska
Ottawa County Museum, Miami
Pawnee Bill Mueum, Pawnee
Philbrook Art Center, Tulsa
Plains Indians and Pioneer Historical Foundation Pioneer Museum, Woodward
Ponca City Indian Museum, Ponca City
Sac and Fox Tribal RV Park and Museum/Cultural Center, Stroud
Seminole National Museum, Wewoka
Sequoyah's Home, Sallisaw
Southern Plains Indian Museum and Crafts Center, Anadarko
Spiro Mounds, Spiro
State Museum of Oklahoma, Oklahoma City
Stovall Museum, University of Oklahoma, Norman
Thomas Gilcrease Institute of American History and Art, Tulsa
Tsa-La-Gi Indian Village, Tahlequah
Western Trails Museum, Clinton
Wichitaw Tribal Cultural Center, Anadarko
Woolaroc Museum, Bartlesville
Yellow Bull Museum, Tonkawa

OREGON

Butler Museum of American Indian Art, Eugene
Collier State Park, Klamath Falls
Coos-Curry Museum, North Bend
Douglas County Museum, Roseburg
Favell Museum of Western Art and and Indian Artifacts, Klamath Falls
Horner Museum, Corvallis
Klamath County Museum, Klamath Falls
Museum of Natural History, University of Oregon, Eugene
Native American Research Center and Museum, Coos Bay
Portland Art Museum, Rasmussen Collection of Northwest Coast Indian Art, Portland

PENNSYLVANIA

American Indian Museum, Harmony
American Indian Museum, Pittsburgh
Atwater Kent Museum, Philadelphia
Carnegie Museum of Natural History, Pittsburgh
E.M. Parker Indian Museum, Brookville
Everhard Museum, Scranton

Hershey Museum, Hershey
Indian Steps Museum, Airville
Museum of the Philadelphia Civic Center, Philadelphia
North Museum, Franklin and Marshall College, Lancaster
Pennsylvania State Museum, Harrisburg
State Road Ripple Site, Clarion State College, Clarion
Tioga Point Museum, Athens
University Museum, University of Pennsylvania, Philadelphia
Warrior Trail Association, Waynesburg
William Penn Memorial Museum, Harrisburg
Wyoming Historical and Geological Society Museum, Wilkes-Barre

RHODE ISLAND

Haffenreffer Museum, Brown University, Bristol
Museum of Primitive Culture, Peace Dale
Narragansett Museum, Exeter
Roger Williams Park Museum, Providence
Tomaquag Indian Memorial Museum, Exeter

SOUTH CAROLINA

Charles Towne Landing–1670, Charleston
Chester County Historical Museum, Chester
Horry County Museum, Consway
Rice Museum, Georgetown
Santee Indian Mounds, Santee State Park, Santee

SOUTH DAKOTA

American Indian Culture Research Center, Marvin
Archaeological Society of South Dakota, Sioux Falls
Badlands National Park, Interior
Buechel Memorial Lakota Museum, St. Francis
Indian Arts Museum, Martin
Indian Museum of North America, Crazy Horse
Klein Museum, Mobridge
Land of the Sioux Museum, Mobridge
Mari Sandoz Museum, Pine Ridge Reservation
Mitchell Prehistoric Indian Village, Mitchell
Old Fort Meade Museum and Historic Research Association, Sturgis
Old West Museum, Chamberlain
Over Dakota Museum, University of South Dakota, Vermillion
Pettigrew Museum, Sioux Falls
Red Cloud Indian Museum, Kadoka
Robinson Museum, Pierre
Sioux Indian Museum, Rapid City
Siouxland Heritage Museums, Sioux Falls
South Dakota Archaeological Society, Vermillion
South Dakota State Historical Museum, Pierre

Standing Soldier Museum, Gordon
Timber of Ages Black Hills Petrified Forest, Piedmont
University of South Dakota Museum, Vermillion
Winona Club Sioux Cultural Center, Rapid City
Yankton Sioux Museum, Marty

TENNESSEE

Chucalissa Village Reconstruction and C. H. Nash Museum, Memphis
Cumberland Museum and Science Center, Nashville
Jeffrey L. Brown Institute of Archaeology, Chattanooga
Lookout Mountain Museum, Chattanooga
McGlung Museum, University of Tennessee, Knoxville
Shiloh Mounds, Shiloh National Military Park, Shiloh
Tennessee Historical Commission, Nashville

TEXAS

Alabama-Coushatta Indian Museum, Livingston
Alibates Flint Quarries National Monument, Fritch
Caddoan Mounds State Historic Sites, Alto
Caddo Indian Museum, Longview
Crockett County Museum, Ozona
Dallas Museum of Fine Arts, Dallas
El Paso Museum of Art, El Paso
Fort Belknap Museum and Archives, Newcastle
Fort Concho Museum, San Angelo
Fort Worth Children's Museum, Fort Worth
Fort Worth Museum of Science and History, Fort Worth
Hueco Tanks State Historical Park, El Paso
Indian Museum, Harwood
International Museum of Cultures, Dallas
Iraan Museum, Iraan
Lubbock Lake Site, Lubbock
Museum of Fine Arts of Houston, Houston
Museum of Texas Tech University, Lubbock
Museum of the Big Bend, Alpine
Museum of the Department of Anthropology, University of Texas, Austin
Native American Cultural Heritage Center, Dallas
Panhandle-Plains Historical Museum, Canyon
Private Caddo Indian Museum, Longview
Seminole Canyon State Historical Site, Comstock
Stone Fort Museum, Nacogdoches
Strecker Museum, Baylor University, Waco
Texas Memorial Museum, Austin
Tigua Pueblo Museum, El Paso

Wilderness Park Museum, El Paso

UTAH

Anasazi Indian Village State Historic Park, Boulder
Anthropology Museum, Brigham Young University, Provo
Arches Overlook, Blanding
Canyonlands National Park, Moab
Capitol Reef National Park, Torrey
Cave Towers, Blanding
College of Eastern Utah Prehistoric Museum, Price
Danger Cave, Wendover
Edge of Cedars State Historical Monument, Blanding
Grand Gulch Primitive Area, Kane Spring
Information Center and Museum, Salt Lake City
Museum of Peoples and Cultures, Provo
Natural Bridges National Monument, Kane Spring
Natural History State Museum, Vernal
Newspaper Rock, Indian Creek State Park, Monticello
University of Utah Anthropology Museum, Salt Lake City
Utah Field House of Natural History, National History State Park, Vernal
Utah Museum of Natural History, University of Utah, Salt Lake City
Ute Tribal Museum, Fort Duchesne
Westwater Ruin, Blanding
William R. Palmer Memorial Museum, Cedar City

VERMONT

Robert Hull Fleming Museum, University of Vermont, Burlington
Vermont Museum, Montpelier

VIRGINIA

Alexandria Community Archaeology Center, Alexandria
Archaeological Society of Virginia, Richmond
Fairfax County Park Authority, Division of Historic Preservation, Annandale
Hampton Institute Museum, Hampton
Hatch Site, Spring Grove
Jamestown Museum, Jamestown
Norfolk Museum, Norfolk
Pamunkey Indian Village, King William
Peaks of Otter Visitor's Center, Bedford
Reul B. Pritchett Museum, Bridgewater
Southwest Virginia Museum, Big Stone Gap
Thunderbird Museum and Archaeological Park, Front Royal
Valentine Museum, Richmond

Virginia Research Center for Archaeology, Williamsburg
Yorktown Visitor Center, Yorktown

WASHINGTON

Anthropology Museum, Washington State University, Seattle
Chelon County Historical Museum, Cashmere
Cheney Cowles Memorial Museum, Spokane
Colville Confederated Tribes, Coulee Dam
Daybreak Star Arts Center, Seattle
Eastern Washington State Historical Society, Spokane
Fort Okanogan Interpretive Center, Brewster
Gingko Petrified Forest State Park, Vantage
Lelooska's, Ariel
Makah Tribal Museum, Makah Indian Reservation, Neah Bay
Maryhill Museum of Art, Goldendale
Marymoor Museum, Redmond
Museum of Anthropology, Pullman
Museum of Man, Ellensburg
Museum of Native American Cultures, Spokane
North Central Indian Museum, Wenatchee
Ozette Village Site, Ozette
Pacific Northwest Indian Center, Spokane
Pioneer Memorial Museum, Port Angeles
Puyallup Tribe, Tacoma
Rocky Reach Dam, Wenatchee
Roosevelt Petroglyphs, Roosevelt
Sacajawea State Park, Pasco
Seattle Art Museum, Seattle
State Capitol Museum, Olympia
Suquamish Tribal Cultural Resource Center, Suquamish
Thomas Burke Memorial State Museum, University of Washington, Seattle
Toppenish Museum, Toppenish
Wanapum Dam Tour Center, Ephrata
Washington State Historical Society Museum, Tacoma
Washington State Museum, Seattle
Willis Carey Museum, Cashmere
Yakima Nation Cultural Center Museum, Toppenish
Yakima Valley Museum and Historical Association, Yakima

WEST VIRGINIA

Archaeology Museum, West Virginia University, Morgantown
Delf Norona Museum and Cultural Center, Moundsville
East Steubenville Site, East Steubenville
Grave Creek Mound, Moundsville
Mound Museum, Moundsville
New River Chapter/West Virginia Archaeological Society, Hinton

West Virginia Department of Culture and History, Charleston

WISCONSIN

Angus F. Lookaround Memorial, Keshena
Apostle Islands National Lakeshore, Bayfield
Arts and Crafts Cultural Center, Bayfield
Aztalan State Park, Lake Mills
City of Kenosha Public Museum, Kenosha
Devils Lake State Park, Baraboo
Gullickson's Glen Petroglyph Site, Black River Falls
High Cliff State Park, Menasha
Hoard Historical Museum, Fort Atkinson
Lizard Mound State Park, West Bend
Logan Museum of Anthropology, Beloit College, Beloit
Man Mound, Baraboo
Menasha Mounds, Menasha
Milwaukee Public Museum, Milwaukee
Museum of Anthropology, Wisconsin State University, Oshkosh
Museum of Natural History, University of Wisconsin, Stevens Point
Nelson Dewey State Park, Cassville
Neville Public Museum, Green Bay
Northland Historical Society, Lake Tomahawk
Ojibwa Nation Museum, Hayward
Oneida Nation Museum, DePere
Panther Intaglio, Fort Atkinson
Sheboygan County Museum, Sheboygan
Sheboygan Mound Park, Sheboygan
State Historical Society of Wisconsin, Madison
Stockbridge Munsee Historical Library and Museum, Bowler
Venne Art Center, Wausau
Winnebago Indian Museum, Wisconsin Dells
Wisconsin Archaeological Survey, Wausau
Wyalusing State Park, Bagley

WYOMING

Arapahoe Cultural Museum, Ethete
Buffalo Bill Historical Center, Cody
Colter Bay Indian Arts Museum, Colter
Fort Bridger Museum, Fort Bridger
Fort Casper Museum and Historic Site, Casper
Fort Fetterman State Museum, Douglas
Fort Laramie National Historic Site, Fort Laramie
Grand Teton National Park, Moose
Guernsey State Museum, Guernsey

Johnson County, Jim Catchell Memorial Museum, Buffalo
The Medicine Wheel, Big Horn Canyon Recreation Area, Lovell
Museum of the Plains Indian, Cody
Obsidian Cliff, Yellowstone National Park
Sweetwater County Historical Museum, Green River
Trail End Historic Center, Sheridan
University of Wyoming Anthropology Museum, Laramie
Wyoming Pioneer Home, Thermopolis
Wyoming State Museum, Cheyenne

CANADA

ALBERTA

Drumheller and District Museum Society, Drumheller
Glenbow-Alberta Centre, Calgary
Homestead Antique Museum, Drumheller
Luxton Museum, Banff
Provincial Museum of Alberta, Edmonton
Writing-on-Stone Provincial Park, Milk River

BRITISH COLUMBIA

Alert Bay Museum, Alert Bay
British Columbia Provincial Museum, Victoria
Campbell River Museum, Campbell River
Kamloops Museum and Archives, Kamloops
Kelowna Museum and National Exhibit Center, Kelowna
Ksan Indian Village and Museum, Hazelton
Museum of Anthropology, University of British Columbia, Vancouver
Museum of Northern British Columbia, Prince Rupert
Queen Charlotte Islands Museum, Skidegate
Thunderbird Park, Victoria
Vancouver Museum, Vancouver

MANITOBA

Manitoba Museum of Man and Nature, Winnipeg
Transcona Regional History Museum, Winnipeg

NEW BRUNSWICK

Red Bank Indian Reserve, Red Bank

NEWFOUNDLAND

L'Anse-Amour, Red Bay, Labrador
Castle Hill National Historic Park, Placentia Bay
Newfoundland Museum, St. John's
Port Au Choix National Historic Park, Port Au Choix
Signal Hill National Historic Park, St. John's

NOVA SCOTIA

The Micmac Museum, Pictou

ONTARIO

Agawa Indian Rock, Lake Superior Provincial Park, Agawa
Bon Echo Provincial Park, Cloyne
Brant Historical Museum, Brantford
Champlain Trail Museum, Pembroke
Chapel of the Mohawks, Brantford
Chiefswood, Six Nations Indian Reserve, Brantford
Huronia Museum and Huron Indian Village, Midland
Joseph Brant Museum, Burlington
Kanawa International Museum of Canoes and Kayaks at Kandolore, Dorset
Museum of Indian Archaeology and Pioneer Life, University of Western Ontario, London
National Museum of Man, Ottawa
Nodwell Indian Village, Port Elgin
North American Indian Travelling College, Cornwall Island
Old Fort William, Thunder Bay
Petroglyphs Provincial Park, Highway 28
Quetico Provincial Park Museum, Atikokan
Rondeau Provincial Park Interpretive Center, Morpeth
Royal Ontario Museum, Toronto
Sainte-Marie Among the Hurons, Midland
Semcoe County Museum, Barrie
Serpent Mounds Provincial Park, Keene
Ska Nah Doht Indian Village, Delaware
Woodland Indian Cultural Education Centre, Brantford

PRINCE EDWARD ISLAND

Fort Amherst National Historic Park, Rocky Point

QUEBEC

Chief Poking Fire Indian Reservation, Caughnawauga
Kanien Kehaka Raotitiohkwa Cultural Center, Caughnawauga
McCord Museum, McGill University, Montreal
Musee des Abenakis d'Odanak, Odanak
Musee de Quebec, Quebec City

SASKATCHEWAN

F.T. Hill Museum, Riverhurst
Saskatchewan Museum of Natural History, Regina
Saskatchewan Western Development Museum, Yorkton
Willow Bunch Museum, Willow Bunch

YUKON TERRITORY

MacBride Museum, Whitehorse

Bibliography

(Earlier dates of publication included only when recent dates vary significantly.)

Adams, James T., and Jackson Kenneth, T. *Atlas of American History*. Scribner, 1978.

Alexander, Hartley Burr. *The World's Rim: Great Mysteries of the North American Indians*. University of Nebraska, 1953.

American Association of Museums. *The Official Museum Directory*. National Register, 1982.

Andrist, Ralph K. *The Long Death*. Macmillan, 1964.

Armstrong, G. H. *The Origin and Meaning of Place Names in Canada*. Macmillan, 1977.

Ashburn, Percy Moreau. *The Ranks of Death: A Medical History of the Conquest of America*. Coward-McCann, 1947.

Axtell, James, L. *The European and the Indian*. Oxford University, 1981.

Baity, Elizabeth Chesley. *Americans Before Columbus*. Viking, 1961.

Bakeless, John. *The Eyes of Discovery*. Dover, 1961.

Bancroft, Hubert Howe. *The Works of Hubert Howe Bancroft*. Arno, 1960s (reprint from 1883–90).

Beckwith, Hiram W. *The Illinois and Indiana Indians*. Arno, 1975.

Benson, Elizabeth P. *The Maya World*. Crowell, 1977.

Bernardo, Stephanie. *The Ethnic Almanac*. Doubleday, 1981.

Billington, Ray Allen. *Westward Expansion*. Macmillan, 1960.

Bolton, Reginald P. *Indian Life of Long Ago in the City of New York*. Friedman, 1971.

Bolton, Reginald P. *New York City in Indian Possession*. Museum of the American Indian, Heye Foundation, 1975.

Boyd, Doug. *Rolling Thunder*. Random House, 1974.

Brandon, William. *The American Heritage Book of Indians*. American Heritage/Bonanza, 1982.

Brebner, John Bartlet. *The Explorers of North America*. World, 1964.

Brennan, Louis A. *American Dawn*. Macmillan, 1970.

Brown, Dee Alexander. *Bury My Heart at Wounded Knee*. Bantam, 1970.

Bryce, George. *The Remarkable History of the Hudson's Bay Company*. Franklin, 1968 (reprint from 1904).

Bureau of Business Research. *Atlas of Mexico*. University of Texas, 1979.

Burt, Jesse, and Ferguson, Robert B. *Indians of the Southeast: Then and Now*. Abingdon, 1973.

Bushnell, G. H. S. *The First Americans: The Pre-Columbian Civilizations*. McGraw-Hill, 1968.

Capps, Benjamin. *The Great Chiefs*. Time, 1975.

Ceram, C. W. *The First American*. New American Library, 1971.

Coe, Michael D. *America's First Civilization: Discovering the Olmec*. American Heritage, 1968.

Coe, Michael D. *Mexico: Ancient Peoples and Places*. Praeger, 1962.

Coe, Ralph T. *Sacred Circles*. Arts Council of Great Britain, 1977.

Collier, John. *Indians of the Americas*. New American Library, 1975 (reprint from 1947).

Cooke, Alan, and Holland, Clive. *The Exploration of Northern Canada*. Arctic History, 1978.

Cotterill, R. S. *The Southern Indians*. University of Oklahoma, 1954.

Craig, Tracey Linton, ed. *Directory of Historical Societies and Agencies in the United States and Canada*. American Association for State and Local History, 1982.

Danziger, Jr., Edmund Jefferson. *Indians and Bureaucrats*. University of Illinois, 1974.

Davies, Nigel. *The Aztecs*. Putnam, 1979.

Davies, Nigel. *The Toltecs*. University of Oklahoma, 1977.

Deloria, Jr., Vine. *Behind the Trial of Broken Treaties*. Delacorte, 1974.

Deloria, Jr., Vine. *Custer Died for Your Sins*. Macmillan, 1969.

Deloria, Jr., Vine. *God is Red*. Grosset & Dunlap, 1973.

Delpar, Helen, ed. *The Discoverers: An Encyclopedia of Explorers and Exploration*. McGraw-Hill, 1980.

Dennis, Henry C. *The American Indian 1492–1970: A Chronology and Fact Book*. Oceana, 1971.

Dillon, Richard H. *North American Indian Wars*. Facts on File, 1983.

Disselhoff, H. D., and Linné, S. *The Art of Ancient America*. Crown, 1960.

Dobyns, Henry F. *Native American Historical Demography: A Critical Bibliography*. Indiana University, 1976.

Driver, Harold E. *Indians of North America*. University of Chicago, 1969.

Dury, G. H., and Chandler, T. J. *North America*. Nelson, 1965.

Eccles, W. J. *The Canadian Frontier*. University of New Mexico, 1983.

Edmunds, R. David. *American Indian Leaders*. University of Nebraska, 1980.

Eliade, Mircea. *Shamanism: Archaic Techniques of Ecstasy*. Princeton University, 1972.

Farb, Peter. *Man's Rise to Civilization*. Dutton, 1968.

Feest, Christian F. *Native Arts of North America*. Oxford University, 1980.

Fell, Barry. *America B.C.* Demeter, 1977.

Ferguson, Linda. *Canada*. Scribner, 1979.

Ferriday, A. *North America: A Regional Geography*. Macmillan, 1965.

Ferris, Robert G., ed. *Explorers and Settlers*. National Park Service, 1968.

Ferris, Robert G., ed. *Soldier and Brave*. National Park Service, 1971.

Fey, Harold E., and McNickle, D'Arcy. *Indians and Other Americans*. Harper & Row, 1970.

Fletcher, Sidney E. *The American Indian*. Grosset & Dunlap, 1954.

Fox, Edward Whiting. *Atlas of American History*. Oxford University, 1964.

Freeman, Milton M.R. *Inuit Land Use and Occupancy Project*. Canadian Department of Indian Affairs and Northern Development, 1976.

Furst, Peter T., ed. *Flesh of the Gods: The Ritual Use of Hallucinogens*. Praeger, 1972.

Gannett, Henry. *The Origin of Certain Place Names in the United States*. Gale Research, 1971 (reprint from 1902).

Garbarino, Merwyn S. *Native American Heritage*. Little, Brown, 1976.

Georgakas, Dan. *Red Shadows*. Doubleday, 1973.

Gibson, Arrell Morgan. *The American Indian*. Heath, 1980.

Gibson, James R. *Imperial Russia in Frontier America*. Oxford University, 1976.

Gilbert, Martin. *American History Atlas*. Macmillan, 1968.

Goetzmann, William H. *Exploration and Empire*. Knopf, 1966.

Hagan, William T. *American Indians*. University of Chicago, 1979.

Hagan, William T. *Longhouse Diplomacy and Frontier Warfare*. New York State Education Department, 1975.

Hale, John R. *Age of Exploration*. Time, 1974.

Haley, James L. *The Buffalo War*. Doubleday, 1976.

Hamilton, Milton W. *Sir William Johnson and the Indians of New York*. University of the State of New York, 1975.

Hanke, Lewis. *Aristotle and the American Indian*. Regnery, 1959.

Harder, Kelsie B. *Illustrated Dictionary of Place Names, United States and Canada*. Van Nostrand–Reinhold, 1976.

Heyerdahl, Thor. *American Indians in the Pacific*. Allen & Unwin, 1952.

Highwater, Jamake. *Fodor's Indian America*. McKay, 1975.

Highwater, Jamake. *Many Smokes, Many Moons*. Lippincott, 1978.

Highwater, Jamake. *The Primal Mind*. Harper & Row, 1981.

Hitchcock, Charles B., ed. *These United States*. Reader's Digest, 1968.

Hodge, Frederick W., ed. *Handbook of American Indians North of Mexico*. Rowman & Littlefield, 1965 (reprint from 1906).

Honour, Hugh. *The New Golden Land: European Images of America*. Random House, 1975.

Hultkrantz, Ake. *The Religions of the American Indians*. University of California, 1979.

Hunt, George T. *The Wars of the Iroquois*. University of Wisconsin, 1940.

Indian Conditions: A Survey. Canadian Department of Indian Affairs and Northern Development, 1980.

Innis, Harold A. *The Fur Trade in Canada*. Yale University, 1962.

Jackson, W. Turrentine. *Wagon Roads West*. Yale University, 1964.

Jacobs, Wilbur R. *Dispossessing the American Indian*. Scribner, 1972.

Jenness, Diamond. *The Indians of Canada*. University of Toronto, 1977 (reprint from 1932).

Jennings, Francis. *The Ambiguous Iroquois Empire*. Norton, 1984.

Jennings, Francis. *The Invasion of America: Indians, Colonialism, and the Cant of Conquest*. Norton, 1975.

Jennings, Jesse D. *Prehistory of North America*. McGraw-Hill, 1974.

Johansen, Bruce, and Maestas, Roberto. *Wasi'chu: The Continuing Indian Wars.* Monthly Review, 1980.

Jones, Charles, ed. *Look to the Mountain Top.* Gousha, 1972.

Josephy, Jr., Alvin M. *The Indian Heritage of America.* Knopf, 1968.

Josephy, Jr., Alvin M. *The Nez Perce Indians and the Opening of the Northwest.* Yale University, 1965.

Josephy, Jr., Alvin M. *The Patriot Chiefs.* Viking, 1961.

Josephy, Jr., Alvin M. *Red Power.* American Heritage, 1971.

Kagan, Hilde Heun, ed. *Pictorial Atlas of United States History.* American Heritage, 1966.

Kellogg, Louise Phelps. *The French Regime in Wisconsin and the Northwest.* Cooper Square, 1968 (reprint from 1925).

Kelsey, Laura. *Cartographic Records of the Bureau of Indian Affairs.* National Archives, 1977.

Kelsey, Laura. *Cartographic Records in the National Archives of the United States relating to American Indians.* National Archives, 1974.

Kerr, D.G.G. *A Historical Atlas of Canada.* Nelson, 1966.

Kickingbird, Kirke, and Ducheneaux, Karen. *One Hundred Million Acres.* Macmillan, 1973.

Kirkham, E. Kay. *A Genealogical and Historical Atlas of the United States of America.* Everton, 1976.

Klein, Bernard, and Icolari, Daniel. *Reference Encyclopedia of the American Indian.* Klein, 1967.

Krickeberg, Walter, et al. *Pre-Columbian American Religions.* Holt, Rinehart and Winston, 1968.

Kroeber, A. L. *Cultural and Natural Areas of Native North America.* University of California, 1963 (reprint from 1939).

La Barre, Weston. *The Peyote Cult.* Archon, 1975 (reprint from 1938).

La Farge, Oliver. *A Pictorial History of the American Indian.* Crown, 1974.

Lamar, Howard R., ed. *The Reader's Encyclopedia of the American West.* Crowell, 1977.

Langnas, I. A. *Dictionary of Discoveries.* Philosophical Library, 1959.

Lavender, David. *The American Heritage History of the Great West.* American Heritage/Bonanza, 1982.

Leonard, Jonathan Norton. *Ancient America.* Time, 1972.

Lord, Clifford, and Lord, Elizabeth. *Historical Atlas of the United States.* Holt, 1953.

Lyttle, Richard B. *People of the Dawn.* Atheneum, 1980.

Maracle, Brant Joseph. *Questions We Indians Are Asked.* Maracle, 1977.

Marquis, Arnold. *A Guide to America's Indians.* University of Oklahoma, 1974.

Marriott, Alice, and Rachlin, Carol. *American Epic: The Story of the American Indian.* Putnam, 1969.

Marshall, S.L.A. *Crimsoned Prairie.* Scribner, 1972.

Martin, Paul; Quimby, George; and Collier, Donald. *Indians before Columbus.* University of Chicago, 1947.

Matthiessen, Peter. *Indian Country.* Viking, 1984.

Matthiessen, Peter. *In the Spirit of Crazy Horse.* Viking, 1983.

Maxwell, James A., ed. *America's Fascinating Indian Heritage.* Reader's Digest, 1978.

McDermott, John Francis., ed. *Travelers on the Western Frontier.* University of Illinois, 1970.

McNickle, D'Arcy. *Native American Tribalism.* Oxford University, 1973.

Miles, Charles. *Indian and Eskimo Artifacts of North America.* Regnery, 1963.

Mohawk, John. *Basic Call to Consciousness.* Akwesasne Notes, 1982.

Morgan, Lewis H. *Houses and House-Life of the American Aborigines.* University of Chicago, 1965 (reprint from 1881).

Morgan, Lewis H. *League of the Ho-de-no-sau-nee of Iroquois.* Dodd, Mead, 1904.

Morison, Samuel Eliot. *The European Discovery of America.* Oxford University, 1971.

National Atlas of the United States of America. Department of the Interior, 1970.

Native American Directory. National Native American Co-operative, 1982.

Naylor, Maria, ed. *Authentic Indian Designs.* Dover, 1975.

Neill, Wilfred T. *Florida's Seminole Indians.* Great Outdoors, 1956.

Nettl, Bruno. *North American Indian Musical Styles.* American Folklore Society, 1954.

Newby, Eric. *World Atlas of Exploration.* Rand McNally, 1975.

Owen, Roger C. et al. *The North American Indians: A Sourcebook.* Macmillan, 1967.

Parkman, Francis. *France and England in North America.* Viking, 1983 (reprint from 1865–92).

Paterson, J. H. *North America.* Oxford University, 1970.

Paullin, Charles O. *Atlas of the Historical Geography of the United States.* Carnegie Institution/American Geographical Society, 1932.

Peterson, Frederick. *Ancient Mexico.* Putnam, 1959.

Pope, Jr., G. D. *Ocmulgee.* National Park Service, 1956.

Pounds, N.J.G. *North America.* Murray, 1966.

Prescott, William Hickling. *The Portable Prescott: The Rise and Decline of the Spanish Empire.* Viking, 1966 (reprint from 1830s–1840s).

Prucha, Francis Paul. *United States Indian Policy: A Critical Bibliography.* Indiana University, 1977.

Quinn, David B. *North America from Earliest Discovery to First Settlements.* Harper & Row, 1977.

Reid, Alan. *Discovery and Exploration.* Gentry, 1980.

Ristow, Walter W., ed. *A la Carte: Selected Papers on Maps and Atlases.* Library of Congress, 1972.

Ritchie, William, and Funk, Robert. *Aboriginal Settlement Patterns in the Northeast.* New York State Museum, 1973.

Roe, Frank Gilbert. *The Indian and the Horse.* University of Oklahoma, 1955.

Royce, Charles C. *Indian Land Cessions in the United States.* Arno, 1971 (reprint from 1899).

Sauer, Carl. *Man in Nature.* Turtle Island Foundation, 1975.

Schwartz, Seymour, and Ehrenberg, Ralph. *The Mapping of America.* Abrams, 1980.

Scott, J.M. *Icebound: Journeys to the Northwest Sea.* Gordon & Cremonesi, 1977.

Secoy, Frank Raymond. *Changing Military Patterns on the Great Plains.* University of Washington, 1953.

Selby, John. *The Conquest of the American West.* Rowman and Littlefield, 1976.

Service, Elman R. *Primitive Social Organization.* Random House, 1971.

Shepherd, William R. *Shepherd's Historical Atlas.* Harper & Row, 1964.

Snow, Dean R. *The Archaeology of North America.* Viking, 1976.

Sorkin, Alan L. *American Indians and Federal Aid.* Brookings, 1971.

Spencer, Robert F. and Jennings, Jesse D. *The Native Americans.* Harper & Row, 1977.

Spicer, Edward H. *The American Indians.* Harvard University, 1982.

Spicer, Edward H. *Cycles of Conquest.* University of Arizona, 1962.

Spicer, Edward H., ed. *Perspectives in American Indian Culture Change.* University of Chicago, 1961.

Steiner, Stan. *The New Indians.* Harper & Row, 1968.

Stewart, George R. *American Place-Names.* Oxford University, 1970.

Stone, William L. *Life of Joseph Brant (Thayendanegea).* Kraus, 1969 (reprint from 1838).

Stoutenburgh, John L. *Dictionary of North American Indians.* Philosophical Library, 1960.

Sturtevant, William, ed. *Handbook of North American Indians.* 20-vol. encyclopedia. Smithsonian, 1978–83.

Surtees, Robert J. *Canadian Indian Policy: A Critical Bibliography.* Indiana University, 1982.

Sutton, Imre. *Indian Land Tenure.* Clearwater, 1975.

Swanton, John R. *Indians of the Southeastern United States.* Scholarly, 1969 (reprint from 1946).

Swanton, John R. *The Indian Tribes of North America.* Smithsonian, 1979 (reprint from 1952).

Symington, Fraser. *The Canadian Indian.* McClelland and Stewart, 1969.

Talbot, Steve. *Roots of Oppression.* International, 1981.

Tanner, Ogden. *The Canadians.* Time, 1977.

Taylor, Theodore W. *The Bureau of Indian Affairs.* Westview, 1984.

Tebbel, John. *The Compact History of the Indian Wars.* Hawthorn, 1966.

Tebbel, John, and Jennison, Keith. *The American Indian Wars.* Crown, 1960.

Terrell, John Upton. *Sioux Trail.* McGraw-Hill, 1974.

Thomas, Davis, and Ronnefeldt, Karin, eds. *People of the First Man.* Promontory, 1982.

Thompson, J. Eric. *The Rise and Fall of Maya Civilization.* University of Oklahoma, 1966.

Thomson, John Lewis. *History of the Indian Wars.* Lippincott, 1887.

Thornton, Russell; Sandefur, Gary; and Grasmick, Harold. *The Urbanization of American Indians: A Critical Bibliography.* Indiana University, 1982.

Thwaites, Reuben Gold. *Early Western Travels.* AMS, 1966 (reprint from 1904–07).

Turner, Geoffrey. *Indians of North America.* Blandford, 1979.

Tyler, S. Lyman. *A History of Indian Policy.* Department of the Interior, 1973.

Underhill, Ruth M. *Red Man's America.* University of Chicago, 1971.

United States Department of Commerce. *Federal and Indian State Reservations and Indian Trust Areas.* Government Printing Office, 1974.

United States History Atlas. Hammond, 1977.

United States Indian Claims Commission. *Final Report.* Government Printing Office, 1978.

Utley, Robert M. *Frontier Regulars.* Indiana University, 1977.

Utley, Robert M., and Washburn, Wilcomb E. *The American Heritage History of the Indian Wars.* American Heritage/Bonanza, 1977.

Vaillant, George C. *Aztecs of Mexico.* Doubleday, 1962.

Van Every, Dale. *Disinherited.* Morrow, 1966.

Voices from Wounded Knee. Akwesasne Notes, 1974.

Von Hagen, Victor W. *The Aztec: Man and Tribe.* New American Library, 1958.

Von Hagen, Victor W. *World of the Maya.* New American Library, 1960.

Walker Art Center. *American Indian Art: Form and Tradition* Dutton, 1972.

Washburn, Wilcomb E. *The American Indian and the United States.* Random House, 1973.

Wax, Murray L. *Indian Americans.* Prentice-Hall, 1971.

Weaver, Muriel Porter. *The Aztecs, Maya, and their Predecessors.* Academic, 1981.

Wesley, Edgar B. *Our United States: Its History in Maps.* Denoyer-Geppert, 1980.

White, Jon Manchip. *Everyday Life of the North American Indian.* Holmes & Meier, 1979.

Whiteford, Andrew Hunter. *North American Indian Arts.* Western, 1970.

Wilbur, C. Keith. *The New England Indians.* Globe Pequot, 1978.

Willey, Gordon R. *Introduction to American Archaeology.* Prentice-Hall, 1966.

Wilson, Josleen. *The Passionate Amateur's Guide to Archaeology in the United States.* Collier, 1980.

Wise, Jennings C. (Vine Deloria, Jr., ed.) *The Red Man in the New World Drama.* Macmillan, 1971.

Wissler, Clark. *Indians of the United States.* Doubleday, 1966.

Woodcock, George. *The Canadians.* Harvard University, 1979.

Index

(Numbers refer to text pagination, except those in italics which refer to artwork or to early maps. Subject matter found on original maps in most cases corresponds closely to text pagination. For further reference to original maps, see list of Maps in front of book.)

Tioga, PA, 112
Tiou(s), 82
Tippecanoe, 115–17
Tiwa(s), 35, 81, 97, 127, 145–6
Tlaloc, 14
Tlatelolco, 12
Tlatilco, 15
Tlingit(s), 38, 72, 83, 124–5, *124*, 173
tobacco, 16–17, 20–1, 28, 37, 45, 60, 88, 171, 186
Tobacco(s), 31, 75, 94
toboggans, 46, 54, *54*
Tohome(s), 80
Tomahas, 130
tomahawks, *77*
Tombigbee River, 106
Tonawanda reservation, 204
Tongue River, 150
Tonkawa(s), 151
Tonto Basin campaign, 129, 141, 143, 146
tools, 3–6, 14, 16, 18, 22–3, *28*, 31, 36, 43, 46–50, 74–5, 98; *see also* technology
Toohoolhoolzote, 134–5
Topiltzen, 11
Tories, 111–13
Tory Rangers, 110–11
totem poles, *37*, *47*
Totonac(s), 8, 15, 80
tourism, 210
Towa(s), 35
toys, 48, 50, *50*
trade and traders, 8–10, 13–15, 18, 20–3, 28, 36, 47–8, 54, 58, 60–1, 65, 71, 74–85, 77, 79–85, 87, 89–90, 93–6, 99, 101–3, 105–6, 108, 124–5, 127–8, 151, 153–4, 159–60, 162, 166–7, 169–73, 175–6, 179–81, 185–6, 188, 190, 211
Trade and Intercourse Act (1834), 182, 190–1
Trade and Intercourse Acts (1790–1802), 78, 190
Trail of Broken Treaties Caravan, 205
Trail of Tears, 120, 122, 127, 145, 178, 183–5
trails, 54, 78, 179–81, 211
transoceanic voyages, 70–2
transportation, 23, 46, 54–6, 70–2, 179–81
Transylvania Land Company, 179
Trappists, 22
traps, nets, and snares, 70–2
travois, 54, *54*
treaties and treaty making, 87, 89, 133, 139, 162, 167, 174, 178, 183–4, 188, 190–1, 194, 198–9, 202–7
Treaty of: Dancing Rabbit Creek, 183; 1804, 118–19; Fort Atkinson, 151; Fort Gibson, 122; Fort Greenville, 115; Fort Laramie (1851), 147, 151, 155–7; Fort Laramie (1868), 149, 156; Ghent, 117, 119; Guadaloupe Hidalgo, 139; Horseshoe Bend, 121; Jay Treaty, 205; Lancaster, 102; Logstown, 102; Medicine Lodge, 149, 156; Paris (1763), 104, 108; Paris (1783), 114, 172, 177; Payne's Landing, 122; Ryswick, 101; Selkirk, 160; Tampa, 122; Utrecht, 77, 101
Tres Zapotes, 8
Trevino, Geronimo, 142
tribes, see by name, maps, tribal list in Appendix, sociopolitical organization
tribal acknowledgment, 199, 201
tribal ethnicity, 199
tribal reorganization and restoration, 192, 194, 210
tribal sovereignty, 123, 167, 190, 198
Trinity River, 32
Truckee River Valley, 136
Tryon County, 110
Tsetsaut(s), 42
Tsimshian(s), 38
Tubatulabal(s), 39
Tubutama mission, 99
Tucson, AZ, 140, 201

Tula, 11–12, *11*
Tule Lake, 132
Tulsa, OK, 200
Tulum, 11
tundra, 1, 41–3
Tunica(s), 82
Turkey Foot, 11
Tuscarora(s), 31, 93, 104, 110, 171, 204
Tuscarora Power Project, 204
Tuscarora War, 99, 104
Tutchone(s), 42
Tututni(s), 128, 137–8
Twiggs, David, 151

Umatilla(s), 128–9, 138–9
Umatilla agency, 130
Umatilla River, 36
umiaks, 55, *55*
Umnak Island, 124
Unalaska Island, 124
Underhill, John, 91, 96
Ungava, 188
Unimak Island, 124
Union Pacific Railway, 181
United American Company, 124, 173
United Nations, 206
United Native Americans, 205
United New Netherland Company, 95, 173
United States, 29, 43, 72–4, 78–9, 83–5, 88, 109–60, 164, 169–70, 173–88, 190–206, 210–11
United States Army, 109–159
United States Commission on Civil Rights, 195
United States Congress, 78, 114, 130, 154, 181–3, 190–2, 194–5, 198–9, 203, 205
United States Constitution, 93, 154, 190, 198–9
Upward Bound, 195
urban Indians and urbanization, 59, 194–5, 200–2, 204–5, 210
Utah, 4, 16–17, 27, 34–5, 128, 138, 181, 194
Utah Lake, 35
Ute(s), 18, 36, 56, 83–4, 129, 138, 145, 204
Ute War, 129, 138

Vaca, Alvar Nunez Cabeza de, 80
Valley of Mexico, 11–15, 58, 63, 65
Van Dorn, Earl, 151
Van Horne, William, 164
Van Twiller, Wouter, 95
Vancouver, British Columbia, 163
Vancouver, George, 83
Vancouver Island, 37–8, 188
Vandalia, IL, 179
Vargas, Don Diego de, 98
vegetation, 23, 31–45; *see also* plants
Venango, PA, 102
Veracruz, 8, 15, *44*
Verde River, 18
Verendrye, Sieur de, 82
Verrazano, Giovanni de, 74, 80
Vespucci, Amerigo, 80
Victoria, TX, 151
Victorio, 142–3
Victorio's Resistance, 129, 142
Vikings, 70–2, 79–80
village life, 6–8, 16–17, 20–1, 28, 33–4, 37–8, 40, 56
Villiers, Coulon de, 102, 108
Vincennes, OH, 112–13, 118
Virginia, 31–2, 62, 89, 102, 105, 109, 112–14, 171, 175, 179, 185
Virginia City, NV, 136
Virginia House of Burgesses, 89
Vista, 195
Vitoria, Francisco de, 168
Voegelin, C.F. and F.M., 66
Voluntary Relocation Program, 194
Voting Rights Act, 195
voyageurs, 75–6, 78, 160

Wabash and Erie Canal, 181

Wabash River, 112, 114, 118
Wahlitits, 133
Wahunsonacock, *see* Powhatan, Chief
Waiilatpu village, 13
Wakenda, 57
Walker, Hovendon, 101
Walker, Thomas, 179
Walker Lake, 35
Walla Walla(s), 128, 138–9
Walla Walla Council, 133, 138–9
Walla Walla Valley, 138
Wallowa Valley, 133, 136
Walpalpi(s), *see* Paiute
Wampanoag(s), 31, 81, 90–3
Wampum, 48, 95, 107
Wamsutta, 92
Wandering Spirit, 164
Wappinger(s), 31, 81, 96, 176
Wappo(s), 39
War Department, 78, 190
War of the Austrian Succession, 99, 101
War for the Black Hills, 129
War for the Bozeman Trail, 129, 150, 155–6, 181
War of 1812, 114, 117, 119, 175, 178–9, 188
War of the Grand Alliance, 99
War of Jenkins's Ear, 101
War of the Spanish Succession, 99
Ward, John, 140
warfare, 8, 10, 12–14, 20–2, 29–30, 34, 45, 53–4, 56–63, 65, 70, 74, 78, 86–165, 167–79, 190, 202, 211, see also wars by name, battles
Warrior, 120
Warrior, Clyde, 205
Wars for the West, 120, 126–59, 189
Wasatch Mountains, 35, 137
Washakie, 137
Washington, 36–7, 128, 130, 133, 136, 138–9, 191, 195, 201, 205
Washington, D.C., 119, 145, *156*, 204–6
Washington, George, 102–3, 110–14
Washo, 35
Watauga village, 32, 179
Waterford, PA, 108
Watershed Age, 4–5, 26
Watkins, Arthur, 194
wattle and daub, 50–2, *51*
Wayne, Anthony, 115
Wea(s), 108, 114, 116
Weapemeoc(s), 31
weapons, *see* by kind
Weatherford, William, *see* Red Eagle
weaving, 5–6, 11, 17–18, 20, 47–8, 144
Webb, Adam Clark, 160
Webster, John, 154
Weippe Prairie, 134
Weiser, Conrad, 82
West, Joseph, 140
West Indies, 60, 74, 93, 101
West Virginia, 19, 32, 105, 179
Western Cattle Trail, 181
Westport, MO, 180
Wethersfield, CT, 90
Wheaton, Frank, 132
wheel, 54
Wheeling, WV, 179
Wheelock, Eleazar, 110
Wheelock–Howard Act, *see* Indian Reorganization Act
Whipple, Steven, 134
White, John, 81
White Cloud, *see* Winnebago Prophet
White Bird, 134–5
White Horse, 148–9
White House Task Force on Indian Health, 195
White Mountain Apache(s), *see* Apache
White Paper (Canada), 207
White River, 138
White Sticks, 120–2
White Woman, 22
Whiteside, Samuel, 118–19
Whitman, Marcus and Narcissa, 128, 130

Whitman, Royal, 140
Whitside, S.M., 158
Wichita(s), 40, 56, 76, 80, 128
Wichita Expedition, 151
wickiups, 50–2, *51*
wigwams, 20, 32, 50–2, *51*, 91
Wilderness Road, 179
Willamette River, 36
Williams, A.T.H., 164
Williams, Roger, 90
Williams Station, 136
Wiltwyck, 96
Wind River reservation, 146
Windigo, 57
Winema, 132
Winnebago(s), 31, 81
Winnebago Prophet, 59, 118–20
Winnebago Uprising, 118
Winnemucca Lake, 35
Winnipeg, Manitoba, 160, 164
Winters Doctrine, 192, 202
Wintun(s), 39
Wisconsin, 22, 106, 118, 120, 194, 201
Wisconsin glaciation, 1–2
Wisconsin River, 118, 120
Wishram(s), *36*
Withlacoochee River, 123
Wolfe, James, 104
Wolfskill, William, 179–80
wolves, 160–2
Women of All Red Nations (WARN), 206
Wool, John, 139
Woodland period, 7, 19–21, 32, 58
woodwork, 3, 5–7, *4*, *6*, 20, 25–6, *31*, 33–4, *36–7*, 41–3, *41*, *43*, 46–7, *46*, 50–5, *54–5*, *86–7*, *92*, *98*, *100*, *151*, *184*
World War I, 192
World War II, 192, 194, 200, 203–4
Worth, William, 123
Wounded Knee (1890), 59, 86, 128, 136, 148, 154–5, 158–9, 178, 205–6
Wounded Knee (1973), 159, 205
Wovoka, 59, 136, 158
Wright, George, 130–1, 139
Wurm glaciation, 1
Wyandot(s), 102, 108, 113–14, 116, 194; *see also* Huron
Wyoming, 35, 40, 129–30, 135, 137–8, 146, 150, 155–7, 178
Wyoming Valley, 111

Yahuskin(s), *see* Paiute
Yakima(s), 128, 130, 137–9, 195
Yakima reservation, 130
Yakima War, 128, 130, 137–9
Yakutat Bay, 125
Yamasee(s), 104–5, 171
Yamasee War, 99, 104–5
Yana(s), 39
Yankton, *see* Sioux
Yanktonai, *see* Sioux
Yaqui(s), 80
Yavapai(s), 18, 35, 81, 129, 142, 146
Yazoo(s), 106
Yellow Bird, 158
Yellowknife, 42
Yellowstone Park, 130, 135
Yellowstone River, 153
Yokut(s), 39, 85, 128, 131, 139
York, ME, 100
York River, 89
Yorktown, 112
Yount, George, 180
Yucatan, 11–12
Yuit(s), 43
Yuki(s), 39
Yukon River, 2, 41, 43
Yukon Plateau, 41
Yukon Territory, 3, 188
Yuma(s), 18, 35, 61, 82, 128, 133, 139
Yuma and Mojave Uprising, 128
Yuma Crossing, 133, 139
Yurok(s), 39, 166

Zapotec(s), 8, 15
Zia Pueblo, 98
Zuni(s), 17, *34*, 35, 61, 80, 97